MW00332567

KITCHEN PLANNING

KITCHEN PLANNING
Guidelines, Codes, Standards

Second Edition

JULIA BEAMISH, PH.D., CKE

KATHLEEN PARROTT, PH.D., CKE

JOANN EMMEL, PH.D.

MARY JO PETERSON, CKD, CBD, CAPS, CAASH

National Kitchen & Bath Association

Cover photographs: (left) Design by Peter Ross Salerno, CMKBD, photograph by Peter Rymwid
(right) Design by Tracey Scalzo, CMKBD, photograph by Tom Harper

Cover design: Anne Michele Abbott

This book is printed on acid-free paper. ∞

National Kitchen & Bath Association
687 Willow Grove Street
Hackettstown, NJ 07840
Phone: 800-THE-NKBA (800-843-6522)
Fax: 908-852-1695
Website: NKBA.org

For general information on our other products and services, or technical support, please contact our Customer Care Department within the United States at 800-762-2974, outside the United States at 317-572-3993 or fax 317-572-4002.

Wiley publishes in a variety of print and electronic formats and by print-on-demand. Some material included with standard print versions of this book may not be included in e-books or in print-on-demand. If this book refers to media such as a CD or DVD that is not included in the version you purchased, you may download this material at http://booksupport.wiley.com.

For more information about Wiley products, visit our Web site at http://www.wiley.com.

Library of Congress Cataloging-in-Publication Data:

Beamish, Julia.
   Kitchen planning : guidelines, codes, standards / Julia Beamish, Ph.D., CKE, Kathleen Parrott, Ph.D., CKE, JoAnn Emmel, Ph.D., Mary Jo Peterson, CKD, CBD, CAPS.—Second Edition.
        pages cm
   Includes index.
   ISBN 978-1-118-36762-9 (cloth); 978-111-8-40458-4 (ebk.); 978-111-8-40462-1 (ebk.);
978-111-8-40464-5 (ebk.); 978-111-8-40466-9 (ebk.); 978-111-8-40468-3 (ebk.); 978-111-8-43860-2 (ebk.)
   1. Kitchens. I. Parrott, Kathleen R. (Kathleen Rose), 1950- II. Emmel, JoAnn. III. Peterson, Mary Jo.
IV. Title.
   TH4816.3.K58B43 2013
   690'.44—dc23
                                                                           2012026250

978-1-118-36762-9

Printed in the United States of America

10 9 8 7 6 5 4 3

Sponsors

The National Kitchen and Bath Association recognizes with gratitude the following companies whose generous contributions supported the development of this second edition of *Kitchen Planning*:

PLATINUM SPONSORS

WWW.FISHERPAYKEL.COM

WWW.FRANKE.COM

WWW.JENNAIR.COM

WWW.MASCO.COM

GOLD SPONSORS

DORNBRACHT

KWC

About the National Kitchen & Bath Association

As the only nonprofit trade association dedicated exclusively to the kitchen and bath industry, the National Kitchen & Bath Association (NKBA) is the leading source of information and education for all professionals in the field.

The NKBA's mission is to enhance members' success and excellence, promote professionalism and ethical business practices, and provide leadership and direction for the kitchen and bath industry worldwide.

A nonprofit trade association with more than 50,000 members in North America and overseas, it has provided valuable resources for industry professionals for more than 50 years. Its members are the finest professionals in the kitchen and bath industry.

The NKBA has pioneered innovative industry research, developed effective business management tools, and set groundbreaking design standards for safe, functional, and comfortable kitchens and baths.

The NKBA provides a unique, one-stop resource for professional reference materials, seminars and workshops, distance-learning opportunities, marketing assistance, design competitions, consumer referrals, employment and internship availabilities, and opportunities to serve in leadership positions.

Recognized as the kitchen and bath industry's education and information leader, the NKBA provides development opportunities and continuing education for professionals of all levels of experience. More than 200 classes, as well as a certification program with three internationally recognized levels, help kitchen and bath professionals raise the bar for excellence.

For students entering the industry, the NKBA offers Accredited and Supported Programs, which provide NKBA-approved curriculum at more than 50 learning institutions throughout the United States and Canada.

The NKBA helps members and other industry professionals stay on the cutting edge of an ever-changing field through the Association's Kitchen & Bath Industry Show (KBIS®), one of the largest trade shows in the country.

The NKBA offers membership in 11 different industry segments: dealers, designers, manufacturers and suppliers, multibranch retailers and home centers, decorative plumbing and hardware, manufacturer's representatives, builders and remodelers, installers, fabricators, cabinet shops, and distributors. For more information, visit NKBA.org

Table of Contents

Acknowledgments

The NKBA gratefully acknowledges the following Peer Reviewers of this book:

Becky Sue Becker, CKD, CBD
Len Casey
Carolyn Cheetham, CMKBD
Dee David, CKD, CBD
Denise Dick, CMKBD
Kathleen Donohue, CMKBD
Pietro A. Giorgi, Sr., CMKBD
Jerome Hankins, CKD
Mark Karas, CMKBD
Martha Kerr, CMKBD
Corey Klassen, AKBD
David Newton, CMKBD
Michael Palkowitsch, CMKBD
Al Pattison, CMKBD
John Petrie, CMKBD
Les Petrie, CMKBD
Betty Ravnik, CMKBD
Klaudia Spivey, CMKBD
Thomas D. Trzcinski, CMKBD
Deleigh Van Deursen, CKD, CBD
Lilley Yee, CKD, CBD

Preface

Kitchens continue to change as new products are introduced to the market, new regulations affect energy and water consumption, and people change in their abilities, cooking preferences, and lifestyles. Therefore, a book on kitchen design needs to be updated periodically, and that is what the National Kitchen and Bath Association (NKBA) has undertaken in conjunction with Wiley publishing. Some of the changes include expanded information on sustainability and environmental issues and more information about universal design, including applications for a variety of users.

In this revised edition, we have maintained an organization similar to that of the original edition. We start with an overview of the history of the kitchen, including the history of research that has been conducted about the design of the kitchen. We also discuss current consumer trends.

We then continue with information about the infrastructure of the home and point out things to consider before the design process begins. The revised section on environmental concerns includes great information on building green and conserving water.

We next approached the design of the kitchen with the understanding that a key component of any designed space is the user, so we discuss universal design and ergonomics. Gathering information about the client and their home is a key first step to pulling things together and planning a great kitchen and is included in the next chapter. Sample forms are provided to assist you.

The next section covers kitchen planning principles and presents each of the NKBA Kitchen Planning Guidelines within the context of a step-by-step consideration of the tasks and activities that occur in the centers in the kitchen. Diagrams and illustrations help explain these basics, and information has been added to help you specify cabinets. We also expand on kitchen planning, including sections on dining, butler's pantries, catering kitchens, outdoor kitchens, and outpost kitchens. The next chapter on mechanical planning continues to highlight some of the technical planning requirements related to systems in the kitchen.

An expanded section on universal design and accessible design provides an in-depth look at the NKBA Kitchen Access Standards and discusses how they can be incorporated into designs when required by the client. In addition, we provided ideas for designing spaces related to kitchens, such as planning centers, laundries, craft, hobby, and social areas. We also walk you through the process of developing the kitchen plan, based on client needs and planning guidelines.

We organized and presented this book as if we were talking to a new designer, just starting a career. At the same time, we offered information, ideas, suggestions and tips for the more experienced kitchen designer. We firmly believe we can all learn something new—as we certainly did in revising this book!

We included many drawings, diagrams, and dimensioned plans to aid you in understanding the concepts presented. We added and updated many photographs to show how the content is integrated into "real-life" settings and to spark ideas of your own.

There are many worksheets and checklists to use in your work and with your clients. Feel free to use them as is or to adapt them to be useful to you.

Our goal and hope continues to be that this book will help you to be a better designer—more creative and more knowledgeable. This is not the type of book that you read cover to cover. It is a book to be used!

We hope that we find this book on a shelf near your drawing board or computer. We hope this book will be in your studio, office, or showroom—wherever you are at your creative best. We envision a book that gets worn from your use, with your comments written in the margin and "sticky notes" coming out in all directions.

Enjoy design and making people comfortable and safe in their homes!

Kitchen History, Research, and Trends

The kitchen and its place in family life have changed throughout history in conjunction with the evolving lifestyles, economic conditions, values, and attitudes of its users. The overall look, feel, location, and relative importance of the kitchen in the home have been emblematic not only of the era, but also of the particular circumstances of the families they served.

So a brief walk through the history of kitchens will help the designer understand the ever-changing and complex interconnection between this room and the various roles it plays in domestic life. Research conducted by various groups has provided valuable guides for designing efficient, functional, and accessible kitchens. As the demographics and attitudes of our society change, so will the kitchen, to keep up with the needs of the users.

Learning Objective 1: Describe how evolving lifestyles have affected trends over time.

Learning Objective 2: Explain how kitchen design research has contributed to the NKBA Planning Guidelines.

A BRIEF HISTORY OF THE KITCHEN

The history of the modern kitchen begins with the need for a place of family food preparation, usually centered on a source of heat and light, which was the hearth (fireplace). This source has changed over time, but for ages the open fire in a hearth reigned supreme. It also served as the sole heat source for the home until late in the seventeenth century. This meant that most family living and activities took place in the one room that contained the fireplace.

The first known kitchen separated from the living area was in thirteenth-century Flanders, along the coast of what is now Belgium. Flemish kitchens contained tables on trestles for food preparation. Horizontal boards placed above the table provided a place to store kitchen utensils. These storage elements developed into display dressers used in fifteenth-century Flanders, where the number of shelves on the dresser was an indicator of social rank. Many of these concepts were eventually brought to North America and incorporated into the early colonial kitchens.

The Colonial Kitchen

The colonists in North America brought many ideas for kitchen design from Europe. Although eventually established as a separate room in many homes, the early colonial kitchen was equipped with perhaps the only heat source in the home, a hearth, and it served as the focus of the family activity. Because it was the most comfortable room in the home, the kitchen was often used for family bathing as well.

Role of the Hearth in the Eighteenth-Century Kitchen

The typical eighteenth-century kitchen was large, and often included a 6-foot wide and 4-foot deep walk-in fireplace (Figure 1.1). The fireplace contained massive wrought andirons with racks for toasting bread, spits for cooking meats, and iron hooks for pots, which were transferred into and out of the fire with lug poles. Beehive ovens were built into the sidewall of the hearth and were used for baking. A trestle table or bench, a storage chest, a corner cupboard, and occasionally a separate worktable were included in the kitchen. These early kitchens were dirty, inefficient, and unsafe, especially for the cook. Long skirts would brush up against the hot embers in the fireplace and catch on fire, and as a result, burns became the second most common cause of death among women, second only to childbirth.

In wealthier households, the kitchen was used only by servants and was often located on the lower level or in a separate building. A summer kitchen—common in the warmer southern colonies, where the heat from cooking was not desirable during warm weather—often consisted of a lean-to or annex to the main house, which kept extra heat out of the house. Eventually, the fireplaces developed a separate chimney, which helped exhaust the excess heat and allowed cooking during hot weather without heating up the house.

Later in the century, wood and coal cast iron stoves, which enclosed the fire and transferred heat through the metal became available. These stoves were less of a fire hazard but provided less heated area for cooking. Benjamin Franklin designed one such stove, which was built to fit into the fireplace.

Most kitchens of the period were enclosed with unadorned wood panels, but by the second quarter of the eighteenth century, paint was used—more as a preservative than for decorative purposes. As paint became more popular, stenciling, marbling, and graining techniques were used on walls, woodwork, and cabinetry to add a decorative touch to the once plain kitchen.

FIGURE 1.1 Colonial kitchens were not only messy places in which to work, but they were also dangerous because the cook was so close to the embers used for cooking.

Photo by Jack E. Boucher. Library of Congress, Prints and Photographs Division, Historic American Buildings Survey or Historic American Engineering Record, HABS VA-1422-7 (CT)

The Modern Kitchen

The modern kitchen has been influenced by two major trends that roughly coincide with the nineteenth and twentieth centuries. The nineteenth century brought industrialization with social and technological changes. In the twentieth century, standardization surfaced with a focus on work simplification and efficiency.

Houses and the kitchens associated with them changed as the country evolved into an industrialized nation. During this time, numerous new products were developed, and the role of women and family life was redefined. In addition, democracy, joined with the industrial age and the rising middle class, discouraged the formation of a permanent servant class, so live-in household help was less available or often not reliable. This meant that the woman of the home had to take on many new roles and activities to manage the house and its occupants.

The Victorian Kitchen

The nineteenth century brought the Victorian era, which coincides with the reign of Queen Victoria of the United Kingdom between 1839 and 1901. Victorian kitchens were large and often located in the rear of the house or the basement. Many homes of the wealthy included a summer kitchen behind the main kitchen, and the family often had servants to perform most of the cooking and household chores. The early Victorian kitchens were not very highly decorated and their walls were simply covered with institutional green or cream-colored enamel paint. Later, the kitchen included wainscoting, plate racks, and glass-door cabinets, but the appearance and efficiency of the kitchen was not the focus of the home. These kitchens were not very comfortable or convenient to work in.

The range, sink, and table in the Victorian kitchen were all freestanding pieces. Gas stoves eventually became available, but many cooks still preferred the wood- or coal-burning stoves (Figure 1.2). These large stoves were kept hot 24 hours a day to provide continuous hot water, instant heat for cooking and baking, a place for flat irons, and space to keep a kettle ready for hot tea. In later kitchens, the pantry, located between the kitchen and dining room, contained large, wall-to-wall and floor-to-ceiling stationary cabinets that served as both a storage area and a preparation area.

FIGURE 1.2 Gas and water are introduced into kitchens that are made up of a hodgepodge of mismatched components.
Courtesy of Keith Clark, Hamilton, Ontario, Canada

These oak "pantry dressers" housed china behind glass doors on the top, with counters and usually a sink below.

The Beecher Kitchen

Recognition that kitchens were not very functional and that servantless households were now the norm led to the work of pioneers in the field of kitchen design during the Victorian period. By 1869, Catherine Beecher and her sister, Harriet Beecher Stowe, a noted author and abolitionist, had written a book, *The American Woman's Home*, which made recommendations for addressing all the concerns of women at the time. The kitchen they advocated used a ship's galley as the model. It featured work centers and used the latest technologies. Storage was close by and compartmentalized. Open shelving was shallow to allow only one row of food items, and bins for flour and other products were planned into the design (Figure 1.3). Two work centers were present in the room for storage/preservation and cooking/serving. The cooking stove stood away from the work areas, while the other area incorporated work surfaces and shelves (Figure 1.4). Windows provided natural light, and painted walls and floors were easier to clean. They recommended placing the pantry between the kitchen and dining room to keep out noise and heat. These recommendations led to the development of kitchens that were a vast improvement over the colonial and Victorian kitchens.

The Plumbed Sink

The development of water and sewer systems in the larger cities began to change the way households functioned. Early in the nineteenth century, the kitchens contained a dry sink, but eventually households were able to hand-pump water, and then the plumbed sink appeared late in the century. The Beecher sisters' model kitchen used a plumbed faucet to distribute water. By the late nineteenth century, campaigns to improve health conditions promoted the idea of cleanliness and sanitation in the home. The ability to obtain water and remove wastewater was critical to this development. Much of the emphasis on kitchen design and materials, too, was focused on sanitation and cleanliness, and innovations and developments during the industrial revolution provided the necessary products.

The food preparation equipment of the 1800s began to reflect the emerging industrial revolution, and goods were designed with more utility and variety. These products were mass produced and made available to the emerging middle class through mail order catalogs.

FIGURE 1.3 Catherine Beecher's intelligent kitchen design.

Beecher and Stowe 1869

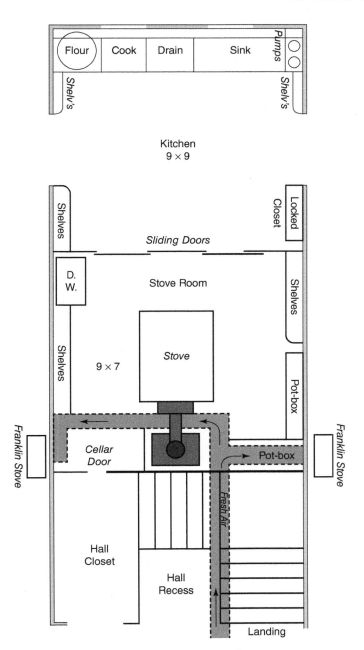

FIGURE 1.4 Here is one example of the Beecher kitchen plan that places the cooking stove in a separate room from the kitchen work area.

Beecher and Stowe 1869

The Beecher sisters encouraged the use of technology to simplify tasks and actually designed a stove that would accomplish multiple tasks efficiently. By the late 1800s, electrification was possible in many locations, but electric rates were not affordable, and most homes were not wired until the next century.

Standardization: The 1900s

Several societal, economic, and technological factors influenced the path of American women and the design of the home at the beginning of the twentieth century. The expansion of industrial jobs resulted in the reduced availability of household labor. Less help in the home was compounded in the 1930s by the economic constraints of the Great Depression. These factors, along with the introduction of improved appliances, led to the designing of more efficient kitchens that were reduced in both size and cost to accommodate the household's head cook, the housewife.

Home economists and others were involved in helping to research and study the equipment and work center concepts and in sharing this information with consumers. Many times labeled "efficiency experts," these home economists studied housework and designed more efficient kitchens with built-in cabinets and abundant storage. These kitchen designs also focused on sanitation for food preparation. More about the development of kitchen design recommendations is presented in the next section on research.

The Laboratory Look

The new kitchens of the era, with their continuous workspace and closed storage, looked very much like a laboratory designed for one person. The concept relied on standardized components that could be bought and added from end to end to produce a kitchen of the desired length. With continuous base cabinets, a sink, and built-in wall cabinets above, these new kitchens began to resemble the former serving pantries. The popularity and demand for the assembled kitchen concept led to growth in the mass production of building materials and kitchen cabinets. The location of the kitchen, however, was still often at the back of the house, isolated from other activity areas of the home.

With electrification came the full mechanization of appliances, which allowed them to be built into the working surfaces as an integral part of this assembled kitchen. These new appliances were unfamiliar to most housewives, and in an effort to sell more electricity and familiarize housewives with the operation of these appliances, utility companies employed individuals who would go into homes to demonstrate the new appliances, as well as provide public programs and educational brochures to explain the new devices. With the increased use of these kitchen appliances, many university researchers were instrumental in studying their efficiency, accuracy, safety, and usage.

Many kitchen-planning guidelines were developed, based on the analysis of kitchen work tasks that recommended counter space and storage requirements. The work triangle concept was developed to provide an efficient arrangement of preparation, serving, and clean-up centers. It utilized the sink, range, and refrigerator to form the centers for an efficient kitchen space. The U-shaped, L-shaped, corridor, and one-wall kitchen were all layouts that could utilize the work triangle concept.

The new modern kitchen perhaps began in suburbia, where the family- and child-centered lifestyle made the kitchen into a place for family interaction. It started to become the hub of home activity, with greater attention being paid to not only usage but also aesthetics. The segregated kitchen of the past was now opening up to other rooms, including the dining and living areas. Designers today are creating kitchens that are efficient and pleasant to work in, and reflect the lifestyle needs of the household. The kitchen has truly become the "hub" of the home.

KITCHEN DESIGN RESEARCH

Creating functional kitchen storage and counter workspaces has been the focus of educators and designers for decades. As early as 1869, Catherine Beecher and her sister, Harriett Beecher Stowe, were making recommendations for homemaking, including how to plan an efficient kitchen (Beecher & Stowe 1869). Their plans included work centers and efficient storage ideas. Around 1912, home economist Christine Frederick was concerned with the efficiency of the home and published articles about home tasks in the *Ladies' Home Journal*. She borrowed the work principles of the factory and applied them to tasks in the home. This analysis of housework moved Christine Frederick to propose kitchen plans that would improve work efficiency (Frederick 1913). In the1930s, motion expert Lillian Gilbreth studied the number of steps necessary to prepare meals within certain kitchen arrangements. She felt that appliance manufacturers knew little about the needs of housewives in the kitchen. As a result of these early studies related to work efficiency, storage, and energy, recommendations for well-planned kitchens were developed.

Early Studies

Some of the earliest known research was conducted by home economists at state universities who were funded by the U.S. Department of Agriculture's Agricultural Experiment Station (AES) to investigate ways to improve rural housing conditions. Findings from their studies were often published in AES Bulletins and then summarized in consumer pamphlets developed by the Cooperative Extension Service. These two agencies together had a large role in developing the first guidelines for the modern kitchen.

A 1932 bulletin by Deane G. Carter reported on several studies of housing that had been conducted by this time. Her work was funded by the AES and the President's Conference on Home Building and Home Ownership. She conducted personal interviews with farm families in Arkansas, reviewed more than 1000 kitchen plans and the catalogs of 20 cabinet manufactures in order to make recommendations for standard cabinet sizes. Some of her recommendations are tied to construction elements. For example, a wall cabinet should be as tall as a standard door height; a kitchen can have a 3-foot-wide work aisle because that allows a door to be placed at the end; counter height should be at the most "commonly preferred height."

In New York, Ella Cushman published several Cooperative Extension bulletins to encourage work efficiency and good household management techniques. Her 1936 bulletin, "The Development of a Successful Kitchen," illustrated numerous ideas that would reduce the time and energy the homemaker spent in the kitchen. In this bulletin, work centers are introduced, work surfaces are at different heights, and cabinets are divided for convenience. The bulletin even illustrated a sink in an island.

By the late 1930s and early 1940s, the work of Maud Wilson began to illustrate a scientific awareness of the study of user needs in kitchen planning. Her analysis, "The Willamette Valley Farm Kitchen" (1938) involved surveys of farm families to determine the size and arrangement of kitchens in the homes of this region of Oregon.

First, the functions of the kitchen and other work areas in the homes were identified, then the equipment and other items used to accomplish the tasks and functions were determined. An analysis was made of the items to group them according to use. Work distances were developed for completing the tasks. Finally, recommendations for the various centers were made according to this analysis. Wilson and Helen McCullough also published the bulletin "A Set of Utensils for the Farm Kitchen" (1940), which encouraged "fewer and better utensils, wisely selected, well cared for, conveniently stored."

By the late 1940s, Maud Wilson developed two reports that focused on the design and placement of kitchen cabinets ("Patterns for Kitchen Cabinets" [1947a] and "Considerations in Planning Kitchen Cabinets" [1947b]) based on her research during the past decade. She recommended workspaces beside the sink and range; various work heights, depending on the task being completed; pull-outs to provide various work heights; and various cabinet arrangements to handle the many different items stored in the kitchen.

Studies at Midcentury

Standards from the 1948 study *Functional Kitchen Storage* (Heiner and McCullough 1948) and the 1949 Small Homes Council (SHC) report, "Cabinet Space for the Kitchen" (McCullough 1949) established the early guidelines for kitchen storage promoted by the Small Homes Council. McCullough (1949) compared the Small Homes Council standards with the Federal Housing Administration (FHA) Minimum Property Standards (MPS). The MPS were based on the number of bedrooms, while the Small Homes Council recommendations were based on family size. Generally, the SHC wall cabinet recommendations were less generous than the MPS, and the base cabinet recommendations were more generous. McCullough cautioned to be sure the MPS were met.

Guides for Arrangement of Urban Family Kitchens

Heiner and Steidel (1951) examined another aspect of kitchen design in their 1951 study of kitchen arrangements. They studied cooks preparing and serving meals and cleaning up in several kitchen arrangements. Some of their findings were: the sink is the most frequently used area (Figure 1.5); the range was second in use, but most often inspected; the mix center was third; and the refrigerator, dining, and serving areas tied for fourth. They recommended keeping work areas together, but cautioned that storage and work areas must be planned into the space.

FIGURE 1.5 Research in the 1950s showed that the sink was the most frequently used area of the kitchen.
Courtesy of Moen

Energy-Saving Kitchen

A study by the Agricultural Research Service of Beltsville, Maryland (Howard 1965), developed and evaluated energy saving kitchen designs. Based on a review of numerous studies of human energy expenditures during cooking activities, three kitchens with three variations each, were developed and built so that cooks could work in them and the arrangements and storage could be studied. The kitchens included seated work areas, carts, and pull-outs, and specially designed storage features, such as revolving base cabinet shelves, slant-front wall cabinets, and floor-to-ceiling open dish storage. The kitchens were demonstrated in magazines and through Cooperative Extension bulletins.

Kitchen Guidelines

During the 1960s, the Small Homes Council continued to issue updated guidelines (Kapple 1964; Wanslow 1965) largely based on the earlier research. They concluded that the optimum kitchen space in a home would depend on a family's belongings and living habits, and be limited by the amount of space available. Thus, multiple standards based on home size (minimum, medium, and liberal) were established according to a wide variety of requirements.

In 1975, NKBA joined the Small Homes Council in issuing the *Kitchen Industry Technical Manual*, Volume 5 (Jones and Kapple 1975), which made recommendations for minimum- and liberal-sized kitchens. The 21 guidelines listed in this publication became the basis for the Certified Kitchen Designer exam. (The technical manuals were issued in a second edition in 1984.)

Kitchen Research in the 1990s

In the early 1990s, NKBA sponsored two research projects that affected their kitchen-planning guidelines. In 1992, Yust and Olsen completed a study entitled *Residential Kitchens: Planning*

Principles for the '90s. They surveyed clients of Certified Kitchen Designers about their kitchens and scored their kitchens based on the 1984 guidelines. A large portion of the kitchens scored poorly, indicating that the guidelines were not reflecting the current trends and needs of kitchen design.

The results of the Yust and Olsen study led NKBA to conduct the Utensil Survey Project (Cheever 1992), the results of which were incorporated into the guidelines used by the kitchen design industry. NKBA's project consisted of:

1. Developing a new core list of items typically found in a North American kitchen
2. Identifying the base/wall cabinet and countertop frontage required to accommodate these items
3. Comparing these new dimensional requirements with the existing information listed in the Small Homes Council *Kitchen Industry Technical Manual*, Volume 5 (Jones and Kapple 1975)
4. Developing new industry standards for acceptable kitchens in two categories: kitchens under 150 square feet and kitchens over 150 square feet

The Cheever study used only 25 households, but it found that the number of items stored in the kitchen had increased 110 percent from the number reported in the research of Heiner and McCullough (1948). The findings from both of these NKBA-sponsored studies resulted in significant changes in the *Kitchen Planning Guidelines* in 1992. The guidelines were updated again in 1996 to incorporate universal design recommendations. Although many space requirements changed, the basic recommendations for the amount and type of storage did not change from the 1992 NKBA recommendations (Cheever 1996).

Virginia Tech Kitchen Research

As the NKBA began to review guidelines in 2000, they recognized a need to reexamine kitchen use and storage requirements. The first study, *Someone's in the Kitchen* (Emmel, Beamish, and Parrott 2001), was actually a combination of several studies: content analysis, interviews, and observations of cooking activities, and a national telephone survey. The second study, *Kitchen Storage Research Study* (Parrott, Beamish, and Emmel 2003) was an inventory of items kept in recently designed kitchens.

Someone's in the Kitchen
The project had the following objectives:

1. To identify the types of foods, utensils, appliances, and products that are stored and used in today's kitchens
2. To identify activities which occur in today's kitchens
3. To determine how kitchen storage and counter space are utilized and organized
4. To classify different styles of food preparation and patterns of kitchen activities
5. To analyze work center and work flow guidelines in relation to the styles of food preparation and patterns of kitchen activities
6. To evaluate current criteria governing the use of cabinets and other storage devices in the kitchen to determine if they meet the needs of today's households

The research project designed to address these objectives had three segments: a content analysis of shelter magazines, a personal interview and cooking activity, and a national random telephone survey.

Content Analysis
One method for evaluating the design and components of contemporary kitchens is to analyze the kitchens featured in popular magazines. From a six-month period in 2000, 19 different shelter-, design-, and kitchen-related magazines were reviewed. A total of 104 articles were analyzed. The findings revealed information about kitchen design features, appliances, and activities, as well as the lifestyle of the households using the kitchens. Islands and wall ovens were two of the most common features. The content analysis provided insight into contemporary kitchen design and usage, important to formulating the interview and telephone survey questions.

Personal Interview and Cooking Activity

A two-phase laboratory activity was developed to assess how families use kitchen space. A personal interview gathered information about the participants' household, food shopping, and food preparation patterns and their present kitchen and its use related to storage, counter space, and appliances. A cooking activity was designed to assess how individuals used kitchen space while preparing a set menu of foods that represented different types of cooking activities. Demographic and anthropometrical data were also collected.

The sample for the laboratory activity was drawn from the local area of Virginia Tech. A purposive sample of males and females of varying heights, ages, and abilities, as well as different household types and cooking partners, was selected. The target sample size was calculated based on 75 menu preparations, but the total number of participants was greater because of multiple cooks sharing some preparation activities.

There were five different menus prepared in the cooking activity. Three different kitchens in the Center for Real Life Kitchen Design at Virginia Tech were used to provide variety. All cooking activities were videotaped for later analysis.

National Telephone Survey

A national telephone survey was conducted to further investigate patterns of kitchen use. The 52-question instrument gathered information about food buying, appliance usage, and cooking patterns, as well as activities that take place in the kitchen. Demographic information about participants was also collected. The survey employed a random sampling design, using a national sampling firm. Telephone interviews, approximately 16 minutes in length, were completed with 630 adults over age 18. The interviews provided a representative sample of adults residing in households in the contiguous United States with a margin of error of ± 3.9 percent at the 95 percent level of confidence.

Results and Implications

The local and national samples in these studies were similar in their demographic make-up. A majority of the respondents in both samples (over 90 percent) were from households of fewer than four people. The most common types of households were a family or adult couple. Both samples included more females than males, within a wide variety of age and income brackets. Approximately 75 percent of each sample lived in single-family residences they owned. There was not a dominance of any particular age or size of residence. The national sample was equally divided among small town, rural, city, and suburban residences.

The researchers found that kitchens are busy places, with frequent cooking and many other household activities (Figure 1.6). Key conclusions from the study can be grouped according to the following questions: What do people do in their kitchens? Who is cooking? How do people cook? What do people have in their kitchen? and What do people want in their kitchens?

What Do People Do in Their Kitchens?
- People cook on a regular and frequent basis, especially in family or couple households. For example, over 70 percent of the national sample prepared a meal five or more times a week.
- People cook, eat, socialize, manage their household, and engage in recreational activities in their kitchens. Around 80 percent talked on the telephone and took medicines and vitamins. Over 70 percent planned meals in the kitchen and had conversations with friends and families.
- Many activities in the kitchen require counter or table space and seating. Multiple people may be in the kitchen, involved in various activities, even if they are not all participating in cooking activities.
- Eating in the kitchen is a common activity (almost two thirds of participants), and most people consider it important to have an eating area in the kitchen. Even people who do not regularly eat in the kitchen consider an eating area important.

Who Is Cooking?
- The most common cooking pattern, in 67 percent of households in the national phone survey, was for one person to do most of the cooking. However, other people may be in the kitchen during food preparation.

FIGURE 1.6 Despite take-out and restaurant meals, researchers have found that people still cook on a regular and frequent basis.
Courtesy of GE

- When there are two cooks in the household, they are more likely to take turns cooking or follow the teacher-student model of cooking. Only a small minority of households (13 percent in the national sample) has members that actually cook together. This trend was reported in both the national phone survey and personal interview with the local sample, as well as being observed during the laboratory cooking activity.
- Two cook patterns of preparation observed in the cooking activity were the teacher-student model and the independent cook model. In the teacher-student model, two cooks stood side by side to work on one task together. The independent cooks worked on separate tasks in separate areas.
- Singles cook less frequently and use their kitchens less than other types of households.

How Do People Cook?

- The microwave oven is a major cooking appliance and is used frequently. For example, 63 percent of the local sample reported using their microwave oven as much or more than the range/cooktop. The microwave oven becomes a central point in the flow of work in the kitchen and adjacent counter space is frequently used for food preparation.

- The sink is also a major focal point for food preparation. People in the laboratory cooking activity used the counter space adjacent to the sink for a variety of food preparation activities as well as for cleanup.
- Most people use and need a generous amount of counter space. Cooks observed in the laboratory typically had a primary and a secondary preparation area. Extra counter space was needed to assemble ingredients.
- The trash is frequently accessed during food preparation. People in the laboratory cooking activity wanted the trash to be centrally located, and easily accessible, preferably under or immediately adjacent to the sink. In addition, many people (approximately one third of the national sample) are storing recyclables in the kitchen.
- Hand dishwashing of at least some items is frequent, especially in smaller households (Figure 1.7). As an example, over half of the local sample did some hand dishwashing daily. Pre-rinsing dishes in the sink, before loading the dishwasher, was common to almost all study participants.

FIGURE 1.7 Hand-washing some dishes at the sink is still a frequent activity, research has shown.

Courtesy of Moen

- The types of food preparation activities were diverse. Preparing food from scratch, baking, and grilling outdoors were the most frequently cited types of cooking. Food preparation activities that were more complex or required special ingredients, techniques, or equipment were less frequent.
- Most people are frequent users of fresh produce. In the national sample, the frequent users of fresh produce were more than twice the number who were frequent users of canned or frozen produce.
- Use of convenience foods was less than might be expected. Close to one half of both samples indicated that they rarely, if ever, use boxed or frozen convenience foods.
- Also surprising was the fact that most people are only occasional users of carryout food, with over 40 percent of the national sample reporting that they "rarely" or "never" use carryout food.

What Do People Have in Their Kitchens?

- Almost every household has a refrigerator, range, and microwave oven in their kitchen.
- Dishwashers and garbage disposers are common in kitchens.
- Built-in ovens and cooktops are found in only a minority of kitchens.
- People have many small appliances (an average of 12 per household), and use some of them frequently. Some small appliances are stored on countertops (four is typical), but many people have to store them outside of the kitchen as well.
- Pantry or tall storage closets are found in over half the kitchens and are considered desirable.
- People store many items on their kitchen counters, only some of which are food preparation tools. Participants in the local sample had an average of seven items stored on their countertops, in addition to the small appliances reported above.

What Do People Want in Their Kitchens?

- People generally express satisfaction with their kitchens, even if they want improvements. People who had input into their kitchen designs, or have had an opportunity to remodel their kitchens, are more satisfied.
- Many people do not "fit" their kitchens. Some people have trouble reaching wall cabinets; others find shelves in base cabinets difficult to access. Standard counter heights may be too high or too low. Better, more accessible, and more efficient storage in the kitchen is a frequently expressed need (Figure 1.8).
- If people had a chance to improve their kitchens, they simply want MORE—more space, more storage, more cabinets, and more counter space. Efficiency and organization are also considered desirable.

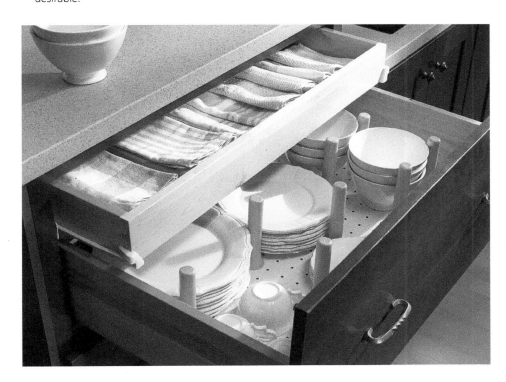

FIGURE 1.8 Research has shown that consumers want more storage, efficiency, and organization in their kitchens.

Courtesy of Diamond Cabinets

Kitchen Storage Research Project
A second Virginia Tech study was conducted to help develop further background for revised kitchen storage guidelines. The purpose of this study was to investigate the number and type of items kept in recently designed kitchens and to determine the amount of shelf and drawer storage needed to store these items effectively.

Kitchen Inventory
An inventory survey instrument was developed to record information about items stored and used in residential kitchens. The instrument included questions about demographic and housing information, kitchen activities, and cooking patterns. A lengthy checklist of items stored in the kitchen was developed to identify the number, location, and frequency of use of the stored items. The inventory checklist listed 550 different items in 16 different categories, plus major appliances.

NKBA cooperated in the study by asking all Certified Kitchen Designers to volunteer to interview recent clients and conduct an inventory of their kitchens. Designers were asked to conduct an interview with a client that had a small kitchen and one that had a large kitchen. The interviews often required several hours to complete. The surveys were conducted in the winter and spring of 2003.

A total of 87 usable inventory surveys were returned. Of these, 81 percent of the respondents prepared five or more meals per week and most often, one person did the cooking (76 percent). The respondents often took medicine in the kitchen (64 percent), did major shopping once a week (63 percent), prepared food from scratch (56 percent), and planned meals in the kitchen (56 percent).

Three kitchen sizes were used in analyzing the data: small kitchen (150 square feet or less) – n = 31, medium kitchen (151–350 square feet) – n = 31, and large kitchen (over 350 square feet) – n = 24. The number of items stored in the kitchen increased with the size of the kitchen. There were an average of 655 items in the small kitchen, 820 items in the medium kitchen, and 1019 items in the large kitchen. As the kitchen size increased, people tended to have both a greater variety of items and multiples of the same items.

Measuring for Storage Needs
After tabulating the surveys, and identifying items stored in 25 percent or more of the kitchens, examples of these items were gathered and arranged in a 12-inch deep x 12-inch high linear mock-up space. This mock-up was used to calculate the amount of storage required for the 16 categories of items and for the total amount of storage needed in the kitchen. The mock-ups with items were photographed. Calculations were made to determine the amount of wall, base, drawer, pantry, counter, and miscellaneous storage needed in the various-sized kitchens.

The total number of linear storage inches required was: 1141 inches in the small kitchen, 1376 inches in the medium kitchen, and 1552 inches in the large kitchens. Storing food required the most space. Other items requiring significant amounts of storage were small appliances, preparation items, small utensils, pots and pans, and baking ware.

Small kitchens had noticeably fewer dishes, baking ware, and bulk storage items, while small and medium kitchens had fewer pots and pans and storage containers than large kitchens. Medium and large kitchens required similar amounts of storage for the following: small appliances, preparation items, baking ware, dishes, flatware, management/home office supplies, and miscellaneous items. Large kitchens needed more storage for food, pots and pans, and serving pieces than the other sized kitchens. Kitchens of all sizes had similar requirements for linens.

Most storage was located in base cabinets, followed by drawer storage, wall cabinets, pantry storage, and counter space. Food, glasses and drinking items, dishes, and serving pieces were most likely stored in wall cabinets. Small utensils, flatware, linens, and management/home office supplies were more likely kept in drawers. Pots and pans were also kept in drawers, especially in large kitchens. Pantries stored food and bulk items. About one fourth of the small appliances were kept on the counter, as well as small utensils, serving pieces, cleaning supplies, management/home office supplies, and miscellaneous items. The amount of counter space used for storage was greatest in the small kitchen where there were fewer storage options. Miscellaneous storage included open shelves, carts, tables, furniture, and wall cabinets above the standard cabinet height.

Implications

Information from this study was used to calculate recommendations for storage. The Kitchen Planning Guidelines discussed in Chapter 6 reflect the findings from the study. The major change calls for the designer to prescribe storage based on a linear shelf/drawer frontage, rather than wall and base cabinet requirements. The new guidelines provide designers with flexibility to plan storage that is both accessible and located where needed. The recommendations are based on kitchen size.

MAJOR KITCHEN TRENDS THROUGH THE 2000s

Throughout the twentieth century, kitchen design evolved rapidly as lifestyles changed, and new products and technologies were developed. Elements of some of these designs are now being revived and adapted for today's kitchens. Following are some of the highlights of kitchen design from the early 1900s to the twenty-first century.

Early 1900s

Simple design: Kitchens were decorated and furnished in a simple manner. Domestic scientists of the time described the kitchen as a gleaming, light-colored laboratory.

Cabinets added: Around the turn of the century a desire and need for more efficient storage appeared and cabinets that did exist were hung high on the wall. Two new types of wooden cabinets appeared: the broom cabinet and the "linen" cabinet. The latter was used to store foodstuffs like cereals and canned goods. Sheet metal cabinets promoted by the metal industry replaced wooden cabinets. These cabinets came to be known as the "Youngstown" cabinets.

The Hoosier: The baking table evolved into a self-contained, upright cabinet work center with all the needed tools for baking. The "Hoosier" (or "Dutch") cabinets, which typically came in oak or painted white enamel, were marketed by manufacturers located mostly in northern Indiana. The list of manufacturers included such names as G. P. McDougall & Sons, Kompass & Stoll Co., the Hoosier Manufacturing Co., Coppes Brothers, and Zook.

Cork flooring: Armstrong Cork Company began production of cork floor tile in 1904 in a limited number of colors. Cork usage declined in the 1930s.

New stoves: For many homes, the fireplace was still the heat source for cooking and heating in the early 1900s. It was soon replaced, however, by coal- and wood-burning stoves and almost immediately followed by gas and kerosene stoves, as well as combination gas and coal ranges.

Electric appliances: Although a prototype of the electric kitchen was exhibited in 1893, the electric stove did not move into the kitchen until 1909. This cooking surface without a flame was quite the novelty to many. By 1915, thermostats made electric and gas stoves "automatic."

Electric lighting: Families with electric lighting were the envy of the neighborhood. If power was available, the lighting typically consisted of a bare, shadeless bulb hanging from the middle of the room on a cloth-covered cord.

The 1920s

Multi-room kitchens: The kitchens of the 1920s (Figure 1.9) were a series of awkwardly connected, dark spaces removed from the family activities with little consideration given to the cook's view. It included as many as three small rooms used for various purposes. Most cabinets and appliances were white, often giving the appearance of a sanitized laboratory.

Variety of countertops: Pine, oak, maple, and fir were favorite countertop materials. Wood was also used as a drain board for the sink. Once tile, steel, and laminate became fashionable, consumers quickly switched from wood.

FIGURE 1.9 Kitchens in the 1920s typically included an electric range with storage and cooking surface, a dish cupboard, and console sink.

Photo by Morris Rosenfeld, NY. Library of Congress, Prints and Photographs Division Washington, D.C. 20540 USA, LC-USZ62-54770

Farmhouse kitchen: The farmhouse kitchen typically included a Hoosier cabinet, lots of open shelves, a pantry, dish cupboard, freestanding range, console sink, and large kitchen table. Countertops and work surfaces were usually covered with enameled sheet metal or linoleum. In some homes, Hoosier or other built-in baking cabinets covered an entire wall. The Hoosier was gone by the 1940s.

Domain for servants: In the homes of the wealthy, the kitchen was the domain of servants. A trash disposal chute, foldout ironing board, bell indicator, and intercom system became part of the more sophisticated kitchens.

Sinks: Cast iron sinks were the most popular, along with earthenware sinks, which were enameled white on the inside and glazed brown on the exterior. Some sinks of the 1920s were made of a copper/nickel mix called Monel, a lightweight, white metal.

Appliances: Appliances of the era included an icebox, gas stove, and the new motor-driven wringer washer. Between 1925 and 1927 ranges came in colors, including black, white, red, green, buff, blue, and gray.

Decorative kitchen: In the late 1920s, the kitchen was first included in the decorative scheme of the home, creating colorful rooms for living and not just working.

Color schemes: Color in the kitchen was attributed to two legendary merchandisers: Abraham & Straus and Macy's. From the 1920s into the 1930s, cobalt blue and silver color schemes were very popular. Black and white with pale tones of yellow and blue were also used. A yellow wall with a double band of blue just under the ceiling molding was one combination.

Linoleum floors: Floors were most often covered with sheet linoleum or linoleum tiles, usually in a black-and-white checkered pattern. Colors also ranged from beige and brown to brilliant scarlet and navy blue. Patterns included Art Deco, Modern, and Colonial Revival. Embossed inlaid linoleum became available in 1925. In 1927, the Formica Company developed its first light-colored faux-wood-grain laminate.

Tudor styling: The Tudor style was popular and included stonework, wood paneling, carvings, decorative moldings, and wooden beams.

Monitor top refrigerator: The first all-steel refrigerator had furniture-like legs for aesthetic purposes, as well as being easier to clean under. The GE Monitor top was built in 1926 and cost

$525. The round-top design was named after the Monitor submarine. In 1929, Kelvinator turned the design into a box with no legs and a concealed compressor.

Accessories: Common kitchen accessories included the electric toaster, coffeepot, Bakelite-handled cutlery, and Clarice Cliff's "Bizarre" line of ceramics.

The 1930s

Work-centered kitchen design: A "typical" 1930s kitchen featured porcelain-topped kitchen worktables and a Hoosier cabinet. An "atypical" kitchen of the time featured the boxy, built-in cabinetry. The built-in, "continuous kitchen" design, with its sequence of workstations and unbroken activity flow, resembled the production line of the modern factory. This highly organized kitchen, beginning in 1935, was known as the "streamlined kitchen." The kitchen began to resemble a scientist's lab more than the heart of the home. Westinghouse ads showed kitchens with three designated work centers: refrigeration and preparation center, range and serving center, and sink and dishwasher center. The breakfast nook was in vogue.

Steel cabinets: Later in the decade, wall-to-wall white steel cabinets, as well as standardized prefab wooden cabinets, were backed by rectangular white tile on the walls. New Porta-Bilt built-in cabinets promoted the idea of being able to build in cabinets and then take them with you when you moved.

Tile on countertop: The introduction of nonporous materials for improved sanitation followed the cleanliness movement taking place in the bathroom. Countertops used oversized hexagonal tiles in olive green, black, and beige. Another look was the white and/or pale yellow 4-inch square tiles on diagonal with accent trim in black, dark blue, green, or maroon.

Black and white floor tile: Black and white tile remained a standard on floors. Linoleum continued to be installed in sheet and tile forms, and tile designs combining different colors began to increase in popularity.

Vinyl flooring: Vinyl made its debut as vinyl/asbestos called Vinylite, but was not widely marketed until the late 1940s.

Center room lighting: Lighting consisted of a single, flush-mount ceiling fixture in the center of the room.

Double sinks: Sinks were large and freestanding. They included a double bowl and drain board.

Pastel colors: Popular colors of the day included Art Deco bright pastels, white, cream, coral red, sky blue, pearl gray, peach, and mint green. Entering a 1930s kitchen, you might see light gray cabinets with light green panels and peach walls.

Modernized appliances: Chromium was widely used on appliances and fixtures. Although the cooling coil-crowned electric refrigerator was available, many households still used the icebox. Chlorofluorocarbon was produced under the name of Freon by DuPont. Electric refrigerators were also shown with legs to allow easy cleaning beneath. Dishwashers were portable and mostly top-loading models. The Tappan "table top" range, a combination of white-enameled range, cupboard, and worktable, was produced. Electric toasters toasted one side of bread at a time. The first electric powered ironer and food waste disposer were introduced.

Accessories: Fiestaware and Harlequin dinnerware were popular kitchen accessories.

The 1940s

Popular colors: Popular colors were white, pale green, light gold, forest green, and gray with maroon accents.

Seamless cabinet look: Kitchens of the era included cabinets that created a seamless, uniform wall of doors and drawers above and below a continuous counter. A range and sink were incorporated into the continuous counter. These modular cabinets were available in painted wood or metal. Custom kitchen cabinets were also marketed.

Variety of materials: Stainless steel became popular for sinks. Linoleum or laminate materials covered the countertops, and linoleum continued to be used on floors. Black-and-white linoleum tile remained popular, but a range of patterns and colors, as well as cork and asbestos tiles, became available after World War II. Vinyl was heavily marketed in the later part of the decade.

Small appliances popular: Appliances in the kitchen included a rounded electric refrigerator, a dishwasher, and an electric range. Auto defrost in refrigerators was developed. In 1947, the Radarange was the first microwave on the market and was used mostly by restaurants and hotels. Disposers, mostly in the batch model, became available. The popularity of small appliances began with the introduction of the electric skillet, blender, and portable mixer.

Accessories: Colonial maple furniture and Priscilla curtains were typical accessories, often in black and white with red accents. Franciscan Dinnerware had its beginning.

The 1950s

Built-in kitchen: New housing of the time formalized the trend for built-in kitchens and often included an informal eating area.

Asbestos and glass: Colorful linoleum reigned supreme until the 1950s, when asbestos and ceramic tiles became the standard. Asphalt-asbestos tile was the most widely used resilient floor covering on the market. Semi-flexible vinyl asbestos tile was also popular. Emerging materials were fiberglass, cast aluminum, acrylics, and resins. Glass became a popular material used in glass-chip terrazzo floors and countertops. Colorful laminates were used on countertops and cabinets.

Factory-built cabinets: Steel cabinets remained popular, but the idea of the factory-built cabinet was born. Merillat Industries and Wood-Metal (now Wood-Mode) cabinet companies were founded, as was the National Institute of Wood Kitchen Cabinets in 1955. (It is now KCMA—The Kitchen Cabinet Manufacturers Association.)

Dramatic colors: Dramatic colors were introduced; among them pink, gray, pastel greens, turquoise, and sky blue.

Self-defrost refrigerators: Refrigerators were large spaceship-like units in bright colors with a top-mount freezer. Bottom freezers were also available, and Amana patented the first self-defrost model in 1954. The first ice maker was introduced in 1953 by Servel and consumed one third of the freezer space. Gas-powered refrigerators were marketed, and GE introduced the "wall refrigerator" to integrate refrigeration with the continuous cabinet look of the kitchen. All cold food storage was now at eye level.

Wall oven: The wall oven was developed, and Tappan produced the first domestic microwave wall oven in 1952. It sold for $1295.

New cleaning appliances: Front-loading, portable dishwashers were developed, followed by built-in models of both the top- or front-loading types. Continuous feed disposers came on the market. In 1953, automatic clothes washer sales topped those of the wringer washer for the first time, and Bendix introduced its Duomatic combination washer/dryer.

Accessories: Accessories included colorful molded plastic furniture with chrome trim, Russel Wright American Modern dinnerware, and Tupperware.

The 1960s

Open kitchen design: Great rooms with an adjacent open kitchen reflected the more casual lifestyle of the time. Although "space age kitchens of the future" were publicized, they were not really taken to heart by consumers.

Pop Art: Pop Art colors, such as acid green, orange, pink, red, yellow, bright blue, black, and white were the look of the 1960s.

No-wax floors: New no-wax, sheet vinyl, and ceramic tile in bright colors and strong patterns covered floors. Brick and wood floors were also used.

Metal cabinets: Furniture designer Paul McCobb designed "Eurostyle" cabinetry with aluminum extruded legs and cabinet dividers from the Mutschler Brothers in the Midwest. Cheerful painted metal cabinets were teamed with laminate surfaces in brightly mixed colors and highly patterned wallpaper.

Self-cleaning oven: In 1963, the self-cleaning oven was developed.

Other appliances: In 1967, Raytheon, after acquiring Amana in 1965, introduced the first countertop microwave oven. By 1969, all built-in dishwashers were of the front-loading type. Chilled water and crushed ice dispensers were now available in refrigerators.

Accessories: Accessories found in the 1960s kitchen were the Smile cookie jar, Pop Art posters, and super graphic Venetian blinds.

The 1970s

Avocado and harvest gold: Colors such as brown, burnt orange, avocado green, and harvest gold were all the rage.

"Euro" cabinets: Dark wood cabinets, as well as cream laminate Euro cabinets with oak trim, were beginning to become popular.

Particleboard: Cabinet companies experimented with wood-like alternatives, and some adopted particleboard for cabinet components. In-cabinet storage accessories, such as the vertical knife holder, were becoming increasingly available.

Energy-efficient appliances: Energy consciousness was imposed because of the oil embargo and the resulting energy crisis. The U.S. government began to look at the energy efficiency of appliances and developed the Energy Guide labels to help consumers find energy-efficient appliances and equipment. Meanwhile, built-in and black glass-front appliances, the trash compactor, the over-the-range microwave oven, and the food processor were introduced. Jenn-Air launched the indoor grill, and microwave oven sales were accelerating.

Solid surface counters: Patterned laminates and butcher block were common on counters. The solid surface counter with integral sink was now available in four colors, which were thought to be the only choices consumers and designers could possibly need. Mylar wallpaper was in style.

Fluorescent lighting: Fluorescent lighting was used to save energy, and track lighting was added for flexibility and to increase the amount of light.

No-wax floors: Floors continue to be covered with no-wax vinyl and ceramic tiles. Indoor/outdoor kitchen carpeting in various patterns appeared in many kitchens.

Accessories: Accessories found in the homes of the 1970s included Styrofoam "wood" beams for the ceiling, Tiffany lamps, and antiques.

The 1980s

Remodeled kitchens: The 1980s were somewhat of a transition period and an era of difficult economic times, high interest rates, and higher energy prices. Because of this, many households were remodeling rather than building and saving costs in their kitchen projects by making cosmetic changes, such as resurfacing cabinets or changing hardware.

The open plan: Kitchens continued to open up into other rooms so that families could spend more time together. The great room became more common. Eating bars on peninsulas became popular as an informal eating space. Some kitchens included islands (Figure 1.10).

Frameless cabinets: Cabinets continued to be influenced by sleek European designs. The Euro-style, frameless cabinet was gaining popularity in the American market. Laminate cabinets with oak trim continued to be in vogue. Appliance garages began to appear. At the opposite end of the spectrum, the 1980s also saw the country look and old-world styling used.

Almond appliances: Neutral and earth tone solid colors with little texture covered surfaces, while almond joined white and black for appliance colors.

FIGURE 1.10 Islands became popular during the 1980s, along with neutral colors.
Courtesy of Wood-Mode, Inc.

Granite countertops: Glass block returned, and granite began to appear on countertops. Overall, solid surface counters gained in popularity. Color-through laminates became available for counter surfaces, and many households chose stainless steel sinks.

Induction cooking: Side-by-side refrigerators, along with ice makers, became the popular style. Trash compactors began to appear in more kitchens, but they never developed into a major trend. The microwave oven became a standard kitchen appliance. Sealed gas burners and halogen heating elements appeared on the market. Induction cooking technology was also available and promoted as the cooking method that would reign supreme, but it never thrived in the North American market.

The 1990s

Large kitchens: Kitchens continued to open up and expand. These larger kitchens accommodated more people and more family activities.

Integrated appliances: Kitchen designs on the upswing included the unfitted kitchen, a look comprised of individual pieces of furniture to replace cabinetry, each serving a specific purpose

FIGURE 1.11 A mix of painted and wood finishes and cabinetry configured to look like unfitted furniture were two style trends that emerged in the 1990s and are still popular today.

Design by NKBA member Julie A. Stoner, CKD, ASID

in the kitchen. Kitchens were also designed with many new shapes and configurations. Islands became highly desirable. The integrated kitchen with hidden major appliances was beginning to emerge.

White cabinetry: White cabinets were widely used, along with the many natural woods, including cherry, oak, maple, and hickory. A combination of painted and natural wood was also popular (Figure 1.11).

Desk work area: Numerous storage and task areas were built into the kitchen cabinetry. Consumers desired a built-in desk or paperwork area in the kitchen.

Under-cabinet lighting: Workspaces were improved with the inclusion of under cabinet lighting to illuminate work surfaces. Low voltage lighting and compact fluorescent lights provided for more flexibility because of their smaller size.

Granite on the rise: Solid surface materials were considered the ultimate in countertops and they were also incorporated into floors and cabinet panels. Granite counters became more common in high-end kitchens.

Universal design: As Baby Boomers looked toward retirement, the idea of incorporating universal design features in their homes gained interest.

Almond to bisque: Almond was a popular appliance color, but it was replaced by a new color called bisque or biscuit. White and black were still strong, with stainless steel emerging.

Drawer appliances: More households installed an additional refrigerator in the kitchen, wet bar, family room, or elsewhere. Drawer configurations were adapted to refrigerators and dishwashers. Warming drawers for residential use came on the market, along with electronic controls.

Professional-style appliances: After a move by consumers to install restaurant-grade appliances into their home, the appliance industry developed professional-style appliances to provide consumers with a safer alternative. For high-end kitchens, the professional look was extremely popular (Figure 1.12).

Retro-look: A return to the look of the 1930s, 1940s, 1950s emerged with retro-styled appliances that contained all of the technologies of modern appliances.

Energy Star: Energy standards demanded that appliance manufacturers design and build models that were increasingly more energy and water efficient. The International Energy Star program began.

FIGURE 1.12 Professional-style appliances were developed in the 1990s and remain popular today.
Courtesy of GE.

The 2000s and Beyond

Hub of the home: Kitchens were becoming larger with the open plan concept and were designed to facilitate a variety of household activities (Figure 1.13). Hobby cooking was a result of popular cooking programs on TV.

Islands a must: Kitchen islands were highly desired and could be designed to include a multitude of kitchen tasks and activities.

Look of furniture: Traditional designs, as well as cabinets and storage that resemble furniture, provided an "unfitted" look to the kitchen. The integrated look remained popular.

Feng Shui: The Asian influence was incorporated through the use of Feng Shui, which created harmony and prosperity in life through the arrangement of their environment.

Multiple appliances: The professional look continued with the liberal use of stainless steel in appliances. A second installation of some appliances in the kitchen provided the necessary equipment for multiple workstations.

Appliance drawers: More appliance manufacturers were incorporating the drawer concept. Speed-cook appliances were offered by more manufacturers.

Three-door refrigerators: The three-door refrigerator was introduced. Water filtration was common and wine refrigerators were found in the kitchen and many other rooms in the home.

Multiple sinks: A smaller salad sink was added in addition to the main sink. Farm sinks were popular, and more sink and faucet shapes were available. Faucets were wall, sink, and counter mounted.

FIGURE 1.13 This kitchen is completely open to a family room area.

Design by NKBA member Gerard Cirrarello, CMKBD

High tech: Appliances incorporated electronic control. Televisions and other electronic devices were common in the kitchen.

Granite: Granite, stainless steel, and tile were used extensively. Natural wood was popular.

Green products: In addition to more energy-efficient appliances, the use of renewable materials such as linoleum, cork, and bamboo was increasing.

Universal design: An increasing number of designers were considering and incorporating universal and/or accessible design into kitchens, especially in kitchens where older adults were present. Universal design included the use of components with varying work heights (Figure 1.14).

FIGURE 1.14 Multiple height counters include an area higher than 36 inches for eating or for workspaces for taller users.

Courtesy of American Woodmark

Multiple kitchens: A second food preparation area was often in an outdoor kitchen or an "outpost" kitchen located in a bedroom suite.

Limited wall cabinets: Fewer wall cabinets allowed for more window area and open floor plans.

Storage: Specialty storage devices came in many configurations, including the popular appliance garage, pot rack, pole storage, backsplash rails, pantries, and drawers.

DEMOGRAPHIC AND POPULATION TRENDS

A study of the demographic and population trends for North America, as well as specific population groups, provides valuable insight into market potential as well as influences on kitchen space use and design. Two major trends emerging are an increasingly more culturally diverse population and a larger number of older people. Another trend of interest would be changes in household composition. All of these affect consumer buying trends, as well as kitchen design considerations.

U.S. Population Growth

The general population of the United States continues to increase, and according to the 2010 census (Mackum and Wilson 2011), it now exceeds 300 million. The population increase from 2000 to 2010 was the third largest in U.S. history, adding 27.3 million people—a 9.7 percent increase. Historically, the highest increase in population was during the "baby boom" years of the 1950s, when the population increased 19 percent, adding 17.5 million people. This current surge in population is often referred to as the "echo-boom" generation (Gen Y), and these are the children of the baby boomers.

Household Growth

Although the general population has increased, household growth has slowed, averaging only 1.12 million households during the 2000s, a full 17 percent below the 1990s according to the 2010 U.S. census (Lofquist et al. 2012). The portion of young adults age 20–24 heading independent households has also dropped by 2.6 percent and for those ages 25–29 by 2.8 percent since 2007. This trend could be very different over the next 15 years, however, as immigration continues and a large percentage of the echo-boom generation (born 1979–2002), numbering around 80.8 million, continue to mature. Even with immigration at only half that rate, the number of these young adults will grow to 86.5 million by 2020 and will produce a higher demand for apartments and smaller starter homes during the next 15 years.

The future of household formation is uncertain. On one hand, the recent drop in home prices and a favorable rental market may encourage more employed individuals to form households of their own. In addition, those doubling up to save expenses are typically in a temporary situation and will eventually seek their own place. On the other hand, the rate of household formation among young adults may continue to decline because of sustained unemployment, home foreclosures, delayed marriage and childbearing, the increased importance of higher education, and the rising cost of going away to college. These young adults will continue to double up or live with their parents.

Not only have the economic and housing situations in the late 2000s decreased household growth, but they have also led to lower mobility. Between 2005 and 2008, overall mobility fell about 12.6 percent with the deepest decline among homeowners (Joint Center for Housing Studies 2010). This trend may continue as financially stressed households find it easier to stay in their current residence rather than experience a financial loss.

Household Composition

Another demographic change that could impact the design market includes changes in household composition as summarized in the 2010 U.S. census (Lofquist et al. 2012). Households are becoming smaller. In 2010, one- and two-person households accounted for more than 63 percent of all households. The share of single-person households rose to 28 percent, with a higher percentage being 65 and older. Married couples, for the first time, represented less than 50 percent of the households (48 percent) and unrelated adults living together made up 6.2 percent. Married couples with children were fewer than 20 percent of all households. The largest change in household composition was an increase in households headed by women without husbands—up 18 percent since 2000.

One other prominent change in households is the return of the multigenerational family household as reported by the Pew Research Center in 2010 (Pew Social Trends Staff 2010). A record 49 million Americans or 16.1 percent of the population in 2008 lived in a household that included at least two adult generations or a grandparent. The rate was only 12 percent in 1980. Multigenerational trends include:

- In 2010, 44.7 percent of the 20–24 year olds who do not live on their own are living with their parents, along with 18 percent of the 25–29 year olds. Since 2005, an additional 1.6 million young adults live at home. Many reasons could account for this increase in adult children living at home, including difficulty with finding a job or launching a career, or they are marrying at an older age. In the 25–34 age group, more men than women are likely to live in multigenerational family households.
- The high rate of immigration since 1970 was dominated by Latin Americans and Asians who are far more inclined to be part of a multigenerational household. Hispanics (22 percent) and Asians (25 percent) are all more likely than whites (13 percent) to be a multigenerational household.
- A significant change in multigenerational composition involves older adults. Once more likely to live in such situations (57 percent of adults 65 and older in 1900), only 17 percent of older adults today live in multigenerational family households because of better health, better financial situations, and better social safety net programs. This number is increasing some in recent years due to the availability of more grown children who are informed caregivers and to recent cuts in Medicare programs. More likely to outlive their spouse, a higher percentage of women are part of this type of household.
- Some 49 million Americans live in a multigenerational family household. Of those, 47 percent are made up of two adult generations of the same family with the youngest adult at least 25 years of age, 47 percent live with three or more generations of family members, and 6 percent belong to a "skipped" generation household with a grandparent and grandchild and no parent.

Different household compositions call for specific design considerations. As designers consider the household for which they are designing, they need to keep in mind the needs specific to that type of household. In some cases, multiple kitchen areas may be warranted to handle the needs of households with multiple generations present.

Population Diversity

According to *The State of the Nation's Housing 2010* (Joint Center for Housing Studies 2010), a publication of the Joint Center for Housing Studies of Harvard University, we continue to see demographic changes because of changes in immigration and the minority populations. Minorities account for 92 percent of the total U.S. population growth between 2000 and 2010, and the growth of the population under the age of 18 was at 1.9 million, driven mostly by racial/ethnic minorities. Immigrants and minorities also account for a large percentage of the household growth in the past decade. Forty-two percent of the echo boom generation is composed of minorities and, over the next 15 years, this diverse generation, along with other minority households, will increase the demand for smaller starter homes, apartments, and remodeling projects. Statistics Canada (2010) places the percentage of visible minority residents in Canada at 16.2 percent (about 5 million people) in 2006, up from 13.4 percent in 2001.

The largest increases for the United States are among Hispanics. Since 2000, the Hispanic population in the United States has increased 43 percent and has doubled since 1990. According to the 2010 U.S. census, there are 50 million Hispanics in the United States, or 1 in every 6 residents and about 16 percent of the population. The U.S. Asian-American population increased

43 percent since 2000, but Asians still make up less than 5 percent of the total population (Humes, Jones, and Ramirez 2010).

Immigration also had a key role in the slowdown in household growth. During the 2000s, not only did the growth of the foreign-born population slow, but the growth of foreign-born households stalled because of the recession. Although the number of households headed by foreign-born citizens increased by about 200,000 from 2004 to 2010, the number of foreign-born noncitizen households declined by the same amount from 2007–2010 (Humes, Jones, and Ramirez 2010).

This increasing diversity means a wider range of lifestyles and design criteria to be considered for clients of varying backgrounds. Out-of-the-ordinary appliances and work patterns may need to be accommodated in their kitchen.

An Aging Population

The 2010 U.S. Census (Werner 2011) places the 65 and older population at 38.6 million, up from 34.9 million in 2000. The U.S. population between ages 65 and 74 is expected to increase 6.5 million over the next decade as more baby boomers reach retirement. The 55 to 64 age group is expected to grow by 3.7 million. Over the next 20 years, the share of 65 and older will rise from 13 percent of the population to 19 percent. Estimates of the Canadian 2011 Census by Statistics Canada (2010) places their 65 and older age group at 14.1 percent of the overall 2011 population number of 34,600,346, with a large portion of the over 65 group living in more rural areas.

Increased life expectancy is credited with some of the increase in this older age group. When the United States was founded, the average American was expected to live to the age of 35, but according to the World Bank, the 2009 life expectancy of U.S. citizens is 78.1 years of age, and it is 80.66 years of age for Canadian citizens.

The State of the Nation's Housing 2010 (Joint Center for Housing Studies, 2010) states that this increasing number of baby boomer retirees has dominated housing market trends for decades and will continue to have a significant impact. As they purchased their first homes and then traded up to bigger better homes, the sheer numbers of individuals in this group has shaped the housing market. Now, as they reach retirement, many are seeking housing to meet their current needs, either by making changes to their current home or by moving to a smaller home.

The number of older homeowners able to move from their current residence has declined sharply in recent years because of the nation's financial crisis, which depressed home equity and reduced retirement income. This trend will open the market for remodeling projects that allow them to "age in place." Those boomers who can relocate tend to downsize to smaller homes with fewer rooms and one-level living.

These demographic trends open up a large market of individuals who will have an increased interest in kitchens that are safe, comfortable, and ergonomically designed, and accessible design will be critical for those with disabilities. See Chapter 8 for additional characteristics of this population and design applications appropriate for them.

Health and Wellness

In today's society, we encounter many health-related issues and trends that connect to the family kitchen. Obesity is very high on the list, especially obesity among children. Storage and preparation of healthy, low-calorie foods is essential. Providing storage and easy access to these healthy foods for children may help change food habits.

In an effort to save money and eat healthier, many households are making use of a home garden or frequenting farmer's markets that provide the household with fresh and healthy foods. An abundance of fresh fruits and vegetables calls for specialized storage to maintain freshness.

A keen awareness of health also prompts consumers to consider other health measures in the kitchen. Materials that deter the growth of bacteria are desired. Households can minimize the use of chemicals in the kitchen through the selection of easy-to-clean surfaces and green cleaning products.

HOUSING TRENDS AND CONSUMER PREFERENCES

Design trends begin with general housing trends. Surveys by the National Association of Home Builders (NAHB) and Better Homes and Gardens (Sullivan 2010) provide a profile of home trends and what people want in their homes. The average home size shrank to 2480 square feet in 2009 as reported by the NAHB. Builders expect homes to continue at this smaller size, averaging about 2152 square feet in 2015. These smaller homes are not only desired by the 65 and older individuals looking to downsize but also the echo boomers interested in smaller, more affordable starter homes (NAHB 2011).

Another focus of builders and consumers alike is "green and sustainable" living. Builders are adding more green features such as insulated front doors, low-e windows, programmable thermostats, and energy-efficient lighting. Water-efficient products and energy-efficient appliances are also included (NAHB 2011). Consumers surveyed by *Better Homes and Gardens* listed their most wanted items in a home as: efficient HVAC systems, Energy Star appliances, efficient design, and natural light. As they plan their choices, consumers are taking more time to research these purchases and projects, and then prioritizing the features they want. Consumers also desire a kitchen with an everyday eating area and comfortable family-gathering space, as well as decks and patios, low-maintenance exteriors, and private backyards (Sullivan 2010).

When it comes to home purchasing, value and needs are driving the decisions, according to an NAHB spokesperson. Households want space they can really use, not spaces that just look nice. Therefore, "luxury and extravagance" are out and "authenticity and dependability" are in. Home trends from builders, as reported by the *Wall Street Journal* (Kalita 2011), are as follows:

- Grand foyers are out and "drop zones" are in. These bigger versions of the mud room serve a place where the family can drop their packs and parcels as they enter the home, and efficient storage helps organize the clutter.
- Formal living rooms are out and open family rooms are in. Little-used formal living rooms and bonus rooms are wasted space.
- A second staircase is out and space for an elevator is in. The baby boom generation is thinking of the future, when they might need an elevator to navigate floors.
- Dad's office is out and a "lifestyle center" is in. People work all over the house, and a lifestyle center near the kitchen can accommodate the activities of many family members.
- The breakfast nook is out and an outdoor living space is in. With open kitchens that incorporate the dining area, an additional nook area is less important. Sliding doors at the back of the house open the house to the outdoors.
- Also included on the "out" list are two-story foyers, cathedral ceilings, and formal dining rooms. A ground-floor bedroom with full bathroom is in for multistory homes.

The American Institute of Architects found similar trends among the residential architects they surveyed (Baker 2010). These architects reported an increased demand for such features as outdoor living space, open-space layouts, and blended indoor/outdoor living, features that correspond to an interest in outdoor cooking and kitchens. In-home accessibility and access into/out of the home were also in demand, important features for "aging in place."

Architects also identified key trends or demands for kitchens. Among the items found to be increasing in popularity are:

- Recycling centers by 52 percent
- Pantry space by 47 percent
- Computer work/recharge areas by 43 percent
- Integration with family space by 41 percent
- Adaptability/universal design by 28 percent
- Double island by 20 percent

Research by many groups, including the Research Institute for Cooking and Kitchen Intelligence (RICKI), Whirlpool, and Masco, has provided insight into consumer preferences and actions related to the kitchen. The RICKI (KBDN 2010b) studied consumers relative to their expenditure on kitchens.

They found that the "ultra-high-end" consumer was considerably more engaged in their kitchens, spent more money on their kitchen project, were most likely to say the look of their kitchen reflected who they were, and wanted the kitchen design to say a lot about them. This group was also more brand conscious and more likely to hire a professional designer to help with their decisions.

Whirlpool (KBDN 2010a) surveyed consumers regarding their feelings toward green products. A majority of the consumers indicated they do their best to be green as long as doing so fits their lifestyle and finances. They want the right product at the right price and will search until they find it. However, over half of those surveyed would rather spend money now to save on energy costs later. Convenience was also important because consumers want the easiest path to energy efficiency and cost savings.

A 2011 study by Masco[1] shed light on the differences between generations related to desires and needs. The three generations compared were Baby Boomer (1946–1965), Gen X (1966–1978), and Gen Y or Echo Boomer (1979–2002). (Date spans for these generations vary among sources.) They found that:

- Baby Boomers desire to age in place with a semi-open or completely open floor plan. They want storage that is easy to reach and well organized. They favor clean, uncluttered lines.
- The Gen X generation is in the middle of raising their families and plan to stay in their current location for another 5–10 years. They place emphasis on the kitchen as a multifunctional space and the hub of the home. They desire an open plan with a computer area and a great room near the kitchen for entertaining and see this as a way to keep an eye on children as they socialize and do homework. If no children are present in the household, they focus on friends, cooking and wine club dinners, and baking.
- The Gen Y or Echo Boom generation uses the Internet for advice and finding the lowest price, and they want it *now*. They prefer an open layout with a simple design that has room for entertaining. When children are present in the household they want storage for children's needs and pull-out drawers for easy access to snacks.

CURRENT AND CONTINUING DESIGN TRENDS

Clearly, styles, designs, colors, and materials go in and out of fashion, often rapidly. New technology is constantly providing new products. Therefore, the professional designer should make a regular practice of attending trade shows, reading trade and consumer publications, and checking online blogs and sites to stay up to date with the newest products and trends. Aside from design and material trends, however, there are overarching demographic and lifestyle factors worth noting that are influencing kitchen planning in this new millennium. Today's casual lifestyle finds more household members working together in the kitchen and carrying on a wider variety of activities. There is often a more relaxed style of entertaining and guests help with the food preparation. Both trends call for a kitchen where people can interact and where two or more cooks can work (Figure 1.15).

Kitchens of today can take on two different looks. One places the appliances as a focal point in the kitchen. Large, stainless steel or colorful appliances make a statement as you enter the kitchen space. Consumers want their high-end appliances to show off, catching the attention of those entering. The other look is the hidden or integrated look. Refrigerators and dishwashers hide behind wooden panels that blend into the adjacent cabinetry (Figure 1.16). This styling creates a simplistic or minimalist look that many households are trying to achieve because it doesn't detract from their other decorating elements. Instead of appliances being the focal point, such things as unique furniture pieces, decorative hoods, or light fixtures attract attention.

A downturn of the economy from 2008 to 2011 has also had an impact on kitchens. As households find their budgets strained, kitchens are becoming smaller and more streamlined to reflect the current economic times. Households are more interested in incorporating function and satisfying needs rather than trying to simply make a design statement.

---

[1]For a discussion of the Masco findings, see "Study details kitchen needs of different types of households," at www.forresidentialpros.com/article/10345270/study-details-kitchen-needs-of-different-types-of-households, retrieved September 15, 2012.

FIGURE 1.15 Household enjoy the flexibility and connectedness of the open design. Here we see the family room and kitchen area linked by an open eating bar that also serves as a kitchen workspace on the side toward the kitchen.

Design by NKBA member Wendy Johnson, CKD, CBD

Space Usage Trends

Command central: As the kitchen continues to be the hub of home activities, the open plan concept, which combines the kitchen with a dining area, family room, and/or den into one large living space or great room remains strong. Sometimes a portion of the great room replaces the formal dining room. Often these spaces become too open and the kitchen is pushed back into a corner. Ellen Cheever, a prominent designer, promotes a new way of looking at the space, putting the kitchen in the center of the space and using walls or partial walls to create activity centers that are somewhat separate yet connected with people able to flow from one space to another.

FIGURE 1.16 With the exception of the professional range, appliances in this kitchen hide behind cabinet doors, which places more of the focal point on the cabinetry rather than the appliances.

Design by NKBA member Sandra Steiner-Houck, CKD

Islands: Consumers' desire for an island in the kitchen remains high, and today's larger kitchens can easily accommodate one. These islands vary greatly in size, shape, and usage and may include multiple levels. The island may be used solely as a prep area or contain a variety of appliances and fixtures, including a cooktop, sink, or microwave oven. One portion may also serve as an eating bar for snacks and informal meals. Double islands, two islands with each serving a different purpose in the kitchen, are also growing in popularity for larger, multi-cook kitchens that support many different activities (Figure 1.17).

Multiple-height counters: More households are becoming interested in universal design features that will help them function more easily in their home. Using multiple counter heights is one way to provide workspace for a variety of activities and users.

Multiple cooks: With the popularity of hobby cooking and shared meal preparation, the multiple-cook kitchen is designed with enough space to accommodate multiple individuals who enjoy cooking together.

More window area: A larger number of windows, as well as larger windows, increase natural light and add to the feeling of openness (Figure 1.18). However, more windows, as well as using more wall space for artwork and the open space design decrease the area available for tall appliances and wall storage.

Environmental Awareness Trends

Recycling: Whether by choice or necessity, many households include recycling in their daily routine. Because the kitchen is the source of many recyclable materials, creating space for temporarily storing bottles, cans, and the like is a growing trend.

Conserving natural resources: Consumers continue to request water- and energy-efficient appliances, and more consumers are aware of the Energy Star–qualified products and look for the Energy Star label.Consumers list energy and water savings as one of the most important factors when selecting new appliances.

Green products: More consumers are concerned about the environment and look for environmentally sound or "green" building products, including those made of recycled materials.

FIGURE 1.17 The use of double islands is on the rise, and this kitchen uses double islands to expand the workspace and incorporate an eating bar. The increasingly popular contemporary styling with its clean lines is also a prominent feature.

Design by NKBA member Laurie Belinda Haefele

FIGURE 1.18 A window wall and corner window open this contemporary kitchen to the outdoors. The beautiful view and abundance of daylight create a pleasant environment for cooks and guests.

Design by NKBA member Laurie Belinda Haefele

Care-free products: Households are seeking low-maintenance products that last longer and minimize the use of harsh chemicals for cleaning.

LED lighting: The more efficient LED lighting is being incorporated by more designers in many areas of the kitchen.

Activity Trends

Hub of the home: The kitchen remains the center of family activities and gatherings. In order to accommodate all of these activities, the space must be multifunctional and flexible.

Hobby cooking: The popularity of television cooking shows has sparked an interest in hobby cooking. Hobby cooking often involves the use of new techniques and appliances for cooking as a form of entertaining, so a large kitchen that accommodates a crowd is necessary. Multiple cooks are often involved so a variety of food preparation stations are planned into the design (Figure 1.19).

Seating areas: Seating areas in and around the kitchen are highly desired (Figure 1.20). These areas serve as gathering areas for family and friends, and can support numerous family activities close to the food preparation activities of the kitchen. Many of these areas include a fireplace and television to accommodate such activities as entertaining, relaxing, Internet surfing, and homework. Audio systems provide background music for numerous activities.

Beverage stations: Beverage stations, such as coffee and wine bars, are showing up in many of today's kitchens.

Lifestyle center: The isolated home office is being replaced with what is referred to as a "lifestyle center." Located near the kitchen, this space has a computer and other electronic equipment that allow children to do homework while being monitored by the parents. It also serves as a space for adults to work at home, pay bills, or plan household meals.

Technology: Our fascination with technology extends to today's kitchens. From improved energy efficiency and water usage to high-tech controls, today's appliances are state-of-the-art devices. Small computer-like components allow the consumer to choose from a wide variety of settings and preset start times. Appliances monitor multiple temperatures at one time, keep refrigerated food at the perfect temperature, sense when food is cooked or when dishes are clean, and even change from a cooling device to a cooking device.

FIGURE 1.19 Generous counter space and two islands in this large kitchen provide spaces for multiple family or hobby cooks to work together without interference.

Design by NKBA member James Howard, CKD, CBD

Location Trends

Outdoor kitchens: The outdoor kitchen concept goes far beyond the backyard grill (Figure 1.21). New appliances and materials allow the designer to develop a complete kitchen outdoors, including grills, burners, refrigerators, beer taps, woks, warming drawers, regular and pizza ovens, ice makers, warming drawers, and even heaters and fireplaces to make the kitchen usable for more of the year. This outdoor space can serve as a secondary dining space when the weather is nice and can allow the household to accommodate more company for holidays and celebrations.

Outpost kitchens: As part of the master or guest bedroom suite, family room, or office space, many households are incorporating a small kitchen space, often referred to as an "outpost

FIGURE 1.20 This open plan kitchen incorporates a casual seating area, as well as a seated counter area. The contemporary styling incorporates interesting shapes and lines and a vibrant color.

Design by NKBA member Tim Scott

FIGURE 1.21 As an extension of the indoors, an outdoor kitchen can expand the home space and provide a second kitchen for preparing meals.
Courtesy of Viking

kitchen" or, "morning kitchen" for preparing food and beverages away from the main kitchen. Such kitchens often include a small refrigerator, a sink, a microwave oven, and storage. House-holds are finding the outpost kitchen a convenient solution to the morning rush, as a support station when a family member is injured or ill, a personal food preparation space for a multi-generational household, or a means for easy access to refreshments by household members.

Appliance Trends

Second appliances: Once a common feature of larger, high-end kitchen designs, the use of duplicate appliances in a kitchen plan has diminished. With a decline in the size of today's homes and a more conservative economic outlook, duplicate kitchen appliances are looked on as excessive. Duplicate appliances, however, might still be found in other areas of the home, especially in homes where multiple generations reside and auxiliary food preparation areas help support the individual needs of household groups.

Variety: With such a large variety of sizes and styles, little is standard today when it comes to appliances. Although many appliances still come in standard sizes, more of the newer models are appearing in both larger and smaller sizes than before.

Controls: Increasing numbers of appliances are incorporating electronic controls that only require a touch of the finger to use (Figure 1.22). Controls are also becoming more sophisticated. Some appear when you touch the surface of an appliance, and others are hidden on the edges of ap-pliance doors. Sensor controls monitor temperatures, and lock-out features limit a child's access.

Gas: Gas is the most popular cooktop fuel in the United States, while the use of gas is on the rise in Canada. Induction is growing in popularity as a clean alternative to the gas.

Ranges: Ranges still dominate in the cooking center, but the use of separate cooktops and ovens is on the rise. Also increasing in popularity are warming drawers and double ovens. Range hoods are becoming more common in Canada, and dramatic, oversized vent hoods create a design statement in U.S. kitchens.

Undercounter appliances: As we move away from using wall cabinets, the use of under-counter appliances is on the rise. This places the appliances next to the storage that might complement their use.

FIGURE 1.22 Electronic controls on appliances provide the user with more programming and control options at the touch of a fingertip. Some controls, like the one on this Jenn-Air oven, even provide photos of foods, such as how meat will appear at various doneness levels.
Courtesy of Jenn-Air

Three-door refrigeration: The three-door refrigerator with a bottom freezer is dominating the market, but the side-by-side model is still popular (Figure 1.23). Chilled wine refrigeration is on the decline, replaced by unchilled wine storage.

Drawers: Drawer appliances, such as the dishwashing drawer, wine storage drawers, the microwave drawer, and the refrigerator and freezer drawers are becoming increasingly more popular.

Convection and steam: Convection cooking modes are almost standard in many mid- to high-end ovens. Steam is being incorporated into many different appliances, including ovens, dishwashers, clothes washers, and clothes dryers.

Disposers: Disposers' use is up, along with the use of trash compactors.

Downsized styles: The commercial or professional look is now available in less bulky models.

Cabinetry Trends

Dark woods: Darker woods and dark stain are popular in both the United States and Canada, but a shift to a medium finish is expected as a safe choice for the current economy. However, some designers are also using light-colored wood finishes extensively (Figure 1.24). With the darker-toned cabinets, homeowners are using lighter floors and counters to lighten up the room.

Wood choices: Cherry is the most popular cabinet wood in the United States followed by maple and alder wood. Mahogany and walnut are also popular. In Canada, popular woods include cherry, dark oak, birch, and maple.

Rustic look: The European farmhouse or rustic elegance look makes use of lighter, gray-toned woods, such as bleached ash, for cabinets as well as floors. These reclaimed or bleached woods add character and weathered imperfections. Mixing these rustic elements with more polished materials is also a hot trend (Figure 1.25).

Shaker styling: Traditional styling continues to be popular and may include influences from France and Sweden. A move away from the very heavily ornamented traditional designs, however, is more reflective of the current economic times where people are seeking a more simplified lifestyle. There is a strong resurgence of the Shaker style.

Fewer wall cabinets: Fewer wall cabinets allow rooms to open up and the use of more windows (Figure 1.26). All of the storage is placed in base cabinets or pantry type storage areas. A lack of or reduction in the number of wall cabinets presents a new way to look at kitchen design.

Furniture pieces: Furniture styled pieces, often with curved lines, serve as storage and work areas.

Lift cabinets: Interest in the lift-style wall cabinet door, which lifts straight up instead of out, is emerging.

Contemporary styling emerges: Geometric lines and shapes, so characteristic of the Euro contemporary style, is a popular look in today's kitchens across the continent (Figure 1.27).

FIGURE 1.23 The three-door or French door refrigerator continues to be one of the most popular refrigerator styles on the market. Newer versions of the style now have water and ice in the door and multiple drawers below that can vary as to use, from refrigeration to freezer.
Courtesy of Jenn-Air.

Elongated, horizontal elements are created with wide drawers and long handles. Cubes of cabinets, arranged geometrically, are clustered on walls. Integrated handles help emphasize the clean lines of the style.

Electronic drawer controls: Electronically controlled drawers open and close with the use of a small motor. Undermount, full-extension glide systems are used on all levels of drawer construction. Soft-close drawers are incorporated into many kitchen cabinets.

Glass shelves: Glass cabinet door panels and glass shelves are popular in Canadian kitchens.

Brushed hardware: Brushed metal hardware has stood the test of time.

FIGURE 1.24 Although dark woods are still popular in kitchen designs, mid-toned woods are making their way into many new kitchens.

Design by NKBA member Tim Scott

FIGURE 1.25 The elements of Tuscany appear in this open kitchen. The casual cabinet styling, rustic metals, and warm colors create the comfortable countryside look.

Design by NKBA member James Howard, CKD, CBD

FIGURE 1.26 Art work and a utensil storage rail replace the upper cabinets in this kitchen to create a minimalist look. Expanded window space and open plans are also reasons for eliminating upper cabinets and opting for the use of large pantries and base cabinets instead.

Design by NKBA member Friedemann Weinhardt

FIGURE 1.27 The clean lines and smooth surfaces present here are typical of a contemporary styled kitchen. European frameless and lift cabinets dominate the look.

Design by NKBA member Lori Carroll

FIGURE 1.28 Dark base cabinets are teamed with white upper cabinets to produce the increasingly popular two-toned look. Light counters help balance the dark cabinet colors, and wood flooring adds warmth to the scheme.

Design by NKBA member Beverley Leigh Binns

Color and Finish Trends

Two-toned look: Canadian and U.S. designers are finding the two-tone look popular (Figure 1.28). This may include painted finishes in two contrasting colors, or a painted surface paired with a natural wood or stone surface.

White and neutrals: White and off-white are still prominent (Figure 1.29). The neutral palettes, including browns as well as beige and bone, are popular. Warm earth tones are used for counters and backsplashes.

The new black: Gray is the new black and is especially popular in Canada.

FIGURE 1.29 White continues to be a popular kitchen color choice, and this large kitchen incorporates it into traditional styling with soft lines. Wood flooring creates a pleasant contrast.

Design by NKBA member Nicholas Geragi, CKD, CBD

FIGURE 1.30 The backsplash's diagonal tile pattern, the pressed tin ceiling, the subtle wall stripe, and the patterned counter all create interest through visual and tactile texture. The color gray, as used here on the cabinetry, is gaining in popularity.

Design by NKBA member Bryan Reiss, CKD, CBD

Vibrant colors: We are seeing a stronger commitment to color with dramatic "pops" of color, such as neon and jewel tones, showing up on walls, as accents, and in appliances.

Texture: Tactile and visual texture is adding interest to the kitchen through the use of line, colors, patterns, mosaic tiles, and glass tiles (Figure 1.30).

International inspiration: Inspirations from Africa, India, Peru, and Turkey incorporate bold pink, orange, turquoise, and green colors into kitchens. Bold patterns are paired with earthy and neutral accessories. Distressed finishes are on the decline.

Tuscany: Design motifs from Tuscany, with their earthy color palettes, multi-style cabinetry, and inclusion of different countertops, materials, and colors are demonstrating that not everything in a kitchen needs to match.

Material Trends

Hardwoods: Hardwoods, including tropical hardwoods, are very popular for cabinetry, furniture, and floors.

Stainless steel: Stainless steel continues to be a hot trend and is used in sinks, on appliances, and as countertops (Figure 1.31). Appliance companies, however, are looking to colors like glossy white, slate gray, and black as up and coming trends.

Natural stone: Ceramic and porcelain tiles, along with natural stone, are desired surface finishes. For the more rustic designs, honed granite or marble create a beautiful contrast against brick and raw-stone walls.

Glass: Designers are using more glass than ever and in many different applications, including glass appliance fronts, glass counters, glass tiles for the backsplash, and glass shelves in cabinets (Figure 1.32).

Antiqued finishes: Canadian designers incorporate antiqued finishes that complement the traditional styling and are moving away from stronger grained woods toward a softer look.

Easy care: Easy to clean and care for finishes are a must.

Mix and match: Designers are incorporating multiple counter materials—one for the island and a different material for the other surfaces.

Green products: Many consumers are interested in materials that are considered "green." These materials are produced with little embodied energy, are easy to care for, durable, and perhaps made from recycled or reclaimed components.

FIGURE 1.31 The popularity of stainless steel is perhaps illustrated to the extreme with this kitchen of stainless steel appliances and surfaces. The large kitchen also has space for multiple cooks and observers.

Design by NKBA member Peter Ross Salerno, CMKBD

FIGURE 1.32 Glass is being used in numerous ways by kitchen designers. A full glass counter, glass cabinet doors, and glass accessories complete this kitchen design.

Design by NKBA member Elina Katsioula-Beall, CKD

FIGURE 1.33 Many types, styles, and sizes of tile are used throughout today's kitchens. This particular design places large tiles on the floor, tiles in a diagonal pattern on the backsplash, and decorative tiles around the room to complete the kitchen's design theme.
Design by NKBA member Cheryl Hamilton-Gray, CKD

Countertop and Floor Trends

Quartz gaining: Granite remains the most popular countertop surface, but it is losing share to quartz or engineered stone. Solid surface is clearly in third place, and the use of laminate is on the decline. Polished concrete is also becoming popular for high-end applications.

Tile backsplash: Popular backsplash materials include ceramic, porcelain, and glass tiles, and backsplashes are lower and less conspicuous. Herringbone mosaic patterns add texture and pattern to the kitchen (Figure 1.33).

Green choices: Bamboo and cork are popular as green product material for floors. Wood flooring in kitchens is increasing in popularity (Figure 1.34).

Slate: Slate is a durable floor covering but it is a less affordable choice and requires resealing on regular intervals. Porcelain tiles are used more extensively and are a better choice for durability. Laminate flooring is also a popular choice, but there are varying degrees of quality.

Heated floors: Radiant heating of floors is popular for the kitchen as well as the entire home. Stepping onto a warm floor adds to the comfort of working or relaxing in a space.

Storage Trends

Specialty storage: Storage features are becoming unique and personalized, including such things as pet supply centers and charging stations. Consumers are looking for ways to eliminate clutter.

Workstations on wheels: Designers find pantry cupboards very popular, as well as workstations on wheels, such as islands and prep workstations (Figure 1.35).

Large pantry: Consumers continue to request pantries more than ever, but a separate, walk-in pantry located in different parts of the kitchen is the most desired style. Many storage devices that make better use of pantry space are available. Some designers see a decline in the use of tall pantries, lazy Susans, pullout racks, and appliance garages.

Barn door: Walk-in pantry areas are making use of a sliding barn-door-style covering for access. The hanging door is mounted from concealed or decorative hardware on the outside of the wall. The door slides along the hardware to reveal the opening. Such doors are also used for openings to laundry rooms or areas.

FIGURE 1.34 Wooden flooring is becoming common in many new kitchens. The lighter colored wooden floors and counter help lighten up this kitchen of dark colored cabinetry.

Design by NKBA member Chris Novak Berry

Fixture Trends

Stainless steel sinks: Stainless steel is as popular for sinks as it is for appliances.

Pull-out faucets: Pull-out faucets are in high demand, with standard and pot filler faucets coming in second. Gooseneck faucets are also popular, even in traditional kitchens. Curving high above the sink, these faucets make it easier to fill pots, and many include a pull-out spray nozzle.

FIGURE 1.35 Placing tables and carts on wheels provides a flexible workspace that can be easily moved to where more counter is needed. The dark cabinetry and open shelves are also popular design features in today's kitchens.

Design by NKBA member Jennifer L. Gilmer, CKD

Multiple sinks: Even though many designers are not including as many multiple appliances in the kitchen, many are still including an additional sink, like a salad sink in the island or in the counter workspace across the kitchen from the main sink (Figure 1.36). This supports the work of two cooks in the kitchen.

Brushed nickel: Brushed nickel and satin nickel are top choices in new kitchens, followed by stainless steel and polished chrome. Venetian bronze finishes are popular in Canada.

FIGURE 1.36 Multiple sinks are frequently designed into larger kitchen plans to provide an additional sink for food preparation activities.

Design by NKBA member Erica S. Westeroth, CKD

SUMMARY

With each subsequent era, new design trends emerged that incorporated the lifestyles and technologies of the time. Research has helped to shape the design of kitchens for many years. Approaching food preparation and cleanup as work and studying how to perform the work more efficiently has guided the study of kitchen design. The planning guidelines for kitchens have consistently reflected the findings from research and continue to keep kitchen design appropriate for the lifestyles of the times. Studies will need to be done more frequently to reflect continually changing food preparation patterns and lifestyles. Although certain styles and designs may go in and out of fashion during various periods of time, the current selection of colors, materials, styles, sizes, and textures offers the consumer and designer an unlimited array of choices for a kitchen design plan. An important part of the kitchen designers' job is to stay abreast of the ever-changing array of products and the evolving lifestyle and design trends that affect their practice. However, regardless of the trends, the designer should always consider the homeowners desires and wishes over their own and over the trends. This information should be gathered during the initial interview process. It is the designers' role and responsibility to lead or influence their client in choosing the most advantageous approach to fit their wants, not push trends and styles on them.

REVIEW QUESTIONS

1. What role did the hearth/fireplace play in early Colonial kitchens and home life? (See "Role of the Hearth in the Eighteenth-Century Kitchen" p. 2)
2. How did the design of the modern kitchen evolve from multiple rooms to today's open floor plan? (See "The Modern Kitchen" to "Standardization: The 1900s" pp. 3–6)
3. How did the industrial revolution and standardization affect early kitchen designs? (See "The Modern Kitchen" to "Standardization: The 1900s" pp. 3–6)
4. How did the Beecher sisters and home economists contribute to the designing of more efficient and functional kitchens? (See "The Beecher Kitchen" p. 4, and "Kitchen Design Research" pp. 6–15)
5. What are some current demographic trends related to household size, diversity, and composition in the United States and Canada? How do they affect kitchen design considerations? (See "Demographic and Population Trends" to "Housing Trends and Consumer Preferences" pp. 24–28)
6. What are the general trends that have had an impact on the look and function of today's kitchens? (See "Housing Trends and Consumer Preferences" pp. 27–28)

REFERENCES

Baker, Kermit. 2010. "Small Talk: Kitchens and Baths Do More with Less." *Kitchen and Bath Business* (May 10), 26–27.

Beecher, C. E. and H. B.Stowe. 1869. *The American Women's Home*. New York: J. B. Ford and Co.

Carter, D.1932. *Studies in the Design of Kitchens and Kitchen Equipment*. Arkansas Agricultural Experiment Station Bulletin 276, Fayetteville.

Cheever, E. M.1992. *Kitchen Planning and Safety Standards*. Kitchen Industry Technical Manuals, Vol. 4. Hackettstown, NJ: National Kitchen and Bath Association.

Cheever, E. M. (1996). *Kitchen Planning and Safety Standards: Kitchen Industry Technical Manuals*, vol. 4 (3rd ed.). Hackettstown, NJ: National Kitchen and Bath Association.

Cushman, Ella. 1936. *The Development of a Successful Kitchen*. Cornell Bulletin for Homemakers 354. Ithaca, NY.

Emmel, J. M., J. Beamish, and K. Parrott. 2001. *Someone's In the Kitchen: Summary of Findings from the Kitchen Space and Storage Research Project*. Blacksburg, VA: Virginia Polytechnic and State University.

Frederick, C.1913. *The New Housekeeping: Efficiency Studies in Home Management*. Garden City, NY: Doubleday, Page and Co.

Heiner, Mary Koll and Helen E. McCollough. 1948. *Functional Kitchen Storage*. Cornell University Agricultural Experiment Station. Bulletin 846. Ithaca, NY: Cornell University.

Heiner, Mary Koll and R. E. Steidel. 1951. *Guides for Arrangement of Urban Family Kitchens.* University Agricultural Experiment Station. Bulletin 878. Ithaca, NY: Cornell University.

Howard, M. S.1965. *Development of the Beltsville Energy Saving Kitchens*, Final report, Project CH 2-14. Beltsville, MD: U.S. Department of Agriculture Agricultural Research Service.

Humes, K. R., N. A. Jones, and R. R. Ramirez. 2011. Overview of Race and Hispanic Origin: 2010– 2010 Census Briefs. Washington, DC: U.S. Department of Commerce, U.S. Census Bureau.

Joint Center for Housing Studies. 2011. *The State of the Nation's Housing 2010*. The Joint Center for Housing Studies of Harvard University. Cambridge, MA: Harvard University.

Jones, R. A. and W. H. Kapple. 1975. *Kitchen Industry Technical Manual*, Vol. 5. National Kitchen and Bath Association and Small Homes Council. Urbana-Champaign: University of Illinois.

Kapple, W. H.1964. *Kitchen Planning Standards*. Small Homes Council—Building Research Council Circular Series C5.32. Urbana: University of Illinois Press.

Kalita, S. M. 2011. "Blueprint for the New American Home." *The Wall Street Journal*, (November 2).

Kitchen & Bath Design News (KBDN). 2010a. "Consumer Buying Trends: Study Uncovers American Consumer Attitudes Regarding 'Green'." *Kitchen & Bath Design News*, 11.

———. 2010b. "Consumer Buying Trends: Upper-end Consumers More Brand Conscious, Survey Reveals." *Kitchen & Bath Design News*, 11.

Lofquist, D., T. Lugaila, M. O'Connell, and S. Feliz. 2012. Households and Families: 2010–2010 Census Briefs. Washington, DC: U.S. Department of Commerce, U.S. Census Bureau.

Mackum, P. and S. Wilson. 2011. Population Distribution and Change 2000–2010. 2010 Census Briefs. Washington, DC: U.S. Department of Commerce, U.S. Census Bureau.

McCullough, H. E.1949. *Cabinet Space for the Kitchen*. Small Homes Council Circular Series C5.31. Urbana: University of Illinois *Press*.

National Association of Home Builders (NAHB). 2011. *NAHB Study: New Homes in 2015 Will Be Smaller, Greener and More Casual*. Washington, DC: National Association of Home Builders. Retrieved on September 15, 2012 from www.nahb.org/news_details.aspx.

Parrott, K., J. Beamish, and J. Emmel. 2003. *Kitchen Storage Research Project*. Blacksburg, VA: Virginia Polytechnic and State University.

Pew Social Trends Staff. 2010. *The Return of the Multi-Generational Family Household*. Pew Research Center. Retrieved from www.Pewsocialtrends.Org/2010/03/18/The-Return-Of-The-Multigenerational-Family-Household.

Sullivan, J. 2010. "Home Sizes Continue to Shrink." *Builder 2010*, National Home Builders Association. Retrieved on January 2, 2012 from www.Builderonline.Com/Design/Home-Sizes-Continue-To-Shrink.Aspx.

Wanslow, R.1965. *Kitchen Planning Guide*. Small Homes Council—Building Research Council. Urbana-Champaign: University of Illinois.

Werner, Carrie A. 2011. *The Older Population: 2010: 2010 Census Briefs*. Washington, DC: U.S. Department of Commerce, U.S. Census Bureau. Available at www.census.gov/prod/cen2010/briefs/c2010br-09.pdf, accessed October 2012.

Wilson, M.1938. *The Willamette Valley Farm Kitchen*. Corvallis: Oregon State University Agricultural Experiment Station.

————. 1947a. *Patterns for Kitchen Cabinets*. Oregon State Agricultural Experiment Station Bulletin 446, Corvallis.

————. 1947b. *Considerations for Planning Kitchen Cabinets*. Oregon State Agricultural Experiment Station Bulletin 445, Corvallis.

Wilson, M. and H. E. Mccullough. 1940. *A Set of Utensils for the Farm Kitchen*. Oregon State Agricultural Experiment Station Circular 134, Corvallis.

Yust, B. L., and W. W. Olsen. 1992. "Residential Kitchens: Planning Principles for the 1990s." In E. M.Cheever, *Kitchen Planning and Safety Standards: Kitchen Industry Technical Manuals*, Vol. 4. Hackettstown, NJ: National Kitchen and Bath Association.

Infrastructure Considerations

Early in the design process, you will need to consider the infrastructure of the kitchen space and related areas in the home. In Chapter 5, "Assessing Needs," Form 7: Job Site Inspection guides you through a needs assessment of many of the infrastructure considerations. No matter what types of structural changes are made, you must take time to carefully plan infrastructure needs and double-check your list so that nothing is forgotten. Mistakes or oversights may not only be difficult to change later, but most likely expensive as well.

This chapter provides an overview of the structural and plumbing elements you should consider while designing or remodeling.

Learning Objective: Identify infrastructure needs assessment issues that can be posed by floors, walls, windows, and plumbing.

CODES

The fundamental guidelines that govern the types of materials that can be used in home construction, as well as how they may be used, are called *building codes*. Although you will be working with a plumber, contractor, or other construction professional who is familiar with these codes, your own understanding of the codes helps you to be aware of restrictions or requirements as you develop a kitchen plan. Building codes are legally binding, and inspectors are required to ensure compliance.

Although a new model international building code, called the International Residential Code (IRC), has been developed to form a set of consistent, correlated, comprehensive, and contemporary building code regulations for homes throughout North America, the code must be adopted by provincial, state, and/or local governments. So becoming familiar with the state and local codes in your area is essential. A few specific items to be aware of are included in this chapter.

In addition to residential construction codes, your kitchen project may be covered by one or more codes targeted at making buildings accessible to people with disabilities. Accessibility codes and laws for the United States and Canada are discussed in Chapter 4, "Human Factors and Universal Design Foundation."

Plumbing codes are a specialized part of the building codes and regulate all aspects of the water supply, drain, waste, and vent system. In new construction, complying with the codes is a matter of the plumbing contractor selecting the materials and methods allowed for the area. For remodeling projects, however, it may take a little more planning to evaluate the situation, decide what changes are feasible, and make certain the changes reflect the current plumbing codes.

Electrical code considerations are discussed in Chapter 7, "Mechanical Planning."

STRUCTURAL ISSUES

Whether you are working with new construction or on a remodeling project, special structural considerations are relevant to each phase and element of the project. Again, a building contractor or other building professional should be well aware of these issues, but careful planning and examination of the current structural components in the kitchen will be critical when making decisions about design options.

If you have the original construction plans, you can begin with them as a guide, but eventually you will need to verify that the structure was actually built as indicated on the plans. Following are some of the structural considerations to keep in mind.

Floors

If the floor will be changed, it is important to know more about the structure and what is hidden within or below that floor. Begin by examining the floor joists to determine how the floor was constructed, if any damage exists, and the size of the framing members. This helps to determine the strength of the floor or its ability to hold weight. If the flooring material is over a slab foundation, check for moisture and cracks that require sealing.

While examining the floor structure, make note of the components contained within the floor structure so that you do not damage them during the remodeling process (Figure 2.1). Concealed air ducts, wiring, or plumbing pipes may already be present. Because some of these items may be difficult and expensive to relocate, knowledge of exactly what is there will help you decide which items you may want to leave as is. Verify the direction and size of the floor joists or trusses to provide a better idea of how to proceed with plans for new plumbing, wiring, or heating components that need to be located in the floor.

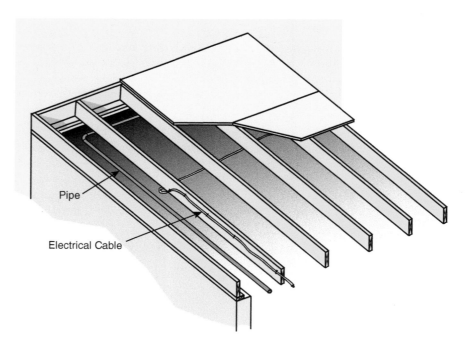

FIGURE 2.1 Piping or wiring contained within the floor structure must be identified before remodeling so that it is not damaged during the process.

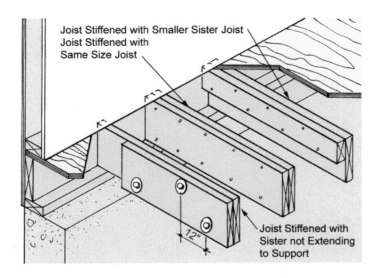

Joist Stiffened with Smaller Sister Joist
Joist Stiffened with Same Size Joist

12"

Joist Stiffened with Sister not Extending to Support

FIGURE 2.2 Extra floor supports may be needed when installing heavy or oversized appliances.

Oversized Appliances

A large professional range, large cast iron range, or oversized refrigerator can exert a great deal of pressure on a floor because of its weight. In new construction, the contractor will need to determine if extra supports must be added in order to handle this extra weight. Floors in older homes were typically not built to hold these extremely heavy, oversized appliances, and therefore reinforcing the floor will most likely be necessary (Figure 2.2).

In older homes, careful evaluation of the present floor structure is essential for determining current strength and condition of the floor for such loads. One way to accurately evaluate the floor structure is to strip the floor down to the joists to see if they are large enough or spaced appropriately to hold these heavy, oversized appliances. While the floor is open, this is an excellent time to investigate the plumbing, ductwork, and other components that may be concealed in the floor joists.

Stability and Evenness

Whether poorly constructed, weakened from age, or sagging because of a settling foundation, floors can become uneven over time. Stable and even floors are essential for many kitchen applications, so modifications may need to take place to improve the floor surface and stability (Figure 2.3).

Cabinets require a sound and flat foundation on which to rest so that all the edges fit perfectly together in a continuous line. Uneven floors may cause gaps to form between cabinets or cabinetry may not line up from front to back. Although shims and fillers can take care of some of these openings or misalignments, a flat and level floor will make the cabinet installation go more quickly and smoothly.

Appliances, like cabinetry, will not fit together properly on an uneven floor. Many appliances are intended to snug up against the cabinetry or another appliance when installed, but an uneven floor causes appliances and cabinetry to tilt to one side, forming gaps between them. Most appliances have leveling legs for adjusting the levelness, but an even floor foundation will save time and tedious adjustments.

Levelness is also important for appliances to function properly and for client satisfaction with the use of the appliance. For example, clothes washers that are not level may begin to vibrate excessively when the washer begins its spin cycle. Your client may also find it frustrating to see the oil run to one side of a pan while cooking on a cooking surface or to discover a lopsided dessert in the refrigerator.

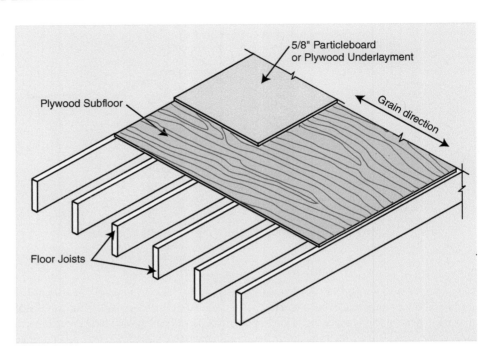

FIGURE 2.3 Uneven floors will have to be leveled to ensure that new cabinets, appliances, and surfacing materials can be successfully installed.

Level, even floors are also important for the successful installation of many surfacing materials. For example, ceramic tile must have a flat surface to avoid tile breakage and cracked grout with use. Uneven floors can also squeak, which is annoying as well as noisy.

Moisture Control

If the kitchen is located on the main floor over a crawl space or on a slab, moisture may migrate through the floor structure and damage the flooring. Vapor barriers should be in place to prevent this migration, but if you are not sure whether a vapor barrier is present, you can conduct a simple test. After the floor is stripped down to the floorboards, tape pieces of plastic sheeting (minimum 12 inches x 12 inches [300 mm x 300 mm]) to the floor in various parts of the room. After about a week, check to see if moisture has become trapped beneath the plastic. If there is no moisture build-up, the floor has probably been sealed against vapor transmission. Signs of moisture mean you need to take measures to seal the slab or the floor and crawl space.

Walls

Often, remodeling projects call for altering the wall or wall surface. Whenever walls are to be removed or exposed, do not break into them until you know what is behind them. Walls may hide wiring, plumbing, drain lines, and vent pipes, and even heating, air conditioning, and air return ducts in some older homes. Any damage to these could not only be expensive, but also disastrous.

Load-Bearing Walls

Walls can be either load-bearing or non-load-bearing. If you are expanding the kitchen or reconfiguring the walls, be aware of the load-bearing walls in your plan. Load-bearing walls are the walls that support the roof and upper levels of the structure. These make up the frame, or skeleton, of the house, which keeps the structure standing even through wind storms and snow loads. The ends of the ceiling joists must connect to the load-bearing walls for support. If this skeleton is not strong and stable, it will shift and cause the walls to crack, floors to sag, and windows and doors to stick and not move smoothly. Over time it can cause the house to become out of square.

Before you remove any walls, determine which type you have—load-bearing or non-load-bearing. Removing non-load-bearing walls is usually not a problem when considering structural support of

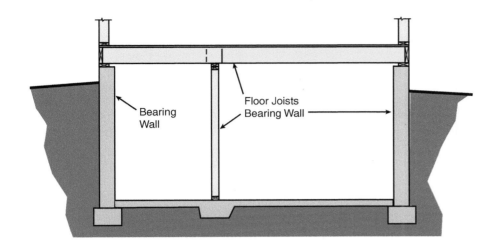

FIGURE 2.4 A load-bearing wall runs perpendicular to the joists.

the floors above. Many times, in an effort to open up space, load-bearing walls may need to be removed. One way to tell whether a wall is load-bearing is to check the ceiling joists above the space, either in the attic or by an access panel to the joists. If the joists run in the same direction as the wall you want to remove, it is probably not a load-bearing wall. Load-bearing walls tend to run perpendicular to the joists (Figure 2.4). If you do not have ready access to the joists, you may either need to remove some molding or to drill holes in the ceiling to determine where the joists are located.

Load-bearing walls can be removed or modified. If your design calls for alterations to this type of wall, work with your contractor to make sure it can be accomplished successfully. When load-bearing walls need to be removed, local codes specify the type and length of header that needs to be used to span the opening for support. Usually wood beams will be sufficient for short spans, but steel I-beams or structural beams made of laminated timbers are needed for longer spans.

Uneven Walls

Uneven walls and out-of-square corners can be a problem in both new and older construction. Such walls may make it difficult to properly install wall finishes and cabinetry. Walls can become uneven for a number of reasons. Over time, old plaster walls crack, and in an effort to restore them, the surface may become distorted. Wallboard may be damaged and not properly repaired. Or, perhaps walls were not installed square when initially built or they have shifted over time.

When these original walls or wall surfaces are to be retained in new projects, problems can arise whenever uneven surfaces interfere with the installation of a product. For example, if you are adding tile or stone to the walls for a backsplash, the pieces may not lay flat to provide an even surface. Stone or tile designed to have an irregular surface may be a good choice here. Cabinets will also not fit flat against the walls and, therefore, will not line up properly. This will either cause gaps to form between the cabinet pieces or the face of the cabinets will not be flat. Once again, fillers and shims may help even out the installation, but it could be a more complex process.

Walls that are not square are especially problematic when installing cabinetry and appliances in corners. Placing a square unit in a less than square corner will surely cause gaps to form somewhere. This problem may be difficult to correct, so you will probably need to rely on cabinet fillers to take care of any gaps that appear. If you do not plan to replace the walls, find surface treatments that will help smooth them out enough to meet your purposes.

Insulation

Wall insulation is beneficial in both interior and exterior walls of a kitchen. For interior walls, insulation produces a sound barrier. The kitchen creates many noises that can echo into the adjoining rooms. In addition, kitchens are typically furnished with many hard surfaces like cabinets and appliances that do not absorb sounds. By insulating the interior walls of a kitchen, you can better isolate the noises that may move into unwanted areas. Most homes, with the exception of those built before energy was an issue, contain insulation in the exterior walls.

The purpose of this insulation is to prevent heat from transferring into and out of the home making the space more comfortable for the occupants. Insulation is rated in R-value, which is a measure of the resistance to heat conductivity of a material. The higher the R-value the more the material resists heat conduction and is therefore a better insulator. The IRC specifies a level of insulation for each climate zone, and in remodeling projects the local energy code may require that the insulation be brought up to this level. An additional benefit of insulated exterior walls is to help control moisture. If exterior walls are cold because of low insulation levels, warm, moist air will be attracted to the walls, condense onto the wall surface, and the water droplets that form can ruin wall, woodwork, and floors. Energy efficiency and moisture control are covered in more detail in Chapter 3, "Environmental and Sustainability Considerations."

Consider adding insulation in all kitchen walls that adjoin another room and extra insulation on exterior walls, and this can take place during remodeling. If the wallboard is being replaced or you are working with new construction, it will be easy to add insulation to the wall cavity. For inside walls that have a closet or other built-in storage that can serve as a buffer for noise, wall insulation may not be necessary. If you want to add additional insulation but do not plan to replace the wallboard on the kitchen walls, you will probably need to use a foam or blown-in type of insulation to fill the walls. Professional installers can do this for you.

DOORS AND WINDOWS

Door and window areas are very important components of the room structure. For new construction, discuss with the client the type and amount of window space they desire and the type of door(s) that best fits their design and room configuration.

For remodeling projects, examine the windows and doors carefully to decide whether they need to be replaced or just refurbished. Use Forms 9 and 10 in Chapter 5 to gather information and measurements on existing doors and windows.

Door Choices

A kitchen can easily have multiple entry or exterior door openings, including those to the garage, patio, or deck. Interior doors may lead to the dining room, family room, stairwell, or other area of the home. It is not uncommon to have as many as six doors opening into the kitchen. Not all of those doorways may have an actual door attached, but some could instead be an opening or archway into another room.

If you include doors as part of your design plan, it is important to consider the direction the doors should swing so that they do not interfere with activities in the kitchen or come into contact with a feature of the kitchen, such as cabinets, appliances, or dining furniture, when opened. When you decide to replace a door or modify a room entry, be sure the new plan fits with the other components of the room or other changes. For example, a new door size may mean a new door swing that could interfere with room features that were not a problem before.

Bifold doors have smaller doors and, thus, may be a good alternative where the door swing space for a standard-sized door is an issue. Pocket doors can also be used. They slide into the wall cavity and are useful for opening up rooms without the worry of a door swing. They do, however, need adequate wall cavity space that is free from plumbing, electrical, or HVAC (heating, ventilation, and air conditioning) components to form the pocket. When a pocket door is not possible, or perhaps too costly, consider a "barn" door—hardware that allows the door to slide along a wall. In this style, you need a span of clear wall space for the door to slide along as it is opened. Figure 2.5 illustrates some of the door style options.

As you select exterior doors, additional factors should be considered. The first is security. Your client may be concerned about how easily someone could access the space through this door. Selecting one that is sturdy with break-resistant glass would be important. A high-quality lock system would also be important. The client may even ask for a screen door that can be locked for added security and also allow the main door to be opened for natural ventilation.

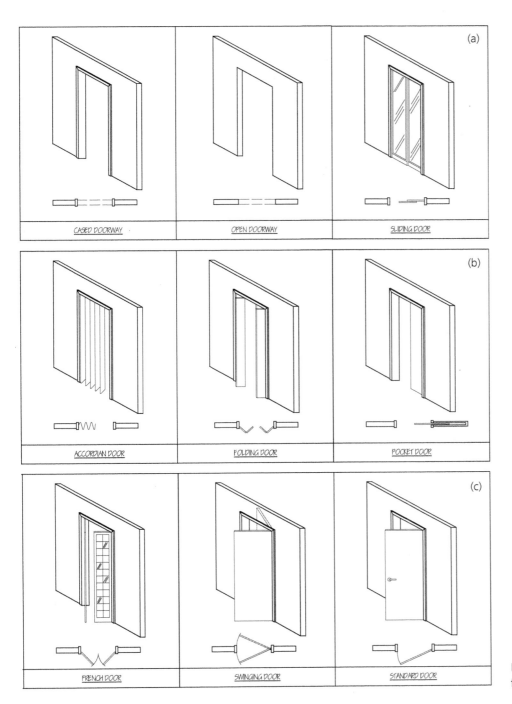

CASED DOORWAY   OPEN DOORWAY   SLIDING DOOR

ACCORDIAN DOOR   FOLDING DOOR   POCKET DOOR

FRENCH DOOR   SWINGING DOOR   STANDARD DOOR

FIGURE 2.5 Select a door style and swing that fit the purpose and design.

The second consideration is energy efficiency. Like windows, doors can vary as to air tightness and insulating value. The most insulating doors are ones that are filled with foam insulation. Solid wood doors may provide the desired look the client desires, but they are not providing the same level of insulating value. A third consideration is style. If the door is a visible feature of the room, you want it to coordinate with the style of the home's exterior as well as the kitchen. Doors can be solid or have varying sizes of windows. Including a window may be an added security risk, but it will add additional light to the room. The client will need to decide the style that is best for them.

Adequate door clearances should be maintained to allow easy access by individuals. See Chapter 6, "Kitchen Planning," for more information on door clearances. Other kitchen modifications can also affect the door fit. For example, some floor covering applications, such as tile or stone, or floor heating systems may raise the floor level enough that the doors will need to be trimmed in order to clear the floor.

Windows

Windows serve many important functions in the kitchen, including providing daylight for the space, supplying fresh air when needed, and allowing a view of the outdoors to watch children play in the backyard or to enjoy the scenery. A window at a sink where the cook may spend a significant amount of time preparing food or cleaning up after the family meal is considered a traditional view. When the sink or cooktop is located in an island, the view is the living area of the home. See Chapter 6 for more sink placement considerations.

For new construction, plan the placement of windows early so that other components of the kitchen can be arranged around them. Once framed in, windows may be difficult to relocate. For remodeling projects, this may be the opportunity to help your client find a better arrangement or sizing for the windows. Carefully examine the current windows and discuss their placement and condition with your client.

Simply replacing a window with one of the same dimensions will not usually require changes in the wall structure. However, if you decide a window needs to be moved or changed in size, carefully examine the wall space where the changes will be made. Be aware of any structural issues that need consideration, such as studs that must be removed or moved, vent stacks that might be present, or headers that need to be modified. The removal of any studs to add a larger window will mean the addition of a larger header over the window to help support the weight of the structure.

With any type of replacement window, consider the fenestration pattern of the windows; that is, the placement of the window openings on the exterior of the home. You want the new window to blend with the other windows of the home, especially if this replacement window faces the street. And, if you modify the size or move the window opening, consider whether exterior surfacing materials can be repositioned or reapplied to blend in.

Selection Considerations

There are numerous window choices and considerations when selecting a kitchen window.

- **Operability:** Windows can be operable or fixed. Clients may wish to add fresh air to a room and desire at least some operable windows. Fixed glass might be found in some decorative or picture windows or sliding glass doors. Place operable windows where they can be easily accessed. If located at a sink, certain types of windows may be difficult to use so select a style that the client can reach and operate.
- **Security:** Vandalism, break-ins, or theft can be a concern for any window in the home. New glass options are available with security glass that is more difficult to penetrate. High-quality lock systems are also important with windows, as they were with doors.
- **Privacy:** If privacy is a concern, especially if the kitchen window is facing a busy street or the house next door, you may need to recommend ways to provide privacy with the addition of an inside window treatment.
- **Cost:** The cost of windows can vary tremendously. The framing materials, size, quality of construction, and energy efficiency can all factor into the cost. It is usually advisable to buy the best windows the client can afford because they will last longer, be easier to operate, and make the home more pleasant and comfortable.

Window Styles

Many different styles of windows would be appropriate for a kitchen. The type, style, and size will depend on the size of the kitchen, the intended use, the view, and where it will be placed. Smaller kitchens may be more limited on window locations. Larger kitchens, however, may have multiple windows or even a sliding glass door to the outdoors. A popular trend is to add a large number of windows to increase daylighting, which will create a kitchen with fewer upper wall cabinets. Whatever the size, windows are an important part of your design plan.

There are a number of common window styles that could be used in a kitchen (Figure 2.6). These include:

- **Single- or double-hung windows:** The single- and double-hung windows are common window styles used in homes. In double-hung windows, both sashes slide vertically, whereas only the bottom sash slides upward in the single-hung window. Many of these windows also have sashes that tilt inward for easy cleaning. These sliding windows generally have higher air leakage rates than hinged windows.
- **Casement windows:** Casement window panels are hinged at the side and crank open to a 90-degree angle, exposing almost all of the window area to the outside. This style has almost double the ventilation area compared to a double-hung window, especially if there is a little breeze. Perhaps a downside to these windows is that the screen is on the inside of the window. Because the sash is closed by pressing against the frame, they have lower air leakage rates than sliding type windows.
- **Hopper and awning windows:** Hopper windows are hinged at the bottom and open inward, and awning windows are hinged at the top and open outward. In both styles, the sash closes by pressing against the frame. They generally have a lower air leakage rate than sliding windows.
- **Single- and double-sliding windows:** Both sashes slide horizontally in a double-sliding window, and only one sash slides in a single-sliding window, opening part of the window at a time. Like the single- and double-hung windows, they have a higher air leakage rate.

Energy Efficiency

The energy efficiency of the window area in the kitchen is extremely important for a number of reasons. More efficient windows will improve energy efficiency, as well as increase comfort. Efficient windows also cut down on moisture accumulation on the window (those frosty windows we sometimes see on cold winter days) because warm, moist air is naturally attracted to cold surfaces like those of poorly insulated windows.

Windows in older homes can be extremely inefficient. First of all, they may have loose-fitting frames and poorly working components that allow air infiltration. Another reason for poor efficiency is the type of frame and glazing present. Uninsulated metal frames and single-glazed windows will allow warmth to be conducted through the materials very easily. If the client insists on keeping the current windows in place, the windows can be tightened up with caulking and weatherstripping. Adding full storm windows is another way to improve efficiency, but your client may not want to deal with storm windows every season.

Windows that are energy efficient will have at least two layers of glazing (glass); a good quality, insulating frame; tight fitting parts; and sometimes argon or other gas between the panes of glazing. Low-emissivity (low-e) glass is another feature that increases the energy efficiency of a window. Low-e window glass has a coating on the glass that can prevent heat loss or gain from radiant energy. The choice of the location of the low-e coating depends on the climate. For heating-dominant climates, the coating is on the inner glass of a multiple pane window, to radiate heat back into the building. This can keep the surface of the glass warmer (Figure 2.7).

One way to identify the most efficient windows on the market is to look for the Energy Star label. Energy Star is an international program to promote energy efficient products and practices. For more information on Energy Star, see Chapter 3.

The National Fenestration Rating Council (NFRC) is a nationally recognized organization that has developed a rating system for windows and skylights. This rating system allows the purchaser to compare different attributes of windows related to energy performance, solar gain, visibility, air leakage, and condensation. Figure 2.8 shows an example of an NFRC label.

The NFRC label contains ratings on the following factors:

- **U-factors for windows and skylights:** U-factor is a measurement of heat conductivity or thermal transfer. This can be heat loss or heat gain. The lower the U-factor, the more energy

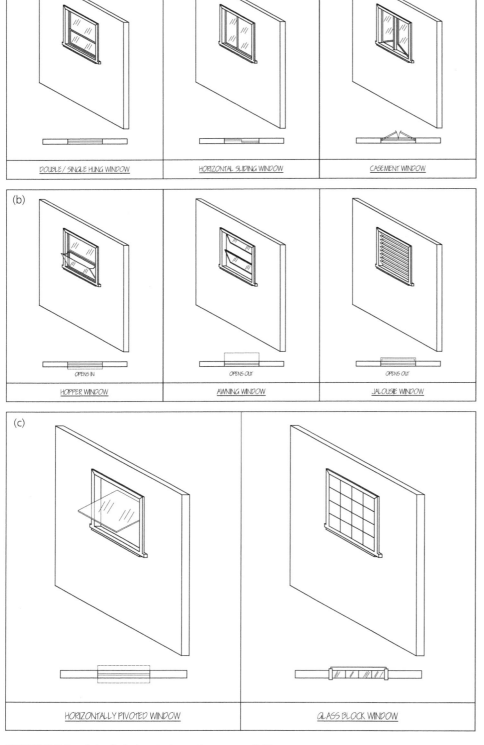

(a)

DOUBLE / SINGLE HUNG WINDOW

HORIZONTAL SLIDING WINDOW

CASEMENT WINDOW

(b)

OPENS IN

HOPPER WINDOW

OPENS OUT

AWNING WINDOW

OPENS OUT

JALOUSIE WINDOW

(c)

HORIZONTALLY PIVOTED WINDOW

GLASS BLOCK WINDOW

FIGURE 2.6 A variety of window design options are available.

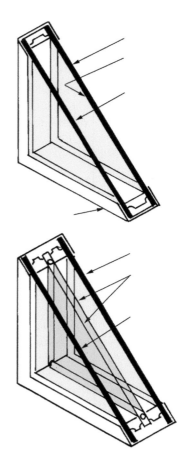

FIGURE 2.7 A low-e–coated surface or low-e coated polyester films improve the energy efficiency of a window by limiting heat gain and reflecting heat back into the home.

NFRC CERTIFIED	
National Fenestration Rating Council®	**World's Best Window Co.** Millennium 2000+ Vinyl-Clad Wood Frame Double Glazing • Argon Fill • Low E Product Type: **Vertical Slider**

ENERGY PERFORMANCE RATINGS

U-Factor (U.S./I-P)	Solar Heat Gain Coefficient
0.30	**0.30**

ADDITIONAL PERFORMANCE RATINGS

Visible Transmittance	Air Leakage (U.S./I-P)
0.51	**0.2**

Manufacturer stipulates that these ratings conform to applicable NFRC procedures for determining whole product performance. NFRC ratings are determined for a fixed set of environmental conditions and a specific product size. NFRC does not recommend any product and does not warrant the suitability of any product for any specific use. Consult manufacturer's literature for other product performance information. www.nfrc.org

FIGURE 2.8 Sample NFRC label.
National Fenestration Rating Council

efficient the window. The U-factor is especially important in heating-dominated climates, but it is also beneficial in cooling-dominated climates as well.

- **Solar heat gain coefficient (SHGC):** SHGC is a measure of how much solar radiation passes through the glass. This is expressed as a number between 0 and 1, and the lower the number the less solar heat it transmits. The rating you need depends on the location of the window and the climate, and the IRC recommends an SHGC level based on the climate zone. For example, a high SHGC is desirable for passive solar heat gain in a cold climate, while a low SHGC is preferred in a hot, sunny climate. West-facing windows can be an issue in most any climate, so low SHGC is important for keeping solar heat from entering through these windows. See Chapter 3 for more details.

- **Visible transmittance (VT):** VT indicates the amount of visible light transmitted through the glass. The NFRC's VT is a whole window rating and includes the impact of the frame. The VT rating varies between 0 and 1, and the higher the VT, the more light transmitted, thus maximizing the amount of daylight through the window. Most double- and triple-pane windows are rated between 0.30 and 0.70.

- **Air leakage (AL):** The air leakage is the amount of heat loss or gain that occurs by infiltration through cracks and openings in the window assembly. The AL is measured in cubic feet of air through a square foot of window area (l/s/m^2 or m^3/h/m). The lower the AL, the less air that will pass through the window assembly, and this rating is optional on the NFRC label. This rating does not measure air leakage between the window assembly and the wall *after* the window has been installed.

- **Condensation resistance (CR):** The CR measures how well a window resists the formation of condensation on the inside surface of the window and is expressed as a number between 1 and 100. The higher the number, the better the resistance to condensation, and this is also an optional rating on the NFRC label.

Window energy efficiency requirements may vary by climate zone, but also by jurisdiction if a variation of the IRC code is adopted.

Framing Materials

Choosing energy efficient, durable, low-maintenance framing materials is important for windows. Following the recommendations of the Energy Star program would be a good suggestion. Energy Star qualified windows come in a variety of framing materials.

- Fiberglass frames are strong, durable, low maintenance, and provide good insulation. Fiberglass frames can be either hollow or filled with foam insulation.
- Vinyl frames are low maintenance and provide good thermal insulation. Sections may be hollow or filled with foam insulation. Wide vinyl sills may be reinforced with metal or wood.
- Aluminum frames are durable, low maintenance, recyclable, and typically have at least 15 percent recycled content. Frame design usually includes thermal breaks to reduce conductive heat loss through the metal.
- Wood frames are strong, provide good insulation, and are generally favored in historical neighborhoods. The exterior surfaces of many wood windows are clad (or covered) with aluminum or vinyl to reduce maintenance.
- Combination frames use different materials separately throughout the frame and sash to provide optimal performance. For example, the exterior half of a frame could be vinyl, while the interior half could be wood.
- Composite frames are made of various materials that have been blended together through manufacturing processes to create durable, low-maintenance, well-insulated windows.

Skylights

Another way to add additional daylight to a kitchen is through the use of a skylight. Skylights bring in natural light, reducing the need for artificial light during the daylight hours. Kitchens in two-story homes may not have roof access for a skylight unless it is under a roof extension, but single-story homes can accommodate a skylight fairly easily. Skylights can be Energy Star–qualified, and they carry NFRC ratings as well. When selecting a skylight for a kitchen, consider many of the same factors you would for other windows. Skylights can come in two basic styles (Figure 2.9):

- **Traditional:** A traditional skylight typically uses the same basic technologies to construct the window as a standard window. Many skylights are fixed, but some are operable (sometimes referred to as roof windows) to let warm air out in the summer. Skylights can be installed horizontal, angled, or perpendicular to the roof joists. Another form of skylight is a plate of glass fixed to an opening in the roof and often covered by an opaque bubble to help shield the glass and add some insulating value. Traditional skylights often have an opening in the ceiling that extends from the glass area on the roof, through the attic to the room below. The ceiling opening can remain the size of the window glass or flare out as it enters the room space to add light to a larger area.
- **Tubular:** The tubular daylight devices (TDD) are tubes that extend from the roof down through the roof /attic to the kitchen space. These devices gather light at the roof and transmit it down to a diffusing lens mounted in an interior surface, usually the ceiling. The opening for these tubes is usually smaller than a typical skylight, so it is a means to add daylight to many areas of the home, including large pantries, butler pantries, or halls that would not have access to sunlight.

The quality of the skylight or tube is important because skylights are usually exposed to the extremes of sun and weather for longer periods of the day, especially those that are installed horizontal to the roof. They could even be covered with snow for periods of time. Skylights have had the reputation of leaking, so careful installation and high-quality products are essential to prevent water damage in the home.

PLUMBING

In addition to the standard kitchen sink and dishwasher, a kitchen may need water for a second sink or dishwasher, steam oven, coffee system, hot water dispenser, water filtration system in a refrigerator, ice maker, or pot filler faucet. To ensure they all function properly, water delivery should be evaluated. If your client is currently having a problem with inadequate water volume,

FIGURE 2.9 (a) Traditional skylights by VELUX America from The No Leak Skylight™ line. (b) Cutaway view of tubular skylight.
Courtesy of VELUX America

water pressure, or the amount of available hot water, help them investigate ways to remedy these issues and, as a result, improve the functioning of kitchen equipment, as well as the water system of the entire home.

Water quality related to water hardness can also affect water delivery when it leads to problems with appliance operation. Chapter 3 provides information on hard water and other water concerns and offers suggestions on how to remedy water problems.

In new construction, the plumbing system can be planned with the new kitchen in mind. If you are working on a remodeling project, however, many decisions will need to be made related to relocating the current fixtures or deciding where new water and drain lines must be added, and the difficulty of that process. Because pipe is bigger and less flexible to work with than wire, it is a good idea to schedule the plumber before you schedule the electrician.

Plumbing Fixtures

A new kitchen means selecting all new fixtures, but when a client is remodeling, you could, on occasion, have a client who wishes to reuse some of the present fixtures. These fixtures may have been recently replaced, or perhaps they are special vintage fixtures that your client wishes to keep in the kitchen design. Reusing current fixtures involves investigating whether or not they can be successfully removed and reinstalled, or relocated if the new plan calls for a new location. Refer to Form 11 in Chapter 5 to collect information and measurements on existing fixtures and water-using appliances.

When new fixtures are desired in the current location, decide if they can be installed using the old plumbing lines or if new lines and fittings need to be added. Talk with the client about the fixtures he or she has in mind and the options that might be available for that fixture. For example, sinks come in many sizes and configurations, and faucets and accessories can vary widely in style, as well as the many mounting locations on and near the sink. Discuss the pros and cons of each type with your client to ensure they end up with the look and function they desire.

Another key consideration is water usage. Be sure to select water-conserving plumbing fixtures such as faucets with aerators. Using these water efficient fixtures may solve or avoid some of the problems or concerns related to high water demand in the home, and the client will be incorporating sustainable measures as well. See Chapter 3 for more information on water conservation and other water issues.

Water Delivery

Consider the following when planning water delivery in the kitchen:

- To help cut costs in new construction or remodeling projects, locate the kitchen near another room with plumbing, like a bathroom or the laundry room, to take advantage of clustered plumbing lines.
- New flexible water supply piping makes it possible to easily reposition fixtures, such as a sink. Before you count on using this type of piping, check local codes to make sure it is allowed.
- Sinks come equipped with water shutoff valves, but when multiple water use appliances are incorporated into the kitchen, also consider locating a central shutoff somewhere in or near the kitchen to control water to that entire area (Figure 2.10).
- Water delivery lines to some appliances, called a supply line, can be merely a small plastic tube. Care needs to be taken so that the line does not kink or is not punctured by other kitchen components. Hard water minerals can also easily clog these lines because they are very small. Be sure to adhere to the manufacturers installation instructions. Many manufactures specify flexible copper lines rather than plastic.
- Outdoor kitchens also include sinks, and so provisions need to be made to ensure that the plumbing lines are protected against freezing in the winter.

Drain/Waste/Vent Pipes

As you examine the plumbing in the kitchen you are remodeling, you may notice that current code requirements for the size, type, and/or height of plumbing drain/waste/vent components may require structural changes (Figure 2.11).

Codes set a minimum diameter for stack and vent pipes in relation to the number of fixtures installed. If the home is quite old, a careful examination may find that the current configuration of vent pipes does not meet these codes, so you must decide what it will take to make the necessary changes. Basically, each sink will need to have a provision for a vent pipe. It may be more difficult to accommodate vents for sinks located on interior walls or in islands.

When relocating a sink, there is a 5-foot (1.5-m) limit for the changeover of a vent. If the distance from the sink to the vent location is greater, you will need to open more wall space to install a new vent or to re-vent.

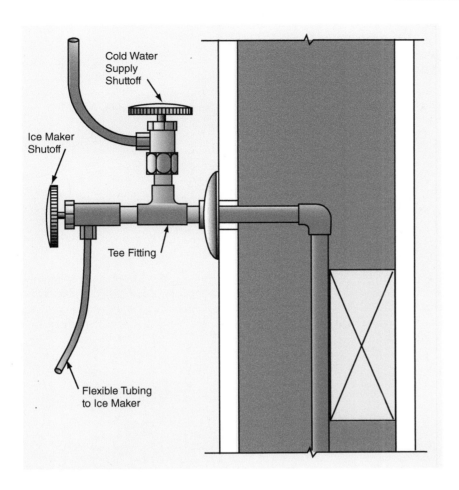

Cold Water
Supply
Shuttoff

Ice Maker
Shutoff

Tee Fitting

Flexible Tubing
to Ice Maker

FIGURE 2.10 Water shutoff valves at the sink stop water delivery when necessary. If an appliance water supply line is connected, such as an ice maker, it must also have a shutoff valve.

If the house is built on a slab, reconfiguring plumbing will involve additional challenges. In order to move or add new pipes, you may need to chip into the concrete to get at the current pipes and/or make channels where new pipe must be laid. In this case, consider changes carefully, as they may make the project more difficult and add to its cost for your client.

Septic Systems

A consideration for clients who are not connected to a municipal waste system is the septic tank. If your client plans to install a garbage disposer, you will need to check the septic system capacity to make sure it can handle the additional water and waste. It may be that you will need to add a larger septic tank to accommodate the extra waste. If the tank is too small, it may need to be emptied more frequently. With too much waste, the system cannot function adequately, leading to a breakdown of the septic system and environmental consequences.

Hot Water and Filtered Water

A dependable and readily available supply of hot water is essential for the kitchen. A large amount of water is wasted when the user needs to open the faucet valve for an extended period of time before hot water reaches the faucet. A nearby hot water supply ensures that appliances like the dishwasher fill first with hot water rather than cold. How quickly that hot water arrives to the kitchen fixtures can vary depending on the location of the water heater in relation to the kitchen. If this appears to be an issue, a second water heater located near the kitchen would be a good idea. Information on water heaters is included in Chapter 7.

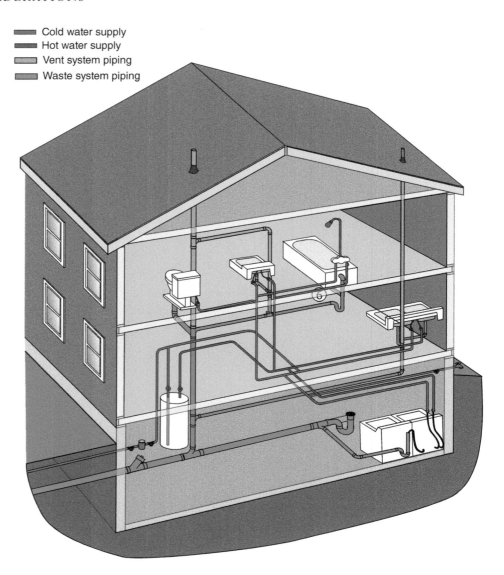

Cold water supply
Hot water supply
Vent system piping
Waste system piping

FIGURE 2.11 The location and size of drain, waste, and vent pipes have to be considered when remodeling a kitchen or bath.

Adapted from Charlie Wing, How Your House Works *(Hoboken, NJ: John Wiley & Sons, 2012)*

Hot water dispensers supply hot water with a separate, smaller faucet to provide nearly boiling water for preparing instant coffee, tea, or instant soups (Figure 2.12). If your client would like to locate this type of hot water dispenser on the sink, an extra hole will need to be ordered or drilled in the surface of the sink. Counter-mounted units will also need to have an opening ready for installation. No matter the type of installation, a water supply line will need to be installed under the sink for the heating unit.

If water filtration is included along with the hot water dispenser in a dual device, space will be needed for the filtration unit as well. Sometimes the space under a sink has become very congested with pipes, a disposer, and an electrical outlet for appliances. If you specify a water heater and filter, make sure there is space to install and service these items. If the space becomes too congested, the client may have little room left for storage of items like a waste basket, dish pan, dish drainer, detergent, or cleaning supplies. Also keep in mind that the filter will need to be replaced periodically, so locate it where the client can access it without too much inconvenience.

NOISE

A kitchen can be a noisy place. Typically, there is a lot of activity, pots and pans banging, appliance motors whirring, water running, and people talking. Even when people are not in the kitchen, appliances can continue to operate, and the sound might be heard in adjacent spaces.

FIGURE 2.12 Hot water dispensers provide instant hot water for many purposes in the kitchen.
Courtesy of InSinkErator

Noise is often defined as unwanted sound. Therefore, controlling noise is a matter of limiting the transfer of sound from one part of the home to another.

Sound moves by vibrations, which are transmitted through both air and building materials. Soft materials, such as carpet and draperies, tend to absorb sound. Hard materials, such as ceramic tile and stone, often found in the kitchen, tend to reflect and/or transmit sounds. Noise is controlled in several ways:

- Reduce the amount of sound or noise that is generated.
- Isolate and buffer the sources of noise by space planning.
- Use construction techniques to insulate and stop sound transmission.

Reduce the Sound Generated

A first step to reducing noise problems in a kitchen is to choose appliances that operate quietly. In particular, specify a dishwasher that is well insulated for sound control. Make sure all appliances are level to reduce noise-generating vibrations.

Kitchen ventilation fans are necessary to control moisture and other air pollutants, yet motors and air movement can be noisy. The quietest fans are those with the lowest *sone* rating. Selecting and installing kitchen fans to minimize noise is discussed in the section on ventilation in Chapter 7. A fan that is too loud simply will not be used by the client. Lack of use may control noise but will lead to air-quality problems, especially with odors and moisture.

Laundry areas (see Chapter 9, "More Than a Kitchen") are sometimes included in or near the kitchen. Noise transmission, especially to the social areas, should be considered when installing washers and dryers near or in the kitchen.

Motors, such as those used in ventilation fans, small appliances, and washing machines, may vary in pitch (hertz). Many people perceive lower pitch noises to be less annoying. However, it is important for your client to "test listen" to different motors to determine his or her reaction to the noise before purchasing.

Another way to reduce kitchen noise is to line shelves in cabinets with cork, rubber, or other sound-absorbing materials to reduce the "clatter" of dishes and other items as they are moved in and out of the cabinet. Cabinet doors and drawers should have cork or rubber bumpers to absorb the banging noise that can occur with closing.

Buffer the Noisy Spaces

If you have the opportunity to influence the home design beyond the kitchen space, look for ways to put sound-absorbing spaces between it and the adjacent quiet areas of the home. For example, a closet situated between a kitchen and a bedroom is an excellent way to buffer noise and to keep sleeping areas undisturbed (Figure 2.13). Built-in cabinets, bookshelves, stairways, and utility closets all make good sound buffers.

Another sound-buffering space-planning technique is to back noisy area to noisy area. For example, put the dishwasher on the wall that is shared with the bathroom toilet, rather than the same wall that is shared with the bedroom.

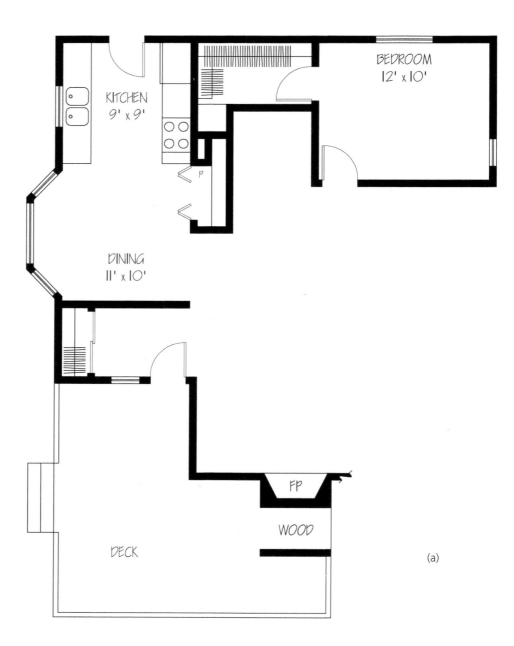

FIGURE 2.13 In plan A, a closet and pantry buffer the kitchen noise from the first floor bedroom. In plan B, the stairway, pantry, and powder room buffer the more formal areas of the home (living room and dining) from the kitchen noise.

(b)

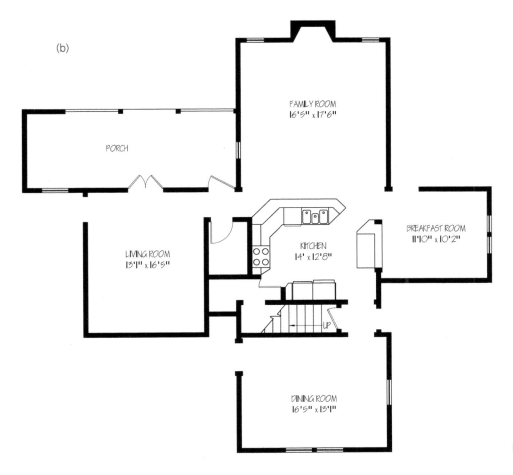

FAMILY ROOM
16'5" x 17'6"

PORCH

LIVING ROOM
13'1" x 16'5"

KITCHEN
14' x 12'8"

BREAKFAST ROOM
11'10" x 10'2"

UP

DINING ROOM
16'5" x 13'1"

FIGURE 2.13 (*continued*)

Sound-Insulating Construction Techniques

In new construction, or renovations that include building new walls, use sound-insulating construction techniques to isolate kitchen noises. One simple approach is to use materials such as acoustical tiles, cork, carpet, and other sound-muffling textiles. However, these softer and absorbent materials may not be the best choices in the kitchen where water, grease, and mold resistance and easy cleaning are important. Therefore, look at wall construction techniques that reduce sound transmission.

To minimize the transmission of sound, avoid air paths between the kitchen and other spaces. For example, use resilient, nonhardening caulk to seal around receptacles, plumbing, light fixtures, and other openings in the walls and ceilings. Also, seal where the wall partition joins the floor and ceiling. If there are switches, receptacles, and other openings on opposite sides of a wall, avoid locating them in the same stud space. If possible, separate these switches and receptacles, horizontally, by at least 24 inches (600 mm).

There are several ways to construct the walls to minimize sound transmission. A standard stud wall could be insulated with fiberglass or a similar material to absorb sound. A sound-deadening gasket could be used between the studs and the drywall to minimize vibration and sound transmission. A double stud wall, with the studs on separate plates, reduces sound transmission by separating the two wall structures and limiting vibration. A staggered stud, double stud wall is another option. Insulating material can be added to any of these special wall constructions (Figure 2.14).

Keep in mind that special, sound-insulating wall constructions do have several drawbacks, and the trade-offs need to be considered. Cost is increased for extra materials and time in construction. Floor space is lost, especially with the double walls. Also, the need to run plumbing, wiring, and ducts in the walls has to be considered, especially with a staggered stud, double wall.

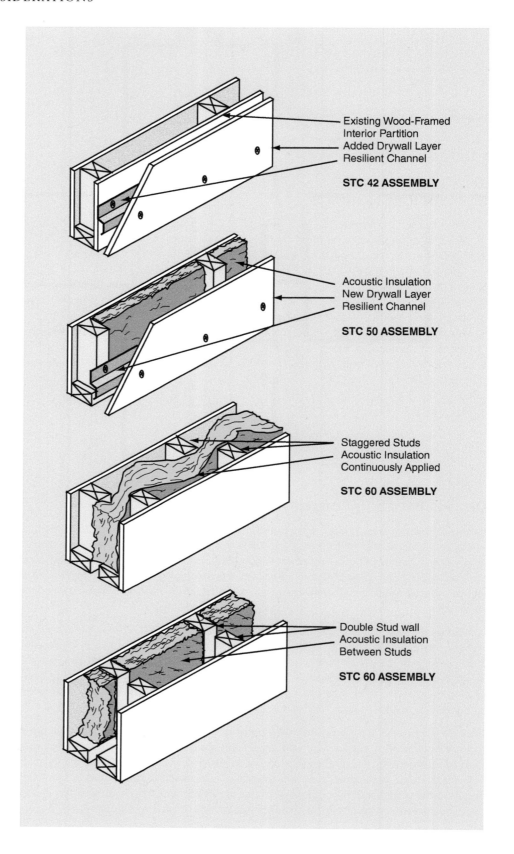

Existing Wood-Framed
Interior Partition
Added Drywall Layer
Resilient Channel

STC 42 ASSEMBLY

Acoustic Insulation
New Drywall Layer
Resilient Channel

STC 50 ASSEMBLY

Staggered Studs
Acoustic Insulation
Continuously Applied

STC 60 ASSEMBLY

Double Stud wall
Acoustic Insulation
Between Studs

STC 60 ASSEMBLY

FIGURE 2.14 Different building techniques can be used to reduce sound transmission through walls, which is measured by sound transmission class, or STC.

SUMMARY

Whether you are helping clients plan a new kitchen or remodel their current one, carefully investigate the basic structural components that are so essential to a successful project.

Floors, walls, windows, and plumbing may pose problems or require special structural considerations that must be identified and dealt with before all the new products are specified and installed. In Chapter 7, additional considerations for mechanical systems are examined. The more you know about these issues, the fewer changes your client will need to make later on and the more functional your plan will become. Your client will also be more satisfied with the results.

REVIEW QUESTIONS

1. Why is it important to check the floor structure for a kitchen remodeling project and what steps should you take to do so? (See "Structural Issues—Floors" p. 48)
2. What information about a window's energy performance is provided on the National Fenestration Council Rating label? (See "Windows—Energy Efficiency" pp. 55–57)
3. How do you identify load-bearing walls? (See "Walls—Load-Bearing Walls" pp. 50–51)
4. Explain how door styles and placement can affect how people function in a kitchen. (See "Doors and Windows—Door Choices" pp. 52–54)
5. How might the installation of a disposer affect cabinet planning and septic tank consideration? (See "Septic Systems" p. 61)
6. What measures may need to be taken when installing cabinets in rooms with uneven and out-of-square walls? (See "Uneven Walls" p. 51)

Environmental and Sustainability Considerations

Good design includes planning spaces that are environmentally friendly and healthy for the user. Good design reflects sustainable use of resources. In this chapter, we will look at important issues of energy efficiency, water quality, waste management, and air quality. We will consider these issues from the choices you, the designer, must make, as well as the impact on your client.

This chapter is a very brief review of environmental and sustainability issues affecting kitchen design. If you as the designer, or your client, need further information on environmental issues, you can contact the U.S. Environmental Protection Agency (EPA). The website www.epa.gov is a good place to start. Other excellent resources are Natural Resources Canada (www.oee.nrcan. gc.ca) and Health Canada (www.hc-sc.gc.ca). Or, contact your Cooperative Extension office, health department, or water authority. Additional resources are included at the end of this book.

After reading this chapter, you may wish to pursue further study and learn more about sustainable and environmental issues. Many of the organizations and agencies discussed in this chapter offer educational classes and opportunities to become a certified professional with special environmental and sustainable knowledge.

Learning Objective 1: Identify and discuss sustainable products and practices for the kitchen.

Learning Objective 2: Identify and discuss policies and practices for the efficient management of energy, water, and waste in the design and construction of the kitchen.

Learning Objective 3: Identify and discuss policies and practices for healthy housing.

SUSTAINABLE DESIGN AND BUILDING

Sustainability, as applied today, has many definitions. It is being energy efficient, but much more. Most definitions of sustainability revolve around the idea of balance, thinking of the future, and minimizing impact today. Sustainability issues in buildings include energy efficiency, water management, air quality, waste management, and recycling. There are sustainable practices, products, and techniques in the design and construction of a building. Sustainability is also a philosophical approach that guides design and business decisions.

Envision a Sustainable Building

The Rocky Mountain Institute (www.rmi.org) offers this description of a sustainable building:

- Makes appropriate use of land
- Uses water, energy, lumber, and other resources efficiently
- Enhances human health
- Strengthens local economies and communities
- Conserves plants, animals, endangered species, and natural habitats
- Protects agricultural, cultural, and archeological resources
- Is economical to build and operate
- Is nice to live in

D. L. Barnett and W. D. Browning, *A Primer on Sustainable Building* (Boulder, CO: Rocky Mountain Institute, 2004).

In recent years, the term *green building* has come to represent policies and practices that are environmentally responsible—sustainable. Sustainable, green building practices are recognized to:

- Promote healthy places to live and work
- Enhance and protect natural ecosystems and biodiversity
- Improve air and water quality
- Reduce solid waste
- Conserve natural resources

For the designer, there are many opportunities to implement sustainable design policies and practices. A general overview follows. This chapter will further detail many opportunities to practice sustainability that are particularly applicable to kitchen design and construction.

- Think small, compact—minimalist (Figure 3.1). A smaller space is a more sustainable space. Fewer materials are used in the constructing of a smaller space. There is less space to heat and cool. Less energy is needed for lighting.
- Specify environmentally healthy building and interior finish materials, including nontoxic, sustainably harvested, recycled, or renewable resource products. Look for opportunities to reuse materials through salvage or repurposing.
- Specify materials and products from local sources to minimize the energy or pollution "cost" for transportation.
- Specify products, including appliances, which are energy efficient.
- Specify plumbing fixtures and appliances that conserve water.
- Maximize the use of daylight and specify energy-efficient light sources.
- Plan window placement to maximize passive solar heat gain through south facing windows and minimize heat loss through north windows in colder months. Limit heat gain though west windows during the cooling season.
- Specify energy-efficient windows (Figure 3.2).
- Plan the layout of the kitchen and auxiliary spaces to maximize the use of standard size materials and products, minimizing the amount of construction waste.
- Investigate and implement opportunities to recycle construction and demolition waste. Encourage clients to donate serviceable cabinetry, appliances, and fixtures removed in renovations to charitable organizations.

CHOOSING SUSTAINABLE PRODUCTS

Product specifications are an important part of any design project. There are many criteria that influence the best choice of materials, fixtures, appliances, lighting, or any of the many items that

FIGURE 3.1 A New Orleans example of a small, compact house.

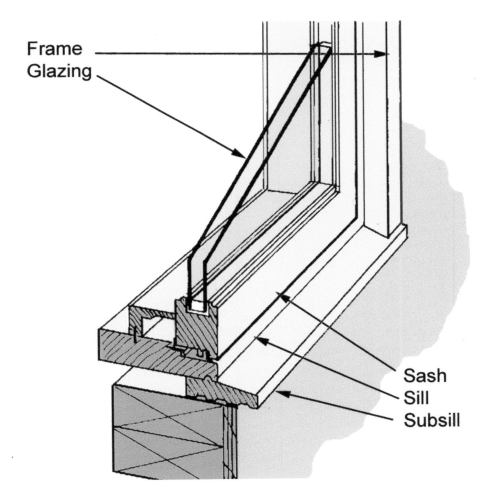

Frame

Glazing

Sash
Sill
Subsill

FIGURE 3.2 Double-glazed windows cut heat loss in half, compared to a single-glazed window.

go into a kitchen or the auxiliary spaces that you are designing. The products must be functional as well as aesthetic, meet the needs of the client, follow the building code, fall within the budget, be compatible with other products being installed—and the list goes on. Add the priority of sustainability, and a complex process is now even more complex.

Evaluating a product for sustainability can be difficult because the criteria are not always clear-cut. Some sustainable practices are easier to accomplish or may be a higher priority for your client. Some sustainable practices have immediate impact, some do not.

Resource use is a basic measure of sustainability. For example, how much energy or water does this product use? Transportation costs are another measure. For example, was the product manufactured locally? However, the picture can then become more complex to evaluate. How sustainable is the manufacturing process for different product choices? Which material has the lesser impact on indoor air quality? Which product can be recycled after use?

There are a growing number of independent and reliable testing, evaluation, and certification programs that evaluate one or more sustainability criteria of products and materials used in kitchens and auxiliary spaces. Many of these programs are discussed in this chapter and can be used to assist you and your client in developing a quality and effective sustainable project.

GREEN BUILDING PROGRAMS

One approach to specifying sustainable products and materials is to become familiar with the criteria for one or more of the programs for certifying residential green buildings. The United States Green Building Council's LEED for Homes, the National Association of Home Builders National Green Building Standards™, and the Natural Resources Canada R-2000 Standard are examples of programs that provide guidelines for certifying homes based on sustainability criteria. In addition, regional and local programs, such as Southface Institute's Earthcraft House, BUILT GREEN® (Canada); Earth Advantage Institute's New Homes; and Austin, Texas's Austin Energy® Green Building provide similar certification opportunities.

A program that certifies a home as a green building sets criteria for products, materials, and practices that are sustainable. Credit toward certification may be given for features such as water-conserving plumbing fixtures, materials with recycled content, or energy-efficient appliances. Therefore, specifying materials and products that meet national, regional, or local green building program criteria contributes to a project's sustainability.

As a designer, you may be part of a team that is seeking a green building certification of a home or building. Careful record keeping and documentation will be required. However, you can take pride in your contribution to a more sustainable world. In addition, completion of a certified green building project is a marketable accomplishment and a valuable addition to your portfolio.

LEED for Homes

LEED, or Leadership in Energy and Environmental Design, is a program of the United States Green Building Council. LEED provides building owners and operators with a framework for identifying and implementing practical and measurable green building design, construction, operations, and maintenance solutions.

LEED certification provides independent, third-party verification that a building, home, or community was designed and built using strategies aimed at achieving high performance in key areas of human and environmental health: sustainable site development, water savings, energy efficiency, materials selection, and indoor environmental quality.

(continued)

LEED-certified buildings are designed to:

- Lower operating costs and increase asset value
- Reduce waste sent to landfills
- Conserve energy and water
- Be healthier and safer for occupants
- Reduce harmful greenhouse gas emissions
- Qualify for tax rebates, zoning allowances, and other incentives in many communities

LEED has multiple rating systems for different situations and buildings. LEED for Homes is targeted to residential buildings (Figure 3.3).

The Canada Green Building Council provides a version of the LEED program that is adapted for the Canadian climate, construction practices, and regulations (www.cagbc.org).

More information about LEED is available at www.usgbc.org.

(a)

(b)

Figure 3.3 A house in Maine (United States) is rated as LEED Platinum, the highest level of performance in LEED for Homes certification. *Courtesy of Creative Commons*

National Green Building Standards™

The creation of the ICC 700 National Green Building Standards™ was initiated by a partnership of the National Association of Home Builders (NAHB) and the International Code Council (ICC) to offer a national rating system and standard definition for green building (Figure 3.4). This building standard has received approval from the American National Standards Institute (ANSI), indicating it was developed through an open, consensus-based process with representative stakeholder participation and ample opportunity for public comment. The standard defines green building for single and multifamily homes, residential remodeling, and land development.

There are four performance point levels: bronze, silver, gold, and emerald. The threshold level (bronze) results in an energy savings approximately 15 percent above code requirements for the 2008 version of the standard. To achieve higher performance levels, the home must meet minimum performance points in each of six areas categories:

- Lot design, preparation, and development
- Resource efficiency
- Energy efficiency
- Water efficiency
- Indoor environmental quality
- Operation, maintenance, and building owner education

An updated version of the NGBS has gone through the consensus development process and is expected to be available in the first quarter of 2013. The draft revision of the NGBS includes a number of changes including more stringent energy-efficiency requirements, as well as the ability to certify small remodeling projects, such as kitchens, bathrooms, and basements.

Figure 3.4 The NAHB Research Center certifies houses, buildings, and developments conforming to the ICC 700 National Green Building Standard™.

R-2000

R-2000 is a voluntary technical performance standard for energy efficiency, indoor air tightness quality, and environmental responsibility in home construction. The program is industry endorsed and administered by Natural Resources Canada. Houses built to the R-2000 standard typically exceed the energy performance requirements of the current Canadian building codes. The standard was introduced over 25 years ago and is continually upgraded to include new technologies as they become established in the marketplace.

R-2000 homes are tested and certified by independent, third-party evaluators.

More information is available at www.oee.nrcan.gc.ca.

SUSTAINABLE CERTIFICATION PROGRAMS

Choosing sustainable products and practices can take time and require research. It will require careful reading of manufacturer specifications and other product information. You may have to become familiar with new terminology. However, there are ways to ways to both make the process easier and more reliable.

Look for products and materials that are certified by an independent organization. A valuable certification will require third-party, independent testing of the product or material to verify that the manufacturer meets the organizations standards or criteria. Certified products or materials will carry a label or logo from the certifying organization. The logo is a clear identification that the product or material meets the certification. This is different than marketing materials that may indicate the product "meets criteria" or is "qualified" but is not actually tested and certified.

Certifications are renewed on a regular basis. New models or types of materials require testing to qualify. Take care to determine what is actually being certified. For example, is the product being certified for some performance characteristic, such as energy use? Or is the manufacturing process being certified for sustainable practices?

This chapter introduces and describes a number of certifications for products and materials commonly used in kitchens. Most certifying organizations maintain websites that describe their programs and include lists of the specific products that are certified.

Specifying Certified Products and Materials

In this section, we describe some of the major certification programs that certify materials and products with respect to sustainability. This list is not exhaustive, but it introduces you to common certifications you might encounter in product literature, marketing materials, or elsewhere. We also discuss some other certification programs throughout this chapter where they fit better with the topic.

Scientific Certification Systems

Scientific Certification Systems works with manufacturers and businesses to offer a variety of certification programs in multiple areas. Some programs are designated under Scientific Certification Systems' own programs, such as the calCOMPliant™ Certification, for compliance with California Air Resources Board requirements on formaldehyde emissions. Other certification programs are developed in conjunction with industry organizations, such as the Resilient Floor

Covering Institute and the Forest Stewardship Council, to offer independent, third-party testing and verification.

Scientific Certification Systems certifications evaluate many construction products of interest to the kitchen designers. In particular, their sustainable certification programs verify recycled content, biodegradability, and chemical emissions. Further information is available at www.scscertified.com.

Cradle to Cradle Certification^{CM}

The Cradle to Cradle Certified Program is a third-party eco-label that assesses a product's safety to humans and the environment from a life-cycle perspective. The Cradle to Cradle framework focuses on using safe materials that can later be disassembled and recycled or composted. Criteria for certification include material health, material reutilization, renewable energy use, water stewardship, and social responsibility.

A wide variety of products have achieved Cradle to Cradle certification. Product categories of particular interest to kitchen designers are countertop materials, flooring, insulation, lighting, and wall coverings. Further information is available at www.c2ccertified.org. Cradle to Cradle Certified^{CM} is a certification mark licensed by the Cradle to Cradle Products Innovation Institute. Cradle to Cradle® is a registered trademark of McDonough Braungart Design Chemisty, LLC (Figure 3.5).

Ecolabel

The Ecolabel is a program of the European Union and is based on a life-cycle analysis of a product or service that is "kinder to the environment." Over 1100 licenses have been granted for products and services meeting the Ecolabel criteria, which starts with the raw material and finishes with disposal.

Currently, floor coverings, light bulbs, paints, varnishes, and some appliances are qualified for the Ecolabel. Taps (faucets) and additional appliances are under evaluation. More information is available at http://ec.europa.eu/environment/ecolabel.

Certifications for Wood Products

There are three different certification programs that certify woods used in cabinetry, flooring, and other products that you might specify in a kitchen.

- **Forest Stewardship Council (FSC):** The FSC Principles and Criteria describe how forests around the world can be managed to meet social, economic, ecological, cultural, and spiritual needs of present and future generations. The FSC offers a **Forest Management Certification**

FIGURE 3.5 The Cradle to Cradle® logo uses two Cs to emphasize the cyclical nature of the model.

for forest operations that are managed in an environmentally appropriate manner. A **Chain of Custody Certification** verifies FSC Certified forest products through the production chain (www.fsc.org).

- **American Tree Farm System® (ATFS):** This program targets small woodland owners. Certification requires implementation of a management plan for sustainable forest stewardship (www.treefarmsystem.org).
- **Programme for the Endorsement of Forest Certification (PEFC):** PEFC is an international organization dedicated to promoting sustainable forest management. PEFC promotes good practice so that forest products are produced with respect for the highest ecological, social, and ethical standards. The PEFC eco-label identifies products from sustainably managed forests. PEFC is an umbrella organization that has endorsed about 30 national certification systems, making it the world's largest forest certification system. PEFC programs of interest to the kitchen designer include its labeling of sustainable forest products and chain of custody certification (www.pefc.org).

Certified Recycled—What Does That Mean?

Using fewer new resources, and maximizing the use of the resources we have, is an important part of sustainability. More and more, sustainable products and materials are those that are made from recycled materials. But is it postconsumer, preconsumer, or postindustrial recycled? And is the material recyclable or compostable or biodegradable after use? If sustainability is based on the full life cycle of the product or material, and considers the impact on the future as well as the present, we need to stop and ask these questions. A few definitions are needed, courtesy of the United States Environmental Protection Agency and Federal Trade Commission.

- **Recycled:** Recycling turns materials that would otherwise become waste into valuable resources (Figure 3.6). Therefore, recycled content is material that has been recovered or diverted from the solid waste stream. Preconsumer (sometimes called postindustrial) recycled content is waste from the manufacturing process that would not normally be reused by

FIGURE 3.6 The universal symbol for recyclable or recycled products.

industry. Postconsumer recycled content is from the waste stream after consumer use. If the entire product or material is not of recycled content, qualifying words on the labeling are required (such as percentage).

- **Recyclable:** A material that is recyclable can be collected, separated, or recovered from the solid waste stream and used again or made into other useful products.
- **Degradable:** Degradable materials will break down and return to nature in a reasonable time frame after disposal. Biodegradable materials are broken down by naturally occurring microorganisms, such as bacteria. Photodegradable materials are broken down by exposure to light.
- **Salvaged or reclaimed:** There is no legal definition for these terms, but they are generally used to describe materials that are reused for a similar purpose in a building project. Often the building materials are taken from buildings, ships, or other sources that are no longer in existence in total. Using salvaged or reclaimed materials is a good way to make sustainable use of existing resources as long as the item being salvaged is safe and appropriate for the new use.
- **Repurposed:** This is a popular term used to describe using a product, material, or item for a new purpose in a project. As with salvage, the repurposed item needs to be safe and environmentally appropriate for the new use.

ENERGY ISSUES AND BUILDING CODES

The *International Residential Code* (IRC) is a model code published by the International Code Council. Although this model code is considered a benchmark in the building industry, it does not have the force of law until adopted by a state or municipal code agency. In 2012, the IRC incorporated the Residential Provisions of the International Energy Conservation Code into the chapter on energy efficiency. The IRC model code requirements represent important standards for energy efficiency in building design and construction. Although not all parts of the energy efficiency code are applicable to kitchen design, it is necessary for a designer to have an overall understanding of an energy-efficient building as represented by the IRC. This understanding prepares you for applying relevant parts of the code to your particular design project.

The 2012 IRC divides the United States and Canada into eight climate zones. Many code requirements are then specific to each climate zone, which is designated by state, province, county, or territory. The energy efficiency chapter of the code emphasizes creating a building structure that has a *thermal envelope* and *air barrier* that minimizes heat loss in winter, heat gain in summer, and air leakage year round. This is done with construction standards that are appropriate and cost effective to the climate.

Of interest to the kitchen designer are the following requirements for windows, doors, and walls:

- **U-factors** for windows, skylights, and exterior doors. A U-factor is a measurement of heat conductivity or thermal transfer. The lower the U-factor, the more energy efficient the window or door.
- **Solar heat gain coefficient** (SHGC) for windows. SHGC is a measure of how much solar heat passes through the glass.
- **R-value of insulation** in floors, walls, and ceilings. R-value is a measure of the resistance to heat conductivity. The higher the R-value, the better the insulation.

The code provides detailed information about sealing the structure to limit air infiltration as well as where to locate insulation. Further information on energy-efficient doors, windows, and walls is found in Chapter 2, "Infrastructure Considerations." In addition, there are requirements related to ventilation, which are further discussed in Chapter 7, "Mechanical Planning." Of particular note is the requirement for whole-house mechanical ventilation to provide adequate fresh air.

From the beginning of the design process, it is important to be aware of the influence of energy-efficiency codes on potential design and space solutions. Issues such as wall thickness and floor area; selection and placement of doors, windows, and lighting fixtures; placement of plumbing pipes and fixtures; and installation of venting systems are examples of design and construction decisions that can be influenced by requirements of the energy code.

EnergyGuide Labels

The bright yellow EnergyGuide label is used to provide information on the comparative energy use and costs on a variety of many appliances (Figure 3.7). This is a tool that can be used to select an energy-efficient appliance. The EnergyGuide label provides the yearly estimated energy costs for an appliance (based on the U.S. national average energy costs) as well as the yearly estimated kilowatt hour usage. The label also provides a graph showing the range of energy costs to operate similar appliances and indicates how the labeled appliance compares to this range. If the appliance is EnergyStar certified, that information is included on the EnergyGuide label.

EnergyGuide labels are found on those appliances where there is the most variation in energy use among models. In the kitchen, EnergyGuide labels can be used to select energy efficient dishwashers, refrigerators, freezers, and, if needed, clothes washers. Note that a dishwasher will have two energy cost estimates: one for water heated by electricity and one for water heated by gas.

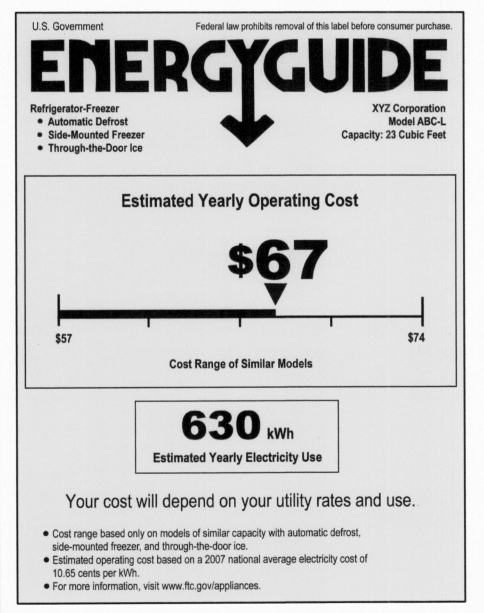

Figure 3.7 The manufacturer's test results of energy use and efficiency are included on a product's EnergyGuide label.

EnerGuide

Federal law in Canada requires an EnerGuide label on all new electrical appliances manufactured in or imported into Canada. The EnerGuide label indicates the amount of electricity used by that appliance. Third-party verification must show that the appliance meets Canada's minimum energy performance levels.

The EnerGuide label is a distinctive black-and-white label, similar in layout to the yellow EnergyGuide label. More information is available at www.oee.nrcan.gc.ca.

WATER

It is important for you, the designer, to discuss water quality with your client. The kitchen faucet is typically the main source of water for cooking, drinking, and washing the dishes. The water must be safe and healthy, as well as smell, taste, and look good. Water should work well for all kitchen uses and not contribute to maintenance problems. At the same time, water is a finite resource, and we have a responsibility to use it wisely and efficiently. The designer is an important influence in sustainable use of water in the kitchen.

Chapter 2 of this book discusses issues of an adequate water supply, water pressure, and the plumbing infrastructure necessary for a well-designed kitchen. This chapter discusses issues of water quality—water that is safe, healthy, and functional for drinking, cooking, and washing. In addition, efficient and sustainable use of water in the kitchen is presented.

WATER QUALITY STANDARDS

There are two types of water quality standards in the United States. The first ensures that water is safe to drink or ingest. These standards are called *Primary Drinking Water Standards* and are enforced by law. The second type of standard is to assure that water is functional and aesthetic for various uses, such as bathing and washing. These standards are referred to as *Secondary Drinking Water Standards*, and they are voluntary.

All municipal or public water systems are required to meet the primary standards that are established by the U.S. Environmental Protection Agency (EPA). These systems must regularly test and, if necessary, treat their water to ensure that it meets the primary standards. Individual or small private water systems (defined by the number of households connected to the water system) are not required to meet any water quality standards. However, owners of private systems are encouraged to use the EPA standards as benchmarks for testing and treatment of their water systems.

Health Canada (www.hc-sc.gc.ca) is the ministry responsible for drinking water standards in Canada and for educating Canadians about the importance of safe drinking water. The *Guidelines for Canadian Drinking Water Quality* addresses many of the same primary and secondary contaminant issues as the EPA guidelines. Similar to the United States, Health Canada works with provincial and territorial governments to ensure that Canadian water is safe to drink as well as functional and aesthetic for household uses. Environment Canada (www.ec.gc.ca) monitors Canadian water quality and provides leadership for water management issues.

Primary Drinking Water Standards

The Primary Drinking Water Standards are based on the *maximum contaminant levels* (MCLs), or highest concentration of pollutants, allowed in public drinking water. The pollutants that are regulated by the primary standards are those that are known to cause adverse health effects and for which there is information available about chronic or acute health risks. There are three classes of pollutants for which there are MCLs.

- **Disease-causing organisms:** Most disease-causing organisms in water come from animal and human waste contamination, including bacteria and viruses. These organisms are very common in water supplies before treatment, especially if the water source is from surface water, such as lakes or rivers.
- **Toxic chemicals:** There are many toxic chemicals covered by the primary standards, including naturally occurring contaminants such as arsenic and copper; heavy metals such as cadmium, lead, and mercury; agricultural byproducts such as nitrates; industrial and manufacturing byproducts and wastes such as asbestos, benzene, and xylene; and pesticides and herbicides such as atrazine and lindane.
- **Radioactive contaminants:** Radium is an example of a radioactive contaminant. In addition, radon can be a radioactive water problem. Radon is a gas that is easily released when

contaminated water is aerated, such as in a faucet sprayer. Radon then is breathed into the lungs, which can be a health threat. Breathing radon gas is usually considered a greater problem than ingesting radon-contaminated water.

Under the provisions of the Safe Drinking Water Act, the Primary Drinking Water Standards are regularly reviewed. As new knowledge about health concerns emerges, or new technology to detect water pollutants is developed, the standards may be modified.

Secondary Drinking Water Standards

Secondary Drinking Water Standards are based on the *secondary maximum contaminant levels* (SMCLs) of pollutants, which affect the aesthetics and function of water. These are contaminants that affect water qualities such as appearance, taste, odor, residues, or staining. Examples of secondary standard contaminants are chloride, iron, manganese, sulfur, and pH. While these contaminants might not present a health threat, they can affect functional water use and can lead to maintenance problems. Secondary standards are voluntary and are not required. A public water system may choose to test and treat for some of the SMCLs.

Other Water Contaminants

Two water contaminants are not covered by the U.S. EPA standards, but can be a concern in the kitchen: hard water and iron bacteria.

Water Hardness

Water hardness is the most common water quality problem in North America. "Hard" water is water with a high mineral content, usually calcium and magnesium. Hard water is usually found in groundwater sources, such as water from wells. Both private and municipal systems can use groundwater.

Hard water creates problems with mineral deposits on fixtures, water-using appliances, and plumbing. As these mineral deposits (sometimes called *lime scale*) build up, pipes can become clogged and water flow is reduced. Heating elements and other parts of appliances and fixtures also can become coated with mineral deposits, reducing effectiveness and leading to mechanical failures. Hard water also reduces the effectiveness of cleaning products, including shampoos and soaps, and increases soap scum deposits (Table 3.1).

However, hard water is safe for drinking and cooking. Some people believe that the minerals in hard water contribute to better tasting, healthier water.

Iron Bacteria

Iron bacteria are a reddish brown slime that can clog pipes and fixtures. It is most likely to result when water is left standing. Typically, it is first noticed in the toilet tank, but it can occur in water left standing in pipes, faucets, and appliances. Iron bacteria are naturally occurring, and more common with well water. They are an unpleasant nuisance that can cause staining.

TABLE 3.1 Hard Water Classifications. Water can be classified from soft to very hard, depending on the amount of calcium and/or magnesium present.

Rating	Grains per Gallon	Milligrams per Liter (mg/L) or Parts per Million (ppm)
Soft	Less than 1.0	Less than 17.1
Slightly hard	1.0–3.5	17.1–60
Moderately hard	3.5–7.0	60–120
Hard	7.0–10.5	120–180
Very Hard	Over 10.5	Over 180

Water Quality Testing

The water in a new or newly remodeled kitchen should not be a health threat. New fixtures and fittings need to be protected from staining, deposits, and other maintenance problems caused by water problems. As part of your design preparation and household assessment (see Chapter 5, "Assessing Needs"), you want to find out if there are any water quality concerns. If the project is a renovation, look for evidence of water concerns in the existing kitchen or a bathroom, such as fixture staining or hard water deposits. Check to see if the household uses filters in the kitchen for drinking water. Draw a glass of water and evaluate how it looks and smells.

If the home is, or will be, on a municipal water system, you can assume that the water is safe for drinking. If the home is on a private water system, ask your client about any testing or treatment they have done. Regular testing is the best method to help maintain a safe water system.

Most experts recommend that private water systems be tested annually for:

- Total coliform bacteria
- Nitrate
- pH
- Total dissolved solids

These contaminants are considered "marker" pollutants, meaning that a problem with one of these contaminants is usually evidence of more extensive problems. Other tests may be recommended, depending on the water source and recent water pollution problems in the area. A financial institution may require water testing before money is lent for any home improvements. The local, state, or provincial health department is an excellent place to contact for further information about water testing.

Additional testing of the water supply may be recommended if there are nuisance problems in the water such as off-color, cloudy appearance, discoloration, unusual taste, odor, or staining of fixtures. These problems can occur with both municipal and private water systems. If water problems are evident, and the home is on a public water system, start by contacting the local water authority. Some nuisance problems are temporary.

The local health department may test for nuisance pollutants or may recommend a private company. An independent company that follows an EPA or Health Canada–approved testing procedure should always do the water testing. Never have a water test done by the same company that wants to sell water treatment equipment. Contact the water testing company and describe the water problem. It can recommend the necessary tests as well as the procedure for gathering the water sample.

Solving Water Quality Problems

There are many options for solving water quality problems. Some may be as complex as having to locate a new water source, such as drilling a new well. Others may be as simple as attaching a filter to a faucet. It is important to match any water treatment equipment to the water problem and the pollutant to be removed (Table 3.2).

Also, the amount of the contaminant in the water may determine the type of equipment as well as the size or capacity. Finally, if more than one water treatment device is needed, the order of installation may be important for the most effective operation.

Water Treatment Equipment

As a kitchen designer, you may need to specify water treatment equipment, or incorporate it into your kitchen design. When single water quality problems are identified, one water treatment device may be adequate. In many cases, however, more than one problem is present, requiring a combination of water treatment equipment. A household water treatment system should take into account the most practical and effective device to treat each problem, the order these devices

TABLE 3.2 Common Types of Water Treatment Methods: A brief summary of water treatment methods for common contaminants in household water.

Water Treatment Method	Typical Contaminants Removed
Activated carbon filtration	Odors, chlorine, radon, organic chemicals
Anion exchange	Nitrate, sulfate, arsenic
Chlorination	Coliform bacteria, iron, iron bacteria, manganese
Distillation	Metals, inorganic chemicals, most contaminants
Neutralizing filtration	Low pH
Oxidizing filtration	Iron, manganese
Particle or fiber filtration	Dissolved solids, iron particles
Reverse osmosis	Metals, inorganic chemicals, most contaminants
Water softening (cation exchange)	Calcium, magnesium, iron

should be placed in the system, and the intended use of the water—for drinking, cooking, laundry, or other household uses.

Most types of water treatment equipment require regular maintenance to be safe and effective. If you specify or recommend this type of equipment, be sure to prepare your client, and assist them in making an appropriate choice in equipment. Following is a brief summary of the more common types of water treatment equipment used in homes.

Filters
Sometimes called carbon or charcoal filters, activated carbon filters are used to treat taste and odor problems, chlorine residue, organic chemicals, and radon. When water flows through the carbon, contaminants adsorb or stick to the surfaces of the carbon particles.

Fiber filters or mechanical filters trap particles in the water, such as sand and soil, reducing turbidity and improving appearance.

Activated carbon filters and mechanical filters may be purchased separately or in a dual unit. Small filters that fit directly onto the kitchen faucet are available. Larger filter units fit under the sink. If desired, a filter can also be installed in a utility area that will treat the whole household water supply.

If a filter is installed in the kitchen, usually only the cold water line is filtered. A bypass feature on the faucet can allow the user to choose filtered or unfiltered water, and extend cartridge life. Sometimes, filters are installed with a dedicated faucet and may be combined with an instant hot water dispenser.

Water Softeners
Water softeners remove the calcium and magnesium that cause water hardness problems. Water softeners are usually installed in a utility area, near the water heater. Because of the extensive problems that occur with hard water, typically all household water is softened.

Sometimes, people are concerned about the health effects of softened water, as the softening process increases the sodium content of the water. In addition, the taste of softened water may not be desirable. A solution to these concerns is to soften only the hot water supply, so that the cold water lines provide untreated water. Another option is to provide a cold water line to the kitchen faucet that bypasses the water softener. These options should be discussed with a plumber.

Iron Removal Equipment
Iron and manganese (which often occur together in water) do not cause health problems but can cause taste, odor, staining, and appearance problems, even if they are present in very small amounts (0.3 mg/L for iron and 0.05 mg/L for manganese). Removal of iron can be complex because it depends on the form found in the water (dissolved or oxidized), the concentration of iron,

and other pollutants in the water. Iron bacteria often occur with iron-containing water. Iron removal equipment is generally installed in a utility area and is used to treat all the water coming into the household.

The options to remove iron include:

- **Iron filter:** Sometimes called a manganese green sand filter, this equipment operates in a way similar to that of a water softener.
- **Water softener:** Depending on the type of resin, a standard water softener will remove some iron.
- **Polyphosphate feeder:** This is effective only on cold water.
- **Chlorinator and filter:** A two-stage process, this also deals with iron bacteria.
- **Aerator and filter:** This is also a two-stage process.

Neutralizers

A neutralizer is used to treat low pH, or acidic, water. As water becomes more acidic, it is more reactive and picks up more pollutants. Acidic water is also more corrosive to plumbing fixtures and water-using appliances. Neutralizers are usually used to treat all household water and are installed in a utility area.

Distillation Units

A distiller provides nearly pure water by boiling water until it evaporates, then condensing it. The resulting distilled water has almost no pollutants but can taste very flat. A distillation unit might be installed in a kitchen, usually under the sink, and the potable water plumbed with its own faucet. Countertop units are also available. Distillers require an electrical connection to provide a heat source. Another consideration is how to vent the heat from the boiling process. Also, the distillation process takes time, so there needs to be a collection and storage container for the water. The size of the distillation unit, and in particular, the storage container, needs to relate to the demand for treated water.

Reverse Osmosis Unit

A reverse osmosis unit (Figure 3.8) will remove many suspended or dissolved pollutants from the water. Usually, a reverse osmosis unit is installed under the kitchen sink, with a dedicated faucet. It is used to treat drinking and cooking water only. A mechanical filter and an activated carbon filter are needed to pretreat the water and to extend the life of the filtering membrane. As with distillation, reverse osmosis is a slow process, so a storage container is a necessary part of the equipment. A connection to a drain is required. Some reverse osmosis units require an electrical connection (to provide a pressure assist and speed the treatment process).

Disinfection Methods

A home on a private water system may need to disinfect water to make it safe to drink. The most common method is an injection pump using liquid chlorine (chlorine bleach). Ozone and ultraviolet light systems are also available. Disinfection methods are usually used to treat all household water and may be installed in a utility area, or even in the well house. Chlorinated water is often treated with an activated carbon filter to remove excess chlorine.

EFFICIENT AND SUSTAINABLE USE OF WATER

As populations expand, finite water resources need to be shared with more people. It is a major community—and taxpayer—investment to collect, treat, and deliver high-quality water to residents, as well as to treat the resulting wastewater.

There are many benefits to efficient and sustainable use of water:

- Reduced pollution caused by excessive water in our waste water systems
- Healthier natural wetlands
- Reduced need for communities to construct water and waste water treatment facilities

FIGURE 3.8 Water filtration devices should be selected so that they eliminate the specific water problems and pollutants encountered by the client.

Charlie Wing, How Your House Works (Hoboken, NJ: John Wiley & Sons, 2012)

FIGURE 3.9 A touchless faucet can save water because it is only activated when hands or an object are under it.

Courtesy of Kohler Company

- Fewer dams and reservoirs needed to provide a water supply
- Reduced energy use to treat both the water supply and waste water

The kitchen designer has a responsibility to be aware of, and plan for, efficient water use. In a well-designed kitchen, water is not wasted, but used where it is most needed and most appreciated.

Faucets

The faucet in the sink or sinks is a major place of water use in the kitchen. Options in faucet control systems make it easier and more convenient to turn the faucet on and off, so that water is not wasted. For example, a faucet with an electronic, motion activator control will turn on only when you put a pot or your hands under the faucet. (Figure 3.9) Touch control faucets can be turned on and off with a light touch anywhere on a large area of the faucet. Foot controls can make it easier to control the faucet, turning it on and off easily, to minimize water use. A leaning bar faucet controller installs beneath the edge of the sink counter, and water flow is controlled by the pressure of someone leaning against it. Many of these control systems also add convenience for the cook with messy hands or foster independence for the cook with limited muscle control.

Some manufacturers offer kitchen faucets with reduced flow rates to conserve water. Most kitchen faucets have a flow rate of 2.2 gallons per minute (gpm) (8.4 liters

WaterSense®

WaterSense is a public-private partnership program between the U.S. Environmental Protection Agency (EPA) and manufacturers to provide water-efficient products. WaterSense products have been independently tested and certified. As a result of meeting the WaterSense standards, the products can bear the WaterSense logo in all packaging, marketing, and promotion (Figure 3.10).

Generally, products that meet the WaterSense standards are 20 percent more efficient than comparable products on the market. In addition, the products must perform their intended function without sacrificing performance, especially to conserve water.

Among the WaterSense products currently available are toilets, bathroom lavatory faucets and accessories, and showerheads. Soon, WaterSense water softeners will be available. New product categories are expected in the future. In addition, through an agreement between the Environmental Protection Agency and Environment Canada, WaterSense products will be available in Canada.

Choosing WaterSense products offers the designer an excellent opportunity to maximize the sustainable use of water.

Figure 3.10 WaterSense makes it easy to find and select water-efficient products and ensures consumer confidence in those products with a label backed by third-party independent testing and certification.

per minute [lpm]). A lower flow rate will conserve water when running water for many kitchen uses, such as preparing vegetables or washing hands. Lower flow rates of 1.8 or 1.5 gpm (6.8 or 5.7 lpm) are typically available. Some faucets come with toggles to offer a higher flow rate for uses such as filling stock pots. When specifying a kitchen faucet, check to see if the local code requires a low flow rate for the kitchen faucet.

A kitchen faucet should have an aerator. An aerator adds air to the water, increasing the pressure. This makes the flow seem greater, so water use is reduced. An aerator also reduces splashing.

Hot Water

Water used in a kitchen is often heated. Wasting hot water would also be wasting the energy used to heat the water. Conserving and reducing the energy used to heat water are part of a sustainable home.

Insulating hot water pipes reduces standby heat loss. Putting a secondary water heater in or near the kitchen minimizes the water that is wasted waiting for the hot water to reach the kitchen as well as the energy lost when the hot water cools in the pipes after hot water is no longer drawn by the kitchen faucet or an appliance. Installing a tankless or on-demand water heater in the home adds the additional savings in energy that is no longer used to maintain a storage tank of hot water.

In this book, installing, locating, and selecting water heaters are discussed in Chapters 2 and 7. It is also important to select a water heater that is energy efficient and sized to household needs. A too large water heater will use extra energy and provide more hot water than is required. There are several technologies and water heater designs that offer particular advantages in energy efficiency. These technologies include high-efficiency gas, tankless, heat pump, condensing, and solar.

If a design project will include the need to specify a new water heater or will include appliances or other features that increase the use of hot water, you should encourage your client to consider an energy-efficient water heater. For example, an Energy Star–rated water heater would be a good choice. In addition, some local codes may specify the type or efficiency of a new water heater for remodeling, replacement, or new construction.

Energy Star®

Energy Star is an international symbol of premium energy efficiency (Figure 3.11). In the United States, Energy Star is a program of the Environmental Protection Agency and the Department of Energy that promotes the protection of the environment through energy-efficient products and practices. Energy Star was established to:

- Reduce greenhouse gas emissions and other pollutants caused by inefficient use of energy.
- Make it easy to identify and purchase energy-efficient products without sacrificing performance, features, and comfort.

Energy Star product specifications are based on the following key guiding principles:

- Product categories contribute significant energy savings.
- Qualified products deliver the features and performance demanded by consumers as well as increased energy efficiency.
- If the energy-efficient product costs more than a less-efficient product, the purchaser recovers their increased cost through utility bill savings within a reasonable period of time.

Figure 3.11 The Energy Star logo is found on qualified products. *Courtesy of the U.S. Department of Energy*

(continued)

- Energy efficiency is achieved through broadly available, nonproprietary technologies.
- Product energy consumption and performance can be measured and verified.
- Labeling effectively differentiates energy-efficient products.

A wide variety of products are certified as energy efficient by Energy Star. Product categories of particular interest to kitchen designers include clothes washers, dishwashers, refrigerators, light bulbs and fixtures, ventilating fans, and water heaters.

Further information and lists of qualifying Energy Star products can be found at www.energystar.gov.

Water-Using Appliances

The dishwasher is usually the major water-using appliance in the kitchen. However, depending on your client's habits, a dishwasher can actually be a more water-efficient method than hand dishwashing. A dishwasher with a choice of cycles allows water use to be matched to the load. Some dishwashers are available with sensors that adjust cycle length and water use to the soil level in the load. An Energy Star dishwasher is a good choice for both water and energy efficiency. According to the Environmental Protection Agency, an Energy Star dishwasher is 12 percent more water efficient and can save over 13,000 gallons of water when compared to a standard model.

If a clothes washer is installed in or near the kitchen, a replacement may be part of your project. When selecting a new clothes washer, look for a water-efficient model, such as an Energy Star–rated model. Adjustable water levels allow less water to be used with smaller loads. Chapter 9 has more information about laundry appliances.

Water Leaks

An important factor in efficient use of water is eliminating leaks. Dripping faucets waste tremendous amounts of water. For example, the EPA estimates a faucet that loses one drop of water per second can waste 3000 gallons (11,356 liters) of water in a year. Talk to your client about selecting high-quality fittings, fixtures, and water-using appliances that are easy to maintain and less likely to develop leaks. These are not only important water conservation measures, but they will also save money and reduce maintenance for the client.

Graywater

So far, the discussion of efficient and sustainable use of water has focused on conserving water. Another approach is to reuse or recycle water. Reusing water is a sustainable practice that has all the same benefits of using less water. *Recycling water* is the term used to describe the practice of treating wastewater, usually in a centralized location, and then using the water for a variety of purposes, including landscaping. Graywater describes the practice of collecting household water from drains and then reusing it on-site for landscaping irrigation or toilet flushing.

The interest in graywater is growing, particularly in the southwestern and western United States, where water is limited. Effective use of graywater reduces the demand for treated drinking-quality water and decreases the water going into waste water treatment facilities or septic tanks.

The model *2012 International Residential Code* (IRC) details the design of graywater recycling systems in the Sanitary Drainage section. Some local codes now require new residential construction to include connections for graywater plumbing. According to the 2012 IRC, discharge water may be collected from bathtubs, showers, lavatories, clothes washers, and laundry trays for a graywater system. The water collected is then used for flushing toilets and urinals or landscape irrigation.

A graywater system can challenge a designer. The system needs to be correctly sized. There are requirements for additional plumbing pipes. A collection reservoir or storage tank is needed. While the opportunity for implementing an important sustainable practice is exciting, advanced and careful planning is needed. Familiarity with all applicable codes and/or permits, and perhaps additional expert advice may be needed.

AIR QUALITY

Another part of the kitchen design process is to provide good indoor air quality, making a space pleasant to be in, healthy for the user, and free of air pollution.

Providing good indoor air quality is a three-step process:

- **Source control:** Minimizing or preventing the sources of indoor air pollution in a room or building.
- **Ventilation:** Providing adequate air exchange, through natural or mechanical ventilation, to dilute the concentration of indoor air pollutants and ensure that the space has a supply of fresh air.
- **Air cleaning:** When necessary, using filters or other devices to remove potentially harmful indoor air pollutants.

SOURCE CONTROL

In the kitchen, there are a number of sources of potential air pollution. Excess moisture is at the top of the list. Too much moisture not only creates a sticky, uncomfortably humid space, but can also lead to structural damage. A high level of moisture creates an environment that fosters the growth of biological pollutants such as molds, viruses, and bacteria. Moisture (71 liters per second) control is discussed in more detail later in this chapter.

Cooking odors, grease, smoke, and by-products from gas combustion in cooking appliances are also common kitchen air pollutants. These pollutants not only affect air quality but can create maintenance problems as well. Effective and easy-to-use ventilation to remove pollutants is a must in a well-designed kitchen. Kitchen Planning Guideline 19 recommends a ducted ventilation system of at least 150 CFM (cubic feet per minute), exhausted to the outside, with each cooking surface appliance. Refer to Chapter 7 for more detailed information about kitchen ventilation systems.

Indoor Air Quality and Construction

Some of the air pollution in a kitchen can also come from building materials and interior finish materials. New building materials, such as paint, manufactured woods, varnishes, and plastics, can off-gas, or emit chemicals into the air, as the materials age or cure. This is especially true of products made from, or with, volatile organic compounds (VOCs), such as some paints, particleboards, or wood finishes. The heat and moisture in a kitchen can increase off-gassing.

Choose building materials that have low amounts of VOCs. Today, many products are identified as low-VOC, and some may be certified as low-VOC emitting. Many alternatives are available, such as latex paints, water-based varnishes, or low-VOC wood products. Some building materials can be ventilated for 24 to 48 hours before installation, so that most off-gassing occurs outside your client's home. Increasing ventilation during and immediately after installation of new building materials is important to good indoor air quality.

Volatile Organic Compounds—VOCs

A common hazardous substance is a *volatile organic compound*, or a VOC.

- *Volatile* means gets into the air easily during use or as it ages. *Organic* means any carbon-based compound.
- VOCs are used in many common household products. VOCs are found in wood preservatives and finishes, composite building materials, glues, adhesives, and solvents.
- They have a strong smell, are easily evaporated, toxic, are potentially harmful, and are flammable.
- Generic names for VOCs include: hydrocarbons, petroleum distillates, mineral spirits, and chlorinated solvents.
- VOCs can have serious health effects.
- VOCs are sensitizers, which are chemicals that may lead to allergic or other serious reactions after many uses.
- Side effects of VOC use can include irritation, drowsiness, headache, nausea, and depression of nervous system, or VOCs can be carcinogenic.

The *Greenguard Environmental Institute* (GEI) focuses on protecting human health and improving quality of life by enhancing indoor air quality. The GEI conducts third-party testing to certify products for low chemical emissions, including cabinetry (www.greenguard.org).

The state of California's Air Resources Board oversees stringent air quality standards. One standard of particular interest to the kitchen industry is for off-gassing of formaldehyde (a VOC) in composite wood products as might be used in cabinetry and construction. Products must meet these standards to be sold in California, but could be marketed as meeting these standards in other locations.

Renovation Hazards

New construction sometimes means removing old construction. Make sure your client is aware of possible air quality problems that can result from demolition. Some things to consider and discuss with both the contractor and your client are:

- Will the demolition area be isolated from the rest of the home? (Figure 3.12)
- Will the heating or air conditioning system be blocked in the demolition area, so that dust and debris are not circulated throughout the home?
- If the home was constructed before 1978, determine if there is any lead paint in the demolition area. Although lead paint was available until 1978, it was especially common in homes built before 1950. Disturbing lead paint can cause serious air pollution and health effects, especially to young children.
- Asbestos is another hazard in building materials in houses built before the late 1970s. Disturbing asbestos-containing materials can create airborne health hazards. If asbestos is a possible hazard, special removal and disposal procedures by a trained contractor may be needed.
- Sometimes demolition uncovers things like dead animals and insects in walls, attics, and other spaces. This is part of the reason it is important to isolate the demolition area from the rest of the home.
- How will demolition waste be removed and disposed? Can any of the materials be recycled? Is any of the waste considered hazardous, such as asbestos-containing materials or preservative-treated wood? Are local regulations for disposal of construction waste being followed?

FIGURE 3.12 Plastic sheeting is essential for isolating the workspace from the living area.

Lead: Renovation, Repair, and Painting Rule

In the United States, the Lead Renovation, Repair, and Painting Rule went into effect in 2010. It applies to all housing built in 1978 or earlier. All contractors performing renovations, repairs, or painting must be trained and certified to follow lead-safe work practices. The focus of these lead-safe work practices is:

- Contain the work area.
- Minimize dust.
- Clean up thoroughly.

The contractor must provide information on the lead-safe practices to property owner.

Lead hazards are not regulated in Canada.

More information is available at www.epa.gov/lead.

Air Cleaning

Air cleaners are often incorporated into the heating, ventilating, and/or air conditioning system of the home, where they are used to filter air, before it is returned, via ducts, throughout the house. Sometimes portable, tabletop, or larger console air cleaners are used in individual rooms. Air cleaners are most likely to be used to control particulate pollutants such as dust, pollen, or tobacco smoke.

A typical air cleaner will use a fan to take air through a filtering medium, and then blow the air back into the room or through ducts. If an air cleaner is desired, choose a filtering medium that is effective for the type of pollutant the client wants removed. Look for information that the air cleaner has been tested and rated against an efficiency standard, such as ASHRAE's (American

Society of Heating, Refrigeration, and Air-Conditioning Engineers) standard for in-duct cleaners and ANSI's (American National Standards Institute) CADR (Clean Air Delivery Rate) standard for portable air cleaners. Finally, make sure the capacity of the air cleaner is matched to the size of the room.

Ventilation Systems and Filters

Most ventilation systems in kitchens are located above the cooktop (called a hood, canopy, or updraft ventilation system) or near the cooking surface (called a proximity or downdraft ventilation system). A fan pulls air through a filter. As you can imagine, the filter catches a lot of grease. Maintenance of the filter is important—many are designed for easy removal and can be run through the dishwasher.

Most kitchen ventilation systems exhaust the air to the outside. However, sometimes a recirculating (ductless) system is used, which puts the air back into the room. An activated carbon type filter may be added, which helps to remove odors and smoke. Recirculating ventilation systems help to control grease and cooking odors, but do not remove moisture, heat, and combustion byproducts. Recirculating ventilation systems are less expensive to purchase and install, but are less effective in controlling indoor air pollution in a kitchen. Therefore, exhaust ventilation systems are the better choice for good indoor air quality.

Refer to Chapter 7 for more detailed information about kitchen ventilation systems.

MOISTURE AND INDOOR AIR QUALITY

An interaction of many factors such as climate, lifestyle, construction, mechanical systems, and ventilation can create moisture problems. There are many potential sources of excess moisture in a home, including cooking, drying clothes, plants, and showering and bathing. The Canada Mortgage and Housing Corporation estimates that the various activities of occupants of a home will generate 2 to 10 gallons (11.4 to 41.6 liters) of moisture every day. Excess moisture is a potential problem for both the building and the people who live in it. Excess moisture in building materials leads to structural problems, such as peeling paint, rusting metal, and deterioration of joists and framing. Damp building materials tend to attract dirt and, therefore, require more cleaning and mainte-nance. Even in a dry climate, excess moisture inside a building can lead to serious problems.

Damp spaces make good environments for the growth of many biological pollutants. Bacteria and viruses can thrive in moist spaces. Pests, from dust mites to cockroaches, need moisture to thrive. Wet building materials can also harbor mold growth, which leads to further structural damage. Mold can be a health threat for some people living in the home. Of course, mold growing on in-terior finish materials smells and is unattractive.

Moisture in Kitchens

Cooking is a major source of moisture in the kitchen. Boiling or simmering food on a cooktop is particularly a problem. In addition, both microwave and conventional ovens remove moisture from food and vent it into the kitchen. The amount of moisture released in cooking depends on the type of food, whether or not the food is covered while cooking, and the length and temperature of cooking. Gas cooking appliances increase the moisture generated, because water vapor is a by-product of gas combustion.

Research conducted at the Cold Climate Housing Information Center at the University of Minnesota estimates that cooking a dinner for a family of four releases 1.22 pints (0.58 liter) of water into the air. The amount of moisture released more than doubles if a gas range is used, to 2.80 pints (1.32 liters) of water. Other moisture sources in a kitchen, identified by the Minnesota research, can include dishwashing (1.05 pints a day) (0.5 liter) and refrigerator defrosting (1.03 pints per day) (0.49 liter). To put this amount of moisture into context, consider that it takes only 4 to 6 pints (1.89 to 2.84 liters) of water vapor to raise the humidity level of a 1000-square-foot (92.9-square-meter) house by 5 percent.

Moisture Basics

Water vapor is present in the air in varying amounts, depending on the temperature. The warmer the air, the more water vapor it will hold. *Humidity* describes how much water vapor there is in air. Relative humidity, expressed as a percent, can be explained by the following formula:

$$\frac{\text{Amount of water vapor in the air}}{\text{Maximum water vapor air can hold at that temperature}} \times 100 = \text{Relative humidity}$$

Note that the temperature of the air is important to understanding relative humidity. For example, on a winter's day, when the temperature is 20° Fahrenheit (– 7° Celsius) and the relative humidity is 70 percent, the air will actually be much drier, and have less moisture, than on a summer's day, when the temperature is 85 degrees Fahrenheit (21° Celsius) and the humidity is 70 percent.

Condensation, the opposite of evaporation, occurs when water vapor returns to a liquid state. As air cools, it can no longer hold as much water vapor, so the water condenses into a liquid. The temperature at which condensation occurs is referred to as the *dew point*. Most everyone is familiar with the experience of fixing a cold glass of ice tea on a warm summer day and then finding that water condenses onto the cold exterior surface of the glass.

In a new or newly renovated kitchen, many building products, such as grout, joint compounds, plaster, and latex paint, contain water. As these products dry and cure, water vapor is released. It is important that the kitchen be well ventilated while these products are drying, to prevent moisture problems.

Many kitchens are open to other living spaces. While this allows some of the water vapor to disperse and reduces humidity in the kitchen, it also allows the water vapor to circulate throughout the home.

Prevention of moisture problems within the kitchen is part of the designer's responsibility. The designer needs to consider problems that might occur throughout the home because of moisture generated in the kitchen. The designer's goal should be to make it as easy as possible to control moisture in the kitchen and to minimize the potential for problems from moisture that is not controlled.

Hidden Condensation

The cycle of water evaporating and condensing in a home can lead to moisture problems. For example, after preparing a meal, a kitchen is a warm, moist place. As the room cools and air from the kitchen moves throughout the home, the water vapor meets cooler surfaces, such as walls and windows, and condensation can occur. Wet materials result in increased maintenance, and eventually, deterioration. This is especially true of any that are absorbent and stay damp, such as drywall and textiles.

The air temperature inside the kitchen can be higher than the air temperature on the other side of the walls, floor, and ceiling. This is especially true in winter of exterior walls and a ceiling with an attic above it. There is a natural tendency for warm air to move to cool air. This is nature's way of trying to maintain equilibrium. In a kitchen, warm, moist air will tend to move through walls and ceilings, moving from warm to cool. As the air moves through the wall or ceiling, it is cooled. When the dew point temperature is reached, condensation occurs (Figure 3.13). This hidden condensation, inside walls and attics, can be a particular nightmare for homeowners. As building materials get wetter, deterioration and mold growth can become extensive before the problem is noticed.

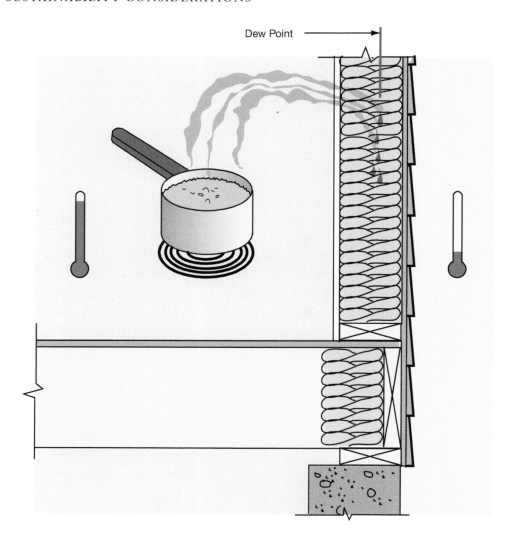

FIGURE 3.13 As warm, moist air moves through a wall, condensation will occur when the air is cooled to the dew point temperature.

Molds, Moisture, and Health

Molds are fungi. There are thousands of varieties of molds. Molds reproduce by spores, which blow out into the air. The spores can be dormant for years. Then, given the right conditions of food and moisture, the spores can begin to grow.

At any given time, there are typically mold spores in the air around us. Molds are a natural part of the ecosystem, and they play an important role in digesting organic debris such as dead leaves and insects. The problem occurs when there is an excess of mold growth and the organic matter they are digesting is part of the building structure.

Molds require moisture, oxygen, and food to grow. How much of each of these elements is required will depend on the mold species. However, most molds start growing at a relative humidity of 70 percent or more. Molds can make food out of almost any organic matter, including skin cells, residues from food, or textile fibers.

Cellulosic building materials such as paper, wood, textiles, many types of insulation, carpet, wallpaper, and drywall make an excellent environment for mold growth (Figure 3.14). The cellulosic materials absorb moisture, providing the right growth conditions, while the materials themselves provide the food for mold growth.

FIGURE 3.14 Growth of various types of mold on wood under flooring.

Molds grow fast. If cellulosic building materials get wet, mold growth will begin in 24 to 48 hours. Mold growth on the surface of noncellulosic materials can start in the same time, as long as food and moisture are present.

Molds can affect people in different ways. Some people are allergic to specific species of mold. Molds produce chemicals that are irritants to most people, and they can cause problems such as headaches, breathing difficulties, and skin irritation as well as aggravating other health conditions such as asthma. Molds can sensitize the body so that the person is more susceptible to health effects from future exposures. Finally, some molds produce toxins. The likelihood of health effects increases with the amount of exposure to mold as well as the sensitivity of the individual.

Preventing Moisture Problems

Household Humidity

Managing the humidity level in a home is a balancing act between comfort of the occupants and protection of the structure. Excess moisture leads to many indoor air quality, structural and maintenance problems, and makes the home's occupants feel "sticky." Too little moisture dries out skin, nasal passages, and throats, as well as wood in furniture and the house's structure. Generally, a relative humidity level of about 40 to 60 percent is a good compromise. At this level, most condensation and mold growth is prevented, but people are comfortable.

One method of controlling household humidity is through exhaust ventilation of moisture-laden indoor air. However, when the outside air is warm and humid, ventilation will not solve the problem. Mechanical air conditioning (cooling) of the air inside the home is effective in dehumidification by condensing water vapor from the air. If the air conditioner is oversized, however, it may cool the home's air quickly, but not operate long enough to provide adequate dehumidification.

Mechanical dehumidifiers may be used in the home to control humidity in moisture-prone areas. A dehumidifier operates on the same principle as an air conditioner. While dehumidifiers can be effective in controlling moisture, they do require regular maintenance and generate heat and noise. A dehumidifier needs to be sized to the space in which it will be operating.

> ## Ventilation Recommendations to Control Moisture
>
> The *2012 International Residential Code* (IRC) details ventilation requirements for houses. The *2012 International Energy Conservation Code*, which is incorporated into the IRC, requires whole-house mechanical ventilation to provide adequate fresh air as well as moisture control. In a whole-house ventilation system, the kitchen would be an area where the air is exhausted directly to the outdoors. The code requirement is:
>
> - 100 cubic feet per minute (47 liters per second) intermittent exhaust or
> - 25 cubic feet per minute (12 liters per second) continuous exhaust
>
> More information on ventilation systems is provided in Chapter 7.

Ventilation

Good ventilation in the kitchen helps to avoid air quality problems. Exhaust ventilation helps prevent moisture problems and mold growth by removing excess moisture and preventing condensation. Ventilation systems are discussed in more detail in Chapter 7. The importance of ventilation and moisture control in a laundry area that might be part of, or adjacent to, the kitchen, is discussed in Chapter 9.

Construction and Finish Materials

Energy-efficient windows are important in preventing moisture problems. The interior surface of an energy-efficient window is warmer, reducing the likelihood of condensation. Look for information on energy-efficient windows by reviewing the National Fenestration Rating Council label on the window. (See Chapter 2 for more information about selecting windows.) In particular, the following features of an energy-efficient window will help prevent moisture problems:

- **U-Factor:** The U-factor measures heat transfer, so a low U-factor usually means an energy-efficient window. The model *2012 International Residential Code* recommends maximum U-factors for windows, based on climate zone.
- **Air Leakage:** This measures the amount of air leakage between the window frame and the sash. It is also important that the window is installed properly to prevent air leakage between the window frame and the rough opening.

Finish materials can contribute to, or help to prevent, moisture problems. After exposure to water and humidity, the more absorbent the material, the longer it stays damp. Specifying hard surface or nonabsorbent materials, such as glazed tiles, solid surfacing, plastic laminate, or engineered stone, reduces the likelihood of moisture problems. Materials that stay damp are much more likely to support mold growth. Specifying sealers for absorbent or porous materials, such as clay tiles, marble, or grout, can also reduce moisture absorption.

It is especially important that wall and ceiling finishes or materials block the flow of moisture into wall cavities or attics. This can be accomplished by selecting materials that are not moisture permeable, such as glazed tiles or vinyl wall coverings. Alternatively, a vapor retarder material, such as plastic sheeting, can be used in the wall construction (Figure 3.15). There are special considerations about the placement of a vapor retarder, depending on whether the climate is dominated by heating or cooling. The vapor retarder is place on the warm side of the wall. In a climate that is dominated by a heating season or has both heating and cooling, that is the interior side. In a hot climate that is dominated by the cooling season, the vapor retarder is usually placed on the exterior side of the wall.

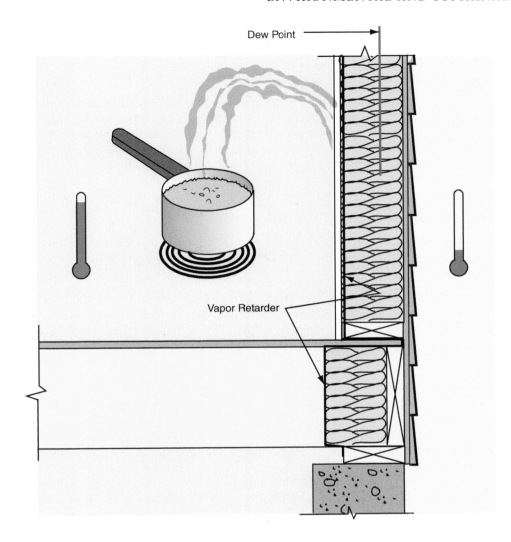

Dew Point

Vapor Retarder

FIGURE 3.15 Place a vapor retarder material on the warm or interior side of the wall, to help prevent moisture condensation inside the wall, in climates with cold winters. In hot, humid climates, where air conditioning is used most of the year, the placement of the vapor retarder may be different.

Low-maintenance materials are also important to preventing mold growth. Materials that are kept clean are less likely to accumulate surface debris that can support mold growth. Avoid appliances, fixtures, and fittings with cracks, seams, crevices, and indentations that can accumulate residue from air borne grease, skin, body oils, spilled foods, and cleaning products. All are organic materials that provide food for molds.

Products are available with various types of antimicrobial finishes or additives. Generally, an antimicrobial finish means that the material is treated with a pesticide of some sort to protect the material or product itself. For example, paints with fungicides prevent mold growth in the paint itself. This does not mean that mold will not grow on the paint, in a moist environment, if a food source were to accumulate on the painted surface. Antimicrobial products may be desirable to minimize mold problems, but they will not be an adequate substitute for good maintenance and moisture control practices. Always follow the manufacturer's directions for safe use of products with antimicrobial finishes or additives.

WASTE MANAGEMENT IN THE HOME

As a kitchen designer, you have a unique opportunity to encourage and facilitate your client's responsible waste management. Research continues to show that convenience motivates waste reduction behavior, in particular recycling. Through supportive design, you can make it easy to recycle.

A great deal of household waste is produced in the kitchen. As part of the preparation process, inedible or unappetizing parts of food—peels, seeds, bones, shells, rinds, fat, gristle, and stems—are removed for disposal. All sorts of metal, glass, paper, cardboard, and plastic packaging is accumulated. After a typical meal, food scraps remain.

Dealing with waste is part of the smooth flow of the food preparation process. For example, in the Virginia Tech research reported in Chapter 1, the location of the trash receptacle was crucial to cooking participants. In Chapter 6, waste and trash collection is addressed from a space-planning perspective. Understanding that different types of waste can—and should—be managed differently creates opportunities for reducing the environmental impact of the waste generated in North American kitchens.

Planning for Waste in the Kitchen

Waste management planning in the kitchen begins by understanding the different types of waste that are generated in the kitchen and the different disposal methods. Waste from kitchen activities can be grouped as follows:

- **Food waste:** Most food waste is organic and so is biodegradable. Much food waste can be composted and need not be put into a landfill.
- **Packaging waste:** Packaging may need to be separated by material to facilitate recycling as much waste as possible.
- **Paper products:** In a typical home, a lot of paper becomes waste in the kitchen, much of which can be recycled, and some can be composted.
- **Miscellaneous Waste:** Because of its central location, the kitchen trash can become the repository for waste from other rooms and activities. Some of this miscellaneous waste can be recycled or composted.

Community Practices and Regulations

Waste management in the kitchen is influenced by community practices and regulations. Some communities require that certain materials be recycled and not be put into trash destined for the landfill. For example, aluminum cans, glass bottles, or newspapers may be prohibited in trash pickups. In other communities, recycling may be voluntary. Some communities provide special containers for recycled items, and pick up recyclables on a regular schedule. Other communities provide collection points throughout the community for residents to drop off recyclable items. Community recycling programs may allow recyclable items to be comingled, such as putting cans, bottles, and newspapers in the same containers for pickup. Other community programs require that recyclable items be separated. Plastic soft drink bottles must be in separate containers from glass bottles, for example.

Some communities encourage recycling by limiting the amount of waste a household can have collected. Households may be limited on the size or weight of their refuse container but may have unlimited amount of recyclables.

Become familiar with your client's community waste-management practices. These practices will influence how much space is needed to collect trash and recyclable items and how many separate containers are needed in the kitchen. Kitchen Planning Guideline 14 recommends two waste receptacles, one for trash or waste, and one for recycling. According to Guideline 14, the recycling receptacle should be located in or near the kitchen (Figure 3.16). Planning a recycling center is further discussed below.

Waste-Management Appliances

Two kitchen appliances can be part of the waste-management process. Garbage disposers installed under the sink drain grind up food waste so that it can be flushed into the sewage system. Trash compactors hold trash and compact it to reduce the volume.

For many people, garbage disposers are a convenient and sanitary way to handle food waste, minimizing odor, and pest problems. However, some communities do not allow garbage disposers.

FIGURE 3.16 Recycling and waste collection systems in kitchens should be planned for flexibility since community requirements will change over time.
Courtesy of KraftMaid Cabinetry

Environmentalists, who favor composting of food wastes, are critical of the amount of water used with garbage disposers.

Trash compactors reduce the volume of trash but not the actual amount. This can be an advantage in a community where trash collection charges are calculated by volume. However, there is no real environmental advantage to the compacted trash. Bags of compacted trash can also become quite heavy, up to 40 pounds (18 kg), so older and smaller individuals may have a difficult time removing these bags from the compactor and taking them to the trash collection location. Smaller households, especially those committed to recycling, are not likely to produce enough waste to find a trash compactor advantageous.

A Recycling Center

When practicing recycling, items to be *recycled* are separated from items that are *thrown away*. Recycled items may need to be disassembled or otherwise prepared, such as separating different materials. Recyclable items usually require temporary storage that is separate from the rest of the waste or trash. These are important distinctions to consider when designing a kitchen space.

Recycling is more than just separating out cans and bottles from regular trash. It is a complex process that includes finding uses for recycled materials and products. This means that the markets for recycled materials are volatile. Therefore, which materials are recycled, and how they must be prepared, will vary from community to community and over time. Flexibility in a recycling system is important!

A recycling center can be a small area of the kitchen set aside for collecting, preparing, and temporarily storing items for recycling. As suggested by Kitchen Planning Guideline 14, this may or may not be in the same location as the kitchen trash receptacle. Here are some suggestions for planning a recycling center.

- The best location for a recycling center is between the primary food preparation area (work triangle) and the exit to the garage, outdoors, or wherever the trash bins are kept.
  - One scenario is that recyclables are collected inside the house for a limited period of time and then taken to the larger storage bin, located in a garage or outside, adjacent to the regular trash bins.

FIGURE 3.17 Recyclable items should be stored in containers that are easily accessible, such as roll-outs. The containers should also be easily removable.

Courtesy of Rev-A-Shelf

- A recycling center could be located in a laundry area, mudroom, or utility room adjacent to the kitchen.
- Make sure that the recycling center is located in a well-ventilated area.
- Keeping the recycling center inside the house, in a heated or cooled space, makes it seem easier to use.
- Storage for recyclable items should be accessible, such as in containers that roll out, pull out, or swing out (Figure 3.17). Containers need to be easily removed to transport the recyclable materials outside of the house.
    - One option for collecting recyclables is to use another container that matches the waste or trash receptacle. This works well if materials can be comingled or do not require much preparation for recycling.
    - An alternative storage arrangement would be to include space for a community provided recycling container that could simply be lifted or wheeled outside for collection. This is a good option if the community container is not too large, unwieldy, or unattractive.
    - Containers for recyclables need to be durable and easy to clean.
- A small sink is desirable in the recycling center or close by. Many items destined for recycling must be rinsed, especially to remove food wastes. A gooseneck or pull-out style faucet adapts to different size containers.
- Storage of items used in preparing recyclables may be needed. Examples include twine for binding newspapers, scissors for cutting packaging, extra paper or plastic bags for sorting items, twist ties for closing bags, a magnet for testing metals, and a can opener for removing lids.
- Provide space for a small trash can for nonrecyclable items removed or discovered in the preparation of recyclable items.
- A small counter area will provide workspace for preparing and sorting recyclables.
- If the household uses and collects returnable bottles, incorporate storage for these into the recycling center.

If your client is interested in composting, try to incorporate some convenience features that encourage the practice. Include a food-scrap collection container in the recycling center. This container needs to be accessible, easily removed, and have a tight-fitting lid when not in use

FIGURE 3.18 A convenient compost bin is recessed into the kitchen counter adjacent to the sink for collecting food scraps.
Courtesy of Rev-A-Shelf

(Figure 3.18). Choose a container made of washable, nonabsorbent material so that odors are not a problem.

Alternatively, the compost scrap collection container might be kept in the food preparation area—where scraps are generated. A pull-out bin under a counter or even a removable section of countertop with a container underneath would make a convenient collection space for peels, trimmings, and scraps. A compost collection container needs to be emptied regularly, so a large container is impractical.

Another idea for collecting food scraps for composting is to keep a container in the refrigerator or freezer. This helps control potential problems with odor or pests, if it is not possible to make an immediate trip to the compost area.

SUMMARY

Sustainable design benefits your client as well as the community as a whole. Sustainability is a philosophical approach that guides design and business decisions. Sustainability in the built environment encompasses energy efficiency, water management, air quality, waste management, and recycling. To be sustainable also means to provide a healthy place to live.

Sustainability can be practiced many different ways. Options include specifying products and materials or following practices that qualify for a national or local green building program. Alternatively, specifying products and materials that have been certified by an independent, third-party organization can be a sustainable choice. Another option is to follow the recommendations of the model *International Energy Conservation Code*.

The designer who makes sustainability a priority uses the various codes, standards, certifications, and guidelines to be informed and knowledgeable on products, policies, and practices. The goal is always to use resources efficiently, to think to the future, and to be concerned about the health and safety of the client.

REVIEW QUESTIONS

1. Describe three building or design practices that incorporate the goals of sustainability. (See under "Sustainable Design and Building" p. 70)
2. Describe a Green Building program. (See under "Green Building Programs" pp. 72–75)
3. If a designer wants to specify sustainable products, how can product certifications assist the process? (See "Sustainable Certification Programs" p. 75)
4. What types of objective information, such as comparative ratings or certifications, are available to assist in selecting energy- and water-efficient appliances? (See "EnergyGuide Labels" p. 79, "EnerGuide" p. 80, "Energy Star" pp. 87–88)
5. What are the government standards for healthy, safe, and functional water quality? Are they required or voluntary? (See "Water Quality Standards" pp. 80–81)
6. What are the steps to providing good indoor air quality? (See under "Air Quality" p. 89)
7. How can the kitchen designer encourage good waste-management practices by their clients? (See "Waste Management in the Home" p. 97)
8. What types of information of use to the kitchen designer would be found in the *2012 International Residential Code*? (See "Energy Issues and Building Codes" p. 78, "Graywater" pp. 88–89 and "Ventilation Recommendations to Control Moisture" p. 96)

Human Factors and Universal Design Foundation

Like most principles and elements of design, universal design is an enduring approach that draws from both science and spirit. It is based solidly on human factors and, along with this quantitative information, places equal value on the aesthetics of a space or product. Universal design responds to our growing appreciation and respect for diversity in the spaces we design, and in the stature, age, abilities, and culture of the people for whom we design. Simply defined, it is the design of products and spaces to be useable by all people to the greatest extent possible.

The study of human dimensions and the design of spaces and products around human factors are solid steps toward good universal design. Traditionally, human-factors-based design seemed to center on two extremes. It was either one-size-fits-all for the nonexistent "average person" or totally custom design for each individual client's dimensions, abilities, and needs. Universal design moves away from these extremes and builds on anthropometry and ergonomics in different ways. It embraces as broad a range of human factors as possible. One example is the placement of a wall switch that is dictated not by the reach range of the average height person, but by overlap of the reach ranges of the shorter and the taller among us. In addition, universal design places equal emphasis on aesthetics, acknowledging the importance of beauty and comfort in design solutions.

In this chapter, you will explore anthropometric and ergonomic information, as well as human factors studies, that help guide design of spaces and the basic concepts of universal design, which have become essential to good kitchen planning. Throughout this book, universal design concepts have been incorporated where applicable. Further information on access and specific user groups will be the focus of Chapter 8, "Accessibility in Practice," which focuses on both universal and access-related design considerations.

Learning Objective 1: Define and describe universal design.

Learning Objective 2: Define and describe anthropometry and its relation to universal design.

Learning Objective 3: Identify and list basic components of universal design as outlined in the Principles of Universal Design.

Learning Objective 4: Recognize some of the sources of information on access available in laws, codes, and related standards

ANTHROPOMETRY

A basic understanding of the human body, including its limitations and capabilities, is helpful in any type of space planning, particularly in a room of such high function and activity as the kitchen. While you will often determine a client's particular dimensions and needs, there are general areas where standards, based on research, are useful. Anthropometry, defined as "the study of human measurements such as size and proportion, and parameters such as reach range and visual range," is a good starting point. While not an exact science, anthropometry uses populations grouped according to specific criteria, such as age, gender, or ability, to collect data on bodies at rest (structural or static) and bodies in motion (functional or dynamic). Much of the information offered here on anthropometric data is sourced from *Human Dimension and Interior Space* by Panero and Zelnick (1979), which is a generally accepted reference for interior space planning in the building industry.

In this chapter, we will discuss various types of anthropometric information. In Chapter 5, which focuses on needs assessment, there is information about collecting anthropometric information on your specific clients. Included in Chapter 5, you'll find Form 1: Getting to Know Your Client, which provides graphics to guide you in collecting anthropometric dimensions (Part 1.2), reach and grasp profiles (Part 1.3), and anthropometric dimensions with mobility aids (Part 1.5).

Structural Anthropometry

Also called static anthropometry, structural anthropometry includes many dimensions relating to the body at rest. Figure 4.1 illustrates those dimensions that clearly have an impact on kitchen space planning and will be important to the design applications detailed in Chapter 6.

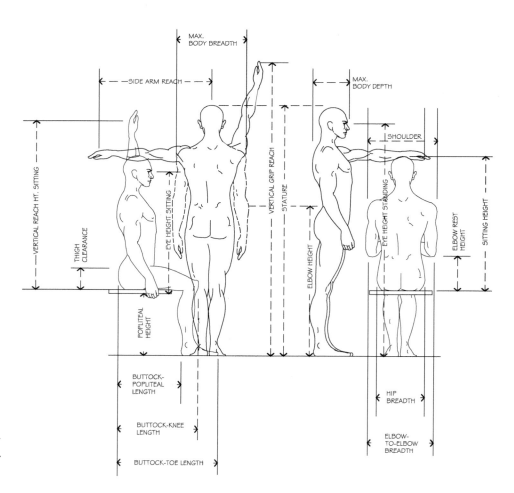

FIGURE 4.1 These are some of the body measurements that influence interior space planning. (Based on Panero and Zelnik 1979, p. 30)

The dimensions presented in Figure 4.1 are defined by Panero and Zelnick as follows:

- Stature is the vertical distance from the floor to the top of the head. It influences such spatial considerations as minimum height of door openings or ceiling.
- Eye height is the vertical distance from the floor to the inner corner of the eye. It dictates and affects such things as sight lines or the height of wall sconces, mirrors, wall art or windows.
- Elbow height is the vertical distance from the floor to the depression formed at the elbow. This affects such things as comfortable counter heights and sink heights.
- Sitting height is the vertical distance from the sitting surface to the top of the head when a person is sitting erect. This influences the height of such things as cabinets over a dining counter.
- Eye height while sitting is the vertical distance from the sitting surface to the inner corner of the eye with the subject sitting erect. This measurement dictates the sight lines that influence dining counter lighting or window mullion heights.
- Mid-shoulder height sitting is the vertical distance from the sitting surface to the point of the shoulder midway between the neck and acromion (end of shoulder blade). It influences the location of neck- or head-rests or backing for seating.
- Shoulder breadth (width) is the maximum horizontal distance across the deltoid muscles, and is important in determining necessary clearance between dining chairs.
- Elbow-to-elbow breadth is the horizontal distance with the elbows flexed and resting against the body, affecting clearances for dining space.
- Hip breadth is the width of the body measured across the widest portion of the hip, and it influences bench or seat width and passageways.
- Elbow rest height, measured from the top of the sitting surface to the bottom of the tip of the elbow, influences such things as armrests and counter heights.
- Thigh clearance is the vertical distance from a sitting surface to the top of the thigh at the point where the thigh and abdomen intersect. This is important when planning full-depth knee spaces, including the apron or drawer height.
- Knee height is the vertical distance from the floor to the midpoint of the kneecap and is useful when planning partial knee space.
- Popliteal height (behind knee) is the vertical distance from the floor to the underside portion of the thigh just behind the knee while a person is seated. This influences the height of benches and seats.
- Buttock to popliteal length is the horizontal distance from the rearmost surface of the buttock to the back of the lower leg. It indicates the necessary depth for benches and seats.
- Maximum body depth is the horizontal distance between the most anterior point, usually the chest or abdomen, to the most posterior, usually found in the buttocks or shoulder. It influences depth of floor space at work surfaces, clearance and passage. To accommodate groups of people who use mobility aids, this measurement must include the aid.
- Maximum body breadth is the distance, including arms, across the body. This measurement affects the widths of aisles, doors, and doorways. To accommodate groups of people who use mobility aids, this measurement must include the aid.

Functional Anthropometry

Functional anthropometry is the measurement of the body in motion. It includes movement of body parts in relationship to one another, as well as measures of strength. Because it is more complex than structural anthropometry, it is more difficult to accurately measure. However, certain aspects are helpful to kitchen planning. This information focuses mainly on the reach range and the functional space of a person using a variety of mobility aids.

- Vertical reach height sitting is the height above the sitting surface of the tip of the middle finger when the arm, hand and fingers are extended vertically (see Figure 4.2). It affects overhead storage.
- Vertical grip reach is the distance from the floor to the top of a bar grasped in the hand, raised as high as it can be without discomfort, while the subject stands erect (see Figure 4.3). It is important in planning the height of bookshelves, storage shelves, or controls. Vertical grip reach from a seated position is also important in a design that accommodates operating from a seated position.

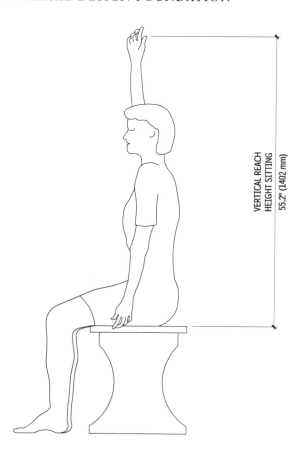

FIGURE 4.2 As a population, women are shorter than men so adult female vertical reach height sitting is indicated. If a design accommodated this shorter reach, it would also include 95 percent of women and others, both men and women with a taller reach. (Based on Panero and Zelnik 1979, p. 100)

VERTICAL REACH HEIGHT SITTING 55.2" (1402 mm)

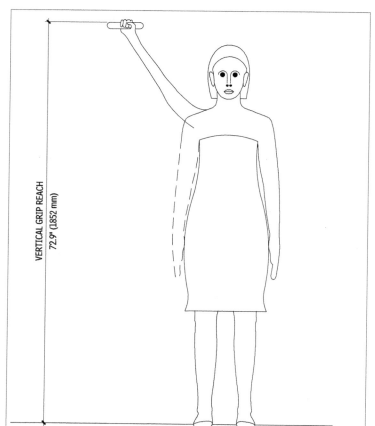

FIGURE 4.3 The vertical grip reach is useful in determining maximum height for readily accessed storage. This drawing and related measurements are again based on the adult female in the fifth percentile, this time in a standing position. (Based on Panero and Zelnik 1979, p. 100)

VERTICAL GRIP REACH 72.9" (1852 mm)

- Side arm grip reach is the distance from the centerline of the body to the outside surface of a bar grasped in the hand, stretched horizontally without experiencing discomfort or strain, while the subject stands erect (see Figure 4.4). Like the vertical grip reach, this measurement helps determine a comfortable location for controls, general storage and the horizontal span of a work area. There seems to be more information available on this dimension for a standing person, but the data and its application involve the seated user as well.
- Forward grip reach or thumb tip reach is the distance from a wall directly behind the person to the tip of the thumb, measured with the subject's shoulders against the wall and the arm extended forward with index finger touching the tip of the thumb (see Figure 4.5). This dimension influences depth and height of work counters and shelves, as well as general storage above the counters.

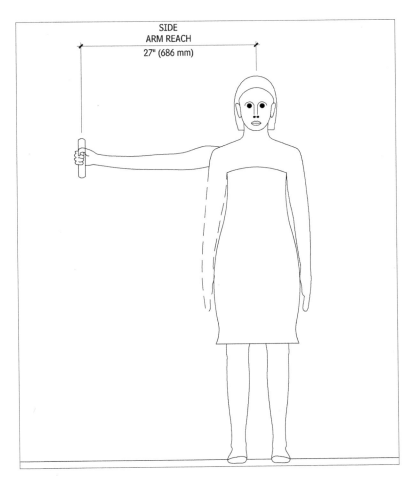

FIGURE 4.4 Whether seated or standing, the side arm grip reach will influence placement of stored items and controls. These numbers are based on a standing adult female in the fifth percentile. (Based on Panero and Zelnik 1979, p. 100)

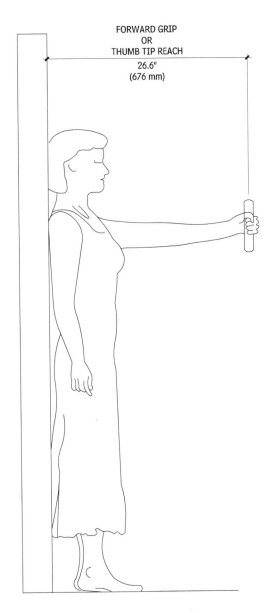

FIGURE 4.5 Using the dimension for forward grip reach based on adult females in the fifth percentile is a good basis for estimating the reach of most people. (Based on Panero and Zelnik 1979, p. 100)

Height and Reach Ranges

Height and reach ranges vary according to stature, physical ability, and obstructions. The height range within a person's reach is useful for planning functional storage, fixtures, appliances, and locating controls in the kitchen.

- The lower end of a forward reach range is 15 inches to 20 inches (381 mm to 610 mm) off the floor, depending on a person's ability to bend. The upper length can go as high as 72 inches (1823 mm), depending on a person's stature and any obstruction, such as a counter or shelf.
- The average person who remains seated to maneuver in the kitchen has a forward reach range of 15 inches to 48 inches (381 mm to 1219 mm).
- A standing person who has difficulty bending may have a forward reach range of 24 inches to 72 inches (610 mm to 1823 mm).
- A person who uses crutches, walker, or in some way needs their hands to maintain balance, has a slightly different reach range, depending on the mobility aid and physical ability.

Combining these reach ranges with the functional limits of reaching over a 25 inch (635 mm) deep counter, a universal reach range of 15 inches to 48 inches (381 mm to 1219 mm) has been suggested. This range is generally accepted and used to guide placement of storage, controls, and more (see Table 4.1).

Range of Joint Motion

Range of joint motion (Figure 4.6) is another aspect of human dimension that affects the design of the space and components within a kitchen. These include: movements of the hands, wrists and fingers; movement and flexibility of the shoulders and elbows; bending or twisting at the waist or spine; and movement of the knees. Because no joint operates in isolation, it is difficult to generate accurate and useful information regarding range of motion of joints. However, understanding the areas to consider will help in developing a space that works for a specific client. If you can observe and estimate a client's range of joint motion, your design and specifications can more accurately meet the client's needs.

Mobility Aids

There is a growing amount of useful data related to movement and maneuvering, including information relating to walking or moving with an assistive device (see Figures 4.7, 4.8, 4.9, and 4.10). Although these data seem less plentiful, Panero and Zelnick do offer minimal parameters. Access guidelines, such as those from the American National Standards Institute (ANSI), the International Codes Council (ICC), or Uniform Federal Accessibility Standard (UFAS), can be helpful. One critical rule: Consider the person and the aid as one. Also, just as for a person who does not use a mobility aid, these figures increase when the person using an aid goes from a static position to motion.

Comfort Zone

Based on psychological factors, we can also identify a body buffer zone or comfort zone (see Figure 4.11). Although this is affected by cultural differences, we maintain this personal space between others and ourselves who are walking, talking, or just standing with us. While we maintain a greater distance with strangers, the personal or close zone will be most applicable to kitchen design.

TABLE 4.1 Working with the functional dimensions and reach ranges of a variety of people, universal design proponents use the universal reach range to accommodate most people.

	Seated	Standing with Mobility Aid	Standing 5' 3"–5' 7"	Universal
Lower Limit–Bending	15" (381 mm)	15" (381 mm)	15" (381 mm)	15" (381 mm)
Lower Limit–No Bending	—	24"(610 mm)	24" (601 mm)	24" (610 mm)
Upper Limit	48" (1219 mm)	72" (1829 mm)	79 1/2" (2019 mm)	48"(1219 mm)

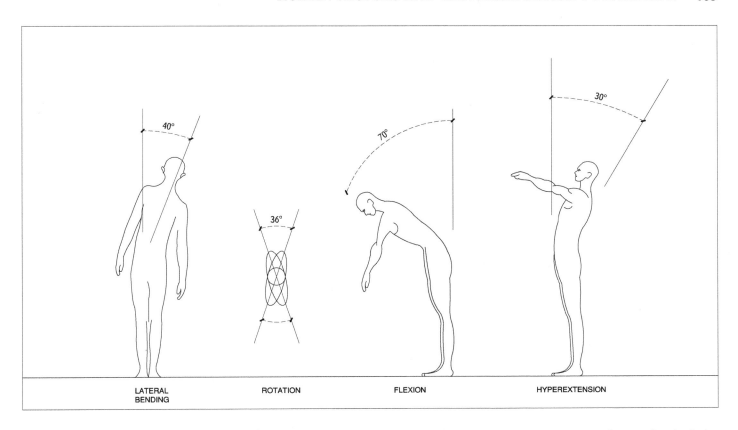

LATERAL
BENKING   ROTATION   FLEXION   HYPEREXTENSION

FIGURE 4.6 A person's range of motion in the spine and shoulders can impact the appropriate size for a work center in the kitchen. (Based on Panero and Zelnik 1979, p. 115)

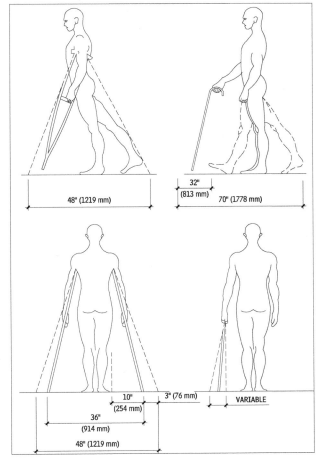

FIGURE 4.7 These minimum allowances will help in planning spatial clearances. Note that in this case, using the larger dimensions of percentile of adult males provides clearances for any human of smaller dimensions as well. (Based on Panero and Zelnik 1979, p. 54)

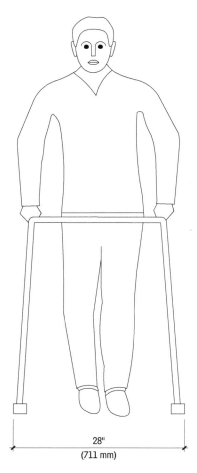

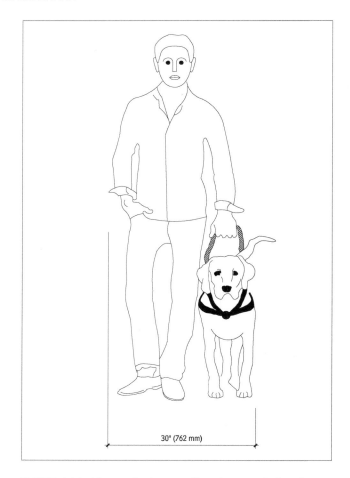

FIGURE 4.8 The width of a walker will determine the minimum clearances needed. (Based on Panero and Zelnik 1979, p. 54)

FIGURE 4.9 In this case, the clearance dimensions must be based on the actual user and dog, but the given dimension of 30 inches could be used as an absolute minimum. (Based on Panero and Zelnik 1979, p. 54)

Anthropometry of Children

Historically, there has been very little anthropometric data available regarding children. However, given the growing national focus on childhood health and safety, we can expect this to change. Although functional data would be most applicable, body dimensions of children are available and can be a starting point for the design of child-oriented spaces (see Table 4.2).

ERGONOMIC AND UNIVERSAL DESIGN

Based on anthropometric data and other human factors, ergonomics is the study of the relationship of people to their environment. Ergonomic design is the application of human factors data to the design of products and spaces to improve function and efficiency. Universal design builds on ergonomics to improve the use of products, spaces, and systems equally for people of a variety of sizes, ages, and abilities. This basis for the kitchen design guidelines and applications is detailed in Chapter 6, "Kitchen Planning," and throughout the book.

Universal design is inclusive and equitable, meeting the needs of a great number and variety of people. It is much more than the misconception that it is design limited to medical solutions for access challenges.

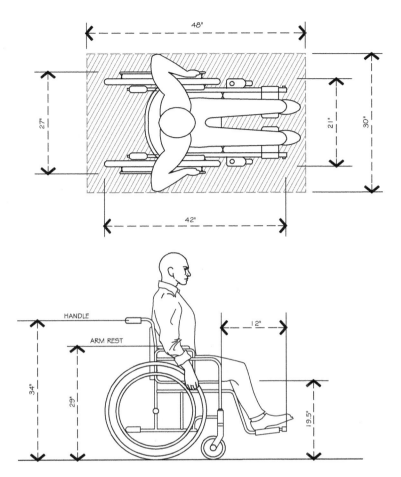

FIGURE 4.10 Although these standards for a person using a chair are useful in general, it is much better to measure the person in the chair. The variables are greatly affected by the person's size and ability, as well as by the design and fit of the chair. (Based on Panero and Zelnik 1979)

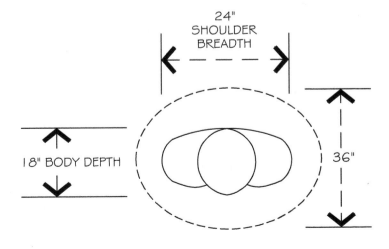

FIGURE 4.11 Based on a shoulder breadth of 24 inches (610 mm) and a body depth of 18 inches (475 mm), a minimum area of approximately 3 square feet (914 mm) per person is a guide in a space to be shared. (Based on Panero and Zelnik 1979, p. 41)

TABLE 4.2 The height and breadth of children, both standing and seated, can be useful dimensions when planning a kitchen that must accommodate them as they grow.

Stature (Height)		6 years	11 years
95 Percentile	Boys	50.4" (1280 mm)	61.8" (1570 mm)
	Girls	49.9" (1267 mm)	62.9" (1598 mm)
5 Percentile	Boys	43.6" (1107 mm) mm)same as??	53" (1346 mm)
	Girls	42.6" (1083 mm)	53.3" (1354 mm)
Sitting Height		**6 years**	**11 years**
95 Percentile	Boys	27.4" (695 mm)	31.7" (805 mm)
	Girls	27.1" (688 mm)	32.8" (833 mm)
5 Percentile	Boys	23.7" (602 mm)	27.6" (701 mm)
	Girls	23.1" (588 mm)	27.4" (697 mm)
Elbow to Elbow Breadth		**6 years**	**11 years**
95 Percentile	Boys	11.3" (288 mm)	14.7" (373 mm)
	Girls	11.1" (281 mm)	14.7" (373 mm)
5 Percentile	Boys	8.5" (217 mm)	10.1" (257 mm)
	Girls	8.3" (211 mm)	9.6" (244 mm)
Hip Breadth		**6 years**	**11 years**
95 Percentile	Boys	9.3" (236 mm)	12" (305 mm)
	Girls	9.3" (236 mm)	13.3" (338 mm)
5 Percentile	Boys	7.1" (181 mm)	8.7" (221 mm)
	Girls	7.1" (181 mm)	8.8" (223 mm)
Popliteal Height **(to knee from floor when sitting)**		**6 years**	**11 years**
95 Percentile	Boys	12.8" (325 mm)	16.3" (414 mm)
	Girls	12.6" (320 mm)	16.4" (417 mm)
5 Percentile	Boys	10.4" (264 mm)	13.3" (338 mm)
	Girls	10.2" (259 mm)	13.1" (333 mm)
Buttock- Popliteal Length **(wall to back of knee when sitting)**		**6 years**	**11 years**
95 Percentile	Boys	14.7" (374 mm)	19" (483 mm)
	Girls	15.2" (386 mm)	19.9" (505 mm)
5 Percentile	Boys	11.3" (287 mm)	14.5" (368 mm)
	Girls	11.3" (287 mm)	15" (381 mm)

Source: Malina, Hamill, and Lemeshow 1973

History and State of the Art

Since the end of World War II, awareness of the need for improved access and universal design has been growing. Currently, we are experiencing unprecedented interest, worldwide, in the design of environments and products that respect the diversity of human beings. Nowhere is this more true than in the kitchen, encompassing activities of daily life critical to everyone.

People are living longer, largely because of healthier lifestyles, better medicine, and vaccines and sanitation that have virtually eliminated many killer infectious diseases. According to the U.S. Census Bureau, life expectancy is projected to be 79.5 years for those born in 2012. We are redefining retirement to encompass active adult living, and our designs must include the support that will enable active lifestyles. In addition, more people are living with disabilities and they want to live better. There is a huge population of veterans with disabilities. Antibiotics and other medical advances have enabled people to survive accidents and illnesses that were previously fatal.

According to the U.S. Census Bureau's *Survey of Income and Program Participation* (SIPP), in 2005, approximately 19% of the population had some level of disability, and approximately 12% had a severe disability. In addition, the National Center for Injury Prevention and Control estimates that 1 out of 3 adults 65 or over falls each year. In short, in response to our current society, universal design concepts must be applied to kitchen planning so that the kitchen will function for, and benefit, all the residents of, and visitors to, a home.

Ron Mace, FAIA, known as the father of universal design, defined it as "the design of products and environments to be useable by all people to the greatest extent possible". From 1994 to 1997, Mace led a research and demonstration project at the Center for Universal Design, funded by the U.S. Department of Education's National Institute on Disability and Rehabilitation Research (NIDRR), which included the development of universal design guidelines or principles.

Following is the Center for Universal Design's current list of the Seven Principles of Universal Design with applications added that apply to kitchens. You might find these principles a good checklist to use in the design process as additional criteria when choosing between options.

1. Equitable Use

Design is useful and marketable to people with diverse abilities. Design provides the same means of use for all users: identical whenever possible; equivalent when not. It avoids segregating or stigmatizing any users. Provisions for privacy, security and safety should be equally available to all users. And the design should be appealing to all users.

Design applications include rocker light switches, motion-sensor lighting, ventilation or faucets, and side-by-side or drawer-style refrigerators (see Figure 4.12).

2. Flexibility in Use

Design accommodates a wide range of individual preferences and abilities. It provides choice in methods of use and accommodates right- or left-handed access and use. The design facilitates the user's accuracy and precision. And it provides adaptability to the user's pace.

Design applications include knee spaces with door and storage options that allow for seated or standing use, 48-inch (1219 mm) work aisles to ensure either a perpendicular or parallel approach to appliances, multiple counter heights and built-in tables (see Figure 4.13), movable storage, and storage for an optional stool.

3. Simple and Intuitive Use

Design is easy to understand, regardless of the user's experience, knowledge, language skills, or current concentration level. It eliminates unnecessary complexity and is consistent with user expectations and intuition. The design accommodates a wide range of literacy and language skills. It arranges information consistent with its importance. And it provides effective prompting and feedback during and after task completion.

Design applications include single-lever faucet operation that is left for hot and right for cold or the use of red to indicate hot and blue to indicate cold (see Figure 4.14), and one-step controls on a microwave for preprogrammed recipes.

4. Perceptible Information

Design communicates necessary information effectively to the user, regardless of ambient conditions or the user's sensory abilities. It uses different modes (pictorial, verbal, tactile) for redundant presentation of essential information. The design provides adequate contrast between essential information and its surroundings. It maximizes "legibility" of essential information. It differentiates elements in ways that can be described (i.e., makes it easy to give instructions or directions). And it is compatible with a variety of techniques or devices used by people with sensory limitations.

Design applications include open or visible storage, digital temperature control that both makes a sound and blinks when temperature limits are reached, or lighting controls that light up in the "off" position and go dark when the light is on. Also included are smoke detectors that sound and light the alarm, and cooking controls that use numbers and pictures to indicate the cooking mode/process (see Figure 4.15).

FIGURE 4.12 Side-by-side refrigeration with bottom freezer drawer provides some storage within everyone's reach.

Courtesy of GE

FIGURE 4.13 Built-in table doubles as an eating area and a lowered preparation counter with knee space.

Design by NKBA member Tim Scott; codesigners: Erica Westeroth, CKD, NCIDQ, and Sheena Hammond

FIGURE 4.14 This single-lever faucet is a great example of universal design, including the fact that right for cold, left for heat is intuitive.
Courtesy of Moen

5. Tolerance for Error

Design minimizes hazards and the adverse consequences of accidental or unintended actions. It arranges elements to minimize hazards and errors, with the most-used elements being the most accessible, and hazardous elements eliminated, isolated, or shielded. The design provides warnings of hazards and errors, and fail-safe features. It discourages unconscious action in tasks that require vigilance.

Design applications include GFCI receptacles that reduce risk of shock, temperature-limiting faucets that prevent accidental scalding, timed automatic shutoff on faucets, ventilation and small appliances, and induction cooktops (see Figure 4.16).

FIGURE 4.15 The controls on this cooktop are placed near the front for safety and offer digital and pictorial communication for perceptible information.
Courtesy of GE

FIGURE 4.16 An induction cooktop offers fail-safe features, such as its ability to shut off if a pan is not on the element or if the pan boils dry. *Courtesy of Wolf Appliance Company*

6. Low Physical Effort

Design can be used efficiently, comfortably, and with a minimum of fatigue. It allows the user to maintain a neutral body position and use reasonable operating forces. It minimizes repetitive actions and sustained physical effort.

Design applications include lever handles; remote controls for operating windows and cooktop ventilation, motion-activated appliances, and controls; D-pulls and cabinetry, and conveniently located storage and appliances (raised dishwashers, counter-height microwaves and ovens) (see Figure 4.17).

7. Size and Space for Approach and Use

Appropriate size and space are provided for approach, reach, manipulation and use, regardless of the user's body size, posture, or mobility. Design provides a clear line of sight to important elements for any seated or standing user. Reach to all components is comfortable for any seated or standing user. Variations in hand and grip size are accommodated. There is adequate space for the use of assistive devices or personal assistance.

Design applications include split double ovens and microwave ovens installed at comfort height (see Figure 4.18); storage accessories installed within the universal reach range; movable (portable) storage; knee space at a sink, cooktop, work counter, or adjacent to tall appliances; and 30 inches x 48 inches (763 × 1219 mm) of clear floor space in front of all appliances.

FIGURE 4.17 Dishwasher and laundry appliances are being designed higher off the floor to minimize bending.
Courtesy of GE

FIGURE 4.18 A microwave installed below the countertop with generous work aisles in front provides for easy approach, reach, and use.
Design by NKBA member Jessica Williamson, AKBD

The field of universal design represents a convergence of several threads of design practice with a focus on usefulness. To this end, the State University of New York (SUNY) at Buffalo is home to the Center for Inclusive Design and Environmental Access, the IDEA Center, an excellent source of information on the current state of universal design. Both the IDEA Center and the recently published book, *Universal Design: Creating Inclusive Environments*, are good sources of information on global and national movement in universal design.

The term universal design is sometimes inaccurately used as the politically correct description of compliance with the Americans with Disabilities Act (ADA) and other access codes or guidelines. While access codes and guidelines are important as a minimum, universal design is a broader approach that works to incorporate the needs of all users, not any one specific group. Universal design is an ideal, a way of thinking, whereas code compliance is often simply following a dictate.

A number of terms are used that relate to universal design, but have slightly different meanings:

- **Lifespan design** refers to the aspect of universal design that provides for the changes that may occur in the lifespan of household members, such as the birth and growth of children or the return home after a skiing accident that resulted in a broken bone.
- **Transgenerational design** refers to the design that acknowledges and supports the multiple generations, commonly living under one roof today.
- **Barrier-free design** is an older term, first used to refer to solutions that removed barriers in the environment. While removing barriers is still one important aspect, in North America universal design has been embraced as a broader, more positive approach and term.
- **Accessible design** or accessibility is a function of compliance with regulations or criteria that established a minimum level of design necessary to accommodate people with disabilities; that is, "wheelchair accessible."
- **Adaptable design** refers to features that are either adjustable or capable of being easily added or removed to "adapt" to individual needs or preferences.
- **Visit-ability** refers to basic accommodations that will allow people of differing abilities to visit a home. In terms of kitchen design, visit-ability requires a minimum 32 inches (813 mm) wide clear passage at the doorway
- **FlexHousing** is a Canadian concept in housing that incorporates, at the design and construction stage, the ability to make future changes easily and with minimum expense, to meet the evolving needs of its occupants. FlexHousing is an approach to designing and building homes based on the principles of adaptability, accessibility, affordability, and healthy housing.

The FlexHousing concept of accessibility is user-friendly, and its features add convenience and practicality to the functions of a home. Another consideration is the reduction of potential hazards. Although the initial cost of FlexHousing is slightly more than that of a conventional home, Flex-Housing features recover their investment over the long term because pre-engineered features allow for easy and inexpensive change and renovation. The integration of healthy building materials and innovative housing technology or Healthy Housing protects both the health of the occupants and the environment.

Dispelling Myths

There are many misconceptions regarding universal design. Let's put an end to the most common ones.

Myth 1: Universal design is nothing more than design for people in wheelchairs.
Fact: The opposite is true. To be considered universal, a design will be accessible not only to people in wheelchairs, but also to people of most sizes, shapes, and abilities. Universal design applies to people tall or short, young or old, left-handed or right-handed, visitors to an unfamiliar city or home, parents with children, people carrying packages, and others.

Myth 2: Universal design only helps people with disabilities and older people.
Fact: Universal design extends the benefits of functional design to many people, including short or tall people, large people, frail people, pregnant women, children, or even people traveling with much to carry or where there is a language barrier—everyone eventually.

Myth 3: Universal design costs more than traditional design.

Fact: Many universal concepts are standard products and cost no more than traditional products. The degree of customization and quality of the products will have the greater impact on cost.

Myth 4: Universal design is stigmatizing because it looks medical.

Fact: The best universal design is invisible. When done well, universal design enhances both the appearance and personality of a space as well as the function of that space for a variety of users.

ACCESS CODES, LAWS, AND STANDARDS

In the United States, most existing access-related laws, codes, and standards are intended as minimum criteria for access for people with disabilities, applicable, for the most part, in other than privately owned single-family residential spaces. While this is not universal design, the related guidelines can serve as a starting point for design parameters that support universal thinking, and in fact, the NKBA Access Standards are based on the ICC (ANSI) standard.

American National Standard for Accessible and Usable Buildings and Facilities (ICC A117.1)

The first edition of the American National Standard for Accessible and Usable Buildings and Facilities (ANSI A117.1) standard was issued in 1961. Since then, the standard has been updated and revised several times; the latest and current revision being the 2009 edition, now called the ICC A117.1, was developed under the International Code Council and approved by ANSI.

Since the International Code Council (ICC) is the current secretariat for the standard, it is referred to as the ICC standard and includes technical design guidelines for making buildings and sites accessible to, and usable by, people with disabilities. The ICC standard is the referenced technical standard for compliance with the accessibility requirements of the International Building Code and many other state and local codes. The 1986, 1992, 1998, and 2003 editions of the ANSI A117.1 standard are also U.S. Department of Housing and Urban Development (HUD) approved "safe harbors" for compliance with the technical requirements of the Fair Housing Amendments Act of 1988 (the Act) when used with the Fair Housing Act, the regulations implementing the Act, and the Fair Housing Accessibility Guidelines (FHAG). The Act is a federal mandate for accessibility in multifamily housing.

Uniform Federal Accessibility Standards (UFAS)

First published in 1984, Uniform Federal Accessibility Standards (UFAS) includes criteria for the design and construction of federally financed buildings to provide access for people with disabilities. UFAS is the technical standard referenced by three federal mandates for accessibility: the Architectural Barriers Act (ABA), Title II of the Americans with Disabilities Act (recognizes UFAS for work prior to March 15, 2012), and Section 504 of the Rehabilitation Act of 1973. The ABA requires access to buildings constructed, altered, leased or financed in whole or in part by the United States, and Section 504 requires that federally financed programs and activities be accessible to people with disabilities. Section 504 also requires access to federally financed newly constructed and altered buildings. The technical provisions of UFAS are largely the same as those of the 1980 ANSI A117.1 standard.

Fair Housing Act Accessibility Guidelines

First published in 1991, the Fair Housing Accessibility Guidelines (the Guidelines) provide architects, builders, developers, and others with technical guidance for compliance with the accessibility requirements of the Fair Housing Amendments Act of 1988 (the Act). The Act covers newly constructed multifamily buildings containing at least four dwellings built for first occupancy on or after March 13, 1991.

Safe Harbors

Standards that are legally recognized as compliance with the requirements of a code or guideline (Chapter 4) are referred to as safe harbors. The following is a list of approved safe harbors for the Fair Housing Accessibility Guidelines:

1. HUD Fair Housing Accessibility Guidelines published on March 6, 1991 and the Supplemental Notice to Fair Housing Accessibility Guidelines: Questions and Answers about the Guidelines, published on June 28, 1994.
2. HUD Fair Housing Act Design Manual
3. ANSI A117.1 (1986), used with the Fair Housing Act, HUD's regulations, and the Guidelines.
4. CABO/ANSI A117.1 (1992), used with the Fair Housing Act, HUD's regulations, and the Guidelines.
5. ICC/ANSI A117.1 (1998), used with the Fair Housing Act, HUD's regulations, and the Guidelines.
6. Code Requirements for Housing Accessibility 2000 (CRHA).
7. International Building Code 2000 as amended by the 2001 Supplement to the International Codes.
8. International Building Code 2003, with one condition.*
9. ICC/ANSI A117.1 (2003) used with the Fair Housing Act, HUD's regulations, and the Guidelines
10. 2006 International Building Code®

Safe harbor standards constitute safe harbors only when adopted and implemented in accordance with the policy statement that HUD published in the Federal Register on March 23, 2000. That policy statement notes, for example, that if a jurisdiction adopts a model building code that HUD has determined conforms with the design and construction requirements of the Act (such as those listed above, then covered residential buildings that are constructed in accordance with plans and specifications approved during the building permitting process will be in compliance with the requirements of the Act.

If the building code official has waived one or more of those requirements or the building code official has incorrectly interpreted or applied the building code provisions, then the buildings are not in compliance. In addition, adoption of a HUD recognized "safe harbor" does not change HUD's enforcement efforts, including conducting investigations when complaints are filed.

Americans with Disabilities Act Accessibility Guidelines and the 2010 Standards for Accessible Design

First produced in 1991, the Americans with Disabilities Act Guidelines (ADAAG) are guidelines for compliance with the accessibility requirements of the ADA. The ADA addresses access to the workplace (Title I), state and local government services (Title II), and places of public accommodation and commercial facilities (Title III). It also requires phone companies to provide telecommunications relay services for people who have hearing or speech impairments (Title IV) and miscellaneous instructions for federal agencies that enforce the law (Title V).

On September 15, 2010, the U.S. Department of Justice published new ADA Title II and III regulations and adopted updated design standards called the 2010 Standards for Accessible Design. On and after March 15, 2012, use of the 1990 ADA as it applied to facilities and entities covered by Titles II and III and the 1991 ADAAG (ADA Access Guidelines) standard was no longer permitted for new construction and for alterations of existing elements conducted after that date.

---

*Effective February 28, 2005 HUD determined that the IBC 2003 is a safe harbor, conditioned upon ICC publishing and distributing a statement to jurisdictions and past and future purchasers of the 2003 IBC stating, "ICC interprets Section 1104.1, and specifically, the exception to Section 1104.1, to be read together with Section 1107.4, and that the Code requires an accessible pedestrian route from site arrival points to accessible building entrances, unless site impracticality applies. Exception 1 to Section 1107.4 is not applicable to site arrival points for any Type B dwelling units because site impracticality is addressed under Section 1107.7."

Canadian Policies and Practices

The National Building Code (NBC) developed by the Canadian Codes Center of the Institute for Research in Construction (a branch of the National Research Center) is the standard on which many of the provincial regulations are based. The Canadian Standards Association (CSA) developed another standard, B651, "Barrier Free Design Standards," in 1975. This standard, now called B651–04, "Accessible Design for the Built Environment," specifies minimum technical requirements, including a section that addresses kitchen and bathroom specifications. It has been revised many times, with the current version reaffirmed in 2010. As is true in the United States, this standard does not have the force of law unless mandated by a particular province. It is based on "average adult" dimension, and to effectively use the concepts, a designer would need to consult with the end user.

Because of provincial jurisdiction, progress has been difficult in Canada in the development and enforcement of national civil rights or legislation related to housing, such as the ADA and the FHA in the United States. In 1982, the federal government enacted the Charter of Rights and Freedoms, including Section 15 prohibiting discrimination on the basis of mental or physical handicap. However, the Charter of Rights has not been as thoroughly implemented into specific enforceable legislation as the FHA and ADA in the United States.

In Ontario, the building code includes specific requirements for accessible buildings, and in 2001, the Ontarians with Disabilities Act (ODA), was passed. The purpose of the ODA is to improve opportunities for people with disabilities and to enable them to become involved in the identification, removal, and prevention of barriers faced by persons with disabilities.

Recognizing the difficulties in mandating change, the Canadian federal government, through Canada Mortgage and Housing Corp. (CMHC), has chosen to assist the development of housing through financial instruments such as grants, loans and insurance arrangements. CMHC assistance helps low-income and older Canadians, people with disabilities and Aboriginals with housing options and expenses.

For example, in 1986 the Residential Rehabilitation Assistance Program (RRAP-D) for Persons with Disabilities was developed to offer financial assistance to homeowners and landlords to undertake accessibility work to modify dwellings occupied or intended for occupancy by low-income persons with disabilities. Another example is the Home Adaptations for Seniors' Independence (HASI) program, which helps homeowners and landlords pay for minor home adaptations to extend the time low-income seniors can live in their own homes independently.

SUMMARY

There is a wealth of information on which we can draw to plan kitchen spaces based on realistic human dimensions. Anthropometric studies give us basic dimensions for people of a variety of sizes and ages. An awareness of this information as we develop a plan for a client's kitchen helps to more accurately determine sizes and spatial relationships in each case.

In this chapter, you have also been presented with a quick summary of federal access laws, codes, and standards. While this overview provides a level of familiarity, each kitchen that you design may fall under specific local regulations and you need to work with your local officials for guidance and technical assistance.

For more information on housing accessibility, contact the U.S. Department of Housing and Urban Development (HUD). For ADA access issues concerning public facilities, contact the U.S. Department of Justice. For issues pertaining to UFAS, ADAAG, and the 2010 Standards, contact the Access Board. To increase your awareness of local access laws, contact the building inspector and consult local homebuilder associations.

As one universal design leader noted, "It is questionable whether accessibility standards will ever encourage designers to practice universal design." However, considering the long-term demographic trends pointing to an increase in older age groups, access needs will not disappear and universal design is a broad and beautiful way to achieve improved access without mandates.

REVIEW QUESTIONS

1. Define universal design, and explain who benefits from it.
2. What is anthropometry, and how does it help determine kitchen-planning guidelines?
3. What is the standard reach range of someone who remains seated to maneuver in the kitchen?
4. What is the referenced technical standard for compliance with the accessibility requirements of the International Building Code and many other state and local codes?

REFERENCES

Malina, Robert M., Peter V. Hamill, and Stanley Lemeshow. 1973. *National Health Examination Survey: Selected Body Measurements of Children 6–11 Years, 1963–1965.* Vital and Health Statistics Series 11, no. 123, DHEW publication no. (HSM) 73-1605. Washington, DC: US Government Printing Office. Available at www.cdc.gov/nchs/data/series/sr_11/sr11_123acc.pdf (accessed September 2012).

Panero, Julius, and Martin Zelnik. 1979. *Human Dimension and Interior Space: A Source Book of Design Reference Standards.* New York: Whitney Library of Design.

Assessing Needs

5

In today's homes, a kitchen is usually much more than a place to cook. It is likely a gathering and social space where many household activities take place. Household management, recreation, socializing, and entertainment are examples of the many activities often accommodated in the kitchen space. However, even in this day of take-out food, restaurant meals, and convenience foods, the kitchen is still very much a place to store, prepare, serve, and eat food.

The multipurpose nature of most kitchens presents a special challenge to the designer. It is a workspace, a personal space, a social space. To design a kitchen, begin by learning about your client(s) and how they use their kitchen.

This chapter focuses on assessing the needs of your client in preparation for developing a design. A needs assessment is the critical first step in the design process. Without knowing what your client wants and needs, you cannot know how to design the space. Listen to your client. Challenge your own assumptions about what is needed in a kitchen, and tune into what your client tells you.

Learning Objective 1: Identify and list the needs of a client in preparation for the development of a design plan for a kitchen.

Learning Objective 2: Describe the purpose and elements of a design program.

THE DESIGN PROCESS

The *design process* is a multistage process in which the designer moves from an idea to a completed product. As part of the design process, the designer can gather and organize information, develop visual diagrams and presentations, refine ideas and ensure accuracy, and manage the installation. In Chapter 10, "Putting it All Together," the design process is discussed in detail and an example of a formal design process is presented. To quote Chapter 10, the design process "involves a lot of going back and forth, checking and rechecking. A . . . design involves a dose of inspiration, a spark of creativity, but mostly a lot of hard work."

A necessary part of the design process is to gather information about your client and the space you will design. This information needs to be organized in a way that is useful to you throughout the design process. You will refer to this information as you develop your design, as you check the details, and as your project is constructed. This organized and documented information is the *design program*. The design program is both your guide through the design process and the inspiration to your creativity.

For a designer to complete the design process with a successful product and a satisfied client, the design programming stage is critical. The design program is built on accurate and complete information about the client, their needs and wants, and the space to be designed. This chapter, on needs assessment, is planned to facilitate design programming and lead to a successful design process.

INTERVIEWING THE CLIENT

From your first meeting with a potential client, you are gathering information. Informal conversations can help you learn more about the client's household, who will use the kitchen, and his or her goals and dreams for a new kitchen. However, you will soon want a more structured needs-assessment interview and information-gathering session with your client.

Prepare for the Interview

You may want to interview your client in your office or showroom. Alternatively, you may set an appointment and visit your client's home, which provides the opportunity to observe it firsthand. Even if your client is building a new home, a visit to his or her existing home can help you better understand what your client wants. Clients may feel more comfortable talking in their home, and their existing kitchen may give them clues about things to tell you. Finally, you may also be able to collect initial measurements (important for a remodel) during the same appointment.

Allow adequate time for the interview. Let the client know ahead of time that a typical interview might take two to three hours, including taking measurements. As you gain experience, you will be able to better estimate the needed time.

Alternatively, you may want to gather the client information in more than one session, so the process is less intense. For example, you may gather information about the client in one interview, and then focus on the home and job site in the second. Again, let your experience and sense of your client be your guide.

Recording the interview on audiotape gives you an accurate record of information and avoids the need to take notes while talking to the client. However, after the interview, it can be time consuming to transcribe information from the recording. Be sure to ask permission before recording the interview

Needs Assessment Forms

Using a prepared interview format is helpful. This ensures that you gather all the information you need and gives you a way to record, and later to organize, the responses. In some cases, you can give your client a checklist to complete and return to you.

The authors have created 11 different needs assessment forms to gather information about your client, his or her home, and the kitchen design project. These forms provide an organized way to complete your interview and job site inspection. These needs assessment forms are discussed and included in this chapter and are also available online at www.wiley.com/go/kitchenplanning.

The needs assessment forms are:

Client Information Forms

> Form 1: Getting to Know Your Client
>
> Form 2: Getting to Know Your Client's Home

Checklists for Client Use

> Form 3: Checklist for Kitchen Activities
>
> Form 4: Kitchen Storage Inventory
>
> Form 5: Cabinetry, Surfaces, and Kitchen Features Checklist
>
> From 6: Appliance Preference Checklist

Job Site and House Information Forms

> Form 7: Job Site Inspection
>
> Form 8: Dimensions of Mechanical Devices
>
> Form 9: Window Measurements
>
> Form 10: Door Measurements
>
> Form 11: Fixture and Appliance Measurements

You might want to adapt the needs assessment forms in this chapter to develop an interview format that works well on a computer and take a laptop with you to record information. The forms can be adapted as needed for your business or a particular client, and used in either an electronic or a printed format.

National Kitchen and Bath Association Kitchen Design Survey Form

The National Kitchen and Bath Association (NKBA) has developed a Kitchen Design Survey form, available to its members. This form, which covers some of the same information as the forms in this chapter, is used by professional designers and students in NKBA-accredited programs. Familiarity with this survey form is necessary for the Certified Kitchen Designer (CKD) certification.

Personal Information

In order to complete a client interview, you need to ask some questions about activities in the home, some of which may seem intrusive to your client. Adopt an open and frank approach to put your client at ease. Explain that some of the questions may seem personal, but the more information you have, the more successful your design will be.

During the interview, you will be asking about physical abilities. This can also be a sensitive subject. A client who is getting older may not recognize or accept the physical changes of aging. People with degenerative conditions may not be willing to yield to the impact of the disease on their bodies. Physical limitations can sometimes be hidden for short periods of time, especially with a relative stranger. Again, be open and stress the importance of fully knowing the client's physical situation, in order to develop the most supportive design. For more information on working with clients with special needs, refer to Chapter 8.

GETTING TO KNOW YOUR CLIENT

(Form 1)

The first thing you want to know is who uses the kitchen? Gather information about the users of the kitchen, their physical profiles, and any specialized needs each may have. For instance, who are the primary cooks? How old are they? How tall are they?

You will want to collect anthropometric (human measurement) information about your individual clients. This is especially important if your clients have any physical limitations or concerns about being able to function independently in the kitchen.

Review Chapter 4 to learn more about the importance of anthropometry and ergonomic design. Form 1: Getting to Know Your Client is a tool to collect anthropometric information about your client. Form 1 is also designed to help you collect information about any of your client's special needs with respect to activities in the kitchen. For example, do members of the household have any special physical needs? Do any of the cooks require a mobility aid, such as a wheelchair or cane?

Food-related activities are central to the design of a kitchen. Therefore, in addition to the anthropometric information and other special needs related to activities in the kitchen, you need to learn about how members of the household do, or do not, share cooking and cleanup activities. Form 1 can assist you in gathering information about cooking patterns.

Another aspect of cooking styles that you will want to discuss with your client is the influences on the types of food they cook. Are there cultural, ethnic, religious, health, or other dietary choices or restrictions that influence household food preparation and eating? For example, designing a kitchen for clients who eat a vegetarian, kosher, or Asian diet requires understanding their food choices and their needs for food preparation space, storage, and appliances. The questions in Form 1 can help you gather the information you need for a successful design.

Form 1: Getting to Know Your Client

This form is an information fact sheet about your client. Use the parts that are appropriate to your design project. A custom design project or a client with special needs may require more detailed information.

1. Users of the Kitchen:

   Name: _____ Age: _____

   Height: _____ Weight: _____ Handedness: ☐ Right ☐ Left

   Special needs or concerns: _____

   _____

   Name: _____ Age: _____

   Height: _____ Weight: _____ Handedness: ☐ Right ☐ Left

   Special needs or concerns: _____

   _____

   Name: _____ Age: _____

   Height: _____ Weight: _____ Handedness: ☐ Right ☐ Left

   Special needs or concerns: _____

   _____

   Name: _____ Age: _____

   Height: _____ Weight: _____ Handedness: ☐ Right ☐ Left

   Special needs or concerns: _____

   _____

   Name: _____ Age: _____

   Height: _____ Weight: _____ Handedness: ☐ Right ☐ Left

   Special needs or concerns: _____

   _____

2. Anthropometric Information (Figure 5.1)

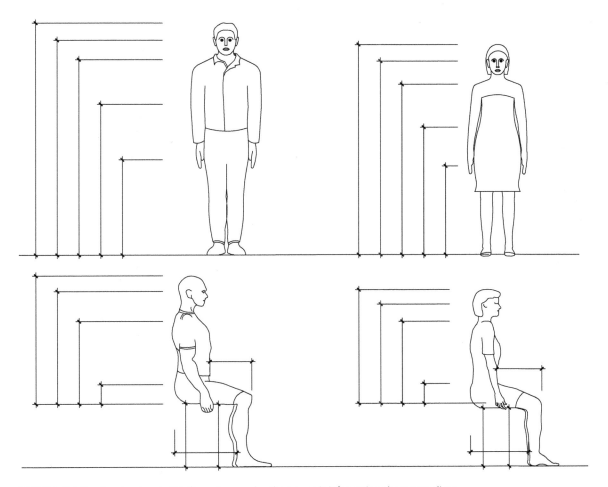

FIGURE 5.1 Use the drawings in this figure to record anthropometric information about your client.

(continued)

3. Reach and Grasp Profile (Figure 5.2)

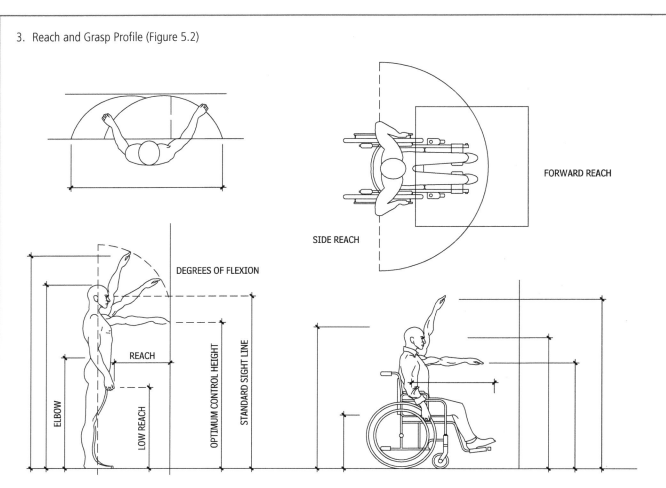

FORWARD REACH

SIDE REACH

DEGREES OF FLEXION

REACH

ELBOW

LOW REACH

OPTIMUM CONTROL HEIGHT

STANDARD SIGHT LINE

FIGURE 5.2 Use the drawings in this figure to record additional antropometric information about your client, including their ability to reach.

4. Physical Profile

Physical characteristic(s) affecting activities in the kitchen:

A. Sight: _____

    Do you wear glasses for: ☐ Reading ☐ Distance

    Are you taking medications that affect your sight? _____

    Are you sensitive to light? _____

B. Hearing: _____

    What issues regarding your hearing will affect your activities in the kitchen? _____

    _____

C. Tactile/Touch: _____

    Can you feel hot and cold? _____

D. Taste/Smell: _____

    What issues regarding your sense of taste or smell will affect your activities in the kitchen? _____

    _____

E. Strength and Function: _____

    What can you lift? _____ Carry? _____

    Do you have more strength on one side than the other? _____

    Do you use both hands fully? _____ Palms only? _____

    How is your grip? _____

    Left side? _____ Right side? _____

F. Balance, Mobility and Assistance: _____

    How is your balance: Standing? _____ Bending? _____

    Does your mobility or balance vary by time of day? _____

    Does an assistant help you: Sometimes? _____ All the time? _____

    What adaptive equipment do you use? _____

    _____

(*continued*)

G. Prognosis: Is your condition stable? Is further deterioration anticipated? Is improvement anticipated?

_____

H. Other Physical Concerns: _____

_____

I. Special Safety Concerns: _____

_____

5. Mobility Aids

If a mobility aid, such as wheel chair, walker, or cane is used, it is important to collect information on the size of the mobility aid, as well as anthropometric information about the client when using the mobility aid.

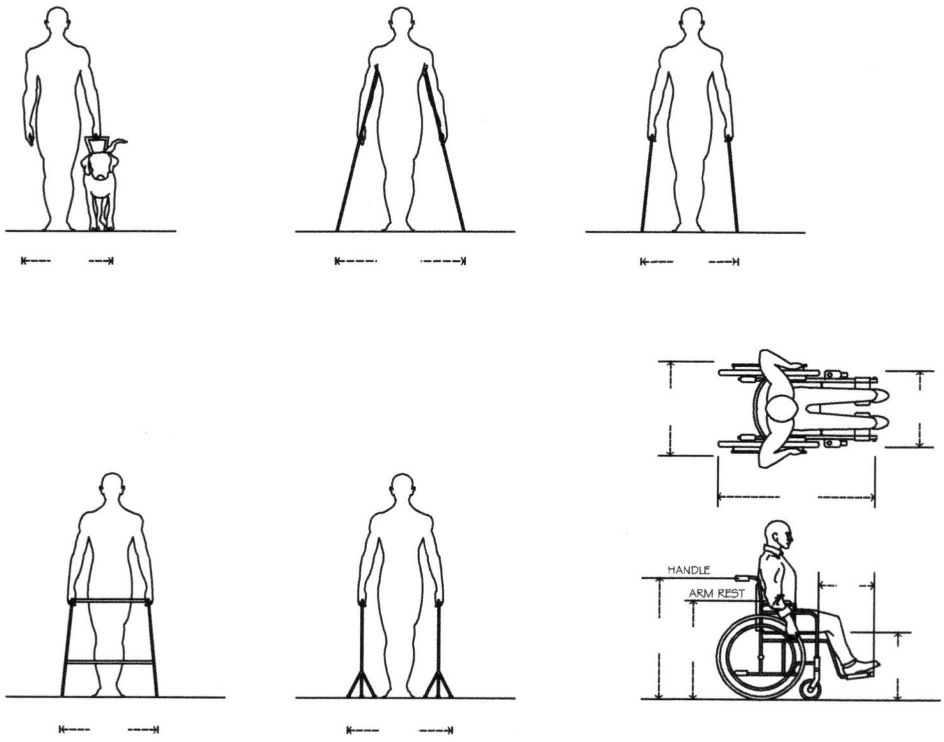

FIGURE 5.3 If appropriate to your client, use the drawings in this figure to record information about your client that includes a mobility aid.

6. Personal Information about the Kitchen

What is the typical pattern of cooking in your household?

☐ One person does most of the cooking. Who? _____

☐ Two or more people share most of the cooking. Describe. _____

_____

_____

☐ One person cooks and another person helps. Describe. _____

_____

_____

☐ Different people take turns doing the cooking. Describe. _____

_____

_____

☐ Another arrangement. Describe. _____

_____

_____

What about clean up?

☐ The cook cleans up.

☐ Cooking and clean-up are shared.

☐ Clean-up is done by someone who does not cook. Describe. _____

_____

☐ Another arrangement. Describe. _____

_____

_____

How often do you or someone in your household:

Do a major grocery shopping? _____

Do a convenience grocery shopping? _____

(continued)

7. General Food and Meal Preferences

How would you describe the food and meals that are prepared in your home?

☐ Most food is prepared using fresh ingredients. Describe. _____

_____

☐ Most food is prepared using convenience and prepackaged ingredients. Describe. _____

_____

☐ We mostly prepare full meals. Describe. _____

_____

☐ We mostly prepare light meals and snacks. Describe. _____

_____

☐ We focus on eating a healthy diet. Describe _____

_____

☐ Most/all food prepared is vegetarian. Describe. _____

_____

☐ We follow a kosher, halal, or other religious diet. Describe. _____

_____

☐ Most food we prepare is influenced by our cultural heritage. Describe. _____

_____

☐ Other

8. Future Plans

How long do you plan to live in this home? _____

_____

Do you anticipate changes in your household size or make-up? _____

_____

Will this affect activities in the kitchen? _____

_____

Is resale value of the home important? _____

_____

GETTING TO KNOW YOUR CLIENT'S HOME (FORM 2)

Start with the big picture. Where is the home located? How will the location influence the design of the kitchen? Location determines climate, telling you whether there are cold winters, hot summers, or long seasons where the windows might be open to the outside air. Are there views of the ocean, a lake, mountains, trees, or a city skyline to be captured in the design? Or does the location determine that the kitchen design needs to be more inwardly focused, sheltered from things such as traffic noise or close-by buildings?

Location of the home can also give you a clue to your client's lifestyle. A kitchen in an urban apartment, a large ranch home in a rural area, or a condominium in a resort community represent different types of homes as well as lifestyles and, thus, different types of kitchen design needs.

Finally, different countries, as well as different regions of the same country, can have variation in design trends. Vernacular housing describes housing styles that are typical or common to a region and that have been influenced by factors such as climate, available building materials, and cultural heritage. Knowing something about the vernacular housing of the area where your client's home is located may give you some ideas about style, color, or materials to use in the kitchen design.

Type of Home

Most kitchen designers work on projects in single-family homes—but not always. Especially in urban areas, a designer may work on a home that is an apartment, townhouse, or other type of multifamily structure. There may be some unique concerns in this type of home. For example, in many multifamily housing communities, plans for remodeling must be approved by a group such as the homeowners' association. You may be limited in making changes affecting the home's exterior. Likewise, plumbing changes may be limited. Carefully consider any possible factors that could occur in a multifamily project.

Often, single-family housing may also be in a community with a homeowners' association with rules that affect home renovations. In addition, sometimes there may be covenants in a property's deed that could influence a kitchen remodeling project, such as the size of an addition or the style and placement of windows.

While you consider these special and legal situations that can affect your design, also bear in mind the impact of the building permit process. Building codes and regulations may vary by location, so make sure you reference the correct codes. You, as the designer, are responsible for knowing the building codes that affect your kitchen project. Further, you need to work with the contractor/builder to see that all building permits are obtained and inspections completed. This process will be easier if you include all building codes and permits as part of your needs assessment and design planning.

Home Tour

If you are working on a remodeling project, ask to take a tour of the existing home. Take along a copy of Form 2: Getting to Know Your Client's Home. This form can be used to gather information about the "big picture" of your client's home and kitchen. Observe the size, and the number of bedrooms and bathrooms. Look at entrances and traffic flow, especially in and around the kitchen space.

A tour of your client's home will also be useful to get a sense of style and color. Ask your client to describe what he or she does and does not like about other rooms in the home. Use this information for clues about design preferences.

During the home tour, note what rooms are on the other side of the kitchen walls. This information might be useful as you think about potentially "borrowing" space from another room or relocating and reconfiguring plumbing. Look for details that might prevent surprises during the construction phase, such as the presence of heating or cooling ducts. You might want to make a sketch of the existing kitchen space, or do this as part of the job site inspection (see Form 7).

A camera can be a useful tool during a home tour. Be sure to ask permission first. Use the camera to make visual notes of features that will be useful to remember during the design process. A digital camera is particularly helpful for this type of documentation as pictures are easily transferred to a computer file. Also, take pictures of family members, favorite accessory items, or views from windows. Later, you may be able to incorporate these items into presentation drawings for a personal touch.

The Home of the Future

Finish your understanding of the big picture by talking to your client about future plans for the home. Is this a home in which he or she plans to retire? Will he or she be likely to remodel or expand this home in the future? Form 1: Getting to Know Your Client and Form 2: Getting to Know Your Client's Home can guide you in gathering this type of information.

While you are learning about future plans for the client's home, you can ask about the future of his or her family or household. "Expanding" households are typically, though not always, younger and are at the life stage where they can expect to add new household members, such as by marriage or birth. Sometimes a new household member is an older relative. "Launching" households are more likely to be older, with children who will soon be leaving. Future changes in household size or composition influence who uses the kitchen, as well as the activities that take place in that space.

ACTIVITIES IN THE KITCHEN
(FORM 3)

Once you know something about who is using the kitchen, gather information about what they actually do there. As the research discussed in Chapter 1 indicates, most activities in the kitchen can generally be grouped as follows:

- Food preparation, cooking, and serving
- Cleanup
- Other food-related activities
- Household management
- Relaxing and recreation
- Socializing

Since the potential kitchen activities are numerous, give your client an activity checklist to complete (Form 3). This can save time and may result in more complete information. Review the checklist with them, and then ask them to complete it at home. Alternatively, mail (or e-mail) the checklist to the client in advance of the interview and then review it during the interview. Use the checklist included in this chapter, Form 3: Checklist for Kitchen Activities. The form also asks about location and frequency of activities—information that is extremely useful during the design process.

In addition to the information provided on the checklist, you may need clarification on certain activities. For instance, ask about activities that your client prefers to do while seated or standing. If your client has completed the checklist in advance, these issues can be discussed at the interview. Form 3 offers space to make notes after the client has completed the checklist.

Form 2: Getting to Know Your Client's Home

This form can be used to collect general information about your client's home to help in developing your design. Specific structural and mechanical information is collected in other forms.

Location of home: _____

Type of neighborhood: _____

Type of home: ☐ single-family home ☐ duplex ☐ townhouse ☐ apartment/flat

☐ other _____

Structure of home: ☐ one-story ☐ two-story ☐ three-story ☐ ranch ☐ split-level

☐ split foyer/raised ranch ☐ high rise ☐ other _____

Approximate size of home: _____

Number of bedrooms: _____ Number of bathrooms: _____

Style of home (exterior) _____

Is the home historic? What time period? _____

Are there historic covenants or restrictions affecting the home?

_____

_____

Is the home part of a homeowner's association? _____

Is there homeowner's association covenants or restrictions affecting the home? _____

_____

_____

Are there any other covenants or deed restrictions? _____

_____

_____

Style of home (interior): _____

_____

_____

(continued)

Colors? _____

_____

Materials? _____

_____

Furniture? _____

_____

Accessories? _____

_____

Future plans for resale or remodeling? _____

_____

Notes:

Form 3: Checklist for Kitchen Activities [Client Checklist]

Instructions: Review the list of activities in each section. If it is an activity that you do, or want to do, in the kitchen, place a check in the first column, then check the appropriate location and frequency columns. Extra lines are left in each section for you to add activities as needed.

Food Preparation, Cooking, and Serving Activities									
		Location						Frequency	
✓ **Activity**	**Sink**	**Cooktop**	**Oven**	**Microwave**	**Refrigerator**	**Prep Area**	**Other (specify)**	**Often**	**Sometimes**
Bake: bread									
Bake: foods made from mixes									
Bake: foods made from scratch									
Bake: frozen prepared foods									
Broil foods									
Can food: for preservation									
Chop, carve, and slice foods									
Cook: breakfast									
Cook: dinner									
Cook: lunch									
Deep fry foods									
Dehydrate foods: for preservation									
Entertain: cook and serve meals for guests									
Entertain: guests help cook									
Entertain: pot luck/shared meals									
Freeze food: for preservation									
Freeze food: large quantity meals for later use									
Freeze food: leftovers									
Fry foods									
Grill foods: indoors									
Grill foods: outdoors									
Hire a caterer: serve foods prepared elsewhere									
Hire a caterer: prepare foods in your kitchen									

(continued)

		Location							Frequency	
✓	**Activity**	**Sink**	**Cooktop**	**Oven**	**Microwave**	**Refrigerator**	**Prep Area**	**Other (specify)**	**Often**	**Sometimes**
	Make candy									
	Pack lunches or food to be eaten away from home									
	Prepare: drinks									
	Prepare: foods from complex recipes									
	Prepare: foods on a griddle									
	Prepare: foods with specialty ingredients									
	Prepare: fresh produce									
	Prepare: frozen convenience foods									
	Prepare: full meals									
	Prepare: items using a rolling pin									
	Prepare: kosher, halal, or similar foods									
	Prepare prepackaged convenience foods									
	Reheat foods in oven									
	Roast meats									
	Serve drinks									
	Serve food: buffet style									
	Serve food: family style									
	Serve food: individual plates									
	Serve food: carryout orders									
	Slow cook or simmer foods									
	Stir fry foods									
	Other activities:									

Food Preparation, Cooking, and Serving Activities, continued

✓	Activity	Location							Frequency	
		Sink	Cooktop	Oven	Microwave	Refrigerator	Prep Area	Other (specify)	Often	Sometimes
	Air dry dishes or utensils									
	Compost food waste									
	Recycle: collect in kitchen									
	Recycle: not in kitchen									
	Recycle: sort in kitchen									
	Rinse dishes or utensils									
	Soak dishes, pans									
	Stack dishes or items for later washing									
	Trash: collect in kitchen									
	Wash dishes: dishwasher									
	Wash dishes: by hand									
	Wash pots and pans: dishwasher									
	Wash pots and pans: by hand									
	Other activities:									

Cleanup and Waste Management Activities

(*continued*)

Other Activities That Occur in the Kitchen										
✓	**Activity**	**Location**							**Frequency**	
		Sink	Cooktop	Oven	Microwave	Refrigerator	Prep Area	Other (specify)	Often	Sometimes
	Food-Related Activities:									
	Eat meals									
	Eat snacks									
	Drink beverages									
	Plan meals									
	Take vitamins, medicines									
	Other:									
	Household Management Activities:									
	Homework/schoolwork									
	Laundry: air dry									
	Laundry: hand wash									
	Laundry: machine wash									
	Laundry: sort, fold									
	Paperwork, pay bills									
	Pet feeding, care									
	Polish shoes									
	Sort mail									
	Use a computer									
	Other:									

Other Activities That Occur in the Kitchen									
✓ Activity	Location							Frequency	
	Sink	Cooktop	Oven	Microwave	Refrigerator	Prep Area	Other (Specify)	Often	Sometimes
Relaxing and Recreation:									
Computer games									
Crafts									
Display collections									
Grow plants									
Listen to music									
Nails: clip, file, polish									
Reading: newspaper, magazines									
Reading: books									
Sewing									
Watch television									
Other:									
Social Activities:									
Conversations with family, friends									
Entertain									
Play with children									
Talk on telephone									
Other:									
Other Activities:									

STORAGE IN THE KITCHEN
(FORM 4)

Talking about activities in the kitchen easily leads to a discussion of your client's storage needs. The number of items to be stored in the kitchen and the volume of space needed for storage can be a major issue in a kitchen design—perhaps the reason for a new kitchen! What does your client want to store in the kitchen? Where will the client use the different items? How frequently does he or she use each item? These are some examples of information that are useful to you, the designer, for planning kitchen storage.

A storage inventory checklist helps to determine your client's storage needs. Form 4: Kitchen Storage Inventory is a storage inventory your client can complete at home. It contains lists of 551 items in 16 different categories:

- Small electric appliances
- Food storage
- Preparation items
- Small utensils
- Pots and pans
- Baking ware
- Glasses and drinking items
- Dishes
- Serving pieces
- Flatware
- Linens
- Storage containers
- Cleaning supplies and tools
- Bulk storage
- Management/home office
- Miscellaneous

The items in this storage inventory are taken from the Virginia Tech Kitchen Storage Research Project (see Chapter 1), and represent those found in at least 25 percent of the 87 kitchens studied in this project. For each item on the storage inventory, there is space to indicate the number stored, the frequency of use, and the type of storage location preferred. Additional space is provided in each category to list other items.

The Form 4 inventory is detailed but is designed for ease of use. The fact that so many common kitchen items are already listed on the inventory saves your client time. This checklist will be helpful in the design process, so encourage your client to be thorough in completing it. As with the activity checklist, it is helpful if the client has completed this inventory in advance of the interview.

Compare Form 3: Checklist for Kitchen Activities with Form 4: Kitchen Storage Inventory. Are supplies needed for an activity that is not included on the storage inventory? Or do some of the storage items suggest activities that are not included on the checklist? If necessary, go back to the client for clarification.

Form 4: Kitchen Storage Inventory [Client Checklist]

Instructions: This inventory is divided into sections representing categories of items typically stored in kitchen cabinets and pantries. Many of the typical items found in kitchens are already listed. Check those items you want to store in the kitchen. Add any additional items needed. Complete the form, indicating how many of each item you have, how frequently you use it, and the type of storage you would like in your new kitchen. Blank lines are included for items you have that are not listed. A space for notes is at the end of each section. Include information about special size or space requirements, items that need to be stored away from children, or other important details.

Small Electric Appliances										
✓	**Item to Store**	**How Many?**	**Frequency of Use**		**Type of Storage**					
			Often	**Sometimes**	**Wall Cabinet**	**Base Cabinet**	**Drawer**	**Pantry/Tall Cabinet**	**Counter Top**	**Other (describe)**
	Blender									
	Can opener									
	Chopper/blender (handheld)									
	Coffee grinder									
	Coffee maker, drip									
	Slow cooker									
	Food processor									
	Food processor blades									
	Fry pan or skillet									
	Juicer									
	Knife									
	Mixer, free standing									
	Mixer, hand									
	Pancake/griddle									
	Television									
	Toaster									
	Waffle iron									
	Additional items:									

Notes:

(*continued*)

Food Storage										
			Frequency of Use		Type of Storage					
✓	Item to Store	How Many?	Often	Sometimes	Wall Cabinet	Base Cabinet	Drawer	Pantry/Tall Cabinet	Counter Top	Other (describe)
	Alcohol/liquors									
	Baking supplies, bottles									
	Baking supplies, boxes									
	Baking supplies, cans									
	Beers/soft drinks/water, bottles									
	Beers/soft drinks/water, cans									
	Beers/soft drinks/water, large bottles/cans									
	Beers/soft drinks/water, small bottles/pouches/boxes									
	Bread/bagels/rolls/muffins									
	Bread, packages									
	Bread, loaf									
	Canned foods, small									
	Canned foods, medium									
	Canned foods, large									
	Cereal boxes, small									
	Cereal boxes, medium									
	Cereal boxes, large									
	Flours/meals, bag									
	Flour/meals, box									
	Food in bags, small									
	Food in bags, medium									
	Food in bags, large									
	Food in canisters, small									
	Food in canisters, medium									
	Food in canisters, large									
	Food in jars, small									
	Food in jars, medium									

Food Storage, continued									
✓ Item to Store	**How Many?**	**Frequency of Use**		**Type of Storage**					
		Often	**Sometimes**	**Wall Cabinet**	**Base Cabinet**	**Drawer**	**Pantry/Tall Cabinet**	**Counter Top**	**Other (describe)**
Food in jars, large									
Food in bottles, small									
Food in bottles, large									
Packaged drink mixes									
Prepared/boxed mixes, small									
Prepared/boxed mixes, large									
Produce, fruit									
Produce, vegetables									
Ready-to-eat boxed foods, small									
Ready-to-eat boxed foods, medium									
Ready-to-eat boxed foods, large									
Rice/grains, bag, small									
Rice/grains, bag, large									
Rice/grains, box									
Spices/seasonings/herbs, bottles									
Spices/seasonings/herbs, cans									
Spices/seasonings/herbs, packages/boxes									
Sugars, bag									
Sugars, box									
Wine									
Additional items:									

(continued)

			Frequency of Use		Type of Storage					
✓	**Item to Store**	**How Many?**	**Often**	**Sometimes**	**Wall Cabinet**	**Base Cabinet**	**Drawer**	**Pantry/Tall Cabinet**	**Counter Top**	**Other (describe)**
	Baking/roasting bags									
	Bread board									
	Colander, small									
	Colander, medium									
	Colander, large									
	Cutting board, small									
	Cutting board, large									
	Measuring cup, 1 cup (wet)									
	Measuring cup, 2 cup (wet)									
	Measuring cup, 4 cup (wet)									
	Measuring cups, set (dry)									
	Measuring spoon set									
	Mixing bowl, small									
	Mixing bowl, medium									
	Mixing bowl, large									
	Mixing bowl, extra large									
	Molds									
	Muffin pan liners (pkgs.)									
	Salad spinner									
	Scale									
	Sifter									
	Storage canister, small									
	Storage canister, medium									
	Storage canister, large									
	Additional items:									

Preparation Items

	Small Utensils									
✓	Item to Store	How Many?	Frequency of Use		Type of Storage					
			Often	Sometimes	Wall Cabinet	Base Cabinet	Drawer	Pantry/Tall Cabinet	Counter Top	Other (describe)
	Apple corer									
	Baster									
	Basting brush									
	Beater (flat rotary)									
	Bottle opener									
	Brush, soft (bottle)									
	Brush, stiff (vegetable)									
	Brushes									
	Can opener (handheld)									
	Cookie cutter									
	Fork (cooking)									
	Funnel									
	Garlic press									
	Grater/shredder									
	Ice cream scoop									
	Juicer (hand)									
	Knife block									
	Knife sharpener									
	Knife, bread									
	Knife, butcher									
	Knife, cake									
	Knife, carving									
	Knife, grapefruit									
	Knife, large									
	Knife, paring									
	Lemon zester									
	Mallet									
	Melon ball cutter									
	Mixing spoon (large)									

Small Utensils, continued

✓	Item to Store	How Many?	Frequency of Use		Type of Storage					
			Often	Sometimes	Wall Cabinet	Base Cabinet	Drawer	Pantry/Tall Cabinet	Counter Top	Other (describe)
	Pancake turner									
	Pasta server									
	Pizza wheel (cutter)									
	Potato masher									
	Rolling pin									
	Scissors (poultry)									
	Skewers									
	Slicer									
	Spatula/scraper									
	Spoon (wooden)									
	Strainer/sieve, small									
	Strainer/sieve, medium									
	Strainer/sieve, large									
	Thermometer, meat									
	Timer									
	Tongs									
	Wine bottle opener									
	Wire whip/whisk									
	Additional items:									

	Pots and Pans									
✓	Item to Store	How Many?	Frequency of Use		Type of Storage					
			Often	Sometimes	Wall Cabinet	Base Cabinet	Drawer	Pantry/Tall Cabinet	Counter Top	Other (describe)
	Double boiler insert									
	Dutch oven lid									
	Dutch oven/stew kettle									
	Griddle									
	Sauce pan, extra small									
	Sauce pan, small									
	Sauce pan, medium									
	Sauce pan, large									
	Sauce pan, extra large									
	Sauce pan lid, extra small									
	Sauce pan lid, small									
	Sauce pan lid, medium									
	Sauce pan lid, large									
	Sauce pan lid, extra large									
	Skillet/frying pan, small									
	Skillet/frying pan, medium									
	Skillet/frying pan, large									
	Spoon rest									
	Steamer, insert									
	Stock pot/pasta pot									
	Stock pot/pasta pot, lid									
	Tea ball									
	Tea kettle									
	Tea strainer									
	Additional items:									

Baking Ware										
✓	**Item to Store**	**How Many?**	**Frequency of Use**		**Type of Storage**					
			Often	**Sometimes**	**Wall Cabinet**	**Base Cabinet**	**Drawer**	**Pantry/Tall Cabinet**	**Counter Top**	**Other (describe)**
	Baking stone									
	Broiler pan									
	Cake pan, angel food									
	Cake pan, bundt									
	Cake pan, rectangle									
	Cake pan, round									
	Cake pan, square									
	Cake rack									
	Casserole dish w/ lid, small									
	Casserole dish w/ lid, medium									
	Casserole dish w/ lid, large									
	Casserole dish w/o lid, small									
	Casserole dish w/o lid, medium									
	Casserole dish w/o lid, large									
	Cookie sheet									
	Custard cups/ramekins									
	Loaf pan, small									
	Loaf pan, large									
	Muffin pan, mini									
	Muffin pan, six									
	Muffin pan, twelve									
	Pie plate									
	Pizza pan									
	Potholder, flat									
	Potholder, mitt									
	Quiche pan									
	Roasting pan w/ lid, medium									
	Roasting pan w/ lid, large									
	Roasting pan w/o lid, medium									
	Roasting pan w/o lid, large									
	Roasting rack									

Baking Ware, continued

✓	Item to Store	How Many?	Frequency of Use		Type of Storage					
			Often	Sometimes	Wall Cabinet	Base Cabinet	Drawer	Pantry/Tall Cabinet	Counter Top	Other (describe)
	Spring form pan									
	Additional items:									

Glasses

✓	Item to Store	How Many?	Frequency of Use		Type of Storage					
			Often	Sometimes	Wall Cabinet	Base Cabinet	Drawer	Pantry/Tall Cabinet	Counter Top	Other (describe)
	Canned beverage insulator									
	Cups, stadium (plastic)									
	Glasses, juice									
	Glasses, highball									
	Glasses, iced beverage									
	Glasses, shot									
	Glasses, stemmed, Champagne									
	Glasses, stemmed, wine (small)									
	Glasses, stemmed, wine (large)									
	Glasses, water tumbler (plastic/ glass)									
	Mugs, beer									
	Mugs, coffee/tea									
	Additional items:									

Dishes (may need to repeat if more than one set is stored separately in the kitchen)

✓	Item to Store	How Many?	Frequency of Use		Type of Storage					
			Often	Sometimes	Wall Cabinet	Base Cabinet	Drawer	Pantry/Tall Cabinet	Counter Top	Other (describe)
	Bowls, individual salad									
	Bowls, large cereal									
	Bowls, small cereal									
	Bowls, soup (w/o lid)									
	Plates, bread and butter									
	Plates, dessert/salad									
	Plates, dinner									
	Plates, luncheon									
	Plates, saucers									
	Coffee/tea cups									
	Additional items:									

			Frequency of Use		Type of Storage					
✓	**Item to Store**	**How Many?**	**Often**	**Sometimes**	**Wall Cabinet**	**Base Cabinet**	**Drawer**	**Pantry/Tall Cabinet**	**Counter Top**	**Other (describe)**
	Basket (wicker), small									
	Basket (wicker), medium									
	Basket (wicker), large									
	Bowl (serving), small									
	Bowl (serving), medium									
	Bowl (serving), large									
	Butter dish, w/ lid									
	Cake plate									
	Cheese board									
	Chip and dip plate									
	Coffee carafe/pot									
	Condiment dish									
	Creamer									
	Hot plate/trivet									
	Ice bucket									
	Pasta bowl									
	Pitcher, small									
	Pitcher, large									
	Platter, small									
	Platter, large									
	Salt and pepper shakers									
	Serving tray									
	Sugar bowl									
	Additional items:									

Serving Pieces

Flatware										
✓ **Item to Store**	**How Many?**	**Frequency of Use**		**Type of Storage**						
		Often	**Sometimes**	**Wall Cabinet**	**Base Cabinet**	**Drawer**	**Pantry/Tall Cabinet**	**Counter Top**	**Other (describe)**	
Forks, dinner										
Forks, salad										
Forks, serving										
Knives, butter										
Knives, cheese										
Knives, dinner										
Knives, steak										
Spoons, condiment										
Spoons, iced tea										
Spoons, serving/table										
Spoons, soup										
Spoons, sugar										
Spoons, tablespoon										
Spoons, teaspoon										
Butter knife/spreader										
Cake/pie server										
Cheese spreader										
Chop sticks										
Corn holders										
Gravy ladle										
Ice tongs										
Salad serving set										
Additional items:										

Linens											
✓	**Item to Store**	**How Many?**	**Frequency of Use**		**Type of Storage**						
			Often	**Sometimes**	**Wall Cabinet**	**Base Cabinet**	**Drawer**	**Pantry/Tall Cabinet**	**Counter Top**	**Other (describe)**	
	Apron										
	Cloth napkins										
	Dish cloths										
	Dish towels										
	Hand towels										
	Placemats										
	Additional items:										

Storage Containers											
✓	**Item to Store**	**How Many?**	**Frequency of Use**		**Type of Storage**						
			Often	**Sometimes**	**Wall Cabinet**	**Base Cabinet**	**Drawer**	**Pantry/Tall Cabinet**	**Counter Top**	**Other (describe)**	
	Aluminum foil										
	Freezer paper										
	Plastic container lids, small										
	Plastic container lids, medium										
	Plastic container lids, large										
	Plastic containers, small										
	Plastic containers, medium										
	Plastic containers, large										
	Plastic storage bags (pkgs.), small										
	Plastic storage bags (pkgs.), large										
	Plastic wrap										
	Spice rack										
	Wax paper										
	Additional items:										

Cleaning Supplies and Tools										
✓ **Item to Store**	**How Many?**	**Frequency of Use**		**Type of Storage**						
		Often	**Sometimes**	**Wall Cabinet**	**Base Cabinet**	**Drawer**	**Pantry/Tall Cabinet**	**Counter Top**	**Other (describe)**	
Brushes, small										
Cleaning supplies, bottles										
Cleaning supplies, boxes										
Cleaning supplies, cans										
Dish cloth, in use										
Dish drainer										
Dish towel, in use										
Dust pan										
Paper towel holder										
Paper towel, in use										
Pot scrubber holder										
Pot scrubber										
Rubber gloves										
Sink strainer										
Sponge										
Trash can										
Additional items:										

Bulk Storage

✓	Item to Store	How Many?	Frequency of Use		Type of Storage					
			Often	Sometimes	Wall Cabinet	Base Cabinet	Drawer	Pantry/Tall Cabinet	Counter Top	Other (describe)
	Coffee filters (pkg.)									
	Napkins, paper (pkgs.)									
	Paper lunch bags (pkgs.)									
	Paper towels, rolls not in use									
	Plastic/paper cups (pkgs.)									
	Plastic/paper, plates (pkgs.)									
	Plastic/paper, utensils (pkgs.)									
	Trash bags, plastic (pkgs.)									
	Additional items:									

Management/Home Office

✓	Item to Store	How Many?	Frequency of Use		Type of Storage					
			Often	Sometimes	Wall Cabinet	Base Cabinet	Drawer	Pantry/Tall Cabinet	Counter Top	Other (describe)
	Calculator									
	Cook book									
	Mail/bills									
	Miscellaneous "junk" drawer									
	Note pad									
	Pencil/pen									
	Recipe file box									
	Scissors									
	Stapler									
	Tape/tape dispenser									
	Telephone									
	Telephone directory									
	Additional items:									

Miscellaneous									
			Frequency of Use		**Type of Storage**						
✓	**Item to Store**	**How Many?**	**Often**	**Sometimes**	**Wall Cabinet**	**Base Cabinet**	**Drawer**	**Pantry/Tall Cabinet**	**Counter Top**	**Other (describe)**
	Batteries									
	Candle holder									
	Candles, birthday									
	Decorative item									
	Fire extinguisher									
	Flashlight									
	Hand soap dispenser									
	Lotion									
	Matches (box)									
	Medications and/or vitamins, bottles									
	Medications and/or vitamins, boxes									
	Nut cracker									
	Plant									
	Straws (pkgs.)									
	Thermos bottle									
	Toothpicks (box)									
	Vase, small									
	Vase, large									
	Additional items:									

YOUR CLIENT'S KITCHEN (FORMS 5 AND 6)

Cabinetry, Surfaces, and Kitchen Features

Once you have the big picture about your client's home, gather specific information about the kitchen project. Ask your client about what he or she does and does not like in a kitchen—and what is feasible for his or her space and budget.

Begin with the client's current kitchen. Ask what he or she does not like about the space. Be very specific. Let your client volunteer information first, such as:

- There is not enough counter space.
- The space feels crowded.
- People bump into each other when sharing cooking activities.

Then, ask about features that they do like, such as:

- The room is open to the family room.
- The location of the refrigerator is convenient.

Ideas suggested by your client, positive or negative, can indicate areas of strong feeling. Remember these ideas as you develop your design.

Next, ask your client to talk about what he or she wants in the new kitchen. Let the client suggest ideas, but be sure to cover the major features. Form 5: Cabinetry, Surfaces, and Kitchen Features Checklist can help you and your client collect and organize information about his or her preferences. Form 5 can be completed during the interview or in advance of your meeting and then reviewed. Be aware—although Form 5 is designed as a client checklist, the number and detail of the choices and decisions on it can overwhelm an unprepared client. You may want to go over the form with your client first.

Appliances

Appliances are such an important part of a kitchen that the need or desire to replace them may be the motivation to remodel a kitchen. There are many choices on the market today. Use Form 6: Appliance Preference Checklist to help determine your clients' preferences for appliances. Note that Form 6 is for new appliances. Form 11 is used to measure any existing appliances slated to remain in the kitchen. Review appliance selection with your client and advise them as to the best choices for their kitchen design.

Client Preferences and Specifications

Many clients think and dream about a kitchen project before it becomes a reality. They read shelter magazines, visit showrooms, or surf the Internet. Many collect ideas about design, products, fixtures, materials, and other features. By asking questions about preferences—or definite specifications—you move from general ideas to the specific decisions to be made about the kitchen design.

In some cases, your client may have an item to include in the new kitchen from the current kitchen, or they may have salvage pieces, such as cabinet or door hardware, to include in the new design. Ask if there are any pieces like this. Get detailed information, such as size, and any mechanical requirements such as plumbing connections.

Some clients may prefer to shop for and to select certain pieces, such as an appliance or a faucet, on their own. If the client is going to provide items for the new kitchen, this information will need to be specified in your contract. You and your client will need to agree on the specifications of the items he or she will provide. Timing will be important as well, so that the installation of the new kitchen is not delayed while waiting for a client-provided item. Forms 5 and 6 will prompt you to collect this information.

Form 5: Cabinetry, Surfaces, and Kitchen Features Checklist [Client Checklist]

Kitchen design is made up of many details. This checklist helps you think about your preferences for many of the products and features for your new kitchen.

Instructions: We start with general questions about your kitchen and features that you might want. We then move to the more specific checklists on kitchen products.

The checklists are divided into sections for different products and materials, such as cabinets, sinks, and floors. Go through each section, indicating what you do and do not want. You will not have information for every column or row—only those that relate to you and your kitchen. If you are not sure about an item, make a note in the "Comments" column to discuss with your designer later.

In places, space is left for you to add information, describing your personal preference—for example, a color choice or an option that is not listed.

General Questions

What ideas do you have about arrangement of your kitchen? _____

_____

_____

Do you have ideas about areas that should be spacious or compact? _____

_____

_____

What areas should be open to another? _____

_____

_____

What will be the focal point? _____

_____

_____

Describe any preferences for style or color that you want to include in your kitchen. _____

_____

_____

Do you have any furniture that you want in your kitchen?

Dining table: _____ Size? _____

Chairs: _____ How many? _____

Hutch: _____ Size? _____

Buffet: _____ Size? _____

Baker's rack: _____ Size? _____

Easy chairs: _____ How many? _____

Sofa: _____ Size? _____

Other items? _____

Do you have special items that you want included in the design that are recycled, repurposed, or have significant meaning to you or your household? _____ Describe. _____ Size? _____

Kitchen Features

Features	Preference			Comments
	Definitely want	**Desirable**	**Definitely do NOT want**	
Separate baking center				
Display area for collections				Describe:
Island				
Pantry				
Closed soffit				
Open soffit				
Raised eating bar (typical 42 inches, 1067 mm)				
Counter eating bar (typical 36 inches, 914 mm)				
Table height eating area (typical 30 inches 762 mm)				
Architectural details				Describe:
Special Features:				

(continued)

Cabinetry				
Features	**Preference**			**Comments**
	Definitely want	**Desirable**	**Definitely do NOT want**	
Construction:				
Framed				
Frameless				
Door Type:				
Full overlay				
Overlay				
Partial overlay/lip				
Inset				
Face Material:				
Wood—species?				
Laminate				
Paint				
Acrylic/thermofoil				
Metal				
Other				
Door Style:				
Describe:				
Color and Finish:				
Describe:				
Hardware:				
Knob				
Pull				
Finger pull				
Material				

Cabinetry				
Features	**Preference**			**Comments**
	Definitely want	**Desirable**	**Definitely do NOT want**	
Storage Accessories or Organizers:				Indicate preferred location of features by circling B for base cabinets, W for wall cabinets, and P for pantry cabinets. Not all types of accessories can be located in all types of cabinets.
Appliance garage				B W P
Bread box				B W P
Cutlery tray				B W P
Door shelf				B W P
Drawer divider/insert				B W P
Knife block				B W P
Lazy Susan/turntable				B W P
Plate rack				B W P
Pot rack				B W P
Pull-out bin				B W P
Pull-out cutting board				B W P
Roll-out cart				B W P
Roll-out shelf				B W P
Spice rack				B W P
Swing-out shelf				B W P
Tilt-down drawer				B W P
Trash can				B W P
Vegetable bin/basket				B W P
Other features:				
				B W P
				B W P
				B W P
				B W P
				B W P

(continued)

Sinks and Other Fixtures and Fittings
SINK 1

Features	Preference			Comments
	Definitely want	Desirable	Definitely do NOT want	
Material:				
Enamel/cast iron				
Composite: granite				
Composite: quartz				
Solid surface				
Stainless steel				
Other:				
Number of Bowls:				
One				
Two				
Three				
Color:				
Describe:				
Mounting:				
Integral				
Self-rimming				
Undermount				
Other:				
Special Features:				

Sinks and Other Fixtures and Fittings				
FAUCET				
	Preference			**Comments**
Features	**Definitely want**	**Desirable**	**Definitely do NOT want**	
Material:				
Brass: antique				
Brass: polished				
Brass: satin				
Bronze				
Chrome: brushed				
Chrome: polished				
Epoxy—color?				
Gold				
Nickel: brushed				
Nickel: polished				
Pewter				
Stainless steel: brushed				
Stainless steel: polished				
Other:				
Style/Features:				
One handle				
Two handles				
Lever handle				
Knob handle				
"Goose" neck				
Pull-out spray				
Automatic operation				
Other features:				
DISPENSERS				
Dish detergent				
Hand lotion				
Hand soap				
Other:				

(*continued*)

Sinks and Other Fixtures and Fittings SINK 2				
Features	**Preference**			**Comments**
	Definitely want	Desirable	Definitely do NOT want	
Material:				
Enamel/cast iron				
Composite: granite				
Composite: quartz				
Solid surface				
Stainless steel				
Other:				
Number of Bowls:				
One				
Two				
Three				
Color:				
Describe:				
Mounting:				
Integral				
Self-rimming				
Undermount				
Other:				
Special Features:				

Sinks and Other Fixtures and Fittings FAUCET 2				
Features	Preference			**Comments**
	Definitely want	**Desirable**	**Definitely do NOT want**	
Material:				
Brass: antique				
Brass: polished				
Brass: satin				
Bronze				
Chrome: brushed				
Chrome: polished				
Epoxy—color?				
Gold				
Nickel: brushed				
Nickel: polished				
Pewter				
Stainless steel: brushed				
Stainless steel: polished				
Other:				
Style/Features:				
One handle				
Two handles				
Lever handle				
Knob handle				
"Goose" neck				
Pull-out spray				
Automatic operation				
Other Features:				
DISPENSERS				
Dish detergent				
Hand lotion				
Hand soap				
Other:				

(continued)

Accessories				
Features	**Preference**			**Comments**
	Definitely want	**Desirable**	**Definitely do NOT want**	
Chilled water dispenser				
Compost bin				
Garbage disposer*				
Instant hot water*				
Pot filler faucet				
Water filter				
Other Accessories:				

*See Form 6 for further information on appliances.

Countertops				
Features	**Preference**			**Comments**
	Definitely want	Desirable	Definitely do NOT want	
Material:				
Bamboo				
Butcher block/wood				
Ceramic tile				
Concrete				
Engineered stone/quartz				
Granite				
Marble				
Metal—stainless steel, zinc, copper				
Paper/resin				
Plastic laminate				
Recycled—glass, paper, metal				
Soapstone				
Solid surface				
Other:				
Color or Pattern:				
Describe:				
Edge Treatment:				
Bevel				
Bull nose				
Square				
Contrast color				
Other:				
Backsplash:				
Match to counter				
Full height				
Backsplash material:				
Describe:				

(continued)

Floors				
Features	**Preference**			**Comments**
	Definitely want	Desirable	Definitely do NOT want	
Material:				
Bamboo				
Carpet				
Ceramic tile				
Cork				
Laminate				
Linoleum				
Vinyl—sheet				
Vinyl—tile				
Wood				
Wood—engineered				
Other:				
Color or Pattern:				
Describe:				

Walls				
Features	**Preference**			**Comments**
	Definitely want	**Desirable**	**Definitely do NOT want**	
Material:				
Ceramic tile				
Paint				
Vinyl wall covering				
Wall paper				
Other:				
Color or Pattern:				
Describe:				

Ceiling				
Features	**Preference**			**Comments**
	Definitely want	**Desirable**	**Definitely do NOT want**	
Material:				
Paint				
Vinyl wall covering				
Wall paper				
Other:				
Color or Pattern:				
Describe:				

(continued)

Lighting				
Features	**Preference**			**Comments**
	Definitely want	**Desirable**	**Definitely do NOT want**	
Light Sources:				
Fluorescent				
Halogen				
Incandescent				
LED				
Xenon				
Light Fixtures:				
Ceiling				
Chandeliers				
Pendant				
Rail				
Recessed				
Sconce				
Track				
Under cabinet				
Special Features:				
Sink area				Describe:
Prep area				Describe:
Refrigerator area				Describe:
Cook area				Describe:
Serve and dining area				Describe:
Other				Describe:

Form 6: Appliance Preference Checklist [Client Checklist]

Selecting and specifying appliances is an important part of a kitchen design. This checklist is designed to help you specify appliances and select the features that you want.

Instructions: In the preference column, simply check the column, or indicate the number of items or the size of the feature. Additional lines are provided to add features not listed. You will not have information in every column or row—only those that relate to your preferences. If you know the brand or model, add that information to the "Comments" column.

Range				
Range Features	**Preference**			**Comments**
	Definitely want	**Desirable**	**Definitely do NOT want**	
Fuel:				
Electricity				
Natural gas				
Propane				
Type:				
Freestanding				
Drop-in				
Slide-in				
Integrated				
Professional style				

(continued)

Range				
Range Features	**Preference**			**Comments**
	Definitely want	**Desirable**	**Definitely do NOT want**	
Electric Surface Units:				
Conventional coil				
Solid disk (electric hob)				
Sealed glass ceramic				
Magnetic induction				
Halogen unit				
Thermostatic controlled unit				
Multiple-size units				
Gas Surface Units:				
Open-air (conventional)				
Sealed				
High Btu				
Surface Controls:				
Electronic				
Conventional knob				
Other cooking surface features:				
Grill				
Griddle				
Oven Features:				
Electric oven				
Gas oven				
Broiler				
Convection oven				
Pyrolytic (self-cleaning)				
Oven Controls:				
Conventional knob				
Electronic				
Other Range Features:				

Cooktop (Separate)				
Cooktop Features	**Preference**			**Comments**
	Definitely want	Desirable	Definitely do NOT want	
Fuel:				
Electricity				
Natural gas				
Propane				
Professional style				
Electric Units:				
Conventional coil				
Solid disk (electric hob)				
Sealed glass ceramic				
Magnetic induction				
Halogen unit				
Thermostatic controlled unit				
Multiple size units				
Gas Units:				
Open-air (conventional)				
Sealed				
High Btu				
Controls:				
Electronic				
Conventional knob				
Other Cooking Surface Features:				
Grill				
Griddle				

(continued)

Ventilation System				
	Preference			**Comments**
	Definitely want	**Desirable**	**Definitely do NOT want**	
Updraft/Canopy:				
Exhaust				
Recirculating				
Hood:				
Match to cooktop				
Match to cabinetry				
Custom design				Describe:
Slim line/telescoping				
Downdraft/Proximity:				
Surface mount				
Pop-up—behind cooktop				
Pop-up—beside cooktop				
Other Ventilation Features				

Oven (Built-In)				
Oven Features	**Preference**			**Comments**
	Definitely want	**Desirable**	**Definitely do NOT want**	
Single				
Double				
Wall installation				
Under-counter installation				
Professional style				
Broiler				
Convection cooking				
Steam cooking				
High-speed cooking				
Microwave/oven combination				
Warming drawer/oven combination				
Pyrolytic (self-cleaning)				
Controls:				
Conventional knob				
Electronic				
Other features:				
Height of installation?				

(continued)

Microwave Oven				
Microwave Oven Features	Preference			Comments
	Definitely want	Desirable	Definitely do NOT want	
Installation:				
Freestanding				
Boxed/built-in				
Integrated				
Drawer				
Microwave-ventilation combination				
Professional style				
Microwave-convection cooking				
Microwave-light cooking				
Features:				
Browning element				
Turntable				
Height of installation?				
Location?				

Refrigerator/Freezer				
Refrigerator/Freezer Features	Preference			**Comments**
	Definitely want	Desirable	Definitely do NOT want	
Type:				
Single-door refrigerator				
Refrigerator Freezer:				
Side-by-side				
Top mount				
Bottom mount				
French doors				
Modular Units:				
All refrigerator				
All freezer				
Refrigerator drawers				
Freezer drawers				
Freezer:				
Upright				
Chest				
Installation:				
Freestanding				
Boxed/built-in				
Integrated				
Under-counter				
Decorative panels				
Professional style				
Features:				
Adjustable shelves				
Humidity controlled compartments				
Ice maker				
Ice dispenser (door)				
Mini-door				
Temperature controlled compartments				
Water dispenser (filter)				
Water dispenser (inside)				
Water dispenser (outside)				
Other Features:				

(*continued*)

Refrigerator/ Freezer				
Other Food Storage Appliances	**Preference**			**Comments**
	Definitely want	**Desirable**	**Definitely do NOT want**	
Beverage center				
Ice maker				
Wine cooler				

Dishwasher				
Dishwasher Features	**Preference**			**Comments**
	Definitely want	**Desirable**	**Definitely do NOT want**	
Installation:				
Freestanding				
Built-in				
Integrated				
Decorative panels				
Professional style				
Drawers				
Size				
Interior Finish:				
Plastic				
Stainless				
Dishwasher Features:				
Adjustable shelves				
Electronic controls				
Flatware trays				
Hidden controls				
Multiple racks				
Special cycles				
Stem storage				
Other Features:				
How many dishwashers?				

Other Cleanup Appliances

Other Waste Management and Cleanup Appliances	Preference			Comments
	Definitely want	Desirable	Definitely do NOT want	
Disposer:				
Batch feed				
Continuous feed				
Trash compactor				

Other Appliances

	Preference			Comments
	Definitely want	Desirable	Definitely do NOT want	
Built-in Small Appliances:				
Other Appliances:				
Computer				
Intercom				
Radio				
Telephone				
Television				
VCR/DVD player				
Warming drawer				
Washer				
Dryer				

Budget

At some point, you will need to discuss the project budget. Unless your client has carefully re-searched the issue before meeting with you, there is a good chance the client's budget is not in the same price range as his or her ideas. The farther clients' ideas are from their pocketbook, the more you will need to focus on priorities. Help your client think about what he or she really needs, wants, and would like to have in the kitchen. The clearer these ideas, the easier it is to make budget decisions.

THE JOB SITE
(FORMS 7 through 11)

Before you can begin the actual design, make a thorough assessment of the job site. Structurally and mechanically, you need to know if your design ideas will work. Unless you are experienced in "reading" a house, and understanding its structural and mechanical systems, you may want to enlist the help of a contractor or other knowledgeable person to assist you before you make sug-gestions about structural changes.

New Construction

If your kitchen project is new construction or an addition, it is best to get involved in the planning before construction begins. Get a copy of all drawings that affect the kitchen design. Make sure that you have all dimensions and mechanical information that relate to the kitchen.

Study the plans for the new space. Find out what is fixed and what is flexible. For example, can an entry door be moved or a window relocated before construction begins? Can an interior wall be increased in width to make it work as a plumbing or "wet" wall?

Although you may or may not be able to inspect the job site when designing for new construction, be sure to review the information in Form 7: Job Site Inspection (discussed later in this section). This helps you review the job site factors what may influence your design.

Remodeling

If you are working on a remodeling project, you need to know all the structural and mechanical information as well, but it may be harder to find. A thorough and detailed inspection of the remod-eled area and surrounding rooms will be necessary. If your client has plans or drawings of the space, this will be useful and can save time. However, you will need to verify that the rooms were actually built as drawn. You may want to make copies of client drawings, so that you can mark them up as needed.

Prepare for your site inspection by making an appointment with your client. Give the client an idea of what you need to do, and make sure that you have access to all the areas of the home. You may do the site inspection at the same time you do the client interview, especially if you have to travel a distance to your client's home. Wear comfortable clothes that allow you to bend and stretch. Bring a sturdy measuring tape, graph paper, pencils, and flashlight. A camera might also be useful to take pictures for future reference.

Your job site inspection needs to cover several areas: overall knowledge about the kitchen and its relationship to other spaces in the home—structure, mechanical systems, access, construction/installation planning, and dimensions (discussed later). As with the client interview, if you use a prepared form or outline, you will be more likely to get all the information you need. Follow Form 7: Job Site Inspection to gain a thorough analysis of the information.

Form 7: Job Site Inspection

The information on this form is collected by a thorough inspection of the existing structure and/or construction documents. Look for detailed information! Some information may appear to repeat some of the questions on other forms, which were asking for client ideas and preferences. However, use this form to verify specifics at the actual site.

Overall Kitchen

Begin with a floor plan sketch to understand the relationship of spaces and to make notes about structural and mechanical details. Use graph paper (4 squares to the inch) and sketch at a scale of 1/2 inch = 1 inch (or sketch in millimeters or centimeters at a ratio of 1:20) for best results. See the questions that follow for additional information to add to your sketch. Use standard graphic symbols on your sketch to minimize clutter.

Note the following information on your kitchen sketch:

- How do people enter or exit the space?
- What rooms are above, below, and around the existing kitchen space?
- Can any of the surrounding space be incorporated into the new plan? If so, how much—exactly?
- What walls can be changed—moved, removed, or otherwise altered?
- Which windows and doors are to remain or be reused?
- What windows and doors can be changed—moved, removed, or changed in size or type?
- What fixtures, appliances, or furnishings are to remain? Are they to be left in the same location, or can they be moved?
- Is there cabinetry that is to be left in place or reused in the new design?
- Is the foundation concrete slab or wood construction?
- Which way do the floor joists run? Does the floor seem sturdy and stiff?
- Are there load-bearing walls to consider? Note location.
- Where does plumbing come into the space?
- Where are the existing gas lines, if any?
- Where are the drain/waste/vent pipes?
- Where are existing ducts and registers located? Can these be moved?
- What is the condition of finish materials—floors, walls, and ceilings?
- Are any of the finish materials to remain unchanged?
- Is there a view from the kitchen?
- Is view from the kitchen important?

Determine the following additional information about the kitchen.

Kitchen is on: ☐ north ☐ northeast ☐ east ☐ southeast ☐ south

☐ southwest ☐ west ☐ northwest

If new fixtures or appliances are to be installed, are they to
be put in the same location as the old fixtures or appliances? _____

If the remodeled kitchen project will affect the exterior
of the home, are there any restrictions to be considered? _____

Will existing doors, windows, siding, or roof materials be easy to match? _____

Are there any home improvements or repairs to be incorporated
into the kitchen project, such as new siding or a roof replacement? _____

(Continued)

If the home is older than 1978, could there be
lead-based paint or asbestos in the existing space? _____

_____

Structure

What is the construction of the house?

_____

What is the condition of the existing structure? Check for sound
and level floors, square corners, and materials in good condition. _____

_____

Is there evidence of water leaks or pest damage?

_____

If home is of wood construction, what size are the joists
and will they be adequate support for the new fixtures? _____

_____

Are windows and doors in good repair and do they operate smoothly? _____

_____

Are new or replacement windows and doors to match the
existing windows with respect to type, size, style, and material? _____

_____

Is the home well insulated? _____
Are doors and windows energy efficient? _____

Mechanical Systems

Can you relocate any plumbing pipes or gas lines? _____

_____

What is the capacity of the plumbing system?

_____

What size are the supply pipes? _____

_____

Is there adequate water pressure? _____
Is the water of good quality? _____
Will you be able to add additional fixtures or appliances, or
higher-capacity fixtures or appliances, to the existing plumbing? _____

_____

Where is the water heater? _____
What is the capacity? _____
Can the drain/waste/vent pipes be relocated if needed? _____

_____

Where are the traps, and what type are they? _____

_____

Is the home on a municipal or private sewage system? _____

Are there any concerns about system capacity, if the amount of wastewater is increased? _____

How many electrical circuits come into the space, and what is the capacity? _____

Do the circuits have GFCI (ground fault circuit interrupter) protection? _____

Is the wiring in good condition? _____

Can existing receptacles be moved? _____

If needed, are 240-volt circuits available? _____
Where is the electrical service panel for the house? _____

How many unused 110/120-volt and 220/240-volt circuits are available? _____

If needed, can additional electrical circuits be added? _____

How is the existing space heated and cooled? _____

Is the current HVAC (heating, ventilating, and air
conditioning) equipment in good condition and adequate in size? _____

If there will be an increase in the size of the kitchen, will the HVAC system be adequate? _____

Is there an exhaust ventilation system? _____
Is it adequate in size? _____
How is make-up air provided? _____

Does all or part of the ventilation system need replacement? _____

Access

What size are any doors between the kitchen and the exterior of the home? _____

Are there narrow hallways or sharp turns? _____

Will there be any problems in removing or bringing in large and/or heavy appliances or cabinetry? _____

Is this an apartment that must be accessed by an elevator? _____

What are the size limitations of the elevator? _____

(continued)

Is there finished living space above or below the kitchen? _____

Will you be able to open up floors, ceilings, or walls to
get access to plumbing, electrical, and HVAC systems? _____

Construction/Installation Planning

What part of the project, if any, do the clients want to do themselves? _____

Is there any part of the project to be done by another professional? Contact information:

_____

_____

What is the time frame of the project? Is there a deadline? _____

Are there specific events that affect the project schedule? _____

Are there specific times when the workers cannot have access to the kitchen space? _____

Can appliances, cabinetry, and materials be stored at the job site? _____

How much space is there? _____

Is the storage secure and protected from the weather? _____

Where will trash be collected? _____

How will workers get into and out of the job site? _____

Is there carpeting or furniture that needs to be protected? _____

Where can workers park? Where can they take breaks or eat lunch? _____

Are smoking, playing music, eating, and drinking allowed at the job site? _____

Will there be bathroom facilities for workers to use? _____

Do community or building restrictions apply to construction projects, such as time restrictions for use of an elevator
for deliveries, construction equipment access and parking, or notification of neighbors? _____

_____

_____

Dimensions

Accurate dimensions of the existing space are critical for a renovation project. This is also true for any fixtures or structural elements that will remain in the newly designed space or will be reused or repurposed. Many designers make a second trip to the client's home to verify all measurements and determine the accuracy of their design.

To collect dimensions of the job site, use:

- Form 8: Dimensions of Mechanical Devices
- Form 9: Window Measurements
- Form 10: Door Measurements
- Form 11: Fixture and Appliance Measurements

As a reminder all the needs assessment forms are also available online at www.wiley.com/go/ kitchenplanning

Following are suggestions on how to collect accurate and complete measurements. Make your drawings at the job site (client's home) on graph paper (four squares to the inch is a good size). Alternatively, take your laptop and enter the drawings directly into a computer-aided design drawing program. Date your drawings and label with the client's name and job site location.

- Measure each wall. Take at least two measurements, one low and one high, on the wall to help determine variations in corners.
  - Prepare a dimensioned drawing, to-scale (1/2" = 1'0" or at a ratio of 1 to 20, using mm or cm) of the kitchen space. Be sure to include wall thickness. Double-check each dimension, and record your numbers carefully.
  - In a complex space, you may wish to prepare more than one dimensioned drawing. One drawing will note the correct dimensions of the space, and additional drawings will be used to note other details, as noted below.
- Measure the ceiling height in several places.
  - Project an elevation of each kitchen wall, verifying the dimensions of each wall. You will use these elevations to note the location of architectural features, mechanical devices (Form 7), windows (Form 8), doors (Form 9), and fixtures (Form 11) to remain.
- Locate each mechanical connection, such as plumbing supply pipes, and electrical receptacles. Locate these features on the floor plan or the elevations as appropriate.
- If needed, prepare a reflected ceiling plan to note features on the ceiling, such as heat registers, beams, or lighting.
- Measure any architectural features in the space, such as columns, arches, or beams. Locate these features on the floor plan or the elevations as appropriate.
- Measure the location and size of each heat register, radiator, or other mechanical device. Include items on the walls, floor, and ceiling. Record these measurements on Form 8, and locate these features on the floor plan and/or elevations.
- Measure each window. Measure the size of the window, size of the frame, and size of the window with the frame. Measure the location of the window from the floor, ceiling, and corners of the room. Include the height of the stool (the sill and trim beneath it) (see Form 9). Note the location of each window on the floor plan and elevations.
- Measure each door, similar to a window. Locate the height of the door handle. Note the location of doors on the floor plan and elevations. Indicate the door swings (see Form 10).
- Measure the size of any appliances or fixtures to be removed. Include height, width, and depth. Note any potential problems with removal (see Form 11).
- Measure the size and location of any appliances, fixtures, or furniture to remain. Include centerline dimensions to determine clearances (see Form 11). Note any details needed for reinstallation.

If the new kitchen design will incorporate any additional existing space that is not now part of the kitchen, that space must be measured and inspected. For example, a porch, closet, or breakfast area may be available to be incorporated into the new design. Follow the preceding guidelines for measuring and inspecting any space that will be part of the new kitchen design.

Form 8: Dimensions of Mechanical Devices

Measure and locate each heat register, radiator, or other mechanical device. Note whether the location of these items is fixed (Figures 5.4, 5.5).

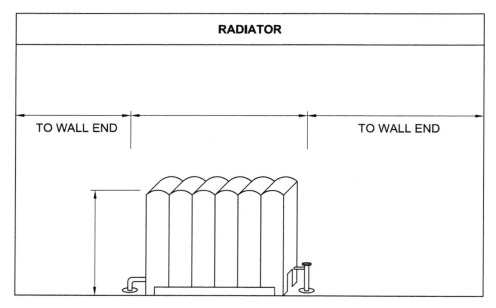

FIGURE 5.4

NO.	A	B	C	D	E	F	G
REGISTER OR FAN - CEILING, WALL OR FLOOR							
1							
2							

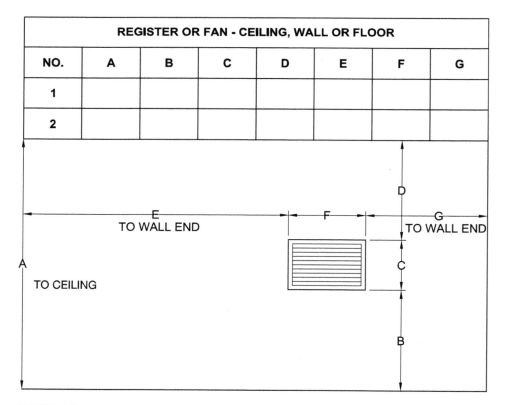

FIGURE 5.5

Form 9: Window Measurements

Note the location of the window in relation to the floor, ceiling, and both wall corners. Include the size of the window frame (Figure 5.6).

WINDOWS										
NO.	A	B	C	D	E	F	G	H	I	J
1										
2										

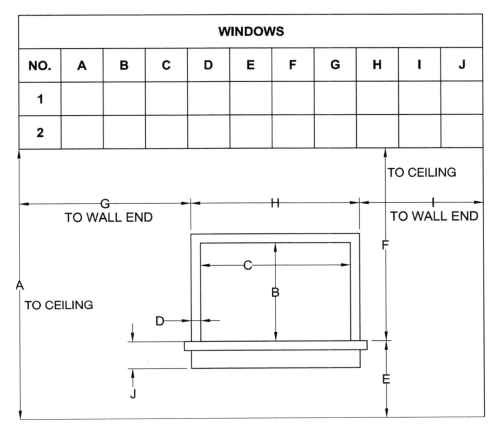

FIGURE 5.6

Form 10: Door Measurements

Note the location of the door in relation to both wall corners and the ceiling. Include the size of the door and the casing (Figure 5.7).

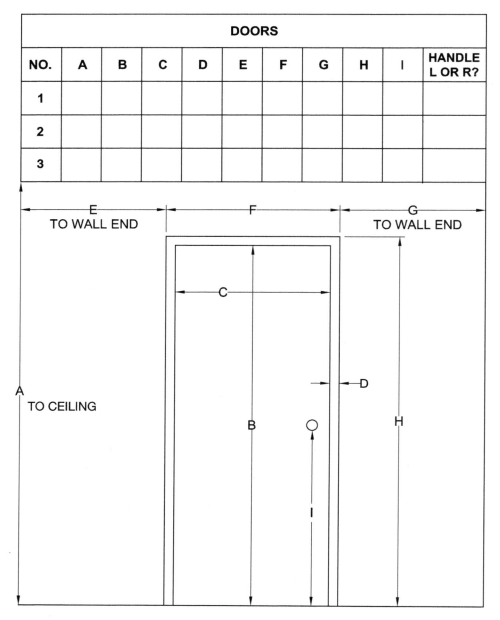

										HANDLE
					DOORS					
NO.	A	B	C	D	E	F	G	H	I	HANDLE L OR R?
1										
2										
3										

FIGURE 5.7

Form 11: Fixture and Appliance Measurements

Carefully measure existing fixtures and appliances that will remain. Also measure depth of handles (Figure 5.8).

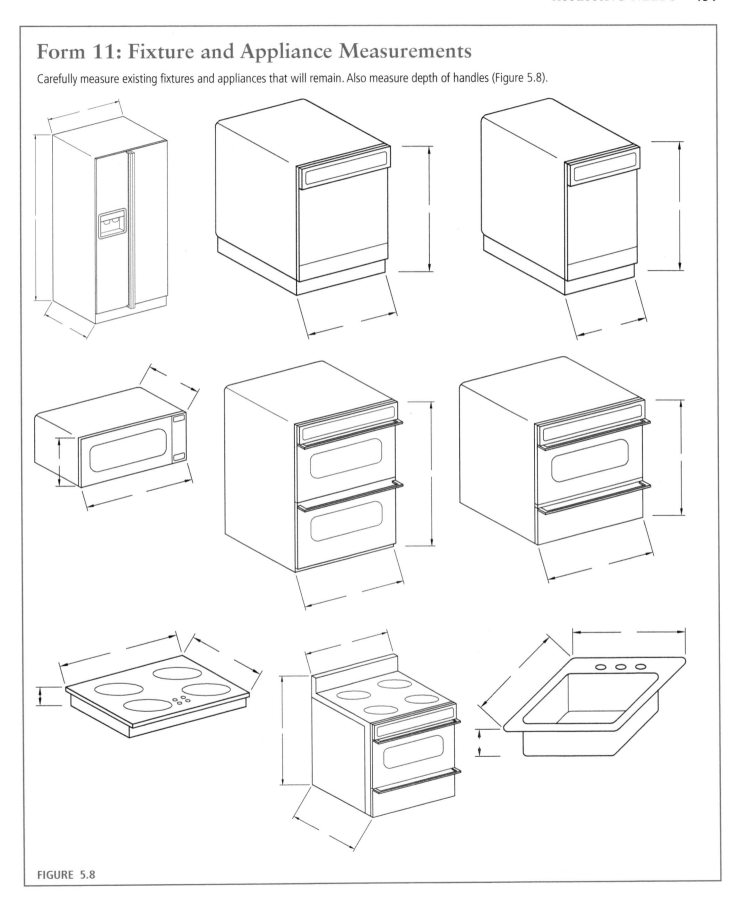

FIGURE 5.8

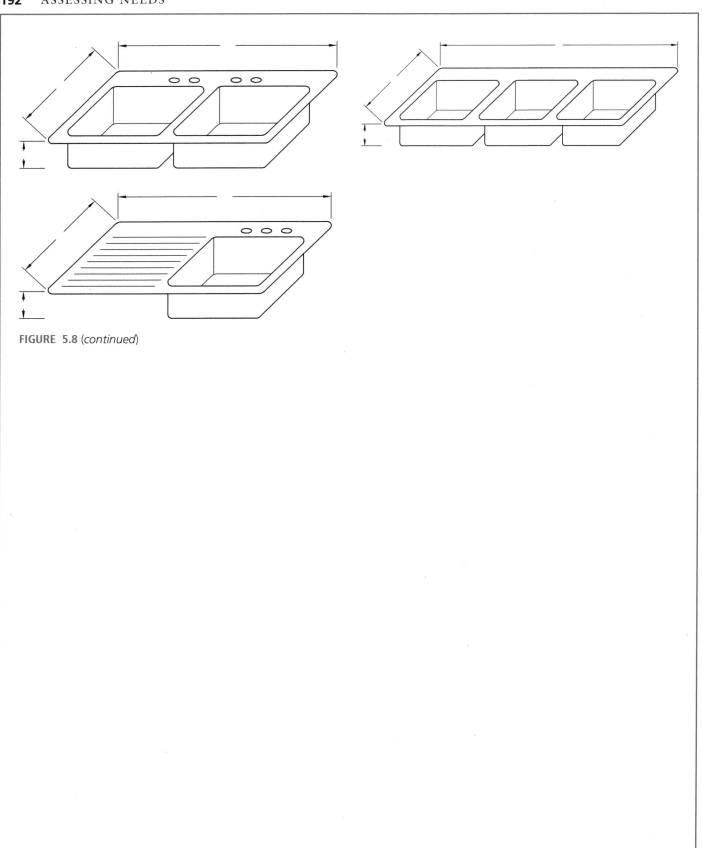

FIGURE 5.8 (*continued*)

PREPARING THE CLIENT

This chapter has detailed a process for assessing the needs of your client and gathering information necessary to design his or her kitchen. That process is extensive, but time spent on preparation will increase your success. Now that you are prepared, it's never too early to start preparing your client. At the end of the interview and/or job site inspection, or when you present your design proposal or contract, discuss both the design process as well as the construction phase with your client.

First, discuss the time frame of the project. Present a realistic plan for each phase of the project. Indicate to your client what factors may delay the project and why. Discuss what you will do to keep the project on target. Suggest what your client can do to keep the project on time, such as minimizing change orders.

Talk to your client about what you will need from him or her. If the client is going to do any of the work, such as tearing out or painting, be clear as to the time frame. At what point will the client be needed to review plans and make color or design choices? When will the client need to make decisions about appliances, fixtures, and accessories? When will he or she need personal items removed from the workspace?

In a kitchen project that involves an addition or remodeling, there will be disruption in your client's home. Emphasize this with your client and reassure him or her that you will do whatever you can to minimize that disruption. Preparing the client requires continuous communication, starting at the interview stage and continuing throughout the project.

READY FOR THE DESIGN PROGRAM?

After completing the needs assessment, you have a detailed picture of your client and his or her ideas about their new kitchen. In addition, you know about the users of the kitchen, activities in the kitchen, and storage needs. You have very specific information about the job site. It might be tempting to rush in and begin laying out your ideas. First, however, think about the next step in the design process. You need to develop a design program.

As you develop the design program, clarify your client's priorities. What does the client need or require in the kitchen project? What does he or she want to have, and what would be desirable? Your goal is to provide all the "needs and requirements," most of the "wants," and some of the "desirables." You will find the time spent on a needs assessment and gathering information about your client will benefit you in the completing the design program. If you and your client are clear on priorities, then it is easier to make compromises or trade-offs because of factors such as budget limitations, product availability, or structural problems.

Consider the design program a working document. After you review the program with your client, you may need to make changes as you fine tune the project plan. Once you and your client agree on the design program, you may ask the client to sign off on the program. This will give you a firm basis for negotiating any change orders as the kitchen project progresses.

You and your client are now prepared for a successful kitchen project.

Design Programming

Design programming is the translation of the information about the client into a plan to guide the design process. Developing the design program allows you to make sure you have gathered—and understand—all the information you need to complete the design. In addition, the design program should be reviewed with your client to ascertain that both you and your client agree on the plan for the kitchen project. A design program can even be the basis of your contract.

Design programming is discussed further in Chapter 10, as part of the design process, and a sample program is shown there. However, a brief review of the parts of a typical design program is included here to help emphasize the need for careful and complete client information gathering.   (*continued*)

Elements of a Design Program

There are many ways to prepare a design program. Here is a suggested outline that has been effective for the authors and their students.

Goal or Purpose. A statement that describes the project and the client, and defines the scope and the parameters of the project.

Objectives and Priorities. A list of the specific features, items, materials, layout, or other details to include in the design project.

Activities and Relationships. A list of the different activities to be accommodated in the kitchen, and the appliances, fixtures, fittings, materials, cabinetry, lighting, furniture, storage, and other details needed to support the activities. An explanation of how the different spaces of the activities relate, in terms of access, circulation, or flow of food preparation activities. Some designers may include charts, matrices, or bubble diagrams in this section to illustrate the different spaces and the relationships among them.

SUMMARY

A *needs assessment* is the first step in the design process. The purpose is to gather detailed information about the client(s) and their home, how they will use the kitchen, storage needs, and the requirements of the job site. Also included in the needs assessment are client preferences, including products, materials, fixtures, appliances, and design features. A variety of methods are used in a needs assessment, including client interview, checklists and assessment forms, photography, observation, and measurement.

A *design program* is a plan to guide the design process. The design program is based on the information gathered in the needs assessment. A typical design program includes the goal or purpose of the project, the objectives and priorities related to the project, the activities to be accommodated in the designed space, and the relationships or adjacencies among the activity spaces. A design program may be presented in various written or visual formats.

REVIEW QUESTIONS

1. What are the advantages of using a prepared interview format when interviewing a client as part of a needs assessment? (See "Needs Assessment Forms" page 124)
2. What is anthropometric information and why is it important to collect this information in a needs assessment? (See under "Getting to Know Your Client" page 125)
3. What are the special considerations when designing a kitchen in a multifamily structure? (See "Type of Home" page 133)
4. Why is a home tour an important part of the needs assessment? What can you learn from a home tour that will assist in the design process? (See "Home Tour" page 134)
5. When conducting a needs assessment, knowing the activities that will take place in the kitchen can provide an understanding of storage needs. Explain this relationship. (See "Storage in the Kitchen" page 142)
6. What is included in a detailed job site inspection? (See under "Remodeling" page 182)
7. What are the steps to taking complete and accurate measurements of an existing space? (See under "Dimensions" page 187)
8. Describe the purpose and function of a design program. (See "Design Programming" page 193)

Kitchen Planning

Kitchens are essential spaces in most homes. In fact, building codes require that dwelling units must have a cooking area. How this indispensable room is designed can determine if the space meets the needs of residents and is truly functional. This chapter presents information to help you consider how to plan the kitchen space to meet the needs of clients. Although each client's needs are unique, the basics of kitchen planning are based on research and the experiences of people preparing food. Anthropometric data and task analysis provide the designer with valuable information in planning kitchens. Also consider the cultural traditions that will influence how and what your client will prepare. Special equipment and methods may dictate specific design solutions.

Learning Objective 1: Identify the right kitchen type for your client and their home.

Learning Objective 2: Describe the various centers (sink, refrigeration and cooking, serving, and dining) and space planning considerations that combine to create the kitchen layout.

Learning Objective 3: Describe how the kitchen planning guidelines and access standards can be used to design kitchens that meet building code requirements and human factors recommendations.

Learning Objective 4: Describe the planning considerations that will influence the design of specialty kitchens.

LOCATION AND TYPES OF KITCHENS

The kitchen has evolved from a workspace that was separate from the social spaces of the home to one that is integrated and vital to the activities of family and friends. There are multiple configurations that the designer can use as a basis for planning a kitchen layout that reflect both closed and open planning.

Location of Kitchen

Some older homes were planned using the zoning paradigm, with the kitchen categorized in the work zone and the other areas of the home characterized as private and social zones. From this perspective, food preparation is a task, along with other household jobs like laundry and mending. These task areas were be grouped together in one part of the house.

However, in many newer homes the kitchen is considered part of an informal social space. While food preparation is still important, other activities are also occurring in the kitchen (and surrounding areas) and should be accommodated by the space. Today's lifestyles seem to require an informal living space where family members and friends gather to share their lives on a regular basis. Time constraints mean that often several activities are occurring in the space at the same time. The kitchen is now often part of a social area.

Work Zone

Originally, the work zone allowed servants to perform household tasks without interruption and observation from the family living in other parts of the house. Even as servants became less common, the work areas remained consolidated into one part of the house. The homemaker was the typical worker and grouping these areas helped to make her job more convenient and remained a good planning concept.

The outcome of this concept was that the kitchen was often placed at the back of the house and close to a utility room or other work area. This location kept the kitchen separated from social and private spaces in the home. It was also close to outdoor play areas so that children could be observed. A formal dining area was adjacent to the kitchen and informal dining might be provided in the kitchen area or in a breakfast nook. The kitchen was located close to a service entry so that groceries and other products could be brought directly into the work area of the home.

Social Area

When the kitchen is considered a part of an informal living space, a different arrangement becomes necessary. More activities occur in the space, not just food preparation. Meals may be served in the social kitchen area regularly. Children's play and homework can take place in this space. It may become the communications headquarters where messages are taken and schedules are kept. Watching television, using the computer, talking, and visiting with friends and family will take place in the kitchen area. The kitchen may be an important space for entertaining as people help with the preparations or visit with the cook/host. The task of food preparation no longer occurs in isolation.

The kitchen can be located in a variety of places within the home, not just the back of the house. It will still need to be located close to a service entry, but access to a guest entry may be important as well. With the many and varied activities taking place, the kitchen requires more space that is adjacent and open to dining and living spaces. Environmental factors, such as noise, moisture, and lighting, must be considered. The aesthetic appeal of materials and equipment may become important since the kitchen will be exposed to people in the social spaces. Often, more than one user will need to access some or all of the kitchen space, influencing the layout and arrangement of the kitchen. Kitchens that incorporate universal design principles can help to meet the needs of a variety of users.

Types of Kitchens

Whether or not the kitchen is considered a work area or a social space may also influence what type of arrangement is planned. Traditional planning has suggested that there were a few common arrangements of kitchen areas and that these could be planned into a variety of spaces. In fact, certain arrangements lend themselves to either a closed arrangement, typical of a work-type kitchen, or an open arrangement, typical of a social kitchen with centers or zones for multiple activities. The physical space and the ability to renovate may dictate which is used.

Closed Arrangements

A closed arrangement indicates that the kitchen is probably best suited for one cook who works in isolation. This arrangement does not lend itself to other family members or guests moving

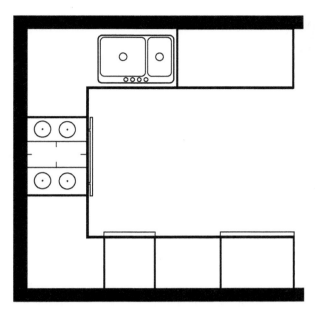

FIGURE 6.1 A U-shaped kitchen has two parallel work areas with a third work area joining them.
Courtesy of American Classics by RSI

about, in or through the space, but it often makes an efficient work space. The following arrangements fall into this category:

- **U-Shaped Kitchen:** This arrangement has two parallel cabinet/counter/work areas with a third area joining them, forming an arrangement similar to a U (see Figure 6.1). Typically, a different type of work area is located on each section: cooking, sink, and refrigeration. This can be a very convenient arrangement for one person moving in between the various areas. Depending on the distance of the work aisle, it can be fairly difficult for more than one person at a time to use it. However, a wide U-shaped kitchen that includes an island can be a good layout for a multi-cook space.
- **Parallel or Galley Kitchen:** This arrangement offers two parallel cabinet/counter/work areas, typically with a wall at the end, so that traffic does not go through the kitchen (see Figure 6.2). At least two work areas have to be on the same side. Again, depending on the size of the work aisle, the arrangement might be best suited for only one cook.
- **G-Shaped Kitchen:** This arrangement is a wide U-shaped kitchen, with a fourth arm turning back into the center of the space (see Figure 6.3). This results in a fairly tight work area that lends itself to one cook, unless secondary work areas are planned along the outer arms.

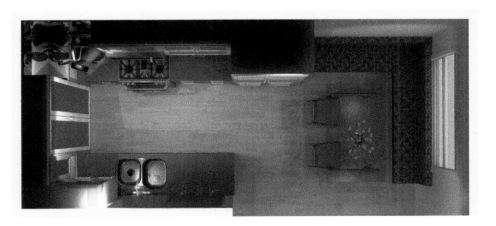

FIGURE 6.2 This parallel, or galley, kitchen locates the range opposite the sink and refrigerator. Tall storage is located at the end wall.
Design by NKBA member Sandra Tierney, CMKBD, CID

FIGURE 6.3 This G-shaped kitchen places the sink and range at a right angle to each other with a peninsula open onto the adjoining space.

Design by NKBA member Rebecca G. Lindquist, CMKBD

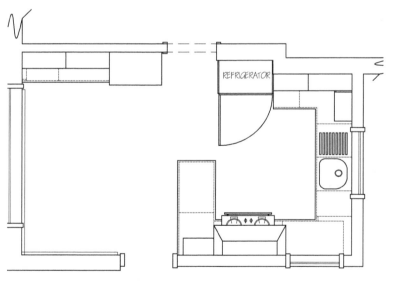

All of these arrangements can be planned to feel more open by increasing the distance between the sides of the space and by creating a pass-through or peninsula counter. Dining areas or other social spaces might be planned at the open end of the arrangements to increase access.

Open Arrangements

Open arrangements are more likely to be used if there are two cooks, or if there will be several people in the kitchen area. Often these arrangements can combine with social spaces to create a multi-use space. These arrangements include:

- **L-Shaped Kitchen:** This arrangement has two arms of work areas joined together at one end to form an L-shape (see Figure 6.4). Often one person could work on one side and another on

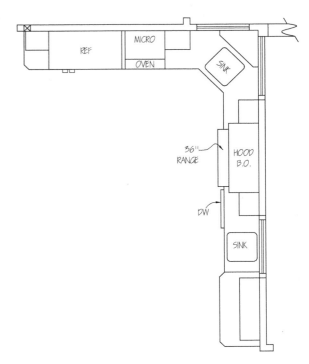

FIGURE 6.4 The L-shaped kitchen has one side open, allowing for another use in the open area, such as dining.

Design by NKBA member Mark White, CKD, CBD

the other side without too much interference. The open side of the arrangement might lend itself to a dining space, a seating arrangement or an island.

- **One-Wall Kitchen:** This arrangement puts all of the work areas on one wall (see Figure 6.5). It can be an inconvenient kitchen because of the distance between the work centers on opposite ends of the wall, or if the distance is not too great, the amount of storage and counter space may be limited. It does allow for an open space opposite the kitchen wall that could be used for dining and social areas.

- **Corridor Kitchen:** This arrangement is similar to the parallel kitchen, except that both ends are open (see Figure 6.6). This allows for traffic through the work areas, which is not desirable. However, if alternate traffic can be arranged so that the traffic is only for the cook(s), then the arrangement may work for single or multiple cooks.

- **Island Kitchen:** A separate work area or island can be incorporated into most of these kitchen configurations, provided there is room for the proper clearances in the work and traffic aisles (see Figure 6.7). Island kitchens can be arranged in many different ways (see Figure 6.8). The island is usually a workspace and may be combined with another activity area, such as dining. At least one side of the island faces a work area with a work aisle in between. The other side is more likely to be a traffic aisle or seating area, but it could be a work aisle as well.

Kitchens may come in even more shapes. Work areas can be placed at 45° angles. Curved arrangements may have no angles. Each work area may be unattached in an unfitted kitchen. No one shape is ideal, and the designer will want to make sure that the needs of the user and the requirements of space are being met (see Figure 6.8).

FIGURE 6.5 This award-winning kitchen has the work areas on one wall and uses an island for seating and storage.

Design by Beverly A. Alig

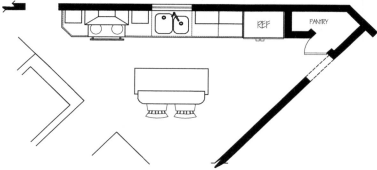

Size of Kitchens

Kitchens come in all sizes. Often this is dependent on the space allocated within a house, but it might also be a factor of the number of cooks or others using a kitchen at one time. Kitchens can be too small to be effective for adequate storage, workspace, and workflow. They can also be too big, with work centers spread out so far that a cook has problems preparing a meal without expending a great deal of energy moving about the space. In some larger spaces, multiple prep centers or zones can be planned to create a smaller work area within the larger space.

Research indicates that Certified Kitchen Designers (CKDs) are designing kitchens in ranges that could be categorized as follows:

- **Small Kitchen:** Less than 150 square feet (13.95 sq. m)
- **Medium Kitchen:** From 151 to 350 square feet (13.95 to 32.52 sq. m)
- **Large Kitchen:** Greater than 350 square feet (32.52 sq. m)

Determining the size of the kitchen you are planning will be an important first step in developing the design and layout of the space. In particular, storage requirements are specified according to

FIGURE 6.6 With both ends of the kitchen open, people can move through the dining area, leaving the kitchen work areas uninterrupted by major traffic.

Design by NKBA member Chris Novak Berry

kitchen size. All food preparation areas of a kitchen arrangement should be measured to determine the size of the kitchen. Figure 6.9 contains an example of how the size of the kitchen should be determined in order to calculate storage requirements.

Sustainability Concerns

While we have identified numerous types and sizes of kitchens, more and more consumers are requesting sustainable options be incorporated into their kitchens. Many ideas and recommendations were included in Chapter 3, "Environmental and Sustainability Considerations," so keep them in mind as you plan the kitchen. Kitchens can use a great deal of water and require substantial amounts of energy to operate cooking, refrigeration, and hot water appliances. Just the size and use of materials in some large kitchens diminish efforts to offer sustainable solutions to the built environment. While we, as designers, would love to create more spacious and high-end kitchens, consider a smaller size, specifying water-efficient fixtures and energy-efficient appliances, and selecting materials that leave a light footprint on the environment, including repurposing items if possible.

FIGURE 6.7 This kitchen features an island with a sink and serving area.

Design by NKBA member Diane Foreman, CKD, CBD

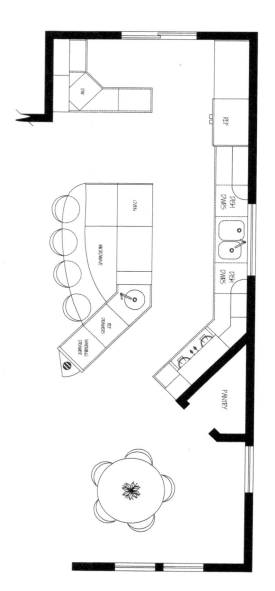

FIGURE 6.8 This kitchen features a triangular pantry and angled island.

Design by Margie Little

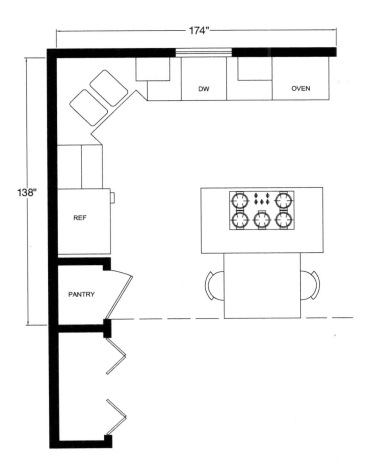

FIGURE 6.9 The main food preparation areas define the size of the kitchen. To calculate the size of this kitchen, include the pantry storage, and the eating area, which is used as a seated preparation area.

THE CENTER CONCEPT

A work center or zone is an area where a particular task occurs. Using the center concept is a comprehensive way to design an area that will be used for a certain task. There are three primary centers in the kitchen for food preparation and cleanup: sink, refrigeration, and cooking. Various secondary centers can be created for certain tasks, such as baking or salad preparation, if the client's activities and the space allow for it. Serving and dining areas should also be provided and are discussed separately. Other areas or centers may be needed for specific tasks that take place in the kitchen: communications, laundry, or office work. Ideas and requirements for these nonfood activities are presented in Chapter 9.

In this book, the approach used to design kitchen work centers considers the following elements: the actual tasks and activities being conducted, the user(s) working in the center, the appliance or fixture that anchors and/or supports the center, required floor space, needed storage for items used, and work surfaces necessary to complete the tasks.

- **Tasks and Activities:** Often multiple activities and tasks are occurring in one center. For example, food preparation and cleanup are two primary tasks that occur at the sink. However, other activities, such as taking medications, also occur within the sink center and should be considered. The tasks and activities may drive decisions about the design requirements that must be met, such as counter height or amount of storage.
- **Users:** Consider the size and abilities of the cook when planning a center. Other user considerations include the number of cooks and the individual tasks they perform. In addition, individuals have different cooking styles that could affect the plan for the kitchen.

    Several anthropometric measurements are explained in Chapter 4, "Human Factors and Universal Design Foundation." The user's reach range over a cabinet is an important measurement

FIGURE 6.10 The average man can reach as high as 72 inches (1823 mm) over a base cabinet, whereas the average woman can reach 69 inches (1753 mm). A comfortable reach range at the kitchen cabinets is between 25 inches and 59 inches (635 mm to 1499 mm). This allows an average standing user to see and to reach the items on the lower wall shelves and to reach the top portion of the base cabinet without excessive bending.

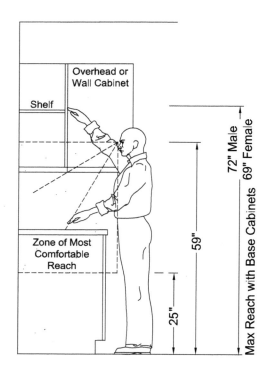

needed for designing a kitchen (Figure 6.10). While the average woman can reach a shelf over a base cabinet that is as high as 69 inches (1753 mm), the most comfortable reach range for most standing users will be between 25 and 59 inches (635 and 1499 mm). A more universal reach range of 15 to 48 inches (381 to 1219 mm) accommodates standing and seated users.

Another important anthropometric consideration is the horizontal work area (Figure 6.11). The average person requires at least 30 inches (762 mm) to stand with elbows slightly extended and can use at least 48 inches (1219 mm) of work surface with a depth of 16 inches (406 mm).

More information about specific user requirements is presented in Chapter 4.

- **Appliance/Fixture:** Each center typically contains a basic appliance or fixture for which it is named. However, some tasks use multiple appliances or fixtures. For example, a range or cooktop may anchor the cooking center and other cooking appliances, such as a wall oven and a microwave may form secondary cooking centers. An auxiliary sink is another example of a secondary center, which can be combined with a work surface to create a second prep area.
- **Floor Space:** Clearances are required at each center to ensure that cooks can move around effectively in the space and operate the appliances and fixtures. These clearances will be discussed later in this chapter.
- **Storage:** All of the tasks that occur in the kitchen require space to store the things that are used in the center. There are several types of storage designed for placement in the kitchen, and the designer can create special storage systems and products if needed (see Figure 6.12). Types of kitchen cabinets include wall cabinets, base cabinets, and tall cabinets. These types of cabinets include drawers, shelves, pull-outs, and other interior configurations that can enhance convenience and accessibility to needed items for the user. Storage and cabinetry are discussed in a later section.
- **Work Surface:** Countertop space provides the work surface needed to perform tasks in the center. Usually, the countertop surface corresponds to the base cabinet depth and will be ± 25 inches (635 mm), depending on the door thickness and countertop overhang needed to clear the cabinetry. Less deep areas are usable for some tasks, because the front 16 inches (406 mm) is the most comfortable work area. The rear 8 inches (203 mm) of the countertop is within reach of most users and is often used for permanent or temporary storage.

While the standard work area is 36 inches (914 mm) high, the ideal work surface height should be planned to be just below the cook's elbow. A comfortable distance is usually considered to be 3 inches (76 mm), but some tasks, such as kneading bread, might require the

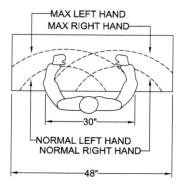

FIGURE 6.11 A work surface should be wide enough to fit the user and the task.

arm to be extended in a way that suggests the need for a lower work surface (see Figure 6.13). Use the client's measurements and cooking style to help you determine what height is best. While some specialized work heights are helpful to specific users or tasks, standard 36 inch (914 mm) high counters should also be provided, since they are considered a standard height that is useable by most people.

Designing Kitchen Centers

In the following sections, some general recommendations for circulation and work aisles are presented. Each center is then discussed separately but comprehensively. The tasks and activities are identified, and requirements associated with completing tasks safely and conveniently are detailed, followed by design recommendations. Combining centers, planning for adequate storage, and recommendations for dining and serving meals are also presented. The National Kitchen and Bath Association (NKBA) Kitchen Planning Guidelines and related Access Standards are important for the safe and comfortable use of the kitchen, and are discussed within these sections. For reference, all of the NKBA Kitchen Planning Guidelines and Access Standards are at the end of this book in Appendix A.

Universal design concepts and ideas are presented and integrated throughout this chapter to encourage you to think about various user needs while planning the space. Thinking broadly about client's needs, now and in the future, can help you develop a thoughtful design that anticipates changes that will occur over the client's lifespan. In Chapter 8 you will find expanded ideas and recommendations for designing for specific user groups.

Background on the Guidelines

The NKBA has been providing information on the design of kitchens since the Kitchen Industry Technical Manuals were first issued in 1975. The Kitchen Planning Guidelines have always had a very strong focus on safety and the building code requirements associated with kitchens. The guidelines have been reviewed and updated periodically to include new information, such as universal design. In 2003, an ad hoc committee of NKBA developed the current guidelines and these are incorporated into this book. The Guidelines and Access Standards were reviewed in 2011 to ensure they were consistent with current building codes and accessibility standards.

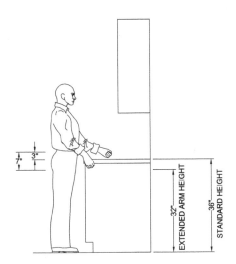

FIGURE 6.13 Standard work-surface height is 36 inches (914 mm). Ideally, the height should be 3 to 7 inches (76 to 178 mm) below the user's elbow.

The examination of the guidelines incorporated a review of current housing trends and an analysis of the *2003 International Residential Code* (IRC). The current guidelines are consistent with the 2012 IRC. Space recommendations are based on documented ergonomic considerations, and code requirements are highlighted. The IRC has been adopted by many states and localities, but designers should check the local building codes in their area to make sure they are in compliance with the jurisdiction in which they are working. The Kitchen Planning Guidelines are intended to serve as a reference tool for practicing designers and an evaluation tool for kitchen designs. Designers taking the Associate Kitchen and Bathroom Designer academic exam will be expected to know the guidelines and designers taking the Certified Kitchen Designer exam will be expected to apply the guidelines to the designs they create for the exam. Students in NKBA Accredited College Programs learn the guidelines and are able to apply them in their design projects.

Access Standards

The NKBA leads the building industry in promoting universal design and awareness. Their 1996 Kitchen Planning Guidelines included recommendations that would make the kitchen universal and accessible, many based on ANSI 117.1 guidelines. Many of the universal points included in the 1996 guidelines continue to be incorporated in the updated guidelines.

In this edition, the Access Standards include planning information that will improve a client's access to the kitchen. Because the International Building Code (IBC) references it, the 2009 edition of *Accessible and Useable Buildings and Facilities* (ICC/ANSI 117.1) has been used as the basis for the specific Access Standards. Following many of the NKBA Kitchen Planning Guidelines, there is a corresponding Access Standard. While these Access Standards and the ICC/ANSI 117.1 standards on which they are based provide a great starting point, designers planning a kitchen for a particular client should closely examine the needs of that client to ensure that the kitchen is truly usable, not just meeting minimum requirements. The assessment forms presented in Chapter 5, "Assessing Needs," should be used to gather information about the client's anthropometric information (Form 1: Getting to Know Your Client), the activities they perform in the kitchen (Form 3: Checklist for Kitchen Activities), and their storage needs (Form 4: Kitchen Storage Inventory). Design suggestions according to user groups and further discussion of the Access Standards are in Chapter 8, "Accessibility in Practice," should help you.

GENERAL KITCHEN DESIGN

In this section, ideas for designing the kitchen work areas are discussed in detail, along with the Kitchen Planning Guidelines and Access Standards that relate to the work area. All the Guidelines and Access Standards are presented in Appendix A.

Design Recommendations for Traffic and Work Aisles

Circulation and movement throughout the kitchen is one of the first areas that must be considered. Adequate traffic and work aisles are important for the safe and efficient use of the other centers. As you analyze the space that you will be designing, consider the traffic flow and the recommended circulation spaces. A specific kitchen layout, such as a U-shape or an island design, may not be possible because there is not enough work or circulation space.

Entry
There will likely be several entries into the kitchen, depending on adjacent spaces that need to be accessed; that is, dining area, social area, service entry, garage, mud room, or outdoor social spaces. Considering the location of these entryways and how they affect the traffic pattern in the kitchen will be an important first step in planning the kitchen. Sometimes the entries have to stay where they are, but often you may be able to move, eliminate, or create entries to enhance the layout of the kitchen.

Door openings should be at least 32 inches (813 mm) wide (see Figure 6.14). This will provide an accessible entry to most people and equipment that will need to be placed in the kitchen.

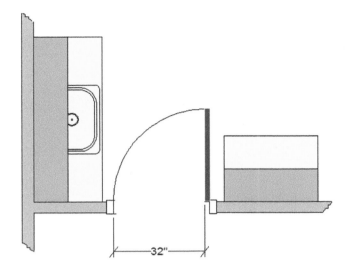

FIGURE 6.14 Allow 32 inches (813 mm) of clear space at each door opening in the kitchen (Kitchen Planning Guideline 1).

The 32-inch (813 mm) clearance is a clear opening and a 2-foot, 10-inch (813 mm) door is required to accomplish this opening. A 36-inch (914 mm) door with a 34-inch (864 mm) clear opening is preferred, especially for persons using a mobility aid.

A door opening without a door can provide good access to the room without taking space for the door swing or clearance beside the door (see Figure 6.15). Space is needed beside the door to ensure that it can be opened. This is especially true for a person using a mobility aid. The Access Standards recommend a clearance on the pull side of a door that extends the width of the door plus 18 inches x 60 inches (457 mm x 1524 mm). A 48 inch (1219 mm) deep clearance is needed on the push side of the door. See Chapter 8 for more information about the Access Standards related to the kitchen door.

Doors should not interfere with the operation of any appliance (see Figure 6.16). For example, make sure an oven placed at the corner of the kitchen does not coincide with a door swing, as this is dangerous to the person using the oven when the door opens. Likewise, appliance doors should

FIGURE 6.15 An opening without a door provides better access to the kitchen work areas.

Design by NKBA member Gerard Ciccarello, CMKBD; Codesigners: Kira Van Deusen and Eric R. Koch, CKD

FIGURE 6.16 An entry door should not interfere with an appliance door opening, and appliance doors should not open into each other (Kitchen Planning Guideline 2).

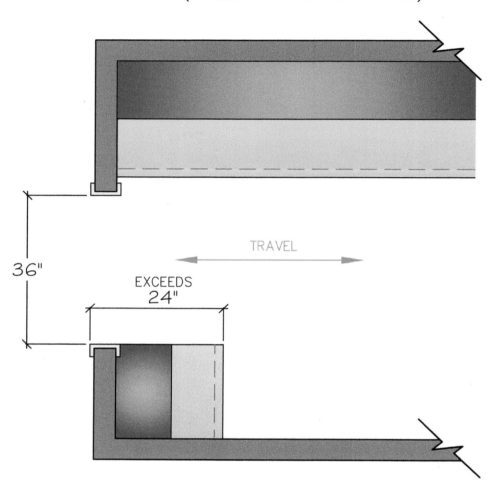

24" DEPTH CLEARANCE
(ACCESS STANDARD 1—ANSI)

not interfere with each other. For example, as you lay out the placement of appliances, make sure oven and dishwasher doors do not open into one another, so that a person cannot use one without closing the door of another.

Work Aisles

Working in the kitchen requires space to move about between work areas. When work areas are across from each other, they create a work aisle. When the kitchen is planned for one cook, at least 42 inches (1067 mm) is required for a work aisle. A 48-inch (1219 mm) work aisle will provide room for the cook to stand in front of an open dishwasher and the oven door. If two cooks are going to be working in the kitchen, then plan at least 48 inches (1219 mm) for the work aisle (see Figure 6.17). A work aisle of 60 inches (1524 mm) to 66 inches (1676 mm) will allow for a standard work aisle and room for someone to pass around the work area. It will also provide an adequate clearance for a cook with a mobility aid to maneuver through a 360° turn.

Either a 42-inch (1067 mm) or a 48-inch (1219 mm) work aisle would be acceptable for access standards that require a 30-inch x 48-inch (762 mm x 1219 mm) clearance at each appliance or fixture for either a parallel or forward approach. Make sure the clear space is planned so that the appliance is usable. For instance, the clear space should be planned beside the dishwasher so that the door can be opened. Similarly, the clear space should be offset at the refrigerator to allow for opening the door and accessing the interior space. See Chapter 8 for more information about planning circulation and clearances for a client with a mobility aid.

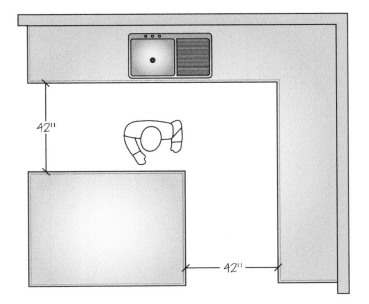

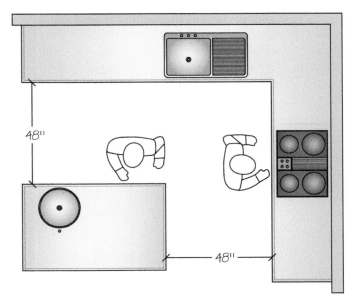

FIGURE 6.17 A kitchen planned for one cook should have 42-inch (1067 mm) minimum work aisles, while a kitchen for two or more cooks should have work aisles of at least 48 inches (Kitchen Planning Guideline 6).

Circulation

Traffic may move through the kitchen in order to access entries and other parts of the room. Ideally, traffic should not interfere with the work aisles of the kitchen to avoid interrupting the cook's work areas (see Figure 6.18). A walkway or traffic aisle that is used only for walking should be a minimum of 36 inches (914 mm) wide to allow for passage by one person (see Figure 6.19). This will allow for the width of the person carrying a tray or other similar object. This width is also acceptable to a person using a mobility aid. If two people will be passing each other in the walkway frequently, then consider a walkway that is 48 to 60 inches (1219 to 1524 mm) wide. A 36-inch (914 mm) walkway that turns at a right angle should have one part that is a minimum of 42 inches (1067 mm) wide to allow a person using a mobility aid easier maneuvering.

FIGURE 6.18 The circulation access to several interior and exterior spaces bypass the kitchen and provide uninterrupted work areas.
Design by NKBA member Jennifer Gilmer, CKD

FIGURE 6.19 A walkway in the kitchen that has no appliances or work centers located along the path needs to be 36 inches (914 mm) wide (Kitchen Planning Guideline 7).

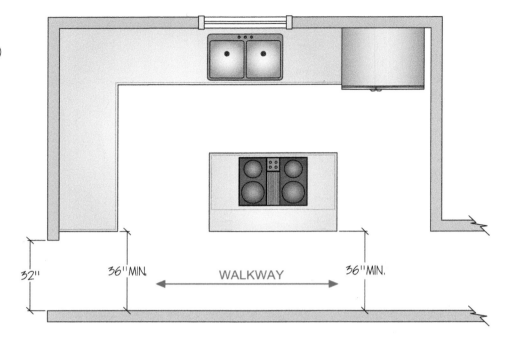

FIGURE 6.19 A walkway in the kitchen that has no appliances or work centers located along the path needs to be 36 inches (914 mm) wide (Kitchen Planning Guideline 7).

Guidelines and Access Standards for Traffic and Work Aisles

The Kitchen Planning Guidelines and Access Standards that are particularly relevant to traffic, circulation, and work aisles are Guidelines 1, 2, 6, and 7. They can be found in Appendix A.

SINK CENTER

The sink center is the most used center in the kitchen because it is the place of both food preparation and cleanup. It is also likely that other household activities will occur at or around the sink. While the requirements for food preparation and cleanup are different, the water source and sink are essential elements for both types of activities, resulting in a sink center that typically accommodates both. In larger kitchens or kitchens that are frequently used by multiple cooks, an auxiliary sink may be planned to reduce the congestion that can occur at the sink when all of these activities are being carried out at the same time.

Activities

Food Preparation

- Washing and drying hands before and during food preparation is important for food safety. Locate hand soap (bar or liquid) and hand towels at the sink.
- Washing fruits, vegetables, and other food items under water at the sink is also important for food safety and quality. The food must be retrieved from its storage (often the refrigerator), brought to the sink, rinsed, and possibly dried with paper or cloth towels. Some foods will be rinsed using a colander or strainer.
- Some of these fruits and vegetables will be cut or chopped, and this will likely occur near the sink. Paring knives, peelers, cutting boards, and bowls or dishes will be needed during this process. Peels and waste will need to be put in the trash, compost container, or garbage disposer.
- All types of food and beverage preparation require water and will involve the sink. Tea kettles, coffee pots, a pasta pot, sauce pans, and several small appliances will be brought to the sink to be filled with water. A pot filler faucet at a range or cooktop may reduce the need to complete these tasks at the sink.

- Mixing and combining ingredients that will be served or cooked is a basic food preparation task that occurs near the sink. Ingredients need to be retrieved from where they are stored in cabinets or the refrigerator. Mixing bowls, casserole dishes, or other pots, pans, and utensils must be brought to the food preparation area. A recipe (often in a cookbook) might be used. Water is often used as an ingredient and will be measured at the sink and brought to where food items are being prepared.
- Used boxes and cans will need to go in the trash or recycling. Besides all the storage that is needed near this area, a large work surface or counter area will be needed for all of the equipment and ingredients for this task.
- After some foods have been cooked using water, the water will be drained from the pot or pan into the sink. A colander or strainer may be used in this process.

Cleanup

- Stacking dirty pots and pans often occurs during the food preparation process. Some cooks wash or put dirty items in the dishwasher as they are preparing the food, but others will get the dirty dishes close to or in the sink and go on to the next task. If they make it to the sink, dirty pots and pans can soak, if needed.
- In the cleanup process, several steps are likely to occur. Food is usually scraped off of dirty dishes (including pots and pans) into the trash, garage disposer, and/or compost container.
- After scraping, dishes go into the dishwasher. Most dishwashers are designed so that the dishes should not be rinsed before being cleaned, but rinsing is a fairly ingrained habit in many households. Dishwashers come in a variety of sizes (18, 24, 30, and 36 inches; 457, 607, 762, and 914 mm) and have cycles for a variety of cleaning situations. The dishwasher will require detergent and other additives.
- Once the dishes are cleaned, they may stay in the dishwasher for a while, but eventually the dishwasher is unloaded and the dishes are put away. Storing dishes, glassware, and flatware close to the dishwasher can make putting things away more convenient.
- Some items will require hand washing rather than being placed in the dishwasher. Small households may find it more convenient to hand wash dishes. Hand dishwashing will require detergents, a drain board, dish towels, and other items, such as scrubbers.

Other

- Getting a glass of water is a common activity that occurs at the kitchen sink. Water filters and hot water dispensers might be added conveniences for preparing beverages. Glasses, mugs, and drink mixes probably need to be stored close by.
- Taking medications in the kitchen was an activity of over 70% of the households surveyed in the Virginia Tech research. Often this will occur at the sink, so planning for medicine storage in this center might be important if this is the pattern in the client's household.
- Sometimes the sink center might be used for other household activities like arranging flowers and repotting and watering plants. The sink might be the water source for some hobby and craft projects. The sink can sometimes become important for household cleaning projects such as hand laundry, mopping floors, and other scrubbing. While we might like separate areas for these activities, often they occur at the kitchen sink.

Design Recommendations for the Sink Center

Placement
Because the sink center is the most used space in the kitchen, place it in a central and accessible spot. Plan to locate the sink in between or across from the major cooking area and the refrigeration storage area (see Figure 6.20).

In traditional kitchens, a window was often planned at the sink so that a view to the outdoors was available while the cook worked at the sink. This made sense in kitchens before dishwashers, when

FIGURE 6.20 If a kitchen has only one sink, it should be adjacent to, or across from, the cooking surface and the refrigerator (Kitchen Planning Guideline 10).

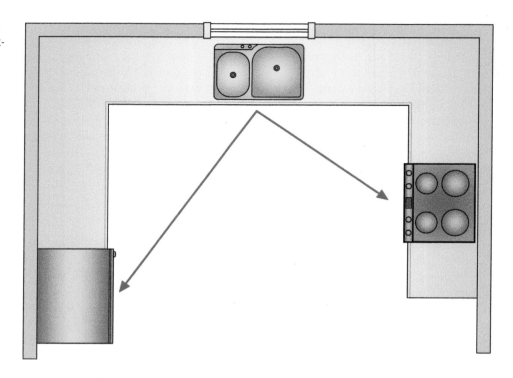

a lot of time was spent standing at the sink during cleanup. It can also be appropriate in today's kitchens if a view to the outdoors is desired or when the cook is supervising children in outdoor play.

A sink placed so that the cook can look into the social areas of an open kitchen may also be appropriate. A sink placed on an island or peninsula encourages the cook to interact with family and guests, supervise homework, or watch television.

The sink drain line must be vented in order to work properly and meet building code requirements. Information on venting options is in Chapter 2, "Infrastructure Considerations."

Landing Area

A certain amount of counter space is needed within each center to serve as a place to put some of the things used there. This is called a landing area.

By definition, a landing area will need to be at least 16 inches (406 mm) deep and between 28 inches (711 mm) and 48 inches (1219 mm) above the finished floor. It is measured along the front edge of the countertop. Because base cabinets are usually about 24 inches (610 mm) deep, the back 8 inches (203 mm) will be available for storing items that are regularly or temporarily kept at the center, but this area is not needed for the counter area to count as a landing area. Clearance will be needed above the landing area to fully access it and to complete tasks. At least 15 inches (381 mm) of clearance will be needed above the landing area for it to count as usable countertop frontage.

FIGURE 6.21 Plan 24 inches (610 mm) of landing area to one side of the primary sink and 18 inches (457 mm) on the other side (Kitchen Planning Guideline 11).

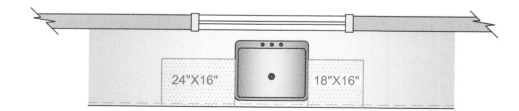

24"X16"   18"X16"

The minimum landing area requirements at the sink are 24 inches (610 mm) on one side and 18 inches (457 mm) on the other (see Figure 6.21). It is not important which side of the sink the areas are on, as long as they are immediately adjacent and on the left and right side of the sink.

The landing area will be used for some of the food preparation tasks mentioned above: a place to sit the pot while the water is being turned on, or where the washed vegetables will be placed or peeled. The landing area will also be important during cleanup since the dirty dishes might be located to one side, or the drain board has to be set on the counter. More generous landing areas might be required to meet the cooking needs for some clients.

If the sink is placed near the corner of the kitchen arrangement, then the 24-inch (610 mm) landing area can be located on the adjacent arm of the counter. Plan 3 inches (76 mm) of countertop frontage between the sink and the corner and then plan at least 21 inches (533 mm) of countertop frontage beside the corner (see Figure 6.22). A sink in or near a corner may restrict access to the sink to just one person at a time and may not be a good choice for a two-cook kitchen, unless a second sink is also planned.

If the countertop areas adjacent to the sink are at different heights, then there should be a minimum 24 inches (610 mm) to one side of the sink and 3 inches (76 mm) on the other at the same height as the sink (see Figure 6.23). For example, if a raised dishwasher is being planned next to the sink on a lowered work area, then there should be at least 3 inches (76 mm) between the sink and the raised area. The raised area will have to serve as the other landing area. If there is only 3 inches (76 mm) between the sink and a vertical surface, problems with water spray and splash will develop, so consider finishing the side of the cabinet as part of the backsplash, using water-resistant materials.

Preparation Area

Counter space will be needed immediately next to the sink for mixing and other preparation activities. This will serve as the primary preparation/work area, sometimes called the prep area.

The recommended size is at least 36 inches (914 mm) measured along the countertop frontage and 24 inches (610 mm) deep. Figure 6.24 illustrates the typical area required for a preparation area. The cook will primarily work within the smaller arc of 16 inches (406 mm) but will be able to

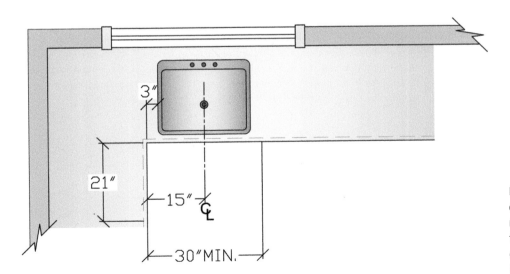

FIGURE 6.22 The 24 inches (610 mm) of recommended landing area can be met by planning 3 inches (76 mm) of countertop frontage from the edge of the sink to the inside corner of the countertop if more than 21 inches (533 mm) of countertop frontage is available on the return (Kitchen Planning Guideline 11).

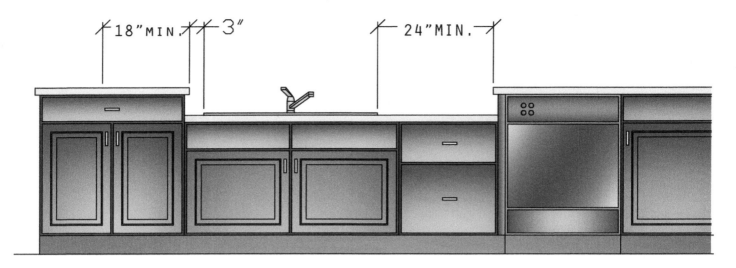

FIGURE 6.23 When raising the countertop at the primary sink, allow for 24 inches (610 mm) of landing area adjacent to the sink and at the same height. Allow 3 inches (76 mm) on the other side of the sink, before the countertop height changes (Kitchen Planning Guideline 11).

reach the larger arc of 24 inches (610 mm). Therefore, the requirement for the preparation area is deeper than the landing area requirements because a cook will use the complete depth of the counter for assembled ingredients and work in the front area.

When planning a kitchen for two cooks, consider how they might use the preparation area. Research has shown that at least two different cooking patterns occur with two cooks. With the student-teacher cooking pattern, one cook helps another. This might occur when a mom helps children bake cookies or one roommate shows the other how to bake lasagna. A preparation area of 60 to 72 inches (1524 mm to 1823 mm) is needed for two persons to stand together to work on one task.

Independent cooks work on separate recipes or foods at the same time. Two separate preparation areas, each at least 36 inches (914 mm), need to be planned for these cooks. When multiple preparation areas are planned, consider varying the heights and providing a knee space to accommodate different cooks.

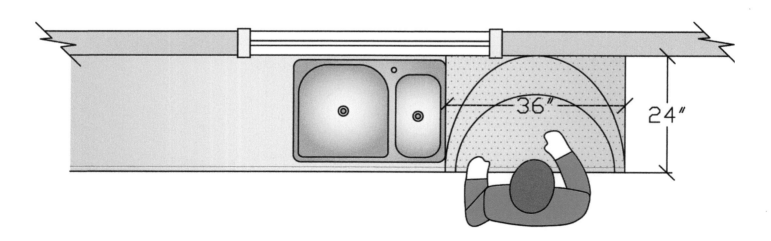

FIGURE 6.24 At least one preparation area should be planned in the kitchen. It must be 36 inches (914 mm) wide and 24 inches (610 mm) deep to allow 16 inches (406 mm) for a clear work area and 8 inches (203 mm) for storage (Kitchen Planning Guideline 12).

Special Preparation Areas

Sometimes a client may request special features to help in a particular food preparation task. In each of these cases, the designer must use the information gained from client interviews to shape the design solution.

- **Baking:** A baking area is the dream of any cook who likes to regularly prepare breads, rolls, cakes, pastries, pies, and tarts. A specialized baking center is a secondary center and should include storage and 36 inches (914 mm) to 54 inches (1372 mm) of counter space for mixing and baking tasks. Store specialized equipment, including mixing bowls, measuring cups and utensils, pans, rolling pins, and ingredients close by.

  Small appliances like blenders and stand mixers are needed here and could be stored on the counter or in an appliance garage. An appliance garage or pop-up mixer stand might add to the convenience of this area (see Figure 6.25). Kneading dough or rolling out pastries requires extended arm movement, so a 32 inch (813 mm) high counter is more ergonomically correct for average-sized users. If the baking center is not located next to the sink, then an auxiliary sink should be considered for this area. An undercounter refrigerator would be a nice addition to the baking center if the primary refrigerator is not close by.

- **Seated Work Area:** Cooks may enjoy sitting to work on some food preparation tasks, such as snapping beans or stirring a cooked pastry cream. Cooks who use a mobility aid or have weak legs may require areas for sitting throughout the kitchen. A typical counter height that allows the cook to sit to work is 32 inches (813 mm). A 30 inch (762 mm) high table height is also

FIGURE 6.25 A pop-up mixer stand is an added convenience in a baking center.

Courtesy of KraftMaid

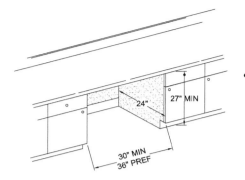

FIGURE 6.26 A knee space at a counter should be at least 30 inches (762 mm) wide (36 inches [914 mm] preferred), 24 inches (610 mm) deep, and 27 inches (686 mm) high.

appropriate. Space beneath the counter should be provided so that legs can pull under the counter and good posture can be maintained. A knee space 30 inches (762 mm) wide minimum (36 inches [914 mm] preferred), 24 inches (610 mm) deep, and 27 inches (686 mm) high provides room for a person in a wheelchair to pull under the counter (see Figure 6.26).

- **Food Preservation:** Some households may conduct food preservation tasks, such as canning, freezing, and drying. Often large quantities of fresh food are brought into the kitchen and prepared by rinsing, chopping, peeling, and shelling. Some food is blanched, drained, and cooled before being put into jars or freezer containers. The preparation area for these tasks, at least 36 to 48 inches (914 mm to 1219 mm) wide, should be located between a sink and cooktop. Consider a surface that is acid and stain resistant. A deep sink might be desirable and a pull-out spray or specialized faucet for filling large pots will be needed.

Dishwasher Placement

The primary dishwasher should be placed within 36 inches (914 mm) of the cleanup sink. Placing the dishwasher immediately adjacent to the sink has some advantages:

- Liquids may remain of dishes and are likely to drip on the floor.
- The person can stand in one place and reach dishes stacked in or near the sink and the dishwasher.
- The 24-inch (610 mm) width of the typical dishwasher ensures a 24-inch (610 mm) countertop area above, which will serve as the sink landing area.

Despite these advantages, the dishwasher may need to be moved away from the sink, but there should be no more than 36 inches (914 mm) from the edge of the sink to the edge of the dishwasher (see Figure 6.28).

Placing the dishwasher some distance from the sink might happen when the sink and dishwasher are being placed at an angle. If a right-angle arrangement is being planned, the designer must allow at least 21 inches (533 mm) for a person to be able to stand at the dishwasher to load and unload the appliance. The standing space between the dishwasher and a perpendicular counter or wall is also needed if the dishwasher is next to the sink (see Figure 6.29). The standing space is measured from the edge of the dishwasher to the countertop, cabinet, or other appliance.

FIGURE 6.27 The cleanup sink and the dishwasher should be within 36 inches (914 mm) of each other.

Design by Joyce Cessar

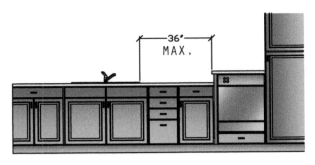

FIGURE 6.28 Locate nearest edge of the primary dishwasher within 36 inches (914 mm) of the nearest edge of a cleanup/prep sink (Kitchen Planning Guideline 13).

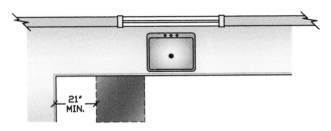

FIGURE 6.29 Allow 21 inches (533 mm) for standing space between the edge of the dishwasher and an adjacent perpendicular counter or wall (Kitchen Planning Guideline 13).

If the sink and dishwasher are placed at an angle other than 90°, the 21 inches (533 mm) is measured from the middle of the sink to the edge of the dishwasher door with the door in the open position (see Figure 6.30). In an installation where the sink is in the corner at a 45° angle to the dishwasher, a small cabinet will need to be specified between the sink and the dishwasher to provide for this space. If a person with a mobility aid will be using this arrangement, increase the size of the cabinet to enlarge the clear floor space at the sink. See Chapter 8 for more information on planning a sink and dishwasher arrangement in the corner.

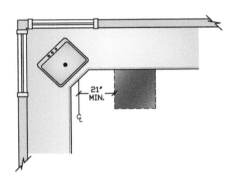

FIGURE 6.30 When a sink and dishwasher are placed at an angle to one another, plan a 21-inch (533 mm) standing space between them by measuring 21 inches (533 mm) from the centerline of the sink to the edge of the dishwasher (Kitchen Planning Guideline 13).

Trash

The trash receptacle is such an ordinary thing that designers might tend to forget about it. However, it is a critical element in both food preparation and cleanup and should be effectively planned into the kitchen. Recycling is also an important activity in many homes and communities. How effective households are in their recycling behaviors can be influenced by how the designer plans for this activity (see discussion in Chapter 3). Many older kitchens were planned before this activity became common, and recycling containers can be found in a closet or the garage. Today, several storage devices have been designed to handle the trash and recycling activities (see Figure 6.31).

It is recommended that the kitchen contain two waste receptacles: one for trash and one for recycling. The trash receptacle should be located near the sink and, while the recycling receptacle can be placed near the sink, it also can be planned elsewhere.

Carefully consider the client's recycling activities and patterns in order to plan the best container design and location.

A trash compactor might be desirable for some clients with large amounts of trash or without local trash collection. Some clients may also compost food waste, and the designer should explore ways to plan for this activity near the sink and preparation areas.

FIGURE 6.31 Base cabinets can incorporate a recycling Lazy Susan or pull-out bins to provide effective waste and recycling storage.
(a) Courtesy of KraftMaid; (b) Courtesy of Crystal Keyline

Auxiliary Sink

A second sink is often desired in today's kitchens. The auxiliary sink can be useful when more than one cook is working in the kitchen. It might be used as part of a secondary preparation area, a place to make salad, or to provide water in a baking area. An auxiliary sink might also serve as part of a beverage center, where family members can get a drink of water, tea, or coffee without interfering with the cook's activities.

An auxiliary sink also could be used as a cleanup sink. If placed close to the serving and dining areas and combined with a dishwasher, a second sink can keep some preparation and cleanup activities separate or provide greater convenience in the cleanup process.

An auxiliary sink can be at a lowered height to accommodate varied users. Provide a knee space below the auxiliary sink and it becomes suitable for sitting to work.

Landing areas are also necessary at the auxiliary sink. The NKBA recommends at least 18 inches (457 mm) to one side of the sink and 3 inches (76 mm) of clearance on the other side (see Figure 6.32). This allows a minimum number of items to be placed next to the sink area, but is not be enough space for some activities that are planned at a second sink, such as major cleanup. Plan for more space if major activities will occur at the auxiliary sink.

Guidelines and Access Standards for Sink Center

The Kitchen Planning Guidelines and Access Standards that are particularly relevant to the sink area are Guidelines 11, 12, 13, 14, and 15. They can be found in Appendix A.

REFRIGERATION CENTER

The refrigeration center can be considered a somewhat passive center. The main activity is storing food items in the refrigerator and freezer. An organized cook may only go to the refrigerator one or two times while preparing a food item, taking out all of the ingredients needed for preparation at one time. A chaotic cook will likely go to the refrigerator several times to take out items one by one as needed. It is probably true that having the refrigerator close to food preparation areas is much more important to the chaotic cook than the organized cook, because the trips to the refrigerator may be numerous and tiring if it is placed too far away.

FIGURE 6.32 A second or auxiliary sink is handy for a variety of purposes. It should have at least an 18-inch (457 mm) landing area to one side and 3 inches (76 mm) of clear space on the other (Kitchen Planning Guideline 15).
Design by NKBA member Savena Doychinov, CKD

The refrigerator will also be used when ingredients and leftovers are stored. Again, this may require several trips or only a few, depending on the cooking style and number of items. Often storage containers for leftovers are kept near the refrigerator, which is a logical place for them. Somehow those plastic freezer cups and containers seem to multiply and can overrun allocated space fairly quickly. Plan accordingly.

Refrigerators are available in several configurations and sizes. These include bottom mount, side-by-side, French doors, top-mount, and column units that are tall refrigeration units with a separate tall freezer unit. Undercounter models are also available in drawers and with doors. Ice makers, wine coolers, and beer kegs also provide refrigeration options.

Design Recommendations for Refrigeration Center

Placement

The refrigeration center is often placed at one end of a kitchen work arrangement. The typically tall unit will not interfere with other work areas if it is placed at the end of the workflow, and often this will make it more accessible to family members getting beverages or preparing to serve the table. However, avoid placing the refrigerator directly beside a wall. There may not be room to open the refrigerator door beyond 90°, making it difficult to access the interior for storage and cleaning. If a refrigerator must be placed adjacent to a wall, plan additional space between the refrigerator and the wall to provide room for the door swing.

Make sure there is adequate floor space in front of the refrigerator for the door to swing open and for a user to maneuver in front of, and around, it. In some wider built-in refrigeration units this could be as much as 48 inches (1219 mm) of clear floor space.

Because the refrigerator is most often used in food preparation, it is a good idea to place a preparation area next to the refrigerator. The 36-inch (914-mm) primary preparation area could be placed between the sink and the refrigerator, or a secondary preparation area could be planned there.

Undercounter refrigerators allow for placing multiple refrigeration units in multiple locations, adding flexibility and improving access. A refrigeration unit might be placed in an area where salads and vegetables are regularly prepared. Alternately, a small unit for beverages might be placed close to the serving area of the kitchen and completely out of the food preparation areas. Wine coolers and beer kegs can help make entertaining convenient. Refrigerator drawers may be particularly useful for placing cold food storage at a height that does not require bending (see Figure 6.33). Refrigeration units require a great deal of energy since they are always on, so you may want to encourage clients to carefully consider the options so that they are mindful of the energy use and operation costs.

The style of refrigerator should be selected based on volume and access needs of the household, as well as the general parameters of the space. Chapter 8 provides more information about selecting refrigeration units that meet client needs.

Landing Area

The landing area at the refrigerator should be a minimum of 15 inches (381 mm) wide, measured as countertop frontage (see Figure 6.34). (Remember a landing area is at least 16 inches [406 mm] deep.) The placement of the landing area can vary depending on the style of refrigerator used. It should be on the door handle side of a top or bottom mount refrigerator-freezer, so that when the refrigerator door is open, an item can be transferred from the refrigerator to the landing area without interference of an open door. In a side-by-side refrigerator, the 15-inch (381-mm) landing area can be located on either (or both) side(s), since both refrigerator and freezer doors are narrow. Because most food will be removed from the refrigerator side of the unit, it is probably best if a landing area is on the freezer side, but other planning considerations may indicate the opposite.

NKBA guidelines allow a landing area to be placed on a counter or island across from the refrigerator. The landing area must be within 48 inches (1219 mm) measured from the front of the appliance to the edge of the landing area. This will allow the user to remove an item and turn to place it on the landing area. It is probably not as convenient as a landing area next to the refrigerator, but it is manageable for most users.

FIGURE 6.33 Undercounter refrigerators are convenient for storing snacks.

Design by NKBA member Thomas David Trzcinski, CMKBD

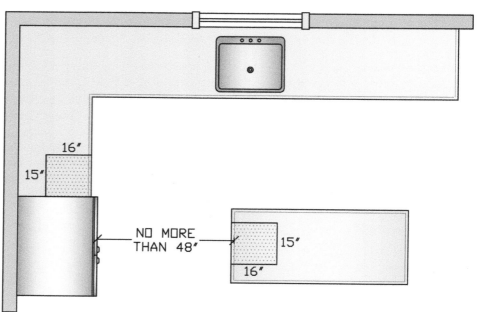

FIGURE 6.34 A 15-inch (381-mm) landing area can be located beside the refrigerator or on a counter no more than 48 inches (1219 mm) across from the refrigerator (Kitchen Planning Guideline 16).

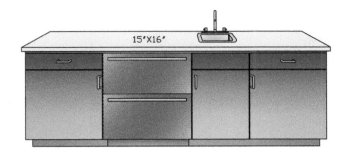

FIGURE 6.35 When an undercounter refrigeration unit is planned, the landing area is planned above the unit (Kitchen Planning Guideline 16).

If undercounter refrigerators are used, a landing space 15 inches (381 mm) wide x 16 inches (406 mm) deep should be planned above the refrigeration unit (see Figure 6.35).

Guidelines and Access Standards for Refrigeration Center

The Kitchen Planning Guideline and Access Standard that is particularly relevant to the refrigeration center is Guideline 16 which can be found in Appendix A.

COOKING CENTERS

While the sink center may be the most frequently used area in the kitchen, the cooking center or centers may be the true heart of the kitchen. People who love to cook will be very particular about the types and features of cooking appliances. They find true self- expression in their cooking techniques, and the quality of the final outcome of the food product and planning for this task is important. How do we cook?

- **Surface Cooking:** This refers to cooking that is taking place on the top of the range or on the cooktop. Frying, sautéing, steaming, and boiling are typical methods of surface cooking. This type of cooking often requires high user interaction. Foods need to be turned and stirred. Ingredients need to be added. Often people check on the progress of the cooking and increase or decrease the amount of heat used. Pots, frying pans, spoons, and spatulas are all needed at this area.
- **Oven Cooking:** Typical cooking in the oven includes baking, roasting, and broiling. This may occur in the oven cavity of a range, or in a separate oven placed in a tall cabinet or under the counter. Ovens may include convection, microwave, speed, or steam options. Often oven cooking is a passive activity, with the cook preheating the oven, putting the food in the oven, setting a timer, and periodically checking on progress before it is done and removed from the oven. Various roasting and baking pans, casserole dishes, and cookie sheets are used here. Hot pads, basters, meat forks, and other utensils are needed.
- **Microwave Cooking:** Over 96 percent of households have a microwave and use it in a variety of ways. Some use it as part of the food preparation process—melting butter or boiling water. Others use it to prepare frozen foods for eating or to reheat leftovers. Still others use it as a major cooking appliance, following microwave recipes for casseroles or other dishes.

  The way the microwave is used will determine where it should be located, what types of items are used with it, and whether a second microwave is appropriate. There may be special cookware used to cook in the microwave, or the same glass dishes used in the oven might be appropriate. Plates, mugs, and measuring cups all might be used in microwave cooking.
- **Speed Cooking:** Several appliances offer higher-speed cooking that combines microwave with convection or light. These ovens may be used like a separate oven or a microwave.
- **Small Appliances:** Numerous small appliances perform some specialized cooking and may be important to the client. Toaster ovens are frequently used in small households to bake rolls or other items. Countertop grills may be used to prepare a hamburger or steak. Toasters, waffle irons, and electric frying pans or griddles may also provide some specialized cooking. Most of the small appliances are placed on the countertop when they are in use, and various types of equipment will be needed, depending on the cooking tasks.

Design Recommendations for Surface Cooking

Planning the cooking center is more complicated today than in the past when the range was the only cooking appliance. With one appliance to anchor the center, it was relatively easy to plan work surfaces and storage that would surround the place of all cooking activities. Today, it is typical to have several cooking appliances, so some of the recommendations must apply to several cooking areas. The recommendations for this center have been arranged according to the type of cooking.

Because of the interaction between the surface cooking appliance and food preparation tasks, this area is often considered the primary cooking center.

Placement

The cooking surface (range or cooktop) should be located with consideration to the other centers, particularly the sink center. Cooks will move most frequently between the sink and the surface cooking appliance, and there should be a clear uninterrupted path between these two areas. This means that the cooking surface will often be placed adjacent to, or across from, the sink center (see Figure 6.36).

Safety is a major concern at the cooking surface because there is danger of scalds, burns, and fire. Several recommendations have been developed to keep this a safe area. These safety requirements are based on building code requirements and are referenced in Kitchen Planning Guideline 20.

If the sink is on an island, there may be a desire to place the cooktop or range beneath the window, the traditional sink placement area. If this is done, the window should not be operable (see Figure 6.37). Trying to open a window by reaching over hot pots is not safe and drafts from the window can affect cooking performance and safety. Fixed windows or a glass block area might be a solution, but consider how hard this area will be to clean. Your client may not thank you. If an inoperable window area is used, and a window treatment is specified, it should not be of a flammable material, which could be a fire hazard.

Plan a fire extinguisher in or near the kitchen. It should not be placed next to the cooking surface or oven because it may not be accessible if there is a fire. Place it close to an exit, in an accessible place, and within the 15- to 48-inch (381 mm to 1219 mm) reach range.

FIGURE 6.36 The range and sink are placed at a right angle to one another in this kitchen arrangement. A preparation area separates the two.

Design by NKBA member Robin Rigby-Fisher, CMKBD, CAPS

UNACCEPTABLE

ACCEPTABLE

FIGURE 6.37 Placing a window behind a cooking surface may mean it is difficult to clean, but it is acceptable to put a nonoperable window behind the cooking surface. An operable window and/or a flammable window treatment would be dangerous (Kitchen Planning Guideline 20).

Cooking appliances that are designated as commercial grade equipment should not be used in a residential kitchen. The high BTU output and difficulty venting the appliances make them a dangerous choice. These ranges are not rated to be placed next to sheetrock walls or residential kitchen cabinets. The pilot lights stay on, adding to the heat of the kitchen and the home. Most home insurance policies and local building codes do not allow this application. Several manufacturers offer "professional style" stainless steel ranges that look similar to commercial ranges and offer high performance, but are permissible under building codes.

Consider the location and design of appliance controls. Controls placed at the back of the appliance may mean that the cook must reach over hot and steaming pots to adjust cooking temperatures, and should be avoided when possible. Controls placed at the front edge of the range provide easy access to seated cooks, but might tempt small children to manipulate them, if they are easily manipulated. Controls on the top of the appliance and/or to the side improve access to most users (see Figure 6.38). Designers and clients are responsible for selecting products that consider the safety needs of all users.

Landing Area

There should be a landing area on both sides of a cooking surface. Not only does the landing area allow for a place to put spoons, pot lids, and ingredients to be added to food being prepared, but it also provides a space to turn pot handles so that they are not hit by passing traffic. Unless the countertop is a heat-resistant material, the landing area is not a place to put hot pots, unless it is an emergency.

There should be a minimum of 15 inches (381 mm) of counter frontage on one side of the cooktop or range and 12 inches (305 mm) on the other (see Figure 6.39). If there are various counter heights at the range, the 12-inch (305 mm) and 15-inch (381 mm) landing areas should be the same height as the cooking surface.

If the cooking surface is on an island or a peninsula that is the same height as the cooking surface, then there should also be 9 inches (229 mm) of counter space behind the cooking surface to

FIGURE 6.38 The controls on this cooktop are located in the center, making them easy to reach, and convenient for two cooks to use at one time.

Courtesy of GE

prevent handles being hit and hot spatters getting onto people standing or sitting behind the cooking surface.

Occasionally, in a small kitchen, a cooking surface will be placed next to a wall or tall obstacle. This should only be done if it is in accordance with manufacturer's instructions for clearances (see Figure 6.40). This closed configuration will not provide an adequate landing area on one side of the cooking center and can restrict the size of pots that will fit on the cooking surface. If no other configuration can be used, then fire-retardant and easy-to-clean wall materials will be necessary.

Ventilation and Clearances

A ventilation system is required for surface cooking. There are several different types of systems available. It is important that the designer match the ventilation system with the features of the surface cooking appliance. More information about ventilation systems is detailed in Chapter 7, "Mechanical Planning."

Besides planning the size and style of ventilation, the designer must plan the placement of the ventilation system. Different cooking and ventilation appliance systems may have different requirements, and manufacturer's specifications should always be followed.

A typical arrangement calls for placing the range hood over the cooking surface. Ideally, the hood should extend at least 3 inches (76 mm) beyond the cooking surface on both sides. A range hood is made of nonflammable materials and is fireproof. It should be placed at least 24 inches (610 mm) above the cooking surface (see Figure 6.41). For a typical application, this would place the bottom of the hood at 60 inches (1524 mm) above the floor. The eye height for a small woman is about 53 inches (1346 mm) and for a tall man it is 69 inches (1753 mm). Consider the client's eye height and overall height when planning the hood placement, so that it does not interfere with the user's view and access to the cooking surface. If a microwave with built-in ventilation is placed above the range, follow manufacturer's instructions for correct clearance.

A proximity ventilation system is located either as part of the cooking appliance or within the counter next to, or behind, the cooking appliance. This type of system allows for a clear open space above the cooking appliance and might be used on an island or peninsula. Check the cooktop and ventilation system manufacturer's specifications for placement and to determine counter depth. A telescoping system placed behind the cooktop may affect the specifications of base cabinets in this area. A cabinet or other flammable object placed above the cooking surface with proximity ventilation should be at least 30 inches (762 mm) above the cooking surface, while a protected or fireproof surface can be located at 24 inches (610 mm) (see Figure 6.42).

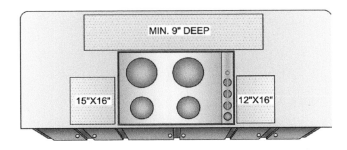

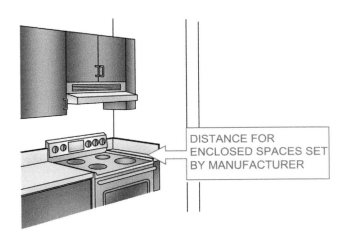

FIGURE 6.39 A 12-inch (305 mm) and a 15-inch (381 mm) landing area should be planned beside the cooking surface. (a) If the cooking surface is on an open island or peninsula at the same height, then
9 inches (229 mm) of counter area should be planned behind it. (b) If the cooking surface is at a height different from the other counter heights, the 12-inch (305 mm) and 15-inch (381 mm) landing areas should be planned at the same height as the cooking surface (Kitchen Planning Guideline 17).

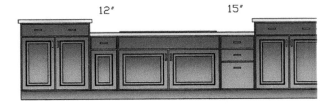

FIGURE 6.40 If a range or cooktop is placed close to a wall, make sure manufacturer's specifications for clearances are followed (Kitchen Planning Guideline 17).

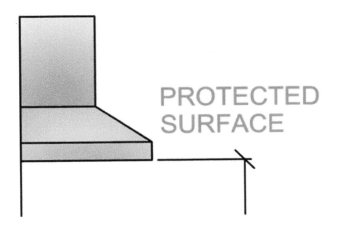

FIGURE 6.41 A protected surface should be at least 24 inches (610 mm) above the cooking surface (Kitchen Planning Guideline 18). This would accommodate a range hood that is 18 inches (457 mm) deep or more without
interfering with the average standing cook's line of vision (Kitchen Planning Guideline 18).

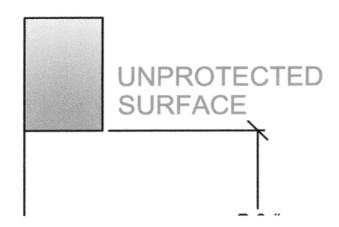

UNPROTECTED
SURFACE

FIGURE 6.42 Cabinets placed over a range with proximity ventilation must be at least 30 inches (762 mm) above the cooking surface (Kitchen Planning Guideline 18).

Design Recommendations for Microwave Cooking

As mentioned previously, people use the microwave oven for a variety of cooking tasks, which can determine where the microwave should be placed in the kitchen (see Figure 6.43). Microwaves come in four different styles: countertop, over-the-range, over the counter, and built-in. The countertop microwave is freestanding and requires open space around it to remove heat from cooking in the microwave. It is typically placed on the counter, but can be placed on a wall cabinet shelf or base cabinet shelf under the counter, as long as adequate open space for removing the hot air from the appliance is provided. Over-the-range microwaves are a special design that not only removes heat from the microwave through vents in the front of the unit, but also includes ventilation to draw heat, smoke, and cooking particles away from the cooking surface (see Chapter 7 for more information about ventilation). In an over-the-counter installation, the microwave is mounted on the wall within the wall cabinet configuration. The vents on the bottom of the unit remove the heat from cooking and should not be blocked. A built-in microwave is designed with a trim kit that helps vent the heat of the cooking microwave out the front of the unit. These can be planned into

FIGURE 6.43 Microwaves can be placed in several locations in the kitchen. (a) This countertop microwave is concealed in a cabinet with a flip-up door and adequate space around the microwave to allow for venting. (b) This built-in microwave pulls out like a drawer under the counter.

(a) Design by NKBA member Thomas Davidom Trzcinski, CMKBD; (b) Courtesy of Dacor

a base or tall cabinet. Drawer microwaves are special built-in units that are placed under the counter and can be placed in a variety of kitchen locations. Typical microwaves have doors that are hinged on the left and open on the right. Microwaves that are part of a speed-cooking appliance often have pull-down doors.

Placement

It might be suitable to place the microwave next to the refrigerator if it will primarily be used to defrost food and reheat leftovers. It could also be placed within a preparation area that is between the sink and refrigerator. This would be convenient for defrosting, reheating, and some food preparation tasks.

Other locations are more suitable for a microwave, microwave/convection combination, or speed-cooking appliance used for major cooking tasks. In this case, the microwave should be part of the primary cooking center. Placing the microwave in a preparation area that is between the sink and surface cooking appliance might be suitable for creating a primary cooking center with food preparation activities.

The over-the-range microwave, combined with a ventilation system, is placed over a cooking surface, placing both appliances at the anchor point of the primary cooking center. This can be efficient in a small kitchen, since the microwave is not taking up counter space or cabinet storage. However, the microwave will not be at a height that is safe and convenient for some users, and the ventilation system may not be adequate. There is one range designed with the microwave in a drawer above the range oven. This locates the microwave in the primary cooking center, but at a safer height.

The built-in microwave located with the wall oven in a cabinet can create a secondary cooking center, and in this case, the cook's height should be carefully considered. This arrangement might be appropriate if the microwave is used in ways similar to the oven. If the microwave cooking process will require frequent checking by the cook, the appliance should not be located outside of the cook's work area.

If the microwave is used for preparing snacks and is not part of the regular food preparation or cooking activities, it might be placed outside of the cook's work area and convenient to users who prepare snacks.

Placement Height

Research has indicated the best body mechanics for using the microwave with a side opening door is for the bottom of the microwave oven to be placed no lower than 2 inches (51 mm) below a primary user's elbow and no higher than 3 inches (76 mm) below the primary user's shoulder height (see Figure 6.44). This will allow the user to see into the microwave to observe food cooking, to see the controls (which often require a visual confirmation of settings), and provide for appropriate leverage when taking hot food out of the oven. The NKBA recommends that the bottom of the microwave be placed no higher than 3 inches (76 mm) below the user's shoulder height.

As a general interpretation of this recommendation, the NKBA guideline states that the bottom of the microwave should be placed no more than 54 inches (1372 mm) off the floor. This will allow a microwave to be placed on the bottom shelf of a wall cabinet. However, this is not a good location if the user's shoulder height is below 57 inches (1448 mm) or if the user has any problem with upper body strength.

If placing the microwave over the cooking surface, follow the manufacturer's instructions for clearances. Keep in mind that 24 inches (610 mm) between the cooking surface and a protected surface is recommended by the NKBA, putting the bottom of the microwave at 60 inches (1524 mm), which is 6 inches (152 mm) above the maximum shoulder height recommendation.

However, more important than either of these recommended distances are the safety concerns of this application. Reaching over hot and steaming food on the cooktop can be dangerous for anyone and a 24-inch (610 mm) clearance does not allow for seeing into a tall pot. Furthermore, the

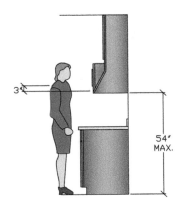

FIGURE 6.44 The bottom of the microwave oven should be placed no higher than 3 inches (76 mm) below the user's shoulder height (Kitchen Planning Guideline 21).

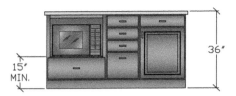

FIGURE 6.45 A microwave can be placed below a 36 inch (914 mm) high counter, when the bottom of the shelf is at least 15 inches (381 mm) off the floor (Kitchen Planning Guideline 21). This may be suitable placement for a seated user or for children.

height of the microwave will place the height of the dish being prepared above eye level, which is also dangerous for users. Also, there is not a convenient counter space below the microwave on which to place a hot food item.

Sometimes a microwave is placed below a raised or even a standard-height counter. This might be appropriate for children or people working from a seated position, again improving access but requiring added attention to safety for toddlers. However, this application may require others to stoop and bend to read controls and to take food out of the oven. The microwave drawer brings the food and controls out from the cabinet providing easier access. The NKBA allows for these types of installation, but the bottom of the microwave should not be below 15 inches (381 mm) off the floor (see Figure 6.45).

Who the users of the microwave are and how they use the microwave will really determine the appropriate placement of the appliance. Make sure you understand the clients' functional requirements (shoulder height, upper body strength, eye height) and their use of the microwave (preparing snacks, cooking casseroles, prepping ingredients) when you plan the placement of the microwave. An arrangement that works for a family with teenage boys might not work for an older couple with physical limitations or a young family with toddlers.

Landing Area

Wherever the microwave is placed, a 15-inch (381 mm) landing area should be provided above, below, or adjacent to the microwave oven (see Figure 6.46). Most microwaves have handles on the right and, ideally, the landing area should be on that side, but it is not always possible to do that. If a landing area is located across from the microwave, it should be within 48 inches (1219 mm) of the front of the appliance. Remember that all landing areas are between 28 and 45 inches (711 mm and 1143 mm) above the finished floor, so evaluate where the landing area will be when a microwave is placed in a 48 inch (1219 mm) high cabinet.

Design Recommendations for Oven Cooking

Oven cooking is a somewhat passive cooking activity, meaning the food is generally prepared in a preparation area and then placed in the oven. Often a timer is set, and the cook comes back when the timer goes off. Of course, some foods and cooking techniques, such as broiling, should be more closely watched, and the cook will return more frequently to check on progress.

Placement

With a range, the oven will be in the primary cooking center and easy for the cook to observe. It is often the client's preference and the only choice for a small kitchen. Some separate ovens are also placed beneath the surface cooking appliance, in the same location as the range oven or below a counter. These applications place the bottom of the oven at an inconvenient height for many people, making bending and lifting difficult.

A separate oven can be placed outside of the primary cooking center, because the cook is not constantly going to the appliance. This might be at one end of the work area or on a separate wall. Be sure to evaluate traffic in this secondary area, to avoid creating a hazardous situation. The oven door should not open into a traffic path.

A separate oven can be placed at a height that is more convenient to the user. A single oven placed with the bottom of the oven at 30 to 36 inches (762 to 914 mm) above the floor allows food to be transferred between the oven and a counter at a similar height. Double ovens typically will have the lower oven at a similar height to a range oven. Some larger kitchens can accommodate two separate ovens designed at comfortable heights. The result is that both ovens can be at a height that places controls no higher than 48 inches and yet high enough to reduce bending. See Chapter 8 for more information on planning oven placement to meet client's needs.

Landing Area

The landing area for an oven is 15 inches (381 mm) and can be placed on either side of the oven. This can coincide with the landing area required for a cooking surface if a range or oven beneath a cooking surface is used. The landing area can be located across from the oven as long as it is within 48 inches (1219 mm) of the front of the oven (see Figure 6.47). A major traffic path should not pass in front of the oven if the landing area is across from oven.

Guidelines and Access Standards for Cooking Centers

The Kitchen Planning Guidelines and Access Standards that are particularly relevant to the cooking center are Guidelines 17, 21, 22, and 23, which appear in Appendix A.

COMBINING CENTERS

Arranging the Centers

As the designer lays out the kitchen, the work flow of the client should be a major consideration in deciding where to place the work centers. An obvious and simple work flow is as follows:

Gather → Prepare → Cook → Serve → Cleanup

Of course, putting a meal together is a series of these steps with back steps, but this basic work flow has been instrumental in our thinking about how to arrange the work centers in kitchens. The work starts by gathering food from the refrigeration center, then moves to a preparation area near the sink center, and then moves to the cooking center. A serving area and eating space (covered in more detail in a later section) should be next and then, after the meal, it all goes back to the main sink center or an additional sink/cleanup zone.

A convenient way to incorporate the basic work flow is to remember the *work triangle*. The work triangle refers to the placement of the refrigerator, sink, and range in a three-point arrangement. The idea has been around for many years, and the consumer seems familiar and comfortable with the concept.

The introduction of additional major appliances, multiple cooks, and other activities has compounded the work triangle. Where does a separate oven or microwave go in the triangle? What about a kitchen with two sinks or two dishwashers? What happens when multiple refrigeration units are placed within centers? We can have multiple work centers or even multiple triangles, often referred to as activity zones.

Because work patterns in the kitchen continue in the traditional order, the NKBA continues to recommend using the three primary centers as points for the work triangle. As previously mentioned, the primary sink center should be in between the refrigeration center and the primary cooking center (surface cooking).

Planning for Two Cooks

The work triangle was originally conceived for and applied to one cook, but in many households more than one cook works in the kitchen. Research has shown that in two thirds of households, one cook still prepares most of the meals. In the other third, two cooks take turns cooking or cook together most of the time. Even when there is only one cook, entertaining and special occasions may bring in additional people to help with some tasks.

When two cooks prepare food together, the work triangle is affected and special consideration should be given to the concept of multiple zones. This is particularly true with independent cooks preparing separate food items at the same time. An auxiliary sink will be an important feature to have, since it will reduce congestion that would occur if there is only a single, primary sink (see Figure 6.48).

If the auxiliary sink is one point on a second triangle, then other points might be the refrigerator and a secondary cooking center, such as the microwave, oven, or grill. When two triangles are planned, examine the relationships carefully in order to avoid as much overlapping traffic as possible.

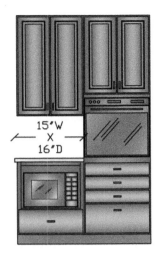

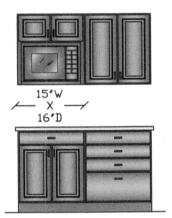

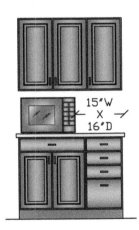

FIGURE 6.46 The landing area for the microwave should be at least 15 inches (381 mm) wide and planned (a) below, (b) above, or (c) beside the unit (Kitchen Planning Guideline 22).

FIGURE 6.47 The landing area for a separate oven should be 15 inches (381 mm) wide and placed (a) beside the oven, (b) on a counter across from the oven, as long as this is not a major traffic path, or (c) on a counter above the oven (Kitchen Planning Guideline 23).

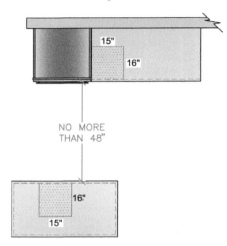

NO MORE THAN 48"

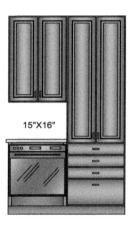

15"X16"

FIGURE 6.48 This kitchen incorporates a large preparation sink and dishwasher into the primary work triangle, and also includes a cleanup sink area with dishwasher. This fourth primary center separates the two major tasks that occur at the sink and also creates a secondary work triangle.

Distance

One of the most beneficial aspects of the work triangle concept is that it provides guidelines for the distance between the various centers. Each leg of the triangle should be no less than 4 feet (1219 mm) and no more than 9 feet (2743 mm) long (see Figure 6.49). These distances ensure that there will be some storage and counter space between each center, but that the distance is not so great that roller skates are needed to move from one center to the other. The sum of the three legs of the triangle should not total more than 26 feet (7925 mm). A work triangle leg should not intersect an island or peninsula by more than 12 inches (305 mm). The distances of the leg should be measured from the center of the refrigerator, sink, range, or other affected appliance (see Figure 6.50).

Separation of Centers

No tall cabinets or appliances should interfere with the work flow between any two primary work centers (see Figure 6.51). The cook should be able to move items along the countertop without having to pull back and around tall features. For example, a pantry or wall oven should be placed outside the work area, not within the work triangle that connects the primary centers.

If a wall cabinet is brought down to the counter, it is not considered a tall unit, and it would not interfere with the work flow. Corner applications of tall units also are permissible if the corner cabinet is recessed back from the counter area (see Figure 6.52). These applications still provide for clear movement of the work flow.

Traffic Interference

No traffic should interfere with the basic work triangle. Traffic interrupts the movements of the cook(s) and is dangerous if cooks are moving with hot pots and pans (see Figure 6.53). Careful consideration should be given if two cooks will be working in the kitchen at the same time, so that

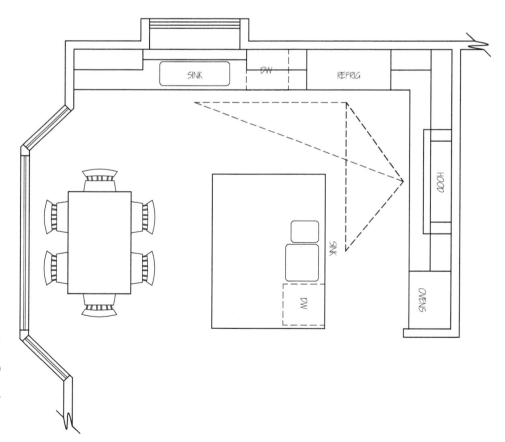

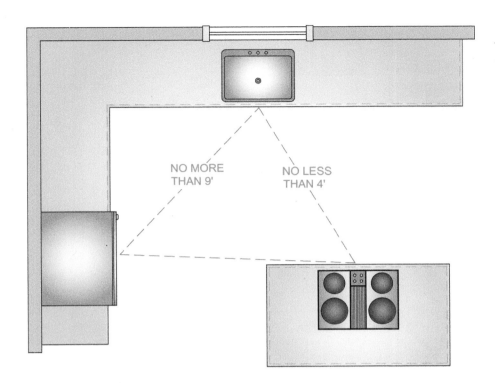

FIGURE 6.49 Plan the primary work centers in the kitchen so that each center is only 4 to 9 feet (1219 to 2743 mm) away from another center (Kitchen Planning Guideline 3).

major traffic between primary centers is not frequently interrupted. Remember to plan work aisles of 48 inches (1219 mm) or greater to ease circulation.

Counter Areas

The counter area is a critical element for working in the kitchen. Insufficient counter space is a common complaint for many people who have not yet remodeled their kitchen. Counter areas are used for landing space, preparation/work, and storage. Carefully review the client's needs for counter space and storage.

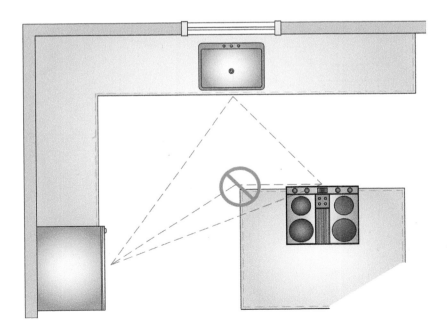

FIGURE 6.50 Measure the work triangle from the middle of the appliance or fixture located in the center. Measure around a counter, if the triangle leg will intersect with the counter by more than 12 inches (305 mm) (Kitchen Planning Guideline 3).

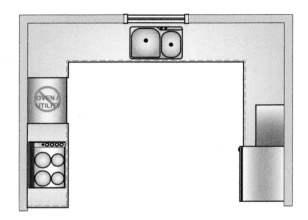

FIGURE 6.51 Place tall obstacles, such as a pantry or wall oven, outside the work triangle (Kitchen Planning Guideline 4).

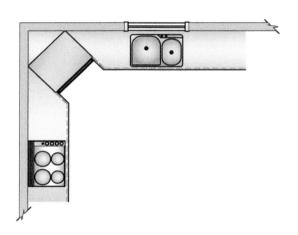

FIGURE 6.52 Tall corner cabinets within the work triangle are acceptable if they are recessed back from the counter edge (Kitchen Planning Guideline 4).

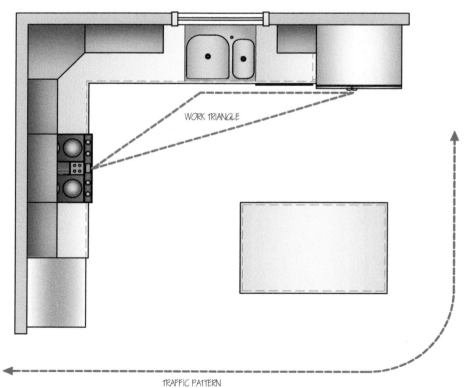

FIGURE 6.53 Plan circulation so that it avoids interrupting the work triangle of the kitchen (Kitchen Planning Guideline 5).

Combining Landing Areas

Each center has minimum landing area requirements. Remember that a landing area specification is given as countertop frontage—at least 16 inches (406 mm) deep and between 28 and 45 inches (711 mm to 1143 mm) high. Recommended landing areas are:

- **Sink:** 24 inches (610 mm) and 18 inches (457 mm)
- **Refrigerator:** 15 inches (381 mm)
- **Cooking Surface:** 15 inches (381 mm) and 12 inches (305 mm)
- **Microwave:** 15 inches (381 mm)
- **Wall Oven:** 15 inches (381 mm)

Landing areas located beside each other can be combined. To calculate the minimum distance in a combined arrangement, take the longest specified landing area in the two centers, and add 12 inches (305 mm) (see Figure 6.54). For example, if a sink center and refrigeration center are next to each other, a minimum amount of landing area for the two centers is calculated by adding the 24-inch (610 mm) landing area of the sink (the longest one) and 12 inches (305 mm). Therefore, a 36-inch (914 mm) area is the minimum that should be planned. If the landing areas from the sink and range are combined on the other side of the sink, the combination would again use the 24-inch landing area from the sink as the longest landing area, and 12 inches (305 mm) would be added.

Total Counter Area

Although the landing areas give the cook some space to place items temporarily and to complete a few tasks, they do not fulfill all of the requirements of the counter area. A preparation area should be provided near the sink, and it should be a minimum of 36 inches (914 mm) wide by 24 inches (610 mm) deep, so that at least one usable work area is provided. This area could overlay the landing areas of the sink and refrigerator centers, if the landing areas are 24 inches (610 mm) deep.

Counter area is also used for storage in nearly all kitchens. For example, the counter area provided 10 percent of the total storage in the small kitchens in the Virginia Tech research. The number of items kept on the counter decreased in larger kitchens, since more cabinet and drawer storage was

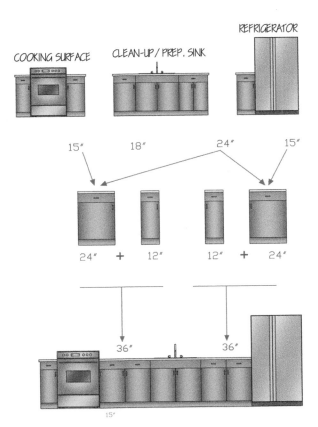

FIGURE 6.54 When combining two landing areas side by side, use the measurement from the longest landing area, and add 12 inches (305 mm) (Kitchen Planning Guideline 24).

available. Although the idea of a clean counter appeals to many, in reality households keep a lot of frequently used things out on the counter, where they are easy to see and reach. Often items like heavy appliances or canisters stay on the counter. The back 8 inches (203 mm) of a 24 inch (610 mm) deep counter provides space that can be used for permanent and temporary storage.

The NKBA recommends that at least 158 inches (4013 mm) of countertop frontage be provided in the kitchen work area to accommodate landing areas, preparation areas and storage (see Figure 6.55). This frontage should be 24 inches (610 mm) deep, so if any landing areas were planned at only 16 inches (406 mm), such as with a mantle-styled hood with columns that extend to the counter beside the cooking surface, those areas cannot count toward the countertop frontage. There should also be at least a 15-inch (381 mm) clear space above the countertop frontage so that a cook can work there.

- **Appliance Garage:** When an appliance garage is placed so that it is parallel to countertop frontage, it can be counted within the total counter frontage, because it is storage (see Figure 6.56). It cannot be placed where landing areas and preparation areas are specified, because it would interfere with the depth of counter space needed for these areas. An appliance garage in the corner would not impact the countertop frontage calculations because it does not parallel countertop frontage, and none of the corner counter area counts as countertop frontage.

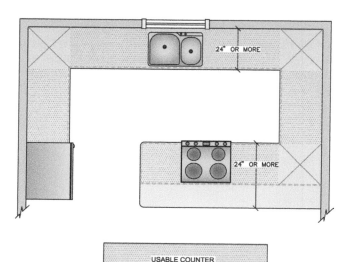

FIGURE 6.55 Plan 158 inches (4013 mm) of counter area to accommodate landing areas, a preparation area, and storage (Kitchen Planning Guideline 25).

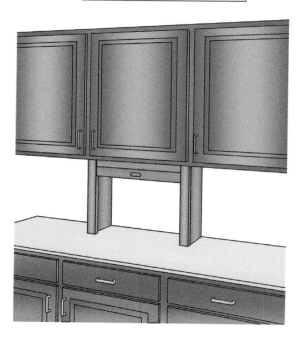

FIGURE 6.56 An appliance garage can be placed on the counter within the 158 inches (4013 mm) of counter space, as long as it does not interfere with landings and preparation areas (Kitchen Planning Guideline 25).

Counter Design

Consider several factors when planning the counter surface. Specify heat-resistant materials at the cooking surface and oven landing areas. Nonglare materials will make the work surface easier to see. Materials that provide a color contrast at the counter edge, or between the counter and the floor, may be easier for people with vision problems to see. Task lighting at the counter area will make it easier for everyone to see their work. See Chapter 7 for more information on lighting requirements and recommendations. Counter corner edges should be rounded or clipped so that there are not sharp edges to bump into (see Figure 6.57).

Guidelines and Access Standards for Work Arrangements and Counter Areas

The Kitchen Planning Guidelines and Access Standards that are particularly relevant to work arrangements and counter areas are Guidelines 3, 4, 5, 24, 25, and 26. They all appear in Appendix A.

STORAGE

All of the food preparation tasks discussed thus far have required "things"—fresh, canned, and boxed foods; equipment and utensils; pots and pans; mixing bowls and baking dishes; dishwashing detergent and dish drainers; and many, many more. Consumer focus groups conducted by Blum identified five categories of storage zones that could help designers plan storage, integrating it into the workflow of the kitchen. The zones are: consumables (edibles), nonconsumables (food serving and storage), cleaning, preparation, and cooking (see Figure 6.58). All of these things (and the things we need for dining and entertaining and managing the home) need a place to stay.

The following storage principles should help the designer plan where, and what types of, storage should be provided in the kitchen to meet a client's needs.

- **Store items at point of first or last use.** Glassware could be stored close to the refrigerator and coffee mugs near the coffee pot. Alternately, they could both be stored near the dishwasher, the point of last use in the cleanup process.
- **Store items in duplicate locations if needed**. Hot pads should be stored next to the cooktop and the wall oven.

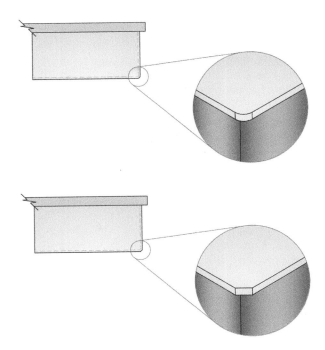

FIGURE 6.57 The corners of counter tops should be rounded or clipped for safety (Kitchen Planning Guideline 26).

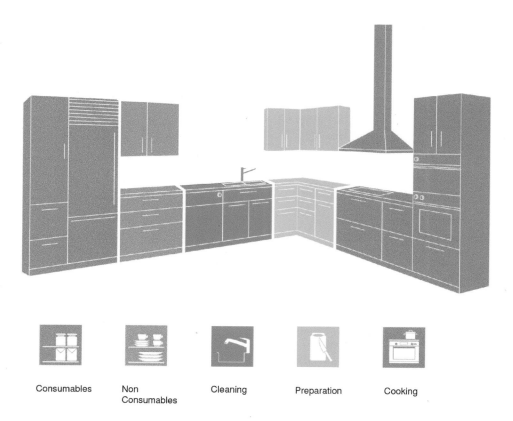

Consumables | Non Consumables | Cleaning | Preparation | Cooking

- **Items that are used together should be stored together.** Measuring cups and measuring spoons should be in the same drawer.
- **Items should be stored so they are easy to see.** Placing spices in a rack at eye level will make it easier to find the right one. Full extension drawers will bring all of the items stored there into view.
- **Frequently used items should be stored so they are easy to reach.** Leaving the coffeepot on the counter may be a good idea, if coffee is prepared every morning and sometimes in the afternoon. The comfortable reach range for the average standing cook is 25 to 59 inches (635 to 1499 mm), which is where most frequently used items should be stored. The universal reach range is 15 to 48 inches (381 to 1219 mm) above the finished floor.
- **Like items should be stored or grouped together.** Dishes, bowls, flatware, or canned goods are often grouped together by stacking.
- **Store hazardous items out of the reach of children or others who might be harmed by them**. Placing knives in a knife block or in a drawer could keep them inaccessible to small children. Often, kitchen cabinets are retrofitted with childproof closures to keep small ones out of the cleaning supplies and breakables.
- **Store items in the appropriate environment.** Items like potatoes and onions are best stored in a dry place with good air circulation, so a basket might be used.

Kitchen Cabinetry

When planning storage, you will specify cabinets in the centers of the kitchen. In order to plan this storage, it is important to understand what types of cabinets are available and how to plan the layout of the cabinets using nomenclature that will call out the selected cabinets.

Cabinetry is available in both *framed* and *frameless* construction. Framed cabinets have a face frame at the opening of the cabinet box, offered in various door styles and configurations. Frameless cabinets are constructed of panels and do not need a face frame. They are also offered in a variety of styles with full overlay doors.

Types of Kitchen Cabinets

Base cabinets: A base cabinet is the bottom cabinet and is usually 24 inches (610 mm) deep and 34½ inches (876 mm) high (see Figure 6.59). When a 1½ inch (38 mm) high countertop is added, it brings the total cabinet height to 36 inches (914 mm). Standard framed base cabinets are typically sized in 3-inch (76 mm) linear measurements, starting at 9 (229 mm) (tray storage) with the largest size of 48 inches (1219 mm). Custom cabinetry can be made in any size.

Typically, a base cabinet has a 4 to 5 inch (102 to 127 mm) high x 3 inch (76 mm) deep toe kick at the base, which allows a user to stand close to the cabinet. Some furniture-type cabinets do not include a toe kick, and the user may need to lean into the cabinet to work at the counter surface. Toe kicks may need to be raised to at least 9 inches (229 mm) and have the depth increased to 6 inches (152 mm) to accommodate the foot rests of a wheelchair or scooter.

Base cabinets can be customized to a lower height to accommodate shorter or seated people.

Drawers: A standard framed base cabinet comes with a drawer approximately 3 inches (76 mm) deep at the top of the cabinet, but a base cabinet can be designed with three to four drawers to accommodate all types of items in an accessible way (see Figure 6.60). Base cabinets also may have pull-out shelves and trays that function like drawers.

Wall cabinets: The standard wall cabinet depth is 12 inches (305 mm), although 13- to 15-inch (330 to 381 mm) depths are also used to accommodate larger plates. The standard framed cabinet height ranges from 30 to 36 inches (762 mm to 914 mm) (see Figure 6.61). Shorter cabinet sizes are used in certain applications, for example, over an appliance or peninsula. Taller or stacked wall cabinets have become more common as ceiling heights have increased. The linear width of standard or stock wall cabinets increases in 3-inch (76 mm) increments. The wall cabinet is placed 15 to 18 inches (381 to 457 mm) above a standard counter height of 36 inches (914 mm). This puts two or three wall shelves within the reach of the average user and leaves a usable clear space above the work surface.

Tall cabinet/pantry/utility: There are several designs and arrangements for a tall cabinet or pantry storage (see Figure 6.62). This storage might be an alternative to a closet or small room that is used for storage. The tall cabinet is 12, 18, or 24 inches (305, 457, 610 mm) deep with shelving and/or pull-outs. There are also fold-out shelving units that increase accessible storage capacity.

Other storage: Base and wall cabinets can include a variety of accessories that enhance the usability of the storage devices. Also, other storage pieces can add to the storage capacity of the kitchen. Pot racks (Figure 6.63), open shelving, and furniture pieces can provide valuable storage areas in some kitchens.

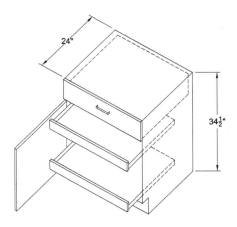

FIGURE 6.59 Base cabinet with pull-outs.

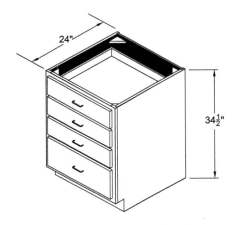

FIGURE 6.60 Drawer base with four drawers.

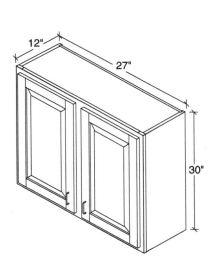

FIGURE 6.61 Typical wall cabinet.

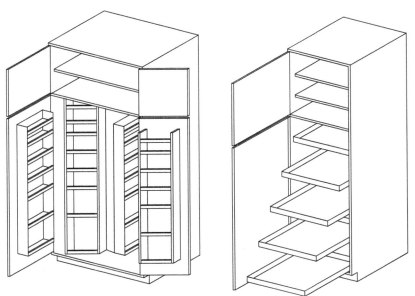

FIGURE 6.62 Tall cabinets can include fold-out storage or pull-out shelves.

FIGURE 6.63 Pot racks can add to the storage capacity of a kitchen.

Design by NKBA member Elina Katsioula-Beall, CKD

Specifying Cabinets

Often, North American–made framed and frameless cabinets use Imperial measurements and are specified using inches, with stock cabinets usually available in 3-inch increments in width. Cabinets are specified using a code of letters and numbers the manufacturer has determined represent their cabinet selections. Although the labeling is unique to each manufacturer, cabinet nomenclature tends to follow similar patterns. The NKBA has provided generic nomenclature to help designers and design students plan kitchens using the basic size and dimensions of cabinetry.

Letters used include B for Base, W for Wall, S for Sink, D for Drawer, and T for Tall, among others. The first one to two numbers reflect the width of the cabinet, the second two numbers reflect the depth, and the third two numbers indicate the height. For example, a SB362434 would be a sink base 36 inches wide, 24 inches deep, and 34 inches high.

European-styled frameless cabinetry built on the metric system is frequently specified in centimeters, which can result in variations in size from framed cabinets. The construction method requires a 32-mm spacing of holes for assembly and installation of hardware.

Amount of Storage

The research conducted at Virginia Tech has led to a new way for the designer to calculate and provide for the storage needs of a client. Base, wall, drawer, and pantry storage are still the main elements of a storage system in the kitchen. However, storage recommendations are given as a total amount of storage capacity for the kitchen, instead of totals for wall, base, and drawer units as in the past. Storage recommendations are based on shelf/drawer frontage, not just cabinet size. Different amounts of shelf/drawer frontage are recommended for small, medium, and large kitchens:

- 1400 inches (35,560 mm) for a small kitchen (less than 150 square feet; less than 13.95 sq. m)
- 1700 inches (43,180 mm) for a medium kitchen (151 to 350 square feet; 13.95 to 32.52 sq. m)
- 2000 inches (50,800 mm) for a large kitchen (greater than 350 square feet; greater than 32.52 sq. m)

The research indicated that newly designed kitchens had similar amounts of storage distributed as in Table 6.1, and the NKBA recommendations suggest that you use these guidelines as a means to calculate the location of storage.

TABLE 6.1 Recommended shelf/drawer frontage for cabinets in small, medium, and large kitchens.

	Small		Medium		Large	
	inches	mm	inches	mm	inches	mm
Wall	300	7620	360	9144	360	9144
Base	520	13208	615	15,621	660	16,764
Drawer	360	9144	400	10,160	525	13,335
Pantry	180	4572	230	5842	310	7874
Misc.	40	1016	95	2413	145	3683

The table indicates the following trends:

- Wall storage needs peak at 360 inches (9144 mm) of shelf/drawer frontage. No more is needed in the large kitchen than in the medium-sized kitchen.
- Base and drawer storage needs increase as the kitchen size increases.
- Pantry storage is an important element in the storage system. Even in small kitchens, a pantry can provide needed and accessible storage.
- Miscellaneous storage is included in every size of kitchen. Miscellaneous storage is storage more than 84 inches (21,334 mm) above the floor. It is also furniture pieces and pot racks, as well as other types of storage that is not wall, base, drawer, or pantry cabinets.

The table recommends the allocation for different types of storage in each size kitchen. However, these specific recommendations do not have to be met as long as the appropriate total shelf/drawer storage is met for kitchen size. For example, it is not necessary for a small kitchen to have 180 inches (457 cm) of pantry storage. The kitchen may have no pantry storage and instead have more base, wall, and drawer storage than indicated on the chart. The guidelines do indicate that only the amount specified as miscellaneous storage can count toward the totals. Since this is pretty inconvenient storage, it would not be a good idea to substitute lots of storage above 84 inches for base storage.

Since all but one of the categories of storage can vary, the designer has great flexibility in planning storage. This flexibility is important in open-plan kitchens that have few walls. It may be impossible to have wall cabinet storage in a room with large windows (Figure 6.64) and island work areas, and it may be undesirable as so much of it is above the reach of shorter or seated cooks.

Fortunately, storage components are changing. Drawers can hold dishes. Open shelves can be placed in front of windows. Peg boards and pot racks can hold utensils and equipment. A narrow but deep pantry can hold more than a wide, shallow wall cabinet. Calculating shelf/drawer frontage, rather than cabinet frontage, opens up the possibilities for creative and innovative storage solutions.

FIGURE 6.64 In this kitchen, base cabinets in the island help fulfill storage requirements.
Design by NKBA member Lance Arnold

Formula for Calculating the Amount of Storage in Cabinets

Cabinets have various shelf and drawer configurations that affect the amount of shelf/drawer frontage the cabinet offers. For example, a wall cabinet with three shelves offers more storage area than a two-shelf cabinet. A base cabinet with two 24 inch (610 mm) deep shelves holds more than one with one 24 inch (610 mm) deep shelf and one 12 inch (305 mm) deep shelf. Use the following formula to calculate the amount of shelf/drawer storage provided per cabinet:

Cabinet size × Number of shelf/drawers × Cabinet depth in feet = Total shelf/drawer frontage

Cabinet size: Standard cabinet width dimensions are usually given in 3-inch (76 mm) increments, for example, 12, 15, 18 inches (305, 381, 457 mm).

Number of shelf/drawers: Each cabinet will have a number of shelves and/or drawers specified. Check the cabinet catalog.

Cabinet depth in feet: Different cabinets have different shelf depths and designs that affect how much space is actually available for storage. Use the following measurement in feet (or fraction of feet) to calculate the actual amount of storage space provided in each cabinet. Wall cabinets of 12 inches (305 mm) have a depth of 1 (12 inch = 1 foot). In most base cabinets, the depth would be 2 (24 inch = 2 feet). Drawer frontage is calculated using the depth measurement as well.

Various cabinet depths provide different capacities for storage and a multiplier based on 1 = 12 inches is used to calculate the depth. For example, a 12-inch deep wall cabinet is 1, a 15-inch deep wall cabinet is 1.25, an 18-inch deep pantry cabinet is 1.5, a 21-inch deep wall cabinet is 1.75, a 24-inch deep base cabinet is 2, a 12-inch deep drawer is 1, and a 24-inch deep drawer is 2.

Example of Storage Calculations

To explain the calculation process, we will calculate the storage available in the kitchen illustrated in Figure 6.73. First, let's examine how to calculate the amount of shelf/drawer frontage in a wall cabinet, a base cabinet, a drawer cabinet, and a tall utility/pantry cabinet.

Wall Cabinet Calculation

The following example provides an application of the formula for the W3630 cabinet (see Figure 6.65):

Multiply the cabinet frontage size (36 inches) by the number of shelves in the cabinet (3) and by the cabinet depth (12 inches = 1):

36 inches x 3 × 1 = 108 inches

Thus, a 36-inch cabinet with three shelves would provide 108 inches of actual shelf frontage.

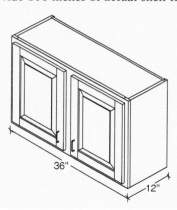

FIGURE 6.65 A 12 inch deep, 36 inch wide wall cabinet with three shelves provides 108 inches of actual wall cabinet shelf frontage.

36"

12"

Base Cabinet Calculation

The following calculation is for the B27 base cabinet with two 24 inch deep shelves (see Figure 6.66). The cabinet also has one drawer. Multiply the cabinet frontage size (27 inches) by the number of shelves in the cabinet (2) and by the cabinet depth (24 inches = 2). Calculate the drawer by multiplying the frontage (27 inches) by the number of drawers (1) by the depth (24 inches = 2).

Cabinet: 27 inches x 2 × 2 = 108 inches
Drawer: 27 inches x 1 × 2 = 54 inches

The 27-inch base cabinet has 108 inches of shelf frontage and 54 inches of drawer frontage storage.

27"   24"

FIGURE 6.66 A 27-inch base cabinet with two 24 inch deep shelves provides 108 inches of base cabinet shelf frontage. Note that a standard base cabinet also provides drawer storage, which is calculated separately.

Drawer Cabinet Calculation

The following calculation is for the BD18D4 with four drawers (see Figure 6.67). Multiply the cabinet frontage (18 inches) by the number of drawers (4) by the depth of the cabinet (24 inches = 2)

18 inches x 4 × 2 = 144 inches

This is the same formula used when calculating a single drawer in a base cabinet.

18"   24"

FIGURE 6.67 An 18-inch cabinet with four 24 inch deep drawers provides 144 inches of drawer frontage.

(continued)

Pantry Cabinet Calculation.

A tall utility cabinet is specified in the plan U242484R (see Figure 6.68). It has three fixed shelves. The following calculation would be used. Multiply the cabinet frontage (24 inches) by the number of shelves (3) and by the cabinet depth (24 inches = 2).

24 inches x 3 × 2 = 144 inches

If pull-out shelves were added, they could be calculated as drawer storage.

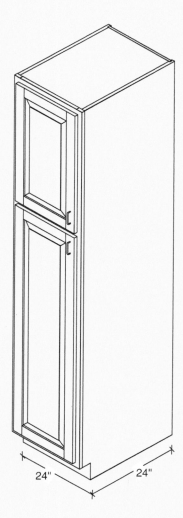

24"   24"

FIGURE 6.68 A 24 inch wide tall utility cabinet with three 24 inch deep shelves provides 144 inches of pantry cabinet shelf frontage.

Corner Cabinet Calculations

Corner cabinet storage can have various configurations that affect the calculation of shelf frontage provided. To calculate the storage provided by the various types of corner cabinets consider the following:

Blind corner: Count the visible cabinet frontage as the cabinet size, then calculate the same as a standard wall or base cabinet. (See Figure 6.69.)

L corner: For an L-shaped wall or base cabinet use the visible cabinet frontage and a shelf/depth multiplier of 1.5. (See Figure 6.70.)

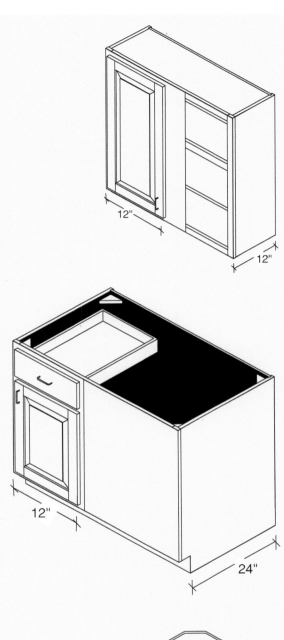

FIGURE 6.69 The blind corner wall cabinet (top) has 12 inches of visible cabinet frontage with three shelves 12 inches deep, for a total of 36 inches of total shelf frontage. The blind corner base cabinet (bottom) has 12 inches of visible frontage and two shelves, 24 inches deep, for a total of 48 inches of base cabinet shelf frontage. The drawer storage provided by the base cabinet is calculated separately.

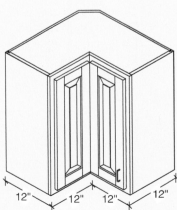

FIGURE 6.70 For an L-shaped wall cabinet use the visible cabinet frontage and a shelf/depth multiplier of 1.5. The wall cabinet would use 24 inches as the cabinet size, 3 shelves, and a multiplier of 1.5, for a total of 108 inches. The base cabinet would use 24 inches as the cabinet size, 2 shelves, and a multiplier of 1.5, for a total of 72 inches of base shelf frontage.

(continued)

L corner with Lazy Susan: For an L-shaped wall or base cabinet with a Lazy Susan, the shelf configurations are usually similar to three quarters of a circle within the L shape of the oversized cabinet. Use the wall side dimension as the cabinet frontage measurement (24 inches or 27 inches for a wall cabinet and 36 inches for a base cabinet) and 1.5 as the shelf dimension, then follow the formula. (See Figure 6.71).

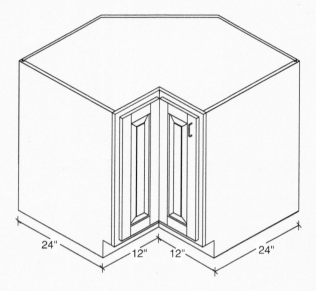

FIGURE 6.71 The L corner base cabinet with Lazy Susan has a wall side dimension of 36 inches that is used as the cabinet frontage measurement. It has two shelves and a multiplier of 1.5. This cabinet will provide 108 inches of base shelf frontage ($36 \times 2 \times 1.5 = 108$).

Diagonal corner with Lazy Susan: In these cabinets, a full circle shelf is fitted within the cabinet. For a wall cabinet, use the wall side dimension (24 inches, 27 inches) and 1.5 as the shelf depth, then follow the formula. For a base cabinet, use the wall side dimension (36 inches) and 1.5 as the shelf dimension, then follow the formula (see Figure 6.72).

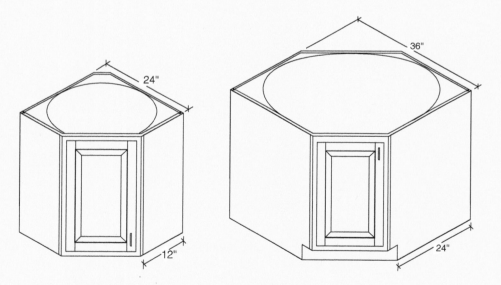

FIGURE 6.72 The diagonal wall cabinet has a side dimension of 24 inches and three round rotating shelves with a shelf depth multiplier of 1.5, for a total of 108 inches of wall cabinet shelf frontage. The diagonal base cabinet has a 36-inch side dimension and 2 round rotating shelves that use a multiplier of 1.5. The total base cabinet shelf frontage is also 108 inches.

Calculating Total Storage

We will use the kitchen in Figure 6.73 to illustrate how to check if enough storage has been provided. First, the size of the kitchen must be calculated. This kitchen is approximately 147 square feet and would be classified as a small kitchen. According to the previous recommendations, a total of 1400 inches of shelf/drawer frontage is needed throughout the small kitchen. Further, we should consider the recommended distribution of this storage in different types of cabinets: 300 inches of shelf frontage in wall cabinets, 520 inches of shelf frontage in base cabinets, 360 inches of drawer frontage in drawers, 180 inches of shelf frontage in pantry cabinets, and 40 inches in miscellaneous storage. Calculations in Table 6.2 indicate how much storage is provided by each category of cabinetry.

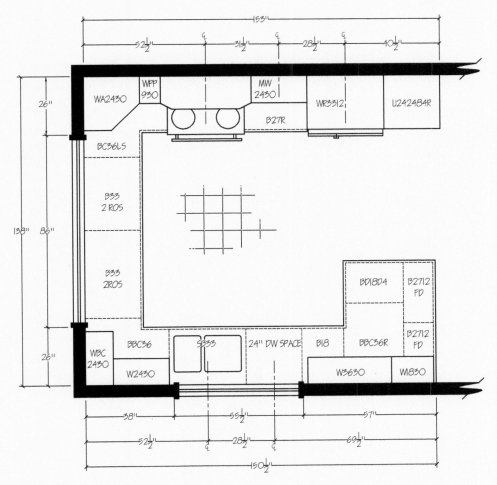

FIGURE 6.73 A variety of cabinets and storage is planned in this small kitchen. Calculations for the amount of shelf/drawer frontage is calculated in Table 6.2.

The calculations indicate that this kitchen has 486 inches of wall cabinet shelf frontage, 672 inches of base cabinet shelf frontage, and 654 inches of drawer frontage, which are all more than the recommended amount. There is only 144 inches of pantry shelf frontage, which is less than the recommended amount and no miscellaneous shelf frontage. The total amount of shelf/drawer frontage is 1956 inches of total shelf/drawer frontage, which is more than 1400 inches that is recommended.

(continued)

TABLE 6.2 As this chart shows, the kitchen in Figure 6.73 has more than the recommended amount of wall cabinets, base cabinets, and drawer storage, but less than the recommended amount of pantry cabinet storage. Overall, the storage exceeds the total recommendation of 1400 inches shelf/drawer frontage for a small kitchen.

	CALCULATIONS	SHELF/DRAWER FRONTAGE
WALL CABINETS		
WR3312	33 × 1 × 1	= 33
MW2430	24 × 2 × 1	= 48
MPP930	9 × 3 × 1	= 27
WA2430	24 × 3 × 1.5	= 108
WBC2430	12 × 3 × 1	= 36
W2430	24 × 3 × 1	= 72
W3630	36 × 3 × 1	= 108
W1830R	18 × 3 × 1	= 54
TOTAL WALL SHELF FRONTAGE		**486**
BASE CABINETS		
B27R	27 × 2 × 2	= 108
BC36LS	36 × 2 × 1.5	= 108
BBC361	12 × 2 × 2	= 48
B181	18 × 2 × 2	= 72
SB33	33 × 1 × 2	= 66
BC36D	36 × 2 × 1.5	= 108
B2712FD	27 × 3 × 1	= 81
B2712FD	27 × 3 × 1	= 81
TOTAL BASE SHELF FRONTAGE		**672**
DRAWERS		
B27	27 × 1 × 2	= 54
BC36L	12 × 1 × 2	= 24
B33/2ROS	33 × 3 × 2	= 198
B33/2ROS	33 × 3 × 2	= 198
BD18D4	18 × 4 × 2	= 144
B18	18 × 1 × 2	= 36
TOTAL DRAWER FRONTAGE		**654**
PANTRY		
U242484R	24 × 3 × 2	= 144
TOTAL PANTRY SHELF FRONTAGE		**144**
TOTAL SHELF/DRAWER FRONTAGE		**1,956**

Cabinet Calculations

Table 6.3 can help organize information from cabinet specifications needed to calculate the amount of shelf/drawer frontage in a kitchen. Enter the cabinet sizes and check specification for the number of shelves and depth of the shelves in each cabinet. Use the following formula to calculate the amount of shelf/drawer frontage provided by the cabinet.

Cabinet size × Number of shelves × Shelf/drawer depth multiplier = Total shelf/drawer frontage per cabinet

Multiply this by the number of cabinets of each size to determine the total amount of shelf/drawer frontage provided by all of the cabinets of a certain size. Add the totals together to determine the total shelf/drawer frontage for the kitchen.

TABLE 6.3 Calculating shelf/drawer frontage.

Standard Wall Cabinets Shelf Frontage—All shelves must be below 84 inches.						
Cabinet Type	**Cabinet Size**	**Number of Shelves**	**Shelf/Depth Multiplier**	**Total Shelf/Drawer Storage per Cabinet**	**Number of Cabinets**	**Total**
30/36/42 inches high/12 inches deep		3	1			
		3	1			
		3	1			
30/36/42 inches high/15 inches deep		3	1.25			
		3	1.25			
		3	1.25			
30/36/42 inches high/18 inches deep		3	1.5			
		3	1.5			
		3	1.5			
21/27 inches high/12 inches deep		2	1			
		2	1			
		2	1			
21/27 inches high/15 inches deep		2	1.25			
		2	1.25			
		2	1.25			
21/27 inches high/18 inches deep		2	1.5			
		2	1.5			
		2	1.5			
21/27 inches high/24 inches deep		2	2			
		2	2			
		2	2			
12/18 inches high/12 inches deep		1	1			
		1	1			
		1	1			
12/18 inches high/15 inches deep		1	1.25			
		1	1.25			
		1	1.25			
12/18 inches high/18 inches deep		1	1.5			
		1	1.5			
		1	1.5			
12/18 inches high/21 inches deep		1	1.75			
		1	1.75			
		1	1.75			
12/18 inches high/24 inches deep		1	2			
		1	2			
		1	2			
Blind corner	Visible cabinet frontage	3	1			
L corner	Visible cabinet frontage	3	1.5			
Diagonal	Wall side dimension	3	1.5			
Other						
Total wall cabinet shelf frontage						

(continued)

Base Cabinet Shelf Frontage

Cabinet Type	Cabinet Size	Number of Shelves	Shelf/Depth Multiplier	Total Shelf/Drawer Storage per Cabinet	Number of Cabinets	Total
32/36 inches high/ 24 inches deep w/ 12-inch–deep shelf		1.5	2			
		1.5	2			
		1.5	2			
32/36 inches high x 24 inches deep w/ 24 inches deep shelf		2	2			
		2	2			
		2	2			
32/36 inches high/ 24 inches deep sink base		1	2			
		1	2			
		1	2			
32/36 inches high/ 21 inches deep w/ 12-inch-deep shelf		1.5	1.75			
		1.5	1.75			
		1.5	1.75			
32/–36 inches high/ 21 inches deep w/ 21-inches-deep shelf		2	1.75			
		2	1.75			
		2	1.75			
32/36 inches high/ 18 inches deep w/ 18 inches deep shelf		2	1.5			
		2	1.5			
		2	1.5			
32/36 inches high/ 12 inches deep w/ 12-inch-deep shelf		2	1			
		2	1			
		2	1			
Blind corner w/ 12-inch shelf	Visible cabinet frontage	1.5				
Blind corner w/ 24-inch shelf	Visible cabinet frontage	2	2			
L corner	Visible cabinet frontage	2	1.5			
L-corner Lazy Susan	Wall side dimension					
Diagonal	Wall side dimension	2	1.5			
Other						

Total base cabinet shelf frontage

Drawer Frontage

Cabinet Type	Cabinet Size	Number of Drawers	Drawer Depth Multiplier	Total Shelf/Drawer Storage per Cabinet	Number of Cabinets	Total
24 inches deep base cabinet drawer		1	2			
		1	2			
		1	2			
		1	2			
3-drawer base cabinet (24 inches deep)		3	2			
		3	2			
		3	2			
4-drawer base cabinet (24 inches deep)		4	2			
		4	2			
		4	2			

Drawer Frontage, continued						
Base cabinet roll-out shelves/ pull out trays (24 inches deep)		2	2			
		2	2			
		2	2			
		2	2			
21-inch-deep drawer		1	1.75			
		1	1.75			
18-inch-deep drawer		1	1.5			
		1	1.5			
12-inch-deep drawer		1	1			
		1	1			
Other						
Other						
Total drawer frontage						

Tall/Utility/Pantry Cabinets Shelf Frontage—All shelves must be below 84 inches

Cabinet Type	Cabinet Size	Number of Shelves/ Drawers	Shelf/Drawer Depth Multiplier	Total Shelf/Drawer Storage per Cabinet	Number of Cabinets	Total
12 inches deep			1			
15 inches deep			1.25			
18 inches deep			1.5			
21 inches deep			1.75			
24 inches deep			2			
Oven —24 inches deep			2			
Other						
Other						
Total pantry shelf frontage						

Miscellaneous Shelf/Drawer Frontage

Cabinet Type	Cabinet Size	Number of Shelves/ Drawers	Shelf/Drawer Multiplier	Shelf/Drawer Frontage per Item	Number of Cabinets	Total
Furniture Piece						
Pot rack						
Shelves higher than 84 inches						
Other						
Other						
Total miscellaneous shelf/drawer frontage						

Total Shelf/Drawer Frontage

Total wall cabinet shelf frontage	
Total base cabinet shelf frontage	
Total pantry shelf frontage	
Total drawer frontage	
Total miscellaneous shelf/drawer frontage	
Total shelf/drawer storage for kitchen	

Storage at the Sink

Because so much activity occurs at the sink, it is important that ample amounts of storage be located there. The Kitchen Planning Guidelines recommend certain amounts of storage be located within 72 inches (1829 mm) of the center of the sink front (see Figure 6.74). At least 400 inches (10,160 mm) of shelf/drawer frontage is needed for a small kitchen; at least 480 inches (12,192 mm) for a medium kitchen; and at least 560 inches (14,224 mm) for a large kitchen. This storage can be wall, base, drawer, or tall/pantry storage and can be located beside or across from the sink, although placing it beside the sink will be most convenient.

The kitchen we have been analyzing (Figure 6.73) includes three wall cabinets and five base cabinets with shelf/drawer frontage within 72 inches (1829 mm) of the sink center. The wall cabinets do not provide the needed storage (216 inches; 5486 mm), but the base cabinets can also be included in calculating the total amount of shelf/drawer frontage needed at the sink. The total amount of shelf/drawer frontage provided by all of these cabinets is 732 inches (18,593 mm), which is more than the 400 inches (10,160 mm) required in a small kitchen.

Corner Cabinet Storage

Corner areas may require some special considerations. In a basic arrangement, two cabinets are perpendicular to each other and there is empty and unusable space in the corner. A blind corner cabinet provides some accessible space, but the user may need to be a contortionist to get to the back areas.

Various Lazy Susan and pull-out designs provide corner storage that is easier to access. If the kitchen will have corner cabinet areas, it is recommended that at least one of the corners include some type of specialized corner cabinet (see Figure 6.75A).

An "unfitted" kitchen with separate counters and furniture pieces may not have any corner units and is not subject to this recommendation (see Figure 6.75B).

Storage Organizers

Storage accessories or organizers enhance the efficiency of cabinetry by increasing access to items (see Figure 6.76). Pull-out shelves and turntables allow the user to fully use a deep cabinet. Pull-out cutting boards add an extra work area and place it at a lower height that is convenient for chopping. Open shelves and backsplash storage make items easy to see and reach. Drawer dividers help keep utensils sorted into an arrangement that keeps them easy to locate. The NKBA recommends that storage accessories be used to enhance storage based on the user's requirements.

Pantry Storage

A pantry is a great storage feature. There are many different styles of pantries, including tall cabinets, closets, and small rooms. Generally, a pantry should be placed outside of the work triangle

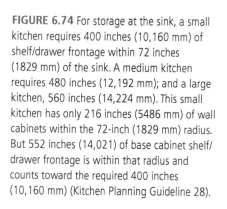

FIGURE 6.74 For storage at the sink, a small kitchen requires 400 inches (10,160 mm) of shelf/drawer frontage within 72 inches (1829 mm) of the sink. A medium kitchen requires 480 inches (12,192 mm); and a large kitchen, 560 inches (14,224 mm). This small kitchen has only 216 inches (5486 mm) of wall cabinets within the 72-inch (1829 mm) radius. But 552 inches (14,021) of base cabinet shelf/drawer frontage is within that radius and counts toward the required 400 inches (10,160 mm) (Kitchen Planning Guideline 28).

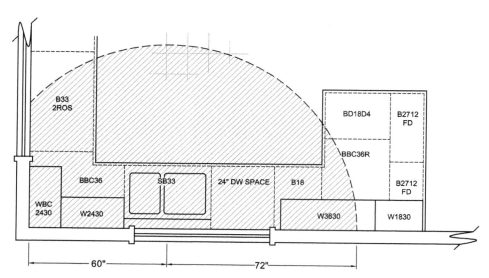

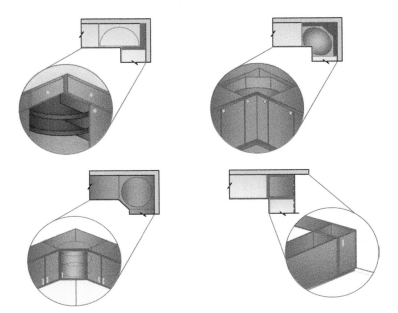

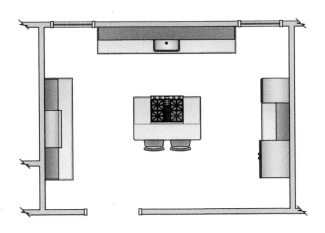

FIGURE 6.75 In a kitchen that features corner cabinets, plan at least one corner cabinet with functional storage (A). An unfitted kitchen may have no corner cabinets and is not subject to this guideline (B) (Kitchen Planning Guideline 29).

so that the tall unit does not interfere with the flow of food preparation. Standard tall cabinet sizes are 12, 18, and 24 inches deep, but custom cabinets can be made at any depth. Different accessories (pull-out shelves and racks, turntables) can be added to increase the effectiveness of the storage unit. Unlike wall and base cabinets, pantry cabinets allow for a large portion of stored items to be within the reach range of users, offering a universal option.

Some clients may really appreciate a walk-in pantry that has open shelving within a small room. This type of storage can accommodate items bought in bulk as well as oversized pots and serving pieces. You should plan shelf depth, which can range from 6 to 30 inches (152 to 762 mm), to accommodate the items being stored. Ideally, the door to a walk-in pantry will allow for a 32-inch (813 mm) clear opening, which will enhance the access to the space and allow for a usable clear floor space in the pantry.

Guidelines and Access Standards for Storage

The Kitchen Planning Guidelines and Access Standards that are particularly relevant to work arrangements, counter areas, and storage are Guidelines 3, 4, 5, 24, 25, 26 27, 28, and 29. They all appear in Appendix A.

SERVING AND DINING

Hopefully, after the food is prepared, it is eaten. There are many ways to serve a meal and dine. The designer should determine the most frequent way the household dines and any special dining and entertaining options. Probably each household will serve and eat meals in a variety of ways, depending on the time of day, the schedules of household members, their ages, and the dining situation. Many lifestyles have become much more informal, but people still like to dress up a table and enjoy using the good china on special occasions.

Serving involves getting the food from the preparation area to the dining area. Some of the ways this might be done are:

- Food is moved from pots and pans into serving bowls and platters and brought to the dining table or buffet area.
- Food could be placed on individual plates and brought to each diner in the dining area.
- For some households with erratic schedules, food might be left in the pots and pans or in warming drawers, and diners help themselves to it when they have time or are hungry.

FIGURE 6.76 A variety of storage organizers are available to help make items easy to see and reach: (a) customizable drawer for dishes and condiments, (b) backsplash rail systems hold cups and a cookbook tray, (c) roll-out tray and lid dividers, (d) rotating shelves.
(a), (b), and (d) courtesy of Hafele America Co.; (c) courtesy of Masterbrand

- Beverages have to be prepared also. Each glass could be prepared and brought to the dining area. Ice could be provided and pitchers brought to the table or buffet. Or everyone could fix his/her own drink before sitting down.

Serving also involves preparing the table and necessary items for the meal. This could include:

- Retrieving dishes, glassware, and flatware for the meal and setting the table or arranging it for a buffet.
- Arranging table linens or paper napkins so the diners can use them during the meal.

- Locating and arranging condiments that will be served with the meal, including salt and pepper.
- Flowers, candles, and special lighting might also be included in a meal.

Design Recommendations for Serving

There are a lot of items needed to serve a meal and, although it is desirable, a special serving area is not required for a well-designed kitchen. However, the components of a serving area should be considered, even if a special area is not planned. The main components are storage and counter space.

Storage

Storage is needed for dishes, glassware, flatware, serving pieces, linens, and accessories. Often this storage is provided in other centers. For example, dishes, glassware, and flatware are stored in the sink center as part of the cleanup activities. This is the last place these items are used, so it is a convenient and suitable storage option. However, the designer should consider the ease of retrieving these items while food preparation is occurring. Ideally, these items should be stored so that they can be accessed without interfering in the work area.

Counter Space

Counter space may be found in all parts of the kitchen and used as part of the serving process. Counter space beside the refrigerator may hold glasses while beverages are being prepared. That same space may be needed to hold items that have been refrigerated, but also needed for the meal (butter, pickles, etc.). Counter space next to the cooking surface and oven will be needed to hold serving platters and bowls.

Past recommendations for a serving area range from 15 to 36 inches (381 to 914 mm) of counter space. Some of this can be combined with the recommended landing area at the cooking surface, oven, and refrigerator. Increasing these areas beyond the minimum landing area requirements would help make any of these areas better suited for serving (see Figure 6.77).

Placement

Whether a special serving area is provided or serving activities occur throughout the kitchen, consider the traffic flow from these areas to the dining area. As mentioned previously, serving should be able to occur without interfering with food preparation work flow. Placing the serving area outside the work triangle would be suitable. If serving is part of the kitchen, consider increasing both the refrigeration center and the cooking center in order to get extra storage and counter area.

Beverage Station or Bar

Planning a beverage station or bar might be a suitable option in some larger kitchens or entertaining areas. The beverage station or bar might include the following: a small auxiliary sink, undercounter refrigerator, ice machine and/or wine cooler, counter area, and storage for glassware and beverages. This separate area allows family members to get beverages anytime, including mealtime, without interfering with the cook. It can be set up and stocked for guests who serve themselves or are served by a host.

The beverage station might be located in a kitchen area, outside the work triangle, but near the dining and social areas. If it will be primarily used to serve guests during entertaining, it could be located in a different room, such as a living or dining area.

Butler's Pantry

A butler's pantry was frequently planned into large homes of the past. It was a staging area between the kitchen and the formal dining room, where food was placed before it was served (by a butler). Typically, it contained storage for dishes, serving pieces, and silver, and a counter area on which the food and dishes were placed both before and after the meal.

A similar area is planned into some homes today (see Figure 6.78). It includes storage and counter space, but it might also include a warming drawer, auxiliary sink, wine cooler, and other items associated with a beverage station. Some also have a second dishwasher so that clean up can occur as the dishes are being removed from the table.

FIGURE 6.77 Serving could be staged on the island or on the counter beside the wall oven. Extra storage for serving pieces is accessible from both areas.

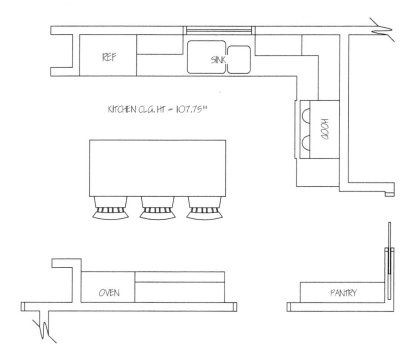

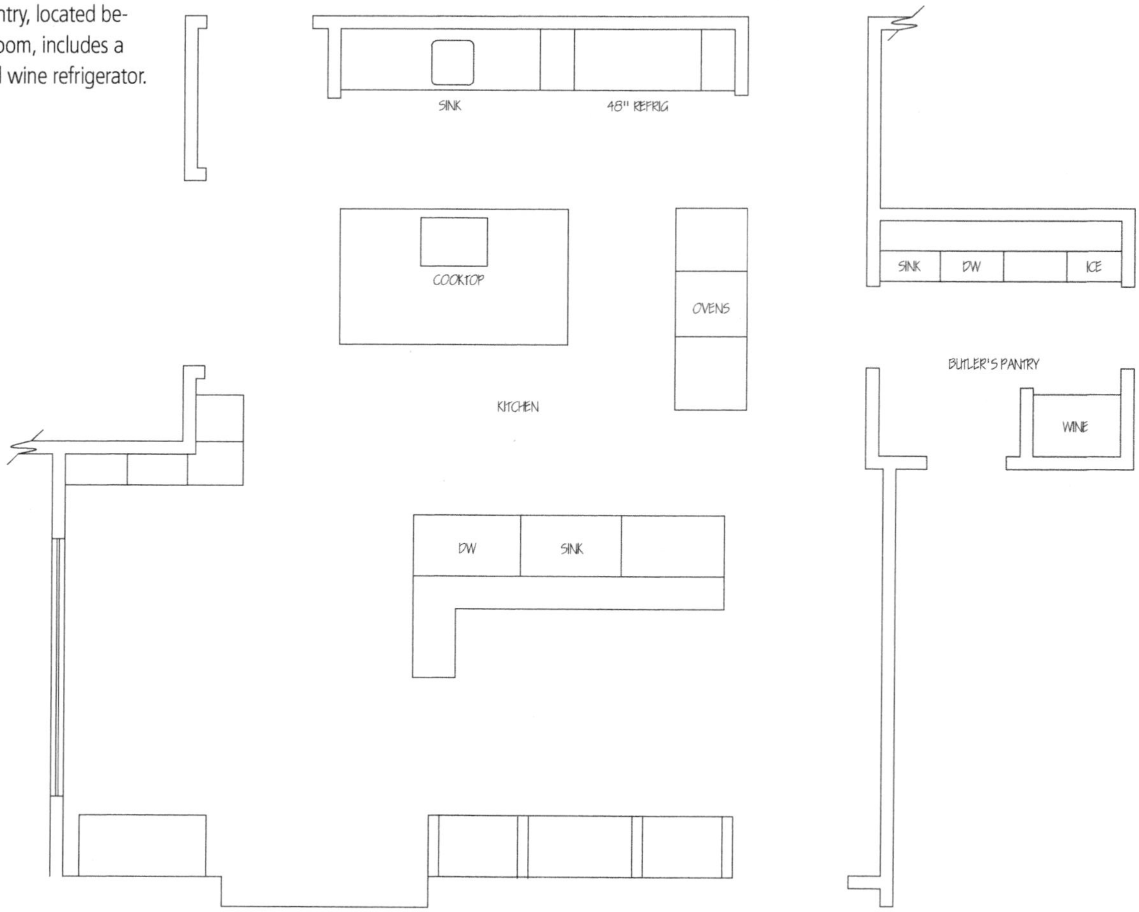

KITCHEN CLG. HT = 107.75"

FIGURE 6.78 This butler's pantry, located between the kitchen and dining room, includes a sink, dishwasher, ice maker, and wine refrigerator.

Another configuration might be to provide only counter space and display storage. This area could be used as a space to serve a buffet or to set out dessert for a meal. Any area used as a buffet area should have between 48 and 60 inches (1219 and 1524 mm) of clear floor space to allow for one person to stand at the buffet line and another to walk behind carrying a plate full of food.

Design Recommendations for Dining

Households may eat in many different locations and ways. Whether it is sit-down dining or eating in front of the TV, the designer should try to plan the kitchen space so that it considers the dining habits and desires of the client.

Placement

As mentioned in previous sections, the kitchen location should be planned with consideration for the formal and informal dining areas, if the house includes both. Location is important to make serving convenient and to have the meal go smoothly.

Consider the view to other parts of the house and to the outdoors while in the dining area. If the cook is the chaotic type who has managed to get everything on the table at the right temperature, but not gotten all the pots in the dishwasher, it may be best to shield the view from the dining area to the work part of the kitchen. Pleasant views to a garden or play space may be more enjoyable. Informal dining spaces in the kitchen can be convenient and encourage socializing among household members and guests (see Figure 6.79).

Seating

Most people enjoy sitting down to eat, although standing up to finish off a bowl of cereal during the morning rush may be common in some households. Several different seating arrangements are common and require minimum clearances for the dining area and the diner.

The minimum space needed for a place setting is 24 inches (610 mm) wide. This allows space for a plate, flatware, and glassware arranged in the typical setting. A more generous space would be 30 inches (762 mm) wide. This would allow for a little more arm space while eating and would allow for a more formal table setting. The 30-inch (762 mm) width would also allow for a person in a wheelchair to sit. See Chapter 8 for more detail on seating.

FIGURE 6.79 Seating in kitchen can be planned into the kitchen for dining and other social activities.

Design by NKBA member Jennifer L. Gilmer, CKD

The size and shape of the table will determine how many place settings and people can be served. A banquette, with some bench seating, can be planned in a corner or bay window area. Figure 6.80 illustrates various sizes of tables and the number of seats that can comfortably fit at the table.

The depth of the place setting depends on the height of the table. For a table height at 30 inches (762 mm), allow 18 inches (457 mm) depth for a seated diner (see Figure 6.81). This depth below the table will provide the knee space to allow the diner to sit comfortably and the top area will provide a generous space for a place setting or serving pieces.

When seating is at a raised counter, allow 15 inches of depth at a 36 inch (914 mm) high counter and 12 inches (305 mm) at a 42 inch (1067 mm) high counter. Clearances below the counter will allow leg room for the tall chairs and stools used at these counter height. Such counters will not be deep enough to accommodate a typical place setting, but can be used to serve snacks and small meals.

Clearances for Dining

The required floor space needed for seating depends on the type of chair and the height of the table or counter. A typical table is 30 inches (762 mm) high, and a person seated in a chair at this height table requires 18 to 24 inches (457 to 610 mm) of clear floor space beyond the table edge, depending on the size of the person and the type of chair used. An eating counter used for dining could be 36 inches high, which is the same as a typical work surface counter, or 42 inches (1067 mm). Seating height should be sized to match the counter height. A knee space depth of 12 to 18 inches (305 to 457 mm) is needed, decreasing as the height increases.

In order for the person to get up out of the chair, a 32-inch (813 mm) space is required from the edge of the table to a wall or other obstruction (see Figure 6.82). If a person must edge past a seated diner or move behind a chair parallel to the table, then 36 inches (914 mm) of space will be needed between the edge of the table and the wall or obstruction. Allow at least 44 inches (1118 mm) if a person needs to walk behind the seated diner. This would allow the person to walk perpendicular to the table and would be the most convenient clearance. A distance of 60 to 72 inches (1524 to 1823 mm) would be generous and allow for a server to serve the table or for a person with a mobility aid to maneuver around the table space.

Guidelines and Access Standards for Serving and Dining

The Kitchen Planning Guidelines and Access Standards that apply to dining areas are Guidelines 8 and 9, which can be found in Appendix A.

THAT'S ENTERTAINING

Entertaining is an important part of many lifestyles today and the kitchen is a crucial element. The aim is to provide good food and conversation in a pleasant setting. Informal entertaining often means the hosts, and sometimes the guests, prepare and serve the food. Kitchens that are open to social spaces facilitate interaction and encourage the guests to participate in the preparations.

Two entertaining trends require some special consideration in kitchen design—using a caterer and outdoor entertaining. When a caterer is used frequently for entertaining, the kitchen might include some special features that can accommodate the caterer's requirements. When preparing food and dining outdoors is a preferred way of informal entertaining, the outdoor kitchen can add to the convenience and ambiance of the event.

Kitchens for Caterers

Caterers provide several different types of services that can help take the worry out of having a party. They typically provide the food, table service, and servers to make sure the event is successful. Often the caterer will prepare much of the food in their facilities and bring it to the home. In

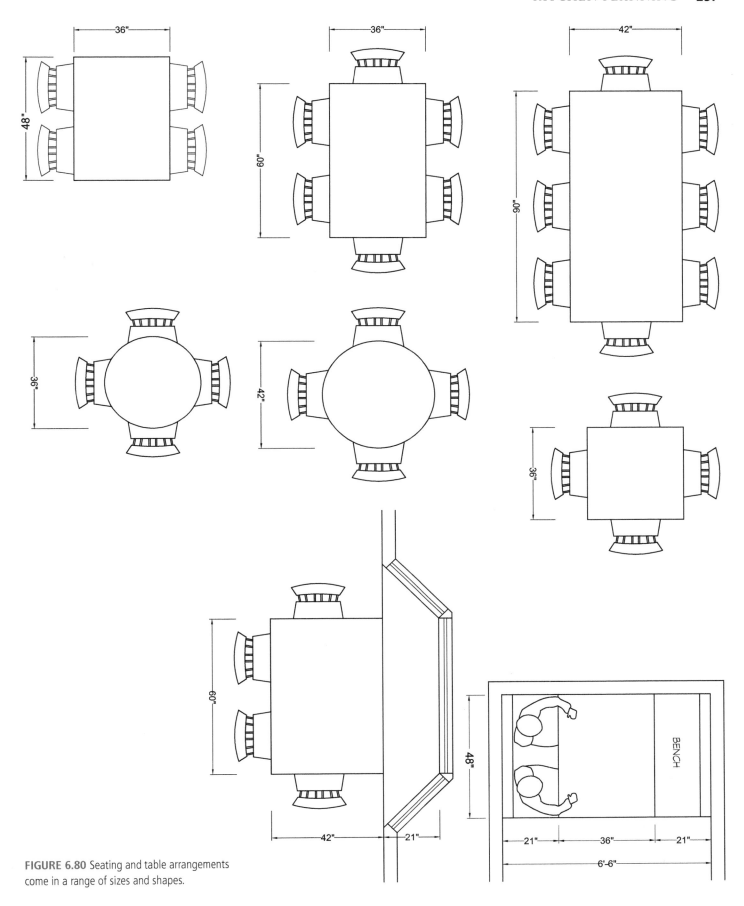

FIGURE 6.80 Seating and table arrangements come in a range of sizes and shapes.

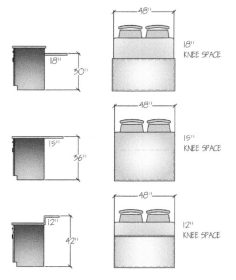

FIGURE 6.81 This chart diagrams the height and depth of different seating options (Kitchen Planning Guideline 9).

other cases, some or all food will be prepared in the host's kitchen. The menu and quantity of food help to determine where and how the food is prepared.

Here are some ideas for a kitchen that a caterer can work in:

- The kitchen should be located with easy access to an outside entrance that can be used for unloading and loading food and supplies.
- A kitchen that is separate from the social areas allows caterers to work in the kitchen without interfering with guests and entertaining. The sight lines and sound insulation need to be considered.
- Wide work aisles, at least 48 inches (1219 mm), help the catering crew circulate and work at different centers simultaneously.
- Larger appliances handle some of the caterers' trays and equipment. Check the interior size of refrigerators and ovens to make sure they can accommodate larger pans and trays.
- A warming drawer holds prepared food at a serving temperature.
- Expanded counter space may be needed for larger preparation tasks.
- A separate beverage station, including an ice machine and extra refrigeration, allows beverages to be prepared outside any food preparation areas.
- A large serving area may be needed for a setup space.
- The caterer may need additional space to store coats, boxes, trays, and supplies.

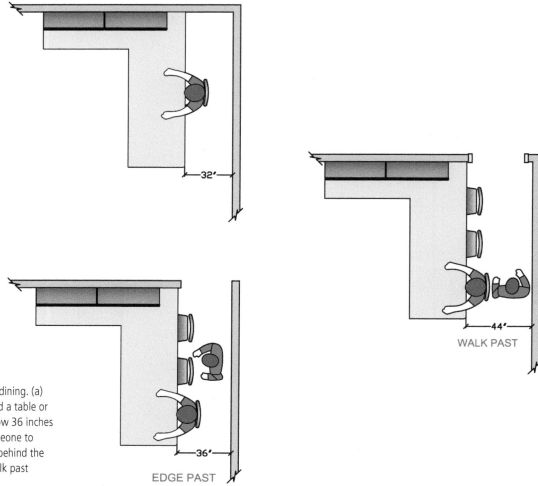

FIGURE 6.82 Traffic clearances at dining. (a) Allow 32 inches of clearance behind a table or counter, if there is no traffic, (b) allow 36 inches behind the table or counter for someone to edge past, and (c) allow 44 inches behind the table or counter for someone to walk past (Kitchen Planning Guideline 8).

Outdoor Kitchens

Cooking outdoors is a great way to entertain and serve a wide variety of meals. Grilling foods is an important food preparation method today and many people prefer to do this outside, to reduce smoke and odors indoors. We can cook outside with just a grill, but there are so many more possibilities that a designer can use to create an exciting cooking experience. The food preparation in an outdoor kitchen may be modified from the typical food preparation sequence, and many of the Kitchen Planning Guidelines we have just examined can be adjusted to suit the requirements of the client.

Location

An outdoor kitchen is often planned next to or close to the kitchen of the house. This will increase the efficiency of extending water, gas, and electrical utilities to the area. It will also be efficient for a cook who prepares part of the meal in the indoor kitchen and brings it to the outdoor eating area.

Examine the overall design of the private outdoor areas to consider how to integrate the kitchen with other outdoor living areas, such as a pool or other landscape feature. Patio or deck areas will be needed for dining and conversation areas if the outdoor kitchen is part of the outdoor entertaining area. Typically, the outdoor area is first a socializing space and second, a cooking area. Safety and separation between the heat of the grill and those who are socializing should be a primary safety concern.

The inclusion of shelter over an outdoor kitchen may depend on the climate and location of the house. How often does it rain? How hot does it get? Is shade needed? Will the clients be using the outdoor kitchen all year long or will they need to winterize the kitchen? Are strong winds an issue that might affect the placement of the outdoor kitchen or the grilling unit and related ventilation needs?

Equipment

The gas grill is an essential element in the outdoor kitchen. The size and features of the grill are varied. Many appliance manufacturers have developed outdoor grill units that have the capacity to act as an expanded cooking center. They have a grill and limited counter areas and warming areas. Other cooking equipment might be warming drawers, smokers, and wood burning ovens or grills (see Figure 6.83). Historically, often no mechanical ventilation was planned, so we have

FIGURE 6.83 This outdoor kitchen includes a large rotisserie grill, warming drawer, sink, gas burner, cooktop, stainless cabinetry, and open shelving.

Courtesy of Viking Range Corp.

learned to consider how the smoke from the grill will be dispersed. An enclosed outdoor kitchen can capture the smoke or even funnel it back into the house. An Underwriters Laboratory (UL)–rated ventilation system for outdoor use should be specified.

An undercounter refrigeration unit is a possibility in an expanded outdoor kitchen. The unit should be UL-rated for outdoor use, well insulated, and made of a weather-resistant material, such as stainless steel.

While a sink may be desirable, it requires connection to water and sewer lines. Dishwashers are also available with ratings for outdoor use. Plumbing connections should be easily accessible, and plans will need to be made for these installations. One option that does not require a complete plumbing installation is a sink with a connection to the outdoor hose system. If the sink is insulated and covered, it can double as a cooler. Make sure any sink that is used is made of a material that can endure outdoor conditions and is easy to maintain. A heavy-gauge stainless steel is often recommended.

Specify cabinets and counters that are weather resistant. Cabinets might be made of a light concrete material, stainless steel, solid surface, or teak. Borrowing from the boating industry, cabinetry is available made from resins that resist weather. Among the countertop choices are granite, slate, concrete, stainless steel, solid surface, or tile. Consider storage for carts that can help in transporting food. Leveling the ground, deck, or patio surface before the installation of cabinets or allowing for the natural irregularities of the outdoor flooring becomes critical.

Heating units might be desirable in some regions. Portable patio heaters that use gas or propane are available, and fireplaces and fire pits might provide a focal point as well as heat to the area. All of these should be designed so that guests are not in danger of being burned. Check local codes to determine if these heating devices are permitted in your client's area.

Often, equipment in an outdoor kitchen will need to be "winterized," meaning it may need to be disconnected and removed from the outdoor area during extremely cold weather. Help the client plan where these items will be stored during this time.

Space Planning

Typically, the grill is located at the center of the work flow in an outdoor kitchen. Landing areas should be planned on both sides of any cooking appliance and on both sides of the sink. If food preparation will actually occur in the outdoor kitchen, provide a 36-inch (914 mm) preparation space.

Because some outdoor kitchens are compact, following the guidelines for a work triangle may not be feasible. However, clear floor space should be provided in front of all of the major appliances and fixtures, and hot grills and appliances should have restricted access from noncooks. Often more than one person is working in an outdoor kitchen and work centers or zones may actually be safer and more functional if they are separated. Follow recommended clearances for work aisles, walkways, and seating. When outdoor decks and patios are planned on several levels, make sure extra-wide traffic space is planned near level changes without rails. Also, give careful consideration to how the level changes are executed for the various abilities of clients and their guests.

A KITCHEN WHERE YOU NEED IT

The modern kitchen continues to represent the heart of the home, but lifestyle considerations and house design have created a need for kitchen components to be planned throughout the house. There are outpost kitchens in areas like the bedroom, bathroom, home office, or studio. If a client is interested in having the convenience of one of these kitchens, carefully consider what specific features are needed. Review local zoning requirements and building codes before planning any outpost kitchen to determine if it will constitute a second kitchen, and if that is permissible or will affect the classification of the home as a single-family house.

Morning Kitchen

A morning kitchen in the bedroom and/or bathroom area provides a place to prepare the first coffee of the day or perhaps an evening snack. Especially if the private area is located a significant distance from the main kitchen, a morning kitchen can add convenience. Coffee, juice, toast, bagels, or pastries can be prepared right in the bedroom while completing the morning routine and without having to go to the kitchen. For some, medicines need to be taken first thing in the morning or at night and with food or beverages that could be stored in a morning kitchen. A morning kitchen is often part of a master suite, but it could also be convenient in a guest suite used by a caregiver or a relative staying for an extended time. A juice bar would provide cold refreshments and could be planned close to an exercise space or home spa.

Mini-Kitchen

Other outpost or mini-kitchens might be located near semiprivate or public spaces in the home. Locating a kitchen at point-of-use in a family or game room adds flexibility and improves access to users of various sizes and abilities. A home office or studio space located in a basement or attic, or in an accessory unit, could benefit from a small kitchen space in which to prepare snacks and beverages for someone frequently working at home. Home recreational areas, such as spaces planned for pool or cards, can benefit from a small, convenient kitchen area that makes entertaining go smoothly.

Considerations

A variety of equipment could be included in an outpost kitchen, and the designer should choose items needed for the planned activities. An undercounter refrigerator can fit into a small space and provide enough capacity to accommodate the needs of the outpost kitchen (see Figure 6.84). In some settings, an ice maker also may be needed.

FIGURE 6.84 A mini-kitchen might be located in a family room, game room, home studio, or office.

Courtesy of U- Line Appliances

A small sink can provide water for drinking, limited food preparation, and help with clean up. Water filters and hot water dispensers might add to the convenience of having a sink, and a small dishwasher could help with cleanup. A small microwave can fit into some spaces and provide a way to prepare snacks. If a one- or two-unit cooktop burner is needed, then ventilation should also be provided.

Small appliances may be the best way to accomplish food preparation in an outpost kitchen. A coffeemaker, toaster, toaster oven, blender, or juicer might be used in certain areas. Extra electrical receptacles should be planned for the kitchen area to accommodate the small appliances that might be used.

Storage will be needed for cups, glassware, dishes, silverware, and utensils. Often, cabinets, open shelving, and counter space are provided to accommodate storage and work areas. The amount of storage and workspace needed will depend on the activities planned.

Particular attention should be given to isolating the noise and odors of an outpost kitchen. Extra lighting may be needed and ventilation and insulation may be required.

SUMMARY

As you have seen, there are many decisions and details involved in creating a space plan for a kitchen that is functional and usable. Not only must you consider your client's needs and the physical space you are working in, but you must also consider the selection of product in relation to some of the spatial requirements. You may find that you have to use a certain style of sink, cooktop, or refrigerator, because of space and planning restrictions. On the other hand, you may have to arrange space to accommodate the appliance or activity desired by the client. There may be several ways that the kitchen could be planned, depending on the choices.

Previous chapters presented assessment tools and background information to help you understand your client's needs and desires. In this chapter, you have been presented with numerous NKBA planning guidelines that will further influence your design decisions. The guidelines provide key criteria for effective space planning. However, you may not always be able to meet every guideline. Budget, time, and space restrictions will influence how you incorporate the guidelines within the parameters of each job. Remember to meet any requirements specified in local building codes.

Throughout this chapter and the rest of the book, improved universal access has been incorporated into recommendations and considerations. As a designer, you will work with clients whose needs are individualized. Refer to Chapter 8 for a more extensive list of universal and accessible design concepts arranged according to user groups. This is a great place to look for ideas that might be useful if your client is older, has children, a unique mobility or handedness requirement, or has sensory or cognitive impairments.

Remember that infrastructure requirements also must be considered in planning the kitchen. There are several decisions related to the mechanical systems that must be made in the design of a kitchen. Lighting, ventilation, and placement of receptacles have been referred to in this chapter, but there are more details (and guidelines) related to these areas in Chapter 7 that will affect the planning of the kitchen. Be sure you are familiar with these recommendations and requirements when you start to design a space.

More information about the design process and steps for the final layout of the kitchen are discussed in detail in Chapter 10, "Putting It All Together." Until you have mastered the planning criteria, be prepared to refer to the guidelines and information presented in this chapter throughout the design and planning process. The NKBA's Kitchen Planning Guidelines and the applicable Access Standards can be found in Appendix A.

REVIEW QUESTIONS

1. Identify and describe three types of closed kitchen arrangements and three types of open arrangements. (See "Types of Kitchens" page 196)

2. What are the sizes for a small, medium, and large kitchen? (See under "Size of Kitchens" page 200)

3. Identify and discuss the elements that make up a work center. (See under "The Center Concept" page 203)

4. Identify and discuss the Kitchen Planning Guidelines associated with the entry, work aisles, and circulation space of the kitchen (See "Design Recommendations for Traffic and Work Aisles" page 206)

5. Identify and discuss the Kitchen Planning Guidelines associated with the sink center. (See "Design Recommendations for the Sink Center" page 211)

6. Identify and discuss the Kitchen Planning Guidelines associated with the refrigeration center. (See "Design Recommendations for the Refrigeration Center" page 219)

7. Identify and discuss the Kitchen Planning Guidelines associated with the cooking centers. (See "Design Recommendations for Surface Cooking" page 222; "Design Recommendation for Microwave Cooking" page 226; "Design Recommendations for Oven Cooking" page 228)

8. Identify and discuss the Kitchen Planning Guidelines that would help in arranging the kitchen work areas and planning the counter areas of the kitchen. (See "Arranging the Centers" page 229)

9. Identify and discuss the storage principles. (See under "Storage" page 235)

10. Identify and describe the Kitchen Planning Guidelines associated with planning the storage in the kitchen. (See "Amount of Storage" page 238)

11. Calculate the amount of storage in a small kitchen. (See "Example of Storage Calculations" page 240)

12. Identify and discuss the Kitchen Planning Guidelines associated with planning the dining areas. (See "Design Recommendations for Dining" page 255)

Mechanical Planning

Planning for electrical and mechanical equipment in the kitchen is more essential than ever. Changing lifestyles, a surge of technology, and an increase in the number of activities, fixtures, and electronic devices in the kitchen result in a space that demands attention to the systems that form the structure for this equipment. Without a clear and detailed plan, necessary components of such a system can be overlooked, leading to disappointment on the part of the client or added costs if features need to be redone. Consider the mechanical features of the kitchen early in the project in order to ensure that they are in place before the installation of cabinetry, fixtures, and finishes is completed.

This chapter describes the general mechanical considerations from a kitchen design and planning perspective. In each section you will find many important factors to keep in mind as you consider the mechanical systems needed for kitchen activities and to meet your client's desires.

Learning Objective 1: Explain the mechanical systems that should be considered in kitchen planning.

Learning Objective 2: Describe important considerations for planning ventilation and lighting systems for a kitchen.

ELECTRICAL PLANNING

The kitchen wiring and electrical system should be designed to meet not only meet current local codes, but also the needs of the individuals using the home. Whether building or remodeling, use the forms in Chapter 5, "Needs Assessment," to evaluate the electrical needs of the client. Then, consult current codes to see what must be implemented and suggest additional ideas for improving the electrical system to address the future needs of the client. Always review the wiring plan before the walls are enclosed.

Codes

Safety is of prime importance in every home, and following the model electric codes will help ensure safe operation in the kitchen. The National Electric Code (NEC) and the Canadian Electric Code (CEC), which are almost identical, ensure a safe electrical system. Checking the code regulations will assist you as you determine the placement of receptacles and other wiring needs. Be sure to familiarize yourself with the specific required codes for your area.

Wiring

One component of older homes that is typically outdated, especially in homes built before 1973, is the electrical wiring. Home wiring added from 1965–1973 might be aluminum, which has been found to develop fire hazards. Copper wire is the wire of choice today, so if aluminum wire is present, the entire home must be rewired as part of the remodeling project. Updating the wiring will ensure that the electrical system is safe and meets current electrical codes.

Signs of inadequate or outdated wiring include:

- The home is over 30 years old.
- A fuse box is present instead of a circuit breaker panel box.
- The system has only two wires and therefore is not grounded.
- Aluminum wire is present.
- No ground fault circuit interrupters are present.
- Lights flicker when an appliance is turned on.
- Motors overheat or sound like they are bogged down.
- Appliances heat slowly.
- Fuses blow or circuit breakers trip often.
- Too few switches, receptacles, or lights are present.
- Extension cords must be used.
- The electrical supply is 100 amps or less.

Wiring requires careful planning because its placement affects both functional and aesthetic qualities of the home (Figure 7.1). Adequate wiring also includes a sufficient electrical supply to meet the household's needs. Even fairly new homes may need a substantial update to the wiring and electrical system.

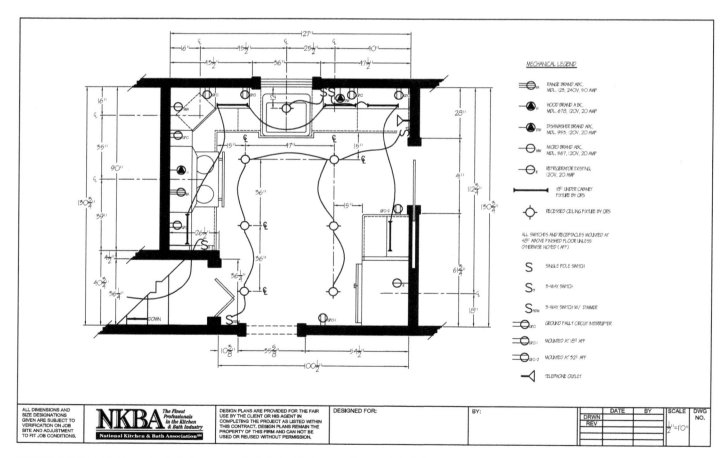

FIGURE 7.1 An accurate mechanical plan ensures that all electrical connections are included.

Source: NKBA

With the addition of more equipment in the kitchen, plan for the wiring needs before walls are finished. Here are a few examples:

- Under cabinet, soffit, and floor lighting
- Built-in appliances
- Toe kick heaters
- Receptacles in an appliance garage or pantry
- Communication equipment
- Computer or laptop

Two terms used when discussing electrical service are voltage and amperes. *Voltage* (volts) is the force that moves the electrons along the wire. *Amperes* (amps) is the quantity or amount of current flowing. At times during storms or power outages your client's electrical system may experience a surge in the voltage when the power flickers or is reinstated. To protect sensitive electronic components in some appliance control panels, recommend a surge protection system for appliances. This is especially important in areas that are prone to power outages or fluctuation.

Begin by determining the size of the electrical service and the number of circuits that service will support. Many existing homes have between a 60- and 100-amp service. For today's homes, a 200-amp service is more appropriate. An electrician can evaluate the service for you, and the level of service should also be stamped on the fuse box or circuit breaker panel.

The circuit breaker panel (or fuse box in older homes) is where the electric service is divided into circuits that supply electricity throughout the home. Each breaker is rated for either 120-volt or 240-volt service and certain amperage. Each room of the home may include a number of different types of circuits and some receptacles may even be serviced by two different circuits. The use of two different circuits, or split wiring, allows continued use of an outlet even if a problem occurs with one of the circuits. Circuits can be of three different types.

General or Lighting Circuits

General or lighting circuits handle lighting and most wall receptacles in the home.

> **Lighting Circuits:** Building codes require 3 watts of light per square foot (300 mm²) of living space. This requirement can be met by:
> - One 15-amp circuit for each 600 square feet (55.74m²) of living space, or
> - One 20-amp circuit per 800 square feet (74.32m²) of living space
>
> **Receptacle Circuits:** The rule of thumb for including receptacles is:

- 12 receptacles for a 15-amp circuit
- 16 receptacles for a 30-amp circuit

Small-Appliance Circuits

These circuits are designed to accommodate small appliances. The recommendation for a kitchen is as follows: receptacles installed in a kitchen to serve countertop surfaces shall be supplied by not less than two small-appliance branch circuits, either or both of which shall also be permitted to supply receptacle outlets in the same kitchen and in other rooms as specified.

Individual or Dedicated Circuits

Circuits designated for an individual appliance are either 120 volt or 240 volt.

Examples of individual circuits:
- 240-volt circuit: Range, cooktop, on-demand water heaters, wall ovens
- 120-volt circuit: Disposer, dishwasher, microwave oven, refrigerator, exhaust fan

Not only are consumers bringing more electrical devices into the kitchen, but also replacement appliances may have different electrical requirements than the previous ones. Newer models of appliances that previously used 120 volts may now require 240 volts. For example, clothes washers that heat water to higher temperatures or small ovens that have large power requirements now need 240 volts. Be sure these new circuits are in place before the finishing work is completed.

Receptacles

Consumers often find that rooms in the home do not have an adequate number of receptacles. In addition to the standard kitchen appliances, such as toasters and coffee makers, many families now have a collection of other small appliances they use for food preparation.

The International Residential Code (IRC) specifies that receptacles should be installed at each wall counter space that is 12 inches (305 mm) or wider, and receptacles shall be installed so that at no point along the wall line, measured horizontally, is more than 24 inches (600 mm) from a receptacle in that space. Receptacles in the kitchen to service countertop surfaces shall be supplied by not less than two separate small appliance branch circuits.

Receptacles shall be located not more than 20 inches (508 mm) above the countertop (such as in an overhead cabinet). If the receptacle assembly is installed in the countertop, it shall be listed for the application. Receptacle outlets shall not be installed in a face-up position in the work surfaces

The universal design reach range recommendation places receptacles below 44 inches (1125 mm) from the floor, which would place the top of the receptacle only 8 inches (200 mm) above the standard 36-inch (900 mm) counter height. Receptacles shall be permitted to be mounted not more than 12 inches (305 mm) below the countertop in construction designed for the physically impaired and for island and peninsular countertops where the countertop is flat across its entire surface and there are not means to mount a receptacle within 20 inches (508 mm) above the countertop, such as in an overhead cabinet. Receptacles mounted below the countertop shall not be located where the countertop extends more than 6 inches (152 mm) beyond its support base. See Figure 7.1 for an example of spacing.

For island and peninsular countertop spaces, at least one receptacle outlet shall be installed at each island countertop space with a long dimension of 24 inches (610 mm) or greater by 12 inches (305 mm) or greater. A peninsular countertop is measured from the connecting edge. Countertop spaces separated by range tops, refrigerators, or sinks shall be considered as separate countertop spaces in applying the requirements. Where a range, counter-mounted cooking unit, or sink is installed in an island or peninsular countertop and the depth of countertop behind the range, counter-mounted cooking unit, or sink is less than 12 inches (305 mm), these appliances have divided the counter top into two separate pieces which must comply with the spacing requirements.

If you are specifying an appliance garage or other appliance cabinets, such as a cabinet with a lift for a large mixer, installing receptacles within those cabinets will make it possible to plug in appliances where they are stored. Receptacles may also be needed in upper cabinets if you are planning to add such items as a built-in television or a microwave shelf. Keep in mind that receptacles that are not readily accessible because of an appliance fastened in place, appliance garages, behind ranges, or where appliances are occupying a dedicated space are not considered in the receptacles required in the space.

Appliance receptacles installed for a specific appliance, such as laundry equipment, shall be installed within 6 feet (1829 mm) of the intended location of the appliance.

Ground Fault Circuit Interrupters

Anytime water and electricity are in close proximity, electrical safety is an issue. To improve kitchen electrical safety, the International Residential Code requires ground fault circuit interrupter (GFCI) receptacles (Figure 7.2) on counter walls as well as near a water source. Check local codes for proper placement. GFCIs reduce the hazards of electrical shock by breaking the circuit when the device senses the slightest disruption in the electrical flow. GFCI receptacles fit in the same space as the standard receptacles, but they need to be appropriately wired. Kitchen Planning Guideline 30 relates to GFCIs and can be found in Appendix A.

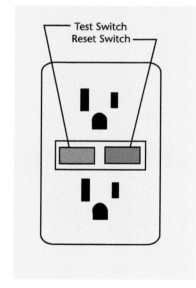

Test Switch
Reset Switch

FIGURE 7.2 The IRC requires that GFCI (ground fault circuit interrupter) protection be in place for all receptacles servicing countertop surfaces within the kitchen.

Communications

Communication systems are becoming a standard component in the kitchen, so consider the wiring needed for these components early in the project. Linking the kitchen to the outside world and other parts of the house requires special wiring and planning. New structured or bundled wiring packages provide all the wiring needed for home communications and entertainment together. It makes installation easier because only one wire bundle needs to be installed rather than installing each wire individually.

Home intercom networks are becoming common, and the kitchen is a logical location. Consider the users when deciding on the most appropriate type and placement of the intercom unit. It should be accessible by all family members.

A telephone or charging station for a cell phone in the kitchen is standard today, so wiring for the telephone may already be available. The new kitchen plan, however, may require moving the phone line, along with the necessary electrical line, to a new location. Your client may wish to have a computer in the kitchen (Figure 7.3), which will probably need an Internet connection, so discuss with your client the type of connection they might need. A base station for wireless Internet capability may be requested. In addition, more appliances are including the capability of being Internet ready, so wiring for the Internet now is advisable. More information about planning for a computer and home office space is included in Chapter 9.

As families include more activities in the kitchen, the television becomes a familiar feature (Figure 7.4). Linking the kitchen to the home cable or satellite system allows family members to keep up with the news while involved with other kitchen activities. Connections for a DVD player and speakers or sound system are also part of the entertainment package. If the client does not want electronic equipment located in the kitchen space, installing speakers in the ceiling or wall, either recessed or wall mounted, that connect to home electronics located elsewhere will allow the sound to be projected into the kitchen.

GAS

Gas is used for many home heating systems and is also a popular cooking fuel in the kitchen. Gas is delivered to homes in one of two forms: *natural gas,* which is delivered to the home through below ground piping, but is not available to all residential areas, and *propane gas* (LP gas), which requires a storage tank on the site that must to be refilled on a periodic basis. If your client desires to have gas cooking equipment in the kitchen, keep the following considerations in mind:

- If your client is installing gas in the kitchen for the first time, make sure gas lines are installed before the finish work on the floors and walls is completed.

FIGURE 7.3 A computer work station in the kitchen.

Design by NKBA member Tim Scott; code-signers: Erica Westeroth, CKD, NCIDQ, and Sheena Hammond

FIGURE 7.4 Televisions are common in to-day's kitchens.

Design by NKBA member Terri Schmidt; codesigners: Linda Eberle, CKD, CBD, and Keven Schmidt

- Current gas lines can be adjusted or relocated without too much difficulty because of the use of flexible pipe. A gas range can generally be relocated up to 6 feet from the old range connection. These changes should be decided early in the remodeling process if you would like the connector concealed behind a wall or under the floor.
- Check to make sure the gas appliances you specify fit the type of gas delivered to the home. Gas ranges and cooktops must be equipped with different orifices according to the type of gas used.
- Don't forget to include space for the gas shutoff valve, which should be located very near the gas device.
- Whenever a gas appliance is moved, be sure to cap the gas line to prevent a gas leak and possible explosion.
- When designing a kitchen with a gas range or cooktop, recommend an outside exhaust ventilation system with the equipment. See the section on Ventilation in this chapter for more details.

HEATING

While there are many ways in which to add heat to a kitchen, if necessary, the first step is to take measures to reduce heat loss by sealing leaks, improving insulation in exterior walls, and upgrading the windows. See Chapter 2, "Infrastructure Considerations," and Chapter 3, "Environmental and Sustainability Considerations," for information on energy-efficiency measures.

Types of Heaters

Heating systems for the kitchen come in a wide variety of types. They vary as to installation needs, space requirements, energy sources, responsiveness, comfort, and heating mode. Some of the most common choices of systems for a kitchen are listed here.

Central Heating Systems

Many homes have a forced air central heating system that also services the kitchen space. Forced air system heating ducts are often used as the cooling ducts as well. Locate central heating duct vents such that they do not interfere with the kitchen design or the user. Some vent location possibilities are shown in Figure 7.5.

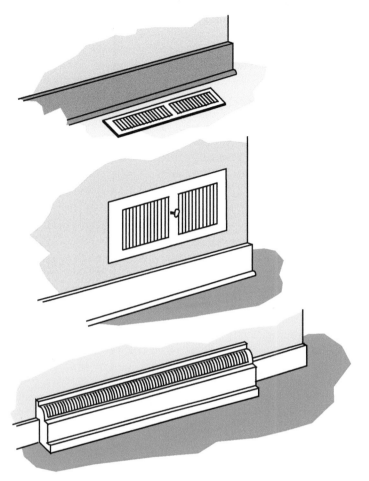

FIGURE 7.5 Locations for central heating and cooling vents.

Electric Toe Kick Heater

A small electric or hydronic heater installed in the toe kick space below the cabinets can provide comfortable supplemental heat to the feet and floor area. Locate these heaters where a little extra heat is needed. Select a heater with a variable temperature setting and on/off switch so that it can be adjusted to the user's comfort level. A provision for this type of heater needs to be made when the cabinet is selected and installed.

Individual Baseboard Heaters

Baseboard heaters used as a permanent installation are typically long heating units attached close to the baseboards at the floor. These heaters are not connected to a central duct system, but instead work individually for room-by-room heating. The heating for each room can be controlled individually, typically with a wall thermostat to make control more convenient. The efficiency of a baseboard system depends on the type of heater used. One drawback is they can take up valuable floor space. If the current kitchen makes use of baseboard heating, other types of electric heating could take their place in your new plan in order to free up that floor space.

- **Electric baseboard heaters** are an inexpensive heating alternative and use electric power to heat coils within the baseboard unit. Often located under a window, a cooler part of the room, it takes the cold air that falls from the window areas, and by using convection the cool air is drawn into the bottom slots and warmed by the heating coils and fins. Warm air then exits from the top slots of the unit. These heaters allow you to control each room separately, so you only need to heat the room you are in. Electric baseboard heaters used extensively in the home, however, are usually more expensive to operate than gas or some more efficient electric central systems.

- **Hot water (hydronic) baseboard heaters** must have a piping system and a central hot water source to provide hot water to the unit. Hot water is piped through individual baseboard heating units, releasing heat into the room as the water flows through. These heaters are typically an efficient heat source if an efficient boiler is used, and they are used widely in Europe. These baseboard heaters are usually a little larger than the electric baseboard style.

Radiators

Radiators are large, flat rectangular units that fit close to the wall. Radiators in older homes are usually larger than more modern units, so if you encounter these older units, they can be replaced by smaller ones. As with hydronic baseboard heaters, hot water flows through the radiator and heat is released to the air, warming the room. The hot water source for these systems can be integrated with the home's hot water system. Be aware that hot water radiators become very hot, so you do not want them in a high-traffic or tight-traffic areas. Radiators also take up valuable floor space.

Hot water heat is usually a little slower to respond when heat is needed, but it is a very quiet and even heat. These systems may not be conducive to zoning, and require a water source and piping system. If the home uses hydronic heating and you are adding heat to a new or renovated space, it may be difficult to find components that you can retrofit to the home's old system. Steam heating is another type of hot water system, and these systems are not used much today but may be found in some older construction.

Floor Heating Systems

Floor heating systems place heating units under the entire floor space and can be of either the electric or hydronic type. Both deliver a very even and quiet heat without drafts. Heat from these systems is very steady because they do not lose heat as quickly as other systems. Heated floors are comfortable to walk on, especially for anyone who comes through in bare feet needing a late night snack or drink of water. When the feet are warm, the whole body feels warm. Young children also like the warm floors because that is where they end up most of the time.

This type of system is a desirable option for the kitchen because it does not take up wall space, require vents, or interfere with cabinet or furniture placement. These systems can also be zoned, allowing flexibility in the temperature in each room. Because this system does not use ductwork, often a cooling system with ductwork will still need to be added to the home.

Electric floor heating systems consist of a series of heating wires placed just below the floor surface. These systems are easy to install during construction, but can also be retrofitted during a remodeling project. Because of the high cost of electricity, this system could be more expensive to operate.

A hydronic system would be a good choice, if there is hot water heat in other parts of the home. It would be a little more difficult to retrofit into an existing home because you would need to add a boiler or other type of water heating system. These systems place piping through which hot water is pumped, either within or under the flooring material. This floor heating system delivers hot water to the floor and returns cooled water to the boiler (Figures 7.6 and 7.7). The cost to install is high, but they are typically very efficient.

Keep in mind that both the electric and hydronic floor units may raise the height of the floor, so door clearances may need to be adjusted. If cabinets are not going to be replaced, they may need to be adjusted to accommodate the added floor height. When selecting a floor covering to place over floor heaters, some manufacturers do not advise installing wood floors that could be damaged by the excess heat. Tile, stone, or poured surfaces are good options. The massive types of flooring materials take a longer time to heat up but retain the heat for extended periods of time.

Considerations for the Kitchen

When selecting a heating system for the kitchen, keep the following in mind:

- Even if the kitchen is part of the central heating system duct network, consider adding some supplemental heat in colder climates to provide flexibility. This is especially important if the kitchen is at the end of the duct run, on the north side of the house, or if the client tends to

FIGURE 7.6 Tubing for radiant floor systems can be embedded in a concrete slab or installed under floor tiles. Metal plates around the tubing help transfer heat from the tube to the wood.

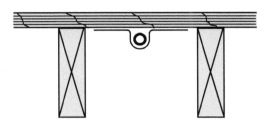

keep the rest of the house cooler than they would like the kitchen. Because the kitchen does produce some of its own heat, in warmer climates you may need to shut off registers and make provisions for more air conditioning in the warmer months.

- When ducting a central heating system into the kitchen, carefully plan in the location of the vents. Floor vents may be difficult to position away from where people will be walking or where food items and dirt will collect. Floor vents may also make it difficult to arrange cabinetry and other kitchen furniture, especially in a small kitchen. Consider the toe kick areas for a duct or register location.
- Registers installed low on the wall will provide heat where cold air collects, but they consume wall space, which is premium in a small kitchen.
- Do not locate the heating vent too close to the kitchen ventilation system as this will reduce the efficiency of both systems.
- Locating vents in the ceiling removes them from the floor and provides a more efficient system for air conditioning, but not all systems allow this option. If ceiling vents are used, locate them so that they do not have a negative effect on the space. For example, do not include vents that direct air down onto a dining table or disperse warm air near the refrigeration units or heating appliances.
- Do not place a heating vent directly over a refrigerator. This adds to the heating load that the refrigerator is trying to disperse.
- If your design incorporates a previously unheated area into part of the kitchen, be sure the central heating system can handle the additional load. If this new space is too far from a central heating system, a supplemental heater may be necessary.

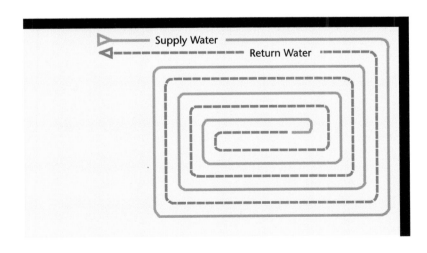

FIGURE 7.7 A simple radiant floor heating system delivers hot water to the floor through one loop, returning cooled water to the boiler through another.

COOLING

Climate will have a substantial impact on which cooling measures are necessary in a kitchen. In cool climates, little, if any, mechanical cooling may be necessary because summertime temperatures may not be extreme enough. In warmer climates, mechanical cooling is, for the most part, an essential component. In addition to cooling, some mechanical units can help remove excess humidity. Cooling systems are not, however, a replacement for good ventilation, as discussed further in this chapter.

Home orientation is another factor that can affect cooling needs. If the kitchen is located on the east or west side of the home, windows, especially large windows or those unprotected by landscaping, can allow excess heat into the space. Therefore, more cooling will be necessary during certain times of the day. Northern windows and southern windows with adequate overhangs should not have the summer time heat gain problems from direct sunlight.

The amount of wall insulation affects cooling needs. Just as an elevated level of insulation will help keep a home warmer in the winter, it will also keep the entire home cooler and require less mechanical cooling in summer.

Appliances can affect cooling needs. Although cooking may add welcomed warmth to the house during cooler weather, it can add to the discomfort in warmer weather. The impact of cooking appliances can be minimized, however, using an exhaust ventilation system to carry away some of the added heat. In addition, other appliances, such as the dishwasher and refrigerator, emit heat that needs to be handled by cooling equipment. Specify well-insulated and efficient appliances to minimize the amount of added heat in a room. In addition, the choice and amount of lighting can affect heat gain in the kitchen.

There are two main types of cooling methods for the kitchen: natural cooling and mechanical cooling. Depending on the climate, one or both methods may need to be incorporated into the plan.

Natural Cooling

The most basic method for natural cooling is to open windows. Heat generated in the home can often be cooled to a comfortable level just by opening a window to let in fresh air. Even on fairly warm days, allowing in cool night air and then closing windows during the heat of the day may be enough to keep a home comfortable. If it is possible to set up cross ventilation, opening windows on two walls of a room or two ends of the home will increase air circulation. A kitchen could also include a door to a patio or deck to open the space to the outdoors for additional fresh air.

Windows with low-e coatings can assist with keeping out the heat from direct sunshine. More information on energy efficient window choices is discussed in Chapters 2 and 3. Your choice of surface materials can affect cooling. Ceramic tile, stone, concrete, and other materials can provide a cool touch to the room. Keep in mind that these materials will also feel cool in colder weather so need to be warmed during that time of year.

Mechanical Cooling

If natural cooling methods cannot give the comfort levels desired, then mechanical means are necessary. The most basic is the fan. Although portable and window fans are available, they are typically not attractive and take up space. A ceiling fan is a better option if the ceiling is tall enough to accommodate one. Ceiling hugger fans are available for standard height ceilings, but above-average-height clients may have an issue with whirling blades just a short distance above their heads. A lighting fixture below the fan will lower the clearance further. Keep in mind that ceiling fans create breezes that will help cool occupants of the room, but the air can also cool food on a table or counter. Avoid placing recessed lighting fixtures above the blades of the fan, because the movement of the blades will create a flickering effect.

Mechanical cooling methods include refrigerated cooling and evaporative cooling. Refrigerated cooling is the most commonly used type of air conditioning in North America. This type of system dehumidifies the air as it cools, which is important for summertime moisture control. For more on moisture problems in kitchens see Chapter 3. Evaporative coolers actually cool by adding moisture to the air and are effective in hot, dry climates. When incorporating either type of cooling system, be aware of how the vent placement may affect the installation of fixtures, cabinetry, and other components. Also evaluate how the vent location will affect the occupants. Cool air blowing directly on people in the rooms will not be very comfortable and cool air blowing on a dining table or counter will quickly chill hot food.

WATER HEATING

The kitchen may not have the hot water demands of a bathroom, but it does use a substantial amount of hot water for various activities. Dishwasher performance depends on very hot water and if the client chooses to lower the hot water tank temperature to save on energy costs, the dishwasher will need to heat the water to make up the difference in temperature. Although most modern dishwashers have a preheater, the user may need to engage the heater on the control panel. Poor dishwashing results may be the result of this feature not being used. Hand washing of dishes also requires hot water, and if you have a laundry area in or near the kitchen, a substantial amount of hot water will be used there. Hot water dispensers are also becoming popular in the kitchen.

Water Heater Location

How quickly hot water arrives to the kitchen appliances and fixtures can vary, depending on the location of the water heater in relation to the kitchen. If the kitchen is located a long distance from the home's water heater, it may take a fair amount of time for the hot water to reach the kitchen fixtures and appliances and waste a large amount of water while waiting for the hot water to arrive. In the case of a dishwasher, if hot water must travel a long distance, the first water entering the dishwasher is probably quite cool, making the starting temperature for water in the dishwasher quite low. Dishwashers function best with 140–150°F (60-66°C) water, so the use of the preheater is even more critical in this type of arrangement.

In many homes, the main water heater is located in the garage and often, but not always, the garage is fairly close to the kitchen for unloading groceries. Therefore, the distance between the water heater and kitchen may not be quite as great as for other rooms like bathrooms.

Selection Considerations

If, after evaluating the hot water situation of your client, you decide you either need to replace or upgrade the hot water source and delivery system, there are a number of factors to consider. These include fuel type, heater type, size, energy efficiency, and cost.

Water Heater Types

Water heaters can be of three basic types—tank, on-demand, and integrated. The type best fits your client's needs depends on their hot water needs, storage space, and home size.

- **Tank:** Tank-type units are what we commonly see in North American homes. This type of water heater keeps water hot on a 24-hour basis, adding more heat when the thermostat is below the set water temperature. Because these standard tank units keep water hot all the time, they are more energy intensive than other types. Some larger households may have one tank located in the garage or basement and a second tank on the second floor or across the house. These tanks vary in size and fuel type and require a space large enough to store the tank.
- **On-Demand:** On-demand water heaters, also called instantaneous or tankless water heaters, are becoming more popular and can also vary in size and fuel type. An on-demand water heater heats the water to a preset temperature as it is used and, therefore, does not require a storage tank. Smaller units, called hot water dispensers, are becoming popular in the kitchen as an

immediate source of near boiling water for instant soups, coffee, tea, and other drinks. These units can be located in a cabinet under the sink or wherever the fixture is located. Whole house on-demand heaters are large units that supply enough water for the entire home and are also wall mounted, typically in the garage or basement. Efficiency ratings of these units can vary. All whole-house units are limited in their capacity, especially the electric type, so be sure to carefully calculate the client's needs if you recommend this type of water heater.

- **Integrated:** Integrated water heating systems heat water for the home heating system as well as general hot water uses. The efficiency of these units depends on how efficiently the water is heated.

Fuel Type

Water heaters can be fueled by a number of different sources, and the type you choose depends on the clients' preferences and where they live. Each has its advantages and disadvantages.

- **Electric:** Electric units are typically less expensive to buy, but an electric unit will generally cost more to operate, unless it is a heat pump heater. If a standard tank-style electric water heater is your only option, it is very important that it be an energy-efficient model. Selecting an efficient model is discussed later in this section. Standard electric units contain two heating elements, one about a third of the way down inside the tank and the other closer to the bottom. If one of the elements burns out, the water heater will not supply hot water at the typical rate.

  The heat pump water heater is a tank-style electric unit that works just like the heat pump home heating systems. It removes heat from the outside air and transfers it to the water to be heated. These are more efficient than a standard electric element tank system but are expensive to buy. They also work best in climates where temperatures are between 40 °F and 90° F. (4.4°–32.2°C) year round.

  On-demand or instantaneous water heaters can also be electric. Whole-house electric units cost about the same as a standard electric tank unit but save on operating costs and last longer. Don't forget that they require an extra circuit for operation.

- **Gas:** Natural gas and propane water heaters are typically more expensive to buy but they cost less to operate. One drawback of the natural gas heater is that you need to have a natural gas pipeline nearby. Propane requires a tank placed in the backyard and is used when gas is desired but natural gas is not available. Gas tank water heaters have a gas burner at the bottom of the tank. The gas burner that heats the tank is ignited by a standing pilot light or a spark ignition. As the gas burns, it heats the water in the tank and releases carbon monoxide (CO) formed during the combustion process. These gas heaters vent out the CO through the center of the water heater to the outside, typically through the roof. This vent can be either a natural draft vent or a forced air vent which boosts the CO release with a fan.

  A more efficient style of tank gas water heater is the condensing heater. Condensing units differ in that they have a sealed combustion chamber inside the tank. As the combustion gases are exhausted, they pass through a coiled steel tube within the water tank, which is a secondary heat exchanger. The hot gases move through the heat exchanger, transferring additional heat to the water. When all of the heat is released the combustion gases cool to a point that water vapor is formed. The resulting vapor is now cool enough to be safely vented through inexpensive plastic plumbing pipe, far less than the stainless steel flues needed for a standard gas water heater. These water heaters have an efficiency of 90–96 percent compared the 60 percent for the average gas tank water heater.

  Most of the larger on-demand heating units are gas fueled. They require a vent to the outdoors and sometimes a large gas line. They are also more expensive to buy than a standard tank gas water heater, but they can save money over time.

- **Solar:** Solar water heaters may be a good option if your client lives in a sunny climate or an area with high electric rates. A typical solar water heating unit has a panel mounted to the roof. The ground is another mounting location, but ground-mounted units are more prone to damage and shading. The solar panels contain tubes where either the water or a heat transfer liquid passes. As the sun strikes the panel, it heats the water or liquid in the tubes. The water then goes to a storage tank for use. The heat transfer liquid passes through a heat exchanger, where the heat is used to heat water in a tank. Keep in mind that solar systems, depending on the climate, may only provide a portion of the hot water needed for a household.

Size

A properly sized water heating unit is essential to provide the necessary quantity of hot water and operate efficiently. Tank-style heaters typically have a capacity of 30–70 gallons (113.6-265 liters) with about 70% of that as usable capacity. Most manufacturers have software that will help you calculate the proper size to install. Sizing will take into consideration the client's flow rate demand, the temperature of the water entering the tank, and the desired output temperature of the water.

The size of on-demand heaters is rated by the maximum temperature rise possible at a given flow rate. To properly size these units you need to know how much water is demanded from each fixture connected to the heater and the starting temperature of the water. Instructions on how to calculate this are on the Department of Energy's (DOE) Energy Savers website, www.energysavers.gov.

For tank-style units, use the water heater's first hour rating (FHR). The first hour rating is the amount of hot water in gallons the heater can supply per hour (starting with a tank full of hot water). It depends on the tank capacity, source of heat (burner or element), and the size of the burner or element. The FHR will be listed as "capacity" on the EnergyGuide label for the product. To determine your FHR, you will need to select a time of day when the maximum amount of hot water is used and then calculate how much water is used during an hour within that time. The DOE's Energy Savers website has more precise calculations for this FHR.

Energy Efficiency

The energy efficiency of a *storage,* demand (*on-demand* or *instantaneous*), condensing, or *heat pump* water heater can be determined through the use of an *energy factor* (EF). The energy factor (EF) indicates a water heater's overall energy efficiency based on the amount of hot water produced per unit of fuel consumed over a typical day. According to the DOE, this includes the following:

- **Recovery efficiency:** How efficiently the heat from the energy source is transferred to the water.
- **Standby losses:** The percentage of heat loss per hour from the stored water compared to the heat content of the water (water heaters with storage tanks).
- **Cycling losses:** The loss of heat as the water circulates through a water heater tank, and/or inlet and outlet pipes.

The standby losses can be minimized with better tank insulation and insulation on hot water pipes, especially those that run through unconditioned space. Heat traps, which allow water to flow into the water heater tank but prevent unwanted hot-water flow out of the tank, will eliminate cycling losses. Other water heater conservation measures, including lowering the water temperature, can be found on DOE's Energy Savers website.

Several labels can assist you in finding the most energy-efficient water heater. The black and yellow EnergyGuide label allows consumers to compare the average yearly operating costs of different water heaters. The Energy Factor (EF) is listed on the EnergyGuide label for the water heaters. The higher the EF number the more energy efficient the unit. See Chapter 3 for more information on EnergyGuide labels as well as the Energy Star program and Canada's EnerGuide appliance labels.

Cost

The cost of heating water will depend on the cost of the unit, installation costs, and the long-term operating cost. To calculate the most cost-efficient option, you need to consider all three. A unit may be inexpensive to buy but will probably be the most expensive to operate in the long run. Calculating the yearly operating cost for a particular type of water heater will help you compare the "actual" cost over the life of the unit. The EnergyGuide and EnerGuide labels are tools to help you compare energy costs.

VENTILATION

Cooking, cleanup, and other kitchen activities can generate moisture, odors, grease, and even smoke. Uncontrolled, these potential air pollutants can lead to both air quality problems as well as maintenance issues. Chapter 3 discusses moisture problems in kitchens and other air-quality issues—and the importance of a mechanical ventilation system in the kitchen.

The kitchen designer is responsible for planning a balanced and efficient ventilation system that does not compromise user comfort and works with the existing mechanical systems in the home. Importantly, the designer needs to provide a ventilation system that will be **used**!

Residential ventilation systems are generally designed with the assumption that inside air is improved by mixing or replacing it with outside air. Air from outdoors is perceived to be fresher. Depending on the location of the home, this may not always be true. If the outside air is polluted, special ventilation systems may be needed that provide additional air filtration. In addition, in very cold climates, a heat-recovery or energy-recovery ventilation system may be recommended to provide more energy-efficient ventilation.

Choosing the Type of Ventilation System

In today's kitchens, there are two common choices in ventilation systems. The first is a fan mounted above the cooktop or range, usually within a hood (*updraft*) (Figure 7.8). The second is a proximity system, installed in the cooktop or adjacent to the cooking surface (*downdraft*). Some kitchens may have a ceiling or wall-mounted exhaust fan, but that is generally not considered as effective as the updraft or downdraft systems (Figure 7.9). In addition, a house with a whole-house ventilation system will typically include an exhaust vent in the kitchen.

Kitchen ventilation systems are usually located near the cooking surface, considered the primary source of odors, heat, combustion pollutants, grease, and moisture. However, other appliances contribute to kitchen air pollution. An oven in a range typically vents through or near a burner on the cook top, putting moisture and odors in the vicinity of the ventilation system. A built-in or wall oven typically vents to the front of the appliance, into the room air, which may or may not be near the ventilation system. A microwave oven, which may vent to the front, side, or back, is often not placed near the kitchen ventilation system. Dishwashers also vent warm moist air.

Canopy or updraft systems can be either a recirculating (ductless) system or an exhaust system. Most downdraft systems are exhaust systems. A recirculating system pulls the air through a filter,

FIGURE **7.8** A variety of hood styles provide ventilation while adding a design element to the kitchen.

(a) Design by NKBA member Nicholas Geragi, CKD, CBD, codesigner Damani King; (b) Design by NKBA member Laurie Belinda Haefele, codesigner Colin Dusenbery

FIGURE 7.9 A proximity ventilaltion system-can be used when it is not possible to have a ventilation hood or when a client does not wish to have the look of a hood in the kitchen design.
Courtesy Sub-Zero Wolf

then returns the air to the room. Thus, a recirculating system is a filtering system, not a ventilation system. The filter may be a simple grease filter screen or include an activated carbon filter to remove odors. Moisture and heat are not removed. Combustion pollutants from gas cooking, including carbon monoxide and water vapor, are also not removed. Recirculating systems are less expensive and easier to install, but less effective. Exhaust systems, on the other hand, remove air as well as heat, moisture, odors, combustion pollutants, and grease from the kitchen to the outside. Generally, a recirculating system should only be used when it is impossible to install the duct work for an exhaust system.

There are many variables involved in designing an effective exhaust ventilation system for the cooking area in a kitchen, including:

- Type of cooking
- Type of cooking appliance
- Type of cooking fuel
- Location of the range and/or cooktop within the kitchen
- Size and location of the hood, if used
- Size, length, and number of turns in the ducts needed to connect the fan to the exterior vent
- Type and size of fan used in the system
- Make-up or replacement air available to the fan

Updraft Ventilation Systems

Generally, a range hood with an exhaust fan vented to the outside (updraft) is considered the most effective system. The hood helps capture the pollutants, such as moisture and grease, before they disperse in the air in the kitchen. There are many styles and designs of hoods available. Some are a focal point in the room; others, such as retractable models, are barely noticeable. The placement of the fan above the cooking area takes advantage of the natural rise of the heated air.

A well-designed and properly placed hood can improve the efficiency of the ventilation system and can reduce the fan size needed (Figure 7.10). A hood should be at least the size of the cooking surface, and preferably 3 to 6 inches (76–152 mm) larger than the cooking surface, in all directions.

FIGURE 7.10 The size and placement of the hood are important to provide effective ventilation.

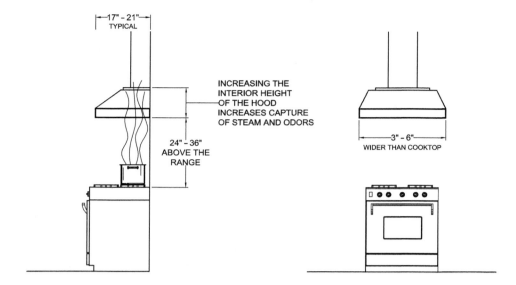

Although ideal, this may be hard to achieve. Hoods are typically available in widths of 24 inches (610 mm) to 54 inches (1372 mm) (in 6-inch [152 mm] increments), so a hood wider than the cooking surface may be selected. However, few hoods have a depth greater than 17 to 21 inches (432–533 mm). Hoods with greater interior height have a larger capture area, which increases efficiency.

The bottom of the hood should be 24 to 36 inches (610 to 914 mm) above the cooking surface. Kitchen Planning Guideline 18 recommends a minimum 24-inch (610 mm) clearance between the cooking surface and a protected noncombustible surface, such as a hood, above it. (See Chapter 6 for further information on this Planning Guideline.) A larger hood can be mounted higher on the wall than a smaller hood, with comparable efficiency. If the same-sized hood is mounted higher on the wall, the fan size may need to be increased to maintain efficiency. Mounting the hood higher on the wall can provide better visibility to the cooking surface and access to large pots, especially on the back burners, and can prevent bumped heads.

When selecting a hood, it is important to know how the ducts will need to be installed to exhaust air outside. Some ducts will run vertically and some will run horizontally. Not all hoods can accept ducts in both directions.

Microwave Ovens and Updraft System Combinations

Some microwave ovens are integrated with an updraft system, so that they can be installed over a cooking surface. The microwave updraft system may be a recirculating system or an exhaust ventilation system. This type of system is not likely to be as effective because the flat bottom of the microwave lacks the canopy shape of a hood, which helps to trap pollutants. In addition, the microwave tends to be shallower than a hood (12 to 13 inches [305 to 330 mm] is typical), giving less coverage of the cooking surface. In addition, the microwave ventilation systems tend to be limited in fan size so may not be appropriate over larger ranges or cooktops.

For the most ventilation efficiency, yet greatest safety, the combination microwave oven and up-draft system should be installed at the 24-inch (610-mm) minimum clearance above the cooking surface (recommended in Planning Guideline 18), typically 60 inches (1524 mm) above the floor (36-inch [914-mm] counter height + 24–inch [610-mm] clearance). However, this would not meet the recommendations in Kitchen Planning Guideline 21 (See Chapter 6, "Kitchen Planning"), which recommends a microwave be installed with the bottom 3 inches (76 mm) below the shoulder of the principle user (which will be less than 60 inches [1524 mm] for many cooks) and no more than 54 inches (1372 mm) above the floor. In addition, the decision to install a microwave oven updraft system combination appliance is often made to visually align the appliance with wall cabinets and for ease of reach. Thus, the appliance is installed 15 to 18 inches (381 to 457 mm) over the cooktop or range.

If your client is interested in a combination microwave oven and updraft/ventilation system, consider the type of cooking surface, the height of the cooking surface, the need for ventilation, the type of cookware and their reach range. Then, be sure to follow all manufacturers' instructions for placement and installation.

Downdraft Ventilation Systems

A downdraft or proximity ventilation system can be an effective alternative for grilling, frying, and other cooking from shallow pots and pans. The downdraft system, including those with "pop-up" vents, captures pollutants near their source (Figure 7.11). A larger fan is required in a downdraft system because there is no hood to help capture the cooking by-products and because the fan must work against the natural tendency for warm air to rise. Before specifying a downdraft ventilation system, determine that there is space for the ductwork.

Ventilation Efficiency

When a cooking appliance is located against a wall, ventilation will be more effective. Ventilation systems for ranges and cooktops that are in open islands or peninsulas require larger fans and/or hoods to compensate for cross-drafts.

Effective ventilation is more critical with a gas cooking system. With gas cooking, there are by-products of combustion, such as carbon monoxide. In addition, gas combustion produces water vapor, so moisture is more of an issue.

Professional-style gas ranges with higher Btu output and gas grills need larger-capacity ventilation systems. One general guideline, used by many manufacturers, is that you need 1 cubic foot per minute (cfm) (.47 liters/sec) for each 100 Btu (50 liters/sec) of output It is important to follow manufacturers' recommendations, as well as local codes, when selecting ventilation systems for larger ranges and grills. It is possible to put in a system that is too large and create an alternate set of problems.

If your kitchen design includes a gas cooking appliance, it is important to recommend that the home have a carbon monoxide detector. This is a safety feature that may also be required by code.

FIGURE 7.11 A "pop-up" or telescoping ventilation fan is almost invisible when not in use and lowered. Such proximity ventilation systems are particularly useful in island applications.

Courtesy of GE

Ducts

Ductwork can alter the efficiency of a ventilation system. A design decision about the location of the cooktop, and thus the ventilation system, will influence the ductwork needed to install the system. Longer duct runs or more turns or angles, reduce efficiency in the system.

- **Length of duct run:** Generally, if the duct run is more than 5 feet (1524 mm) from the intake vent in the kitchen to the exhaust vent in the wall or roof, the size of the fan should be increased to compensate for the resistance of a longer duct run.
- **Elbows or bends in the ducts:** Generally, if there is more than one elbow or bend in the duct, the size of the fan should be increased to compensate for the greater resistance. Three 90-degree elbows are considered the maximum.

Smooth ducts with sealed joints offer less resistance to air movement and provide quieter, more efficient operation. Any duct that must go through spaces that are not heated or cooled should be insulated to help prevent moisture condensation. The ducts should not terminate in the attic or basement but continue to the outside. Warm, moist air exhausted into the attic can lead to condensation and eventual structural problems.

A back-draft flap on the exhaust vent is important to the fan system. This prevents infiltration of outside air, or loss of conditioned air from inside the home, when the fan is not operating. Also, the flap can prevent insects, birds, and other animals from getting into the fan duct.

Fan Size and Ventilation Capacity

Ventilation fans are sized in cubic feet per minute (cfm) or l/s (liters per second). These terms both describe the volume of air the fan can move in a period of time.

In addition to the National Kitchen and Bath Association (NKBA), there are several sources for sizing kitchen ventilations fans, including the Home Ventilating Institute (HVI), the American Society of Heating, Refrigeration, and Air-conditioning Engineers (ASHRAE), and the model 2012 International Residential Code (IRC). Although the ventilation requirements are determined somewhat differently, the resulting recommendations are similar in practice. Finally, the recommendations of the manufacturers of the primary cooking appliances in the specific kitchen must be considered in the final ventilation decision.

The model 2012 IRC identifies a minimum exhaust rate in the kitchen for intermittent exhaust systems, such as that found in an updraft range hood or downdraft proximity system, of 100 cfm (47 l/s). A ductless or recirculating range hood is allowed only if there is sufficient other mechanical or natural ventilation in the kitchen. A similar recommendation of 100 cfm (47 l/s) minimum exhaust is found in the ASHRAE Standard 62. These minimum standards, however, do not allow for variations in types of cooking appliances and cooking styles.

Kitchen Planning Guideline 19 recommends a minimum size fan of 150 cfm (71 l/s). This increased fan capacity allows for larger ranges and better moisture control.

The ventilation recommendations of the Home Ventilating Institute (HVI) (Table 7.1), an industry organization that test and certifies ventilation equipment, are shown in the tables below. HVI also recommends ventilation rates above the code minimum for improved air quality (Table 7.2). In addition, fan sizes are increased for cooking surfaces in an open island.

TABLE 7.1 Ventilation recommendations from the Home Ventilating Institute.

Location of Range Hood	HVI Recommended Ventilation Rate per Linear Foot of Range	Minimum Ventilation Rate per Linear Foot of Range
Against a wall	100 cfm	40 cfm
In an island	150 cfm	50 cfm

Courtesy of the Home Ventilating Institute (www.hvi.org)

TABLE 7.2 Ventilation rates increase with the size of the range and the accompanying hood.

Width of Hood against a Wall	2.5 Feet (30 Inches) (762 mm)	3 Feet (36 Inches) (914 mm)	4 Feet (48 Inches) (1219 mm)
HVI recommended rate	250 cfm 118 l/s	300 cfm 141 l/s	400 cfm 188 l/s
Minimum	100 cfm 47 l/s	120 cfm 56 l/s	160 cfm 75 l/s
Width of hood in an island			
HVI recommended rate	375 cfm 176 l/s	450 cfm 212 l/s	600 cfm 282 l/s
Minimum	125 cfm 59 l/s	150 cfm 71 l/s	200 cfm 94 l/s

Courtesy of the Home Ventilating Institute (www.hvi.org)

Whole House Ventilation

The 2012 International Energy Conservation Code, which has been incorporated into the 2012 International Residential Code (IRC), requires whole-house mechanical ventilation to provide adequate fresh air, as well as moisture control, in the tightly constructed, energy-efficient homes built to the code. With a whole-house mechanical ventilation system, the system operates continuously, providing a constant stream of fresh air to ventilate the home. Advantages to whole-house ventilation also include quiet operation, better moisture control, greater comfort, and less need for motivation to use ventilation fans.

In a home with a whole-house mechanical ventilation system, the requirement for ventilation in the kitchen is different. The 2012 IRC requires a minimum of 25 cfm (12 l/s) of *continuous* exhaust ventilation from the kitchen.

The need for additional ventilation systems in the kitchen of a home with a whole-house ventilation system will depend on several factors, including what type of cooking appliances are selected, the type of cooking fuel, the style of cooking, the foods cooked, and the frequency and volume of cooking. An exhaust ventilation system may still be needed at the cooktop for specific cooking activities. However, the capacity of the fan must be considered in the balance of the whole-house ventilation system. Alternatively, a recirculating or ductless system may be selected to filter grease and odors.

Whole-House Ventilation System

There are different types of whole-house ventilation systems. In some cases, the design of the system needs to be matched to the type of climate—heating or cooling dominated. An effective and popular type of whole-house ventilation system is a balanced mechanical ventilation system. This type of system is available as a heat recovery ventilation (HRV) system or an energy recovery ventilation (ERV) system. HRV and ERV systems work similarly and are effective in all types of climates.

In a balanced mechanical ventilation system, fans are used to exhaust air from the home as well as to bring it into the home (Figure 7.12). Exhaust vents are located in areas of the home where moisture and pollutants are most likely to be generated, including kitchens. Fresh air intake vents are centrally located but away from main living areas, such as in an entry way or closet. Exhaust and intake air pass through a heat exchanger. During the heating season, exhaust air preheats the incoming intake air. In the cooling season, the exhaust air is cooler than the intake air, so the reverse process occurs, and the incoming air is cooled. Thus, the house is ventilated and energy is conserved as well.

(continued)

The HRV system transfers heat between incoming and outgoing air. The ERV system also provides moisture management by dehumidification or humidification, providing further energy savings.

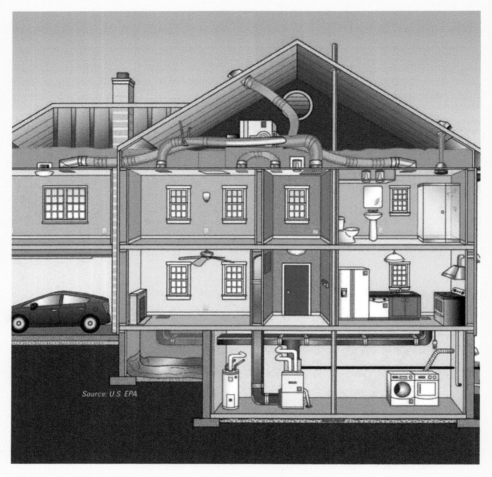

FIGURE 7.12 This diagram illustrates an HRV system for ventilation in a home.
Courtesy of EPA

Replacement Air

A final, often overlooked factor in kitchen ventilation system efficiency is make-up or replacement air. Exhaust ventilation systems remove air from the kitchen, and this air must be replaced. If replacement air is not provided, the fan will not operate effectively. In addition, negative pressure in the home could be created. With a larger ventilation fan, such as might be paired with a professional-style range, there is a greater possibility of depressurizing the home.

If the home has negative pressure, there can be problems with other combustion appliances that need to exhaust to the outside, such as a gas furnace or water heater. Combustion by-products will not be able to exhaust from the home through the chimney or flue. Instead, these byproducts will spill back into the interior of the home. This situation is referred to as *back-drafting.* When back-drafting occurs, dangerous combustion pollutants, such as carbon monoxide, as well as excess moisture, will be pulled into the home. In extreme cases, back-drafting could lead to fatal carbon monoxide poisoning of the residents.

In older homes, make-up air would usually come from natural air leakage. In newer or renovated, more tightly constructed and energy-efficient homes, this replacement air must be provided. A simple solution could be opening a window slightly when operating the kitchen exhaust fan. A supply vent could be installed in the soffit or toe kick, to provide make-up air. In this type of vent, an in-line heater could be included to preheat the incoming air as needed. Other solutions include a whole-house mechanical ventilation system that balances airflow in the home.

The model 2012 IRC requires that exhaust hood systems in kitchens capable of exhausting 400 cfm (0.19 cubic meters per second or 188 l/s) or more must be provided with a makeup at an approximate rate to the exhaust rate. The code requires that the makeup air vent be automatically controlled to operate with the exhaust system and to close down when not in use. It is important for you the designer to know if your locality has adopted this, or a similar code requirement, and plan for an adequate makeup air system.

Noise

Although the noise of a kitchen ventilation system is not a factor in efficiency, it is a major concern of the users. Noise is a frequent reason for not using kitchen exhaust fans.

The noise level of fans is rated in sones. Ventilation fans will vary in their sone rating. The fewer the sones, the quieter the fan. Larger fans and longer or more convoluted duct runs can increase noise. Axial or propeller fans are noisier than centrifugal or "squirrel-cage" fans, although the axial fans are usually cheaper.

Installing the fan in a remote location such as the attic instead of the kitchen, reduces noise. Installing the fan on rubber gaskets or similar cushioning will reduce vibration, and the fan will operate more quietly.

Controls and Features

A multispeed fan is a desirable feature. The fan can be used at a high setting if needed for quick or powerful ventilation, but the lower, quieter setting will encourage regular use. Some fans feature heat sensors that will increase fan speed automatically if there is extra heat.

The ventilation fan filter should be easily removed for cleaning. A convenient feature is a filter that can be washed in the dishwasher. The smaller the diameter of the filter mesh, the more effective it is in catching grease.

Most ventilation hoods come with lights, typically incandescent or halogen lamps. Some feature dual lamps or high/low settings. Make sure that the hood lighting is consistent with the overall plan for kitchen lighting.

The Kitchen Planning Guideline and Access Standard that applies to ventilation, Guideline 19, can be found in Appendix A. In summary, a kitchen ventilation system needs to be carefully designed to provide good control of moisture, heat, grease, odors, and other by-products of cooking. However, ventilation systems are only as effective as their frequency of use. Therefore, quiet, convenient ventilation systems are most desirable.

LIGHTING

Many tasks take place in the kitchen, all requiring the appropriate lighting. As more activities move into the kitchen area, lighting must be more varied and flexible to accommodate them.

Your client will be the main source of information for determining lighting needs. Once you have determined the client's kitchen activities in Chapter 5, "Assessing Needs," and made note of any special vision needs (as determined in Chapters 4, "Human Factors and Universal Design Foundation," and 8, "Accessibility in Practice"), you will have a better idea of the required light sources and types. Also, investigate the client's likes and dislikes regarding lighting and light fixtures.

In addition to considerations for activities, the lighting plan should take into consideration the number and size of the windows, the ceiling height, the size of the room, and the room's style.

The focus of this section is on planning considerations. After you identify needs and research the options, consider the budget and then get creative with your lighting plan. A good lighting design does not rely on just one light source but uses light layering to incorporate all of the functions you would like the room's lighting to perform. Begin by considering the basic types of lighting and how you might use them. These include daylighting, general or ambient, task, decorative, and accent lighting.

Natural or Daylighting

Daylighting makes use of windows, glass doors, and skylights to add natural light to a space. When planning daylighting, first determine when the kitchen is most used. Emphasizing natural light when the kitchen is only used in the evening or very early morning may not be logical or cost effective. Use these ideas to help plan daylighting in a kitchen:

- Too much natural light can lead to glare. If the window area faces a sunny direction, incorporate window treatments that can help control the bright sunlight.
- Large windows can provide adequate daytime lighting needs, plus visually open the room to the outdoors (Figure 7.13). Select windows that have a high insulating value to keep the kitchen more comfortable year around. Chapter 2 includes more details on energy-efficient windows.
- Skylights can provide about five times as much light as comparably sized windows on a wall, without sacrificing wall space (Figure 7.14). If the ceiling is not at the roof line, a shaft will need to be added. The shaft can be straight, angled, or wider at the ceiling line. Consider adding artificial light to the shaft for the evening hours to eliminate the dark hole formed by the shaft. Select high-quality skylights and have them installed properly to avoid leaks and condensation. When positioning a skylight, decide where the direct light will enter the space. Avoid adding extra heat to a dining area or the refrigerator, or creating glare onto a glossy surface.
- Privacy may be another consideration when incorporating a large amount of glass. Privacy measures such as glass block on the exterior or adequate window treatments may be necessary.
- If there is a view from the kitchen, be sure to take advantage of that feature when you plan the window placement.

Artificial Lighting

Natural lighting often does not provide enough illumination for the kitchen's activities, so artificial means must be incorporated. When sizing artificial light, decide what is needed to supplement the natural light during the day, and then consider the needs in the room after dark. No single type of fixture can produce the light needed for enjoying a cup of coffee at breakfast, mixing a batch of cookies, and reading a cookbook, so many different sources need to be considered. Artificial lighting should be thought of as light layers, and these layers can be incorporated through ambient, task, accent, and decorative lighting sources (Figure 7.15). With the input of your client, decide if the light sources will be a prominent feature of the room, ones that grab the attention of people as they enter. Or, would the client prefer to have lighting fixtures that disappear into the background with only the effects of the lighting evident in the room.

General or Ambient Lighting

When daylighting is not adequate, artificial lighting is needed to illuminate traffic paths, see into cabinetry, and prevent accidents. Provisions for general lighting can be accomplished through a variety of sources, including ceiling fixtures, table lamps, track lighting, pendants, linear rail or cable systems, wall sconces, recessed lights, and indirect or cove lighting.

The best-quality ambient lighting adds a soft, general illumination to the room. It should fill the room with a glow that softens the shadows on faces in the space. The best ambient lighting is created by light sources that bounce light off of light-colored surfaces like ceiling and walls to give that soft glow. Ambient lighting fixtures can contribute to the style of the period the design is creating (Figure 7.16).

FIGURE 7.13 Large windows add quality daylighting to a kitchen.

Design by NKBA member Chris Novak Berry and Co-Designer Emily Castle

FIGURE 7.14 Skylights are another way to add daylighiting.

Design by NKBA member Cheryl Hamilton-Gray, CKD

How many light fixtures it will take to achieve the desired level of lighting will depend on many factors. The height of the ceiling affects how much light a fixture delivers to the area. Dark and more textured surfaces absorb more light than light and smooth surfaces and, therefore, need to be considered in the formula. A kitchen with dark surfaces will need about one third more light than a kitchen with light surfaces. The recommended footcandle (fc or lux) level for general lighting is 30–40 fc (323–431 lux) depending on the reflective value of the kitchen surfaces.

It is possible to add too much light to a space. Multiple light-colored surfaces and excessive amounts of light can produce glare, which makes the space uncomfortable for working. Too much light can also wash out room features you would like to showcase, as well as negatively affect the ambience of the room that the light layering is trying to create. Also keep in mind that some light

sources are high-heat producers and add to the discomfort of the room as well as significantly increase the cooling load for the room.

Task Lighting

Based on how the family uses the kitchen, plan lighting for each task or activity. At a minimum, plan to incorporate task lighting for the cooking surface, at the sink, over the counters, and over any table or other work surface. A lighting level of 75–100 fc (807–1076 lux) on work areas is recommended for kitchens. Task lighting may be in the form of a pendant over a table, a hood light over a cooktop, light sources under the cabinets, or a recessed light positioned over a sink. High-quality task lighting should be placed between the head and the work plane or work surface. This eliminates the possibility of creating shadows on the work surface.

Low-voltage systems are widely used for undercabinet lights that illuminate the counter work surface as well as illuminate the backsplash to serve as accent lighting (Figure 7.17). Some under cabinet lights can be simply attached to the bottom of the cabinet and plugged into the wall. However, this application features dangling cords that look unattractive and can get in the way of kitchen activities. A preferred application is to hard wire the lighting into the electrical system so that all cords are hidden. Although these lights can usually be hard wired as a retrofit, it is much easier to conceal the wiring during the kitchen construction or renovation project.

Some precautions should be taken when selecting and specifying under cabinet lighting. Be careful of using under cabinet lights with plastic diffusers above a toaster or toaster oven. They may be damaged by heat from the appliances. Lighting sources that become extremely hot, like recessed halogen puck lights, should not be used below food cabinets because the added heat will shorten the shelf life of many foods. When light fixtures are mounted too far to the back on the bottom of the cabinet, it will become more visible and shine into the eyes of those seated in the room. Task lighting can also be hidden. Designers are using lighting in such spaces as closets, pantries, cabinets, and drawers that use jamb switches, which control lights as the doors/drawers are opened and closed. This added light helps the occupants more easily see the contents of these areas.

Task lighting can be created using many different types of fixtures. The table below lists guidelines from the American Home Lighting Institute for areas of the kitchen and suggested task lighting for that area (Table 7.3).

FIGURE 7.17 Undercabinet lighting provides high-quality task lighting.

Design by NKBA member Anastasia Rentzos, CKD, CBD

TABLE 7.3 Recommended task lighting for kitchen spaces provided by the American Home Lighting Institute.

Kitchen Area	Fixture Placement	Incandescent Lamping	Fluorescent Lamping
Counter	Mount incandescent or fluorescent fixtures under cabinets, as close to the front of the cabinet as possible. Consider putting under cabinet lighting on a dimmer separate from other lighting in your kitchen.	Use low-voltage halogen, xenon, or LED light strips (bulbs 2" apart) or puck lights (18" or 450 mm apart). Some require a transformer.	Tubes long enough to extend 2/3 the length of the counter
At the range or sink	Built-in hood light for range	800 lumens	
	With no hood or at sink, place recessed or surface mounted units 15"–18" (15–18 mm) apart over the center of the range.	Minimum of two 1,100 lumen flood lamps	Two 36" (750 mm) 30 W or three 24" (600 mm) 20 W
General lighting	Recessed lighting placed around perimeter of room approx. 30 inches (750 mm) from wall. Chandeliers can be used in addition to other lighting in space		
Over kitchen table	Pendant centered 30" (750 mm) above table. Size - 12 inches (300 mm) narrower than diameter of round table and 12 inch (300 mm) narrower than smallest side of square or rectangular table.	One 1600 lumen or two 800 lumen or three 450 lumen lamps	
Island counters and breakfast bars	Add a group of miniature pendants. Mount each so that the bottom is approx. 66 inches (1.7 m) above the floor. If shades are not deep and there is seating at the island, install pendants 60 inches (1.5 m) above the floor.		

Accent Lighting

The purpose of accent lighting is to highlight various features of the kitchen (Figure 7.18). Accent lighting can also contribute to the task and ambient lighting, such as pendants over a peninsula. Following is a list of ways you might consider adding accent lighting to your client's lighting plan layers:

- Illuminate the soffit area above the wall cabinetry where a collection of items can be displayed. Use rope lighting either in front of the opening to shine onto the items or at the back of the space to backlight the decorative items in a continuous line of light. Individual fixtures can also be used to illuminate the open space but may create a spottier lighting pattern.
- Light open shelves filled with decorative items.
- Glass-door cabinets are a popular trend and are used to hold special dishes or decorative serving pieces that the client may want people to notice. A simple solution is to place single light at the top or bottom of the cabinet, but a single light may only illuminate one shelf because most cabinet shelves are solid. If the client would like all of the shelves lit, either use glass shelves or place lighting strips along the front edge of the cabinet along the entire length of the cabinet.
- Use light to highlight wall art or a decorative piece in the room.
- Emphasize surface textures, such as a textured wall or a special texture on the backsplash.
- Highlight architectural features such as bookcases, crown molding, or elaborately carved cabinetry.
- Track lighting, recessed lights, and wall-mounted lights can all be used to provide the accent lighting you desire for an area, but be careful that directional lights do not shine into the occupants' eyes.
- Accent lights can vary from small intense spotlights to the soft glow of a rope light. Select the light that gives the desired effect.

FIGURE 7.18 Accent lighting in this kitchen highlights objects in the glass front cabinets.

Design by NKBA member Peter Ross Salerno, CMKBD

Decorative lighting is becoming more popular in today's kitchens as consumers incorporate more detail and design features into their kitchen. This lighting adds a little touch of sparkle to the room through small bright lights and decorative fixtures. Decorative lighting can serve more than one purpose, especially in smaller kitchens. For example, a chandelier is a very decorative fixture, but it also provides ambient lighting to the space (Figure 7.19). A small table lamp may add a little sparkle as well as accent light for a corner. Decorative pendants can add an artistic element to the design, but they can also serve as ambient and task lighting.

Lamps

Light sources that we commonly call bulbs are referred to as "lamps" by the lighting industry. What is the correct lamp to choose will depend on the fixture you select, the space it will light, and the

FIGURE 7.19 Chandeliers in kitchens as decorative and ambient lighting.

Design by NKBA member James E. Howard, CKD, CBD

effect you want to create or achieve. Even though you may consult a lighting designer to help you create a lighting plan for your client, having some knowledge of lighting terms and applications will give you a base for thinking through the possibilities.

Lamp Sizing

Lamps are sized in ⅛-inch (3 mm) intervals. For example, if you see a lamp labeled as PAR30 means a lamp that is 30 × ⅛ inches (762 mm x 3 mm) in diameter. An MR16 lamp is 16 × ⅛ inches (3 mm) in diameter. Fluorescent tubes are also measured in ⅛ of an inch. The original standard T12 (12 × ⅛ inches (3 mm)) tube is being replaced by T8 and T5 tubes which are smaller in diameter. This sizing system will help you decide if a lamp will fit into a fixture.

Lighting Terms

The lighting industry uses many terms to describe various aspects of lighting related to lighting quantity, quality, and efficiency. Although not a complete list, discussion of the following terms will help you become familiar with some of the concepts used in lighting selection.

Quantity

Lumens: Lumens is a measure of the lamps light output. Most lamps are rated in lumens, and by comparing the lumen ratings of various lamps you can select the one that has the light level you desire.

Footcandles: Footcandles are a measure of the light levels on a surface or work plane, the place where activities needing light take place. Footcandle levels can also be stated in "lux" and one footcandle equals 10.76391 lux. A footcandle meter can be used to measure the light levels. Standard kitchen counter work planes are 2.5ft–3 ft (762 mm–914 mm) from the floor, and a reading work plane is typically 2.5 ft (762 mm). Footcandle levels vary by activity. The footcandle level for general conversation in a kitchen is 10–20 fc (108–215 lux); for general kitchen or laundry tasks, 20–50 fc (215–538 lux); and for preparing food or removing laundry stains, 50–100 fc (538–1076 lux). Other areas of the home will vary, depending on the activity to take place. The goal is to select lighting sources that will provide the appropriate level of lighting for the space.

Candelas or candle power: The intensity of the light beam in one direction is measured in candela or candle power. This figure is taken into consideration when calculating the lamps needed to achieve a certain footcandle level onto a surface at a certain distance. If 10-foot (3 m) ceilings are present, for example, more intense light is needed than with 8-foot (2.4 m) ceilings.

Quality

Color temperature: This is the term used to specify the color of light coming from a lamp. All lamps emit some color ranging from warm oranges to cool blues (Figure 7.20). Some lamps come close to neutral or white but may still have a small amount of color. The lamp color affects how the colors of object appear in your room. Color temperature is rated in kelvin (K) and can range from 1500 to 9000K; the higher the number the bluer the light. Color temperatures in the 3000–3600K range are closer to neutral and create little or no effect on the room colors. Warm lamps in a room with blue hues will make the blue color appear gray. Lamps placed in the same room or area should have the same color temperature to help them blend together. Because kitchens often contain many colors in the materials and furnishings, color temperature is an important factor.

Color rendering index (CRI): Color rendering is the lamp's ability to accurately show the colors of objects illuminated by that lamp. CRI peaks at 100, and the higher the number the more accurately the light will reproduce color, the more natural and normal colors appear. Daylight is very close to 100, and that is why many people will take fabrics over to a window to view them. Colors will appear differently under various lamps, and this is usually even more critical to color appearance than color temperature. Lamps may have the same color tempera-ture but different CRI. Find lamps with the highest CRI as possible, and in most rooms a CRI of

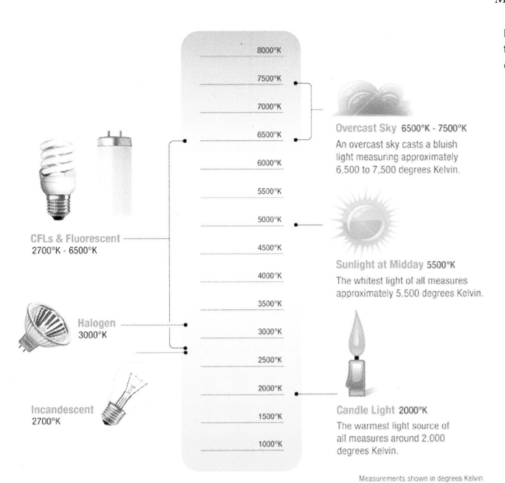

FIGURE 7.20 Color temperatures of various types of light.

Courtesy of American Lighting Association

85–90 is good. Incandescent lamps typically have the highest CRI, but some newer fluorescent lamps are around 90.

Efficiency

Efficacy: *Efficacy* is a term typically used to quantify how efficiently a lamp turns electricity into light; the higher the efficacy, the more efficient the lamp. Calculate efficacy by dividing the lumen rating by the watts used to operate the lamp. Both figures are usually found on the lamp's package. Halogen lamps are more efficient than the standard A-type lamp, and fluorescent and LED lamps are more efficient than halogen.

Types of Lamps

Lamp choices have changed significantly in recent years with more variations in light quality, lamps shapes and sizes, voltage requirements, and efficiency. The lamps you select for your client's lighting needs will depend on the purpose of the light source, the effect you want to achieve, and the fixture in which the lamp will be placed. The following is a brief discussion of the most common lamp types used in the home.

Incandescent

The incandescent lamp has been around since 1859 and many homes have used this type of lamp in a majority of their lighting fixtures. The most common type of incandescent lamp that most people think of as a "light bulb" is the A-bulb or "arbitrary" lamp. This lamp is very inexpensive to buy, but it is a big heat producer with 90 percent of a standard A-bulb's energy used to produce heat. Because only 10 percent of the energy goes light, these are very inefficient lamps, and the reason many of these lamps have new energy efficiency requirements. The new energy requirements state lumen levels for various wattages of lamps and thus the current standard incandescent A-type lamps may not meet these new efficiency levels. Instead of purchasing a certain wattage of lamp, a lamp with a specific lumen level will be purchased. Canada has similar energy efficiency regulations. Beginning January 1, 2011, in California and January 1, 2012, throughout the United States, incandescent lamps must meet the lumens/watt requirements given in Table 7.4.

An incandescent lamp produces light by heating a tungsten filament, and as it heats, it glows and gives off light. These lamps give off a warm light and come in a wide variety of shapes and sizes. The life of these lamps is 750–1500 hours. They can be dimmed, and their light becomes warmer as they are dimmed.

Other types of more efficient incandescent lamps, halogen and xenon, are now on the market. These can serve as replacements for the standard incandescent lamps and are available in the low-voltage type as well.

- **Halogen:** Halogen lamps were introduced in the 1950s and are 25 to 30 percent more efficient than standard incandescent lamps. A halogen is designed a little differently from the standard incandescent, and provides a soft warm light but less warm than the standard incandescent. Halogen lamps are delicate to handle and emit ultraviolet rays (UV). Covers are available to filter out the UV. They come in a wide variety of shapes, sizes, and wattages, and the lamp's life is close to 3000 hours. These lamps cost more to purchase and become very hot with use.
- **Xenon:** Xenon lamps can be used interchangeably with halogen but they come in fewer varieties than the halogen. They are only low-voltage at this time. The xenon have many advantages over the halogen in that they operate cooler, do not need special handling and last about 5000–8000 hours. Xenon lamps may cost more than halogen and they do not emit UV rays.
- **Other Styles of Incandescent Lamps:**

  - *Spot lamps.* These lamps focus the light energy into a narrow beam of concentrated light. They are often used as accent lighting.
  - *Flood lamps.* Flood lamps spread the light beam and flood an area with a lower level of light.
  - *PAR, or parabolic aluminized reflector lamps.* These lamps have a heavy glass casing and reflective surface. They are often used for outdoor settings, and some low-voltage MR-16 lamps are available in the PAR casings.

TABLE 7.4 New requirements for lamp efficiency.

Clear, Frosted, and Soft White General Service Incandescent Light Bulbs

Current Wattage	Lumen Range	New Max Wattage	Minimum Lifetime	Effective Dates
100	1490–2600	72	1000 hours	1/1/2012
75	1050–1489	53	1000 hours	1/1/2013
60	750–1049	43	1000 hours	1/1/2014
40	310–749	29	1000 hours	1/1/2014

Modified Spectrum General Service Incandescent Bulbs (Like GE Reveal)

Current Wattage	Lumen Range	New Max Wattage	Minimum Lifetime	Effective Dates
100	1118–1950	72	1000 hours	1/1/2012
75	758–1117	53	1000 hours	1/1/2013
60	563–787	43	1000 hours	1/1/2014
40	232–562	29	1000 hours	1/1/2014

Source: American Lighting Association

- *Reflector lamps.* Reflector lamps are incandescent lamps with a reflective coating to reflect more of the light out the front of the lamp. These have been a popular source for recessed can lights but are being replaced by more efficient halogen, LED, and compact fluorescent lamps.

Fluorescent

Fluorescent lamps were introduced in the 1930s. They use a ballast to feed electricity through glass tubes filled with gas and a small amount of mercury, creating UV light that turns visible when it hits a phosphor coating on the inside of the tube. The newer electronic ballasts have replaced the magnetic ballasts, eliminating the former problems of slow start-up, flickering, and humming. Fluorescent lamps, in general, are more efficient than incandescent lamps, last longer, and operate cooler. Fluorescent lamps contain a small amount of mercury so should be recycled properly. You will find three styles of fluorescent lamps on the market.

- **Tube:** This was the first style of fluorescent lamp, and they now come in a variety of sizes. Tubes are excellent for ambient or some task lighting, they can be dimmed, and they last around 10,000 hours. For many locations, it is important to pay attention to the lamps color temperature and CRI.
- **Compact fluorescent lamps (CFL):** CFLs use the same fluorescent technology only the tube is designed into a compact style, the now familiar corkscrew style. This style has a screw-type base, so they can be used in fixtures to replace some incandescent lamps. Dimmable lamps are available, and compact fluorescents come in different color temperature and CRI ratings. The ballast for these lamps is contained in the lamp base, and they last around 10,000 hours. Compact fluorescents are also available with a glass bulb around them to make them appear the same as incandescent lamps, which is a good alternative if your client does not like the appearance of the corkscrew lamp (Figure 7.21). Be aware that some compact fluorescent lamps take time to warm up, so when they are first turned on they are very dim but after a period of time achieve their full brightness. This too may not be popular with your clients.
- **Circline:** These fluorescent lamps are built with the tube forming a circle or ring. They operate like other fluorescent tubes and are designed to fit in many center room light fixtures for ambient lighting.

Light-Emitting Diode (LED)

The LED lamp was developed in the 1960s and is fast becoming the energy-efficient lamp of choice. An LED lamp is a very small light source, ¼ inch (6 mm) or smaller. In order to generate a large amount of light, these small dots are clustered together in various configurations. The light waves are only emitted in one direction so the configuration will determine how light is distributed. These lamps require a driver to operate, and the color temperature and CRI depend on the lamps selected. LEDs can be either line voltage or low voltage and are currently rated to last about 50,000 hours, but the life expectancy is expected to increase far beyond that as more efficient LEDs are developed. LEDs come in an almost unlimited number of colors, and they have recently been able to produce a white wavelength as well. They are temperature tolerant and durable, but currently carry a high cost. The applications for LED are increasing and the quality is improving. Many feel this will be the energy-efficient lamp of choice in the future.

FIGURE 7.21 Examples of LED, compact fluorescent, and halogen lamps.

Clean Energy Resource Teams (lighting. mncerts.org)

Fiber Optics

Fiber-optic lights send light along a glass fiber and are, therefore, very delicate. Fiber-optic lights are quite expensive and are often used in decorative lighting to create a dramatic effect.

Following is a comparison chart developed by the Department of Energy and listed on their EnergySavers.gov website to show how the various types of lamps compare to one another (Table 7.5).

New Package Labeling

The U.S. Federal Trade Commission (FTC) is requiring manufacturers of incandescent, compact fluorescent and LED lamps to use new labeling on packaging to help consumers select the most efficient lamps. Natural Resources Canada (NRCan) has also proposed new packaging labels for general service lamps and CFLs.

The front of the new U.S. label displays the lamp's brightness as measured in lumens, rather than watts, as well as the estimated yearly energy cost of that particular lamp. The back of the package will contain "Lighting Facts", including life expectancy, light appearance; wattage and mercury content (Figure 7.22). The proposed Canadian label will be bilingual, and include the model number, the wattage, lumen rating, expected life, and an energy saving tip.

Lighting Fixtures

Lighting fixtures come in a wide variety of styles, mounting types and sizes. When deciding which type to use, consider the size of the space you are lighting, the type of light you want, the design theme of the space, and the tasks that must be illuminated. Following are a few important points to consider concerning light fixtures.

TABLE 7.5 Lighting comparison chart.

Lighting Type	Efficacy (lumens/ watt)	Lifetime (hours)	Color Rendition Index (CRI)	Color Temperature (K)	Indoors/ Outdoors
Incandescent					
Standard "A" bulb	10–17	750–2500	98–100 (excellent)	2700–2800 (warm)	Indoors/ outdoors
Energy-saving incandescent halogen	12–22	1000–4000	98—100 (excellent)	2900–3200 (warm to neutral)	Indoors/ outdoors
Reflector	12–19	2000–3000	98–100 (excellent)	2800 (warm)	Indoors/ outdoors
Fluorescent					
Straight tube	30–110	7000–24,000	50–90 (fair to good)	2700–6500 (warm to cold)	Indoors/ outdoors
Compact fluorescent lamp (CFL)	50–70	10,000	65–88 (good)	2700–6500 (warm to cold)	Indoors/ outdoors
Circline	40–50	12,000			Indoors
Light-Emitting Diodes					
Cool white LEDs	60–92	25,000– 50,000	70–90 (fair to good)	5000 (cold)	Indoors/ outdoors
Warm White LEDs	27–54	25,000– 50,000	70–90 (fair to good)	3300 (neutral)	Indoors/ outdoors

Courtesy of the Department of Energy (www.energysavers.gov)

FIGURE 7.22 New Package Label.
Courtesy of American Lighting Association

Location

- **Lighting needs:** Locate the light fixtures where they can deliver the maximum amount of light for their purpose. Think through the needs for each area and decide how the lighting should be positioned to achieve the effect you want.
- **Center lighting:** General lighting might involve one or two lights in the center of the room, or a number of recessed lights around the perimeter. Provide enough light to cover the floor area so that dark corners do not form. Be aware of fixtures that can get in the way of the users—for example, wall sconces in the walkways of very small kitchens, hanging lights that are too low or in the traffic area, or central ceiling fan lights in average height ceilings.

- **Dining tables:** A pendant light or chandelier over the dining table should be no lower than 25 to 30 inches (625–750 mm) above the table and 7 feet (2 m) to 7 feet 6 inches (2.3 m) above the floor. These lights can also be in the way if they do not allow for location flexibility. Fixtures over a table may be a problem when the client decides to move the table, for example.
- **Accent lighting:** As discussed previously, accent lighting is located where it can highlight a desired feature of the room and achieves the effect your client desires. The soffit is a good example. Decorative items can be highlighted from the front, back, or both. The light can be continuous or in the form of spot lights. Accent lighting can also take the form of a night light near the floor. Placed in the toe kick area of the cabinetry, this soft glow is just the right level light for nighttime visitors to the kitchen. Highlighting too many features can create a busy or cluttered look to the room. Only highlight the items you truly want people to focus on as they enter the room.
- **Task lighting:** Place task lighting where additional light is needed for working or reading. Place the task lighting between the head and work plane/work surface to eliminate shadows on the surface where tasks are taking place. The work plane in a kitchen can be a counter top, table, eating bar, or desk area.
- **Other uses:** Do not forget to place some general lighting in all compartments of the kitchen, including large pantries and laundry areas. Consider illuminating the ceiling to expand the feel of the room.

Recessed Lighting

Recessed lights, sometimes called recessed cans, come in a variety of styles. Some have the lamp located a few inches up inside the cylinder, which may have a white, black, or reflective coating. Other recessed fixtures are closed and flush with the ceiling, while still others have an eyeball design for adjusting direction. Place recessed lights about 24 to 42 inches (600–1075 mm) apart and position them so that the beams overlap, according to the manufacturer's specifications. These lights are described by how they distribute light—wide, medium, or narrow beam, so choose the style that fits your needs. Recessed lights are often positioned above islands, peninsulas, sinks, or countertops.

If you are using recessed lighting to illuminate a work plane or counter area, the fixtures should be mounted so that they cast light onto the task area without causing glare, direct contact with users' eyes, or shadows. For example, a pot rack should not interfere with the functional lighting, which could be recessed lights placed over the island area where a pot rack might be located. In this case, either use cross-illumination or have a light included in the pot rack. Many times it's difficult to avoid shadows from people working at the task area, which is why under cabinet lighting is a better choice of task lighting for work surfaces. Recessed lights alone should not be considered the total solution for task lighting.

Recessed fixtures must be selected and installed so that they do not pose a fire hazard. The housing or covering of some recessed fixtures must not come into contact with insulation because the heat from the fixture could be a fire hazard. However, the housing for insulating ceiling fixtures (IC) serves as a protective shell, which allows these fixtures to be covered with insulation. Select the type that is most appropriate for the job and check local codes. Some jurisdictions require that all recessed fixtures be the IC type, but not all fixtures are available with IC housings.

There are also different recessed fixtures for new construction and for remodeling projects. Consult with your supplier to obtain the correct type fixture for your needs.

Controls

A key factor of a lighting design is control over the light sources, whether it is a window/glass area or artificial lighting. Controls should be conveniently located, easy to use, and offer flexibility to your lighting plan.

Controls for general lighting should be located where users enter the room so that they do not walk into a dark room. If the kitchen has multiple entries, such as those from a deck, hall, dining room, garage, and perhaps a living area, use a combination of three- or four-way switches to control lights from multiple locations. For large kitchens, planning two separate general lighting circuits will provide more options for lighting control. Additional rooms within or near the kitchen, such as a pantry, wet bar, or laundry room, typically have their light controls at the room entrance rather than the main kitchen entrance.

Other lighting controls need to be close to where the light is used. In addition to the controls for general light fixtures that illuminate the space, help your client decide which other lights should be controlled individually. As an example, it is probably not desirable to have one switch for turning on all of the task and accessory lighting in the room. Instead, you may wish to have separate switches at the point of use for the under cabinet lighting, soffit lighting, shelf and glass door cabinet lighting, and floor lighting.

Because every kitchen has many lights to control, try, as much as possible, to consolidate the controls into banks of switches to avoid having the wall dotted with switches. When grouping controls, some professionals recommend only two switches in one location. If more need to be grouped together, four switches is the maximum in one location. When arranging the switches, try to make it easy for your client to remember which switch controls which fixture(s). This may be difficult, but devise a logical order so that a light switch is nearest the corresponding light fixture. The general surface lighting should be the first accessible switch for the room. The recommended universal reach is for controls to be placed less than 48 inches (1200 mm) from the floor or 44 inches (1125 mm) when over a counter.

Many different types of controls are now available for lighting. Select the type your client could use easily, as well as the style they prefer. The flip switches are perhaps the most common. You may also choose a toggle or rocker switch, a motion sensor switch, or even a remote control switch for adjusting light levels on elevated ceiling lights. The remote control switches are especially nice for ceiling fans that also include lights.

Controlling the amount of light is important in some areas of the kitchen. For lighting over a table, in a bar area, or over a peninsula, consider adding a dimmer. A dimmer can help create a soft, low light to give the kitchen a glow when not being used. Be aware that different types of light sources such as fluorescent, halogen, and xenon can be dimmed, but each requires a different type of dimming device, or ballast in the case of fluorescent.

Low-Voltage Lighting

Low-voltage lighting systems have many uses in a kitchen lighting plan. These light sources can be in the form of a small strip that easily disappears behind the molding above or below a cabinet. Above the cabinets, lights give off indirect light for the room, and below the cabinet lights provide good task lighting for the countertop. Other low-voltage design options are the round puck light, which can be placed either under or inside cabinets, and the smaller track lighting units with self-contained transformers for a minimal visual effect. In addition to small track and recessed lights for general lighting, low-voltage units can light shelves, floors, and art work. Low-voltage lights also make good night lights.

These lighting systems use a transformer, either as a separate unit or built into the lighting fixture, to transform the 120-volt service to the lower voltage (usually 24, 12, or 6 volts). Larger-capacity transformers are used to control multiple applications of low-voltage lights installed in one area. These transformers can be fairly large (5 × 5 × 9 inches) (125 × 125 × 225 mm), so you need to decide where they will be hidden, which may be in or above a cabinet or in the ceiling. Transformers incorporated into a fixture make the fixture a little larger and more difficult to conceal.

Low-voltage lights come with halogen, xenon, or LED lamps (bulbs), which give off a crisp, clear light. Halogen lights burn at a high temperature, and even though the low-voltage bulbs are small, added together they can still produce a significant amount of heat. Therefore, keep them out of reach of users and flammable objects.

Lighting Safety

All lighting fixtures and components should have a safety approval label by a recognized testing laboratory (Underwriters Laboratories [UL], Canadian Standards Association [CSA], etc.), which most codes require. Although most lighting systems are generally tested and safe to use, follow proper installation instructions and place fixtures in locations away from contact with people to prevent light fixture hazards. If an uninsulated recessed light is installed too close to combustible materials, the heat from the light could ignite the materials around it. Many recessed fixtures are designed as IC fixtures with built-in air spaces to help cool the lamps.

Installing the incorrect lamp into a fixture can also increase the chances of a fire. When a fixture is selected, it may be difficult to tell how much light it will emit into a room. Most fixtures specify the size of lamp that is safe to use in a fixture. The size of the room, and the colors and textures used, can affect the available light. If your clients find the fixture is not producing the amount of light they desired, they may increase the wattage of the lamps. This will provide more light, but at the same time, the larger lamps will give off more heat than the fixture can handle. The fixture becomes hot to the point where it could crack or ignite. Excess heat also shortens the life of the lamp. Many types of light fixture lamps, like incandescent and halogen, produce a significant amount of heat. Be careful to locate these where your client cannot easily come into contact with the bulbs, for example, while walking through the room or reaching for something. Think through your client's lighting needs carefully to avoid this mistake.

The Kitchen Planning Guideline and Access Standard regarding lighting, Guideline 31, can be found in Appendix A.

SUMMARY

As the kitchen becomes the hub of the home, the expanding number of activities requires multiple equipment, system, and connection considerations. Evaluating the client's activities, as well as desires, in the space will help the designer plan for every need. A key factor is flexibility. The kitchen systems must accommodate user activities from cooking tasks, to reading and entertaining. Flexible lighting, as one example, can set the mood and light levels for various times of day and uses. Attention to code requirements will produce a kitchen that is safe and accessible with high environmental quality. Accurate information and an attention to detail will provide you, the designer, with the information needed to design a successful project and a kitchen that your client will enjoy for years to come.

REVIEW QUESTIONS

1. What are the signs of an outdated or inadequate wiring system for a home? (See "Wiring" page 266)
2. How do general, small appliance, and individual (dedicated) circuits differ? (See "General or Lighting Circuits," "Small Appliance Circuits," and "Individual or Dedicated Circuits" page 267)
3. What considerations are important when incorporating a heated flooring system into a kitchen? (See "Floor Heating Systems" pages 272-273)
4. How are water heaters rated for efficiency? (See "Water Heating: Energy Efficiency" page 277)
5. What variables are important when deciding the type of exhaust system you need for the kitchen range? (See "Choosing the Type of Ventilation System" pages 278-281)
6. What considerations are important when designing task lighting for a kitchen? (See "Task Lighting" pages 289-290)

Accessibility in Practice

The goal of this chapter is to first clarify the differences and overlaps between universal design and design for accessibility, and then to provide examples for customizing the kitchen to your client, with respect for their sensory, cognitive, or physical abilities. To do this, we will tie together Chapter 4, "Universal Design and Human Factors"; Chapter 5, "Assessing Needs"; and Chapter 6, "Kitchen Design," and we will refer back to these chapters often.

The tools presented in Chapter 5 give you a great start to gathering information that can help you identify and plan for each client's needs. When a specific chronic condition or disability is involved, the client will often be your best source of information regarding unique needs and solutions. In addition, health professionals involved with your client, such as occupational or physical therapists, make great team members. Their expertise is the human body and its workings, whereas yours is the space and its function and components. Keep in mind that should specific medical equipment be involved, your role as designer may be to provide appropriate space planning and to involve the equipment expert to execute the plan.

> *Learning Objective 1: Describe the differences between universal design and accessibility.*
>
> *Learning Objective 2 : Provide examples of the universal design principles that apply to variations in abilities, grouped as follows: sensory, cognitive and perceptual, and physical characteristics and needs.*
>
> *Learning Objective 3: Identify kitchen design concepts for addressing sensory, cognitive and perceptual, and physical characteristics and needs.*

UNIVERSAL DESIGN VERSUS ACCESSIBILITY: FURTHER CLARIFICATION

These two categories of design certainly overlap, but they are not the same thing. By definition, universal design improves access and function for most people, with respect for differences in ability, size, or age, and as these concepts are tried and found successful, they are adopted into standard practice. For these reasons—that UD works for most people and that the concepts are embraced as they are used—universal design has been included throughout the book. To the greatest extent possible, you will incorporate universal concepts into every kitchen you design in order to meet the needs of clients throughout their life span and the changes and variety in their physical conditions.

In contrast, in some cases, you may be asked to design all or part of a kitchen that responds to the particular requirements of a person with specific characteristics and needs—sometimes going beyond what would be considered universal design. This is accessible design (see Table 8.1). In response to demand, this chapter will expand on access issues and options, first by citing some of the variations in human factors and abilities that we may be called on to address. We'll go on to review the centers of the kitchen with a focus on design concepts that can respond to those variations and improve the kitchen experience. Finally, for each center, we will summarize the concepts according to the three categories previously used: sensory, cognitive/perceptual, and physical characteristics and needs. Where appropriate, concepts will be explored in more depth to broaden your understanding, or additional resources may be mentioned to enable you to go further in accessibility solutions.

The good news is that in the course of creating access solutions, we often find concepts that will work well for many types of people, and they can be adopted into universal practice, as was the case with oven placements. Traditionally, ovens were typically stacked in a tall cabinet or incorporated into the range. To improve access for a seated cook, we began to split the ovens, placing each at a height within easier reach. Today it has become common practice to place single or double ovens at what is now referred to as a comfort height, as many of us would prefer to reduce bending and lifting—once an issue of access and now universally accepted. To further clarify the difference between access and universal design, consider the sink or sinks in a kitchen. To accommodate a cook who operates from a seated position or one who is shorter, a sink might be planned at a lower height with a knee space, accessible design for the specific user. A universally designed kitchen might include two sinks, one at the lower height and as described, and a second at the traditional height for others using the space.

CHARACTERISTICS OF SPECIFIC USERS

According to some sources, we grow and change to our physical prime at around age 16 and then have a long period of gradual changes in our bodies and abilities. As we age, a broad range of environmental issues affect our abilities, such as broken bones and activity-related injuries, pregnancy, parenthood, increased responsibilities and related stresses, and caring for parents and children. During this time, many of us experience increased strength, stamina, balance, and dexterity, with decreased time for activities and conflicting demands for our attention.

Changes in vision, hearing, and memory are a common thread in our aging process. We reach a point in the growth process where a number of our abilities begin to change again, decreasing as we continue to age and grow. We adapt ourselves to the changes as we age and may not notice any difference until the environment is no longer adequate to support us.

Better design for access related to these changes can alter our life experience, and the user groups and design recommendations listed here, while in no way complete, will provide a good start in this effort.

TABLE 8.1 Comparison of universal and accessible design.

Universal Design	Accessible Design
An approach that accommodates a wide range of human performance characteristics.	It responds to the particular requirements of a person with specific characteristics and needs.
It is invisible.	While it can be attractive, it targets a narrow audience.
It is attractive.	
It has broad market appeal.	
It is flexible for ease of use with respect for the natural diversity in people.	

There is much overlap because, for example, the knee space that allows access at the sink for a person using a wheelchair also provides for seated use by a pregnant woman experiencing fatigue. It can also function as a storage place for a step stool for a child. In some cases, information is repeated, and in others different sections of the chapter and book are referenced.

Sensory Characteristics

Hearing
Have you ever tried to have a conversation on a cell phone with background noise? Or tried to have a conversation in a noisy bar or restaurant?

In this user group are people who are fully or partially deaf, from birth or from a loss of hearing as a result of illness, disease, blockages in the inner ear, damage from prolonged exposure to excessive noise, head injuries, stroke, or other causes. Again, people may not identify a change in hearing as a disability, but a space can be designed to be more accommodating, if you examine common needs and possible responses.

A common occurrence in aging is some level of hearing loss, usually beginning with difficulties with high frequencies and progressing to lower frequencies. Ringing in the ears is also common. Hearing loss and the inability to communicate can cause significant emotional stress, and potential negative effects can be reduced through design. Wall, floor, and window treatments, such as cork, carpet, and fabrics can absorb some of the room's noise to reduce noise from reverberation off the hard surfaces of the space, improving a person's ability to hear as needed.

Concerns with hearing impairments include both the social isolation and difficulty communicating, and also, the safety issues related to not hearing audio cues. Whether hearing loss is a congenital issue or one that occurs later in life, it frequently leads to greater reliance on the other senses to compensate, especially visual skills. Pay attention to design concepts such as noise control, clear sight lines, redundant cuing and visual cuing on all equipment, sound-absorbing materials, quiet ventilation and appliances, line of sight, good lighting, and safety. These and other design considerations are detailed in the sections to follow.

Vision
Have you ever driven west into a setting sun or struggled to focus when entering a dark theater from a bright lobby or tried to pour a black cup of coffee into a dark mug sitting on a dark counter in a poorly lit kitchen?

Because vision changes are a natural part of the aging process, many people would not consider themselves disabled but would benefit from responsive design. This user group also includes anyone who is blind or who has partial vision loss because of cataracts, glaucoma, retinitis, macular degeneration, or eye injuries, as well as anyone with congenital vision impairments or those caused by other conditions. Depending on their condition, user needs will be different.

Physical changes in the eyes increase with age and can lead to vision impairment, such as difficulty seeing in dim light, increased light sensitivity, difficulty focusing on moving objects, and a decrease in peripheral vision. More time is needed for the eyes to adjust when transitioning between light and dark areas. Reading glasses become a common need beginning in the forties, and lenses begin to yellow, causing difficulty in distinguishing some colors.

A concern among people with vision impairments is their depth perception and the ability to distinguish foreground from background. Their needs might also differ from day to night or summer to winter. As eyes age, difficulty differentiating colors with minimal contrast increases, such as navy, black, brown, or pastels and varying whites. Again, if a person has vision issues, he or she will rely more heavily on other senses, particularly auditory abilities.

Pay attention to design concepts such as redundant cuing, eliminating clutter, tactile indicators, intuitive operation, increased and adjustable general and task lighting, careful use of color, contrast, and pattern, and the selection of materials and lighting to reduce glare. These and other design considerations are detailed in the sections to follow.

Other Sensory Characteristics

We often will experience a general and gradual decline in other senses as we age. We may have a change in our ability to taste, including a decline in the recognition of sweet, sour, and salty foods, and a common complaint relates to a bitter taste in the mouth or food tasting bland. Many of us experience a decline in olfactory capacity, which affects our ability to recognize such odors as smoke and leaking gas. This decrease in our ability to smell what's cooking also directly affects our taste and has a negative impact on our appetite. Our sensitivity to touch may decline as well; more specifically, we may not feel the pain of a bump or burn as quickly, so our ability to recognize contact with something too hot or sharp is decreased. Add to this our slowing response time, and there are definitely design decisions that will help us function more safely and comfortably. Consider that we move more slowly and recover from changes in light levels or temperature in a space or in the water we are using, and you'll begin to recognize appropriate design responses.

For a person with tactile or olfactory impairments, pay attention to design concepts such as rounded edges, temperature control that maintains a steady temperature, temperature-limiting faucets, covered heating pipes or elements to prevent burning, and an emphasis on the social aspects of cooking and eating to improve appetite. These and other design considerations are detailed in the sections to follow.

Some key examples of the universal design principles in Chapter 4 that become more critical when responding to a client with sensory issues include:

- Provide effective prompting and feedback during and after task completion.
- Provide adequate contrast between essential information and its surroundings.
- Use multiple modes (pictorial, verbal, tactile, auditory) for redundant presentation of essential information.
- Provide warnings of hazards and errors.
- Provide a clear line of sight to important elements.
- Maintain clear and well-lighted traffic and work areas.

Perception and Cognition Characteristics

Have you ever been in a country where a language foreign to you is spoken and tried to use the phone or to get on the right train, or driven through the day and night and then, while exhausted, tried to follow oral directions to the nearest motel or gas station?

This user group includes anyone with limited comprehension or memory, some confusion, or reduced reasoning. A few of the contributing factors include injury, illness, learning disability, stroke, general aging, using a foreign language, or youth/limited vocabulary and reasoning skills. With a client who has cognitive impairments, safety is a primary concern, and involving caregivers in the design process is critical. Some memory loss or occasional forgetfulness, as opposed to overall mental decline, is very common as we age. The ability to learn does not decrease with age, but stereotypes cause many to fear the loss of mental ability as one ages. Reaction time generally is longer. Reduced physical and reaction abilities cause many to prefer home where things are familiar, allowing for a sense of security.

At the other end of the age spectrum, children are in the process of developing cognitive skills and often share needs with those advancing in age, and they deserve attention as well. A child's language and reasoning skills are only just beginning to develop. Children see the world differently from adults and often do not understand danger or the consequences of their actions. In addition, they have a short attention span and, occasionally, a lack of body function or control. In designing spaces they will inhabit, it is critical to acknowledge their limited awareness of risk/safety factors and lack of understanding.

A concern in planning for children arises when placing potentially dangerous items, such as the microwave oven, within reach of an older child, which are still off-limits to a younger child or toddler. Detailed conversation with the supervising adult is needed to determine what responsible safety precautions must be taken. Children will be learning to participate in the preparation, serving, eating, and cleanup in the kitchen, so it is important that the space be planned to stimulate and enhance their safe learning experiences. Another concern in planning for any client with cognitive issues is clarification as to how involved the client will be in the design and use of the space. Will he or she use the space independently, and are there unique opportunities to enhance the living experience for the client? Or will a caregiver be involved at all times, and are there unique safety concerns? Are there aspects of the space that should be made more accessible and some that should be off limits?

Pay attention to design concepts such as security, lock-out for off-limit cleaning supplies or medications, judicious use of contrast, provision for visual ordering of items to be used regularly, simple communication, preprogramming for controls or intuitive or one-step operations, and creating familiar spaces. These and other design considerations are detailed in the section to follow.

Some key examples of the universal design principles in Chapter 4 that become more critical when responding to a client with cognition issues include:

- Eliminate unnecessary complexity.
- Be consistent with user expectations and intuition.
- Accommodate a wide range of literacy and language skills.
- Arrange information consistent with its importance and its order of use.
- Provide effective prompting and feedback during and after task completion.
- User different modes (pictorial, verbal, tactile, auditory) for redundant presentation of essential information.
- Arrange elements to minimize hazards and errors.
- Provide fail-safe features.

Physical Characteristics

Mobility
Have you ever tried to walk a straight line on a moving airplane or train, or use steps that are slippery with water or ice? Have you ever tried to pass through a space not big enough to accommodate you?

Changes in mobility include body stiffness and rigidity, as well as diminished strength, stamina, balance, and range of motion, usually in the spine, legs, and/or lower body. This includes those who use a wheelchair, scooter, walker, crutches, braces, or other mobility aids. Less obviously, this group also includes those whose mobility is challenged, sometimes temporarily, by pregnancy, excess weight, cardiovascular or respiratory problems, injury, or fatigue. It also includes people who have difficulty bending or stooping.

Measurements used to plan the kitchen should include any assistive device the client uses. The wheelchair or mobility aid should be measured, just as you would document a client's height or body breadth. Standard dimensions for a person using a mobility aid are listed in Chapter 4, but in fact, each client and each mobility aid is unique. In the assessment tools in Chapter 5, you will find several diagrams to use when measuring people and their mobility aids.

Pay special attention to design concepts such as clear floor space for passage and storage of an assistive device, reach ranges, sight lines, selection of drawer pulls, supports, and controls for ease of use and safety. These and other design considerations are detailed in the section to follow.

Dexterity, Strength, Balance, and Stamina
Have you ever tried to lift a mixer out from the back of a base cabinet or to balance and lift a stack of china above your head?

Included in this user group are those who are fatigued or frail from illness or age, and the multitudes of people with limited upper body strength. Also included are individuals with pain, or limited joint or muscle motion, including the ability to grip or grasp, because of temporary or minor injuries and illness. Specific conditions include arthritis, carpel tunnel syndrome, asthma, allergies, chemical sensitivities, post-polio syndrome, stroke, Parkinson's disease, multiple sclerosis, ALS, cerebral palsy, and numerous additional unique physical conditions.

As we age, we experience a decrease in strength because of bone density and muscle loss, causing an increase in accidents and fractures. Decreased mobility can be caused by changes in joints, stooped posture, and/or decrease in height, and common disorders such as arthritis, osteoarthritis, and osteoporosis. As we "shrink" in height, our reach ranges become shorter than those of middle-aged people, moving closer to the range of children.

Changes in internal functions can cause increased incidence of high blood sugar, gallstones, diverticulitis, constipation, and loss of bowel control. Changes in kidney and bladder function can inhibit urinary control and cause dehydration. Changes in the nervous system result in slower movements, and decreased balance and coordination because of inefficiency of the nervous system and central brain processes. Many people experience a sleeping pattern change, requiring less sleep or experiencing less sound sleep.

A concern with this client is the prognosis and how the condition will likely change, another critical issue that can be informed by involved medical professionals. Strength and pace may vary throughout the day. If a cane, walker, or other mobility aid is needed, the ability to carry things is often compromised. Observe your client's balance, and how he/she lifts and moves his or her feet.

Pay special attention to design concepts such as clear floor space, options to sit or stand, reach ranges, design of supports, drawer pulls, and controls for ease of use, particularly the strength/dexterity needed for operation and safety. These and other design considerations are detailed in the sections to follow.

Stature

Do you remember, as a child, trying to reach the faucet at the sink? Children and others small in stature have reduced reach. In addition, children have less stamina, balance, strength, and dexterity, coupled with huge spurts of energy and a much shorter attention span. A child's stature at age six is closer to that of a seated adult than it is to even the shortest of standing adult females (see Figure 8.1).

In contrast, those taller than average height can experience fatigue from operating in a stooped position at fixtures, appliances, and work surfaces planned for the comfortable use of an average height person.

Pay special attention to design concepts such as reach ranges, with and without obstruction, selection of supports, including step stools, drawer pulls, and controls for ease of use and safety, and sight lines. These and other design considerations are detailed in the section that follows.

Some key examples of the universal design principles in Chapter 4 that become more critical when responding to a client with physical issues include:

- Avoid segregating or stigmatizing any users.
- Make the reach to all frequently accessed components comfortable for any seating or standing user.
- Allow user to maintain a neutral body position.
- Provide clear line of sight to important elements for any seated or standing user.
- Provide space for the use of assistive devices or personal assistance.
- Use reasonable operating forces.
- Minimize sustained physical effort.
- Accommodate variations in hand and grip size.

ADDRESSING DIFFERENCES

In any client/designer relationship, a mutual respect and a comfort level must be established. A considerate approach to a client who has different abilities than yours requires that you pay careful attention to your attitude and that you work harder at dropping your own assumptions and listening to your client's needs and priorities. Raising one's voice does not help a person who speaks another language or one who is blind understand you, yet we often experience this. For example,

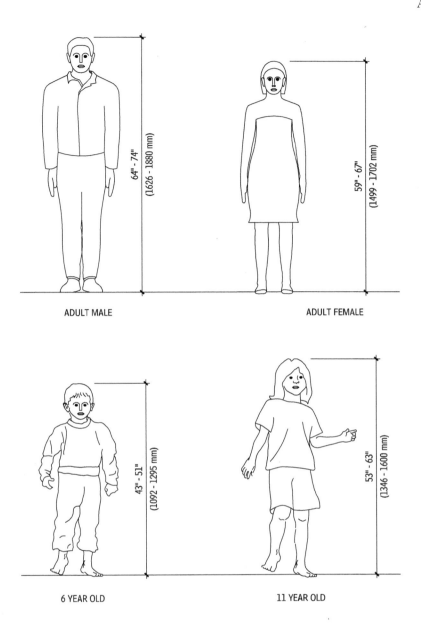

ADULT MALE

64" - 74" (1626 - 1880 mm)

ADULT FEMALE

59" - 67" (1499 - 1702 mm)

6 YEAR OLD

43" - 51" (1092 - 1295 mm)

11 YEAR OLD

53" - 63" (1346 - 1600 mm)

FIGURE 8.1 1 Differences between a child and even the smallest of adult females (fifth percentile) require adjustments to the location of the faucet, storage, controls, support, and more.

assuming that a client who uses a wheelchair must have a separate oven and cooktop with a knee space could be incorrect if that client does not want or need to use the cooktop.

When speaking or referring to a person with a disability, refer to the person first and avoid negative descriptions—not confined to a wheelchair, but a person who uses a wheelchair. For many of us, the word handicapped conjures up negative images of institutional settings, and today the word is used with care to avoid any suggestion of a person being less than whole or "normal." If you are not sure how to refer to a disability, ask your client and if you feel you've misspoken, apologize—in other words use positive references and honest conversation. Emphasize abilities not limitations.

The following suggestions are fairly evident and universal. Position yourself to speak at the client's eye level. Respect a client's assistive devices and do not interfere with their use by moving them or positioning yourself between the person and his or her aide. Respect your client's privacy by accepting what the client may choose not to discuss with you. Keep in mind that these suggestions are intended to help you focus on the person and the space, and not the disability, to achieve the most positive results.

ACCESS DESIGN CONSIDERATIONS

Kitchen space planning considers the given parameters of the job, the NKBA Kitchen Planning Guidelines and Access Standards found in Appendix A, and a client's preferences and budget. Although true in every kitchen design project, when a client has a unique condition, it becomes more critical to carefully consider traffic flow, work aisles, clear floor space, and knee space based on the client's needs and abilities in each of the work centers. Also more critical, lighting and contrast, product and control specifications, surfaces, and all aspects of the room can affect the success of the space in relation to a client's specific sensory and cognitive needs and abilities. For example, reverberation of noise off hard surfaces makes it more difficult for a person with limited hearing to perceive sound, so incorporation of sound-absorbing materials, such as a cork floor or absorbent fabric for a window treatment or a banquette to improve acoustics, becomes more critical.

The centers of the kitchen are reexamined here, with an emphasis on access modifications for a client with an injury, a disability, or abilities and characteristics that are otherwise unique. These centers have been discussed at length in Chapter 6, and the intent here is simply to add concepts that address specific user needs. Design concepts will focus on three areas of human performance: sensory, perceptual/cognitive, and physical. To use this information successfully, it is imperative that you start with a full assessment of the person's current and future functional capabilities and, again, this is where the OT (occupational therapist) or other medical professional will be useful.

Kitchen Configuration, Entry, and Circulation

In Chapter 6, design of the kitchen and its centers is discussed, including many references to design for the differences in people. The intent here is to supplement that chapter's discussion with only that information that is specific or unique to a client with exceptional needs. For a complete review of kitchen planning relating to entry and circulation, please refer to Chapter 6.

Doorways to the Kitchen

Although most issues in designing the entry and doorway to the kitchen relate to physical characteristics and needs of the people who will use the space, there are considerations that relate to sensory and perceptual/cognitive aspects of the client.

Depending on your client and their family, the kitchen may need to be closed off with a door and lock for someone with cognitive impairments or disabilities, or it may need to be open for a watchful eye.

The use of contrast to indicate the entry can help with way-finding, but this contrast must be used judiciously when perceptual/cognitive impairments are a concern, as the contrast that highlights the doorway can be perceived as a wall or an obstruction to those of us with cognitive issues. Another option to make the doorway leading to the kitchen safe is to plan responsive lighting concepts for nocturnal visits, such as motion sensor lighting, night lighting that fades on and off rather than operating only in full on or off, or toe kicks lighted by LEDs (see Figure 8.2).

While the entry to the kitchen from the living area is very often an open arrangement, the following recommendations can be used for doors from the kitchen to adjacent spaces including garages, laundry rooms, pantries, and the outside. In some cases, a door that swings out of the room or pockets into the adjacent wall will be desired, as it will allow for an aide to enter the room if assistance is needed. Planning so that the door swing does not interfere with open appliance doors or cabinet doors or drawers, and storage so that passage aisles are clutter-free is particularly important for a client with visual issues (see Figure 8.3).

Repetition in the process and order of entry to the kitchen can make passage and function easier for those of us with perceptual/cognitive issues—in other words, if the door opens to lighting switches and controls, and the storage inside the door is ordered as it will be used, it can reinforce intuitive practices in the entry and kitchen activities.

FIGURE 8.2 **FIGURE 8.2** Lighted toe kicks can help with night lighting in the kitchen for mood or for way-finding.

Design by NKBA member Tracey Scalzo, CMKBD

Although a 32-inch (813 mm) clear door opening is allowed in access standards, entry doors into the kitchen should maintain a clearance of 34 inches (864 mm), which is the typical clearance of a 36-inch (914 mm) door minus the thickness of the door and doorstop (see Figure 8.4). When you consider that the standard clear floor space for a person in a wheelchair is 30 inches (645 mm) wide, this seems a bare minimum.

When feasible, clear passage can be improved by removing the door between the kitchen and adjacent spaces to avoid conflict with the door swing. Swing-away hinges allow the door to swing

FIGURE 8.3 There is a trend toward sliding and tambour doors. These door types reduce risk of injury by staying out of the way.

Design by Vernon Applegate

FIGURE 8.4 Access Standard 1: The clear opening of a doorway should be at least 34 inches (864 mm), requiring a 36-inch (914-mm) door to allow for passage by a person using a mobility aid, and there should be 18 inches (457 mm) of clear floor space adjacent to the latch side of the swing side of the door.

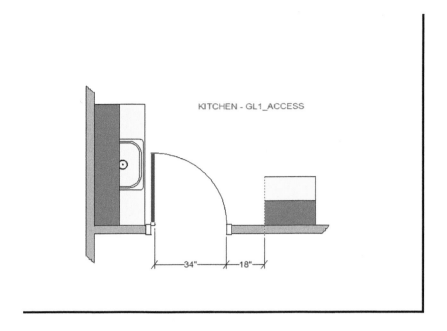

out of the door opening and increase the clear space by 1 inch to 1½ inches (25 mm to 38 mm), the thickness of the door (see Figure 8.5).

Access guidelines vary in the clearances required at a door or door opening, but several general guidelines can be helpful. First, a minimum clear floor space of the door width plus at least 18 inches (457 mm) beyond the latch by 60 inches (1542 mm) perpendicular to the door on the pull side of a standard door is called out as necessary to permit a person using a mobility aid to position him- or herself next to the door, beside the handle/lever, and out of the way of the door swing, in order to pull it open. In addition, on the push side of the door, a minimum clear floor space of the door width plus 12 inches (330 mm) beyond the latch by 48 inches (1219 mm) (when there is a closer and latch) is called out. This clear space is detailed in Appendix A, the Access Standards, Guideline 2. This dimension varies based on the type of door and the approach.

In door openings when the cabinetry or other fixtures of the kitchen butt up against the door opening, if the total depth of the opening is 24 inches (610 mm) or deeper, the clear space is called out as a minimum 36 inches (914 mm), to provide easier passage for a person using a mobility aid (see Figure 8.6). This wider clearance is rarely difficult to achieve in a kitchen plan, and beyond the improved passage, it can contribute to the open sense of the kitchen.

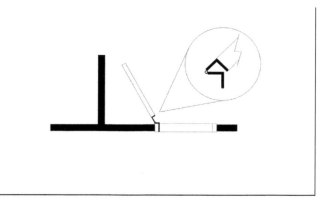

FIGURE 8.5 A swing-clear hinge can help to widen the clear space of the door opening by the thickness of the door.

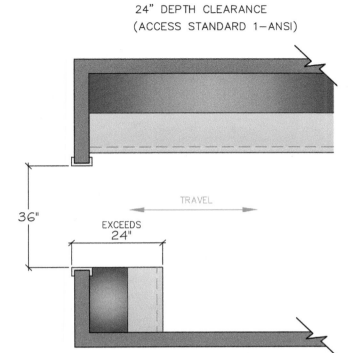

24" DEPTH CLEARANCE
(ACCESS STANDARD 1—ANSI)

FIGURE 8.6 Access Standard 1: If the depth of a passage into the kitchen is 24 inches (610 mm) or greater, the clear width must be a minimum 36 inches (914 mm).

Work Aisles and Clear Floor Space in the Kitchen

As with the doorways, most issues in designing the circulation in the kitchen relate to physical characteristics and needs of the people who will use the space, but there are considerations that relate to sensory and perceptual/cognitive aspects of the client.

For those of us with hearing impairments, a clear line of sight will make entering and using the kitchen more comfortable. When planning, determine a client's preferences and main work areas so that you can plan the most used spaces, whether the sink and prep area, or the cooking appliances facing out to a snack counter or table to encourage face-to-face contact. Increased and adjustable, nonglare lighting and tactile cuing, such a change in texture around the door trim, will help those of us with vision impairments.

Colors and patterns should be chosen with consideration of the total room in terms of contrast and light. Color contrast can be used to highlight edges or borders, as in the edge of a counter or a border around the floor. Overuse of contrast, particularly on walls and floor borders, can block a person with perception impairments from maneuvering and must be carefully planned.

Use easy-to-maneuver and easy maintenance flooring, such as slip-resistant tile or vinyl. Commercial-quality resilient flooring resists wear, is easy to maintain and clean, and in some cases, has raised dots or granular materials to improve slip resistance. Slip-resistant coatings can be applied to some flooring materials. Given the popularity of wood and tile, whether stone, ceramic, or porcelain, it is good to consider a rug or padding placed at frequently used work areas to relieve discomfort, provided it is recessed so that it maintains a level floor.

In the challenge to match sufficient clear floor space for work aisles and functional passage with the wish list of the client and the space available, the physical characteristics and needs of the people who will use the kitchen will have critical impact. Bigger kitchens are not always the answer. As strength, stamina, and balance decrease, minimal passage clearances, a compact work triangle and continuous counters, as found in a U-shape arrangement, can help to give people support as they move through a small kitchen. With a mobility aid, more generous spaces are mandatory and fewer or no sharp turns are desirable. An occupational therapist or medical professional working with the client can be a good source of information in determining current and future needs. As discussed in Chapter 5, if a client uses a mobility aid, the person and the aid must be measured to accurately design the space.

FIGURE 8.7 Access Standard 6: Access standards call for a minimum 30 × 48 inch (762 × 1219 mm) clear floor space at each fixture or appliance, and these clear floor spaces can overlap.

30" x 48"
CLEAR FLOOR SPACES AND
KNEE SPACES MAY OVERLAP

Once in the kitchen, a minimum of 42-inch (1067 mm) wide walkways (48 inches [1219 mm] for multiple cooks) and a space with few right-angle turns provide easier maneuvering (see Chapter 6). At each appliance, the 30 inch × 48 inch (762 mm × 1219 mm) clear floor space that is standard for a person using a wheelchair should be planned (see Figure 8.7), although this dimension will vary with the client and the aid, so it is always best to measure your client, as outlined in Chapter 5. Remember that wheelchairs are unique, and that scooters and other mobility aids will have different measurements. The suggestion is that either a parallel or front (perpendicular) approach is functional, but this varies tremendously from client to client; preferences and ability must be taken into account, with the front approach being best for most people. Clearance recommendations will also be based on the appliance specified and will be detailed as the centers of the kitchen are discussed in the ensuing sections. These clear floor spaces can overlap as long as there is no interference with the entry to the room, and this is generally not difficult to work into a kitchen plan.

Depending on the kitchen arrangement, turning may or may not be necessary, but it is typically an important part of safety and function in the kitchen. Kitchens with an open arrangement allow fluid circulation throughout the space. In a closed arrangement such as a U-shape, G-shaped, parallel, or galley kitchen (see Chapter 6), there must be space to allow the person using a wheelchair to turn around. A 60-inch (1524 mm) turning circle is preferred; however, it is possible to plan for a person using a chair to turn via a T-turn, measuring a minimum 36 inches × 60 inches × 36 inches (914 mm × 1524 mm × 914 mm) (see Figure 8.8) at floor level, with the needed clearance decreasing at heights above the floor (Figure 8.9). The T-turn can sometimes be the better answer in a small kitchen, using the knee space under the sink or prep area (for the stem of the turn). The U-shaped kitchen is unique in that it will need to include a minimum 60 inches (1524 mm) clear space between opposing counters or appliances, or other protrusions, to provide for turning (see Figure 8.8a).

Beyond this, increasing walk aisles and reducing the number and depth of obstructions by planning shallow storage areas with open shelves, and tambour, sliding, up-lifting, or other doors that will not protrude will increase and improve the clear floor space. It is good to remember that a person using a wheelchair needs the greatest amount of clear space at floor level and that, if storage or any obstruction can be planned off the floor, it will be easier to create that needed clear space. If a knee space or a toe kick raised to 9–12 inches (229–305 mm) is planned, this space can be used for a portion of the clear floor space at floor level.

Although 90° turns are less common as we trend to more open plans, they still deserve discussion. If you imagine yourself driving a car and making such a turn, you'll be better able to appreciate the maneuvering required by a person using a wheelchair in making these turns. Although the standard minimum width for a walkway is 36 inches (914 mm) as discussed in Chapter 6, when two walkways are perpendicular to each other, one walkway should be at least 42 inches (1067 mm) wide to allow for a person using a wheelchair to make the turn (see Figure 8.10).

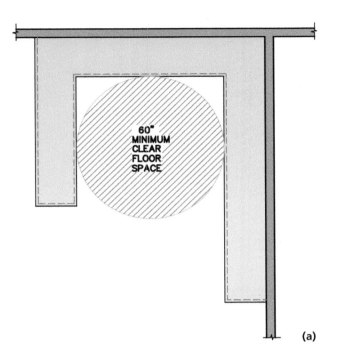

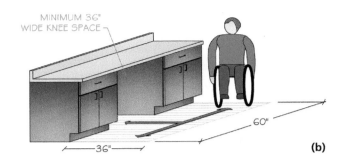

FIGURE 8.8 Access Standard 6: Two methods for turning in a wheelchair: (a) the preferred 60-inch (1524 mm) circle or (b) the t-turn.

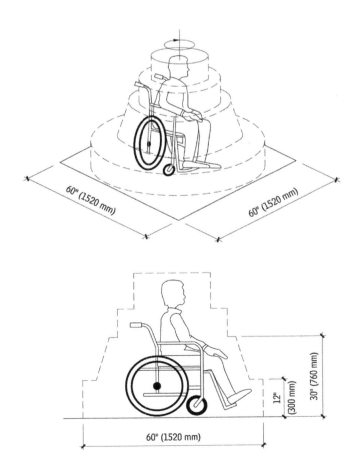

FIGURE 8.9 Clear floor space needed for 360° turns.

FIGURE 8.10 Access Standard 7: If two walkways are perpendicular to each other, one walkway should be at least 42 inches (1067 mm) wide.

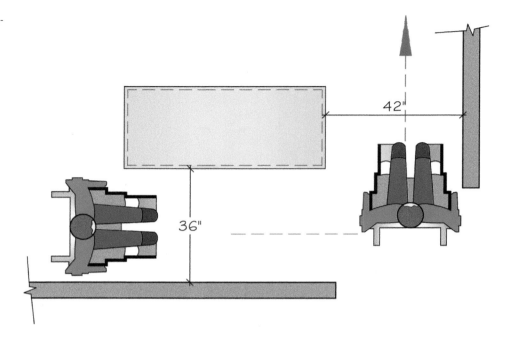

Traffic Clearance at Seating

Clearances around snack bars and tables or lowered work areas are discussed at length in Chapter 6. Beyond that discussion, clearance behind seated cooks or diners must of course be increased to accommodate any person using a mobility aid. Dimensions and design concepts relating to this will be discussed further in this chapter under "Serving and Dining."

Access Standards

The NKBA Kitchen Planning Guidelines and Access Standards that relate to the entry and circulation are 1, 2, 3, 6, and 8.

Responsive Design Summary: Entry and Circulation

- Sensory
  - Universal Design Recommendations
    - Plan so no entry doors interfere with appliance doors (Guideline 2).
    - Specify eased counter edges and rounded corners, which are helpful in reducing bumps and bruises (Guideline 8).
    - Increase tactile and audio cuing for way-finding, function, and warnings.
    - Carefully plan color contrast to highlight edges or borders, as in the edge of a counter or a border around the floor.
    - Reduce the number and depth of obstructions that protrude into the passage space.
    - Provide clear sight lines for clients of various heights throughout the space (improves function for all, especially useful to those with hearing issues).
    - When possible, place sink, cooking appliances, and/or preparation centers facing out to a snack counter or table to encourage face-to-face contact.
    - In multiple-cook kitchens, plan adjacent or facing work and avoid back-to-back interaction.
  - Access Recommendations
    - Plan needed allowance for a service dog or other service pet.
    - Provide clear floor space according to the dimensions of the client, his or her assistive device and/or caregiver, and maneuvering needs.
    - Organize space and storage in the kitchen so that it follows logical steps in using the space.
- Cognition
  - Universal Design Recommendations

- Depending on your client and his or her family, the kitchen may need to be closed off with a door and lock, or it may need to be open for a watchful eye.
- Carefully plan color contrast to assist in comprehension of the workings of the space, but take care not to overuse so that it confuses and inhibits.
  - Access Standard Recommendations
    - Organize space and storage in the kitchen so that it follows logical steps in using the space.
- Physical
  - Universal Design Recommendations
    - No entry doors should interfere with appliance doors (Guideline 2).
    - Reduce hallways and right-angle turns to provide easier maneuvering, particularly for a person using a wheelchair or other mobility aid.
    - Reduce/eliminate the number and depth of obstructions that protrude into the passage space.
    - Consider the relationship of the kitchen door to an express exit route to allow egress for the client with longer reaction times.
    - Increase the range for sight lines, especially if the client is seated or exceptionally tall.
    - Organize space for minimum movement and reduced strength and bending.
    - Provide clear floor space/opportunities to operate from a seated position to preserve strength.
    - Include support for passing through a space to relieve demands on balance, stamina, and strength.
    - Increase clear floor space to ease maneuvering, with particular attention to the door.
  - Access Recommendations
    - Plan minimum door/entry clearance of 34 inches (864 mm) (Access Standard 1).
    - Plan a minimum 18 inches (457 mm) beyond the latch by 60 inches (1524 mm) clear floor space on pull side of door, and 12 inches (305 mm) beyond the latch by 48 inches (1219 mm) on the push side of the door (Access Standard 2, Code Reference).
    - Provide a minimum clear floor space of 48 inches by 30 inches (1219 × 762 mm) at each fixture (Access Standard 6).
    - In a U-shaped kitchen, plan a 60-inch (1524 mm) clear floor space between the opposing arms to allow someone in a wheelchair to turn around.
    - Consider a 36 inch x 36 inch x 60 inch (914 × 1524 × 914 mm) T-turn, especially in closed parallel or galley arrangements (Access Standard 6, Code Reference).
    - Plan 42-inch (1067 mm) wide walkways (Access Standard 7).
    - Include space to store and recharge mobility aids, with consideration of the associated noise.
    - Consider the strength and coordination of the client when choosing the door operating system.

Lighting and Electrical in the Kitchen

Whole volumes have been written about the impact of lighting on our success at integrating with our immediate environment. In this section, a few of the considerations that relate specifically to a client's sensory, cognitive, and physical characteristics will be mentioned. First, we need more light as we age, and depending on the condition of our eyes, it may be beneficial to turn down certain lighting and turn up other lighting—turning down the ambient light and up the task light, for example, so adjustability is key. Diffused and natural light sources are best and should be generous, but attention must be paid to reduction of glare with the use of shades, blinds, or opaque surface treatments. Reducing glare and shadowing is especially important to those of us with aging eyes or impaired sight, so the location and direction of light, as well as the amount of light, is important. Increased light that is indirect, or at least diffusing the source will help with this. Given the reduced ability to adjust to changes in lighting that comes with age, it is important that the lamp or light source be filtered or recessed out of the line of sight, and motion-activated lighting that fades on and off can be effective. Selecting light-colored, matte surfaces for their reflective qualities can be one way to avoid the shadows and make best use of the available light. As eyes age, it becomes difficult to differentiate colors with minimal contrast, such as navy, black, brown, or pastels. The contrast created by placing light objects against darker backgrounds, or vice versa, can be useful on controls, work surfaces, and storage. Better control of lighting with dimmers will enable the user to adjust the lighting to his/her needs depending on the time of day, and also allows a variety of users to customize to suit their vision and their lighting needs.

Regarding electrical issues beyond the coverage in Chapter 6, access to outlets can be an issue. Given that the standard for reach by a seated user over base cabinets is 44 inches (1118 mm), GFCI* plug molding placed up under the wall cabinets may look good, but it will not be accessible. Instead the plug molding can sometimes be planned under the overhang of the counter at the top of the base cabinets if the cabinetry or trim are planned to accommodate this. Pop-up outlets and outlets built into the sides of base cabinets can also be options, but care must be taken that there is no risk of exposure to water.

Regarding appliances, the control-lock-out feature on many computerized appliances can increase safety in use by children or cooks with cognitive issues. In the case of the dishwasher or the continuous feed disposer, the switch can serve as further protection, provided it is clearly marked and readily identified. There are a number of appliances that incorporate redundant cuing—for example, the microwave that blinks and beeps when a function is complete—and these improve the numbers and variety of people who can operate the appliance. In addition, there are supplemental products will add the visual or auditory notice for operation. For safety, fire alarms with dual cuing should be included in the kitchen.

Sink and Preparation Center

In Chapter 6, the design of the sink and preparation center is discussed in detail, including many references to design for the differences in people. The intent here is to supplement that chapter's discussion with only that information that is specific or unique to a client with exceptional needs. For a complete review of kitchen planning relating to the sink center, please refer to Chapter 6.

The sink center is typically the beginning of the task of food preparation. It is also the end of the food preparation and dining cycle when it serves as the cleanup center. Finally, it is the fixture most frequently duplicated in a kitchen, sometimes to provide a second prep center or to separate prep from cleanup, and we'll examine each of these concepts in relation to unique client needs.

Clear Floor and Knee Space at Sink/Prep Center

The sink/prep center is an ideal location for a knee space because it is the primary work center in most kitchens and is often the center of the kitchen, socially and literally. It can be a relief to a tired cook, and beyond simple comfort, being able to sit at the sink/prep center preserves strength and energy and improves balance, so this is a concept that suits many users. The open knee space can also provide flexibility, as it allows a person to sit or stand, as well as providing storage for a waste bin, chair, or step stool for those not tall enough to comfortably reach the sink and controls. If it is to accommodate a client who must sit to use the sink, you will need to plan a clear floor space for approach and use. While a parallel approach is allowed by access codes and standards (see Figure 8.11), a perpendicular approach with an open knee space is much preferred.

Because the sink is used so much and by so many, it is desirable to plan it not in a corner, but in a straight run of counter to allow for multiple approaches. This becomes more important when a cook has greater strength or dexterity on one side than the other. There is an exception to the corner sink guidance and that is when the main cook operates from a seated position and the entire corner area can be planned as open knee space, providing a more generous maneuvering space with less loss of desirable storage (see Figure 8.12).

When planning an open knee space for someone who uses a wheelchair, it is best to measure the client in the chair that will be used, and when this is not possible, the recommended dimensions are cited in Access Guideline 6 (see Figure 8.13). The width of an open knee space should be a minimum of 30 inches (762 mm), with the preference being 36 inches (914 mm), as this is the minimum needed to serve as one leg of a T-turn.

*A device that monitors the electric current on a circuit to make sure the amount of current going out is the same as that returning to the electric receptacle. Serving as a safety device, the slightest difference in current will shut off the circuit.

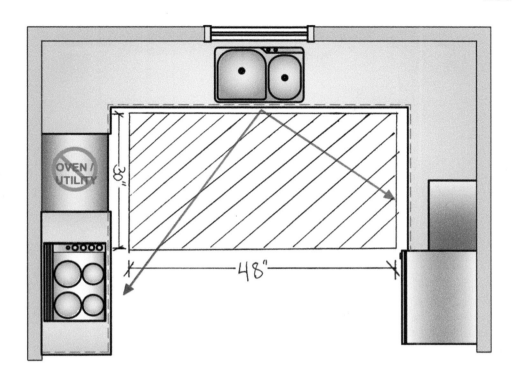

FIGURE 8.11 Guideline 4: Clear floor space at sink.

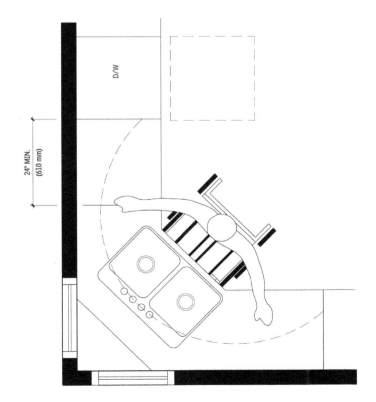

FIGURE 8.12 A corner sink with full knee space can provide generous maneuvering space.

FIGURE 8.13 Access Standard 6: Recommended knee space dimensions.

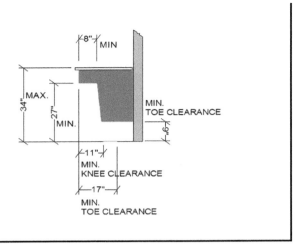

The height of the counter, or the top of the sink should be designed to fit the user, usually between 27 and 34 inches (686 mm and 864 mm) for seated use. This dimension will best be determined by measuring the clearance needed in the knee space and considering the depth of the sink. With this in mind, a sink of no more than 6½ inches (165 mm) depth is best. The height of the counter surface and sink is often a compromise, as seated users work well with the lowest height their lap will accommodate, but allowances must be made for the depth of the sink.

The lowered counter height at the sink must also be considered in relation to the rest of the kitchen. Although the main cook might operate from a seated position and benefit from the lowered work surface, there will usually be others using the space as well, calling for a variety in counter heights. When this is the case, care must be taken so that there is sufficient adjacent landing counter on either side of the sink at the same height. This creates both a functional and an aesthetic issue and must be carefully planned. While the preferred landing space would be as stated in kitchen Guideline 11, 24 inches (610 mm) on one side and 18 inches (457 mm) on the other, this can be difficult with the lowered sink area. In this case, it may be preferable to plan the sink to one side of the available counter to get a usable surface on the second side, and the NKBA recommends a minimum of 3 inches (76 mm) and 24 inches (610 mm) (see Figure 8.14).

The depth of the knee space can vary from floor to counter with 19 inches (483 mm) being desirable, but most needed at the floor where the feet of the seated user will be positioned, and often the clearance slopes back from the work surface to accommodate the sink depth. Shallow sinks with the drain placed at the rear provide the greatest knee space. The sink must be supported and the plumbing must have protective coverings, including material to match surrounding cabinetry or the sink, or designed from custom railing systems to coordinate with the accessories. These coverings protect both the plumbing and the user and will need to be durable.

A garbage disposal does interfere with the knee space. If a garbage disposal is necessary, consider a compact model and offset the knee space to the opposite side (see Figure 8.15).

Although today's designs have a high level of comfort and beauty in the open knee space, there may be times when a client prefers or a design dictates concealing the open area, and this can be done in a variety of ways (see Figure 8.16). Retractable doors are the most common, but the overall width of the knee space will need to grow to allow for the area the doors take up in the retracted position, and this can be as much as 3 inches (76 mm) per side. Bifold doors are another option. Adaptable design might involve finishing the space as an open knee space and then installing a cabinet face frame and doors to be used until that point at which a client wishes to remove them and use the open knee space.

Placement Considerations

A preparation center with enough work surface to spread out and do the work of food preparation is needed somewhere in the kitchen, called out in the guidelines as a minimum 36 inches (914 mm)

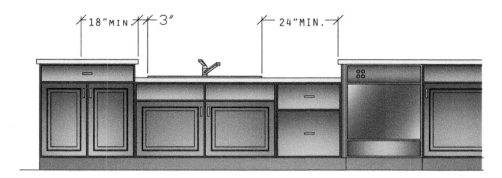

FIGURE 8.14 Guideline 11: Planning the sink a minimum of 3 inches (76 mm) from one end of the work surface allows a reasonable work area of at least 24 inches (610 mm) on the other side, also a possible space for a knee space when combined with the sink.

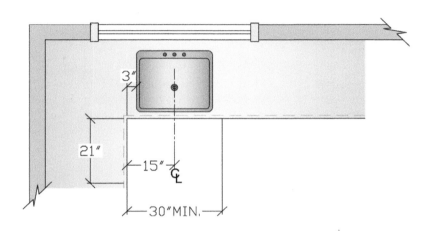

wide, and when possible it is adjacent to a sink. To improve access, this space adjacent to the sink and at the same height is another opportunity for a knee space and, in this case, a rolling cart, a waste receptacle on castors, or rolling storage can be a way to maintain storage while allowing for the knee space when desired (see Figure 8.17). If rolling storage is planned to allow for a knee space, it is important to plan a secondary parking space for the cart when the knee space is in use. The cart can also be useful for those of us who have limited strength, stamina, or balance to move items from one part of the kitchen to another. Between knee spaces and appliances, storage can run short, and the rolling cart can also transport supplies from the pantry to the prep area. The cart can be designed to match cabinetry or, today, there are a number of carts on the market.

When planning counter heights, multiple height work surfaces are recommended in the kitchen, with one being between 28 inches (711 mm) to 36 inches (914 mm) and the other being 36 inches (914 mm) to 45 inches (1143 mm) above the finished floor (see Figure 8.18). The three most

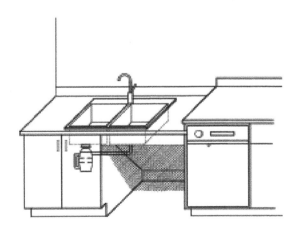

FIGURE 8.15 Combining a garbage disposal and a knee space successfully.

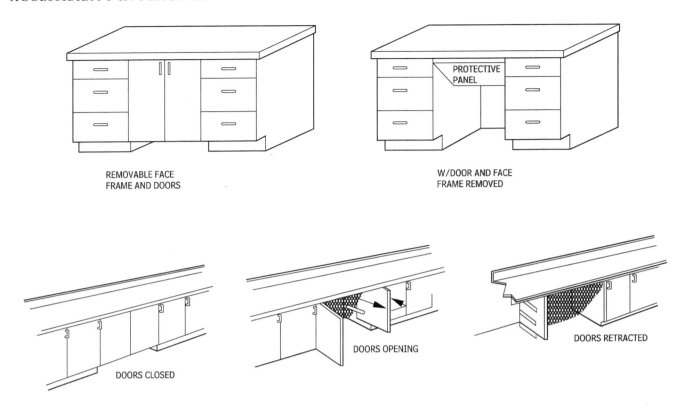

REMOVABLE FACE
FRAME AND DOORS

W/DOOR AND FACE
FRAME REMOVED

PROTECTIVE
PANEL

DOORS CLOSED

DOORS OPENING

DOORS RETRACTED

FIGURE 8.16 Options for a concealed knee space in the kitchen.

FIGURE 8.17 Rolling storage creates flexibility.
Courtesy of Kitchen Source

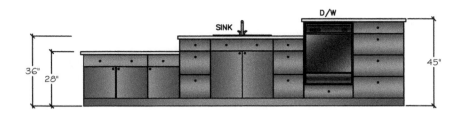

FIGURE 8.18 Access Guideline 25: Recommended variations in counter height include one at 28 inches (711 mm) to 36 (914 mm) and the other at 36 inches (914 mm) to 45 inches (1143 mm).

commonly used heights are 30 inches (762 mm), which is standard table height; 36 inches (914 mm), which is standard counter height; and 45 inches (1143 mm), which is standard bar height. These heights will fit standard seating options, but other heights can be more beneficial and even necessary to a particular client.

Remember that, while varied heights accommodate cooks of various heights, a continuous counter at one height is useful for sliding things that your client may not be able to lift to transport. Pull-out work surfaces add flexibility to countertop heights (see Figure 8.19).

Beyond the knee space, the location and number of sinks in the kitchen can have access implications. When possible, the sink should be placed so that the cook will face the serving or breakfast bar, the view, or the social area of the kitchen. For those of us who have lost olfactory ability or otherwise lost interest in food and eating, this social aspect can help encourage healthy eating (see Figure 8.20).

When possible a second sink can be an asset, especially if it can be planned at a second height. Given the standing and seated heights of the different cooks, this can help to accommodate not just the seated cook, but the taller one. When planning for a kitchen that includes a seated cook, one option is to plan the lowered height sink at one end of a built-in table or eating area, placing it at a comfortable height for the seated user and allowing the lower surface to serve multiple purposes. Options exist for adjustable height sinks when appropriate.

FIGURE 8.19 Pull-out work surfaces can provide a lowered work area without breaking up a length of counter at the same height.
Courtesy of Hafele America Co.

FIGURE 8.20 The sink center opposite the eating area encourages face-to-face conversation.

Design by NKBA member Cameron M. Snyder, CK

Fixture, Fittings, Appliances, and Controls in the Sink/Prep Center

The design of the sink itself presents many opportunities, with product manufacturers creating accessories that create a prep center right in the sink (see Figure 8.21). The option of a remote control for the drain can reduce frustration and improve safety in that it reduces the need to grip/grasp, and it eliminates the need to reach blindly into a full sink. While most of these sinks are too deep for a full knee space, they can be good applications when the client will benefit from concentrating the work area and reducing the need to travel back and forth in the kitchen.

When selecting faucets and fittings for the sink, concerns for someone with cognitive impairments include the risk of scalding and leaving the water on, and specifying an anti-scald faucet and

FIGURE 8.21 Sinks accessorized to become full prep zones, and faucets that can be installed and positioned where needed as needed.

Courtesy of Kohler Co.

FIGURE 8.22 Touch controls improve fittings for a variety of needs.
Courtesy of Delta Faucet

electronic-sensor faucet controls help ensure that the water is not left running. The anti-scald feature will also help those of us with slower reactions times and reduced sensitivity to the temperature changes. In some cases, the addition of instant hot or filtered water dispensers at the sink can reduce the need to involve the use of other appliances, but again, consideration must be given to the user's ability to use the hot water safely. Electronic sensor controls on faucets and lighting help ensure that things are shut off when the user is finished. Motion-sensor light switches and touch-control faucets eliminate the use of hands for operation (see Figure 8.22).

In addition the controls should be lever or loop handles, or at a minimum, not smooth round knobs. The single-lever faucets with pull-out spray heads and the introduction of faucets that can be installed and positioned wherever needed have greatly improved function in this regard. Changing the location of the faucet from the back of the sink to an offset location to one side of the sink can put it within reach, especially when the space is limited or there is no knee space at the fixture.

There are a number of appliances showing up in the sink and prep center, and with them, features and concepts that can improve access and function. In general, placing controls and the operating and moving parts of any appliance within comfortable reach of the cook is critical, and at the dishwasher, two concepts support this. When the design for the space lends itself, the dishwasher can be elevated, which certainly reduces bending for standing cooks and can improve access for seated cooks who have the balance to lean and reach (see Figures 8.23 and 8.24). Some cabinetry lines offer a standard cabinet or you may need a custom cabinet or one built on site with stock parts and pieces. You will need to carefully consider this concept because the raised dishwasher can become an obstacle when it interrupts the flow of the work area. When the dishwasher is raised, a landing counter between it and the sink will need to be at the height of the sink. The 30 inch x 48 inch (762 mm × 1219 mm) clear floor space required at the dishwasher should be measured adjacent to the door so that the open door will not interfere with the clear space (see Figure 8.25).

Another option is dishwasher drawers, either stacked or, better yet, the single drawer, as this greatly reduces the need to bend and the obstruction that the open door can become (see Figure 8.26). When considering a drawer, be sure to discuss with your client his or her comfort level and ability to reach over the side of the drawer and access the inside.

FIGURE 8.23 Raised dishwasher: This raised dishwasher reduces bending.

Courtesy of Poggenpohl US, Inc.

Dishwasher controls should be raised to offer tactile and redundant cuing. While controls on the top of the door are convenient for a standing person, they may confuse someone with visual or cognitive impairments because they are hidden when the door is closed. Another feature that reduces effort on the part of the cook is the automatic dispensing of detergent within the dishwasher. The noise level of dishwashers has been greatly insulated, so be sure to review the noise level as described on the specification sheet and chose the quietest to minimize background noise distortion, particularly for the client with hearing issues.

FIGURE 8.24 This raised dishwasher is placed at the end of the cabinet and counter length, making it aesthetically and functionally right.

Courtesy of Mary Jo Peterson, Inc.

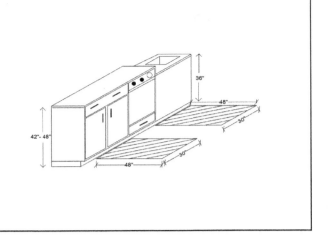

FIGURE 8.25 Access Standard 13: Clear floor space at dishwasher.

Small appliances are frequently stored and used in the sink/prep center, and access to them can be challenging to those of us with sensory, cognitive, or physical issues. Whenever possible, storage of frequently used, small appliances should be in the position where they might be used, not tucked away and requiring unpacking and moving before use. Appliance garages are constantly being redefined and with the added influence of technology, there are a number of options (see Figure 8.27).

Waste containers and recycle centers may include compactors or compost appliances and they will also have to follow the same guidance to be accessible, designed within the reach of the client and so that they can be accessed with minimum bending or reaching. If a compactor is specified, the ability to lock it when not in use can reduce the misuse by a child or one with cognitive issues. In these appliances or storage units, it is important to consider how they will be emptied and proximity to the garage or waste collection point is critical. Given the limits on storage, there are some products that help with this process and reduce the amount of space needed in the prep area.

When specifying a garbage disposer, discuss the options with the client to determine if a continuous feed can be safely switched. The benefit of the continuous feed is that the cook does not have

FIGURE 8.26 Single-drawer dishwashers reduce bending.

Courtesy of John Salmen, Universal Designers and Consultants, Inc.

REACH RANGE (ACCESS STANDARD 22)

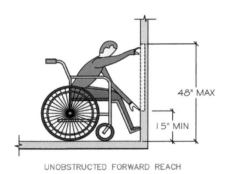

48" MAX

15" MIN

UNOBSTRUCTED FORWARD REACH

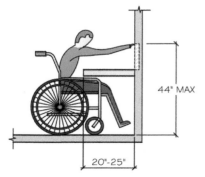

44" MAX

20"-25"

OBSTRUCTED HIGH FORWARD REACH
FIGURE 8.28 Access Standard 27: Standard reach ranges for a seated person.

to maneuver the cover to operate the appliance, but safe use will require a clear indication of the control switch.

Storage and Accessories, in the Sink/Prep Center

On cabinetry, touch latches eliminate the need for grasp or strength and the risk of anything being hooked by the hardware, but they may be confusing for someone with visual or cognitive impairments. Contrast can be used to visually highlight the controls. Assisted automatic opening and soft close can be beneficial in many ways, but whatever the method, it should be used throughout to reduce confusion. The design of the hardware should be easy to grasp and require minimum pressure to open. Locking hardware may be desirable where cleaning supplies, medications, or other items that might be a risk to children or family members with cognitive issues are to be stored. Raising toe kicks on sink and storage cabinets 9 inches to 12 inches (229 mm to 305 mm) provides clearance for wheelchair footrests and other mobility aids, increasing clear floor space. When planning for a particular client, measure their footrest clearance to confirm height. As a first step toward improved access, drawers on full extension slides are the most basic and successful storage design concept.

Thoughtful design can often result in storage right where it is needed, in the sink/prep center or throughout the kitchen. Storage should be placed at the point of use and within easy reach with as much as possible stored between 15 inches to 48 inches (381 mm to 1219 mm) above the floor (see Figure 8.28). Tall storage takes advantage of the full reach range. When planning storage above the sink base or sink where reach is obstructed the guideline for high reach is 44 inches (1118 mm) maximum, an interesting dimension, given that wall cabinets typically begin at 54 inches (1372 mm), completely out of reach of the seated cook.

As always, the best approach is to work with your client to determine his or her comfortable reach range, ability to bend and to grip and lift or carry, and priorities for storage. Chapter 5 offers a number of aids for collecting and confirming this information, and it is worth emphasizing that a client's ability to grip, lift, and carry is best confirmed by demonstration (use a heavy fry pan or a bag of potatoes). Chapter 6 discusses storage concepts and features in detail, but there are a few accessories and concepts that change and improve access tremendously, and they should be mentioned here. To begin with, shallow storage reduces reaching, improves visibility, and consumes less clear floor space, so depth should always be considered. For example, in a walk-in pantry, reducing the shelf depths to 18 inches (457 mm) from the standard 24 inches (610 mm) can increase the clear passage into the pantry and will hold much of what is to be stored. Be creative and plan storage in the sink center that is more than just out-of-reach wall cabinets for glasses. Plan shallow storage areas with open shelves, tambour, sliding, bifold, up-lifting, or other doors that will not protrude into the clear space. Limiting cabinet door size to 18 inches (457 mm) wide will limit interference. Shallow hutch storage 12 inches to 15 inches (305 mm to 381 mm) deep will accommodate most kitchen glassware and dishes and will minimize obstruction of clear floor space, while providing storage at the point of use.

A cook using a knee space at the sink will also need tools and products to function, and there are base cabinet accessories that take great advantage of shallow or narrow spaces of as little as 3 inches (76 mm).

Open shelves are easy to access and provide easy view of stored items—helpful when memory fails or vision is impaired. Open storage, such as a backsplash rail system, is easy to view and access.

If open storage is not possible or desired, lighting the interior of storage cabinets improves visibility. Storage of items in the order in which they will be used can be helpful to those of us with memory or other cognitive issues. Drawers on full extension glides and roll-out shelves are a straightforward way to make access easier. When organizing storage, those items used most and that are the heaviest should be stored to reduce bending and lifting.

As previously mentioned, storing small appliances on the counter eliminates the need to lift and carry. Provided balance is not an issue, most seated cooks can reach 24 inches (610 mm) to the backsplash area beyond standard base cabinetry, so generous counter depth can hold frequently used small appliances, either visibly or behind doors, so that they can be pulled forward for use but do not interfere with the working area. With careful electrical planning, appliances should be stored "ready to use." For safety, this can require outlets that will be automatically shut off when the door or other storage space is closed. When locating outlets, reach range and safety mush be considered, as discussed in Chapter 6.

In some cases wall cabinets can be lowered 3 inches (76 mm), so they are 15 inches (381 mm) above the counter and easier for someone short in stature to reach. However, for some users this storage may still be beyond the reach range, and there are accessories that allow this storage to be pulled down and it should be installed so that the handle is easily grasped by the cook. When this is planned carefully it can increase accessible storage.

Storage options in the cabinet that houses the sink have expanded, and when no knee space is planned in this cabinet, cleaning supplies and sometimes waste or compost can be easily stored and accessed here.

Accessories such as paper towel holders and towel bars should be placed within reach of the sink and within the 15-inch to 48-inch (381 mm to 1219 mm) reach range. Keep in mind that, for a person who needs a support for use or passage in the sink center, anything within reach will be used, and consider specifying only those accessories that will hold the weight and function as grab bars if called on to do so.

When specifying waste and recycle receptacles, consider a unit on a rolling shelf that can be removed by sliding it off laterally, rather than lifting it up. When planned into cabinetry on full extension glides, these units do not protrude into the clear floor space except when in use. If the knee space under the sink is flexible in use, the waste container can be placed there. Towel and dish cloth storage should be planned so the contents can be accessed within the 15-inch to 48-inch (381 mm to 1219 mm) reach range. Hand and dish soap dispensers built into the counter reduce confusion and reinforce the order of tasks, and they should be easy to fill.

Access Standards
The NKBA Guidelines and Access Standards that relate to the sink and preparation are 10, 11, 12, 13, 14, 15, 25, 27, 28, and 31.

Responsive Design Summary: Sink and Preparation Center
- Sensory
  - Universal recommendations
    - Specify an anti-scald faucet device.
    - Specify eased counter edges and rounded corners, helpful and useful as a tactile guide (Guideline 8).

- Use both visual and tactile cuing when possible to improve comprehension, such as to identify hot or cold water, or on the edge of a counter to aid in way-finding.
- Provide task lighting.
- Provide the ability to adjust lighting levels.
- Use contrast carefully to highlight edges or borders, such as the edge of a counter or a border around the floor.
- Use reflective surfaces, pattern, and contrast judiciously to avoid visual confusion and issues with depth perception.
- Plan shallow storage areas with open shelves, and tambour, sliding, up-lifting, or other doors that will not protrude into the clear space.
- Light storage interiors to improve visibility.
- Consider the line of sight of user when planning height of bottom of glazing (Access Standard 15).
- Plan a batch feed disposer or a continuous disposer with a clearly marked switch to eliminate confusion with other switches.
- Access recommendations
  - Include the appropriate assistive devices for redundant cuing for safe use of appliances and the space.
- Cognition
  - Universal recommendations
    - Specify electronic sensor controls on faucets to help ensure that things are shut off when the user is finished.
    - Evaluate intuitive cuing and operation, such as using a blue color for cold and a red color for hot, to assure ease of use.
    - Consider instant hot water dispensers to eliminate the use of cooktop or microwave for some food and beverage preparation.
    - Consider a filtered drinking water faucet within child's reach to encourage children to get their own drinks.
    - Avoid cabinet panels on integrated dishwasher and trash compactors which can cause confusion.
    - Plan a dishwasher with a shutoff switch or a model that has programmable lock-out to prevent accidental operation of the appliance.
    - Plan disposer and dishwasher switches out of the reach range of younger children.
    - Specify a trash compactor with a lock to keep children out. Some manufacturers offer a removable key lock.
    - Incorporate open storage and generous counters to allow for easy view and ordering of stored items, which may be helpful when memory fails.
    - Plan storage for medications that is out of the reach of children or others not able to use them as directed.
  - Access recommendations
    - (Note: all access considerations have been accepted as general universal design.)
- Physical
  - Universal recommendations
    - Plan multiple-height sinks and work surfaces with opportunities for flexible knee spaces below (Guideline 7).
    - Plan clipped or eased counter edges to reduce potential hazards for one's hip or head, particularly that of a toddler or busy child (Guideline 8).
    - Avoid any controls that are difficult to grasp or operate, particularly smooth, round knobs. Consider an electronic or battery-operated motion-sensor faucet to reduce the dexterity required for operation and save water.
    - Include a step stool at the sink base to eliminate the need to climb on the counter to use the sink or access storage, reducing safety risks.
    - Select a sink with integrated accessories, like chopping blocks and strainers/colanders, so both hands can be used to cut or pour.
    - Install soap dispensers into the sink or counter within reach of the user to reduce needed strength and dexterity.

- Evaluate dishwashers with adjustable racks to make loading more convenient.
- Dishwashers with automatic soap dispensing eliminate the need to add soap in every wash.
- Plan a waste receptacle on a rolling shelf so it can be removed by sliding it off laterally, rather than lifting it up.
- Consider line of sight of user when planning height of bottom of glazing.
- Access recommendations
  - Plan a minimum clear floor space 48 inch × 30 inches (1219 mm × 762 mm) centered on the sink (Access Standard 6).
  - Plan the minimum size of a knee space 36 inches × 27 inches high × 17 inches deep (914 mm x 686 mm high × 432 mm deep) with protection for exposed pipes (Access Standard 6 and 10).
  - Choose sink controls that are operable with one hand and not require tight grasping, pinching, or twisting or the wrist (Access Standard 19).
  - Elevate the dishwasher for less bending and improved access from a seated or standing position, when the space allows (Access Standard 13).
  - Maintain a minimum 24 inches (610 mm) of landing counter at the sink height when planning a raised dishwasher (Access Standard 11).
  - Position the 30 inch × 48 inch (762 mm × 1219 mm) of clear floor space so the dishwasher door does not obstruct it (Access Standard 13 Code Reference).
  - Plan two counter heights in the kitchen—one at 28 inches to 36 inches (711 mm to 914 mm) and the other at 36 inches to 45 inches (914 mm to 1143 mm) (Access Standard 25).
  - Plan at least one 30 inch wide (762 mm wide) section of counter 34 inches (864 mm) high or lower, or adjustable from 29 inches to 36 inches (737 mm to 914 mm), for food preparation (Access Standard 12).
  - Place storage of frequently used items, accessories, and controls 15 to 48 inches (381 mm to 1219 mm) above the floor (Access Standard 27 and 28).
  - Specify lighting controls between 15 inches and 48 inches (381 mm and 1219 mm) and operable with a closed fist and with minimal effort (Access Standard 19).

Refrigeration Center

In Chapter 6, the design of the refrigeration center is discussed in detail, including many references to design for the differences in people. The intent here is to supplement that chapter's discussion with only that information that is specific or unique to a client with exceptional needs. For a complete review of kitchen planning relating to the refrigeration center, please refer to Chapter 6.

Placement and Clearance Considerations at the Refrigeration Center

In the case of the refrigerator, the required minimum 30 inch x 48 inch (762 mm x 1219 mm) of clear floor space should be positioned in front of or offset up to 24 inches (610 mm) on the handle side of the refrigerator so the door minimally obstructs it (see Figure 8.29). While access standards recommend a parallel approach, additional clear space to allow for either parallel or perpendicular approach, or a 48-inch x 48-inch (1219 mm x 1219 mm) total adds greater flexibility. Given the

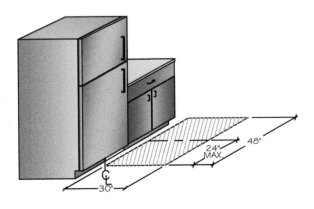

FIGURE 8.29 Access Standard 16: Clear floor space for parallel approach to the refrigerator.

current trends to French door refrigerators and drawers, this added clear floor space becomes more critical, and is typically done anyway when planning a multiple-cook kitchen.

For a seated cook, the space adjacent to the refrigerator is ideal for a knee space, and it should be planned on the handle side of a side-hinged model. Because storage is also critical here, this knee space may be immediately adjacent or at the prep center, which often falls between the refrigerator and the sink. The dimensions and details of the knee space are discussed above in the sink/prep center. The clear floor space should not be obstructed by a refrigerator that is deeper than adjacent cabinetry, and designing a pocket into the wall behind the refrigerator can eliminate this challenge, as can specifying a counter depth or integrated refrigerator. Another option that can be worked into some spaces with multiple benefits is to block out adjacent cabinetry 6 inches (152 mm), which will create a deeper cavity for the refrigerator. The added depth can also be added to the adjacent counter space, providing room for small appliances and other storage at the back of the counter, still within reach, but without compromising the work surface.

When possible, refrigerator placement between two tall elements should be avoided, as this eliminates the option of an adjacent landing counter. Placing the minimum 15 inch wide (381 mm wide) landing counter immediately adjacent to the handle side of the refrigerator rather than across the work aisle makes it more usable by a person who has strength, grip, or balance issues, or a person who uses a mobility aid, as it allows food to be removed from the refrigerator directly onto the counter without the need for carrying. If this is not possible, a pull-out work surface or rolling cart, as illustrated earlier in this chapter, can help assist the user. With a side-by-side refrigerator, the landing counter should first be accessible to a person who is using the fresh food side.

In addition to the main refrigerator, smaller auxiliary refrigerators can be useful in creating storage at the point of use and in reducing traffic in the work aisles, as well as helping to create multiple prep centers (see Figure 8.30). When planned, these units must also have the clear floor space for approach and the work or landing surfaces incorporated into the plan.

Appliance Features in the Refrigeration Center

Of the popular styles of refrigerator available, the side-by-side, column, French door, and drawer units all offer some benefits, and careful review of client needs and wishes, as well as reach range and abilities should guide the decision. The side-by-side models have smaller doors, so they are easier to maneuver around, and they place some storage within everyone's reach. The French door refrigerators have the same advantage as to door size, and they have the benefit of drawer storage, which can be easier for most people to access, but they put more freezer storage and less refrigerator storage within the reach of most people, particularly those operating from a seated position. Column refrigerators offer the greatest benefit of the three in that they can be sized for specific use, have full-height storage in each compartment, and they can be installed so that both doors hinge to the advantage of the client.

Two specification options that will make any of these models more usable are the ability to convert to a 180° hinge and the ability to reduce the suction on the vacuum seal of the doors/drawers.

Drawer refrigerators provide chilled storage that can be easily accessed and hold great appeal, provided your client has the balance and strength to reach over and into the drawers, and lift and carry contents. While this is easy for many of us, it can be a challenge for a cook operating from a seated position and with limited lower body control or balance. Newer models with division of space within the refrigerator include a shallow drawer above the main deeper drawer. This shallow drawer at no-bend height is ideal storage for anyone, and can be put to good use with those items used most frequently. This discussion can be applied to other refrigerator types that have similar characteristics, and for some the smaller, top-mount refrigerator can be the answer, from a convenience and a cost perspective.

Once the style or model is chosen, there are some things to consider in the hardware, accessories, and lighting of the refrigerator. Handles that are longer will put the ability to open the unit into more hands. There should be enough space between the handle and the door to allow a hand to pass through and grip the handle, and the surface should be nonslip. For the cook with limited strength, it can also allow for a towel or other assistive device to pass through so that the cook has more leverage when opening the door. Taking this a step further, some manufacturers can provide

(a)

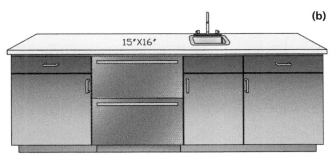

(b)

FIGURE 8.30 When undercounter refrigeration is planned, the landing area is planned above the unit.

(a) courtesy Sub-Zero Wolf

a small device that weakens the vacuum seal on the door, making it easier to open, but care must be taken to do this with the blessing of the manufacturer. Ice and water dispensers on the door are convenient features that require the use of one hand and less movement/maneuvering. Although they negatively affect the appliance's energy rating, they eliminate the opening/closing of the door by children and they keep water seekers out of the work flow at the prep/cleanup sink.

Light and temperature control and even the lamps should be located toward the front of the unit to make operation and lamp replacement easier to access. LED-sourced lighting is good for its longevity and flexibility as we can now find lighting at the front and at the point of use within the appliance. Web-connected refrigerators can assist with home care and monitoring and at the very least; they can reduce maintenance issues for the client.

Shelves and drawers that roll out to the cook are ideal. Deep storage on the door of a refrigerator and a counter depth overall, put most things in easier view and reach, and the improved food storage benefits everyone but is of special value to the cook with sensory or cognitive issues. Automatic closing and/or alarms that indicate when a door is ajar can be helpful, and those alarms should be both visual and audible. Appliances with large, easy-to-read controls facilitate use, and your client may need to determine if green or blue or yellow digital clocks and indicators are easier to see. While the invisible nature of integrated appliances is beautiful, it can cause confusion, so this should be reviewed with the client and the planning team.

Storage and Accessories in the Refrigeration Center

As discussed in the sink/prep center, there are a number of accessories available that make the needed storage in the refrigerator center easier to access. In addition, this is often where some pantry storage is created. If a tall pantry cabinet is planned, the space adjacent to the hinge side of a single-door refrigerator is a good place for it. The fact that this blocks adjacent landing area can, to some degree, be compensated for with the use of a rolling cart and by substituting opposing counters. There are a variety of pantry configurations that allow the user to easily pull the storage out within sight and reach. When planning a tall cabinet or a deep cabinet over the refrigerator, tray storage can sometimes make reachable storage out of that portion of the cabinet.

When the pantry is a walk-in pantry, the clearances required for passage can reduce the resulting storage, and there may be times that a cabinet pantry simply nets more usable and accessible space. Keep in mind that shallower shelves are easier to see and reach, and that the door opening must be a minimum 32 inches (813 mm) clear if a cook using a wheelchair is to enter. This can be a great place for a sliding door, as it eliminates the obstacle a swing door can become.

Access Standards

The NKBA Guidelines and Access Standards that relate to refrigeration are 6 and 16.

Responsive Design Summary: Refrigeration Center

- Sensory
  - Universal recommendations
    - Specify refrigerators that have large, easy-to-read controls, and ask manufacturers if there are options for larger print read-outs.
    - Select refrigerator controls that are intuitive; that is, with a visible arrow or line that points to red or blue to help determine how to adjust the temperature.
    - Specify refrigerators with light and temperature controls located in front portion of interior for improved view.
    - Consider programmable controls to simplify consistent operation.
  - Access recommendations
    - (Note: all access considerations have been accepted as general universal design.)
- Cognition
  - Universal recommendations
    - Specify a refrigerator with doors that close automatically and have open door alarms to help ensure that the door is not accidentally left open.
    - Use caution in specifying cabinet panels on integrated refrigeration, as they can cause confusion.
    - Consider ice and water dispensers on the refrigerator door because they direct children away from the prep/cleanup sink, reduce the opening of the full door, and can be used with one hand.
    - Consider Web-connected refrigerators that maintain themselves and reduce user maintenance tasks.
    - Look for refrigerators with intuitive and redundant cuing, such as using a blue color for cold and a red color for hot.
  - Access recommendations
    - (Note: all access considerations have been accepted as general universal design.)
- Physical
  - Universal recommendations
    - Place the recommended minimum landing counter without obstruction and immediately adjacent to the refrigerator, when possible.
    - Consider a side-by-side refrigerator with handles that extend the full length of the doors to accommodate cooks of different heights. Consider the ease with which the refrigerator door can be opened.
    - Look for refrigerators with light and temperature controls located in front portion of interior for improved access and view.
    - Consider an easily accessible, undercounter unit, in addition to the main refrigerator.
    - Consider ice and water dispensers on the refrigerator door.
  - Access recommendations
    - Position a minimum 30 inch x 48 inch (762 mm x 1219 mm) of clear floor space in front of or offset up to 24 inches (610 mm) on the handle side so the door minimally obstructs it (Guideline 16 Code Reference).
    - Consider a 48 inch × 48 inch (1219 mm x 1219 mm) of clear floor space for more flexibility in approach and use.

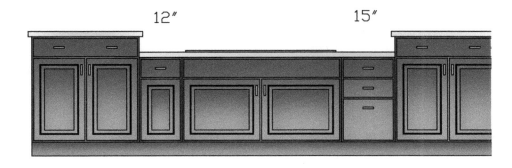

12"   15"

FIGURE 8.31 Guideline 17: A cooktop and the adjacent landing counters must be at the same height.

- Plan a knee space adjacent to the refrigerator 36 inches wide × 27 inches high × 17 inches deep (914 mm × 686 mm high × 432 mm deep) (Guideline 6 Access Standard).
- Choose appliance handles that are operable with one hand and do not require tight grasping.
- Select a refrigerator that puts most of the storage between 15 inches and 48 inches (381 mm to 1219 mm) AFF.

Cooking Center

In Chapter 6, the design of the cooking center is discussed in detail, including many references to design for the differences in people. The intent here is to supplement that chapter's discussion with only that information that is specific or unique to a client with exceptional needs. For a complete review of kitchen planning relating to the cooking center, please refer to Chapter 6.

Particularly with the numbers and variety of cooking appliances today, we can be designing multiple cooking stations within one kitchen. Depending on a client's habits, preferences, and needs, we may incorporate a surface cooking center, an oven center or centers, a microwave and/or speed cooking center, and space for smaller cooking appliances, so the following information will include a look at each in relation to sensory, cognitive, and physical abilities of the client.

This center is where safety risks and improved access sometimes conflict; the cooktop that is lowered for access by a seated cook becomes accessible also to the young child, or the knee space at the cooktop that puts access and use within the reach of a seated cook also exposes that cook to burn risk that had been out of reach. While the concepts and products here are presented as steps toward an improved accessible cooking experience, the need to discuss and evaluate decisions in this area cannot be overemphasized.

Placement and Clearance Considerations in the Cooking Center

The area surrounding and including the cooktop is what we will call the surface cooking center. In some cases, this will be the surface cooking portion of a range, but when possible, having a separate cooktop and oven(s) is more flexible and allows a more personalized approach to the placement of the appliances, so the separate cooktop will be considered first.

Surface Cooking

Second only to the sink center in time spent here, the surface cooking center should also be faced to the social area whenever possible, a benefit to most and more essential to those of us with hearing impairments or issues around eating. However, safety and ventilation needs will sometimes dictate that it face a wall. The standard minimum 30 inch × 48 inch (762 mm × 1219 mm) of clear floor space can be planned for either a parallel or perpendicular (front) approach, centered on the appliance. As discussed in Chapter 6, there are minimum landing space dimensions on either side of a cooktop and behind it in an island or peninsula configuration for safety and convenience (see Figure 8.31). When planning for a shorter client or one who cooks from a seated position, this area may be lowered, and when it is, these minimums must remain at the same height as the cooktop, again for safety and function.

This is an ideal place for heat-proof counters, providing a place for the cook who may not be able to lift heavy pots to slide them to the side. Controls should be designed at the side or front or

FIGURE 8.32 Side controls on the cooktop, a sink to one side, and a generous knee space improve access and function.
Courtesy of Mary Jo Peterson, Inc.

remote to the cooktop for easier and safer access. In addition, a pot-filler faucet and a sink or drain in the area complete a plan that allows the cook to fill and empty pots without ever having to lift them (see Figure 8.32).

Whether a plan includes a second sink in the cooking area or a single main sink, the cooktop should have an uninterrupted path to the sink and when possible a continuous stretch of counter to again allow for sliding heavier pots.

As with most work areas, a knee space can increase the options for use by a seated cook, and this concept in this area generates strong arguments for and against. An open space below the cooktop can double as a knee space or as storage for a rolling cart, rolling waste container unit, or a stool. As at the sink or prep area, a knee space allows for closer access and easier use by a seated cook. This same access creates serious risk of the cook leaning on/reaching over hot elements or even open flames. In addition, if a seated cook is to travel from the cooktop with hot food or equipment, it is likely that cook will place the items in his/her lap, creating another hazardous situation. There are features in a cooktop to reduce these risks, which will be discussed in the next section.

Basic knee space guidelines were discussed in the sink center section of this chapter, but there are design considerations when the knee space is at a cooktop, which will be examined here. When lowering the work and cooking surface, measure your client's clearance and consider the "thickness" of the cooktop, counter, and protective panels to determine the best height, recommended between 28 and 34 inches (711 mm and 864 mm). Although the recommended clearance for the height of the knee space is 27 inches (686 mm), the exact counter height for a specific client will be determined by the height of his or her wheelchair arm or his or her knees if the wheelchair arms are not an issue. An apron and underpanel must be planned to cover any rough surfaces and to insulate the appliance workings from the cook, as well as protecting the cook from burns, abrasions, or electric shock (see Figure 8.33).

As mentioned, the cooktop knee space is a good place for a rolling cart, as the cart can help many of us to transfer heavy items to and from the cooking area. While this knee space is typically

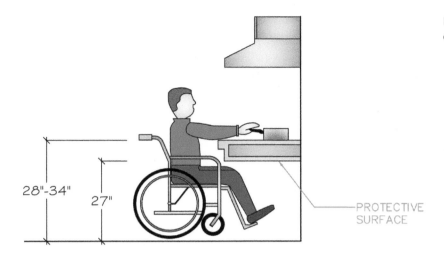

supported by cabinetry on either side, it is also critical to build in sufficient support as the front edge because that counter may be used for support as one approaches the cooktop.

Oven

Oven placement is a good example of a concept that began as access for a specific need and evolved to good universal design as it benefits so many. Where once we had ovens stacked in tall cabinets, today we see more of ovens split and designed at heights that reduce bending and lifting (see Figure 8.34).

The 30 inch × 48 inch (762 mm x 1219 mm) of clear floor space at the oven should be positioned so that the oven door does not obstruct it. When possible the minimum landing space should be immediately adjacent to the oven, and in the case of a side swing oven door, on the latch side (see Figure 8.35). A knee space next to the oven can benefit the user, and the space can double as storage for a rolling cart, convenient for transporting roasted or baked items. This landing surface or the top deck of the rolling cart should be heat resistant to receive hot items, even more essential for those of us with limited strength or balance. If adjacent landing space is not possible, another option is a pull-out work surface at or near the oven, provided it is not obstructed by the oven door.

In some cases, the total space available, budget, and the cook's preference may dictate that a range is the appropriate appliance for a given design, and in this case, an adjacent knee space can make a major difference in access by a person using a wheelchair. One of the obstacles to selecting

FIGURE 8.34 Ovens placed next to each other, rather than stacked, can be placed at a comfortable height. *Design on left by NKBA member Jennifer L. Gilmer, CKD; Design on right by NKBA member Lori Carroll*

FIGURE 8.35 Access standard 23: Landing space at the oven.

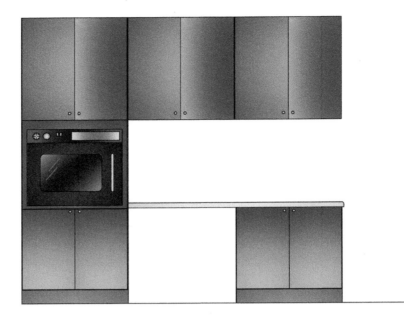

a range is that the oven is low and the oven door can be a significant obstacle, especially for shorter or seated cooks. Newer ranges with a smaller oven just under the cooktop have made this access issue go away (see the "Appliance Features" section in the "Cooking Center" later in this chapter).

There is a unique challenge that is not always obvious when planning the clearances and layout in the cooking center. First, when a tall oven cabinet or a range is installed in a recessed corner, a person of shorter stature or one operating from a seated position may not be able to access the oven (see Figure 8.36). When the oven door is open, the door itself holds the cook away from its interior and in this corner installation, that cook cannot stand or sit to the side of the door, making the interior unreachable.

Microwave

A microwave hung immediately below a wall cabinet may be outside the user's reach range, and placing the microwave on the counter or below the counter may be a more comfortable height. The 15-inch (381 mm) landing counter can be placed above, below, or adjacent it, depending on its placement. For a side swing oven door, the heat-resistant landing counter should be adjacent to the latch side. If this is not possible, a pull-out work surface below the microwave can be the landing counter. Even better, placing the microwave on a continuous counter allows items to slide

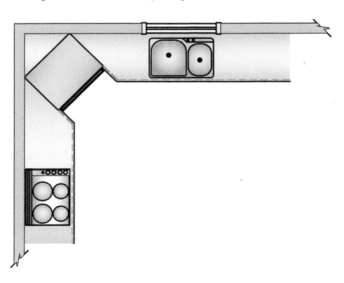

FIGURE 8.36 Access Standard 4: Recessed corner designs can be difficult or impossible for a person of shorter stature or one operating from a seated position.

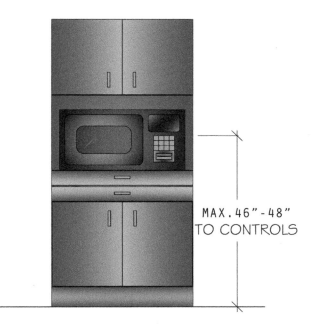

MAX.46"-48"
TO CONTROLS

from the food preparation center into the microwave, and then the items can slide from the microwave to the serving center.

The height of the microwave can be debated and, with the heavy use by children, it has moved lower. The access standard is that you avoid placing the microwave controls above 48 inches (1219 mm) (see Figure 8.37), which eliminates an over-the-range installation, and another consideration is the line of sight of the cook. Lowering the oven so that more cooks can reach it, but then creating the need to bend to read the controls is a challenge to be discussed with your client.

The microwave oven can be located in the cooking center, near the refrigerator, or in the serving center, and it is not uncommon that there be more than one, especially when one of the cooks has cognitive or physical issues. Because it can be portable, is fairly straightforward in its function, and small, it is a good option when planning a secondary cooking or reheating station (see Figure 8.38).

FIGURE 8.38 A microwave placed under the counter is convenient for children to use.
Courtesy of KraftMaid Cabinetry

Appliance Features in the Cooking Center

It's a natural consequence of aging that our tactile sensitivity decreases and thermoregulation becomes less efficient, and for those of us with cognitive impairments, the cooking experience can be intimidating. For clients with virtually any sensory, cognitive, or physical issues, there is increased risk of injury from hot surfaces and items. Features that address safety issues and those that make use and maintenance easier will be at the top of the list when selecting appliances and related equipment for the cooking center.

The appliances and controls should be easy to understand. Although some feel color cuing takes away from the beauty of the appliance, it can be used to reinforce understanding, with red for hot and blue for cold. One challenge to this is in the case of a black glass or reflective cooktop or oven control panel. The color red can be very difficult to see against the black by the aging eye, so look for better contrast or redundant cuing, such a beep or a blinking light, or an icon or image. These multiple indicators provide an additional way for a cook with sensory or cognitive impairments to determine on/off, when a cycle is complete, if a surface is still on or hot, when the correct temperature setting has been reached. Intelligent appliance controls are changing our interface and opening the opportunity for programmed favorites, brainy appliances that judge when more or less heat or time should be provided, and when the item is cooked to desired doneness, at which point the appliance communicates that it is shutting down and does so. The ability to use this communication with our appliances for health monitoring is also growing in practice, although not mainstream. The options are endless.

Cooking surface and ventilation controls should be offset toward the room for easy operation, within reach, at a height that works for the cook. Ventilation controls can be a particular challenge, and they should be planned between 15 and 44 inches (381 mm and 1118 mm) above the floor (see Figure 8.39).

In the case of cooktops, the controls should be at the front or to one side of the unit to eliminate the need to reach across heating elements to operate the controls. Lever controls are easier to grasp and turn than smooth round knobs, and touch controls that include a tactile cue, a raised or textured surface, and logically follow the burner configuration are more easily interpreted and used. Contrast in color or lighting around the control can also be an asset. Creating this contrast or adding visual or tactile reinforcement can be done when an existing appliance controls are not clear or intuitive. A cabinet door bumper pad or a brightly colored dot can be added to the button on the microwave for heating morning coffee, or the temperature setting used most often at the oven. In some cases, contact with the manufacturer may reveal an accessory label available in larger, bolder print, or an adjustment to the programming of the control panel that will increase the size or light of the indicators.

Cooking surface configurations can go far to improve safe access and use, beginning with the location of the controls. As previously mentioned, the controls must be positioned so that a cook

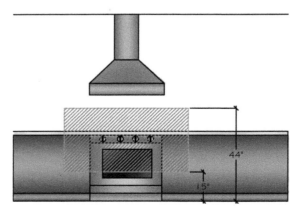

FIGURE 8.39 Ventilation controls should be placed 15–44 inches (381–1118 mm) above the floor.

VENTILATION CONTROLS
WITHIN 15"–44"
REACH CONTROL

FIGURE 8.40 Electric cooktop safety features include a universal off switch that lets the user shut down all the cooktop elements at once, a lock key that childproofs the unit, and an integral hot surface indicator for each element, which stays lit until the element has cooled.
Courtesy of Wolf Appliance, Inc.

need never reach over heating elements or open flames to operate them. Cooktop modules can serve this design need as they can be placed so that the burners are side by side rather than in front and behind, and while not common, there are unique configurations that offer a more linear or curved placement of the elements.

For most of us, induction cooktops reduce the risk of burns and fires. For those of us who are forgetful, the automatic temperature sensor and shut off is a risk reducer. In newer models, there is a natural mapping feature that activates the cooking surface according to the size pan being used. For those of us more susceptible to air impurities or with reduced sense of smell, this technology cooks more cleanly. The smooth glass surface is great for sliding rather than lifting pots and pans, but the main benefits come from the fact the surface can get warm but not hot. The only heat on the surface is that transferred back from the pan, and we even have a answer for that in the "coaster," available from some manufacturers, that can be placed between the glass and the pan to eliminate this heat on the cooktop. This means that the risk of burns is greatly reduced and cleanup is much easier, as nothing is burned on. As they gain in popularity, the options are expanding and include a single burner unit that can be placed anywhere, useful when a temporary or permanent lowered cooking area is needed,

In general, cooking surfaces with smooth glass top or continuous grates allow items to slide across the surface. Cooking surfaces with a control lock-out program keep children or those with cognitive issues from accidentally turning on the appliance (see Figure 8.40).

For ventilation, compare the noise level on different types of ventilation appliances, including in line or remote motors, and chose the quietest to minimize background noise, more important for someone with partial hearing, or those who relies on hearing to find their way. Electronic sensor controls on ventilation activate the system when the temperature reaches a certain point, and help ensure that things are shut off after the user is finished. Proximity or downdraft ventilation or shallow, retractable overhead ventilation systems with eased or radius edges do not obstruct the cook and reduce the risk of collision with the cook's head (see Figure 8.41), an issue when planning the cooking area for cooks of serious variations in height. Remote switching for ventilation, traditionally a custom installation but now more readily available, provides needed flexibility to get the controls within reach of the shorter or seated cook.

When a range is the chosen option, the first feature to confirm is the location of controls, as a backsplash location for the control panel is not uncommon and less than ideal. To eliminate the need for a cook to reach over the burners, be sure to select a range that has controls at the front or side (see Figure 8.42).

FIGURE 8.41 Overhead ventilation with eased and curved edges reduces the risk of head bumps for users who are tall or who have issues with vision.
Design by NKBA member Siri Evju

There are interesting variations on the traditional range that are making it more flexible and functional for the shorter or seated cook. As mentioned, the shift in configuration places the smaller

opening just under the surface cooking and the main or larger oven nearer the floor. The top smaller cavity is available from some manufacturers as an oven, a microwave, or a warming drawer. While this configuration puts the larger oven at a disadvantaged height, the smaller oven can be used for much of what we seem to be doing in ovens from day to day, and it is a door or drawer that most cooks can manage much easier than the door to the larger oven. If this does not meet client needs, there is also a model available with two equal-sized ovens, reducing issues with the smaller cavity. If the upper smaller cavity is specified as a microwave, it also shows wonderful access progress, as it reduces the need to consider the over-the-range microwave which is at a height that challenges many cooks.

For microwaves, there are many differences in auditory indicators (beeps) in different brands of appliances. For example, a microwave that beeps 5 times at completion might be better choice than one that beeps only once. The pitch of beep should also be evaluated. Technology has greatly simplified the options for microwave habits. While a cook can do elaborate recipes, he or she can also push button #1 for reheating coffee, or a labeled button for popping corn, all requiring less cognitive engagement and less hand manipulation.

The option of a drawer microwave has brought the installation under the counter and to a convenient height for many. There is an issue with standing cooks having to bend to read the controls, so specify a model with an angled panel to eliminate this problem. When considering ovens, the controls and handles should be operable with one hand, require only a minimal amount of strength for operation, and not require tight grasping, pinching, or twisting of the wrist. A field trip to an appliance showroom would be a good way to confirm that your client has the strength, dexterity, and balance to reach and lift into and out of the drawer.

Ovens are available in a great variety of sizes and shapes, and with varied functions and door designs, all to be tailored to your client's needs. Some of the same features for control and lighting for the refrigerator apply to ovens: large, easy-to-read controls, interior lighting near the front of the cavity, and redundant cuing to indicate the setting, when temperature limits are reached and the end of a cycle with sound and light. Ovens with automatic shutoffs reduce the dangers of a hot oven accidentally left on. An oven with a central lock-out program can keep children and those with cognitive issues from accidentally turning it on. Again, the technology-related intelligence of ovens and other appliances is changing rapidly to improve their function and ease of maintenance in the lives of clients. Given that anything with a "chip" in it can help monitor a cooks movement and activity if equipped to do so, these appliances are also entering the areas of social and personal health.

In terms of design, the biggest news might be in door design. Side-swing oven doors can eliminate the need for a cook to maneuver around the hot door to access the interior of the oven, but they do still require care and distance in a new location. Side-swing oven doors allow the cook to get closer to the interior and are less of an obstacle. French or split side-swing doors are another option with similar benefits and disadvantages. Drawer configurations eliminate the door issue altogether. There are many choices that improve access for some and careful examination with the client will be the best way to determine the best option.

Storage and Accessories in the Cooking Center

As in the other centers, adequate storage in the cooking center can be enhanced by the myriad of accessories that bring the stored items to the cook. Probably the heaviest equipment in the kitchen, pots and pans should be carefully sorted and prioritized so that those used frequently are stored within reach with minimal bending or lifting, and in close proximity to the place they will be used. This may involve hanging storage in or out of cabinetry or it may be in base cabinetry or shelves. It is best to avoid stacking pots, particularly those used most often, as this necessitates lifting multiples to get to one pot.

Smoke and fire alarms and extinguishers should be within easy reach, and they should incorporate dual or redundant cuing, so that whether the cook sees or hears the alarm, he or she receives the message. When considering fire safety, multiple and direct routes of egress should take into account the abilities and challenges of the client. A small thing, but worth mentioning, is the fire-resistant apron, which can help to reduce risks for the seated cook.

When working to make the contents of pots on surface burners visible, a demonstration mirror, angled over the cooktop, can help. The seated cook can look up and see the reflection of the contents of the pots and pans. If planning for this concept, include a plan for its cleaning and maintenance.

As mentioned, the pot-filler faucet comes in many sizes and shapes and can greatly reduce the need to carry heavy filled pots. To further reduce this challenge, the use of a built-in steamer allows the cook to steam the vegetables or fish and then drain and clean the appliance in place, requiring no lifting of the filled appliance.

Access Standards

The NKBA Kitchen Planning Guidelines and Access Standards that relate to cooking are 6, 17, 18, 19, 20, 21, 22, 23, and 27.

Responsive Design Summary: Cooking Center

- Sensory
  - Universal recommendations.
    - Request cooking appliances with large, easy-to-read controls to facilitate use.
    - Specify heat indicator lights on smooth surface electric cooktops.
    - Select cooking appliances with redundant cuing to indicate the setting, when temperature limits are reached the end of a cycle with sound and light.
    - Consider raised controls to provide tactile cuing.
    - Consider electronic backlit controls or glow-in-the-dark controls to provide better contrast.

- Consider proximity or downdraft ventilation or shallow, retractable overhead ventilation systems with eased or radius edges that do not obstruct the cook and avoid possible contact with the cook's head.
- Explore the addition of tactile cuing to identify a frequently used setting on the microwave, such as beverage or popcorn setting.
- Specify interior oven lighting that is near the front of the cavity for better view.
- Specify a smoke alarm with dual cuing, both audio and visual.
- Access recommendations
  - Choose quiet ventilation to minimize background noise for a client with hearing issues (Access Guideline 26).
- Cognition
  - Universal recommendations
    - Specify cooktops with a control lock-out program to eliminate accidental activation of the appliance.
    - Consider induction cooktops that sense the presence of a pan and include automatic shutoff.
    - Consider electric cooktops with a heat indicator light to help users recognize that the cooktop is hot.
    - Consider cooking controls that use numbers and pictures to indicate the cooking mode or process.
    - Look for redundant cuing that indicates the setting, when temperature limits are reached and the end of a cycle with sound and light.
    - Take advantage of technology with easy programming options.
    - Specify ovens with automatic shutoffs to reduce the dangers of a hot oven accidentally left on.
    - Specify an oven with a central lock-out program.
    - Specify electronic sensor controls on ventilation to help ensure that it comes on when needed and shuts off after the user is finished.
    - Place fire extinguishers 15 inches to 48 inches (381 mm to 1219 mm) above the floor (Access Standard 20).
  - Access recommendations
    - (Note: all access considerations have been accepted as general universal design.)
- Physical
  - Universal recommendations
    - Separate cooktop and oven appliances when possible to provide more flexibility in their position and location.
    - Specify controls, handles, and pulls that are operable with one hand, require only a minimal amount of strength for operation, and do not require tight grasping, pinching, or twisting of the wrist.
    - Consider task specific gas cooking element accessories such as wok support accessories to help stabilize a wok.
    - Store heavy and commonly used pots close to the cooking surface.
    - Plan a pot-filler or a faucet with retractable spray head in a main or secondary sink near the cooking surface to allow pots to be filled outside the sink with less lifting.
    - Specify microwaves with one-touch easy programming options that require less hand manipulation.
    - Plan the microwave at counter height or below so it is within reach of more cooks.
    - Avoid stacked double ovens; rather, use two separate single ovens, both at a comfortable height when possible.
    - Plan oven heights to reduce the need to bend or lift.
    - Consider side-swing oven doors to allow the cook to get closer to the interior.
  - Access recommendations
    - Plan a minimum clear floor space of 30 inches × 48 inches (762 mm × 1219 mm) at each appliance for approach for a person using a wheelchair (Access Standard 6).
    - Plan a knee space below the cooktop or next to the oven or range. When planning a knee space, the *minimum* dimensions are 30 inches wide by 27 inches high by 17 inches deep (762 mm x 686 mm high x 432 mm deep) (Guideline Access Standards 6 and 17).

- Lower the cooktop to 34 inches (864 mm) high or lower (Guideline 17 Access Standard) to improve the view into tall pots for a seated user.
- Maintain 12-inch and 15-inch (305 mm and 381 mm) landing counters at the same height as a lowered cooktop (Guideline 17).
- Specify a range or cooktop appliance with controls placed at the front to avoid reaching over burners (Guideline 17 Code Reference).
- Consider an angled mirror above the cooktop to make it easier for shorter or seated cooks to see into the pots, but recognize the maintenance challenge.
- Locate ventilation controls within 15 inches to 44 inches (381 mm to 1118 mm) above the floor so that they can be used by a child or seated person (Access Standard 19).
- Place the microwave oven at least 15 inches (381 mm) above the finished floor, and locate the controls below 48 inches (1219 mm) (Access Standard 21).
- Plan a heat-resistant landing counter adjacent to the handle side of the oven (Access Standard 22).
- For a side-swing oven door, the heat-resistant landing counter should be adjacent to the handle side (Access Standard 23).
- When the appropriate landing surface is not possible, a pull-out work surface below the appliance can be the landing counter.
- Position the 30 inch by 48 inch (762 mm × 1219 mm) of clear floor space, so the oven door does not obstruct it.

Serving and Dining Center

Placement and Clearance Considerations

The serving and eating centers of the kitchen are thoroughly examined in chapter 6, but there are a few things to emphasize in relation to access.

For dimensions per person at the eating area, the numbers will increase when a person is using a mobility aid. In a seating area where no one will need to pass by a seated diner, a minimum of 36 inches (914 mm) of clearance will allow a person using a wheelchair to move into the dining space, provided there is enough clearance in the knee space to make any required turns. When traffic will pass beyond the diner, the minimum increases to 60 inches (1525 mm), to allow a person in a chair to pass behind the diner, and it is critical that this passageway be maintained free of obstacles (see Figure 8.43).

It can become difficult to accomplish this clear floor space, and the space can seem "empty," so a shallow furniture piece is sometimes placed in this passage until such time as the full clearance is needed. The current trend to building in the table or a portion of the seating can help save space (see Figure 8.44). When a table is built in, room for a diner on one side of the table is lost, but the space that might have been needed to pass along that side of the table is saved. When banquette seating is used, the space required to pass behind that seated diner is saved.

The space and knee space allowed for each person will also increase when planning for those of us using a mobility aid and in particular, a wheelchair we will occupy to travel and while at the table. The width of the space allowed will grow from the basic allowance of 24 inches to 36 inches (610 mm to 914 mm). Beyond that, the dimensions are similar to those specified for a knee space elsewhere, 36 inches (914 mm) wide by 27 inches (686 mm) high by 19 inches (483 mm) deep as a minimum. While the height of the knee space must clear your client and their chair, the standard being 27 inches (686 mm), the actual table or work surface height should be close to 30 inches (762 mm), as this is standard table height and seating will typically fit this height (see Figure 8.45). However, a diner who operates from a seated position will often function best when the work surface height is as low as possible, so again, this is a point of exploration with your client.

The idea that seating should encourage face-to-face conversation becomes more critical when one of the diners has lost appetite or has hearing issues, and the social aspect of dining can reinforce good habits and improve communication. For example, a square or round table, rather than a long rectangle, and curved eating bars, rather than straight and long ones, make this not just more pleasant but more supportive.

FIGURE 8.43 Access Standard 8: Passage for a person using a wheelchair.

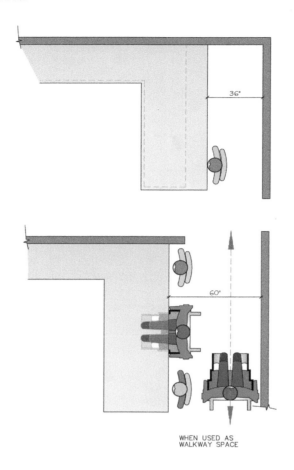

WHEN USED AS
WALKWAY SPACE

FIGURE 8.44 This banquette saves clear floor space in the dining area.
Design by NKBA member Dana Jones, CKD

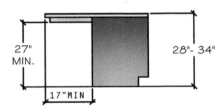

FIGURE 8.45 Access Standard 9: Seating area dimensions.

If they are to be part of the dining experience, be aware of radio, television, and computer placement. Perhaps the background noise of the television is distracting or the opposite: it may need to be directly visible for the diner who must use the closed-captioning. Specify eased counter edges and rounded corners, forgiving for those of us who bruise easily and may not be as visually attentive, and it can be helpful and useful as a tactile guide for way-finding. As elsewhere, carefully planned color contrast can be used to highlight edges or borders, as in the edge of a counter or a border around the floor.

Plan clear sight lines and windows with the client in mind, especially if they are seated, exceptionally tall, or if they have hearing issues.

Storage in the Serving and Dining Center
When planning storage and surface areas in the serving space, consider proximity to cleanup and storage of dishes and remember the guidance relating to the reach range of your client. Sometimes, shallow storage on the back of an island or peninsula can store dishes and tableware in close proximity to the eating area and within reach of most who will access the storage. Because of the difficulties many clients have reaching to the height of storage in wall cabinets, there are some storage features that accommodate in base cabinets those items traditionally stored in wall cabinets, and the dish stacks in holders are particularly good for many table setters. It is also useful to plan pull-out resting surfaces wherever you can, as a cook who needs his or her hands to operate a mobility aid, does not have hands free to easily organize or transport anything (see Figure 8.46).

Access Standards
The NKBA Kitchen Planning Guidelines and Access Standards that relate to serving and dining are 8, 9, and 31.

FIGURE 8.46 Storage for dishware and glasses convenient to the dining counter. *Courtesy of Rev-A-Shelf*

Responsive Design Summary: The Serving and Dining Center
- Sensory
  - Universal design recommendations
    - Plan passage or maneuvering space clear of clutter and obstructions.
    - Specify eased counter edges and rounded corners.
    - Plan color contrast carefully to highlight edges or borders, as in the edge of a counter or a border around the floor.
    - Provide clear sight lines throughout the space so a person who has limited hearing will be able to see throughout the space.
    - Plan seating at counter or table to encourage face-to-face contact when possible.
    - Design lighting that does not interfere with line of sight to other diners.
  - Access recommendations
    - Plan lighting controls from multiple sources and adjustable (Access Standard 31).
    - Plan needed allowance for a service dog or other service animal.
- Cognition
  - Universal design recommendations
    - Plan layout to encourage social interaction
  - Access standard recommendations
    - Store frequently used items in sight and/or in the order in which they will be used.
- Physical
  - Universal design recommendations
    - Plan passage or maneuvering space clear of clutter and obstructions.
    - Consider the relationship of the kitchen door to an express exit route to allow for longer reaction times.
    - Plan sight lines, especially if the client is seated or exceptionally tall.
  - Access recommendations
    - Allow 36 inches (914 mm) of clearance from the counter or table edge to any wall or obstruction behind the seating area.
    - Plan 60 inches (1524 mm) to allow passage for a person in a wheelchair if traffic passes behind the seated diner.
    - Plan seating areas 28 to 34 inches (711 mm to 864 mm) high with knee space, 27 inches (686 mm) high by 30 to 36 inches (762 mm to 914 mm) wide by 19 inches (483 mm) deep (Access Standard 9).

SUMMARY

In this chapter, you have been presented with information on various sensory, cognitive, and physical characteristics of people, and related design concepts to help stimulate and streamline your process when working on a space that is to accommodate a client with a specific disability. It is worth repeating that just as there is no average person, no two people with disabilities are alike. These general groups have been formed simply to help pull together and further explore the design concepts discussed throughout the book and particularly in Chapter 6. You will have noticed repeated concepts and concepts that might fall into either the universal design column or the access column. As time passes and we embrace more and more of the access solutions, more concepts will be moved from the access to the universal category, creating true equity in our design. Hopefully, you will continue to build on the lists and grow your library of access-related design. As you do, you'll discover that most of the access solutions are better for everyone and you'll be experiencing that "Aha" of universal design.

REVIEW QUESTIONS

1. Design that responds to the particular requirements of a person with specific characteristics and needs is (See "Universal Design vs. Accessibility" pages 301-302)
   - Universal design
   - Accessible design
   - Barrier-free design
   - Lifespan design
2. What are three kitchen design concepts or practices that will improve the function of the space for a client with hearing issues? (See "Sensory Characteristics, Hearing" page 303)
3. What are three design concepts or practices that will improve the function of the space for a person with vision impairments? (See "Sensory Characteristics, Vision" page 303)
4. What are three concepts or practices that will improve the function of the space for a person with tactile or olfactory issues? (See "Sensory Characteristics, Other Sensory Characteristics" page 304)
5. What are three concepts or practices that will improve the function of the space for a person with cognitive impairments? (See "Perception and Cognitive Characteristics" pages 304-305)

More Than a Kitchen

Today's kitchen is more than just a place to cook and to eat. In fact, the kitchen may function like command central for the household. Sometimes it's a gathering place that allows busy family members to work and play near each other. Activities may merge here, allowing one or more household members to perform multiple tasks, such as laundry, cooking, homework, and bill paying, all at the same time. The kitchen may be the place where household members come and go and keep their lives organized.

As a kitchen designer, you may be called on to design activity spaces in the kitchen or other areas of the home that include social, home management, or hobby activities. In this chapter, we discuss designing these auxiliary spaces to integrate with the primary food preparation and eating areas of the kitchen. Specifically, we will discuss a family foyer or mudroom, a home planning center, a laundry area, a craft/hobby area, a gardening area, and social spaces. It is unlikely that you will design all these spaces into one kitchen project, but hopefully, you will find many suggestions and ideas that will be beneficial to your clients.

> *Learning Objective: Discuss auxiliary spaces that are adjacent to or within the kitchen that include: a foyer, planning center, laundry area, craft/hobby area, gardening area, and other social spaces.*

THE FAMILY FOYER OR MUDROOM

Many American homes have beautiful foyers or front entrance areas. These ceremonial entrance areas may be grand, vaulted spaces or simple but defined designs. However, many of them share an important characteristic—the members of the household seldom use them on a regular basis. Instead, most homes have another, more casual entrance to the back, side, or rear of the home that is used for the daily comings and goings of household members. Typically, this entrance is off the garage or parking area, and often opens directly into the kitchen or an area adjacent to the kitchen. Therefore, a busy household has people coming and going through the kitchen, not to prepare and eat food, but to enter and exit the home.

As part of the design of the kitchen, it may be important to think in terms of a family foyer or a mudroom. These terms are both applied to an informal entrance to the home, used by members of the household and perhaps close friends. This is where groceries come into the house and the trash/recyclables are removed. It might be where backpacks, briefcases, and a charged cell phone wait in readiness for a quick morning departure. Winter coats and boots, sun hats, and gardening gloves might find temporary homes in such a space. Perhaps the baby's stroller or a snow shovel is kept in this space. Because groceries arrive in the family foyer, pantry storage might also be included.

The family foyer or mudroom is also a communication space. Messages and reminders might be left there. Outgoing mail, recyclables, or dry cleaning may wait in the space for the next person to take it out. Depending on the household, some of the functions of the home planning center may overlap with the family foyer or mudroom. Be sure to read the section on the home planning center for further ideas about designing a communication center for the home.

A family foyer is likely a simple space, a transition between outside and inside. A mudroom is usually a more detailed space, including storage and activity spaces, and may be a separate room. Part of the decision as to what is appropriate to a particular home will depend on what other spaces are available, such as a garage, laundry, or hobby area. A family foyer might include:

- A passageway in and out of the house, without interfering with kitchen work areas
- Space to put on and remove outer clothing, such as coats, boots, or hats
- A bench or other seated area to use when putting on or removing boots or shoes (Figure 9.1)

FIGURE 9.1 A family foyer can include a bench with storage underneath and pegs for hanging hats and other garments.
Courtesy of American Woodmark

- Storage space for items carried in and out of the house, such as backpacks, briefcases, purses, and packages
- An idea borrowed from the preschool classroom: individual cubbyholes for household members; things can be left for picking up before leaving or to be put away later
- Storage space for items frequently used outside, such as an herb-gathering basket or snow shovel. Shelves, hooks, or bins are good options
- Tack space for messages, reminders, notes, or coupons
- Charging station for cell phone or laptop computer, especially those that are used primarily for work or travel
- Hooks for frequently used items such as keys, flashlights, the dog's leash, or umbrellas
- Hanging space for outer wear, such as coats, scarves, or hats
- Baskets or bins for mittens, gloves, scarves, or other small items
- Storage space to leave wet coats, boots, shoes, or umbrellas until they dry
- A mirror for a quick check of appearance before leaving the house
- Easy-to-clean materials that are not damaged by water, mud, or sand

A mudroom might include many of the same features of the family foyer and one or more of the following:

- A wall- or floor-mounted utility sink that might be used for activities such as washing garden produce, washing up after working in the yard, or cleaning muddy shoes (Figure 9.2)
- A laundry area (more about laundry areas later in this chapter)
- An indoor gardening, house plant, or potting area (more about indoor gardening areas later in this chapter)

FIGURE 9.2 A mudroom incorporated into the informal entrance includes storage, a sink and work area, a place for shoes and boots, and durable, easy-to-clean materials.
Courtesy of American Standard

- A pet washing, feeding, or sleeping area
- Storage for outdoor tools, gardening equipment, or outdoor recreation equipment
- A shower, lavatory, and/or toilet facilities, so that someone working or playing outside could use the toilet or cleanup without going into the main area of the house
- Overflow storage from the kitchen, such as bulk paper goods storage, a pantry for home pre-served foods, a beverage or snack refrigerator, or a separate freezer
- Collection area for recyclable items (See Chapter 3, "Environmental and Sustainability Considerations")

Designing the Family Foyer/Mudroom

There are many possible configurations for a family foyer or mudroom, depending on the flow of people through the space and its relation to the kitchen. Is this a separate space, closed off from the kitchen? Or, is it integrated with the kitchen? Does the space match the kitchen stylistically?

First, think about the space as a circulation area. Here are some important dimensions for you to keep in mind:

- Any doorway should have a minimum of a 32-inch (813-mm) clear opening (refer to Kitchen Planning Guideline 1 in the Appendix).
- A minimum of 36 inches (914 mm) is needed for a walkway (refer to Kitchen Planning Guideline 7 in the Appendix). This is adequate for one person. Additional space is needed if several people will be passing through the area at the same time.
- A wheelchair requires a 60-inch (1524-mm) circle to turn around (refer to the Kitchen Planning Access Standards in the Appendix). Providing a clear area will help make the space accessible for current and future household members and guests who might use mobility aids.

Coats, Jackets, Hats, and Other Outerwear

A typical family foyer or mudroom will include space to store coats, jackets, rain slickers, boots, hats, scarves, mittens, and other items of outerwear. This is also the space where these items are likely to be put on or taken off. What exactly is kept in this area will depend on the climate as well as other storage areas in the home (Figure 9.3). A house in a cold climate is likely to need more space for bulky winter clothes, while a house in a warm climate may need space for items like rain wear and sun hats.

If a coat closet is planned, here are some useful dimensions:

- A typical closet is 24 inches (610 mm) deep, with the rod placed 12 inches (305 mm) from the wall. However, coats and jackets are bulkier, and need 26 inches to 28 inches (660 mm to 711 mm) to hang perpendicular to the rod. Bulky outerwear, such as parkas or ski jackets, may need 30 inches (762 mm) of depth. If closet rod depth is inadequate, clothes will hang at an angle, and additional rod storage length will be needed.
- Heavy coats may take 4 to 5 inches (102 to127 mm) width or more on a rod. The amount of rod length needed will depend on the number of coats and jackets to be stored.
- The height of the rod needs to be reachable by the user, but high enough that the coats clear the floor (Table 9.1).

If the household for which you are designing includes a person who uses a wheelchair or mobility aid, a person with limited reach, or a shorter person, lower rods will be appropriate. Although 48 inches (1219 mm) is considered the upper limit of the universal reach range for a seated person, this may vary with individual abilities. Refer to Form 1: Getting to Know Your Client in Chapter 5, "Assessing Needs," for specific information about your client. Chapter 4, "Human Factors and Universal Design Foundation," also has general information on reach ranges for different people.

Children cannot reach a full height closet rod. However, every parent wants to teach their children to hang up their coats! The solution might be adjustable rods that can be increased as children grow, their clothes get bigger, and they can reach higher.

If boots or shoes will be kept on the closet floor, be sure that the rod is high enough for adequate clearance. A drip pan or rack for boots and shoes can be useful.

- Adequate space to access hanging coats is important to well-planned coat storage. A clearance of 36 to 38 inches (914 mm to 965 mm) is recommended in front of the hangers in order to remove hangers (Figure 9.4). This clearance gives space for activities such as turning, holding up coats and jackets, or removing items from a hanger.

It takes an area equal to about a 42-inch (1067-mm) circle to put on or remove a coat. Therefore, increasing the clearance or access space in front of the closet to 42 inches (1067 mm) is preferable.

If a shelf is placed above the rod, a clearance of 2 to 3 inches (51 to 76 mm) is needed to allow space to remove the hangers from the rod.

TABLE 9.1 Functional rod heights will depend on who uses the closet and what type of coats and garments will be stored.

Age and Type of Garment	Suggested Rod Height
Children, ages 2–6	30–40 inches (762–1016 mm)
Children, ages 6–12	40–54 inches (1016–1372 mm)
Teens, ages 12–16	54–63 inches (1372–1600 mm)
Adults, jackets, and parkas	45–48 inches (1143–1219 mm)
Adults, topcoats, and dress coats	54–63 inches (1372–600 mm)

Hook Storage. Instead of a coat closet, hooks can hold coats and jackets for easy access. This might be desirable for frequently used garments, in season. Hooks are also easy to use for children, provided they are at a height they can reach. Use large and sturdy hooks or pegs that can hold bulky outer garments.

- A minimum height for a hook would be the length of the garment or item to store, plus 6 inches (152 mm) of clearance beneath. For multiple hooks, space them about 12 inches (305 mm) apart, to allow for the bulk of coats and jackets.
- Make sure that hooks are clear of passageways so that there is no danger of people walking into them when not in use.
- Provide 33 to 36 inches (838 to 914 mm) of clear space in front of the hook (for removing or hanging up items on the hook) or, preferably, 42 inches (1067 mm) (for putting on or removing a coat or jacket).

Seating Area

A seating area in the family foyer or mudroom is helpful for putting on or removing boots and shoes. This can help prevent tracking dirt into other areas of the home and save time on maintenance.

- A typical chair seat is 16 to 20 inches (406 to 508 mm) high. However, when designing seating for people to put on or remove shoes or boots, you may want to lower the height. The lower height will also be better for children.

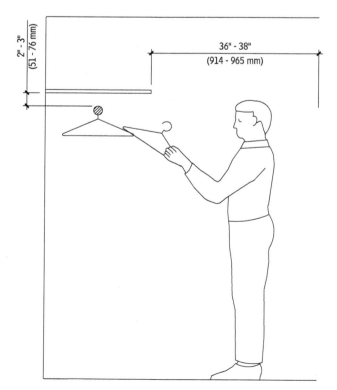

FIGURE 9.4 Adequate clearance space allows access to hangers.

- Consider putting a handrail or handle near the seating area to aid in getting up and down from the seat.
- Allow at least 24 inches (610 mm) in width and 18 inches (457 mm) in depth for a person to sit on a bench seat.
- An oversized seating area could double as a bench or shelf area to hold packages, backpacks, or briefcases while putting on or taking off coats.
- An open area underneath a seating bench can be used to temporarily store boots and shoes. Alternatively, a box bench can open up to provide storage inside.

Design Details

The design for the family foyer or mudroom is not complete until you have selected materials and planned for mechanical systems. By definition, this is a busy space in the home, and one that will get a lot of wear and tear.

Materials

Whether designing a family foyer that is just an area off the kitchen, or a separate mudroom, choose materials that are durable and easy to maintain. Think about the traffic through the space. Select materials that can withstand the bumping and scraping of backpacks, briefcases, packages, and other assorted items.

The flooring materials will be particularly important in this space. As a designer, you may not often think about what type of soil is in an area. However, for the floor of a mudroom, this can be important. Depending on the location of the home, you may need to select flooring that is resistant to the grit of sand, the staining of iron-rich soil, or the corrosion of salt used to melt icy sidewalks. In some climates, the floor of the entry area may often be wet, and this is an important design challenge for both safety and maintenance. Nonslip surfaces will be important. In some cases, such as a beach or farm home, or in a snowy climate, you may consider a floor with a drain system.

Mechanical Systems

The electrical and lighting requirements of the family foyer or mudroom will be dependent on the activities that will take place there. In general, make sure that there is adequate lighting for people coming in and out of the space. Be generous with receptacles and circuits to allow future additions of electrical equipment.

Pay special attention to the placement of switches. Since this is a transition space between inside and outside, there are likely to be multiple switches for both interior and exterior lights. Group switches logically so that it will be easy to remember which switch goes with what light.

Since the family foyer or mudroom is an entrance to the home, consider planning for security or automatic lighting, both inside and outside the entrance. Lights can be on timers, photocells, or motion detectors and be set to turn on and off, according to the client's preferences. A low-level "night light" might be appreciated.

In addition to security lighting, your client might have a home alarm system, fire monitoring, weather monitoring, or other security systems. These may need to be included in your plans as well.

HOME PLANNING CENTER

Many activities important to the management of a busy household are conducted from the kitchen. With the kitchen as a central gathering place in the home, it follows that management and planning activities—the business of the household—are also handled in this space. Therefore, it becomes necessary that a planning or management center be part of the kitchen, separate from the food preparation area but integrated into the overall design.

A home planning center can be a communication center for the household members. The mail may be collected, a calendar posted, and reminders or messages left. Perhaps a telephone or telephone/cell phone charging station is located in the area.

At the other end of the spectrum is the home planning center that functions like a home office. There may be a computer, a laptop docking station, electronic charging station, or other electronic equipment. Files may be needed to store household papers and records. Space may be needed for working on a laptop, bill paying, making out grocery lists, or completing correspondence.

Most likely, the home planning center will include elements of both a communication center and a home office. Start with an understanding of how your client will use the space. Refer to Chapter 5 for Form 3: Checklist for Kitchen Activities, especially the "Other Kitchen Activities" section for ideas about the types of activities to be accommodated in a home planning center. In addition, refer to Form 4: Kitchen Storage Inventory, and the "Management/Home Office" and "Miscellaneous" sections for information on what your client may want to store in the home planning center.

Locating the Home Planning Center

The home planning center is not part of the flow of food preparation activities and, thus, should be located outside of the primary work triangle. In addition, the planning center is usually not part of the traffic flow from the food preparation to serving or eating area.

In many households, while one person is cooking, another member of the household might be using the desk or work area of the home planning center for activities like reading the newspaper, doing schoolwork, or paying bills. These people like to be able to easily communicate, so the planning center should be convenient to the food preparation areas (Figure 9.5). The home planning center is where a phone might be located and cookbooks stored—another reason there should be convenient access from the food preparation areas to the home planning center.

Often, the home planning center is a collection area for things like the day's mail, school papers, house or car keys, and messages. Therefore, the center should be convenient to entrances and exits to the home, especially those used most frequently by household members. In some homes, the planning center may be part of the family foyer or mudroom, and these spaces may overlap in function.

Later in this chapter, we will discuss a kitchen sitting area as part of a social space. In some homes, a planning center, especially the planning desk, may be located in a casual sitting area that is part of, or adjacent to, the kitchen.

FIGURE 9.5 A small home planning center has enough space for a laptop and is located near the secondary sink center so that the user can converse with the primary cook.
Courtesy of American Woodmark

The Desk Area

A typical home planning center is anchored around a desk or work surface area with a chair. The size of the desk area will vary, depending on the type of activities. For example, meal planning may require work surface space to open several cookbooks at the same time, whereas bill paying may only require space for the checkbook and a few pieces of paper or a laptop.

Often, a planning center desk is 24 inches (610 mm) deep because this matches the depth of the kitchen counters. However, a 30-inch (762-mm) depth would be preferable for a desk (Figure 9.6). The full 30-inch (762 mm) depth provides space for office supplies and equipment without compromising the work area. Likewise, a width of 60 to 72 inches (1524 to 1829 mm) is recommended for the desktop to provide both work area and convenient surface storage.

Some of the area under the desk may be used for storage, but adequate space for sitting at the desk must be allowed. Following the recommendations used in Kitchen Planning Guideline 9 (See the Appendix) for seated areas at a 30 inch (762-mm) high counter or table (similar to a desk height), maintain clear knee space under the desk that is at least 18 inches (457 mm) deep and 24 inches (610 mm) wide.

The recommended height of a desk is 29 to 30 inches (737 to 762 mm) (Figure 9.7). An adjustable height chair is recommended, with a seat that varies in height from 14 to 18 inches (356 to 457 mm) above the floor. This type of chair will adapt to different users but will still allow at least 7 inches (178 mm) of clearance under the desk for the user's thighs. A footrest may be needed to accommodate users with shorter legs.

Desk Area Storage

In addition to the work surface, a desk area usually includes storage. As suggested, refer to Chapter 5 and Form 4: Kitchen Storage Inventory for the kinds of items your client will want to store in the desk area. Keep in mind the principles of storage as you plan storage in the desk area. Make items easily accessible, visible, and near the point of use.

Items stored in the desk area are likely to include the usual office supplies, such as paper, tablets, pens, pencils, markers, paperclips, rubber bands, scissors, tape, stapler, and hole punch. Shelf

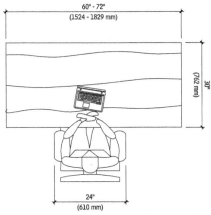

FIGURE 9.6 A 30 inch (762 mm) deep and 60 to 72 inch (1524 to 1829 mm) wide desk top allows a generous work area and provides space for supplies and equipment. Clear knee space, 24 inches (610 mm) wide by 18 inches (457 mm) deep, is needed under the desk.

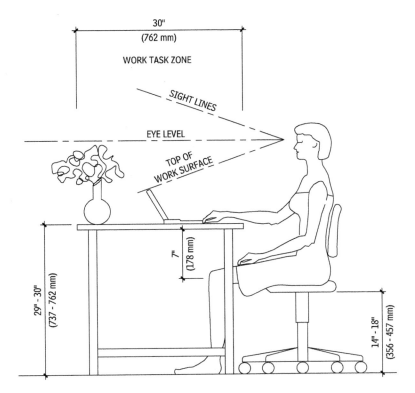

FIGURE 9.7 A chair with adjustable height allows different-sized people to use a standard-height desk.

space may be needed for items such as cookbooks, directories, address books, and a dictionary. File space may be needed for items such as appliance instruction booklets, warranty information, and recipes.

Some people may want to have display space in the home planning center to show personal items such as mementos, family pictures, antiques, collections, or decorative items. Shelf space or wall space can provide options for these special pieces. Glass door cabinets are another option for display.

In today's electronic age, you can expect that the desk area may include several different pieces of equipment. Typically, the planning center will include a phone, but this might be a charger base for a portable phone or a cell phone, and an answering machine. A fax machine may be connected to the phone system. Other items might include a printer, shredder, electric pencil sharpener, electric stapler, clock, CD or DVD player, television, and radio. Perhaps charger bases for items like flash lights or the base station for wireless Internet connections are kept in the planning center. Determine what items will be kept on the desk and which items need to be permanently connected to a power supply. Plan for the cords! Check to see if any items have special utility requirements, such as connections for cable or satellite communications.

Many households have one or more laptop computers that are used in different parts of the home, such as in a casual sitting area, at the snack bar, or even in a bedroom. These clients may not want a seating area for laptop use in the planning center. Other clients might want the convenience of using a laptop in the planning center. If so, include a work surface space at a convenient height, easy access to a power supply connection, and an Internet connection. A charger or docking station for the laptop might be needed.

Clearance around the Desk Area

Kitchen Planning Guideline 8 in the Appendix recommends that 44 inches (1118 mm) be allowed from the edge of a counter or table to a wall or obstruction, in order to walk behind someone seated at that counter or table. However, if there is a file in the desk, the user often wants to move in front of an open file drawer for more convenient access. Therefore, the clearance behind the desk should be increased by the depth of the file drawer, which can be from 12 to 24 inches (305 to 610 mm) (Figure 9.8). If there is no traffic or passage behind the person seated at the desk, Kitchen Planning Guideline 8 recommends 32 inches (813 mm) of clearance from the edge of a counter or table to a wall or obstruction. This allows enough space to sit at the desk and to get up or down from the chair. Although 18 to 24 inches (457 to 610 mm) of that space is needed for the seated person, 32 inches (813 mm) would not allow enough room to access most file drawers, except from the side (Figure 9.8).

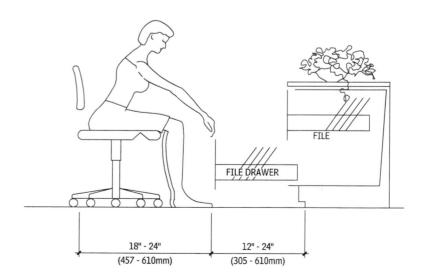

FIGURE 9.8 A file drawer will add 12 to 24 inches (305 to 610 mm) to the clearance needed in front of the desk.

Lighting

Good lighting is important in the home planning center, especially when it is used for desk work. Task lighting should be provided at the desk area and be shielded from the eye level of a seated user. Lighting in the planning center should be on separate switches from other kitchen lighting. For more information on kitchen lighting, see Chapter 7, "Mechanical Planning."

A Standing Desk

Not every household wants a sit-down desk area in the home planning center. For some households, perhaps the center is more of a communication area. Maybe a counter that works well at a standing or podium height, such as 36 to 42 inches (914 to 1067 mm), is a better choice. Great for jotting down messages and giving the mail a quick read, this type of counter would allow space for files, bins, or drawers underneath. Wall space above the counter provides vertical storage and display space. A standing desk could be designed to be as shallow as 12 inches (305 mm), to take advantage of an otherwise unused, narrow space.

Household Communications

The home planning center is often "communication central" for the household. Often, the planning center may be the spot that everyone passes going in and out of the house. Therefore, car keys, briefcases, backpacks, school books, messages, and reminder notes may be left there to be picked up or dropped off as people come and go. The day's mail may be deposited until someone has time to review and sort it. Phone messages may wait to be claimed. Perhaps the home has an intercom system or audio system with controls in the planning center. This may also be the place where the monitor for the alarm or security system or the readout for the electronic weather-monitoring system is located.

All of the items that contribute to the activity of the household and its communications activities can become a clutter problem if not organized properly. It is a design challenge to make items in the home planning center accessible and easy to use, yet to avoid an area that is messy and unsightly. Here are some ideas you can incorporate into the planning center to help manage the "stuff" that moves through it on a daily basis or that tends to accumulate!

- Provide a message board. Include a tack surface to pin notes and messages as well as special school papers. Magnetic surfaces work well for the same purpose. A dry erase or chalkboard can be used to write messages or reminders. Hang message boards on walls or integrate them into the doors of cabinets, pantries, closets, or the refrigerator.
- A flat writing surface, such as a small counter area or pull-out board, is useful for making notes.
- Provide hooks. Small hooks hold car and house keys; heavy-duty hooks hold bags and backpacks. Make sure that hooks do not protrude into passageways.
- Think of the old-fashioned pigeon-holed desk and provide places to sort items such as mail, bills, coupons, recipes, and messages.
- Use glass door cabinets to store items, which are then easy to find when needed.
- Pull-out bins and drawers can be divided into sections to sort items for easy access.
- Frosted or colored glass doors can be used to enclose storage areas of desks, bins, and other areas that are visible from social areas of the room when they are not in use. Rolling or retracting doors will move out of the way for easy access to the enclosed areas.

Computer Workstation

In the household where the planning center functions as the home office, it usually includes a computer workstation (Figure 9.9). If a computer will be added to the planning center desk area, there are additional design considerations. Is this the only computer in the home? How will the computer be used? Are recipes saved and grocery lists accumulated? Are family bills and records managed on spreadsheet software? Are school work essays written and class assignments completed on word processing programs? Do people play games and shop online? The frequency and type of use, as well as the number of users are important in designing the computer workstation. It is even possible that the client will want more than one computer workstation in the home planning center.

FIGURE 9.9 A computer work station and planning desk provides this household with the flexibility to accomplish different activities in the kitchen area.

Source: Courtesy of Pennville Custom Cabinetry

First, determine what type of computer will be used. Will there be a table or console model computer located permanently in the desk area? Or, will there be a laptop computer that is sometimes moved someplace else? Will there be a laptop docking station left on the desk?

As you design for a computer area, here are some factors to consider:

- Measure all components of the computer system. There are no standardized sizes in the computer industry. You may choose to custom design the space to fit particular computer components or to be flexible to adapt to different components, as it is likely a new computer will be selected in the future.
- In addition to a computer, your client may have or plan to add peripheral equipment, such as a printer, scanner, speakers, or digital camera dock. Plan space to accommodate these items.
- Think carefully about the placement of computer components with respect to switches, disk bays, CD and DVD trays, USB ports, and other parts of the computer components that need to be accessed during use of the computer.
- The computer keyboard should be placed so that the hands, wrists, and forearms are level and parallel to the floor (Figure 9.10). This is usually achieved through a combination of an adjustable height chair (with foot rest, if needed) and lowered keyboard surface. A keyboard height of 26 to 27 inches (660 to 686 mm) is often recommended for typing surfaces.
- The mouse is usually placed next to the keyboard, on the right or left, depending on user preference. The surface height of the mouse is comparable to the keyboard.
- The monitor or viewing screen should be 20 to 28 inches (508 to 711 mm) in front of the user, or about an arm's length away. The location should be 10° to 60° below horizontal eye level.

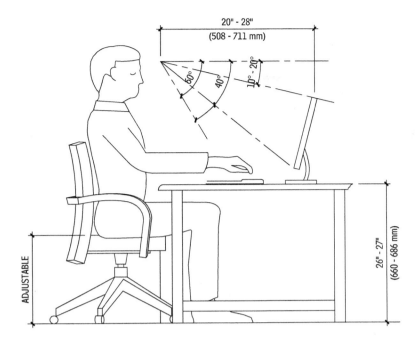

FIGURE 9.10 Adjust the computer workstation so that the forearm, wrist, and hand are parallel to the floor and the monitor is at or below eye level.

- If the computer station will include a printer, consider how the printer will be placed in relation to the rest of the equipment. Usually, the printer is used after the primary computer work is completed, so the printer may not need to occupy immediate work space. Will it need to be connected to the computer or is it wireless? Plan enough space to load printer trays, retrieve printed papers, and change ink cartridges.
- In addition to the space for the computer equipment, most people need some work surface space adjacent to, in front of, or beside the computer equipment to accommodate notes, papers, books, and other reference materials.
- Storage space is needed in a computer work area to accommodate items such as disks, CDs, DVDs, computer instruction manuals, printer paper, cartridges, and files of projects in progress.
- Most households that have a computer workstation in the home planning center will want an Internet connection. Discuss with your client the type of connection he or she will have. If the home has wireless Internet capability, determine whether the base station will be located in the home planning center or elsewhere.
- Computer components need to be well ventilated during use. Avoid enclosing computer components in cabinets or drawers that limit air circulation.
- Typically, a computer system requires a lot of electrical cords. Consider how you will manage these so that the system is functional but the cords will not be problematic. Cable channels or raceways can be used to hide cords at the back of desktops, underneath counters, or in other inconspicuous places.
- The electrical requirements for a computer station depend on the requirements of the computer equipment. Typically, one or more dedicated circuits with surge protection will be necessary. Determine which components of the computer system or peripheral pieces of equipment need their own power supply. Consider planning extra receptacles for future expansion. See Chapter 7 for more information about electrical wiring.

A LAUNDRY AREA

A laundry area in or near the kitchen is a convenience. Laundry can be sorted, washed, and dried while doing other activities in the kitchen. Mechanical connections for plumbing, electricity, and perhaps gas are readily available in the kitchen area, which can reduce construction costs. The challenge to the designer is to consider how to design a functional laundry area, providing adequate space and needed storage, that is compatible with the other kitchen activities, including cooking and eating.

What Type of Laundry?

Some people like the idea of having a complete laundry area centrally located near the kitchen. This may be the only laundry area in the home, or the household may have another "mini-laundry" near the bathroom or bedroom for washing towels or doing quick loads of laundry while bathing, grooming, or dressing. Some people may only want to use the kitchen to rinse out or hand wash single items, and then hang them up to drip-dry, in the kitchen or elsewhere in the home.

Your client needs assessment (Chapter 5) should reveal what type of laundry area your client might like, in or near the kitchen. In addition, the checklists and questionnaires in the assessment will help you determine what type of laundry activities, equipment, and supplies will need to be accommodated in your design. This section will give you some specific information about planning a laundry area.

A laundry area in or near the kitchen can be convenient, but there are some factors to consider first:

- Who will use the laundry area?

  A laundry area used by different members of the household needs to be centrally located for easy access.
- Is there adequate space for laundry equipment?

  A laundry area is more than a washing machine. A well-designed laundry includes storage, hanging and folding space, a sink, and adequate clearance to move and complete tasks. Will laundry area space interfere with other activities and space needs associated with kitchen activities?
- What about access to the laundry?

  Door and hall width clearance for carrying laundry baskets and hanging clothes needs to be considered. If an outside clothesline is used, there needs to be a direct route to the outdoors. Access to the laundry should not interfere with cooking activities.
- What about noise associated with laundry equipment?

  A busy kitchen may already be a noisy place, with food sizzling, water running, and people talking. The sound of laundry equipment located in or near the kitchen for convenience should not be an annoyance. This is especially true if the kitchen opens onto social areas.
- Is it feasible to provide the infrastructure for a laundry area in or near the kitchen?

  Water supply and drainage for the washing machine and electrical or gas connections, as well as exhaust ventilation for the dryer, need to be considered in planning. The floor structure may need reinforcing for the weight or vibration of the laundry equipment. A floor drain is good protection in event of a leak or other water problem. These features may be easy to provide in new construction, but more of a problem in a remodeling project.
- A laundry area can be messy.

  Laundry areas seem to collect clothes waiting for special treatment, or to be washed, folded, ironed, or repaired. This is a utility area of the home and may not be the most aesthetically pleasing. Will the laundry area be closed or open, especially when not in actual use?

Laundry Equipment

A washing machine and automatic dryer will anchor most laundry areas. A typical American model washer or dryer is 27 to 29 inches (686 to 737 mm) wide (across the front) and 25 to 32 inches (635 to 813 mm) deep. Most are about 36 inches (914 mm) high, but some are as high as 45 inches (1143 mm). European and some Asian models tend to be smaller. Always check the exact size of the equipment in the manufacturer's specifications or by measuring the actual equipment. Keep in mind that the installed depth of the appliance will usually be greater, because of the utility hook-ups at the back.

A washer can either be a front-loading or top-loading model. Most dryers are front-loading. Washer doors can be hinged on either side, depending on the model. Some top-loading models may have a door hinged at the back. Dryer doors can also be hinged on either side, and some models are hinged on the bottom.

Front-loading laundry appliances are usually the easiest to use for people using mobility aids or with limited reach range. The location of the appliance controls, typically on a back control panel, is also important to consider for universal access. Front-loading laundry appliances with front controls are desirable to improve access within the universal reach range.

Knowing the location and swing of the door is important for efficient placement of laundry equipment. It should be convenient to remove wet laundry from the washer and place it in the dryer without interference from the open door of either piece of equipment. This movement of laundry between appliances determines how the appliances are placed in relationship to each other.

Front-loading washers and dryers require the user to bend down to load and unload. Some models of front-loading washers and dryers are available with a 12- to 15-inch (305 to 381 mm) pedestal for easier access. The pedestal also provides storage (Figure 9.11). An alternative is to install the equipment on a raised platform so that the door is easier to access. Planning the equipment at this height cuts down on bending and allows the door to swing open clear of the armrest or lap of a person using a wheelchair. While this is an advantage in access to the appliance, the top of the washer and dryer is no longer easily accessible to use as folding space. If the equipment is raised, be sure that the user can still reach and read the controls.

If you will be placing laundry equipment in a closet, cabinet, or under a counter, check manufacturer's specifications. Typically, there are requirements for clearances on the sides, front, back, and top of the equipment to allow for ventilation and equipment connections. Doors to closets and cabinets must have a specified area and location of ventilation screening or be louvered for air circulation.

FIGURE 9.11 Raising a front-loading washer or dryer, up to about 15 inches (381 mm), reduces bending and makes access easier but still allows most people to reach the controls. Some washer and dryer manufacturers sell a pedestal to raise the appliance, as an accessory. *Courtesy of Whirlpool Corp.*

Stacked Washer and Dryer

If space is limited, a stacked washer and dryer can be a good choice (Figure 9.12). A stacked washer and dryer takes up about the same floor space as a single washing machine (approximately 30 inches by 30 inches [762 mm by 762 mm]), yet provides the capacity for full loads of laundry. While stacked equipment saves floor space, the height of the equipment precludes locating any accessible storage above it.

If a stacked washer and dryer are selected, be sure that the user can access all controls and door openings. Check model specifications to make sure that stacking is an option. Careful planning of water connections, shutoffs, and dryer venting will be required.

Smaller stacked washers and dryers with integrated controls and reduced capacity are available. These machines are good choices for a secondary laundry area or a smaller household.

FIGURE 9.12 A stacked washer and dryer can save floor space and be a good choice for a laundry in a kitchen.
Courtesy of GE

Utility Service

Utility service requirements for laundry equipment are specified by the manufacturer and may be controlled by local building codes. Utility shut-offs should be located for quick and easy access. Consult the product specifications and installation information for the selected laundry equipment. Following are typical requirements.

Washing Machine

- Hot and cold water supply
  - Check distance from water supply to washer.
  - Check that water pressure is adequate.
- Vented drain
- 120-volt, 15- or 20-ampere dedicated electrical circuit
  - Some European-style washers require a 240-volt circuit

Electric Dryer

- 240-volt, 50-ampere dedicated electrical circuit
- Exterior ventilation for dryer exhaust outlet; distance from dryer to outside vent is dependent on number of elbows

Gas Dryer

- Natural or LP gas connection
- 120-volt, 15- or 20-ampere dedicated electrical circuit (may be able to share electrical circuit with the washer if a 30-ampere circuit is used)
- Exterior ventilation dryer exhaust outlet; distance from dryer to outside vent is dependent on number of elbows
- Cold water supply if dryer has steam feature

One or more additional electrical circuits are recommended in the laundry area to use additional clothes care equipment, such as irons, sewing machines, or clothes steamers. An electrical circuit for lighting is also needed. A sink in the laundry area is common, and water supply and drains are needed for this. Alternatively, the laundry area may not need a separate sink, if the primary or secondary kitchen sink is convenient to use.

Exterior ventilation of the dryer is important, even though there is sometimes consideration of venting dryers to the inside. The thought behind venting a dryer to the inside is that heat is retained, which is seen as an advantage in cold climates in the winter. However, the problems with this practice far outweigh the energy savings. The excess moisture can lead to serious condensation and mold problems in the home (see Chapter 3). Odors from laundry products can be a problem. Lint in the exhaust air presents maintenance problems. Gadgets are available to add to the dryer exhaust vent to filter lint. However, these filters require regular maintenance, and failure to maintain them results in clogging the exhaust vent. This puts strain on the exhaust motor and can lead to a fire.

If venting is a problem, condensing dryers, which do not require an outside vent, are available. A condensing dryer may require a drain.

Manufacturer's specifications typically require vinyl, rubber, or other moisture-resistant flooring under laundry equipment. A floor drain near the washing machine is a desirable feature, to minimize the problems with water leaks. If this cannot be provided, the washer can be installed in a floor pan, which will contain leaks and overflows.

Laundry and the Environment

Everyone wants laundry equipment that is high performance, easy to use, and quiet in operation. However, today we also want laundry equipment that contributes to our goals of sustainability and "green" design. If you are designing a laundry area, recommending a high-efficiency washer results in a laundry system that minimizes the use of both energy and water.

- **Energy Star–Qualified Washer:** Energy Star–qualified equipment is more efficient, uses less energy, saves money, and helps protect the environment.
  - The *Modified Energy Factor (MEF)* is a performance factor based on washer capacity, electricity use, energy required to heat the water, and energy that will be used to remove water from the clothes (dry the clothes). The higher the MEF, the more efficient the washer.
  - The *Water Factor (WF)* measures water per cycle. The lower the WF, the more water conserving the washer.

- **CEE (Consortium for Energy Efficiency) Tier Rankings:** The CEE uses the MEF and WF performance factors to rate clothes washers. A Tier I ranking is equivalent to an Energy Star–qualified washer. Tier II and Tier III rankings result in a more efficient appliance.
- **Equipment Capacity:** Match the capacity of the washer and dryer to the size and frequency of the household laundry needs to encourage the efficient use of energy and water.

Space Planning in the Laundry Area

Adequate space is needed in the laundry area to move, turn, bend, and twist while moving laundry in and out of the equipment. Space for a laundry basket or cart is also needed. A clearance of 42 inches (1067 mm) in front of a washer, dryer, or stacked washer and dryer is recommended (Figure 9.13A). This will provide adequate space to access either front- or top-loading machines, allowing space for door swings and a person to kneel or bend. Whether this 42-inch (1067 mm) clearance can overlap with other workspace clearances in the kitchen will depend on how your client envisions laundry activities overlapping with food preparation, serving, and cleanup activities.

When the washer and dryer are placed side by side, the 42-inch (1067 mm) clearance space should be 66 inches (1676 mm) wide (Figure 9.13B). If front-loading appliances are being used, check to see that this dimension allows adequate clearance for a door swing. If appliances are placed at right angles or across from each other, the clearance space for each machine overlaps (Figures 9.13C and 9.13D).

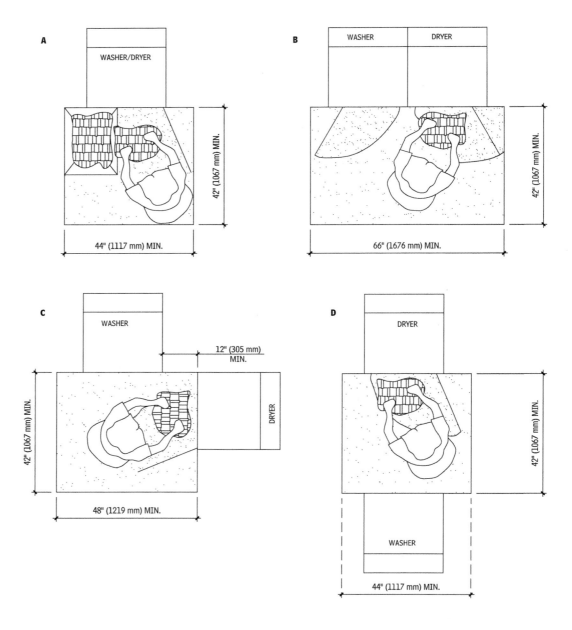

FIGURE 9.13 (A) Clearance in front of laundry equipment provides space for bending and kneeling, as well as for door swings and a laundry basket or cart. This illustration shows clearances for a single washer or dryer or a stacked washer and dryer. Figure 9.13(B) shows clearances for a side-by-side washer and dryer. Figure 9.13(C) shows clearances for a washer and dryer at right angles. Figure 9.13(D) shows clearances for a washer and dryer arranged on opposite sides.

If the person doing the laundry uses a mobility aid, such as a wheelchair or cane, these clearances will need to be increased. Refer back to Form 1: Getting to Know Your Client, in Chapter 5, for information on collecting clearances for mobility aids your client might use.

Laundry in Transition

Designing a laundry area is more than installing equipment with clearance space. The flow of laundry in and out of the space needs to be considered. Dirty laundry is brought into the area; clean laundry is moved out. During the transition, clothes, towels, bed linens, and other items may spend time "hanging out" in the laundry area. To help organize the laundry area, smooth the flow of laundry, and minimize clutter, consider the following ideas:

- **Dirty laundry needs to be collected.** Hampers, bins, or baskets in the laundry area can be used for short-term storage of dirty laundry. Good ventilation of the dirty laundry containers is necessary to dispel dampness and odors.

Several containers might be used to presort laundry. For example, white socks, T-shirts, and underwear might go into one container, jeans into another. (The effectiveness of this system depends on cooperation of everyone in the household.) Or, if several members of the household do laundry separately, each person can have his or her own container, using it to accumulate enough laundry for a washer load.

- **Dirty laundry needs to be sorted before washing.** A table or counter surface works well for this task and then can later be used for folding and sorting clean laundry. A work surface 24 to 36 inches (610 to 914 mm) deep and 32 to 36 inches (813 to 914 mm) high would work for most people. The length of work surface depends on how much laundry is typically sorted and how much space is available. The work surface should be smooth so that it will not snag fabrics, durable, nonabsorbent, resistant to damage if laundry products such as detergent are spilled on it, and easy to clean and sanitize. If laundry and cooking are not done at the same time, the prep counter area might work well for this task.

Several bins or baskets might be used to sort laundry. These items might rest on a work counter, or pull out from underneath a counter or from inside a cabinet.

Avoid using the kitchen or laundry room floor for sorting dirty laundry, which can create congestion and clutter.

- **Hanging up items removed from the dryer minimizes wrinkles.** Provide a space to hang shirts, blouses, pants, dresses, and similar items. This hanging space should be convenient to the dryer. Garments on hangers should not block work areas or passages. Good ventilation is needed to allow garments to cool without wrinkling.

Refer to information presented earlier in this chapter on coat closets for suggested space clearances for hanging garments.

- **Not everything goes into the dryer.** Some items, like sweaters, need to lay flat, on a clean, smooth surface to dry. Other items are hung up to drip-dry—and they may drip while drying— so a waterproof area is needed. Delicate items, such as lingerie, may be put over a drying rack. The amount of space devoted to these activities will depend on your client.

If your client frequently air-dries laundry items, be sure that the area is adequately ventilated to prevent moisture problems.

An air-dry area may be elsewhere in the house, but consider how wet clothes are moved to this area without dripping. A laundry cart might be desirable, but consider where the cart will be kept when not in use.

- **Clean laundry needs to be folded.** A table or counter work surface, such as that used for sorting dirty laundry, will provide a space to fold clean laundry. Provide a knee space for seated work when possible. If laundry is folded fresh from the dryer, wrinkles are minimized. Many people want space to sort clean laundry, by type of garment or item, or by its owner. Clean laundry may be stacked in a basket or cart for transport to storage areas in the home.

Several bins or baskets might be used to sort laundry by its owner. Household members can then come claim their own laundry.

- **A sink in the laundry area is a desirable feature.** Some laundry products need to be diluted. Pre-rinsing may be helpful in removing stains. The sink can also be used for hand washing items or soaking soiled items.

A laundry sink is typically placed next to the washer to facilitate plumbing connections and for convenience of workflow. Unless your client does a lot of hand laundry, an extra-deep utility or laundry type sink is not necessary. A small bar-type sink can work well. Select a gooseneck or pull-out faucet for fitting bulky items under the water flow. Look for controls that are easy to operate with one hand or even hands-free.

Depending on the kitchen layout and its proximity to the laundry, a secondary sink in the kitchen can double as the laundry area sink.

- **A laundry needs adequate lighting that is conveniently switched.** Good color rendition in the light sources is important for noting stains and other problems on fabrics—and for matching socks. See Chapter 7 for more information about lighting.

Storage

Easily accessible storage is needed for laundry supplies. Items such as detergent and fabric softener are used almost every time something is washed and need to be easily reached. Other laundry supplies, such as stain removers, special detergents, bleaches, wrinkle removers, and fabric fresheners, may be used less frequently but still need to be convenient to the laundry equipment. Most of these items will fit on 8-inch to 10-inch (203 mm to 254 mm) deep shelves.

Storage in laundry areas is often placed over the laundry equipment. However, the depth of the washer or dryer reduces the height of the user's reach. Bringing a shelf forward makes items more accessible, as long as they will not get "lost" at the back of extra-deep shelves. Keep in mind that some laundry products, such as detergent, come in large, heavy containers that are awkward to lift, especially for people with limited strength. These items should not be stored above shoulder height (52 to 57 inches [1321 to 1448 mm] for most people) and are best stored within the universal reach range of 15 to 48 inches (381 to 1219 mm). Finally, shelves above laundry equipment should not interfere with door openings for top-loading equipment or access to controls. For all these reasons, storage areas adjacent to laundry equipment may be more desirable for the most frequently used items.

As previously mentioned, front-loading washers and dryers are available with pedestals that raise the machines 12 to 15 inches (305 to 381 mm) for easier access. These pedestals are usually drawers that provide additional storage. Other items may be stored in the laundry area, including hangers, clothespins, measuring cups for laundry products, stain removal guides, sponges, brushes, rags, and cleaning supplies. A divided drawer or small bins work well to collect items found in garment pockets or buttons that pop off. Some people keep basic sewing supplies in the laundry area so that repairs can be made on the spot.

Open storage in the laundry area increases accessibility by making it easier to see stored items and eliminating cabinet doors that might not swing out of the way. However, the desirability of this depends on how open the laundry area is to view from the kitchen and other spaces in the home.

Laundry storage can be messy. Containers of detergents and other laundry products may drip when being used. Spills are inevitable. Storage areas, in fact all of the laundry area, should be made of durable, easily cleaned materials that are not damaged by exposure to water, detergents, and other laundry products. Vinyl, ceramic tiles, and plastic laminates are popular materials used in laundry areas.

Ironing

Despite permanent press fabrics and finishes, many people still want a place to iron clothes and household linens. The laundry area is a logical place to put an ironing area. Built-in ironing boards fold down from wall cupboards or pull out from underneath a countertop, yet are out of the way when not in use (Figure 9.14). Many of these include storage space for the iron as well. Placement of a built-in ironing board must consider the side of the board from which you client prefers to work. Racks are available to hang freestanding ironing boards, or ironing boards can fold up to store in utility closets.

FIGURE 9.14 An ironing board and iron can be hidden in a kitchen cabinet or drawer when not in use, but be convenient when the need arises.

Courtesy Pennville Custom Cabinetry

Include adequate space in the laundry area to use the iron and ironing board (Figure 9.15). The amount of space may need to be increased if the user requires a mobility aid. Because an iron is hot and the cord could be a tripping hazard, the ironing area should not be in a passage or walkway. Most ironing boards adjust in height to allow a person to sit or stand to work.

A CRAFT/HOBBY AREA

Hobbies and crafts encompass many different activities as varied as scrapbook making, sewing, stamp collecting, model building, jewelry making, or crossword puzzles. These activities can be done by adults or children. Hobbies and crafts can be done on a regular basis, such as children's school projects, or they can be occasional activities, such as a family get-together to make holiday decorations.

In Chapter 5, your client may have indicated "crafts" on Form 3: Checklist for Kitchen Activities. If they checked this as a frequent activity, you might want to get more detail. What type of craft activities? Who participates? How often do they do these crafts? How much space is needed? What supplies and equipment do they use? There may be specialized space needs for a particular craft activity.

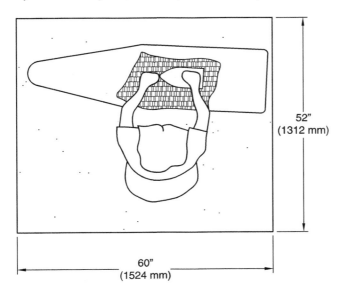

52"
(1312 mm)

60"
(1524 mm)

FIGURE 9.15 A typical ironing area requires a space that is 60 inches by 52 inches (1524 mm by 1321 mm).

Consider the other auxiliary areas that we have discussed in this chapter as possible areas for hobby and craft activities. For example, the laundry area may be a convenient place to add a sewing space. The mudroom may be a good place for messy activities, such as painting, working with clay, or indoor gardening as discussed later in this chapter. The planning desk can also be used as a writing surface for hobbies (Figure 9.16). Even the kitchen counter can get called into service as a good surface for wrapping packages or making a collage. Later in this chapter, we will discuss a kitchen sitting area, which might include a table and chairs that would make a great place for school projects, jigsaw puzzles, or scrapbook assembly.

For the household that wants to use the kitchen or related space for general hobby or craft activities on an occasional basis, here are some design suggestions.

- Kitchen counters make an excellent area for many hobby activities because they provide a level surface and adapt to both seated and standing activities. Durable, nonporous materials that are easily cleaned help ensure that food residues and craft materials will not get mixed.
- If a counter area will be used for standing activities, make sure that there is adequate toe kick space on all open sides.

FIGURE 9.16 A planning desk can double as a craft area, and nearby storage can hold supplies.

Courtesy of Country Home—Meredith Corp.

- Plan for a seated work counter in or near the kitchen to be used for craft activities. This can also double as the eating counter, prep area, or serving bar. Chapter 6 provides detailed information on space allowances for seating in the kitchen.
- If the household includes children, be sure that there are chairs or stools that have adjustable-height seats, with foot rests, so that the children can use the work counters comfortably along with the rest of the household.
- Many craft and hobby activities need a water source or are messy enough to require hand washing and water for cleanup. A sink near the area used for crafts or hobbies will be convenient. If chemicals are used in the hobby activity, make sure that the sink material is resistant to those chemicals.
- Make sure that the craft or hobby area is well lit with adjustable light levels. Many hobby activities can require a lighting level that is brighter than would usually be used for eating or social activities. Chose light sources with good color rendition, which is especially important for art activities. See Chapter 7 for more information about lighting.
- Plan electrical receptacles or power strips convenient to the hobby or craft area. Ask your client about specialized equipment or electrical needs. For example, many craft patterns are now available in digital form, so a person may want a laptop available. Electric scissors, soldering irons, and hot glue guns are just a few examples of tools requiring electrical connections. See Chapter 7 for more information about electrical wiring.
- Plan storage for craft or hobby supplies, tools, and equipment in or near the kitchen. This storage area can be cupboards, drawers, or shelves, depending on what will be stored. This storage area should be out of the primary work triangle and separate from food storage. In some cases, hobby supplies may need to be stored in childproof cabinets. In other situations, hobby supplies will be stored so that young children can independently access them.
- Temporary storage may be needed in or near the kitchen. For example, newly crafted items may need to be hung up or laid out flat to dry. Equipment may need to be set aside to cool before being put away. This type of storage may be in the kitchen or in an auxiliary area, such as the mudroom.
- Consider planning some display space for finished craft projects in or near the kitchen. Depending on the activity, this might be a tack board, magnetic board, hooks, a plate rack, open shelves, or a glass-door cabinet.
- Make sure that the kitchen has an exhaust ventilation system with adjustable fan speeds. Many hobby activities involve glue, paint, and other chemicals that could contribute to indoor air pollution. The kitchen ventilation system can help remove these vapors from the air. See Chapter 3 for information about indoor air quality hazards, and Chapter 7 for information about kitchen ventilation systems.

A GARDENING AREA

Indoor gardening may be a desirable activity in a kitchen or nearby area. Typically, the space will be used for potting plants, trimming house plants, watering and fertilizing potted plants, arranging flowers, and similar tasks. An area for growing herbs and starting cuttings or seeds may be included. Storage will be needed for pots and vases of various sizes, potting soil, fertilizer, scissors, spades, and assorted tools for indoor gardening.

A gardening area may be included in the kitchen proper, but not in the primary work triangle, or a garden area may be incorporated into other areas that are adjacent to the kitchen, such as the family foyer, mudroom, laundry area, or a sunroom. The gardening area may be a defined space. Alternately, you may design a multipurpose space, such as a laundry area, recycling center, or pet-washing area that can also work for indoor gardening. The amount of space, and the complexity of the gardening area, will depend on how important gardening is to your client.

Planning the Indoor Garden Area

One approach to planning an indoor garden area is to think of it as another prep area—but for plants. Using this approach, the garden area would include work counter area, a sink, and storage for tools and supplies.

Work Counter Area

Most indoor garden activities will occur with the person standing. Therefore, a comfortable height at, or slightly below, the gardener's elbow is recommended. The standard 36-inch (914-mm) height of a kitchen counter is a good compromise but may not work as effectively for a tall or short person or someone in a wheelchair (Figure 9.17).

As in the prep center in the kitchen, approximately 16 inches (406 mm) of counter depth is used as work area. Additional depth becomes storage or landing area for tools and supplies. Therefore, a standard 24-inch (610-mm) counter would work well for a gardening area. If the work counter is also used to hold pots with growing plants, a deeper counter may be desired.

The amount of counter space will vary with the type of gardening activities and the size of pots used most frequently. Counter frontage of 36 inches (914 mm) would likely be considered a minimum.

The counter needs to be durable and easy to clean. Choose a nonabsorbent material that will resist garden chemicals as well as abrasion from rough pots. Glazed tile, solid surface, engineered stone, sealed concrete, and sealed masonry are possible choices.

Even the most careful gardeners will sometimes get potting soil, plant cuttings, or debris on the floor instead of the work counter. Durable, easy-to-maintain flooring—much like that for the mudroom—is important in the gardening area.

A Garden Sink

Water is used on plants, to mix fertilizer and other plant chemicals, and for cleanup. A water source is needed for the gardening area. If at all possible, provide a separate sink.

A single-bowl sink will serve most garden area needs. When repotting, many gardeners like to water a plant and then let it drain in the sink, so make sure the sink is large enough to handle the pots the gardener will use. A large sink will actually become a work area for most gardeners (Figure 9.18). Also, choose a sink of a durable material that is not easily scratched by rough pots.

FIGURE 9.18 A large garden sink, surrounded by a ledge, becomes a potting area in a rustic enclosed porch.

Courtesy of American Standard

A clever idea is to fit the garden sink with a slatted insert, so that pots rest on the insert for draining, and the sink is protected from scratching (Figure 9.19). A slatted drain board over the sink is an alternative idea.

Think about the relationship of the faucet to the sink, and plan for room for pots and large containers, such as watering cans. Consider a gooseneck faucet or a wall-mounted faucet to provide adequate clearance. A faucet with a spray attachment makes it easier to water plants, especially in large pots. A pot-filler faucet could be adapted to a garden sink. Another option is a touch or hands-free faucet for easy operation with dirty hands.

Storage

Start planning storage in the garden area with simple open shelves to accommodate pots, baskets, vases, trays, and similar items. Provide some storage for heavier or bulkier items that does not require the gardener to lift the item above shoulder level. Bookshelf space can be used for gardening books and reference manuals.

FIGURE 9.19 A slatted sink insert makes a great place to drain plants or fill pots.

Courtesy of Kohler Company

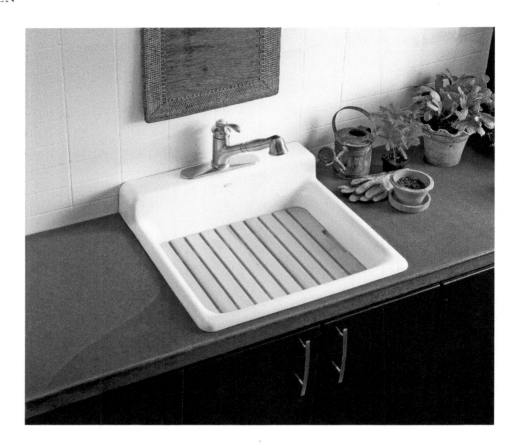

Drawer storage is desirable for small items, such as scissors, spades, and twist ties. Pull-out baskets or bins can also be used to store pots and oddly shaped items. If the gardener buys or mixes potting soil in large amounts, a tilt-out bin for ready access to the soil would be a great convenience.

In a household with small children, there needs to be secure storage in the gardening area for garden chemicals such as fertilizer and insecticides, as well as sharp tools, such as scissors. A locked cabinet or a drawer with a childproof latch is recommended.

A Growing Area

Many gardeners also want an area in the kitchen or nearby where they can grow indoor plants, especially herbs. Most herbs need a window area that gets full sunlight at least five hours a day (or up to 15 hours a day of fluorescent/grow light artificial light). Usually this means a southern or western exposure, although in some climates, the western exposure may be too hot. Most herbs prefer cooler temperatures (60 to 65° F; 16 to 18°C) and need to be protected from strong drafts. Before planning a growing area, be sure that these ambient conditions can be provided.

There are many ways to provide a growing area in a kitchen, such as a greenhouse-style window that "bumps out." Another idea is to pull the cabinets out from the wall, creating a deeper countertop, and use the extra depth as a plant area. Hanging baskets can provide plant space, but they must be clear of passageways and "head space" for people working in the kitchen. Sometimes, extra deep window sills are available. Or, in homes with high ceilings, plants on top of partial height partitions can thrive under well-placed skylights.

SOCIAL SPACES

Throughout this book, we have talked about the kitchen as a gathering space. How many times have you heard a client say something like: "no matter what is planned, guests always seem to gravitate to the kitchen?" How many clients want to design their kitchen so that being in the kitchen is part of the entertainment? In Chapter 6, we discussed many aspects of kitchen design related to guests, entertaining, and socializing in the kitchen: serving centers, dining areas, butler's pantries, beverage bars, and caterer's kitchens. So why, in a chapter that is about "more than a kitchen," are we talking about social spaces?

First, let's think about how the kitchen is part of the social or community area of the home. How does the kitchen, as a unit, relate to other social spaces of the home, such as a family room, den, or great room? Many homes today are designed or remodeled with the kitchen as central and open to the living or social areas of the home. Some homes may have another separate, more formal, social and/or dining space, but these are typically not used on a daily basis.

Options for Kitchen Social Spaces

Some kitchens may have a small sitting area adjacent to the primary kitchen work area. This area might function as a casual eating area, a place for morning coffee or afternoon tea. Maybe it is a place for one household member to sit and read the newspaper or share the day's events while another person takes his or her turn to cook. Perhaps this area includes a fireplace, a sunroom, or an enclosed porch. Sometimes these areas are expanded to a breakfast room, or they may be called a hearth room, country kitchen, or inglenook. People in these social spaces usually feel part of the kitchen but are out of the primary work area.

Another arrangement is a kitchen that is adjacent to the family living area. The kitchen space has one or more sides in common with the family living area. There may be a partial barrier between the kitchen and living area, such as a counter or bar. There is a visual and usually an auditory link between the spaces. This type of arrangement is designed so that the two spaces flow into each other, but there is a sense of separate areas. Activities occur simultaneously in the kitchen and living areas, and people can communicate, but people in the living areas are not in the kitchen.

Thus, the kitchen that is open to a social or community area of the home can both be defined as a separate space and unified with the larger area. The amount of integration and separation depends on your design choices. Visual definition or separation of the kitchen comes by:

- A change in flooring material between the kitchen and the social space.
- A change in ceiling material or height between the two spaces. The kitchen space could be defined by a lowered soffit.
- Separate lighting system for the kitchen, especially the lighting that defines the food preparation areas or an eating area within the kitchen.
- A counter, bar, or partial wall that physically defines the parameters of the kitchen (Figure 9.20).
- Backsplash color, design, or material that is unique to the kitchen area.

FIGURE 9.20 The different finishes on the wall, and the orientation of the living area furniture to the focal point of the fireplace, establish the social area as a separate space.

Design by NKBA member Wendy F. Johnson, CKD, CBD; codesigner: Alex Esposito

Alternatively, unity of the larger space, integrating the social area with the kitchen (Figure 9.21), can be achieved by:

- Using the same or coordinating flooring materials throughout
- Using the same ceiling finish or height
- Coordinating wall finishes in color, texture, or material
- Using the same cabinetry style and material as in the kitchen for features, such as a computer desk area, games storage, or media center, in the social area
- Coordinated window styles and treatments throughout the space

Designing the Kitchen Sitting Area

An adjacent sitting area is usually stylistically coordinated and integrated with the kitchen. There is usually a sense of a single space. However, people need to be able to walk into and out of the sitting area without interrupting the work triangle in the food preparation area.

Start planning the kitchen sitting area by considering the following questions:

- What is the capacity of the sitting area? Will just members of the household use it or is this also an area for entertaining?
- Will the sitting area be used for eating meals? Often a sitting area and casual eating or breakfast area are integrated together. What about lap-meals or snacks?
- What type of seating will be included—couches, loveseats, easy chairs, or rockers? Figure 9.22 gives the typical dimensions, in plan, of common types of furniture.
- What will be the focal point of the area—a fireplace, a view to the outside, a television, or media center—or into the kitchen?
- How will the seating arrangement be oriented—toward the kitchen or away from it?
- How will the kitchen be oriented to the seating area—across the sink, the cooktop, the prep area, or an eating counter?

Here are some suggestions to consider when designing a kitchen sitting area:

- Pay very close attention to sight lines and eye height.

    Most people in the kitchen will be looking into the sitting area from a standing eye level. Be aware of cabinetry and other structures that might interfere with sight lines into the seating

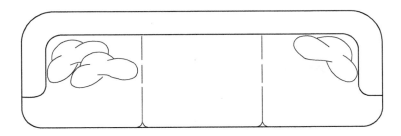

COUCH
30"-36" x 72"-90"
(762 - 914 mm × 1829 - 2286 mm)

CHAIR
18" x 18"
(457 mm × 457 mm)

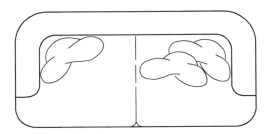

LOVESEAT
30"-36" x 60"
(762 - 914 mm × 1524 mm)

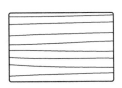

END TABLE
18" x 26"-30"
(457 mm × 660 - 762 mm)

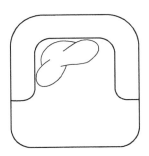

EASY CHAIR
30"-32" x 34"-36"
(726 - 813 mm × 864 - 914 mm)

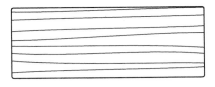

COFFEE TABLE
18" x 48"
(457 mm × 1219 mm)

FIGURE 9.22 Furniture sizes are not standardized, but these examples will give you an idea of the approximate size of common pieces of furniture that might be used in a sitting area.

[Source: NKBA]

area. Wall cabinetry that is installed at the usual height of 15 to 18 inches (381 to 457 mm) above the counter will be 51 to 54 inches (1295 to 1372 mm) above the finished floor and block most people's sight lines.

People in the sitting area will more likely be at a seated eye level. This can be used to advantage if you wish to partially screen kitchen work areas. However, remember to consider seated eye level for placement of other features, such as muntins on windows. Also, people in the sitting area will see up underneath wall cabinets, so avoid glare from under cabinet lighting.

- Keep the conversation circle in mind. Group furniture for easy conversation by keeping distances less than 10 feet (3 m).

  Plan traffic so that it goes around the conversation circle, not through it. Also, people find it easier to converse when someone is at a right angle, or across, from them, rather than directly beside them.

- Since this sitting area is part of the kitchen, assume that people using it will often have drinks or snacks. Plan landing space convenient to each seat, such as a side or coffee table.
- A sitting area may include a table and straight-back chairs, even if there is another eating area. These can be used for casual meals, snacks, homework, menu planning, or any number of activities that are facilitated by sitting at a table surface. Refer to Chapter 6 for guidelines on seated table space and clearances.
- A planning desk, as described previously in this chapter, may be part of the kitchen sitting area.
- If a television will be located in the sitting area, determine who will be watching it. Will it be located for prime viewing by someone working in the kitchen, or someone sitting in an easy chair? An adjustable viewing location may be desirable.

  Viewing distance for a television is related to the size of the screen. The 10-foot (3-m) distance for conversation is often used as a guide for television viewing, but a large screen television can be viewed from a greater distance.

  Volume can be an issue with the television. A television speaker in the sitting area may not be loud enough to be heard in the kitchen area. Consider a system with multiple speakers for the most flexibility. A sound specialist may need to be consulted to ensure effective placement of speakers.

- Plan for storage in the sitting area. Often, cabinetry matching or coordinating with the cabinetry in the kitchen work area is used. Shelves for books, mementos, decorative items, and plants are often desired. Games, CDs, DVDs, videos, puzzles, magazines, and craft and hobby supplies are examples of additional items that might be stored in the sitting area. Depending on the relationship of the sitting area to the dining area, china, silver, and linens may also be kept there.
- Control of noise from kitchen activities will be important so that it does not interfere with conversation and other activities in the sitting area. Carefully consider whether hard surface materials that reflect sound are appropriate. Review the information in Chapter 2 on noise.
- Good ventilation will be important in the kitchen so that grease, smoke, and odors are removed effectively from the cooking area and do not linger in the sitting area. Review the information on ventilation in Chapter 7.
- The kitchen sitting area is an everyday space, a gathering place for members of the household. Plan to use durable, easy-to-maintain materials that resist the wear and tear of frequent use and spills from drinks and food.
- The kitchen sitting area may also relate to an outdoor kitchen, deck, or patio area for indoor-outdoor activities and entertaining. Plan for circulation space and access to these additional spaces.

SUMMARY

A family foyer or mudroom provides an informal entrance and communication and storage space. The home planning center may be a communication and management space, or a complete home office. A laundry in or near the kitchen allows convenient management of this household task.

With advance planning, the kitchen, with counters, water and utility connections, good lighting, and storage, makes an excellent craft, hobby, or indoor gardening space. People gravitate to the kitchen and joining social spaces to food preparation spaces integrates household activities in the community area of the home.

The kitchen, and the auxiliary spaces adjacent it to it, are truly the heart of a home. Many activities—from managing the home to socializing with family and friends, from keeping track of busy lives to engaging in pleasurable hobbies—all take place in these spaces. As a designer, your expertise and creativity can help ensure that the auxiliary areas of the kitchen are well planned to accommodate and support these activities as effectively and efficiently as the food preparation and eating activities of the primary kitchen area.

REVIEW QUESTIONS

1. Describe at least five activities that might take place in a family foyer that would need to be accommodated by the designer. (See under "The Family Foyer or Mudroom" page 349)
2. What are the important dimensions and planning considerations for a computer work station in or near the kitchen? (See under "Computer Workstation" page 360)
3. A "communication center" can be important to a household with multiple people coming and going. Describe several ideas for designing a communication center in or near the kitchen. (See "The Family Foyer or Mudroom" "Home Planning Center," "Household Communications" pages 355 and 359)
4. What criteria can be used to recommend energy- and water-efficient laundry appliances? (See "Laundry and the Environment" page 365)
5. Discuss several considerations in designing a craft/hobby area in or near a kitchen that will be used by children. (See under "A Craft/Hobby Area" page 369)
6. How is designing an indoor garden area like designing a prep area? Give multiple examples. (See "Planning the Indoor Garden Area" page 371)
7. What design techniques can be used to visually separate adjacent social areas from the kitchen? Likewise, how can these areas be visually integrated? (See "Options for Kitchen Social Spaces" page 375)

Putting It All Together

Design is a process—but not a neat, tidy, linear process. Moving from the idea, or the wish, for a new kitchen to the finished product involves a lot of going back and forth, checking and rechecking. Developing a kitchen design involves a dose of inspiration, a spark of creativity, but mostly a lot of hard work.

Throughout this book, we presented a considerable amount of information about kitchens, what to include and how to arrange the space. We talked about appliances, cooking styles, where to eat, and the many activities that take place in a kitchen. We even talked about designing auxiliary spaces around a kitchen. We emphasized how to gather client information to help focus your design to meet their needs and desires.

In this chapter, we show you how to organize this wealth of information and translate it into an actual kitchen design. First we discuss the overall design process and how to move from an idea to a complete design. Next we focus on the design program, the part of the process where you organize all your information and ideas into a plan for the kitchen design. Finally, we address the design drawing and present a method to move from a concept to an actual layout. Throughout the chapter, we will supplement the text with an example of a basic kitchen design, from the design program to the design drawing.

In this chapter, the focus is to develop a single design drawing through the use of the design process. In reality, you will probably use this design process to develop several alternative plans to present to your client. Then, these plans will be evaluated by you and your client before making the final selections for the kitchen design.

Learning Objective 1: Describe and explain the stages of the design process.

Learning Objective 2: Identify and describe the parts of a typical design program.

Learning Objective 3: Use a design program to develop a completed design drawing.

THE DESIGN PROCESS

There are many different ways to approach design, probably as many as there are designers. As designers gain more experience, they develop a method and unique style that is personally successful.

Summary of the Design Process

- Identify and describe the client.
- Organize the information.
- Identify the activity spaces.
- Visualize the activity spaces.
- Develop the visual diagram.
- Refine the visual diagram.
- Think in three dimensions.
- Evaluate the plan.
- Think about details, details, details.

If you are a new designer, you can benefit by following a formal structure for the design process. This will help you become adept at sequencing the steps in developing a kitchen design and ensure that no parts of the process are forgotten.

If you are an experienced designer, reviewing a formal design process may give you a fresh approach and spark new creativity in your designs. What follows is a brief discussion of the design process that is used by the authors:

- **Identify the client**. Gather information about the client. This is both the tangible, such as anthropometric information and a list of items for storage, and the intangible, such as ambience desired in the space or style preferences. Chapter 5, "Needs Assessment," is a detailed guide to gathering information and assessing client needs, and provides forms and checklists to facilitate the process. You may also need additional research at this stage, learning about things such as appliances, products, or materials that the client wants. You also want to make sure that you are informed on issues that will influence design decisions, such as the need for accessible design, sustainable product choice, or multiculturalism.
- **Organize the information.** Develop the first part of your design program by determining the goals and objectives for the design. Prioritize the needs and wants of the client and identify the limitations of the project. (Design programming will be discussed in more detail later in this chapter.)
- **Identify the activity spaces.** Develop the second part of the design program by preparing the *user analysis.* The user analysis is a chart or table that groups design requirements by the major activities that will take place in the kitchen space. An example of a user analysis chart is presented later in this chapter when we discuss the design program. In most cases, this will mean that you are organizing information by the activity centers that were described in Chapter 6, "Kitchen Planning."

Check your user analysis against the client needs assessment information (Chapter 5) to make sure that you have accommodated the client's priority needs. You may even want to share the user analysis with the client, as a double-check.

- **Visualize the activity spaces.** This is the stage when you are moving from verbal and quantitative information to visual ideas. Many designers use bubble diagrams to represent activity spaces or various centers and to explore the relationships of the different spaces. For example, you may have one bubble for the cooking center (representing a cook top and the surrounding cabinetry and counter space), another bubble for the refrigerator area, and so on. (See Figure 10.1 for an example of a bubble diagram.)
- **Develop the visual diagram.** Select the best one or two bubble diagrams for refinement. Prepare a room outline, to scale (1/2" = 1'0" or a ratio of 1 to 20 using mm or cm) and note project parameters, such as windows or doors that are fixed in location. Start using templates for each center or activity space and place them on your room outline, using the bubble diagrams as your guide. A design template is a scale drawing representing the appliances, cabinetry,

and clearances for a center or activity space. (See Figures 10.4, 10.5, and 10.6, later in this chapter when we talk about the design drawing, for examples of design templates.) Templates allow you to see how spaces fit together and how your design ideas will work in the actual kitchen space. Templates can be created by hand drafting or with computer-aided design software. Remember that appliances and fixtures come in different sizes and the template should reflect the size that is to be specified.

Check your visual diagram against the user analysis. Have you included all the requirements?

- **Refine the visual diagram.** You will be moving from the bubble diagram to the arrangement of templates to a sketch of a floor plan. Work in scale. Evaluate your visual diagram against the project parameters.
- **Think in three dimensions.** Use elevation or perspective sketches to develop the vertical elements for your design. Changes in the floor plan may be required.
- **Evaluate the plan.** Check the preliminary design against the design program. Review the relationship of the centers. Evaluate zoning and circulation within the kitchen as well as in relationship to adjacent rooms. Evaluate your plan against the Kitchen Planning Guidelines Checklist and if appropriate, the Kitchen Access Standards Checklist. These checklists are presented later in this chapter. Check your plan against any additional building code requirements.
  - Review the preliminary plan with the client. You may be working with more than one design option at this point, so gather feedback from the client.
- **Think about details, details, details.** Lay out the preferred design of the kitchen in dimensioned drawings. Select and specify the actual appliances, cabinetry, materials, fixtures, and other items in the space, so that you can verify sizes, installation requirements, clearances, and other details. Review product specifications against client priorities and realities as determined in the needs assessment and your research. Check dimensions to make sure that everything will fit as you envision.
  - Review the final design with the client. Prepare appropriate contract documents as needed for construction, code review, cost estimates, and bids.

The design process may not be complete at this point. For example, client review may require you to revise your plan. Or, products specified may, in fact, not be available. However, thinking through the parts of the design process does allow you to be thorough and careful, and results in a better design in the long run.

THE DESIGN PROGRAM

Let's imagine that you have just completed an exciting meeting with your client. Lots of ideas were shared back and forth. Enticing possibilities for a unique kitchen design were explored. You are eager to sketch, pull out material samples, and develop your thoughts into a new design. Ready to go? What? Start by writing a design program? No, you say, let's just go straight to the design. You can incorporate your client's needs as you go along.

If you skip the design program, how will you know what to design? Design programming is an important and necessary part of successfully completing the design. When we discussed the design process, did you note how often we recommended you check your developing design against the various parts of the design program? Think of the design program as the contract between you and your client. It is an organized directory of all the client's needs, wants, and wishes for the kitchen design, plus the important parameters of the total design.

In Chapter 5, we talked about the design program as "both your guide through the design process and the inspiration to your creativity." Developing the design program allows you to make sure you have—and understand—all the information necessary for the kitchen design. A typical design program has three parts:

- Goals or purpose.
- Objectives and priorities.
- Activities and relationships.

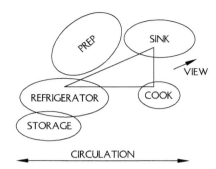

FIGURE 10.1 A bubble diagram is a simple sketch to show how different activity areas can be arranged in a kitchen space. Each "bubble" is an activity area. This is an example of a bubble diagram for a remodeled kitchen, designed for our clients Rosa and Vincente. The same kitchen design will be used in Figures 10.1 through 10.20 as the basis for our design and drawing examples in this chapter.

Goals and Purpose

Can you briefly describe the goals of a design project? Think of this part of the design program as the overview. It should include a description of the client(s), the type and scope of the project, the budget, and your role and responsibilities in the project. Include the major criteria for the kitchen design and any unique aspects of the project. Needed information can come from Form 1: Getting to Know Your Client as well as Forms 3, 4, 5, and 6, which gather information about your client's preferences and desired activities in the kitchen. All forms are found in Chapter 5.

You might want to share your goal statements with your client to determine if you have interpreted the project correctly. The statements could also be included in your contract.

Objectives

Objectives are used to operationalize your goals. If goals tell what you want to do, objectives tell how you are going to do it. Objectives are written with active verbs, and the outcomes can be measured. Here is an example.

- **Goal:** The kitchen will be a social space.
  - **Objective:** Install a raised counter area across from the cook-top with seating for three.
  - **Objective:** Design two prep areas.
  - **Objective:** Provide an open view from the sink area into the family room.

Write objectives to identify the client's major wants and needs. Use the development of the objectives to sort out priorities—must have, should or want to have, and desire or would like to have.

Activities and Relationships

This section is the crux of the design program. Focus on the various activities that will take place in the kitchen and what is needed in the design to support the activities. You may want to group activities together into centers. For example, kneading bread, assembling pies, packing a lunch box, and preparing vegetables for a stir-fry all have similar workspace requirements, and could be grouped together as part of the food preparation center. Form 3: Checklist for Kitchen Activities and Form 4: Kitchen Storage Inventory, found in Chapter 5, are arranged in sections by center, so you can collect activity and storage information in an organized fashion.

Since the focus is on the activities taking place in the space, the emphasis is on who is doing what. Organize the activity information into a user analysis chart. You might want to prepare a user analysis for each center in the kitchen or group of related activities. The user analysis can include the following information:

- Activities that take place in the space
- Who will be doing the activities; the users
- Frequency of activities
- Appliances, fixtures, fittings, furnishings, accessories, and any other physical items needed to support the activities, including special sizes or characteristics
- Storage needed to support the activities
- Amount of space needed for the activities, including clearances; and relationships to other spaces
- Ambience requirements
- Special requirements, such as safety features
- Future changes to be accommodated
- Summary of the NKBA Kitchen Planning Guidelines or Access Standards relevant to the activities and requirements of the client and their kitchen

Preparing the user analysis as a chart or table helps to organize the information into an easily referenced format to which you can refer during the development of your design. Using a spreadsheet program or the table function in a word processing program on your computer makes it easy to prepare a user analysis. However, it is a good idea to leave some open space for extra notes if changes are needed.

TABLE 10.1 An example of a user analysis chart, showing information for a sink center. This will be used in the design templates shown in Figures 10.4, 10.5, and 10.6, and in the sample kitchen design shown in Figures 10.7 through 10.20, for our clients Rosa and Vincente.

Activity Space	Users	Frequency	Appliances, Fixtures	Storage, Fittings, Furniture, etc.
Sink Center: Automatic dishwasher; hand wash large items; produce prep; primary water source for kitchen	Vincente, Rosa	Daily	Dishwasher, 24" (610 mm) energy-efficient, quiet Garbage disposer Two-bowl sink, 33" (838 mm), 18-gauge stainless steel Pull-out spray faucet, single lever Hot water dispenser	Drawer storage Cleaning supplies Vegetable prep tools Tea and mugs Ice tea maker Coffee pot and supplies Everyday dishes Waste receptacle

Space Relationships	Ambiance	Special Needs	Furniture Needs	Guidelines and Access Standards
42" (1067 mm) work aisle, 48" (1219 mm) preferred Adjacent to prep center 21" (533 mm) minimum clearance by dishwasher 18" and 24" (457 and 610 mm) landing space by sink, more preferable	Night light at sink	Sink below window 36" (914 mm) window to be added Pull-out cutting board Toe kick step by sink	None noted	Kitchen Planning Guidelines 2, 3, 6, 10, 11, 13, 14, 26, 28, 30, 31

As you develop your user analysis, you will be relying on the client interview and needs assessment to determine what activities will take place in the kitchen. Using a prepared assessment form, such as Form 3: Checklist for Kitchen Activities, can help ensure that all activities are considered. However, you will want to review your user analysis to make sure that it is inclusive. Some activities are so common and routine that we might not think about them. For example, your clients might tell you that they frequently chop and dice vegetables for salads and stir-fry (requiring a cutting surface at an appropriate height, counter space for assembling ingredients, and convenient storage for knives) but assume that you know that they also wash and drain the vegetables first (requiring a water source near the cutting surface, an area to drain the vegetables, and storage for a colander). Further, did you think about refrigerated and nonrefrigerated storage for these vegetables?

As you develop the user analysis, it is a good time to review the Kitchen Planning Guidelines and Access Standards that apply to the spaces you are designing. You can note the number of the Guidelines that apply, as we did in our example, or note a detail, such as "increase light level." This also creates opportunities to determine if the design will meet both current and future accessibility needs of the client.

Reviewing the user analysis also gives you an opportunity to consider other aspects of the design that were not initially identified by the client. For example, in the user analysis in Table 10.1, Vincente and Rosa (the clients) noted that they wanted an energy-efficient dishwasher. However, there is no mention of the energy efficiency of the new window or the environmental sustainability of the materials to be selected. You, the designer, could then recommend a window with a low U-factor, or countertops from a certified recycled glass product. (See Chapter 3, "Environmental and Sustainability Considerations," for more information.)

Relationship or Adjacency Matrix
The detail you include in your user analysis will depend on the complexity of the project. For a larger project, especially if it involves multiple spaces, you may want to use a relationship or adjacency matrix (see p. 386). A relationship or adjacency matrix is a graphic method of organizing the relationships of multiple spaces. The matrix can help you more easily see the types of relationships among activity spaces and assist in determining how to group and separate activities into different centers and spaces. You can also use a matrix to graph relationships between the kitchen and other spaces in the home.

Relationship or Adjacency Matrix

This is an example of a matrix showing physical access between centers and other areas in the kitchen. Similar matrices could be developed for visual access or auditory access. Or the same matrix approach could be used to study access between the kitchen and other spaces within the home. This matrix was used in developing the bubble diagram (Figure 10.1) and the visual diagram (see Figure 10.9, found later in this chapter) for the sample kitchen design for the clients Rosa and Vincente.

Matrix

Sink			
1	Prep		
2	1	Cook	
2	2	2	Refrigerator/Storage

1 = Direct access needed
2 = Partial or indirect access desirable
3 = No access necessary

To read the matrix: read down a column and across a row from the right to the cell where the column and row meet. For example, the yellow highlighted cell is in the Sink column and the Cook row. There is a number 2 in the cell. That tells us that partial or indirect access is desirable. However, if we look at the blue highlighted cell, in the Prep column and the Cook row, we see that there is a 1, which means that direct access is needed. Using the matrix can help you prioritize relationships between centers or other areas within your design.

The Four-Stage Interior Design Project

The discussion in this chapter is focused on the *design process*, from idea to product. We have emphasized the completed design. However, the design process can also include project management, including construction supervision and installation coordination.

A four-stage approach to the design process is commonly used by interior designers, who may also be kitchen designers. The four-stage interior design project includes both the development of the design and management of the project, and it is similar in many ways to the design process and design programming presented in this chapter. However, review of the four-stage interior design project is another way to examine and expand our understanding of the design process.

Stage One

- **Program Design and Analysis:** The first designer-client meetings establishes the relationship and allows the designer to prepare a detailed *design analysis* of the project.
- **Proposal:** The *proposal* details the stages of the project, services and products to be provided, and fee structure.

Stage Two

- **Survey and Analysis:** Stage two begins with a comprehensive *survey and measurement* of the space.
- **Creativity and Concept:** A *creative concept* is developed, then analyzed, detailed, and evaluated.
- **Space Planning and Design:** Rough sketches of the design are explored until a *drafted presentation* and other visual material is prepared.
- **Client Presentation:** A *professional presentation* is made to the client, supported by various visual materials of the proposed design.
- **Client Approval:** The client provides *written approval* of the proposed design.

Stage Three

- **Contract Documents:** *Working drawings* and all *contract documents* are prepared, including:
  - Specifications for all interior elements
  - Bids
  - Cost estimates
  - Contracts
- **Permits:** Designer obtains all necessary approvals for *codes and regulations*.

Stage Four

- **Project Management:** The designer may *manage the project*, or may coordinate with a project manager, to implement the design project. Responsibilities include:
  - Schedule
  - Procurement
  - Site supervision
  - Construction management
  - Installation planning
  - Completion and client turnover

Reference: Gibbs, J (2005). *Interior Design: A Practical Guide.* New York, NY: Harry N. Abrams, Inc.

THE DESIGN DRAWING

Moving from the design program to the completed design solution is an exciting and creative process. It is also a process that requires accuracy and verification.

In this section, we discuss how to move from the design program to a dimensioned design drawing of your solution. We will emphasize the importance of checking and rechecking dimensions to verify that your design solution will work in "real space." This section tells you how to manage the technical details—you supply the creativity.

Templates

As you begin refining your conceptual ideas, it is important to begin working to scale. First, this gives you a realistic picture of space relationships and possibilities—very important in the complex spaces of a kitchen. Second, it helps prevent you from making mistakes. If you work with the right proportions and sizes from the beginning, you tend to "see" the space relationships more clearly and you are less likely to misjudge clearances and space needs.

A helpful way to develop your visual diagram is to use design templates. A design template is used to represent an activity space or a center, and includes any appliances, fixtures, or equipment, plus the clearances needed (Figure 10.2 and Figure 10.3). For example, you can have a sink center template, which would show the sink in its cabinet, associated counter space, the dishwasher, and the clearances needed for door swings and access. Or a refrigerator center template would include the appliance, landing space countertop, door swings and clearances, and perhaps note where water and electrical connections are required.

It is a good idea to prepare design templates in both plan and elevation view (Figure 10.4). This can be very useful as you evaluate your design in three dimensions. You may want to prepare several elevation views, as you experiment with different arrangements of wall cabinets, or to be prepared to work with different ceiling heights.

Draw your design templates in a scale of 1/2" = 1'0" or a ratio of 1 to 20 in mm or cm. Since these are the typical scales for kitchen drawings, starting in one of these scales will be a time saver.

Based on your design program, you will want to develop a number of design templates for a particular kitchen design. Consider the special needs and requests of your client. You may develop

FIGURE 10.2 This drawing is a *plan view design template* of a basic sink center, including a sink cabinet (36 inches or 914 mm) and dishwasher (24 inches or 610 mm) to the right of the sink. Landing areas of 18 inches (457 mm) and 24 inches (610 mm), a preparation area of 36 inches (914 mm) next to the sink, and a work aisle of 42 inches (1067 mm) are included. Clearances are based on recommendations for sink landing area (Planning Guideline 11), prep area (Planning Guideline 12), dishwasher placement (Planning Guideline 13), and work aisle clearances (Planning Guideline 6). Additional clearances to meet the Access Standards could be added.

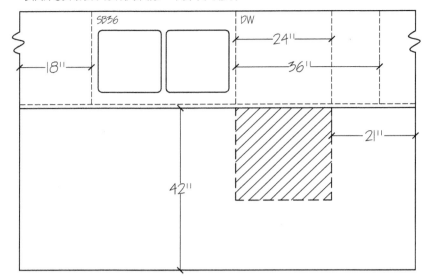

SINK CENTER TEMPLATE - PLAN VIEW

alternative templates for the same activity space. For example, you may develop two design templates for different sized refrigerators and then determine which size refrigerator will fit best in the final design.

Label your design templates. This will facilitate using them to develop the kitchen plan. It will also help you develop a timesaving file of design templates for future use. For example, if you have design templates for 33-inch (838 mm), 36-inch (914-mm), and 39-inch (991-mm) refrigerators with clearance, from one project, you can likely use them on many other kitchen designs. Depending on your preferred style of working, design templates can be saved in computer files or on sturdy paper.

Room Outline

An important foundation for producing your visual diagram, and eventually your design drawing, is the room outline. The room outline is a scaled drawing of the perimeter of the kitchen space.

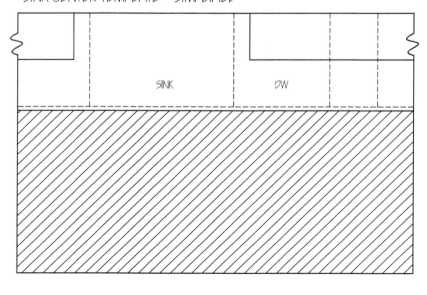

SINK CENTER TEMPLATE - SIMPLIFIED

FIGURE 10.3 This illustration is a *simplified design template* of the sink center, in scale, with wall cabinets blocked. This template would be useful in experimenting with different design layouts.

SINK CENTER TEMPLATE - ELEVATION

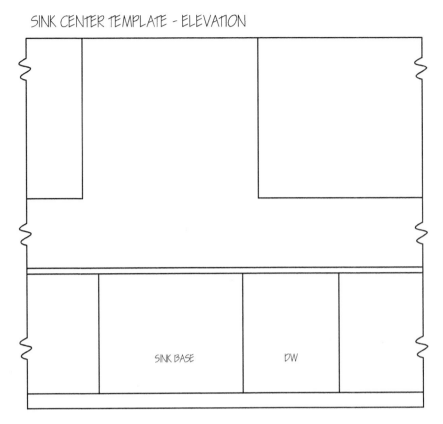

SINK BASE

DW

FIGURE 10.4 This *elevation design template* is a simplified view of the sink center, using a 96-inch (2438 mm) ceiling.

Prepare a drawing of all walls and fixed structural or architectural features, such as windows and doors. The information you need to complete the room outline should be found on the following needs assessment forms from Chapter 5, Form 8: Dimensions of Mechanical Devices; Form 9: Window Measurements; Form 10: Door Measurements; and Form 11: Fixture and Appliance Measurements.

In some kitchen design projects, walls, windows, doors, and other structural features are fixed, and cannot be moved or altered. For example, moving windows affects the exterior design of the home, and the client may not want to change this. In other projects, you may have some options to relocate some features or even expand the space. Perhaps a doorway can be moved or an interior wall removed. This is the type of information recorded on Form 7: Job Site Inspection.

You may find it useful to prepare two room outlines. One room outline shows the existing room space as it is (Figure 10.5). The second drawing removes features that can be changed but retains the fixed features. The second drawing will help you see the possibilities of the space (Figure 10.6).

You may have other limitations on your design that should be noted on your room outline. All mechanical, electrical, and plumbing parameters need to be noted. For example, the location of one or more plumbing fixtures or appliances may be predetermined. Or, the location of heating and cooling vents may be fixed.

Add any additional information to your drawing that will help in design decisions. Note what types of spaces surround the kitchen. Note interior and exterior walls. The height of windows or any fixed structural features will be useful to know. Important interior or exterior views can be noted.

It is important to note all constraints and options on your room outline. Noting these features on your room outline helps ensure that your design will remain within the parameters of your project.

Verify all room measurements and check your room drawing. The room outline must accurately represent the space of the kitchen.

FIGURE 10.5 The existing kitchen space with project parameters for our clients Vincente and Rosa.

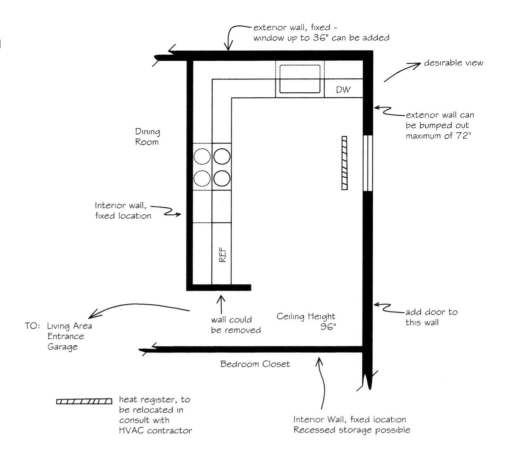

FIGURE 10.6 The room outline as altered. Nonfixed features are removed, the exterior wall is bumped out, fixed features are included, and dimensions are shown. This room outline will be used to develop the visual diagram shown in Figure 10.7.

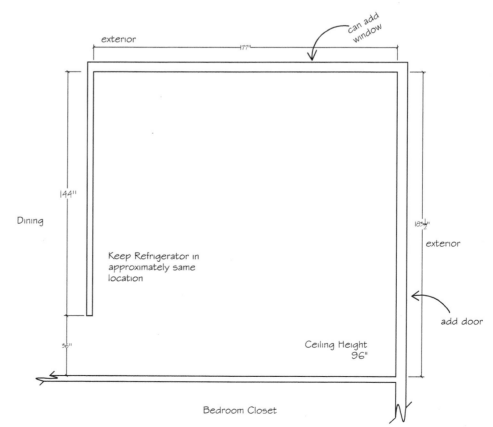

Visual Diagrams

Your bubble diagrams suggest ways to arrange the spaces in the kitchen. Now it is time to see if these ideas can be translated into a design that will work in the actual space. This is the development of the visual diagram.

Using the design templates that you developed, place them in the room outline. Use the ideas generated by the bubble diagrams to guide your work. Refer to the information on the room outline to see if your design ideas are possible within the existing space.

You will want to try a number of different layouts before you decide on the best solution. As you consider a possible layout, review the information on your room outline that details project parameters. Refer back to the design program, especially the user analysis, to remind yourself of what the design layout needs to accomplish.

If you are having trouble getting everything into the space, reconsider the templates you are using. Could space clearances overlap without compromising function or safety? Could a smaller fixture be used and still meet client needs?

Three Dimensions and Vertical Relationships

Very early in the design process, think in three dimensions. For example, placing the wall oven next to the refrigerator may work fine in plan, but how will it look vertically? We experience space in multiple dimensions, so we must design for all perspectives.

After you have developed one or more visual diagrams that appear to work in plan, develop some three-dimensional sketches. Elevation sketches of a wall, to scale, are useful to evaluate spatial relationships of appliances, fixtures, cabinetry, and structural features (Figure 10.8). Design templates of elevation views can speed the process. You may wish to make notes on your elevations, as you did on the room outlines.

Many computer programs used in design drawing will generate perspective views of a design. This technology is an excellent way to view your design from different angles and evaluate its effectiveness. Keep in mind, however, that these perspectives are interpretive—they give you a sense of the space but do not show all the details.

After reviewing your visual diagrams, in plan and vertical views, select the best design layout. Review your design program to determine that the layout meets the goals and objectives. Verify that the design layout is appropriate to the structural and mechanical parameters of the project. For a renovation project, refer back to your on-site measurements of the existing space for verification. If you are working with new construction, consult project documents.

Now you are ready to detail your design solution in a complete dimensioned drawing.

A SAMPLE DESIGN DRAWING

Priority Areas

Start your dimensioned design drawing with the priority areas of the plan. These are the elements of your plan that are not moveable, demand the most space, or are most important to the client. For example, you might start your dimensioned drawing with the sink center because plumbing connections or a window dictate the location. Or, you might start with the placement of a commercial-style range because of its large size and because it is going to be a focal element of the kitchen design.

To best explain how to use priority areas to layout a design drawing, we will take you through an example. The visual diagram in Figure 10.7 and elevation sketch in Figure 10.8 got us started on the kitchen design for Rosa and Vincente that is being used throughout this chapter.

FIGURE 10.7 The visual diagram for Rosa and Vincente's project uses the room outline from Figure 10.6 and bubble diagram from Figure 10.1. Four design templates were used to develop the visual diagram, with landing space and clearances determined by Kitchen Planning Guideline recommendations.

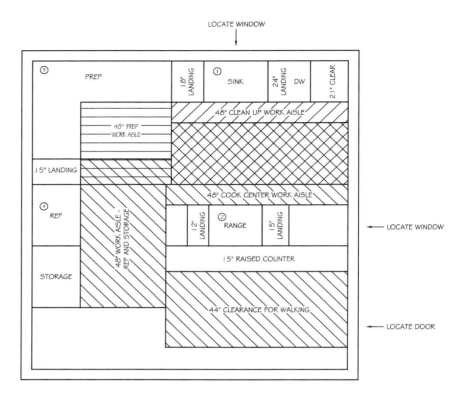

① SINK STORAGE (DESIGN TEMPLATE)
* SINK IN 36" CABINET
* 24" DISHWASHWER
* 18" LANDING SPACE TO LEFT & 24" LANDING SPACE TO RIGHT OF SINK
* 21" CLEARANCE BETWEEN DISHWASHER AND WALL
* 48" WORK AISLE

② COOK CENTER (DESIGN TEMPLATE)
* 30" RANGE
* 12" LANDING SPACE TO RIGHT AND 15" LANDING SPACE TO LEFT
* 15" RAISED COUNTER
* 48" WORK AISLE AND 44" CLEARANCE FOR WALKING

③ PREP AREA (DESIGN TEMPLATE)
* COUNTER SPACE ADJACENT TO SINK
* 48" WORK AISLE

④ REFRIGERATOR CENTER
* 36" REFRIGERATOR
* 15" LANDING AREA
* 48" WORK AISLE

FIGURE 10.8 A computer-generated elevation sketch of the wall with the sink center, in Rosa and Vincente's kitchen design, shows vertical relationships and encourages you to begin thinking about details such as the placement of specific cabinets and drawers.

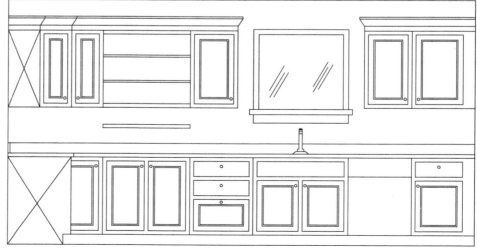

For our example, we are going to start with the sink or cleanup center wall. The clients (Rosa and Vincente) want to add a window to that wall and the location of the sink will determine the placement of the window. First, we draw the room walls to scale. We lightly add the wall thicknesses and overall dimensions (Figure 10.9). We may need to modify walls as we add windows and doors, or move dimensions to complete the drawing. However, it is important to start with an accurate drawing of the space.

We will start detailing our drawing at the corner, where the two exterior walls meet, to the right of where we expect to place the sink. Referring to the design template and the visual diagram, we know that we want to have at least 21 inches (533 mm) of clearance before we place the dishwasher and that we have generous wall space to fit in the cleanup center. We choose to place a 21-inch (533-mm) base cabinet with a 3-inch (76-mm) extended stile on the right and label the cabinet with appropriate nomenclature (Figure 10.9).

Next, we draw the centerline, to place a 24-inch (610 mm) dishwasher next to the base cabinet. Continuing, we place a 36-inch (914 mm) sink base cabinet next to the dishwasher, label it with correct nomenclature, and draw the centerline for the sink (Figure 10.10).

Now, we have a decision to make. We know that we need at least 18 inches (457 mm) of landing space next to the sink. However, from our visual diagram, we know that we have room for a generous amount of counter space for the prep area to the left of the sink. So, we choose to put a 24-inch (610-mm) drawer base next to the sink, which will balance the dishwasher on the other side of the sink (Figure 10.11).

The following three figures show the sequence of placing the base cabinets and dishwasher in the sink or cleanup center for clients Rosa and Vincente. These are the first steps in developing the design drawing based on the visual diagram in Figure 10.7.

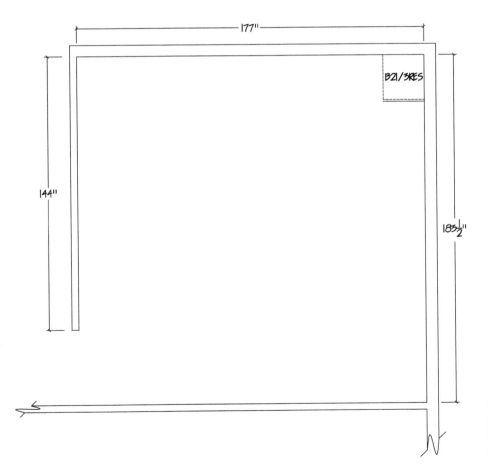

FIGURE 10.9 This drawing shows the whole room with the first cabinet (a 21-inch or 533-mm cabinet with 3-inch or 76-mm extended stile) in place.

FIGURE 10.10 This drawing shows the 36-inch (914 mm) sink base cabinet and 24-inch (610 mm) dishwasher in place.

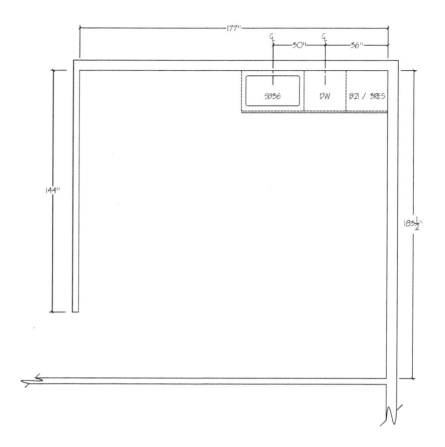

FIGURE 10.11 This drawing adds the 24-inch (610 mm) drawer base next to the sink.

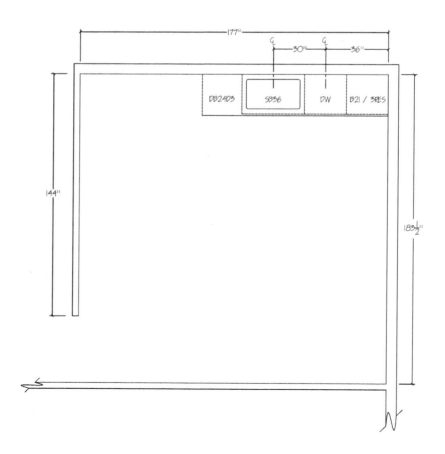

The base cabinets and counters of the sink or cleanup center are now placed. There are several options to continue working on our design drawing. We may choose to place all the base cabinets in the kitchen and then work on wall cabinets. We could lay out the peninsula with the range next, so that its design will relate to the cleanup center.

The best advice is to work on priority areas. The next priority, in our example, is to place a corner cabinet with a lazy Susan in the prep (preparation) area. This corner cabinet will determine the remaining cabinetry placement and sizes on both kitchen walls, so it should be placed next. There-fore, we will draw a 36-inch (914 mm) base corner cabinet in the prep area, and label it with cabinet nomenclature (Figure 10.12).

The next priority area in our design drawing is most likely the placement of the refrigerator. This is a large appliance and has a strong vertical presence. In addition, the client has expressed a desire that the refrigerator remain in approximately the same location as in the original kitchen. For func-tion and a compact work triangle, we decide to put the refrigerator a little closer to the prep area and sink/cleanup center, yet still along the same wall as its current location. On the wall shared with the dining room, we place the 36-inch (914 mm) refrigerator, a 24-inch (610 mm) pantry, and open shelves (turned 90 degrees to face the walkway) at the end of the wall. We label the pantry with nomenclature and draw the centerline for the refrigerator (Figure 10.13).

We know that we need to place a base cabinet next to the refrigerator and that we need to provide at least 15 inches (381 mm) of landing space. However, we are going to wait to place that cabinet until we can evaluate it in the design of the whole prep center and determine the best size and function of cabinet for the space.

As shown, we have the basic plan for the L-shaped portion of the kitchen design. Before we go any farther, let's block in the location of the peninsula that will hold the range and raised eating counter (Figure 10.14). We may adjust the exact size when we detail the cabinets, but, for now, we will block the maximum dimension based on work aisle clearances. Our kitchen design is start-ing to take shape!

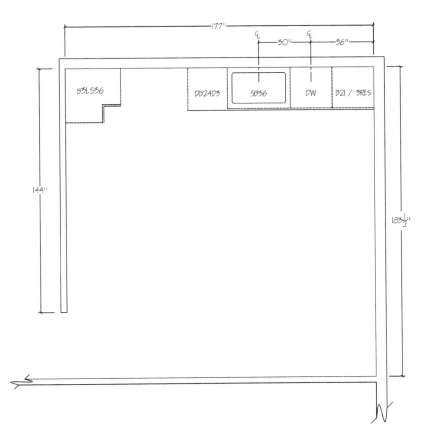

FIGURE 10.12 To continue the design draw-ing for Vincente and Rosa's kitchen remode-ling, begun in Figure 10.9, we add a base corner cabinet.

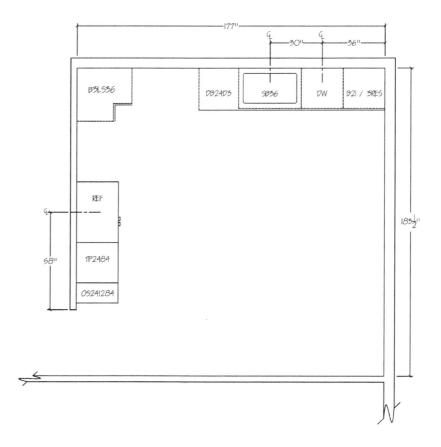

FIGURE 10.13 With the addition of the pantry storage and refrigerator to our design drawing, the L-shape of Vincente and Rosa's kitchen plan becomes apparent.

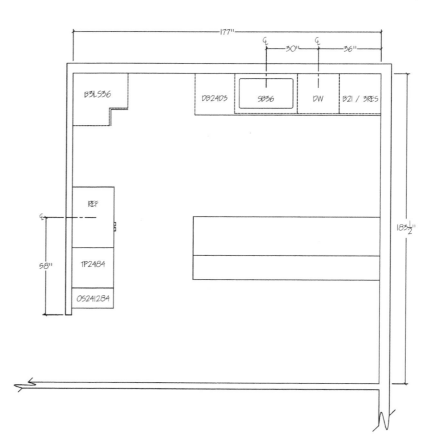

FIGURE 10.14 The next step in developing the design drawing for clients Rosa and Vincente is to block in the location of the peninsula that will include a range and eating counter.

It is time to look at some specific details of dimensions and cabinet sizes. As we make final decisions on placement of the remaining cabinets, we need to consider many things, such as: storage needs of the client; functional arrangements of work centers; types of storage, such as drawers or roll-out shelves; and the visual relationship of vertical and horizontal design elements. Next, we will focus on making sure that everything fits in place.

Let's look at the window wall of the kitchen with the sink or cleanup center. First, we will calculate the total amount of wall space used in the cabinets placed so far, then we can determine what additional cabinetry can be placed. To help ensure accuracy, we will start with the total wall length and subtract for each cabinet or appliance:

177 inches	**Total wall length**	**4496 mm**
− 24 inches	21-inch (533 mm) base cabinet with 3-inch (76 mm) extended stile	− 609 mm
153 inches		**3887 mm**
− 24 inches	Dishwasher (610 mm)	− 610 mm
129 inches		**3277 mm**
− 36 inches	36-inch (914 mm) sink base cabinet	− 914 mm
93 inches		**2363 mm**
− 24 inches	24-inch (610 mm) drawer base	− 610 mm
69 inches		**1753 mm**
− 36 inches	36-inch (914 mm) base corner cabinet	− 914 mm
33 inches		**839 mm**

Using this method, we can determine that we have 33 inches (839 mm) remaining on the wall for base cabinetry. Given that the space is in the prep area, let's put a 33-inch (839 mm) base cabinet with rollout shelves for easily accessible storage. Now, the base cabinets are complete on this wall (Figure 10.15). We can verify the accuracy of our calculations by adding the dimensions together.

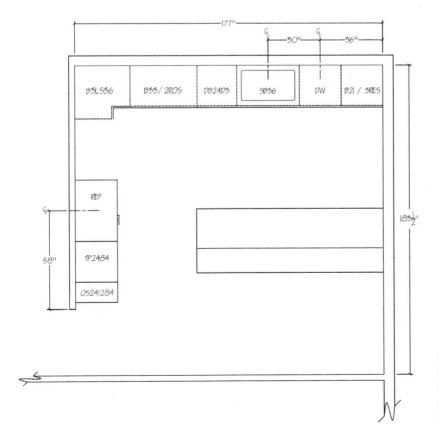

FIGURE 10.15 With the addition of a 33-inch (839 mm) base cabinet, the placement of base cabinetry on the cleanup/sink center wall is complete in the plan for Rosa and Vincente's kitchen remodel.

The next priority step in completing our dimension drawing would most likely be to determine the wall cabinet placement for the same wall—the window or exterior wall where the sink center is located. This allows us to coordinate wall cabinets with base cabinets and determine if any changes are needed. We started by placing a 24-inch (610 mm) diagonal corner wall cabinet and then coordinating the remaining wall space with the base cabinets. Figure 10.16 shows the placement and nomenclature for wall cabinets along that wall.

We can now check the dimensions on the wall cabinets. Again, it is good to start with the total wall length and subtract the various measurements, in order. Double-check the results by adding them up working in the opposite direction.

177 inches	**Total wall length**	**4496 mm**
− 24 inches	21-inch (533 mm) wall cabinet with 3-inch (76 mm) extended stile	− 609 mm
153 inches		**3887 mm**
− 18 inches	18-inch (457 mm) wall cabinet	− 457 mm
135 inches		**3430 mm**
− 6 inches	Setback for window and allowance for window casing (153 mm)	− 153 mm
129 inches		**3277 mm**
− 36 inches	Clearance for 36-inch (914 mm) window	− 914 mm
93 inches		**2363 mm**
− 6 inches	Setback for window and allowance for window casing (153 mm)	− 153 mm
87 inches		**2210 mm**
− 18 inches	18-inch (457 mm) wall cabinet	− 457 mm
69 inches		**1753 mm**
− 33 inches	33-inch (839 mm) wall cabinet, no doors	− 839 mm
36 inches		**914 mm**
− 12 inches	12-inch (304 mm) wall cabinet with spice rack	− 304 mm
24 inches		**610 mm**
− 24 inches	24-inch (610 mm) diagonal corner wall cabinet	− 610 mm
0 inches		**0 mm**

Finishing the Floor Plan

After the priority areas are placed and dimensioned, add the other centers, appliances, cabinetry, fixtures, and features in the plan. Continue checking dimensions by subtracting the amount of space for each item placed in the plan from the remaining wall space. Be sure to verify dimensions in each direction.

As you check dimensions, allow for door swings and clearances for hardware. In some places, you might need to plan on fillers or extended stiles on cabinetry to provide the space to open doors or pull out shelves and drawers. In our example, we had originally planned to put 21 inches (533 mm) between the dishwasher and the wall, to provide the minimum clearance recommended in Kitchen Planning Guideline 13. However, we decided to increase that to 24 inches (610 mm) by using a 21-inch (533 mm) cabinet with an extended stile. The extended stile pulls the cabinet out of the corner, providing more space for the door swing and hardware.

Now that you have worked through some examples of placing the cabinetry and appliances as well as checking the dimensions, finish the sample plan. Complete the placement of cabinetry along the wall with the refrigerator. Be sure to evaluate the design of the prep area—you may want to make some changes in the choice of cabinets that we have already made. Next, work on laying out the peninsula with the range and raised eating counter. Place the windows and doors that will be added in the remodeling. Remember to verify that everything will fit.

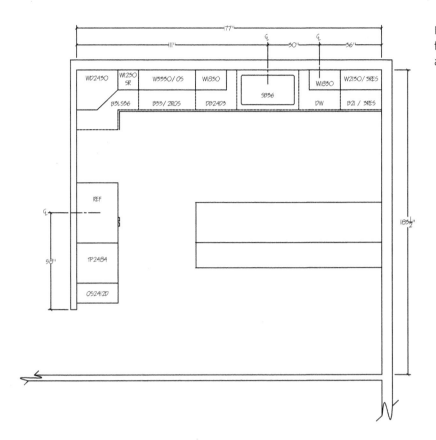

FIGURE 10.16 Continuing the design drawing for clients Rosa and Vincente, the wall cabinets are shown on the sink/cleanup center wall.

Adjusting the Dimensions

Sometimes, at this point, the dimensions do not work out. You may find that your total space for appliances, cabinetry, and other features adds up to more or less than the length of a wall. If this is the case, you need to consider alternatives.

If you have extra space, you may decide to increase the size of selected cabinets or add additional cabinets. This is a good solution if you do not have a lot of extra space. For example, a 33-inch (838 mm) cabinet can be substituted for a 30-inch (762 mm) cabinet. Using one or more fillers or extended stiles may also solve the problem. Another alternative, if appropriate to the client's needs, would be to use a larger fixture, such as 36-inch (914 mm) sink instead of a 33-inch (838 mm) model.

Be sure to consider how these size changes affect the balance, visual impact, and function of your design. If you have a large amount of additional space, you might want to reconsider your design to determine if you have chosen the best solution.

If you are short on space, the solution can be more challenging. As you consider each alternative, review your design program to make sure that changes in your design do not compromise important needs of the client. Some ideas for alternatives:

- Reduce the amount of cabinetry or countertop space in a center. If you have allowed generous space for landing areas or prep areas, you could reduce it a bit. For example, if you have planned a cooktop with 18 inches (457 mm) of landing area on both sides, you could reduce this to 16 or 17 inches (406 or 432 mm) on one or both sides. This would still meet the Kitchen Planning Guidelines recommendation for landing areas.
- Use smaller appliances or cabinetry. For example, instead of a 33-inch (838 mm) wall oven, use a 30-inch (762 mm) oven. Or substitute a 15-inch (381 mm) drawer base for an 18-inch (457 mm) drawer base. Again, make sure that you try to meet recommendations of the Kitchen Planning Guidelines.

- Choose alternative design elements. For example, a range that includes both cooktop and oven uses less space than a separate cooktop and wall oven. Specifying the single range may allow you to choose a larger appliance, yet conserve space, as compared to two separate appliances. Another example is to choose a full-height, pantry-style cabinet to provide the same amount of storage as two base cabinets, but in less floor space.
- Choose cabinetry or appliances with smaller doors, to reduce door swings. This might mean going from a single door 24-inch (610 mm) cabinet to a two-door, 27-inch (686 mm) cabinet, or choose a side-by-side refrigerator instead of a bottom-mount model. However, consider the functionality of the size of the door opening, the continuity of cabinet spacing, and client preferences when making size alterations.

You may need to try several alternatives to make sure your layout fits the actual space. As you are exploring alternatives, be sure that you are working with the actual dimensions of the various appliances, fixtures, cabinets, and other items to be placed in the kitchen. Do not depend on the size shown on a drawing template or a generic example in a computer program.

Vertical Relationships

Dimensioned elevation drawings of each wall of the kitchen are needed to determine the vertical relationships of the design. You may choose to place all items on the floor plan and verify the dimensions before drawing the elevations and verifying vertical placement and dimensions. Alternatively, you may choose to work with one wall at a time—place the cabinets, appliances, fixtures, clearances, and other elements on the floor plan and then draw the elevation. If you are developing your design using computer software, you will likely find it easy to develop elevations as you go along.

Begin drawing the elevation of a wall by drawing an outline of the wall, showing the length and height of the wall. Include any architectural and structural features. Dimension these basic elements of the elevation.

Just as you did with the dimensioned drawing of the floor plan, start with the priority areas. For example, if you started with the sink and cleanup center, project the centerline of the sink and dishwasher onto the elevation. Project the cabinets onto the elevation. Mark the height of the cabinets, countertop, appliances, and other features—as determined from actual measurements or product specifications, and dimension this on the elevation. Show other details, such as the backsplash and toe kicks.

Continue drawing the elevation by adding items from the floor plan, for which the height is known, such as cabinets and appliances. Dimension the heights of each item. Detail items that are important to the design and visual continuity of the elevation design, such as cabinet doors and hardware placement.

Now, place items that were not identified in your dimensioned drawing of the floor plan, such as cabinet hardware, light fixtures, and moldings. Make sure cabinetry details, such as placement of doors and drawers, size of doors, and door style, are determined, considering client needs, function, and design impact. Review the elevation for both the vertical and horizontal relationships of line and shape.

Consider the functional placement of items, such as switches, undercabinet accessories, or towel racks. In some cases, you may need to do a detail drawing, such as for an island.

Check all dimensions on the elevation drawing. Verify that individual items are dimensioned correctly and that all vertical dimensions are correctly added.

In our sample kitchen drawing, for our clients Rosa and Vincente, we started with the sink center. That is where we will start the elevation drawing (Figure 10.17). First, we block in the whole wall. Then, we locate the centerlines for the sink and dishwasher and draw the base cabinets. Next, we locate the wall cabinets. Next, we place the rest of the cabinetry along the wall. We also need to draw the window, verifying the specifications.

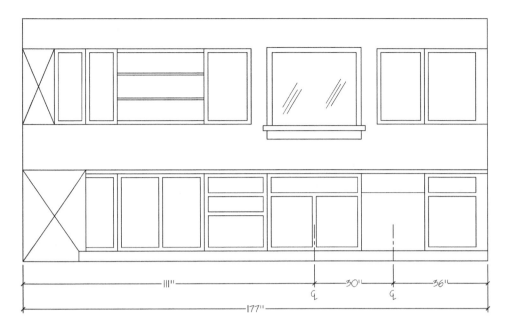

FIGURE 10.17 Begin drawing the elevation of the sink/cleanup center wall by transferring information from the design drawing floor plan to an elevation view. This continues the development of Vincente and Rosa's design project.

Now consider details and design decisions that were not in the floor plan. However, you may find it useful to block out elevations of all the walls in the kitchen before working on details. Thus, you get a better sense of the total design, before spending time on details. You may also choose to make some modifications in the cabinet arrangement or placement at this stage.

To complete the elevation of the cleanup center wall, consider details such as a valence over the sink area and molding above the wall cabinets. We might draw hardware on the cabinetry to give our client an idea about style, scale, and placement (Figure 10.18).

It is useful to develop all the wall elevations and then compare them. Consider how your eye will be drawn across the room and the horizontal relationships from one wall to the next. Is there a unity to your design? What type of rhythm is established by the vertical and horizontal elements in the space? Are all the functional requirements of the design program met?

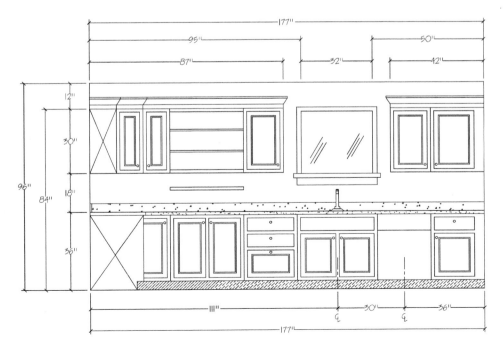

FIGURE 10.18 The elevation drawing for clients Rosa and Vincente is completed by adding details not found in the floor plan. In addition, the elevation is dimensioned to verify all the cabinet specifications.

If you are working with computer-aided design software, you may also want to look at different perspective views at this stage of the design process. If you are skilled at sketching, you may also prepare perspective sketches of several views of the design drawing. This can be helpful in giving a realistic view of the kitchen and a sense of the space. However, do not rely on these perspective drawings as your only review of vertical relationships in the space. Perspective views can be distorted, depending on where the view is taken. In addition, they cannot be used to verify dimensions.

Evaluating and Checking

Begin the evaluation of your plan by scoring your design against the NKBA Kitchen Planning Guidelines. This is an important step to make sure that you have developed a design that is functional as well as safe. On the following pages is a checklist that you can use to score your plan against the Kitchen Planning Guidelines. Review your plan against each guideline on the checklist. Your design should meet all the "Must Haves," which are Planning Guidelines based on code requirements and are shown unshaded on the following checklists. Also, your design should meet the "Recommended" Planning Guidelines, unless there are extenuating circumstances that prevent this.

Depending on your clients and their needs, review your plan against the Access Standards checklist. In your user analysis, you will have noted the relevant Access Standards.

The final step in developing the design drawing is to check all dimensions. Double-checking for accuracy is critical.

- Verify all job site dimensions. If necessary, return to the job site and re-measure. The success of your final design is dependent on working from accurate information.
- Verify the construction constraints. Review all mechanical, electrical, and plumbing information for accuracy. Consult the plumber, electrician, or contractor, if needed. Review any structural limitations that impact your design, such as load-bearing walls.
- Verify that the actual dimensions of the space were transferred to the room outline that was the starting point of your dimensioned drawing.
- Verify the placement of all centerlines of appliances and fixtures. Verify the sizes of all appliances and fixtures from actual measurements or product specifications and determine that there is adequate space. Make sure that you are using current literature and that the appliances you are specifying will be available at the time of installation.
- Review the landing space and clearances that are recommended and/or required in the Kitchen Planning Guidelines, and verify that you have met these.
- Verify the size of the cabinets, both vertically and horizontally. Check the dimensioned sizes on your drawing against the most current product literature or actual measurements. Check clearances for door swings.
- Verify all vertical relationships. Double-check the heights of appliances and other features, and review the clearance above and below items and verify that it will be adequate.

Once your design has been finalized, you will create all the necessary contract documents for your client and all trades people involved in the project.

PUTTING IT ALL TOGETHER—A SAMPLE PROJECT

Meet Leah and Matthew. Their kitchen remodeling project is being used as an example of how to prepare a design program. We interviewed Leah and Matthew at their home. We used the various forms and checklists from Chapter 5 to collect information for their design project. Then, we developed this design program.

After you read the design program, look at the design that was prepared for Leah and Matthew. Do you think the design meets their needs? Is the design solution functional, safe, and convenient? Use the Kitchen Planning Guideline and Access Standards Checklists to evaluate the plan.

Kitchen Planning Checklist—Guidelines

Use this checklist to determine that a kitchen design meets all code requirements and incorporates the recommended Planning Guidelines.

Kitchen Planning Guidelines Checklist	Must Have (meet or need)	Recommended
1. Door entry is 32" (813 mm) clear opening		
2. Door does not interfere with safe operation of appliance		
Appliance doors do not interfere with one another		
3. Distance between three primary work centers is no more than 26' (7.9 m)		
No leg less than 4' (1.2 m) or more than 9' (3.3 m)		
Leg intersects island/peninsula or other obstacle by no more than 12" (305 mm)		
4. Tall obstacle does not separate two primary work centers		
5. No major traffic should cross through the work triangle.		
6. Work aisle is 42" (1067 mm) for one cook, 48" (1219 mm) for two cooks.		
7. Walkway width is 36" (914 mm).		
8. 32" (813 mm) behind seated diner if no traffic		
36" (914 mm) behind seated diner to edge past		
44" (1118 mm) behind seated diner to walk past		
9. 30"-high (762 mm) table/counter: allow 24" (610 mm) wide x 18" (457 mm) deep per diner		
36"-high (914 mm) counter: allow 24" (610 mm) wide x 15" (381 mm) deep per diner		
42"-high (1067 mm) counter: allow 24" (610 mm) wide x 12" (305 mm) deep per diner		
10. One sink adjacent to or across from cooking surface and refrigerator		
11. Sink landing area if level counter height: 24" (610 mm) and 18" (457 mm)		
Sink landing area if varied counter height: 24" (610 mm) and 3" (76 mm)		
12. Continuous countertop 36" (914 mm) wide x 24" (610 mm) deep next to sink for prep area		
13. Dishwasher within 36" (914 mm) of sink edge		
21" standing space to side of dishwasher		
14. Two waste receptacles: one at sink; one for recycling		
15. Auxiliary sink countertop frontage: 18" (457 mm) and 3" (76 mm)		
16. Refrigerator landing area: 15" (381 mm) on handle side, or on either side of a side-by-side, or above, or within 48" (1219 mm) across from the refrigerator		
17. Cooking surface landing area: 12" and 15" at height of cooking surface		
On island or peninsula include 9" (229 mm) behind the cooking surface		
18. 24" (610) behind cooking surface and protected noncombustible surface		
30" (762 mm) between cooking surface and an unprotected/combustible surface		
Follow manufacturer's specifications for a microwave/hood application		
19. Correctly sized, ducted ventilation system, at least 150 cfm (71 L/s)		
Minimum required exhaust rate for ducted hood: 100 cfm (47 L/s)		

Kitchen Planning Guidelines Checklist	Must Have (meet or need)	Recommended
20. Cooking surface not under operable window		
No flammable window treatments over cooking surface		
Fire extinguisher located near exit of kitchen		
No commercial cooking appliances		
21. Microwave bottom 3" (76 mm) below user's shoulder, between 54" (1372 mm) and 15" (381 mm) off the finished floor		
22. Microwave landing area: 15" (381 mm) above, below, or adjacent to handle side		
23. Oven landing area: 15" (381 mm) beside or within 48" (1219 mm) across from oven		
24. Combine landing areas by using longest measure and adding 12" (305 mm)		
25. Total countertop frontage: 158" (4013 mm) long, 24" (610 mm) deep, with 15" (381 mm) clearance above		
26. Counters have clipped or rounded edges		
27. Shelf/drawer frontage total: 1400" (35,560 mm) for small kitchen (150 sq. ft. [13.9 m^2] or less)		
1700" (43,180 mm) for medium kitchen (151–350 sq. ft.) (14.02 m^2–32.5 m^2)		
2000" for large kitchen (50,800 mm) (351 sq. ft. [32.6 m^2] or more)		
28. Shelf/drawer frontage at sink: 400" (10,160 mm) for small kitchen (150 sq. ft. [13.9 m^2] or less)		
480" (43,180 mm) for medium kitchen (151–350 sq. ft.) (14.02 m^2–32.5 m^2)		
560" (14,224 mm) for large kitchen (351 sq. ft. [32.6 m^2]or more)		
29. One corner cabinet includes a functional storage device		
30. GFCI outlets at countertop receptacles		
31. Task lighting at work surfaces		
General lighting with at least one switch at entry		
Window/skylight area equals 8% of kitchen square footage		

Kitchen Planning Checklist—Access Standards

Use this checklist to determine that a kitchen design meets all code requirements and incorporates the Access Standard appropriate to meet the client's needs.

Kitchen Planning Access Standards Checklist	Must Have (meet or need)	Recommended
1. Door entry is 34" (864 mm) clear opening		
2. Door does not interfere with safe operation of appliance		
Appliance doors do not interfere with one another		
Clear floor space for maneuvering (pull side of door, width of door + 18" × 60" [457 × 1524 mm]; push side, width of door × 48" [1219 mm])		
3. Distance between 3 primary work centers is no more than 26' (7.92 m)		
No leg less than 4' (1.2 m) or more than 9' (3.3 m)		
Leg intersects island/peninsula or other obstacle by no more than 12" (305 mm)		
4. Tall obstacle does not separate two primary work centers		
5. No major traffic should cross through the work triangle		
6. Work aisle is 42" (1067 mm) for one cook, 48" (1219 mm) for two cooks		
Work aisle is minimum clear floor space: 30" × 48" (762 × 1219 mm) at each appliance		
60" (1524 mm) turning diameter or T-turn space of 36" × 36" × 60" (914 × 914 × 1524 mm)		
Knee space 36" (914 mm) wide × 27" (686 mm) high × 17" (432 mm) deep		
60" (1524 mm) between opposing counters in U-shaped kitchen		
7. Walkway width is 36" (914 mm)		
8. 60" (1524 mm) behind seated diner if traffic; 36" (914 mm) behind seated diner if no traffic		
9. Allow 30"–36" (762–914 mm) wide × 28"–34" (711–864 mm) high × 19" (483 mm) deep per diner		
10. One sink adjacent to or across from cooking surface and refrigerator		
Sink 34" (864 mm) high, or adjustable 29"–36" (737–914 mm)		
Knee space 36" (914 mm) wide × 27" (686 mm) high × 17" (432 mm) deep at least one sink		
Sink bowl 6 1/2" (165 mm) deep		
Exposed pipes covered		
11. Sink landing area if level counter height: 24" (610 mm) and 18" (457 mm)		
Sink landing area if varied counter height: 24" (610 mm) and 3" (76 mm)		
12. Continuous countertop 36" (914 mm) wide x 24" (610 mm) deep next to sink for prep area		
30" (762 mm) wide section of counter, 34" (864 mm) high with an adaptable or permanent knee space		
13. Dishwasher within 36" (914 mm) of sink edge		
When appropriate, install the dishwasher 6–12" (152–305 mm) above floor		
30" x 48" (762 × 1219 mm) clear floor space adjacent to dishwasher door		
14. Two waste receptacles: one at sink; one for recycling		
15. Auxiliary sink countertop frontage: 18" (457 mm) and 3" (75 mm)		
16. Refrigerator landing area: 15" (305 mm) on handle side, or on either side of a side-by-side, or above, or within 48" (1219 mm) across from the refrigerator		

Kitchen Planning Access Standards Checklist	Must Have (meet or need)	Recommended
30" × 48" (762 × 1219 mm) clear floor space offset 24" (610 mm) from centerline of refrigerator		
17. Cooking surface landing area: 12" (305 mm) and 15" (381 mm) at height of cooking surface		
Consider lowering the cooktop and adjacent counters to 34" (864 mm) maximum height and creating a knee space		
On island or peninsula include 9" (229 mm) behind the cooking surface		
18. 24" (610 mm) behind cooking surface and protected noncombustible surface		
30" (762 mm) between cooking surface and an unprotected/combustible surface		
Follow manufacturer's specifications for a microwave/hood application		
19. Correctly sized, ducted ventilation system, at least 150 cfm (71 L/s)		
Minimum required exhaust rate for ducted hood: 100 cfm (47 L/s)		
Controls no higher than 44" (1118 mm) if obstructed or 48" (1219 mm) unobstructed and easy to use		
20. Cooking surface not under operable window		
No flammable window treatments over cooking surface		
Fire extinguisher located near exit of kitchen no higher than 48" (1219 mm)		
21. Microwave controls no higher than 48" (1219 mm)		
22. Microwave landing area: 15" (381 mm) above, below, or adjacent to handle side		
23. Oven landing area: 15" (381 mm) beside or within 48" (1219) across from oven		
24. Combine landing areas by using longest measure and adding 12" (305 mm)		
25. Total countertop frontage: 158" (4013 mm) long, 24" 610 mm) deep, with 15" (381 mm) clearance above		
Include at least two counter heights, one 28–36" (711-914 mm) and one 36–45" (914–1143 mm)		
Include a minimum 30" (762 mm) wide, maximum 34" (864 mm) or variable in height, preferably with a knee space		
26. Counters have clipped or rounded edges		
27. Shelf/drawer frontage total: 1400" (35,560 mm) for small kitchen (150 sq. ft. [13.9 m²] or less)		
1700" (43,180 mm) for medium kitchen (151–350 sq. ft.) (14.02 m²–32.5 m²)		
2000" for large kitchen (50,800 mm) (351 sq. ft. [32.6 m²]or more)		
28. Shelf/drawer frontage at sink: 400" (10,160 mm) for small kitchen (150 sq. ft. [13.9 m²] or less)		
480" (43,180 mm) for medium kitchen (151–350 sq. ft.) (14.02 m²–32.5 m²)		
560" (14,224 mm) for large kitchen (351 sq. ft. [32.6 m²]or more)		
29. One corner cabinet includes a functional storage device		
30. GFCI outlets at countertop receptacles		
31. Task lighting at work surfaces		
General lighting with at least one switch at entry		
Window/skylight area equals 8% of kitchen square footage		

Note: This sample design program will focus on space planning, the emphasis in this book. If you were developing a design program, you might want to give additional attention to color, style, and visual impact.

A Sample Design Program

Goals and Purpose

Client description: Leah and Matthew are in their late 20s and have a 4-year-old son, Ethan. Both Leah and Matthew are employed in child advocacy professions. They live a family-centered lifestyle. Extended family, especially grandparents Caitlin and David, are frequent visitors. The couple bought their first home about a year ago, knowing that the kitchen would require some work. Matthew hopes to do at least part of the renovation work himself.

Project description and goals: After years of tiny apartment kitchens, Matthew and Leah dreamed of an efficient and spacious kitchen in their own home. While their existing kitchen is light-filled and opens to the family living area, there is limited counter, storage, and circulation space (Figure 10.19). It is difficult for two people to cook at the same time, and even harder to encourage Ethan's growing interest in helping with meals.

Leah and Matthew would like a kitchen with two prep areas. They would consider borrowing some space from the family and/or living room to expand the kitchen area. However, they want to keep the kitchen visually connected to the family living area. Adding a baking center would be desirable.

Scope of the Project
- Develop a design that meets the client needs.
- Select all appliances, fixtures, fittings, and finish materials.
- Prepare drawings and specifications for completion of the project.
- Supervise construction and installation of the project.

Objectives and Priorities
- Create room for at least two people to work in the kitchen at the same time.
- Create a baking area with easy access to the oven and sink.
- Relocate the wall between the living room and kitchen to expand the size of the kitchen.

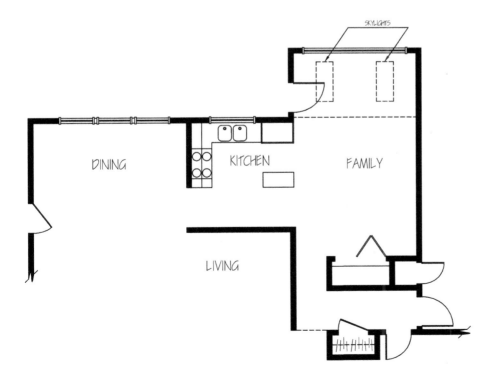

FIGURE 10.19 Leah and Matthew's existing kitchen is limited on counter space and storage.

TABLE 10.2 This user analysis highlights the design requirements for the baking center. More information about materials, color, and style could be added.

Activity Space	Users	Frequency	Appliances, Fixtures	Storage, Fittings, Furniture, etc.
• Baking center: mix cookies and bread; make pies; cool baked goods	Leah, Ethan, Caitlin	2–3 times a week; Caitlin less often	• Large stand mixer • Food processor	• Counter storage for appliances • Vertical storage for cookie sheets and cooling racks • Spice rack • Drawer storage • Pie safe cabinet • Roll-out shelves for bowls, baking pans, etc.

Space Relationships	Ambiance	Special Needs	Future Needs	Guidelines and Access Standards
• 42" (1067 mm) work aisle, • 48" (1219 mm) preferred • Easy access to sink and oven • 42" (1067 mm) counter frontage, more desirable	Good lighting	• Non porous, heat-proof surface • Lower counter 2"–3" (51–76 mm) • Pull-out cutting board	None noted	Kitchen Planning Guidelines 6, 26, 30, 31

- Reorient the kitchen sink so that it faces toward the family living area.
- Provide increased refrigerator storage, including space for produce, convenient to both cooking and family living spaces.
- Design a bar counter seating space for casual eating to seat 2–3 people that also provides visual and conversation access between family room and kitchen.
- Provide a dual-fuel range with hood ventilation system.
- Expand window area in exterior wall.
- Specify Energy Star appliances if they are available.
- Specify low-maintenance materials and select recycled flooring and countertop products.

Activities and Relationships

A user analysis was prepared for Leah and Matthew's remodeling project. The user analysis for the baking area is shown in Table 10.2.

The Design Solution

From Leah and Matthew's design program, we developed several bubble diagrams before choosing the one that seemed to work best (Figure 10.20). We then drew design templates and a room outline. We explored borrowing some space from the family and living rooms to expand the kitchen—which fit with the design program. We laid out the templates within the expanded room outline. After choosing the best layout for the visual diagram (Figure 10.21), we tried some elevation sketches and then refined the dimensioned design drawing (Figure 10.22). Finally, we carefully checked all our dimensions and clearances. We developed elevations (Figure 10.23) and a perspective (Figure 10.24).

We evaluated the kitchen design against the Kitchen Planning Guidelines using the checklist on page 407. As we developed our design, we checked for clearances and landing spaces. Looking at the plan, we can verify that there are over 158 inches (4013 mm) of counter space (Guideline 25) and an effective work triangle (Guideline 3). The storage calculations (Guideline 27) are

FIGURE 10.20 The chosen bubble diagram presents a workable plan for activity spaces in Leah and Matthew's remodeled kitchen.

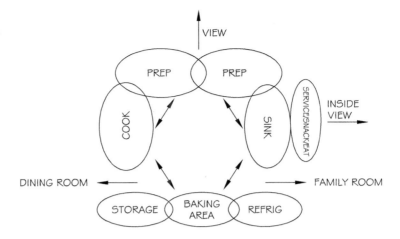

presented in the next section (Table 10.3) and show that the kitchen has more than the recommended minimum amount.

Storage Calculations

The basis for the storage calculations is:

- Kitchen size = 160 square feet (14.9 square meters) (156" x 148"), (3962 mm x 3759 mm) a medium-size kitchen.

The calculation formula was:

- Frontage (inches) x number of shelves/drawers x depth (feet) = storage inches.

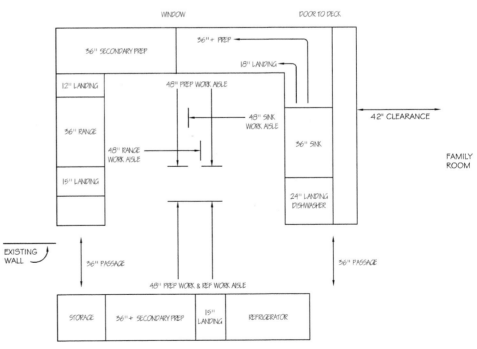

FIGURE 10.21 The visual diagram shows the layout for Leah and Matthew's kitchen, using an expanded room outline. Clearances and landing areas are verified.

FIGURE 10.22 The design drawing presents many details for the design for Leah and Matthew's new kitchen.

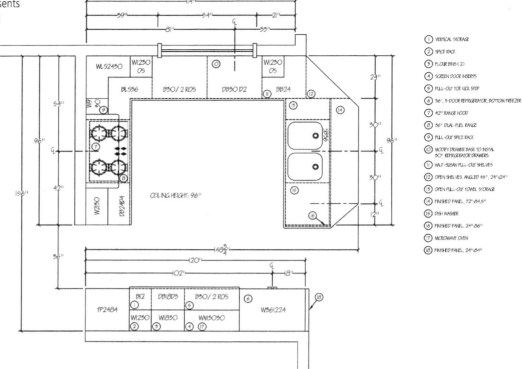

① VERTICAL STORAGE
② SPICE RACK
③ FLOUR BINS (2)
④ SCREEN DOOR INSERTS
⑤ PULL-OUT TOE KICK STEP
⑥ 36", 3-DOOR REFRIGERATOR, BOTTOM FREEZER
⑦ 42" RANGE HOOD
⑧ 36" DUAL-FUEL RANGE
⑨ PULL-OUT SPICE RACK
⑩ MODIFY DRAWER BASE TO INSTALL 30" REFRIGERATOR DRAWERS
⑪ HALF-SUSAN PULL-OUT SHELVES
⑫ OPEN SHELVES, ANGLED 45°, 24"×24"
⑬ OPEN PULL-OUT TOWEL STORAGE
⑭ FINISHED PANEL, 72"×34.5"
⑮ DISH WASHER
⑯ FINISHED PANEL, 24"×36"
⑰ MICROWAVE OVEN
⑱ FINISHED PANEL, 24"×84"

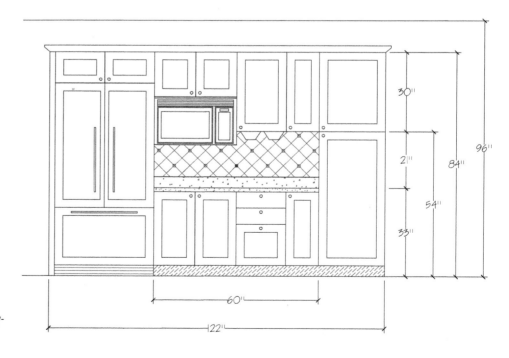

FIGURE 10.23 An elevation of the baking area in Leah and Matthew's kitchen shows many of the client requests from the user analysis in Table 10.2.

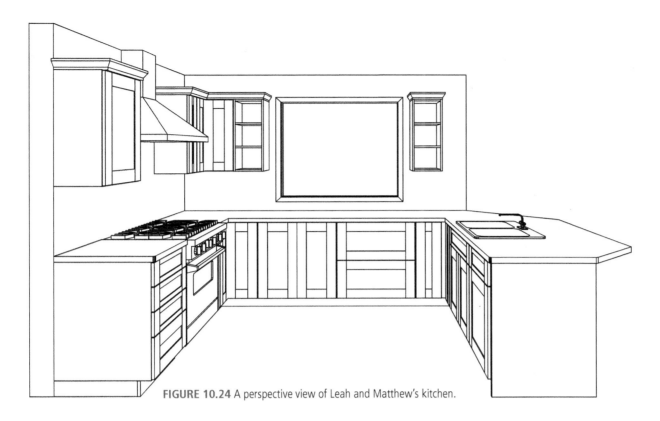

FIGURE 10.24 A perspective view of Leah and Matthew's kitchen.

Leah and Matthew's New Kitchen

Leah and Matthew's new kitchen appears to meet their goals and the objectives of the design program. Bumping a peninsula 24 inches (610 mm) into the family room and taking 48 inches (1219 mm) along the living room wall gained additional space for the kitchen. The peninsula between the kitchen and the family living area contains the sink and dishwasher, as well as an eating counter. Family members can sit at the counter to chat with cooks in the kitchen or the counter can be used for serving snacks.

A generous counter area between the sink and range provides a prep area for two cooks, a refrigerator drawer for additional produce storage, access to either the sink or the range, and a view to the deck. A baking area is located next to the refrigerator center, providing a lowered counter, microwave oven, specialized storage for baking pans and racks, flour and sugar bins, a ventilated cabinet for baked goods, and a pantry.

Critique. Throughout this chapter, we have emphasized that design is a process. At the beginning of the chapter, we discussed the back and forth nature of the design process: going forward, but returning to check ideas against the design program, for example. The same is true with a finished design. A critique can help you learn to improve and create better designs, each and every time.

Can you critique Leah and Matthew's kitchen? What are some weaknesses, or less than successful parts of the design? We have noted a few concerns, places where we made compromises between the ideal design and the reality of the existing space.

- There is a traffic pattern through the work triangle (Planning Guideline 5). Although this traffic pattern (not a primary path) only goes to the formal dining area, it does separate the sink/cleanup, prep, and cooking areas from the refrigerator. This was necessary in order to enlarge the size of the kitchen and maximize the size of the prep areas.

TABLE 10.3 Storage calculations for Leah and Matthew's kitchen design.

Drawer/Roll-out Shelf Storage	
DB 2424	24 × 4 × 2 = 192
BS30/2ROS	30 × 3 × 2 = 180
(cabinet has 2 roll-out shelves + 1 drawer)	
DB30D2	30 × 2 × 2 = 120
BS30/2ROS	30 × 3 × 2 = 180
(cabinet has 2 roll-out shelves and 1 drawer)	
DB18D3	18 × 3 × 2 = 108
TP2484	24 × 4 × 2 = 192
(pantry has 4 roll-out shelves & 3 fixed shelves)	
	Total: 972

Base Cabinet Storage	
BLS36	36 × 2 × 1.5 = 108
BB24	12 × 2 × 2 = 48
SB36	36 × 1 × 2 = 72
B12	12 × 2 × 2 = 48
	Total: 276

Wall Cabinet Storage	
W2130	21 × 3 × 1 = 63
W930	9 × 3 × 1 = 27
WLS2430	24 × 3 × 1.5 = 108
W12300S	12 × 3 × 1 = 36
W12300S	12 × 3 × 1 = 36
WM3030	30 × 2 × 1 = 60
W1830	18 × 2 × 1 = 36
W1230	12 × 3 × 1 = 36
	Total: 402

Pantry Storage	
TP2484	24 × 3 × 2 = 144
Miscellaneous Storage	
Open towel storage 12″	= 12
W361224	36 × 1 × 2 = 72
	Total = 84

Summary	Kitchen	Guideline 27
Drawer/Roll-out	972″ (24,689 mm)	400″ (10,160 mm)
Base cabinet	276″ (7010 mm)	615″ (15,621 mm)
Wall cabinet	402″ (10,211 mm)	360″ (9144 mm)
Pantry	144″ (3658 mm)	230″ (5842 mm)
Miscellaneous	84″ (2134 mm)	95″ (2413 mm)
Total:	1878″ (47,701 mm)	1700″ (43,180 mm)

- Only part of the refrigerator has a full 48-inch (1219 mm) work aisle in front of it (Planning Guideline 6). This resulted from positioning the refrigerator to maximize the size of the baking area. A French door model refrigerator, with narrower doors, was chosen to limit this concern.
- The U-shaped kitchen has two corners, which can be problematic and limit accessible storage. To address this concern, we put a Lazy Susan (BLS36) in one corner. In the other corner, we installed a blind base cabinet (BB24), with half-Susan pull-out shelves, and then used the back-side of the corner to put angled shelves that open to the family room area.
- The microwave oven is installed above the counter, in the baking area, to be conveniently located yet give maximum work surface area. The height of the microwave shelf is in accordance with Planning Guideline 21 (no more than 54 inches [1372 mm] above finished floor). However, the controls are above the universal reach range of 48 inches (1219 mm) (Access Standard 21).

Can you suggest other improvements? Perhaps you have ideas that would better meet Leah and Matthew's needs, create a more functional space, be more economical to build, or be easier to maintain. After all, this is where creativity is at work.

SUMMARY

Design is a process in which an idea is turned into a finished product. In order for this to happen, creativity and inspiration are needed. At the same time, organization, attention to detail, and hard work underlie the process. The design process involves gathering information about the client, the space to be designed, the activities that will occur in the space, and the materials that will be used to create the space. The design process also includes the translation of design information and ideas into visual and technical documents that communicate the design to the client and guide the construction and installation of the final product.

The design program is critically important documentation that defines what will be designed. Although a design program can take many formats, it is the basis for the creation of the design, the contract with the client, and the evaluation of the success of the final product.

The design drawings are the visual representations of the design. A variety of scale drawings are prepared as part of the design process, based on the design program, to communicate the details of the design. Attention to detail and accuracy are necessary in preparing design drawings that are part of the contract documents, including the basis of product specifications, bids, code compliance, construction decisions, and fee determination.

REVIEW QUESTIONS

1. Describe the steps of a design process. (See "Summary of the Design Process" page 382)
2. What is a bubble diagram? (See "The Design Process: Visualize the Activity Spaces" page 382)
3. What is a user analysis and why is it an important part of a design program? Give several examples of the type of information found in a user analysis (See under "Activities and Relationships" page 387)
4. Describe an adjacency matrix, and give an example of where you would find it helpful to use one in preparing a kitchen design. See "Relationship or Adjacency Matrix" page 386)
5. What are design templates, and how can they be useful in preparing visual diagrams and drawings. Describe or sketch several types of templates. (See "Templates" page 387)
6. Sometimes, when laying out a design drawing, your dimensions do not work out correctly, and you have too much or too little space. What are some ideas for adjusting the space, to make your dimensions work accurately, without having to make major changes in the design? (See "Adjusting the Dimensions" page 399)
7. Describe a process for checking your dimensions in a drawing to make sure you have placed everything correctly. (See "Evaluating and Checking" page 402)

Kitchen Planning Guidelines with Access Standards

The National Kitchen & Bath Association developed the Kitchen Planning Guidelines with Access Standards to provide designers with good planning practices that consider the needs of a range of users.

The code references for the Kitchen Planning Guidelines are based on the analysis of the 2012 International Residential Code (IRC) and the International Plumbing Code.

The code references for the Access Standards are based on ICC A117.1-2009 Accessible and Usable Buildings and Facilities.

Be sure to check local, state, and national laws that apply to your design and follow those legal requirements.

KITCHEN PLANNING GUIDELINE 1

Door/Entry

Recommended:

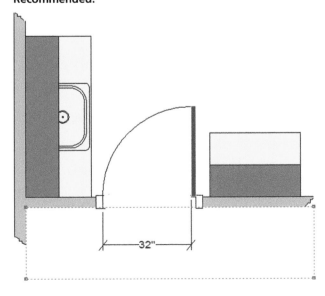

- The clear opening of a doorway should be at least 32" (813 mm) wide. This would require a minimum 2'-10" (864 mm) door.

Code Requirement:
- State or local codes may apply.

Access Standard

Recommended:

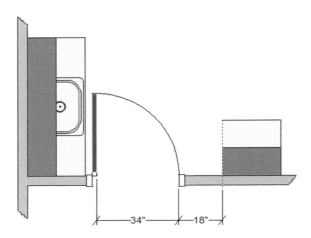

- The clear opening of a doorway should be at least 34" (864 mm). This would require a minimum 3' 0" (914 mm) door.

ICC A117.1–2009 Reference:

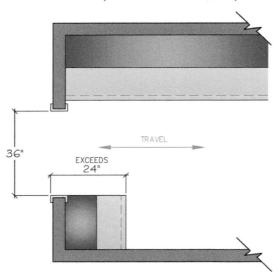

- Clear openings of doorways with swinging doors shall be measured between the face of door and stop, with the door open 90°.

    (404.2.2)
- When a passage exceeds 24" (610 mm) in depth, the minimum clearance increases to 36" (914 mm).

    (404.2.2)

KITCHEN PLANNING GUIDELINE 2

Door Interference

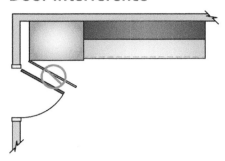

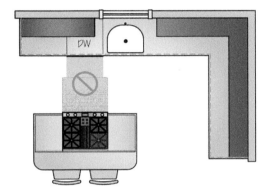

Recommended:

- No entry door should interfere with the safe operation of appliances, nor should appliance doors interfere with one another.

Code Requirement:

- State or local codes may apply.

Access Standard

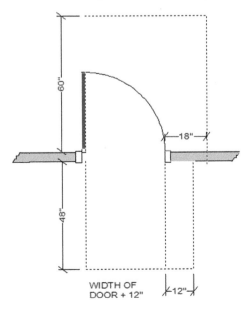

FRONT APPROACH TO SWING
DOORS (ACCESS STANDARD 2)

Recommended:

- In addition, the door area should include clear floor space for maneuvering, which varies according to the type of door and direction of approach.

ICC A117.1–2009 Reference:

- For a standard hinged door, the clearance on the pull side of the door should be the door width plus 18" by 60" (457 mm x 1524 mm).

  (404.2.3)

- The clearance on the push side of the door should be the door width by 48" (1219 mm).

  (404.2.3)

KITCHEN PLANNING GUIDELINE 3

Distance between Work Centers

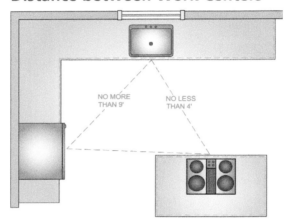

Recommended:

- In a kitchen with three work centers* the sum of the three traveled distances should total no more than 26' (669 mm) with no single leg of the triangle measuring less than 4' (1219 mm) nor more than 9' (2743 mm).
- When the kitchen plan includes more than three primary appliance/work centers, each additional travel distance to another appliance/work center should measure no less than 4' (1219 mm) nor more than 9' (2743 mm).

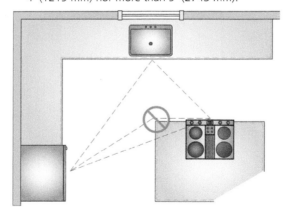

- Each leg is measured from the center-front of the appliance/sink.

---

* A major appliance and its surrounding landing/work area form a work center. The distances between the three primary work centers (cooking surface, cleanup/prep sink, and refrigeration storage) form a work triangle.

- No work triangle leg intersects an island/peninsula or other obstacle by more than 12" (305 mm).

Code Requirement:

- State or local codes may apply.

Access Standard

Recommended:

- Kitchen guideline recommendation meets Access Standard.

KITCHEN PLANNING GUIDELINE 4
Separating Work Centers

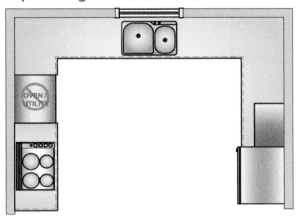

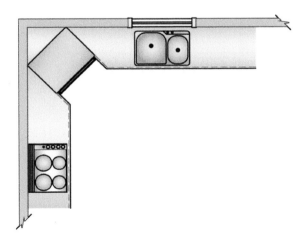

Recommended:

- A full-height, full-depth, tall obstacle* should not separate two primary work centers.
- A properly recessed tall corner unit will not interrupt the workflow and is acceptable.

Code Requirement:

- State or local codes may apply.

---

* Examples of a full-height obstacle are a tall oven cabinet, tall pantry cabinet, and refrigerator.

Access Standard

Recommended:
- Kitchen guideline recommendation meets Access Standard.

KITCHEN PLANNING GUIDELINE 5
Work Triangle Traffic

Recommended:

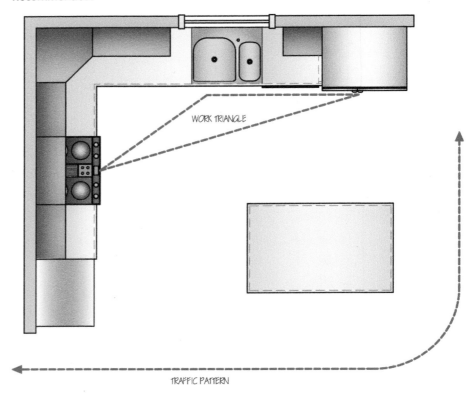

- No major traffic patterns should cross through the basic work triangle.

Code Requirement:
- State or local codes may apply.

Access Standard

Recommended:
- Kitchen guideline recommendation meets Access Standard.

KITCHEN PLANNING GUIDELINE 6
Work Aisle

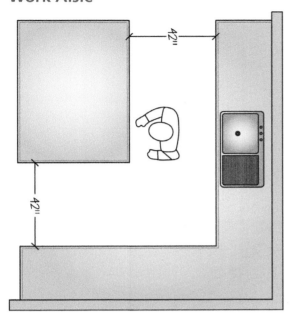

Recommended:
- The width of a work aisle should be at least 42" (1067 mm) for one cook and at least 48" (1219 mm) for multiple cooks. Measure between the counter frontage, tall cabinets, and/or appliances.

Code Requirement:
- State or local codes may apply.

Access Standard

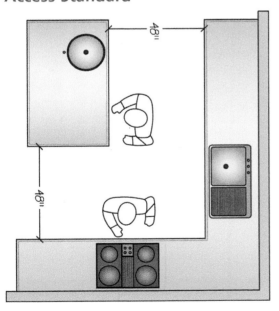

Recommended:

Kitchen guideline recommendation meets Access Standard recommendation. See Code References for specific applications.

ICC A117.1–2009 Reference:

- A clear floor space of at least 30" by 48" (762 mm x 1219 mm) should be provided at each kitchen appliance. Clear floor spaces can overlap.

  (305.3, 804.5)
- In a U-shaped kitchen, plan a minimum clearance of 60" (1524 mm) between opposing arms.
- (804.2, 1003.12)

30" x 48"
CLEAR FLOOR SPACES AND
KNEE SPACES MAY OVERLAP

- Include a wheelchair turning space with a diameter of at least 60" (1524 mm), which can include knee* and toe** clearances.

  (304.3).
- A wheelchair turning space could utilize a T-shaped clear space, which is a 60" (1524 mm) square with two 12" wide x 24" (305 mm x 610 mm) deep areas removed from the corners of the square. This leaves a minimum 36" (914 mm) wide base and two 36" (914 mm) wide arms. T-shaped wheelchair turning spaces can include knee and toe clearances.

  (304.3)

---

* Knee clearance must be 30" (762 mm) wide (36" (914 mm) to use as part of the T-turn) and maintain a 27" (686 mm) high clear space under the cabinet, counter, or sink. At 27" (686 mm) AFF, the depth must be a minimum 8" (203 mm). At 9" (229 mm) AFF, the depth must be a minimum 11" (279 mm). The space from 9" (229 mm) to the floor is considered toe clearance and must be a minimum of 17" (432 mm) and a maximum of 25" (635 mm).

** Toe clearance space under a cabinet or appliance is between the floor and 9" (229 mm) above the floor. Where toe clearance is required as part of a clear floor space, the toe clearance should extend 17" (432 mm) minimum beneath the element. (306.2)

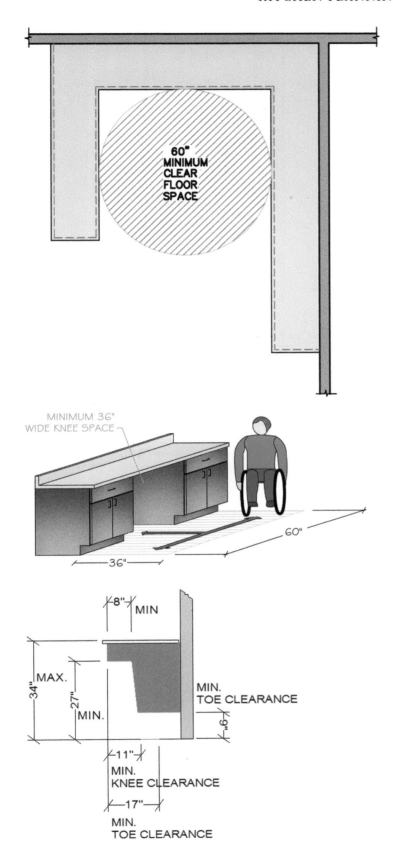

60"
MINIMUM
CLEAR
FLOOR
SPACE

MINIMUM 36"
WIDE KNEE SPACE

60"

36"

8" MIN

34" MAX.

27" MIN.

MIN.
TOE CLEARANCE

6"

11"

MIN.
KNEE CLEARANCE

17"

MIN.
TOE CLEARANCE

Code Requirement:

• State or local codes may apply.

KITCHEN PLANNING GUIDELINE 7
Walkway

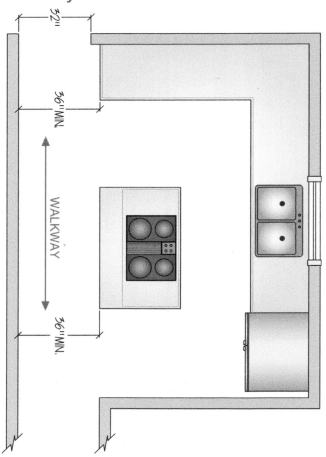

Recommended:

• The width of a walkway should be at least 36" (914 mm).

Code Requirement:

• State or local codes may apply.

Access Standard

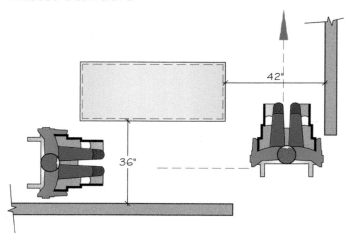

Recommended:
- If two walkways are perpendicular to each other, one walkway should be at least 42" (1067 mm) wide.

KITCHEN PLANNING GUIDELINE 8

Traffic Clearance at Seating

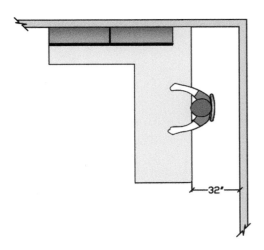

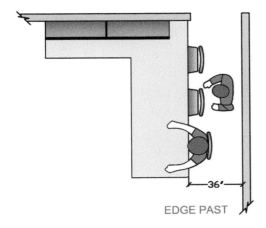

EDGE PAST

Recommended:
- In a seating area where no traffic passes behind a seated diner, allow 32" (813 mm) of clearance from the counter/table edge to any wall or other obstruction behind the seating area.
    - a. If traffic passes behind the seated diner, allow at least 36" (914 mm) to edge past.
    - b. If traffic passes behind the seated diner, allow at least 44" (1118 mm) to walk past.

Code Requirement:
- State or local codes may apply.

Access Standard

Recommended:
- In a seating area where no traffic passes behind a seated diner allow 36" (914 mm) of clearance from the counter/table edge to any wall or other obstruction behind the seating area.

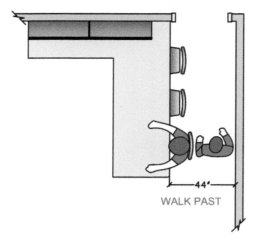

WALK PAST

• If traffic passes behind the seated diner, plan a minimum of 60" (1524 mm) to allow passage for a person in a wheelchair. This will be affected by the depth of the knee space.

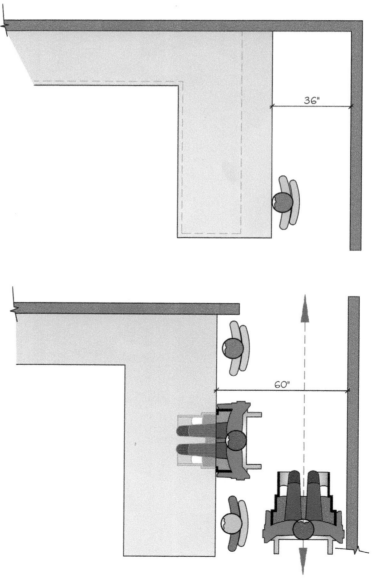

WHEN USED AS
WALKWAY SPACE

KITCHEN PLANNING GUIDELINE 9
Seating Clearance

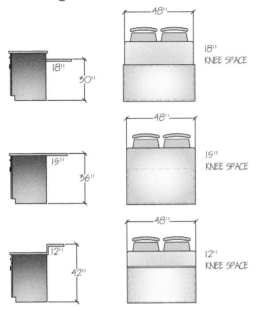

Recommended:
- Kitchen seating areas should incorporate at least the following clearances:
    a. 30" (762 mm) high tables/counters: allow a 24" wide x 18" deep (610 mm x 457 mm) knee space for each seated diner and at least 18" (457 mm) of clear knee space
    b. 36" (914 mm) high counters: allow a 24" wide x 15" deep (610 mm x 381m) knee space for each seated diner and at least 15" (381 mm) of clear knee space.
    c. 42" (110 cm) high counters: allow a 24" wide x 12" deep (610 mm x 305 mm) knee space for each seated diner and 12" (305 mm) of clear knee space.

Code Requirement:
- State or local codes may apply.

Access Standard

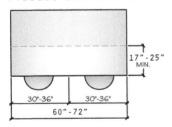

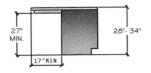

Recommended:
- Kitchen seating areas should be 28"–34" (711 mm x 864 mm) high x 30"–36" (762 mm x 914 mm) wide x 17" x 25" (432 mm x 635 mm) deep to better accommodate people of various sizes or those using a mobility aid.
- Recommended minimum size for a knee space at a table or counter is 36" wide x 27" high x 17" deep (914 mm wide x 686 mm high x 432 mm deep).

KITCHEN PLANNING GUIDELINE 10
Cleanup/Prep Sink Placement

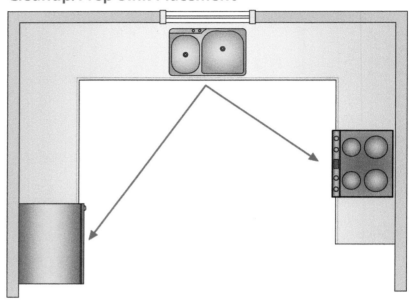

Recommended:
- If a kitchen has only one sink, locate it adjacent to or across from the cooking surface and refrigerator.

Code Requirement:
- State or local codes may apply.

Access Standard

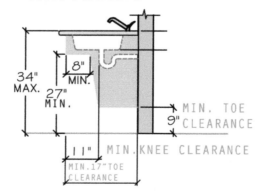

Recommended:
- Plan knee spaces at the sink to allow for a seated user. Recommended minimum size for a knee space is 36" wide x 27" high x 8" deep (914 mm x 686 mm x 203 mm), increasing to 17" (432 mm) deep in the toe space, which extends 9" (229 mm) from the floor. Insulation for exposed pipes should be provided.

ICC A117.1–2009 Reference:

- The sink should be no more than 34" (864 mm) high or adjustable between 29" and 36" (737 mm and 914 mm).

  (1003.12.4.2)

- Exposed water supply and drainpipes under sinks should be insulated or otherwise configured to protect against contact. There should be no sharp or abrasive surfaces under sinks.

  (1003.12.4.4)

KITCHEN PLANNING GUIDELINE 11

Cleanup/Prep Sink Landing Area

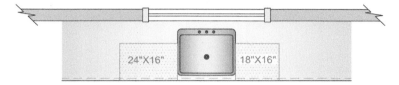

RECOMMENDED:

- Include at least a 24" (610 mm) wide landing area* to one side of the sink and at least an 18" (457 mm) wide landing area on the other side.
- If all of the countertop at the sink is not the same height, then plan a 24" (610 m) landing area on one side of the sink and 3" (76 mm) of countertop frontage on the other side, both at the same height as the sink.

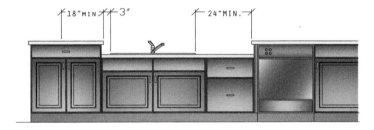

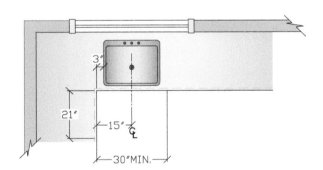

- The 24" (610 mm) of recommended landing area can be met by 3" (76 mm) of countertop frontage from the edge of the sink to the inside corner of the countertop if no more than 21" (533 mm) of countertop frontage is available on the return.

Code Requirement:

- State or local codes may apply.

---

* Landing area is measured as countertop frontage adjacent to a sink and/or an appliance. The countertop must be at least 16" (406 mm) deep and must be 28" to 45" (711 mm to 1143 mm) above the finished floor to qualify.

Access Standard

Recommended:

Kitchen guideline recommendation meets Access Standard.

KITCHEN PLANNING GUIDELINE 12

Preparation/Work Area

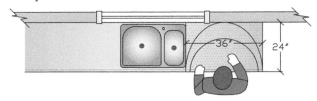

Recommended:
- Include a section of continuous countertop at least 36" wide x 24" deep (914 mm x 610 mm) immediately next to a sink for a primary preparation/work area.

Code Requirement:
- State or local codes may apply.

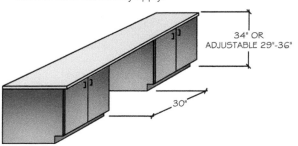

Access Standard

Recommended:
- A section of continuous countertop at least 30" (762 mm) wide with a permanent or adaptable knee space should be included somewhere in the kitchen.
- See Access Standard 6 for knee clearance specifications.

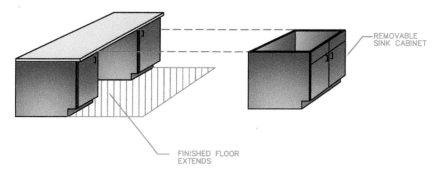

ICC A117.1–2009 Reference:
- In a kitchen, there should be at least one 30" (762 mm) wide section of counter, 34" (864 mm) high maximum or adjustable from 29" to 36" (737 mm to 914 mm). Cabinetry can be added under the work surface, provided it can be removed or altered without removal or replacement of the work surface, and provided the finished floor extends under the cabinet.

  (1003.12.3)

KITCHEN PLANNING GUIDELINE 13

Dishwasher Placement

Recommended:

- Locate nearest edge of the primary dishwasher within 36" (914 mm) of the nearest edge of a cleanup/prep sink.

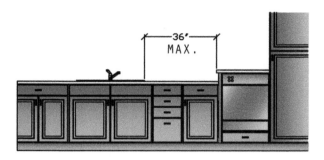

- Provide at least 21"* (533 mm) of standing space between the edge of the dishwasher and countertop frontage, appliances and/or cabinets, which are placed at a right angle to the dishwasher.

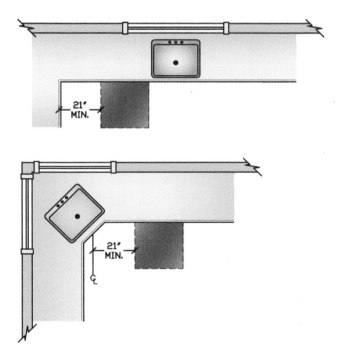

Code Requirement:

- State or local codes may apply.

Access Standard

Recommended:

Raise dishwasher 6"–12" (152 mm–305 mm) when it can be planned with appropriate landing areas at the same height as the sink.

---

* In a diagonal installation, the 21"(533 mm) is measured from the center of the sink to the edge of the dishwasher door in an open position.

ICC A117.1–2009 Reference:

- A clear floor space of at least 30" x 48" (762 mm x 1219 mm) should be positioned adjacent to the dishwasher door. The dishwasher door in the open position should not obstruct the clear floor space for the dishwasher or the sink.

  (1003.12.5.3)

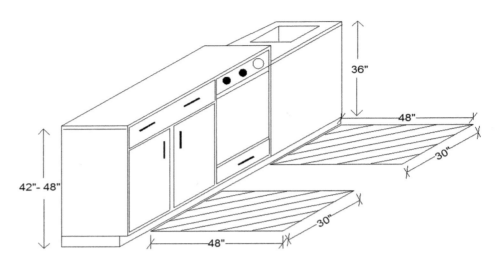

KITCHEN PLANNING GUIDELINE 14

Waste Receptacles

Recommended:

- Include at least two waste receptacles. Locate one near each of the cleanup/prep sink(s) and a second for recycling either in the kitchen or nearby.

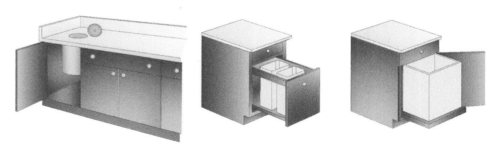

Code Requirement:

- State or local codes may apply.

Access Standard

Recommended:

- Kitchen guideline recommendation meets Access Standard.

KITCHEN PLANNING GUIDELINE 15

Auxiliary Sink

Recommended:

- At least 3" (76 mm) of countertop frontage should be provided on one side of the auxiliary sink and 18" (457 mm) of countertop frontage on the other side, both at the same height as the sink.

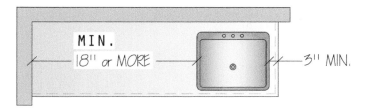

Code Requirement:
State or local codes may apply.

Access Standard

Recommended:

- Plan a knee space at, or adjacent to, the auxiliary sink.
- See Access Standard 6 for knee clearance specifications.

KITCHEN PLANNING GUIDELINE 16

Refrigerator Landing Area

Recommended:

- Include at least:
    a. 15" (381 mm) of landing area on the handle side of the refrigerator or
    b. 15" (381 mm) of landing area on either side of a side-by-side refrigerator or
    c. 15" (381 mm) of landing area which is no more than 48" (1219 mm) across from the front of the refrigerator or
    d. 15" (381 mm) of landing area above or adjacent to any undercounter-style refrigeration appliance.

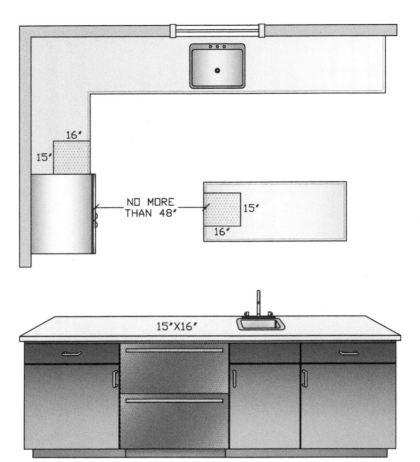

Code Requirement:

• State or local codes may apply.

Access Standard

Recommended:

• See Code Reference

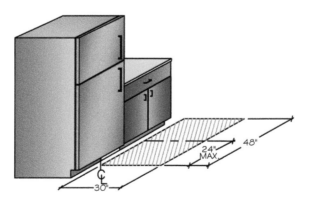

ICC A117.1–2009 Reference:

• A clear floor space of 30" x 48" (762 mm x 1219 mm) should be positioned for a parallel approach to the refrigerator/freezer with the centerline of the clear floor space offset on the handle side 24" (610 mm) maximum from the centerline of the appliance.

(804.6.6, 1003.12.6)

KITCHEN PLANNING GUIDELINE 17

Cooking Surface Landing Area

Recommended:

- Include a minimum of 12" (305 mm) of landing area on one side of a cooking surface and 15" (381 mm) on the other side.
- If the cooking surface is at a different countertop height than the rest of the kitchen, then the 12" and 15" (305 mm and 381 mm) landing areas must be at the same height as the cooking surface.

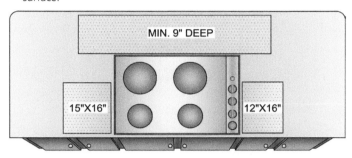

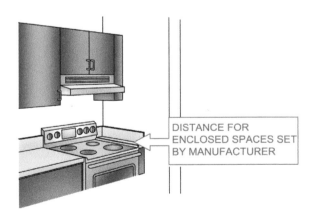

- For safety reasons, in an island or peninsula situation, the countertop should also extend a minimum of 9" (229 mm) behind the cooking surface if the counter height is the same as the surface-cooking appliance.
- For an enclosed configuration, a reduction of clearances shall be in accordance with the appliance manufacturer's instructions or per local codes. (This may not provide adequate landing area.)

  (IRC M 1901.2)

  (IRC E 4101.2)

Code Requirement:
- State or local codes may apply.

Access Standard

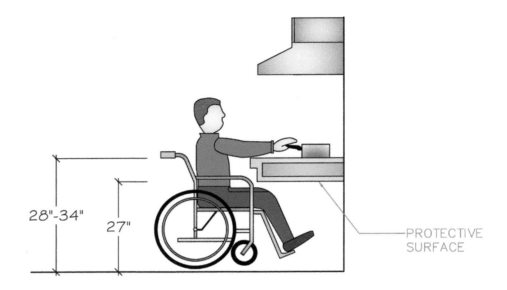

Recommended:
- Lower the cooktop to 34" (864 mm) maximum height and create a knee space beneath the appliance.

See Access Standard 6 for knee clearance specifications.

ICC A117.1–2009 Reference:
- When forward-approach clear floor space is provided at the cooktop, it should provide knee and toe clearance, and the underside of the cooktop should be insulated or otherwise configured to prevent burns, abrasions, or electric shock.

  (1003.12.5.4)
- Where the clear floor space is positioned for a parallel approach, the clear floor space shall be centered on the appliance.

  (1003.12.5.4)
- The location of cooktop controls should not require reaching across burners.

  (1003.12.5.4)

KITCHEN PLANNING GUIDELINE 18

Cooking Surface Clearance

Recommended:

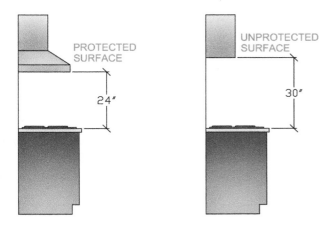

- Allow 24" (610 mm) of clearance between the cooking surface and a protected noncombustible surface above it.

Code Requirement:

- At least 30" (762 mm) of clearance is required between the cooking surface and an unprotected/combustible surface above it.

    (IRC M 1901.1)

    (IRC G 244705)

- If a microwave/hood combination is used above the cooking surface, then the manufacturer's specifications should be followed.

    (IRC M 1504.1)

    (IRC G 2447.5)

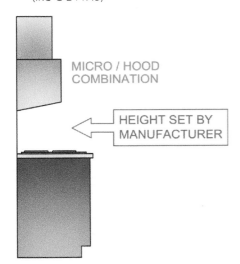

- Refer to manufacturer's specifications or local building codes for other considerations.

Access Standard

Recommended:

Kitchen guideline recommendation meets Access Standard.

KITCHEN PLANNING GUIDELINE 19

Cooking Surface Ventilation

Recommended:
- Provide a correctly sized, ducted ventilation system for all cooking surface appliances. The recommended minimum is 150 cfm.

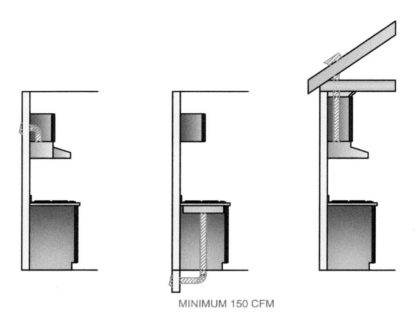

MINIMUM 150 CFM

Code Requirement:
- Manufacturer's installation instructions and specifications must be followed.

  (IRC G 2407.1, IRC G 2447.1, IRC E 4101.2)
- The minimum required exhaust rate for a ducted hood is 100 cfm and must be ducted to the outside.

  (IRC M 1507.3)
- Exhaust hood systems capable of exhausting in excess of 400 cfm shall be provided with make-up air at a rate approximately equal to the exhaust air rate. Such make-up air systems shall be equipped with a means of closure and shall be automatically controlled to start and operate simultaneously with the exhaust system.

  (IRC M 1503.4)
- Refer to local codes for more restricted requirements.

Access Standard

Recommended:
- Ventilation controls should be placed 15"–44" (381 mm–1118 mm) above the floor, operable with minimal effort, easy to read, and with minimal noise pollution. Plan storage of frequently used items 15"–48" (381 mm–1219 mm) above the floor.

ICC A117.1–2009 Reference:
- Operable parts should be operable with one hand and not require tight grasping, pitching, or twisting of the wrist. The force required to activate operable parts should be 5 pounds (2 kg) maximum.

  (309.4)

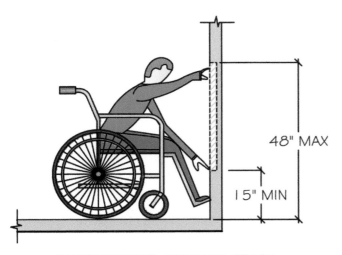

UNOBSTRUCTED FORWARD REACH

- Where a forward or side reach is unobstructed, the high reach should be 48" (1219 mm) maximum, and the low reach should be 15" (381 mm) minimum above the floor.

  (308.2.1, 308.3.1)
- Where a forward or reach is obstructed by a 20" – 25" (508 mm–635 mm) deep counter, the high reach should be 44" (1118 mm) maximum.

  (308.2.2)
- When a side reach is obstructed by a 10"–24" (254 mm–610 mm) counter, the high reach should be 46" (1168 mm).

  (308.3.2)

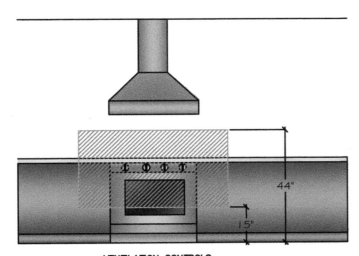

VENTILATION CONTROLS
WITHIN 15"–44"
REACH CONTROL

KITCHEN PLANNING GUIDELINE 20
Cooking Surface Safety

UNACCEPTABLE

Recommended:

- Do not locate the cooking surface under an operable window.
- Window treatments above the cooking surface should not use flammable materials.
- A fire extinguisher should be located near the exit of the kitchen away from cooking equipment.
- Commercial cooking appliances are not to be installed in residential kitchens.

  (IRC M 1901.3)

  (IRC G 2447.2)

ACCEPTABLE

Code Requirement:

- State or local codes may apply.

Access Standard

Recommended:

- Place fire extinguisher between 15" and 48" (381 mm and 1219 mm) off the finished floor.
- Select cooking appliances with the controls located so that there is no need to reach across burners to operate.

  (1003.12.5.4.4)

KITCHEN PLANNING GUIDELINE 21

Microwave Oven Placement

Recommended:

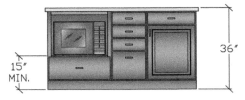

- Locate the microwave oven after considering the user's height and abilities. The ideal location for the bottom of the microwave is 3" (76 mm) below the principle user's shoulder but no more than 54" (1372 mm) above the floor.
- If the microwave oven is placed below the countertop the oven bottom must be at least 15" (40 cm) off the finished floor.

Code Requirement:

- State or local codes may apply.

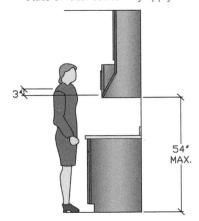

Access Standard

MAX.46"-48"
TO CONTROLS

Recommended:
Locate the microwave controls no higher than 46"–48" (1168 mm–1219 mm), depending on approach and reach range. (See Access Standard 19).

KITCHEN PLANNING GUIDELINE 22

Microwave Landing Area

Recommended:
- Provide at least a 15" (381 mm) landing area above, below, or adjacent to the handle side of a microwave oven.

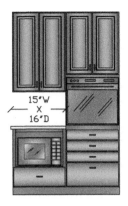

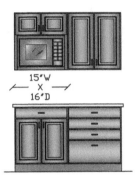

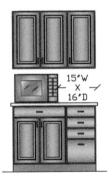

Code Requirement:
- State or local codes may apply.

Access Standard

Recommended:
- Provide landing area in front of or immediately adjacent to the handle side of the microwave.

KITCHEN PLANNING GUIDELINE 23

Oven Landing Area

Recommended:
- Include at least a 15"(381 mm) landing area next to or above the oven.

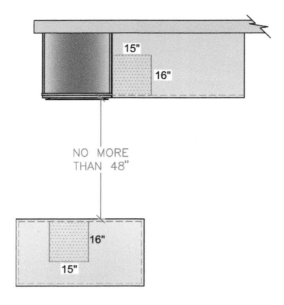

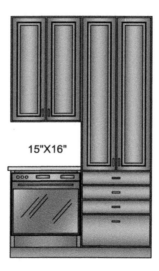

- At least a 15" (381 mm) landing area that is not more than 48" (1219 mm) across from the oven is acceptable if the appliance does not open into a walkway.

Code Requirement:
- State or local codes may apply.

Access Standard

Recommended:
- See Code reference

ICC A117.1–2009 Reference:

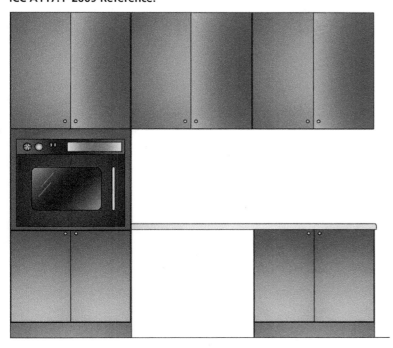

- For side-opening ovens, the door latch side should be next to a countertop.
  - (1003.12.5.5.2)

KITCHEN PLANNING GUIDELINE 24

Combining Landing Areas

COOKING SURFACE   CLEAN-UP / PREP. SINK   REFRIGERATOR

Recommended:

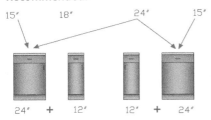

15″   18″   24″   15″

24″ + 12″   12″ + 24″

- If two landing areas are adjacent to one another, determine a new minimum for the two adjoining spaces by taking the longer of the two landing area requirements and adding 12″ (305 mm).

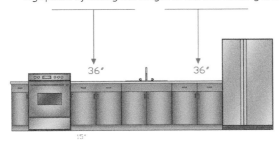

36″   36″

15″

Code Requirement:
• State or local codes may apply.

Access Standard

Recommended:
• Kitchen guideline recommendation meets Access Standard.

KITCHEN PLANNING GUIDELINE 25

Countertop Space

Recommended:

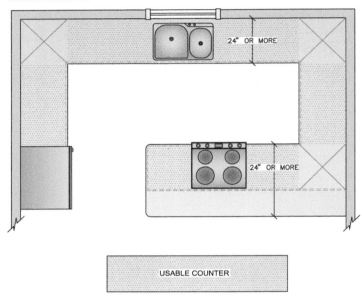

- A total of 158" (4013 mm) of countertop frontage, 24" (610 mm) deep, with at least 15" (381 mm) of clearance above, is needed to accommodate all uses, including landing area, preparation/work area, and storage.
- Built-in appliance garages extending to the countertop can be counted towards the total countertop frontage recommendation, but they may interfere with the landing areas.

Code Requirement:

- State or local codes may apply.

Access Standard

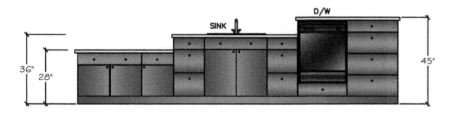

Recommended:

- At least two work-counter heights should be offered in the kitchen, with one 28"–36" (711 mm–914 mm) above the finished floor and the other 36"–45" (914 mm–1143 mm) above the finished floor.

KITCHEN PLANNING GUIDELINE 26

Countertop Edges

Recommended:

Specify clipped or round corners rather than sharp edges on all counters.

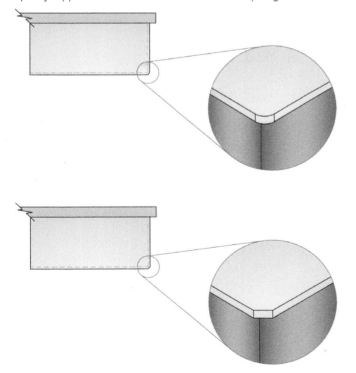

Code Requirement:
- State or local codes may apply.

Access Standard

Recommended:
- Kitchen guideline recommendation meets Access Standard.

KITCHEN PLANNING GUIDELINE 27

Storage

Recommended:
- The total shelf/drawer frontage* is:
    a. 1400" (35560 mm) for a small kitchen (less than 150 square feet) (3810 square cm);
    b. 1700" (43180 mm) for a medium kitchen (151–350 square feet) (3835 mm–8890 square mm);
    c. 2000" (50800 mm) for a large kitchen (greater than 350 square feet) (8890 square mm).

SHELF/DRAWER FRONTAGE IN INCHES

	Small	Medium	Large
Wall	300"	360"	360"
Base	520"	615"	660"
Drawer	360"	400"	525"
Pantry	180"	230"	310"
Misc.	40"	95"	145"

SHELF/DRAWER FRONTAGE IN MILLIMETERS

	Small	Medium	Large
Wall	7620 mm	9144 mm	9144 mm
Base	1320 mm	15621 mm	16764 mm
Drawer	9144 mm	10160 mm	13335 mm
Pantry	4572 mm	5842 mm	7874 mm
Misc.	1016 mm	2413 mm	3683 mm

- The totals for wall, base, drawer and pantry shelf/drawer frontage can be adjusted upward or downward as long as the recommended total stays the same.
- Do not apply more than the recommended amount of storage in the miscellaneous category to meet the total frontage recommendation.
- Storage areas that are more than 84" (2134 mm) above the floor must be counted in the miscellaneous category.

---

* Shelf and drawer frontage is determined by multiplying the cabinet size by the number and depth of the shelves or drawers in the cabinet, using the following formula: Cabinet width in inches x number of shelf and drawers x cabinet depth in feet (or fraction thereof) = Shelf and /Drawer Frontage

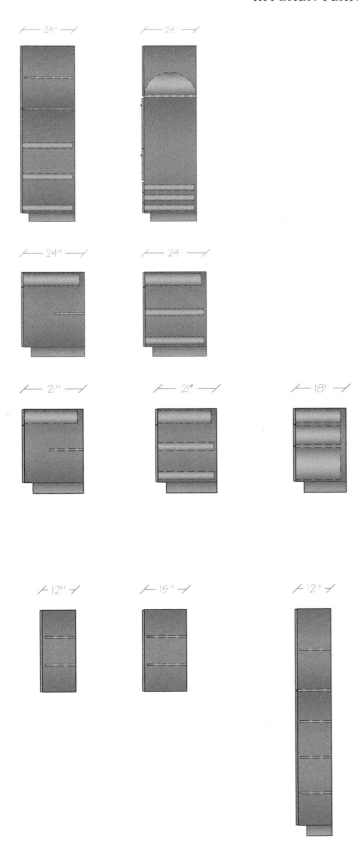

- Storage/organizing items can enhance the functional capacity of wall, base, drawer, and pantry storage and should be selected to meet user needs.

Code Requirement:

• State or local codes may apply.

Access Standard

Recommended:

• See Guideline 19.

ICC A117.1–2009 Reference:

• Where a forward or side reach is unobstructed, the high reach should be 48" (1219 mm) maximum and the low reach should be 15" (381 mm) minimum above the floor.

  (A117.1 308.2.1, 308.3.1)

• Where a 20"–25" (508 mm–635 mm) deep counter obstructs a forward reach, the high reach should be 44" (1118 mm) maximum.

  (A117.1 308.2.2)

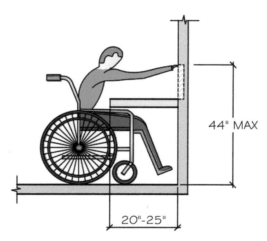

44" MAX

20"-25"

OBSTRUCTED HIGH FORWARD REACH

• Where a 10"–24" (254 mm to 610 mm) counter obstructs a side reach, the high reach should be 46" (1168 mm) maximum.

  (A117.1308.3.2)

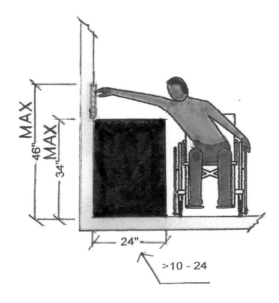

46" MAX

34" MAX

24"

>10 - 24

KITCHEN PLANNING GUIDELINE 28

Storage at Cleanup/Prep Sink

Recommended:

- Of the total recommended wall, base, drawer, and pantry shelf/drawer frontage, the following should be located within 72" (1829 mm) of the centerline of the main cleanup/prep sink:
    - at least 400" (10160 mm) for a small kitchen.
    - at least 480" (12192 mm) for a medium kitchen.
    - at least 560" (14224 mm) for a large kitchen.

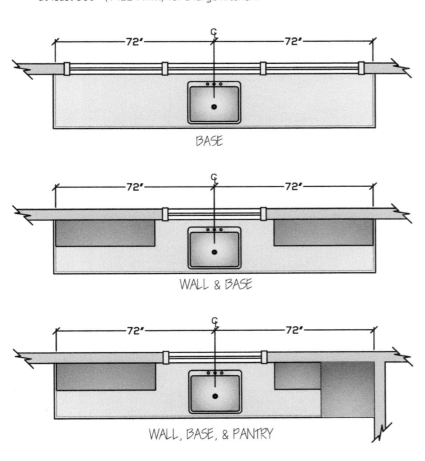

BASE

WALL & BASE

WALL, BASE, & PANTRY

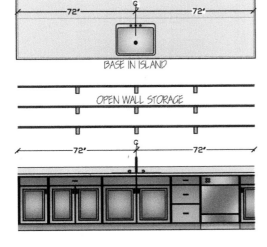

BASE IN ISLAND

OPEN WALL STORAGE

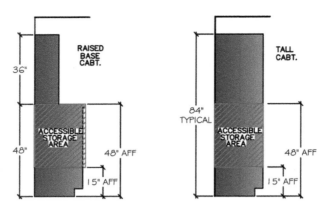

Code Requirement:

- State or local codes may apply.

Access Standard

Recommended:

- Plan storage of frequently used items 15"–48" (381 mm to 1219 mm) above the floor.

ICC A117.1–2009 Reference:

- See Access Standard 19 for reach specifications.

KITCHEN PLANNING GUIDELINE 29

Corner Cabinet Storage

Recommended:

- At least one corner cabinet should include a functional storage device.

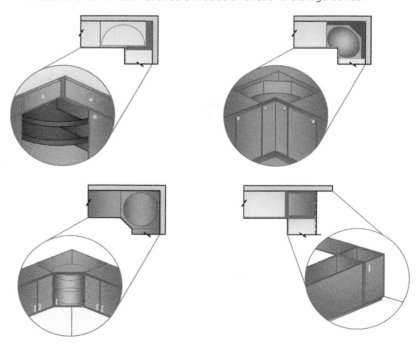

- This guideline does not apply if there are no corner cabinets.

Code Requirement:

- State or local codes may apply.

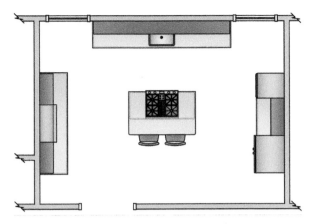

Access Standard

Recommended:

- Kitchen guideline recommendation meets Access Standard.

KITCHEN PLANNING GUIDELINE 30

Electrical Receptacles

Code Requirement:

- GFCI (Ground-fault circuit interrupter) protection is required on all receptacles servicing countertop surfaces within the kitchen.

   (IRC E 3902.6)

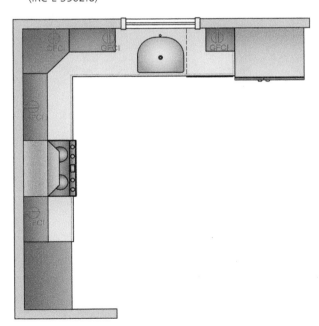

- Refer to IRC E 3901.3 through E 3901.4.5 for receptacle placement and locations.

Access Standard

Recommended:

- See Code Reference.

Code Reference:

- See Access Standard 19 for reach and control specifications.

KITCHEN PLANNING GUIDELINE 31

Lighting

Recommended:

- In addition to general lighting required by code, every work surface should be well illuminated by appropriate task lighting.

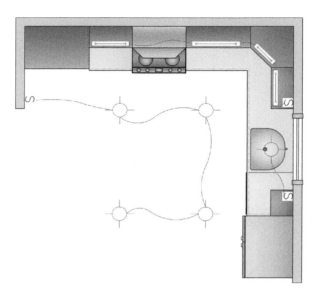

Code Requirement:

- At least one wall-switch-controlled light must be provided. Switch must be placed at the entrance.

  (IRC E 3903.2)

- Window/skylight area, equal to at least 8% of the total square footage of the kitchen, or a total living space that includes a kitchen, is required.

  (IRC R 303.1, IRC R 303.2)

Access Standard

Recommended:

- Lighting should be from multiple sources and adjustable/

ICC A117.1–2009 Reference:

- See Access Standard 19 for reach and control specifications.

Glossary

A

Accent lighting:
Lighting that emphasizes displayed items, such as artwork or china cabinets.

Accessible design or accessibility:
Characteristics of spaces or products that meet prescribed requirements for particular variations in ability, for example "wheelchair accessible."

Acromion:
A human body measurement of the two large triangular bones on the upper back that function to support the shoulders.

Adaptable design:
Features that are either adjustable or capable of being easily added or removed to "adapt" the unit to individual needs or preferences.

Adjacency matrix:
Also called a Relationship Matrix, this is a graphic method of organizing relationships of multiple spaces, including various types of relationships, such as visual or auditory; a step in design programming.

A.F.F.:
Above the finished floor; sometimes written O.F.F. for over the finished floor.

Aging in place (design for):
Design that considers the changes that occur as one ages, supporting the ability to live in one's own home and community safely, independently, and comfortably, regardless of age, income, or ability level.

Air barrier:
Materials or products used to control air leakage out of, or air infiltration into a building, to minimize heat loss or gain.

Air leakage (AL):
This air leakage rating is the amount of heat loss or gain that occurs by infiltration through cracks and openings in the window assembly.

Americans with Disabilities Act Accessibility Guidelines (ADAAG):
Guidelines for compliance with the accessibility requirements of the Americans with Disabilities Act (ADA).

Ambient (general) lighting:
General lighting diffused within an entire room.

Ambient:
The environment surrounding us. In the context of buildings, the environmental conditions in the room.

ANSI A117.1 Accessible and Usable Buildings and Facilities:
Original American National Standards Institute (ANSI) guidelines for accessible design in commercial and residential spaces. Now the International Code Council (ICC)/ANSI A117.1 is the referenced technical standard for compliance with the accessibility requirements of International Building Code and many other state and local codes. The 1998 edition is used as reference for NKBA Access Standards.

Anthropometrics:
The study of human measurements, such as size and proportion, and parameters, such as reach range and visual range.

Antimicrobial finish:
A material that has an applied finish, or ingredient in the product that inhibits the growth of microorganisms, such as bacteria or fungi.

Auxiliary sink:
Second sink in the kitchen providing additional work area for either cleanup or food preparation, or other activities such as hobbies.

B

Back-drafting:
Used to describe a situation where combustion by-products, from furnaces, gas water heaters, fireplaces, stoves and other fuel-burning appliances, are pulled back into the house instead of exhausting through the flue or chimney; the situation can occur when the air pressure inside the home is less than outside, and is usually the result of running exhaust fans and appliances without providing adequate make-up air.

Ballast:
A device that controls the current in a fluorescent lamp.

Banquette:
A built-in table with chairs in an alcove.

Barn door:
Hardware that allows the door to slide along a wall. Useful when a pocket door is too costly or not possible.

Barrier-free design:
An older term for universal design, based on the concept of solutions that removed barriers in the environment.

Base cabinet:
A base cabinet is the bottom cabinet and is usually 24 inches (610 mm) deep and 34½ inches (876 mm) high with a 11/2-inch (38 mm) high countertop bringing the total cabinet height to 36 inches (914 mm). These cabinets typically have a 4 to 5 inch (102–127mm) high x 3 inch (76 mm) deep toekick. A standard cabinet has a drawer at the top and two shelves behind a cabinet door.

Baseboard heater:
A type of heating equipment made up of shallow panels that are mounted along the baseboard of a room. The system could distribute heat through the use of electricity or hot water.

Beecher kitchen:
A kitchen plan that advocated used a ship's galley as the model. It featured work centers and used the latest technologies. Storage was close by and compartmentalized. Open shelving was shallow to allow only one row of food items, and bins for flour and other products were planned into the design. The concept relied on standardized components that could be bought and added end-to-end to produce a kitchen of the desired length.

Biological pollutants:
Indoor air pollutants that originate from living sources, including molds, insects and animals; more likely to be found in moist places.

Btu:
British Thermal Unit, a measurement of heat quantity in countries using the British system. One Btu is the amount of heat energy required to raise the temperature of one pound of water by one degree Fahrenheit.

Bubble diagram:
A simple visual or sketch where each "bubble" represents an activity area in the space to be designed; used to help organize activity and space relationships at an early stage of design programming.

Building code:
Community and state ordinances governing the manner in which a home may be constructed or modified.

Butler's pantry:
A small room or passageway between the kitchen and dining area used for storage of serving pieces and preparations for serving and clearing the table.

C

Cabinet nomenclature:
A code of letters and numbers that designate a cabinet's size, use, and placement. Manufacturers typically have their own code for their products. The National Kitchen and Bath Association (NKBA) has developed a generic nomenclature for kitchen and bath cabinets.

CADR (clean air delivery rate):
A measure of the efficiency of a portable air cleaner, based on the percentage of particles removed from the air and the speed at which the particles are removed.

Canadian Electric Code (CEC):
A code for electrical safety adopted by Canadian political jurisdictions. The CEC is almost identical to the National Electric Code (NEC).

Candelas or candle power:
The intensity of the light beam in one direction is measured in candela or candle power.

Canopy ventilation systems:
See Updraft ventilation systems

Casement window:
Panels are hinged at the side and crank open to a 90-degree angle, exposing almost all of the window area to the outside.

Center:
Area where a task occurs, including the fixture, clear space, storage and other components that support the function of the task. In the kitchen the centers are: preparation, cooking and cleanup.

Certified Kitchen Designer (CKD):
NKBA designation for a kitchen designer who has passed the certification examination.

CFM:
Cubic feet per minute; used as a measure of the amount of air a fan can move in one minute. See L/s for the metric equivalent.

Circuit breaker:
A device that is designed to protect electrical equipment and people from damage caused by overload or short circuit. It can be reset to resume operation.

Circline:
These fluorescent lamps are built with the tube forming a circle or ring. They operate like other fluorescent tubes and are designed to fit in many center room light fixtures for ambient lighting.

Clear floor space:
Area which is free of obstruction within an overall space, typically used in reference to the recommendations for clearances at an appliance or work center.

Color rendering index (CRI):
A method for describing the effect of a light source on the color appearance of objects compared to a reference source of the same color temperature.

Color temperature:
An index of how the light source, itself, looks to us, measured in degrees Kelvin (K).

Comfort zone:
Refers to a body buffer zone that people maintain between others and themselves.

Compact fluorescent (CFL):
A type of fluorescent lamp with the fluorescent tube coiled into a compact shape in a size similar to an incandescent bulb.

Condensing dryer:
A condensing dryer uses either air or water to cool the hot air from inside the dryer, thus condensing the moisture collected from the clothes, which is drained away; condensing dryers do not require an exhaust vent to the outside; depending on the model, the dryer may add heat to the room or require a plumbing connection.

Condensation:
The process whereby water, in the form of steam, changes from a gaseous stage to a liquid stage; heat is released by condensation.

Condensation resistance (CR):
The CR measures how well a window resists the formation of condensation on the inside

surface of the window and is expressed as a number between 1 and 100.

Congenital:
A condition existing at birth or dating from birth, such as "congenital deafness."

Conversation circle:
A conversation circle has an approximate diameter of 10 feet (3 meters); when planning social spaces, consider that it is easy for people to converse within the area of a conversation circle, but it is difficult to talk to people who are at a farther distance

Cycling losses:
The loss of heat as the water circulates through a water heater tank, and/or inlet and outlet pipes.

D

Daylighting:
Using light from the sun to illuminate the interior of a building.

DC:
Direct current, commonly supplied by batteries and photovoltaic generating systems.

Decorative lighting:
The lighting jewels that dress up a home, like chandeliers and sconces. They can also contribute to the general lighting in a room.

Design process:
Multistage process where a designer moves from an idea to a completed product, usually with the help of a design program. The design process is both a verbal and visual process.

Design program:
Organized and documented information about a client and their proposed project that guides the design process. Design programming includes the various steps of gathering, organizing, and analyzing the information to develop the plan of the design program, which is critical to the execution of the design.

Dew point:
The temperature at which water vapor condenses; the dew point temperature is a function of humidity: when the relative humidity is 100%, the air is saturated and can hold no more water vapor, therefore, if there is more water vapor, or the temperature drops below the dew point, condensation occurs.

Downdraft ventilation systems:
A kitchen ventilation system that pulls air with the by-products of cooking down through a vent and exhausts it to the outside; typically the ventilation system is integrated with the cooktop or installed immediately adjacent to it.

Drawer cabinet:
A base cabinet with two to three drawers.

Drinking water standards:
Governmental standards for water quality to ensure that water is safe to drink. In the United States, drinking water standards are established and enforced by the Environemntal Protection Agency while in Canada these standards are the responsibility of Health Canada.

Dual cuing:
Also called redundant cueing, refers to the use of different modes (pictorial, verbal, tactile) to communicate necessary information effectively to the user, regardless of ambient conditions or the user's sensory abilities.

E

Efficacy:
The energy efficiency of a lighting source or lighting output per watt of power in lumens per watt (LPW).

Egress:
A path or opening from a room or building.

Electric toe kick heater:
A small electric heater installed in the toe kick below the cabinet.

EnerGuide label:
A distinctive black and white label required on all appliances sold in Canada that shows the amount of energy used and verifies that the appliance meets the Canadian minimum energy standards.

EnergyGuide label:
A bright yellow and black label required by the U.S. Department of Energy and is used to provide information on the comparative energy use and costs on a variety of appliances.

Energy Star:
An international program to promote protection of the environment through energy efficient products and practices; qualifying products are identified with the easily recognized Energy Star logo.

Energy recovery ventilation system:
See Whole house ventilation system.

Ergonomic design:
The application of human factor data to the design of products and spaces to improve function and efficiency.

"Euro" cabinets:
Cream colored laminate flat panel cabinets with oak trim were popular in the 1970s and 80s.

F

Fair Housing Accessibility Guidelines (FHAG):
Accessibility regulations affecting the design of multifamily housing built since 1991. The FHAAG make up the technical guidance for compliance with the accessibility requirements of the Fair Housing Amendments Act of 1988.

Fenestration:
The arrangement of windows in a building.

Feng Shui:
The Chinese art or practice of positioning objects based on a belief in patterns of yin and yang and the flow of chi have positive and negative effects.

Fiber optic lighting:
An illuminating system composed of a lamp source, fiber and output optics to remotely light an area or object. Light traveling along a fiber.

Filler:
Wood or veneer strips inserted merely to occupy space.

Fitting:
A term used for a device that controls water entering or leaving a fixture. Faucets, spouts, drain, controls, water supply lines and diverter valves are all considered fittings.

Fixture (lighting):
The assembly that includes the mounting base or socket and any features that reflect or dispense the light from a lamp fitted into the fixture.

Fixture (plumbing):
Any fixed plumbing feature that is part of the structural design, such as the primary and auxiliary sinks.

FlexHousing:
Housing that incorporates, at the design and construction stage, the ability to make future changes easily with minimum expense to meet evolving needs of occupants.

Floor heating systems:
Floor heating systems can be either electric or hydronic and will incorporate heating coils or tubes directly under the flooring materials.

Floor joists or floor trusses:
Beams used to support floors.

Floor-mounted radiators:
In homes where hydronic heat is used throughout the home, the hot water heat is often distributed through radiators mounted on the floor next to walls.

Fluorescent:
Light produced by arcing an electrical current between electrodes at opposite ends of a gas-filled tube.

Footcandle (fc):
A measurement in the American System (AS) for the amount of light that falls on a surface. One footcandle is the amount of light that falls on a surface one foot square, placed one foot from the source. A footcandle of illumination is a lumen of light distributed over a 1-square-foot (0.09-square-meter) area.

Foyer:
An area that serves as an entrance to the home; a transition space between outside and the living areas of the home.

Framed cabinets:
Cabinets constructed with a face frame which provides the primary support for the cabinet. Doors and drawers fit in one of three ways: flush with the frame, partially overlying the frame, or completely overlaying the frame.

Frameless cabinets:
The case part of the cabinet does not need a front frame for stability. Doors and drawers cover the entire face of the cabinet.

Functional anthropometry:
The measurements of the body in motion.

Fuse:
A device that can interrupt the flow of electrical current when a circuit is overloaded.

G

General (ambient) lighting:
See "Ambient lighting"

Glazing:
Industry term for a pane of glass in a window.

Ground fault circuit interrupter (GFCI):
A device that monitors the electric current on a circuit to make sure the amount of current going out is the same as that returning to the electric receptacle. Serving as a safety device, the slightest difference in current will shut off the circuit.

Green design, green building:
Generally, the term green is applied to policies and practices that are environmentally responsible and sustainable.

Graywater:
Water that has been used in the household and has the potential to be reused or recycled. Graywater may come from bathtubs, showers, sinks, lavatories, and washing machines, and does not contain sewage (black water).

H

Halal:
Halal is an Arabic word meaning lawful or permitted and can be applied to foods that are permitted to followers of Islam. Dietary practices can influence kitchen design. Foods meeting halal specifications may be difficult to find in some areas, necessitating special long-distance shopping trips and extra storage space.

Halogen lamp:
A gas-filled tungsten filament incandescent lamp with a lamp envelope made of quartz to withstand the high temperature. This lamp contains some halogens (namely iodine, chlorine, bromine, and fluorine), which slow the evaporation of the tungsten. It is also commonly called a quartz lamp. Halogen lamps can be either low voltage or operate with a standard 120V electrical source.

"Hard" water:
Water with a high content of minerals, usually calcium and magnesium; often leads to plumbing problems from mineral deposits.

Hard wired:
A permanent electrical connection for an appliance or device (as opposed to a cord with a plug).

Hearth:
Another term for fireplace; also the floor of a fireplace and area that extends into the room.

Heat pump water heater (HPWH):
A heat pump adapted to heat water for domestic use.

Heat recovery ventilation system:
See Whole house ventilation system.

Homeowner's association:
An organization of the property owners in a specific housing development or neighborhood; responsibilities of the association will vary, but often include management of common areas and oversight of requirements affecting the community as a whole; requirements for membership and dues may be a condition of property ownership.

Hoosier:
The baking table evolved into a self-contained, upright cabinet work center with all the needed tools for baking. The "Hoosier" (or "Dutch") cabinets was one popular style which typically came in oak or was painted white enamel.

Hopper and awning windows:
Hopper windows are hinged at the bottom and open inward and awning windows are hinged at the top and open outwards

Humidity:
The amount of water vapor in the air.

Hybrid water heater:
Hybrid water heating systems heat water for the home heating system as well as general hot water uses.

Hydronic systems:
A heating system that uses circulating hot water as the heat source; the water is distributed through tubes in the floor, baseboards, or freestanding radiators.

I

Incandescent:
Light produced when an electrical current runs through a poor conductor, such as a tungsten carbide filament in an incandescent bulb.

Individual or dedicated circuits:
Circuits designated for an individual appliance and are either 120-volt or 240-volt.

Induction cooking:
A technology that heats cookware made of a magnetic material, without heating the surface of the cooktop, through the use of magnetic energy.

International Residential Code (IRC):
Building code developed by the International Code Council for single-family housing and

used as a reference for the NKBA Kitchen and Bathroom Planning Guidelines.

J

Joists:
A level or nearly level member used in a series to frame a floor or ceiling structure.

K

Kilowatt-hours (kWh):
A measurement of power consumption over time. One kWh is the power consumed by a 1000w device operating for one hour.

Kilowatts (kW):
One thousand watts.

Kosher:
In Judaism, the term kosher can be applied to foods that meet a series of dietary laws. The ease of meeting some of these dietary laws, such as the separation of meats and dairy products, can be enhanced by the design of the kitchen.

L

L/s:
Liters per second; metric measurement used to rate the capacity of a ventilation fan.

Lamp:
Industry term for a light bulb. An interchangeable bulb or tube that constitutes the lighting source in a fixture.

Landing area:
Measured as countertop frontage adjacent to a sink and/or appliance. Must be at least 16 inches (406 mm) deep and 28 to 45 inches (711 to 1143 mm) above the finished floor.

Lazy Susan cabinet:
Tray carousels are added to a base or wall cabinet that fits into the corner of a kitchen arrangement. The circular shelves may rotate 360 degrees or be pie-shaped and attached to the cabinet doors.

LED:
Light emitting diodes are diodes (electronic components that let electricity pass in only one direction) that emit visible light when electricity is applied, much like a light bulb.

Life cycle analysis:
A life cycle analysis, perspective, or assessment looks at a product from a long term or life cycle view. This perspective considers all the costs (purchase, energy, maintenance, disposal, etc.) as well as all the impacts (type of energy, pollution, disposal, etc.) of the product.

Lifespan design:
The aspect of universal design that provides for the changes that occur in the lifespan of the home and its owners.

Linoleum:
A floor covering make from renewable materials such as solidified linseed oil or pine rosin, usually on a burlap or canvas backing.

Load-bearing wall:
Exterior and interior walls of the home that support the structure vertically. Openings in any load-bearing wall must be reinforced to carry the live and dead weight of the structural load.

Low-emissivity (low-e) coating:
A low-e coating consisting of a thin, virtually invisible metal or metal oxide layer deposited on a window-glazing surface primarily to reduce the U-factor by suppressing radiant heat flow.

Low-voltage:
A system that uses less than 50-volt current (commonly 12-volt), instead of 110-120 volt, the standard household current. A transformer is used to convert the electrical power to the appropriate voltage.

LP gas:
Liquid propane (see "Propane").

Lumen:
The amount of light, measured at the lighting source.

Luminaire:
See "Fixture (lighting)".

Lux:
A measurement in the International system (IS) for the amount of light that falls on a surface. One lux is the amount of light that falls on one square meter placed one meter from the source.

M

Make-up air (replacement air):
Air brought into a building (such as a home) from the outside to replace exhaust air.

Mechanical cooling:
If natural cooling methods cannot give the comfort levels desired, then mechanical means are necessary. The most basic of mechanical devices is the fan. Other mechanical cooling methods include refrigerated cooling and evaporative cooling.

Mobility aid:
A device, such as wheelchair, cane, or walker, used by a person for assistance with movement through a space.

Modified energy factor (MEF):
A performance factor for clothes washing machines based on capacity, electricity usage, energy to heat the water, and energy to remove water from the clothes. A higher MEF is more efficient.

Mold:
Fungi that grow in moist environments and will use organic materials, especially cellulosic building materials, as a food source.

Monitor top refrigerator:
One of the first refrigerators designed by General Electric, the round top designed was named after the Monitor submarine.

Motion detectors
Motion detectors use electronic sensors to detect motion which triggers an electric signal; motion detectors are often used to turn on lights

Muntins
Muntins are the small bars that hold the panes of glass in a window sash; contemporary windows are often made of a single piece of glass with fake muntins to make the window appear to be made of smaller panes of glass.

N

National Electric Code (NEC):
A code for electrical safety adopted by states and local jurisdictions in the United States.

Natural cooling:
Cooling by opening windows to let in fresh air during the cooler part of the day or night.

Natural gas:
A gaseous mixture of hydrocarbon compounds, the primary one being methane, that is delivered under pressure through an underground gas line.

Needs assessment:
Gathering information about the client and their needs, wants, and desires for the design project as well as the physical characteristics of the jobsite.

O

Off-gas:
A term used to describe the release or evaporation of chemicals into the air from building materials as they dry, cure, or age. The process can be more rapid if temperature and/or humidity are increased.

On-demand/instantaneous water heater:
A gas or electric unit that heats water, with no waiting as it is needed by the user.

Outpost kitchen:
Small kitchen located away from the primary food preparation area, such as in the bedroom/bathroom area (morning kitchen) or a living or recreation area.

P

PAR or parabolic aluminized reflector lamps:
These lamps have a heavy glass casing and reflective surface. They are often used for outdoor settings, and the low voltage MR-16 lamps can be PAR style lamps as well.

Pendant:
A lighting fixture containing one or more lamps and hung from the ceiling.

Peripheral vision:
Scope of vision on both sides of the eyes. Range often diminishes with age.

pH:
A scale used to measure acidity or alkalinity, with values from 1 to 14; neutral is 7; decreasing numbers below 7 mean greater acidity and increasing numbers above 7 mean greater alkalinity.

Photocell
Photocells use light to activate the flow of electricity; photocells are typically used in homes to turn on and off safety and security lighting

Planning desk
A small desk that is often included in a kitchen to provide a space to sit for non-food activities such as planning menus, paying bills, and correspondence; a planning desk typically matches the cabinetry in material and style

Pocket door:
A door that slides horizontally on a track and is typically concealed inside a wall for storage.

Popliteal:
A human body measurement relating to the back part of the leg behind the knee.

Preparation center:
Long, uninterrupted span of countertop used to make food. Typically placed between the sink and the cooking surface, or the sink and the refrigerator.

Primary center:
One of the three main work centers; these include the main sink, cooking surface, and refrigeration storage.

Primary cleanup/prep sink:
The sink used most frequently. If only one sink is planned it will be used for both cleanup and food preparation. A kitchen with primary and auxiliary sinks may separate these tasks.

Primary Drinking Water Standards:
Federally mandated standards for acceptable levels of certain pollutants in water; used to ensure that water is safe to drink or ingest.

Professional-style appliances:
Restaurant-style appliances, typically made of stainless steel, designed for residential installations.

Propane:
A type of gas delivered to home storage tanks by trucks.

Proximity ventilation systems:
See downdraft ventilation systems.

Pullout faucets:
A faucet that has a retractable spray hose hidden inside the traditional fixed spigot.

R

Radiators:
Large, flat rectangular heating units that fit close to the wall and heat spaces using circulating hot water.

Radon:
A naturally occurring radioactive gas found in soil and ground water; tasteless, odorless, colorless, and detectable only through testing equipment; can seep into homes and build to levels that can be a health threat; long-term exposure can lead to lung cancer.

Reach range:
The measured distance off the floor within which a person can reach and grasp an item. The universal reach range refers to the distance where most people can reach an item, which is 15 to 48 inches (381 to 1219 mm) off the floor.

Receptacle (outlet):
An electrical fitting that is connected to a source of electrical power and equipped to receive an insert such as a plug from an electrical device.

Recirculating (ductless) system:
A kitchen ventilation system installed in a hood that pulls air through one or more filters, then exhausts the filtered air into the room; a metal mesh filter to remove grease is typical; an activated carbon filter to remove odors may be included.

Recycle:
Recover or divert material from the solid waste stream.

Recovery efficiency:
A measure of how efficiently the heat from the energy source is transferred to the water in water heating systems.

Redundant cuing:
Repetition of a message in more than one sensory mode, such as a smoke alarm that flashes a light, sounds a buzzer, and vibrates to alert in case of fire or smoke.

Reflector lamps:
Reflector lamps are incandescent lamps with a reflective coating to reflect more of the light out the front of the lamp.

Relationship matrix
See Adjacency matrix.

Repurpose:
Use a material, product, or item for a new purpose in a project.

Retro-look:
A return to the look of the 1930s, 1940s, 1950s emerged with retro- styled appliances that contained all of the technologies of modern appliances.

R-value:
A measure of the resistance to heat conductivity of a material; the higher the R-value, the more the materials resists heat conduction or the better an insulator.

S

Safe harbors:
Standards that are legally recognized as compliance with the requirements of a code or guideline.

Salvage:
Generally used to describe materials that are reused in a building project, typically for a purposed similar to their original use; may also be described as reclaimed.

Sconce:
A light fixture that is fixed to the wall.

Sealed combustion appliances:
Appliances, such as a furnace or water heater, where the air needed for combustion is pulled from an outside vent and then the flue gases resulting from combustion are exhausted to the outside; the combustion process is thus "sealed' from room air.

Secondary center:
A work area established for a specific task, such as baking or salad preparation. It may include an appliance or fixture, storage, and counter space, but is not calculated as part of the work triangle.

Secondary Drinking Water Standards:
Voluntary standards for acceptable levels of certain pollutants in water; used to ensure that water is functional and aesthetically pleasing for typical household uses, such as bathing and laundry.

Self-defrost refrigerator:
A refrigeration feature that uses small heaters to periodically melt frost that accumulates on the inside surfaces of a refrigerator/freezer eliminating the need for manual defrosting.

Septic tank:
A large holding tank where solid matter or sewage from a home is disintegrated by bacteria.

Service entry:
A second, informal entrance to the home, used for bringing in groceries and supplies. It is often close to the kitchen and to garage or carport.

Shaker styling:
A style produced by the Shakers that is simple, unornamented, functional, clean angled, and gently curved design. It is often referred to as the "Amish" furniture style.

Shelf/drawer frontage:
Calculation of cabinet size x number of shelves or drawers x cabinet depth in feet. Used to determine adequate storage in a kitchen.

Shutoff valve
A valve control that allows the user to shut off the water entering a fixture. These valves are usually located close to the fixture.

Sight lines:
The range or visual field in direct line with a person's eyes, affected by the position a person will be in when the space or product is being used. This is useful in planning heights of fixtures, fittings, lighting, windows and more.

Single- or double-hung windows:
In double-hung both sashes slide vertically whereas only the bottom sash slides upward in the single-hung window.

Single- and double-sliding windows:
Both sashes slide horizontally in a double-sliding window and only one sash slides in a single-sliding window.

Skylight:
Skylights are typically located on the roof area and bring in natural light, usually eliminating the need for artificial light during the daylight hours.

Small appliance circuit:
These electrical circuits are designed to accommodate small appliances.

Solar:
Using the sun's energy.

Solar heat gain coefficient (SHGC):
A measure of how much solar heat passes through glass, used in matching window glass to climate and location of the windows.

Sound transmission class (STC):
A measure of the absorption of sound as it passes through building materials (transmission loss); a higher STC will reduce the transmission of sound.

Sone:
A unit of loudness, which is a subjective characteristic of a sound; the sone scale is based on data from people judging the loudness of pure tones; as an example, a noise at four sones is perceived to be four times as loud as a noise of one sone.

Standby losses:
For water heaters with a storage tank, it is the percentage of heat loss per hour from the stored water compared to the heat content of the water.

Static or structural anthropometry:
The study of the measurements of the body at rest.

Storage principles:
A series of recommendations, developed through research, to increase both the efficiency of storage space and the ease of use. The most common principles are:

1. Store items at the first or last place of use.
2. Store items in duplicate locations, if needed.
3. Items used together should be stored together.
4. Items should be stored so they are easy to see.
5. Frequently used items should be stored so they are easy to reach.
6. Like items should be stored or grouped together.
7. Hazardous items should be stored out of reach of children.
8. Store items in the appropriate environment.

Surge protector:
Also surge suppressor; an electrical device used to protect electronic equipment, especially computer systems, from surges or spikes in electrical current or voltage.

Sustainability, sustainable design:
As used in this book, sustainability is a philosophical approach to the built environment that emphasizes balance, thinking of the future, and minimizing the impact today.

T

Tactile cuing:
Using textural elements to communicate necessary information through touch to the user.

Tall cabinet:
A cabinet that is typically the height of the base cabinet, the wall cabinet and the distance between the base and wall cabinet. The cabinet can come in several depths and widths. They may be used as a pantry or utility cabinet or to hold a built in appliance such as an oven. Tank water heater: Tank type units are what we commonly see in U.S. homes. This type of water heater keeps water hot on a 24 hours basis, adding more heat when the thermostat is below the set water temperature.

Task lighting:
Lighting focused on a work area.

Thermal envelope:
In a house, the thermal envelope is the boundary between the conditioned (heated and/or cooled) space and the non-conditioned spaces. For example, the bathroom is part of the thermal envelope, but a garage or attic is usually not.

Third-party verification:
A practice used in many certification and accreditation programs in which an independent organization or qualified professional evaluates compliance with program requirements.

Toe kick:
An intentional space in cabinetry near the floor to accommodate the feet while standing next to a cabinetry.

Transformer:
An electrical device by which alternating current of one voltage is changed to another voltage.

Transgenerational design:
Another term for universal design, referring to design that acknowledges and supports the multiple generations more commonly living in a home.

Truss:
A framework of beams forming a rigid structure such as a roof or floor truss.

Tubular daylight devices (TDD):
This type of skylight is a tube that extend from the roof down through the roof /attic to the interior space.

Tudor styling:
An architectural style of the Tudor era (1485-1603) that incorporated the perpendicular style that focused on building with exposed timbers and brick.

Tuscany:
A region of west central Italy that is noted for its use of tile flooring and rustic color palette.

U

U-factor:
U-factor is a measurement of heat conductivity or thermal transfer in windows and skylights. This can be heat loss or heat gain. The lower the U-factor, the more energy efficient the window. U-factor recommendations vary by climate zone.

Ultraviolet:
An invisible portion of the light spectrum that fades fabrics.

Uniform Federal Accessibility Standards (UFAS):
The technical standard referenced by two federal mandates for accessibility for federal buildings; the Architectural Barriers Act (ABA) and Section 504 of the Rehabilitation Act of 1973 (Section 504).

Universal design:
The design of products and environments to be usable by all people to the greatest extent possible.

Updraft ventilation systems:
A kitchen ventilation system that includes a hood over a cooking surface to capture the airborne by-products of cooking and a fan to pull air up; captured air is either exhausted to the outside or filtered and recirculated into the room, depending on the system.

User analysis:
A chart or table that groups design requirements by major activity spaces; an organizational tool used in design programming or as part of the design process.

V

Vegetarian:
The term "vegetarian" is generally applied to people who restrict meat or animal products in their diets. Today, people who call themselves vegetarian may range from those who limit their meat consumption to maybe once a week to those who eat no animal products at all (usually called vegans). People may choose vegetarianism for many reasons, with health concerns being the most popular. Most vegetarians consume more fruits, vegetables, legumes, and/or grains, which influences their need for food storage and preparation space.

Vapor retarder:
A building material that limits the flow of moisture. Vapor retarders are especially important in the construction of the building envelope to prevent moisture condensation within the building structure.

Vernacular housing:
Housing styles that are typical or common to a region and have developed over time in response to factors such as available building materials, climate and cultural heritage.

Victorian era:
A period which coincides with the reign of Queen Victoria of the United Kingdom between 1839 and 1901.

Visible transmittance (VT):
Visible transmittance indicates the amount of visible light transmitted through the glass.

Volatile organic compounds (VOCs):
A class of organic compounds that are easily evaporated into the air and used in the manufacturing, installation, and maintenance of many building products; many VOCs are toxic and may contribute to urban smog, the greenhouse effect, and global warming.

Voltage, Volts:
Voltage is the electrical force, or pressure that pushes the current over the conductors. Volts are the measurement units.

W

Wall cabinets:
Cabinets that are typically 12 to 18 inches (305 mm to 457 mm) deep and placed on the wall 15 to 18 inches (381 mm to 457 mm) above a base cabinet.

Waste pipe:
The pipe that carries water and waste away from a water-using fixture.

Water factor:
Measures water used per cycle in a clothes washing machine. The lower the water factor, the more efficient.

Water vapor:
Water in its gaseous form.

Wattage, watts:
The unit of measurement for electrical power. The power in watts equals the voltage times the amperage.

Wet wall:
A wall containing supply lines and soil and waste lines.

Whole-house ventilation system:
A mechanical ventilation system that continuously ventilates the home by pulling outside air into the house and exhausting indoor air; heat recovery or energy recovery ventilation systems increase energy effi-

ciency by using heat exchangers (sometimes called air to air heat exchangers) to preheat or precool the incoming air with the exhaust air.

Work aisle:
Space needed to function at the kitchen centers.

Work center:
Composed of an appliance or sink, surrounding landing/work area and storage.

Work triangle:
The distance between the three primary work centers (cooking surface, cleanup/prep primary sink and refrigeration).

X

Xenon:
Xenon lamps are similar to halogen lamps in their characteristics and are made with electrodes in a small tube filled with an inert gas. These lamps do not burn as hot as halogen lamps and are not as fragile. They operate at a lower voltage than the standard 120V, and thus require a transformer.

Z

Zone:
A section of a building that is served by one heating and cooling loop to meet distinct heating and cooling needs; (b) A section of the home where similar activities occur such as social, private and work; (c) A kitchen center.

Resources

CHAPTER 2

National Association of Home Builders
1201 15th Street NW
Washington, D.C. 20005
www.nahb.com

National Fenestration Rating Council
6305 Ivy Lane, Suite 140
Greenbelt, MD 20770
www.nfrc.org/about.aspx

CHAPTER 3

American Lung Association
1301 Pennsylvania Avenue NW
Washington, DC 20004
www.lung.org

American National Standards Institute
1899 L Street NW, 11th Floor
Washington, DC 20036
www.ansi.org

American Society of Heating, Refrigeration
and Air-conditioning Engineers
1791 Tullie Circle NE
Atlanta, GA 30329
www.ashrae.org

American Tree Farm System®
1111 Nineteenth Street NW, Suite 780
Washington, DC 20036
www.treefarmsystem.org

Association of Home Appliance
Manufacturers
1111 19th Street NW, Suite 402

Washington, DC 20036
www.aham.com

Austin Energy Green Building
721 Barton Springs Road
Austin, TX, 78704
www.austinenergy.com

Canada Mortgage and Housing Corp.
Housing Information Center
700 Montreal Road
Ottawa, ON, Canada K1A 0P7
www.cmhc-schl.gc.ca

Children's Environmental Health Network
110 Maryland Avenue NE, Suite 402
Washington, DC 20002
www.cehn.org

Cradle to Cradle Certification Program
MBDC, 1001 E. Market Street, Suite 200
Charlottesville, VA 22902
www.mbdc.com

Earth Advantage Institute
Director Building
808 SW 3rd Avenue, Suite 800
Portland, OR 97204
www.earthadvantage.org

Ecolabel
www.ecolabel.eu

Energy Star (see also: U. S. Environmental
Protection Agency)
www.energystar.gov

Environment Canada
Inquiry Centre
10 Wellington, 23rd Floor

Gatineau QC, K1A 0H3
www.ec.ga.ca

Health Canada
Address Locator 0900C2
Ottawa, ON, Canada K1A 0K9
www.hc-sc.gc.ca/

Forest Stewardship Council
www.fsc.org

Greenguard Environmental Institute
2211 Newmarket Parkway, Suite 110
Marietta, GA 30067
www.greenguard.org

International Code Council
500 New Jersey Avenue NW, 6th Floor
Washington, DC 20001
www.ixxsafe.org

National Green Building Program
www.nahbgreen.org

NAHB (National Association of Home
Builders) Research Center
400 Prince Georges Boulevard
Upper Marlboro, MD 20774
www.nahbrc.com

National Center for Environmental Health
Centers for Disease Control
1600 Clifton Road
Atlanta, GA 30333
www.cdc.gov/nceh

National Institute of Environmental Health
Sciences
111 T.W. Alexander Drive
Research Triangle Park, NC 27709
www.niehs.nih.gov

Natural Resources Canada
www.oee.nrcan.gc.ca

Programme for the Endorsement of Forest
Certification
www.pefc.org

Rocky Mountain Institute
2317 Snowmass Creek Road
Snowmass, CO 81654
www.rmi.org

Scientific Certification Systems
2000 Powell Street, Suite 600
Emeryville, CA 94608
www.sccscertified.com

Southface Energy Institute
241 Pine Street NE
Atlanta, GA 30308
www.southface.org

U.S. Environmental Protection Agency
Ariel Rios Building
1200 Pennsylvania Avenue, NW
Washington, DC 20460
www.epa.gov

U.S. Green Building Council
2101 L St., NW, Suite 500
Washington, DC 20037
www.usgbc.org

Water Quality Association
4151 Naperville Road
Lisle, IL 60532–3696
www.wqa.org

CHAPTER 4

Accessible and Usable Buildings and
Facilities, ICC A117.1-2009
International Code Council
500 New Jersey Avenue NW, 6th Floor
Washington, DC 20001
www.iccsafe.org

American National Standards Institute
www.ansi.org (see Chapter 3)

Barrier Free Architecturals, Inc.
2700 Dufferin Street, Unit 24
Toronto, ON, Canada M6B 4J3
www.barrierfree.org

Center for Inclusive Design and
Environmental Access (IDEA Center)
School of Architecture and Planning
University of Buffalo
378 Hayes Hall
Buffalo, NY
www.ap.buffalo.edu/idea

Concrete Change-Visitability
600 Dancing Fox Road
Decatur, GA 30032
www.concretechange.org

Fair Housing Accessibility First
www.fairhousingfirst.org
(see U. S. Department of Housing and Urban
Development)

Institute on Human Centered Design
(Adaptive Environments)
200 Portland Street
Boston, MA 02114
www.adaptenv.org
www.humancentereddesign.org

Mace Universal Design Institute
410 Yorktown Drive
Chapel Hill, NC 27516
www.udinstitute.org

National Resource Center on Supportive
Housing and Home Modifications
Andrus Gerontology Center
University of Southern California
Los Angeles, CA 90089-0191
www.homemods.org

U.S. Access Board
1331 F. Street, NW, Suite 1000
Washington, DC 20004–1111
www.access-board.gov

U.S. Department of Housing and Urban
Development
Tech. Assistance on Section 504 & Fair
Housing: 800–827–5005
Publications Center: 800–767–7468
www.hud.gov

CHAPTER 7

American Lighting Association
2050 N. Stemmons Freeway, Unit 100
Dallas, TX 75207-3206
http://www.americanlightingassoc.com/

CHAPTER 8

American Association of Retired Persons
(AARP)
601 E Street NW
Washington, DC 20049
www.aarp.org

Abledata
8630 Fenton Street, Suite 930
Silver Spring, MD 20910
www.abledata.com

Access One
25679 Gramford Avenue
Wyoming, MN 55092
www.beyondbarriers.com

Alzheimer's Association
225 North Michigan Avenue, Suite 1700
Chicago, IL 60601–7633
www.alz.org

Alzheimer's Disease Education & Referral
Center
ADEAR Center
P.O. Box 8250
Silver Spring, MD 20907–8250
www.alzheimers.org

American Foundation for the Blind
11 Penn Plaza, Suite 300
New York, NY 10001
www.afb.org

American Heart Association National Center
7272 Greenville Avenue
Dallas, TX 75231
www.americanheart.org

American National Standards Institute
1819 L Street NW, 6th Floor
Washington, DC, 20036
www.ansi.org

American Occupational Therapy Association
4720 Montgomery Lane
P.O. Box 31220
Bethesda, MD 20850
www.aota.org

American Stroke Association
National Center
7272 Greenville Avenue

Dallas, TX 75231
www.strokeassociation.org

Amputee Coalition of America
900 East Hill Avenue, Suite 285
Knoxville, TN 37915–2568
www.amputee-coalition.org

Area Agencies on Aging
www.aoa.dhhs.gov/agingsites/state.html

Arthritis Foundation
1330 West Peachtree Street
P.O. Box 7669
Atlanta, GA 30309
www.arthritis.org

Barrier Free Architecturals, Inc.
2700 Dufferin Street, Unit 24
Toronto, ON, Canada M6B 4J3
www.barrierfree.org

Center for Inclusive Design and

Environmental Access (IDEA Center)
School of Architecture and Planning
University of Buffalo
378 Hayes Hall
3435 Main Street
Buffalo, NY 14214–3087
www.ap.buffalo.edu/idea/

The Center for Universal Design
North Carolina State University
50 Pullen Road
Brooks Hall, Room 104
Campus Box 8613
Raleigh, NC 27695
www.ncsu.edu/project/design-projects/udi/

Council for Exceptional Children
1110 North Glebe Road, Suite 300
Arlington, VA 22201
www.cec.sped.org

Cystic Fibrosis Foundation
6931 Arlington Road
Bethesda, MD 20814
www.cff.org

Disability Rights Education Defense Fund
1730 M Street NW, Suite 801
Washington, DC 20036
www.dredf.org

Disabled American Veterans
807 Maine Avenue SW
Washington, DC 20024
www.dav.org

Easter Seal Society
230 West Monroe Street, Suite 1800
Chicago, IL 60606
www.easter-seals.org

Eldercare Locator
c/o Administration on Aging
220 Independence Avenue SW
Washington, DC 20201
www.eldercare.gov

Harris Communications, Inc.
15155 Technology Drive
Eden Prairie, MN 55344–2277
www.harriscomm.com

Home Modification List Serve
Homemodification-list@listserv.acsu.buffalo.edu

Independent Living Research Utilization Project
2323 South Shepard Street, Suite 1000
Houston, TX 77019
www.ilru.org

Institute for Human Centered Design
(Adaptive Environments)
(see Chapter 4)

Lifease Inc.
2451 15th Street NW, Suite D
New Brighton, MN 55112
www.lifease.com

Lighthouse International
111 East 59th Street
New York, NY 10022–1202
www.lighthouse.org

Mace Universal Design Institute
(see Chapter 4)

Muscular Dystrophy Association
3300 East Sunrise Drive
Tucson, AZ 85718
www.mdausa.org

National Association of the Deaf
814 Thayer Avenue
Silver Spring, MD 20910–4500
www.nad.org

National Council on Independent Living
1916 Wilson Boulevard, Suite 209
Arlington, VA 22201
www.ncil.org

National Institute on Aging
Building 31, Room 5C27
31 Center Drive, MSC 2292
Bethesda, MD 20892
www.nia.nih.gov/

National Institute on Deafness and Other
Communication Disorders
National Institutes of Health
31 Center Drive, MSC 2320
Bethesda, MD USA 20892–2320
www.nidcd.nih.gov

National Institute on Disability and
Rehabilitation Research
US Department of Education
400 Maryland Avenue, SW
Washington, DC 20202–2572
www2.ed.gov/about/offices/list/osers/nidrr/
index.html?%20src=mr

National Kitchen & Bath Association
687 Willow Grove Street
Hackettstown, NJ 07840
www.nkba.org

National Rehabilitation Information Center
4200 Forbes Boulevard, Suite 202
Lanham, MD 20706
www.naric.com

National Resource Center on Supportive
Housing and Home Modifications
Andrus Gerontology Center
University of Southern California

3715 McClintock Avenue
Los Angeles, CA 90089–0191
www.homemods.org

Paralyzed Veterans of America
801 Eighteenth Street, NW
Washington, DC 20006–3517
www.pva.org

ProMatura Group, LLC
142 Hwy 30 E
Oxford, MS 38655
www.promatura.com\

Rehabilitation Engineering and Assistive
Technology Society of North America (RESNA)
1700 North Moore Street
Suite 1540
Arlington, VA 22209–1903
www.resna.org

Trace Research and Development Center
University of Wisconsin
2107 Engineering Centers Bldg.
1500 Highland Avenue
Madison, WI 53706
www.trace.wisc.edu

U.S. Dept. of Justice Tech. Assist. on ADA
950 Pennsylvania Avenue, NW

Civil Rights Division
Disability Rights Section—NYAV

Washington, DC 20530
www.usdoj.gov/crt/ada/adahom1.htm

Visitability List Serve
visitability-list@ACSU.buffalo.edu

Volunteers for Medical Engineering
2301 Argonne Drive
Baltimore, MD 21218
www.toad.net/~vme

CHAPTER 9

Consortium for Energy Efficiency, Inc.
98 North Washington Street, Suite 101
Boston, MA 02114-1918
www.cee1.org

Energy Star
(See Chapter 3 resources)

CHAPTER 10

NKBA, *Kitchen and Bathroom Planning
Guidelines with Access Standards*, Hoboken,
NJ: John Wiley & Sons, 2012.

Index